PETRA
REDISCOVERED

Lost City of the Nabataeans

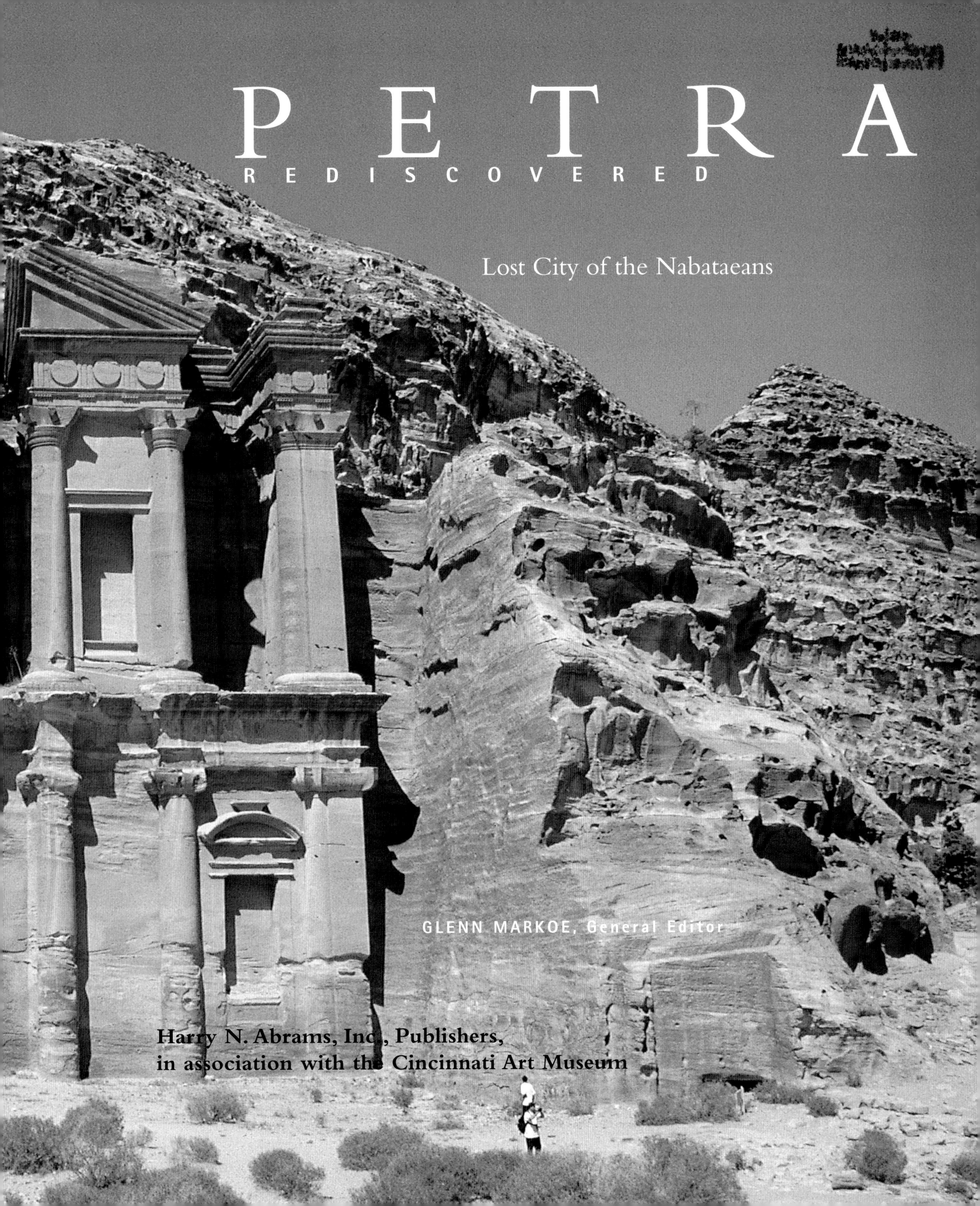
PETRA
REDISCOVERED
Lost City of the Nabataeans
GLENN MARKOE, General Editor
Harry N. Abrams, Inc., Publishers,
in association with the Cincinnati Art Museum

Editor: Elaine M. Stainton
Designer: Antony Drobinski, Emsworth Design, Inc.
Production Manager: Maria Pia Gramaglia

LIBRARY OF CONGRESS CATALOGING-IN-PUBLICATION DATA

Petra rediscovered : lost city of the Nabataeans / Glenn Markoe, general editor.
p. cm.
Includes bibliographical references and index.
ISBN 0-8109-4537-1 — ISBN 0-8109-9128-4 (pbk.)
1. Petra (Extinct city)—Exhibitions. 2. Nabataeans—Exhibitions. I. Markoe, Glenn, 1951-

DS154.9.P48P49 2003
939'.48—dc21

2003006209

Published in 2003 by Harry N. Abrams, Incorporated, New York.

Printed and bound in China

10 9 8 7 6 5 4 3 2 1

Harry N. Abrams, Inc.
100 Fifth Avenue
New York, N.Y. 10011
www.abramsbooks.com

Abrams is a subsidiary of

Cincinnati Art Museum
953 Eden Park Drive
Cincinnati, Ohio 45202

Half title: Architectural fragment with lion mask, Petra. h: 35.0 cm. Department of Antiquities, Amman, Jordan.

Pages 2–3: View of "Royal Tombs" at Jebel el-Khubthah ridge, looking east from Colonnaded Street, Petra.

Title spread: Ed-Deir (Monastery), Petra.

Table of Contents

Foreword

HER MAJESTY QUEEN RANIA AL-ABDULLAH

ACROSS THE CENTURIES, the Nabataeans continue to fascinate and intrigue the world. Although in many ways they remain a mystery obscured by the mists of antiquity, they also strike us as remarkably contemporary. Jordanians are justly proud to be the custodians of this amazing heritage. Indeed, many of our Jordanian national characteristics are notably similar to those of the Nabataean people. Like the ancient Nabataeans, Jordanians value our traditional roots but are also forward-looking. We, too, have carved out a special and unique place as a bridge between diverse regions and as a peaceful culture committed to international commerce and dialogue.

In ancient days, desert caravans transported people and exotic goods over the fabled trade routes of Arabia to converge in Petra and to be transferred on to the wider world. These commercial caravans carried with them not just a constant exchange of currency and commerce but also one of ideas and culture. Today, modern business people may travel trade routes in cyberspace instead, but the transfer of goods and cultures is no less vital and essential. The magical rose-red city of Petra, the center of the Nabataean civilization, prospered for centuries, not as a result of war and conquest, but as a center of honorable trade. This miracle of the ancient world still demonstrates to us how economic prosperity and peaceful interchange can encourage human artistry and creativity.

Modern nations can learn from the wisdom and the technological acumen of the Nabataean people. From a simple pastoral society, they transformed themselves into a stunningly accomplished civilization through their scientific and practical adaptation to a challenging environment. Their success in architecture, hydrology, irrigation, and agriculture sustained a remarkable level of prosperity and culture despite the starkly inhospitable terrain. This genius for innovation can be seen in everything from the awesome splendor of the Petra monuments to the smallest sherds of finely crafted Nabataean pottery decorated with images of flourishing fruit trees.

Their advances were not limited solely to scientific and environmental successes, but also reflect an admirable level of social and humanitarian development as well. In their inscriptions, we find the words "peace" and "blessing" liberally and prominently featured. Nabataean coins indicate the respected position of women in their culture – often depicting the wife, sister, or mother of the king along with the ruler himself.

Scholars and dreamers alike still continue to journey to Jordan to study, to learn, and to wonder at the awesome historical and archaeological treasures left to us by the Nabataeans. Excavations and academic research, carried out jointly by Jordanian and international experts, continue to unearth new knowledge of this ancient people. Tourists and travelers come by the hundreds of thousands each year to share in the unique experience of Petra, our UNESCO World Heritage site. To assure the protection and preservation of the Petra basin, the Jordanian government has officially declared it a protected natural reserve.

Petra Rediscovered is a special opportunity for Jordan to share these Nabataean treasures with the people of the entire world, so that they, too, will come to know the diversity and ingenuity of this fabled people.

1. The Khazneh ("Treasury"), Petra.

Preface

FAWWAZ AL-KHRAYSHEH

Director-General, Department of Antiquities, The Hashemite Kingdom of Jordan

THE LAST TWENTY-FIVE YEARS have brought extraordinary advances to our understanding of the Nabataeans, the great traders and agriculturalists of the southern Levant. Nowhere are these achievements more evident than at the site of Petra, the capital and center of Nabataean civilization. Here, thanks to the cooperation and involvement of many nations, the story of this great city is now being elucidated through scientific research and excavation carried out under the active supervision of the Department of Antiquities of the Hashemite Kingdom of Jordan.

The archaeological importance of Petra cannot be underestimated. Designated a World Heritage Site in 1985, Petra has furnished a wealth of archaeological data about the city and its Nabataean occupants—from its establishment in the last centuries of the first millennium BC through its final florescence in the Byzantine era. Research at Petra has taken a number of different forms, among which physical excavation is only one. Efforts in recent years have also concentrated on scientific analysis of the site's ecology through extensive survey and mapping, and through examination of ancient Nabataean barrage-damming and terracing methods. Such ecological work, together with recent efforts at conserving Petra's rock-cut tomb façades, have been conducted with an eye toward the long-term preservation of the site, which has been prioritized on UNESCO's list of endangered archaeological locales.

2. Interior view of the Siq, the gorgelike entryway into Petra

To insure the safe passage of visitors and to protect its monuments from the effects of flash floods, the Siq of Petra was recently excavated down to its Roman-period pavement level. This project, which was carried out from 1996 through 1999 by the Petra National Trust in close cooperation with the Jordanian Department of Antiquities and the Petra Regional Planning Council, resulted in the clearance of about 30,000 cubic meters of rubble. The cleaning enabled the restoration and reconstruction of several components of its original Nabataean hydraulic system, consisting of barrage dams that controlled the entry flow of water through its thirty-four wadis, or tributaries.

Our understanding of Nabataean civilization has been elucidated through archaeological work not only at Petra but at a host of other sites in Jordan, Israel, Arabia, and Syria. Of particular importance, as summarized in chapters of the present volume, are excavations in the Negev, the Syrian Hauran, and in southern Jordan southeast of the Dead Sea. In the latter region, attention may be drawn to the site of Khirbet edh-Dharih, where recent excavations have documented a major Nabataean sanctuary and accompanying settlement. Of especial relevance to the present volume and exhibition are the sculptural finds from neighboring Khirbet et-Tannur, which was excavated in 1937 by the Jordanian Department of Antiquities and the American School of Oriental Research in Jerusalem. Highlights of these finds, which were divided between the respective authorities, have now been physically reunited for display for the first time since their discovery, thanks to the joint efforts of the Cincinnati Art Museum and the Jordanian Department of Antiquities. It is in this spirit of cooperation and exchange that the present exhibition, which has been organized by the Cincinnati Art Museum and the American Museum of Natural History, New York, has been undertaken.

It is my privilege to have been involved in facilitating work on this book and accompanying exhibition, which are devoted to recent archaeological and art historical research on the Nabataeans. I wish to express my sincere thanks to the above-named institutions, not only for organizing the present exhibition, but for cleaning and conserving a number of important antiquities from Petra in collaboration with the American Center of Oriental Research in Amman. I hope that the publication of this volume will serve as a catalyst for future research and for the continued exchange of expertise and ideas so essential to a further understanding of the Nabataeans and their great civilization.

Introduction

GLENN MARKOE

Curator of Classical and Near Eastern Art, Cincinnati Art Museum

As its title suggests, this volume and accompanying exhibition celebrate the rediscovery of a lost city and a civilization on a number of different levels. Petra's physical rediscovery by the Swiss explorer Johann Burckhardt occurred in 1812—after a hiatus of more than a thousand years, during which knowledge of the city's existence was lost to the West. Burckhardt's accomplishment ultimately led to Petra's scientific rediscovery through systematic mapping and survey of its monuments, beginning in 1898 with the classification work of R. E. Brünnow and A. von Domaszewski; this process continues today with the Petra Survey Project, which has now identified and recorded more than three thousand of Petra's monuments and man-made features.

Burckhardt and the many nineteenth-century artist-explorers who followed in his wake knew of Petra only from its rock-cut tombs and monuments. It was only in the second half of the twentieth century that Petra's urban fabric was rediscovered through controlled excavation of its built temples, theaters, shops, and houses. Such archaeological research, initiated in the 1950s, has accelerated greatly in the last two decades; a number of ongoing scientific projects have now succeeded in documenting important aspects of the city during its Nabataean, Roman, and Byzantine periods.

The last decade has now witnessed a rediscovery of Petra's ecological landscape through concerted exploration of its ancient terraces, dams, and irrigation channels. In antiquity, these helped to convert Petra from an arid, rocky retreat (Petra in ancient Greek actually means "rock" or "ledge") into a city lush with fertile gardens, pools, and orchards. Recent excavations have, in fact, revealed traces of an enormous pool-complex and garden terrace situated in the very heart of the city. A modern re-acquaintance with ancient Nabataean soil conservation and water engineering methods should now help archaeologists preserve the site for future generations.

3. Over-lifesize limestone bust of a bearded male deity, probably Dushara or Serapis. Area of Temenos Gate, Petra. Department of Antiquities, Amman, Jordan.

As history has revealed, the Nabataeans were great traders, agriculturalists, and skilled engineers and builders. At their height, from the second century BC through the third century AD, they interacted commercially with the great civilizations around them—Greek, Roman, Near Eastern and Egyptian—venturing, through trade, as far afield as India and China. A thriving marketplace in its heyday, Petra was situated at the crossroads of several major trade routes, east-west, north-south. From Arabia came its most valuable commodities: costly perfumes and incense, such as frankincense and myrrh. From the east came other treasures, such as silk, spices, and ivory. The source of the latter has now been dramatically documented in the hundreds of carved stone elephant heads that graced the monumental capitals of Petra's Great Temple (see p. 219, figs. 236, 37).

Through their mercantile activities, the Nabataeans were well known in antiquity. References in the Bible allude to their wealth and commercial prominence. Relations were particularly strong between the Judaean and Nabataean dynasties: as a symbol of such alliance, the Judaean prince Herod Antipas even married a Nabataean princess. Yet, despite their ancient acclaim, the Nabataeans have remained largely a mystery; even their origins remain enshrouded in mist. Much of this is due to the loss of their own written records, which were penned on perishable materials such as leather and papyrus. Nearly all that remain today of their writings are a small number of rock-cut inscriptions. Yet, despite this historical loss, our understanding of Nabataean culture has progressed enormously in recent years, thanks to varied archaeological research conducted both at Petra itself and at a variety of Nabataean sites in Jordan, Israel, Syria, Egypt, and Saudi Arabia. The twenty-two essays in *Petra Rediscovered* are the product of such archaeological and historical enquiry, much of it undertaken in the last few decades. Indeed, such research has now made it possible, for the first time, to survey the history of Nabataean culture in its broad parameters.

The objective of this book is to address the current state of research in Nabataean studies, focusing on new interpretation and analysis made possible by recent discoveries. The twenty-seven scholars solicited for this publication have been asked to take a broad view of their respective subjects and to look at their fields in a synthetic fashion, identifying vexing problems and issues and offering direction on future avenues of enquiry. In sum: how has recent research influenced our understanding of the Nabataean cultural landscape and what still remains to be done?

This book consists of two parts. The first section deals with the Nabataeans as a societal whole, surveying their cultural, technical, and commercial accomplishments in language and writing, religion, art, architecture, and trade. Included in this section are current overviews of Nabataean cultural presence in focal areas of their settlement—in southern Jordan, northwestern Arabia, the Israeli Negev, and Syria. The second half of the book surveys recent research at Petra itself, based upon field archaeology, survey, architectural analysis, art history, and epigraphy. Included are studies and reviews of current archaeological research on private dwellings, sanctuaries, and other monuments of Petra, including the Khazneh, or "Treasury." The work surveyed in these studies covers the full chronological spectrum of Petra's history—from its Nabataean origins through its final, Byzantine florescence. The first two chapters of the second section address the story of Petra's rediscovery in the nineteenth century—by Johann Burckhardt and the many artist-travelers who followed in his wake. Their extraordinary accomplishments are documented through excerpts from their own writings and by original renderings in surviving prints, drawings, and paintings.

The present volume differs from previous works on Petra in its emphasis on the artistry and craftsmanship of the Nabataeans, as revealed in their art and architecture. The *Nabatu* (as they were known in antiquity) were master stonecarvers and sculptors; their technical virtuosity may be seen, above all, in the extraordinary, monumental rock-cut tombs that they carved throughout Petra. This same technical expertise allowed the Nabataeans to produce exquisite sculpture (fig. 3), fine painted ceramics, metalwork, and jewelry, as well as painted architectural stuccowork of extraordinary caliber. Select examples of such workmanship are illustrated throughout the volume and in the accompanying exhibition by photography specially commissioned for this project.

Petra Rediscovered is also distinguished by its focus on architecture from two outlying Nabataean sanctuaries located northeast of Petra and southeast of the Dead Sea: Khirbet et-Tannur and Khirbet edh-Dharih. Both sites, which are closely situated to one another, have produced a wealth of architectural sculpture in a style distinct from that of metropolitan Petra. Major finds from the first, Khirbet et-Tannur, are discussed and illustrated for the first time since their original publication in 1965.

The Cincinnati Art Museum, the co-publisher of this volume, is privileged to possess half of the architectural finds from this hilltop site, which housed a major Nabataean sanctuary to the storm god Qaws and his consort Atargatis, goddess of fertility (fig. 4). The product of American excavations undertaken in 1937 with the Jordanian Department of Antiquities, these objects constitute the most extensive holdings of Nabataean sculpture outside of Jordan. In the accompanying exhibition, highlights from Cincinnati's collection will be reunited, for the first time since their discovery, with associated finds from Khirbet et-Tannur in the Jordan Archaeological Museum, Amman. This display will feature the reassembled statue depicting the bust of Atargatis in her guise as Tyche, goddess of fortune, surrounded by the signs of the zodiac (see pp. 188–190, figs. 197–99).

The second outlying sanctuary is the recently excavated temple at Khirbet edh-Dharih, the focus of ongoing excavations by the French and Jordanians. The role and importance of this sanctuary and its adjoining settlement have been assessed in the context of its neighbor, Khirbet et-Tannur, an isolated pilgrimage site. As their respective essays illustrate, both sanctuaries have revealed remarkable evidence for Nabataean cultic worship centered on the celestial sphere.

As general editor of this volume and as organizer of the accompanying exhibition, my appreciation goes to a great number of individuals who have helped make both projects a reality. First and foremost, I would like to acknowledge the generous assistance offered by the Jordanian Department of Antiquities under the able supervision of Dr. Fawwaz al-Khraysheh, its Director-General. A great debt is owed to him and to his predecessor, Dr. Ghazi Bisheh, the former Director. I would also like to acknowledge the generous assistance of Suleiman Farajat, Director of the Petra Archaeological Park; Dr. Ziad al-Saad, Director of Archaeology and Anthropology, Yarmouk University; and Mohammad Shoubaki, of the Department of Antiquities, Petra.

Further gratitude is due to H. E. Nader Dahabi, the Minister of Tourism and Antiquities, and to Samer A. Majali, President and CEO of Royal Jordanian. The latter is to be thanked for his generous support of the exhibition in the form of subsidized air transport for the Jordanian antiquities. My sincere appreciation also goes to Malia Asfour, Director of the Jordan

4. Limestone tympanon panel with the bust of Atargatis. Khirbet et-Tannur. Department of Antiquities, Amman, Jordan.

Tourism Board, North America, for her cooperation in promoting *Petra Rediscovered*.

In facilitating on-site work in Jordan and at Petra, I owe an enormous debt of gratitude to Drs. Pierre and Patricia Bikai of the American Center of Oriental Research, Amman. Both have assisted not only with a myriad of logistical matters concerning the exhibition, but have overseen the critical conservation and restoration work required for many of the antiquities on display, including their own recent discoveries from the Byzantine Petra Church and adjacent Blue Church.

Closer to home, I would like to thank the staff of the Cincinnati Art Museum for their commitment and support for these two projects. An especial debt is owed to Director Timothy Rub and Deputy Director Stephen Bonadies for their invaluable support and assistance. The exhibition would not have come to fruition without Mr. Rub's guidance and encouragement. Stephen Bonadies's tenacious oversight and input, too, were instrumental in guiding this complicated project through its various stages. An enormous debt is due to Chief Registrar Kathryn Haigh for her deft supervision of the exhibition's organization, transport, and tour development. In addition, I would like to express my personal thanks to former Museum Director Barbara K. Gibbs for her encouragement and critical support on both projects in their early stages of development.

Needless to say, *Petra Rediscovered* would not have taken place without the active involvement and support of the American Museum of Natural History, New York, co-producer of the exhibition. An especial debt is owed to Museum President Ellen V. Futter and Dr. Craig Morris, Senior Vice-President and Dean of Science. Special thanks go to Dr. Morris for his invaluable input and assistance as exhibition co-curator. Special thanks are also due to Melissa Posen, Senior Director of Exhibition Operations, and David Harvey, Vice-President for Exhibitions. My sincere thanks go to both of them for their able oversight of the design, development, and production of *Petra Rediscovered*.

On matters directly relating to the book, a great number of individuals and institutions have helped in various ways. First and foremost, I would like to thank the many scholars and specialists who contributed to this volume; its publication would not have been possible without their expertise and input. A debt of appreciation is due to the Joukowsky Family Foundation for its generous financial support for the publication. The Museum is equally grateful to Peter John Gates, FBIPP, ARSPS, for his excellent photography work, including nearly all of the images of the sculpture and artifacts in the book, which were photographed on site. The following individuals and institutions are also to be thanked for their assistance in providing photography, maps, and line drawings for the volume: N. Baker; U. Bellwald; C. Bissell; A. R. Cassidy; A. Caubet; Cincinnati Art Museum; Cecil Higgins Art Gallery, Bedford; Cooper-Hewitt, National Design Museum, New York; J. M. Ferrant; Z. Fiema; E. Fontan; T. Gagos; S. Gibson; Houghton Library, Harvard College Library; P. Hammond; S. Hisey; K. Horton; A.W. and M. S. Joukowsky; G. King; A. Kitzinger, L. Koenen, B. Kolb; F. Larché, N. Lewis; B. Llewellyn, M. Macdonald; J. McKenzie; Musée du Louvre, Paris; The National Trust, London; G. Naughton; A. and E. Negev, L. Nehmé; Olana State Historic Site, Hudson, New York; P. Parr; D. Politis; J. Rothwell; S. Schmid; S. Sidebotham; T. Springett; A. Stewart; J. H. Stucky; V & A Picture Library, London; F. Villeneuve; R. Wenning; and F. Zayadine.

In the preparation of the manuscript, an especial debt of gratitude is due to Jong Son, Departmental Curatorial Assistant, who helped in innumerable ways, particularly in compiling the glossary, endnotes and extensive bibliography for the book. This project could not have taken shape in its present form without her untiring assistance. Thanks are also due to Kristin Spangenberg, Curator of Prints, Drawings, and Photographs, for her scholarly expertise, and to Linda Pieper, former Curatorial Secretary, for her expert typing of much of the volume's text. The staff of Harry N. Abrams, Inc., is to be commended for their excellent work; especial thanks are due to Robert Morton, former Head of Special Projects, for his early assistance and encouragement on the project; and to Elaine Stainton for her adept editorial work on the volume.

A few comments about the book's presentation are in order. In rendering most Nabataean personal and place names, the standard Arabic diacritical markings have been employed. This convention has sometimes been broken for site names that occur commonly throughout the book. Depending upon their context and usage, both the ancient classical and the modern Arabic spellings for such locations have been used. Bibliographic references in the endnotes (which are grouped by chapter at the end of the book) employ the "Harvard" system of abbreviation (with author's last name and publication date, followed by the page citation.) For ease of reference, the illustrations, which have been carefully keyed to the text, have been numbered sequentially throughout. For the reader's edification, a glossary of architectural terms employed in the text has been included.

Above all, the Cincinnati Art Museum would like to express its heartfelt appreciation to the Royal Family of the Hashemite Kingdom of Jordan for its gracious support of these two projects. An enormous debt of gratitude is owed to Her Majesty Queen Rania Al-Abdullah for her patronage of this volume and the accompanying exhibition. Her generous advice and assistance have proved invaluable on many levels. Additional thanks are due to the Queen's Chief of Staff Rania Atalla and to Hanan Kurdi in the Office of Her Majesty. In acknowledging the support of the Royal Family, we should not forget Her Majesty Queen Noor Al-Hussein, whose timely assistance proved invaluable to the exhibition's early development. It was from initial discussions with Queen Noor, on the occasion of her visit to Cincinnati in 1994, that the groundwork for this ambitious project was laid.

The present volume is dedicated to the memory of Dr. Nelson Glueck, distinguished biblical archaeologist and former President of Hebrew Union College in Cincinnati. May the spirit of his early pioneering work on the Nabataeans serve as an inspiration for future archaeological research in Jordan.

5. Limestone head of a Nabataean dignitary. Provenance unknown. h: 37 cm. Department of Antiquities, Amman, Jordan.

Based upon its distinctive soft-pointed cap, this sculpted head probably depicts a Nabataean priest.

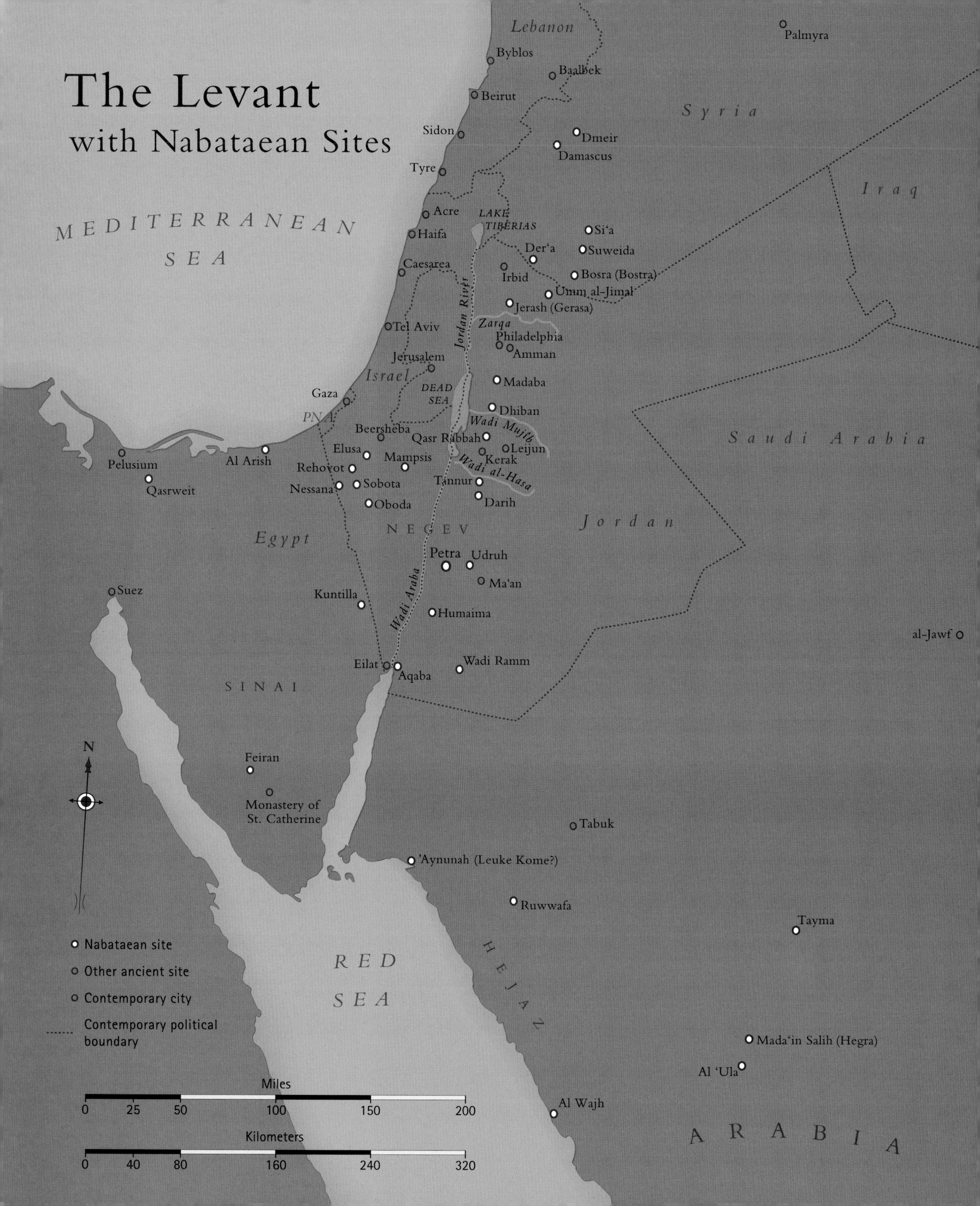
The Levant
with Nabataean Sites
MEDITERRANEAN
SEA
Lebanon
Syria
Iraq
Israel
PNA
Egypt
Jordan
Saudi Arabia
NEGEV
SINAI
HEJAZ
ARABIA
RED
SEA
LAKE
TIBERIAS
DEAD
SEA
Jordan River
Zarqa
Wadi Mujib
Wadi al-Hasa
Wadi Araba
Palmyra
Byblos
Baalbek
Beirut
Sidon
Dmeir
Damascus
Tyre
Acre
Haifa
Si'a
Der'a
Suweida
Caesarea
Irbid
Bosra (Bostra)
Umm al-Jimal
Jerash (Gerasa)
Tel Aviv
Philadelphia
Amman
Jerusalem
Madaba
Gaza
Dhiban
Beersheba
Qasr Rabbah
Elusa
Leijun
Pelusium
Al Arish
Mampsis
Kerak
Rehovot
Tannur
Qasrweit
Nessana
Sobota
Oboda
Darih
Petra
Udruh
Ma'an
Suez
Kuntilla
Humaima
al-Jawf
Eilat
Aqaba
Wadi Ramm
Feiran
Monastery of
St. Catherine
Tabuk
'Aynunah (Leuke Kome?)
Ruwwafa
Tayma
Mada'in Salih (Hegra)
Al 'Ula
Al Wajh
N
Nabataean site
Other ancient site
Contemporary city
Contemporary political
boundary
Miles
0
25
50
100
150
200
Kilometers
0
40
80
160
240
320

1 | The Nabataeans in Historical Context

GLEN W. BOWERSOCK

The people we know as the Nabataean Arabs held a place on the historical stage for some eight hundred years. During this time they lived uninterruptedly alongside Jews, Greeks, Romans, and other Arabs, both nomadic and sedentary, throughout the long pre-Islamic centuries after Alexander the Great. Between the conquests of Alexander and Muhammad they occupied the territory of Transjordan (the modern Hashemite Kingdom of Jordan) as well as the northwest corner of the Arabian Peninsula, southern Syria, and the Negev. For approximately the first half of the eight hundred years in which they can be tracked, the Nabataeans had an autonomous kingdom of their own, and for the second half they lived within provinces of the Roman Empire, notably the province of Arabia and a later configuration of two provinces called Third Palestine and Arabia. They were present, although in modest numbers, in Greek cities of the Decapolis at the margins of their homeland.[1] The territorial extent of Nabataean culture across this long period remained essentially the same, bringing the people into close contact with their neighbors in Palestine and Syria. In the third century AD the deified Nabataean king Obodas was still worshipped at Avdat in the Negev, and in documents from the fourth century AD the northern Nabataean city of Bostra can still be described as a city of Syria.[2]

The longevity, tenacity, and regional distribution of the Nabataeans made them one of the most influential peoples in the Near East after Alexander the Great. Their first appearance in the historical record, in 312 BC, is a dramatic demonstration of their ability to withstand the attempt of Alexander's successor Antigonus to overwhelm them in their rock-girt city of Petra. In the centuries that followed they substantially affected the fortunes of aspiring rulers outside their kingdom by lending their support to one side or another. The Hasmonaean Jews found to their cost that a union of Nabataeans with Greeks could be devastating, and the Roman army under Augustus could not even have contemplated its adventurous mission into south Arabia without the help of a Nabataean guide.[3] In the early imperial period Rome, in the person of Germanicus Caesar, found it prudent to accept the hospitality of the Nabataean king, and the early emperors all supported the dynasty as an independent kingdom for over a century before it was incorporated as a province.[4]

The archaeological and documentary record of the Nabataeans begins somewhat later than their confrontation with Antigonus in 312 BC, but there is no reason to doubt that they already had a base in Petra at that date. Diodorus Siculus, who records the episode on the basis of a report from Alexander's officer Hieronymus of Cardia, leaves no doubt that the Nabataeans were nomadic at the time and used the impregnable site of Petra mainly for annual assemblies and for thwarting enemies.[5] They lived under tents and had no houses of their own. They had camels and sheep, but their principal occupation was traffic in the perfumes and spices that passed from the southwestern corner of the Arabian Peninsula up into the Jordanian Hisma and thence across the Wadi Araba on to the Mediterranean ports of Gaza and Rhinocolura. They also did a brisk business in harvesting bitumen from the Dead Sea on the side.

No source reveals the origins of the Nabataeans.[6] Linguistic considerations guarantee that they were not the Nebayoth mentioned in the Bible, although they might conceivably be the Nabaiati of Assyrian chronicles. How long they had operated in the vicinity of Petra cannot be divined. It is often assumed that they came out of the Arabian desert and gradually assumed the commercial role that they already had by the end of the fourth century. When the Nabataeans became a sedentary people is no less obscure than their origins. The Hellenistic work of a certain Glaucus, entitled *Arabian Archaeology*, appears not to have mentioned the Nabataeans at all, although Glaucus knew about Petra and its adjacent city

6–7. Monumental Roman marble cantharus with panther handles. Petra Church. h: 86.5 cm. Department of Antiquities, Amman, Jordan.

of Gaia (al-ji).[7] By the middle of the third century BC there were Nabataeans in the Hauran of southern Syria, as a papyrus document from the Zeno Archive in Egypt demonstrates, and the earliest Nabataean inscription, probably from the second century, proves that the people had a king by that date and had made their way to Elusa in the Negev, where the inscription was found.[8]

The Elusa text shows, as does the extensive repertoire of later Nabataean epigraphy, that the Nabataeans employed Aramaic for all public documents. This perhaps facilitated communication with their immediate neighbors in Palestine, while the borrowing of Greek military terms in Nabataean texts reflects the ever-increasing Hellenism in the region. But the personal names of the Nabataeans themselves and some peculiarities of their dialect of Aramaic have suggested to some scholars that they were speaking a kind of early Arabic.[9] A graffito from the Negev in the imperial period actually lapses into Arabic in the midst of a Nabataean text.[10] Obviously in the commercial enterprises of this people their multilingual talent would have served them well.

A younger contemporary of Diodorus, the geographer Strabo, also described the Nabataeans at length, and it is probably no accident that the two fullest accounts of them that we possess both come from the second half of the first century BC. Both Antony and Augustus had realized, as Pompey had earlier, that the Nabataeans effectively controlled trade and communication from the Arabian Peninsula to Syria in the north and to Mediterranean ports in the west. It was undoubtedly in this period that their decisive role was recognized by the Roman government, and hence some effort must have been made to learn about them. Diodorus went back to Hieronymus of Cardia, but Strabo turned to an eyewitness of his own day, Athenodorus of Tarsus, who had been to Petra.[11] His picture of Nabataean life is utterly different from the one that Diodorus provided from nearly three centuries before. Athenodorus reported that the Nabataeans inhabited stone houses, enjoyed banqueting, and conducted their affairs prudently and peaceably. He observed a thriving international community with many Romans and other foreigners present. They, it seems, were the sole parties to whatever litigation occurred in the city.

Athenodorus praised the democratic instincts of the Nabataean king. In commenting on the burial customs of the people, he noted that the dead were judged no better than dung and that the remains of kings were placed beside dungheaps. This curious report was, as Clermont-Ganneau brilliantly suggested over a century ago, undoubtedly based upon a misunderstanding of the Nabataean word for tomb, *kpr*, which would have sounded to Greek ears like the Greek word for dung (*kopros*).[12] Another of Athenodorus's observations imputed to the Nabataeans an acquisitiveness so ingrained that they publicly fined those who diminished their possessions and honored those who enlarged them. The most plausible explanation of this report is that the possessions at issue here were collective tribal possessions, not personal property.[13]

In addition to Athenodorus, Strabo had another eyewitness source for his knowledge of the Nabataeans. This was his friend and patron, Aelius Gallus, who led the audacious campaign into South Arabia on behalf of Augustus in the 20s BC. Gallus's guide on this mission was a leading courtier of the Nabataean king by the name of Syllaeus, who has been judged, on Strabo's testimony, responsible for the apparent failure of Gallus to complete his campaign successfully. But, like it or not, we must accept that Augustus himself represented this expedition as a triumph in which Arabs were humbled.[14] The Nabataeans were Rome's allies in a war against the affluent Arabs of the south, who were from a different cultural tradition and who spoke and wrote an entirely different, though related, language. Had the Roman invasion of the South been more successful than it was, it is unlikely that the Romans would have wanted to administer it as an exceedingly remote province. The Nabataeans would undoubtedly have been the gainers from the expedition, and that is presumably why they offered help to the Romans. In the twenties, well before Strabo wrote, Syllaeus was manifestly a trusted ally of Rome.

Syllaeus was, in fact, a major Near Eastern diplomat of the early decades of the Augustan principate. He went twice to Rome, and inscriptions prove that among his stops along the way were Miletus and Delos.[15] A newly published Safaitic graffito from northern Jordan provides eloquent witness to the local fame attached to his contact with Rome.[16] Strabo's representation of Syllaeus as cunning, devious, and unhelpful undoubtedly reflects the troubled years after 9/8 BC, when the king Obodas, whom Syllaeus served, died. The turmoil over the succession led in 6 BC to Syllaeus's disgrace before the Roman authorities and his execution. The geographer, whose allusion to Syllaeus's fall from grace proves that he was writing after it, must have chosen to describe the Arabian campaign as he did because Aelius Gallus's reputation would not have been well served at that time by a positive representation of collaboration with Syllaeus.

The local winner in the power struggle that ended in 6 BC was the new king of the Nabataeans, Aretas IV (Ḥāritat), who went on until 40 AD to preside over the efflorescence of Petra and the Nabataeans for decades to come. His name is regularly accompanied on coins and inscriptions by the expression *rḥm ʿmh*, "who loved his people."[17] Some of the most glorious monuments in the city, such as the Khazneh and the Qasr al-Bint, appear to have been created in his reign. His kingdom extended southward into the Hijaz of the Arabian Peninsula, where a magnificent series of inscribed rock-cut tombs from the early first century AD at Madāʾin Ṣāliḥ, ancient Hegra or Egra, provide the only important parallels in existence to the great tombs at Petra.[18] Aretas IV sent ambassadors to Rome where they and their king were commemorated in a grand marble inscription on the Capitoline.[19] From the New Testament's account of Paul's visit to Damascus there is explicit evidence of a Nabataean representative of Aretas (an *ethnarch*),[20] which may conceivably (although not necessarily) show that the kingdom had recovered, for a time, the territory it had formerly possessed north of the Hauran in the previous century. The commercial activity of the Nabataeans in this age of prosperity is documented for the reign of Aretas's successor, Malichus, in the Greek trader's manual known as the *Periplus of the Red Sea*.[21]

Malichus's successor, Rabbel II, acceded to the throne in 70 AD and proved to be the last of the Nabataean kings. He appears to have relocated the center of government to Bostra in the north, where an inscription shows he had his seat.[22] The precise nature of the elevation of Bostra within the administrative structure of the kingdom is unclear. Petra continued to be a major urban center. But the internal trade route out of the Arabian Peninsula up the Wadi Sirhan from al-Jawf led straight into the Hauran at Bostra. Rabbel evidently fostered the cult of the Nabataeans' chief divinity, Dushara (Greek, Dusares), at Bostra, perhaps as a counterbalance to the prominence of al-ʿUzza (identified with Aphrodite) at Petra.[23]

In 106 AD the emperor Trajan annexed the Nabataean kingdom through the agency of the governor of Syria, Cornelius Palma, apparently without any armed confrontation.[24] At least there is no clear evidence of resistance in either the textual or archaeological material for the annexation. The easiest supposition is that Rabbel died, and that Trajan, who had an expansionist temperament, saw an opportunity to close the one remaining gap in the provincial system in the Near East between the Anatolian plateau and the Arabian Peninsula. A legion (*III Cyrenaica*) was stationed in the new province, which was called simply Arabia, and it went immediately to work on building a good Roman road along the ancient route that joined Bostra to Aila (Aqaba) at the head of the Gulf of Aqaba.[25]

There is a lively debate as to whether Petra or Bostra served as the administrative center of the first governor of the new province, Claudius Severus.[26] The three points that bear upon this issue do not allow an easy answer. First, Petra received from Trajan the honorific title of Metropolis, which it already displays in a Greek inscription from 114 AD.[27] Second, the legion was clearly based at Bostra, where its camp has been identified. Third, a Nabataean inscription dates the era of the new province with the anomalous expression "year three of the eparch [governor] of Bostra."[28] The first item might well suggest that the governor sat in Petra, but the second and third would naturally put him in Bostra (in the place of the late Rabbel). Since Severus was both commander of the legion and governor of the province at the same time, the argument for Bostra would appear more compelling, particularly since there is no doubt that from the mid-second century onwards Bostra was indisputably the seat of the governor.

The transition from kingdom to province subjected the homeland of the Nabataeans to Roman jurisdiction, but an extraordinary collection of private documents from the Judaean desert shows that daily life in the region was not dramatically altered for those who lived there.[29] A Jewish woman called Babatha, who lived peaceably together with the Nabataeans in a settlement south of the Dead Sea, was involved in considerable petty litigation over property and multiple husbands throughout a period that extended from the last decade of Rabbel into the third decade of the province. The language of the documents changes from Nabataean to Greek as a result of the new government, and oaths that once had to be sworn in the name of the king had later to be sworn in the name of the Roman emperor. But the mixed society of the area is everywhere apparent in the whole range of the documents, with signatories writing in Nabataean and Greek. Both the cities of Petra and Rabbathmoba appear as venues for hearings and judgment, but there is no indication as to where the governor was normally established. Babatha's precious documents were hidden away when she took refuge in the Judaean hills during the revolt of Bar Kokhba. Knowledge of her cruel and miserable end in a cave gives poignancy to the mundane, if vexing, legal problems that seemed to have pursued her in her lifetime. No ancient archive provides such eloquent and abundant testimony to a multicultural, multiethnic, multilingual society.

In the current excavations at the so-called Great Temple on the south side of the main street in Petra, a fragment of a monumental Latin inscription with an evident piece of imperial titulature suggested to its editor that this was a commemoration of the emperor who turned the Nabataean kingdom into a province.[30] Since Trajan made the city a metropolis, this is not an unreasonable supposition. But fresh evidence from the vicinity of the Qasr al-Bint, the greatest of the Nabataean temples in the city, would imply another emperor in the second century. A fragment of a large Greek inscription records the titulature of Lucius Verus, and a head of that ruler's father has turned up in the same area as well.[31] (fig. 8) Verus was a potent presence in the Near East at the time of his ambitious Parthian campaign. The dedication of the temple in Ruwwafa in the formerly Nabataean territory of the Hijaz was carried out under the auspices of the governor of Arabia at precisely the time of Verus's presence in the East.[32] The surviving inscription, with its reference to the governor's role, is proof that this southernmost part of the old Nabataean kingdom had been included in the new province. It illustrates the enthusiastic response of the local population to the imperial intiative against Parthia. A similar recognition of Verus's presence is implied by a Palmyrene inscription concerning the imperial cult.[33] For Petra to have joined in these commemorations makes excellent sense, and in view of the inscription and head at the Qasr it might be reasonable to associate the fragment of the grandiose Latin text with Verus rather than Trajan.

8. Marble portrait of Aelius Caesar, Petra. h: 50 cm. Department of Antiquities, Amman, Jordan.

It might have been at this time that some dramatic changes

9. Theatron. Great Temple, Petra.

were made along the south side of the main street of Petra in the enigmatic complex where that Latin text was found. What had long seemed to be a temple with a large forecourt suddenly turns into a theater for some six hundred people or so (fig. 9).[34] The excavators have documented the building of seats and proscenium, facing north. The theater area of the supposed temple has produced sculpted masks and astonishing column capitals with elephants (p. 219, figs. 236, 237).[35] It has now become difficult to interpret the whole complex as a temple, since it would be implausible to postulate an abrupt secularization of a sacred space. Furthermore, the area adjacent to the complex on the east appears to have been provisioned with water. Although a garden or *paradeisos* of some kind has been suggested,[36] a better possibility might be a pool for the celebration of the Maioumas water festival that enjoyed such popularity in the East. The recent discovery of a pool for this purpose (as guaranteed by an inscription naming a Maioumarch) could provide an interesting parallel.[37] In any case, the Great Temple looks more and more like a secular building, perhaps even the site of the litigation for which Babatha's documents provide such moving testimony.

The distinctively Nabataean contribution to life in the province of Arabia becomes increasingly hard to make out, as the evidence for the Roman military and administrative presence proliferates. But from time to time we catch a stunning glimpse of this local culture thriving under Roman rule and participating in its international culture. Recent excavations of the Petra church have brought to light a magnificent vase (*cantharus*) in Phrygian marble with handles in the form of panthers standing on their hind legs to peer into the interior of the vase.[38] (figs. 6, 7) This luxurious object, imported from Asia Minor, evokes the cult of Dionysus, for whom the panther was a favorite companion. Of all the Greek divinities Dionysus was arguably the most popular and widespread in the Semitic Near East. The Petra cantharus, from the late second or early third centuries, was clearly a treasured object and later took its place in the nave of the Christian church. Its Dionysiac associations were easily submerged in its service of providing water for the faithful.

Arab emperors often understandably provided the inspiration for a reassertion of Nabataean character and language. Under Elagabalus, for example, the city of Areopolis (Rabba) suddenly proclaims itself on its coinage as Arsapolis, reviving the Arabic name of the deity Arsu, with whom Ares had been identified.[39] Under Philip the Arab the coinage of Bostra represents an anthropomorphic Dusares, who had traditionally been worshipped in an aniconic form, and the image is clearly that of a Nabataean, with curly locks and eastern profile.[40] It is only a little after this that we find the cult of the deified king Obodas, who ruled centuries before, revived at the old Nabataean center of 'Avdat in the Negev.[41] An inscription from the early fourth century produces for the first time since the graffito in the Negev a text in Arabic written in Nabataean script.[42] The last surviving Nabataean inscription dates from 356 in the mid-fourth century, at a time when a tantalizing item in Epiphanius's *Panarion* records a Nabataean religious ceremony celebrating the infant Dusares in an Arabic liturgy.[43]

The notice in Epiphanius might have alerted us to the continuity of Nabataean culture in the later fourth century, but the devastating earthquake of 363, which put an end to Julian's plan to rebuild the Jewish temple, has been traditionally seen as the death knell of Petra and the Nabataeans. The excavation of a Christian church on the northern side of the colonnaded street at Petra changed all that through the sensational discovery of a cache of approximately 150 carbonized papyrus rolls.[44] When these were expertly opened, the documents were seen to contain details of property and people at Petra in the middle of the sixth century. It became immediately obvious that the city, perhaps with a diminished population, was still a vigorous community in touch with its Nabataean past. Names such as Obodianus and Dusarios evoked a distant king (Obodas) and the principal deity of the Nabataeans (Dusares). The greater Arab world in the region is reflected in the name of a woman, Thaaious.[45] The standard Syriac term for nomadic Arabs in late antiquity was *tayyaye,* which Libanius had reproduced in Greek as *Taienoi*.[46] It was the local equivalent of the Graeco-Roman term Saracen. The woman in Petra may be presumed to have been an Arab of non-Nabataean stock.

Another new discovery reinforces the impression from the papyri that Petra was still thriving in the sixth century. A ten-line verse inscription in Greek, which manages to squeeze the name of the province of Palaestina Salutaris into dactylic hexameters, celebrates a local benefactor for building walls.[47] The commemoration is not merely in verse, but in Homeric verse, with an obvious borrowing from the opening lines of the *Odyssey*. So Hellenism too was alive and well in the old Nabataean capital.

By raising the curtain on late antique Petra we can now see, for the first time, the historical context in which the late Greek historian Uranius composed his work on the Arabs under the title *Arabica*.[48] This writer was highly esteemed by Stephanus of Byzantium, who comments on his admirable character as well as his writings and therefore perhaps knew him personally. He appears to have been writing in the sixth century and to have taken a special interest in the history of the Nabataeans. He knew about the cult of the old king Obodas, and he is familiar with the name *Taienos/Taïnos* for Saracen. Perhaps the most startling item among all the fragments of Uranius is his statement that the name of the eponym of the Nabataeans, *Nabates*, means in Arabic a person born out of wedlock. This betrays accurate knowledge of the Arabic use of the word Nabataean to mean a bastard or, more generally, a despicable person.

Such intimate knowledge of Arabic suggests that Uranius's *Arabica* must have been a work of exceptional erudition, and in fact the surviving fragments all demonstrate an unusual familiarity with Arab customs, toponyms, and onomastics. The late antique Petra that has lately seen the light of day for the first time in a millennium and a half must have been a place that Uranius would have known well. His *Arabica* from the sixth century AD marked the terminus and summation of the Nabataean culture that had dawned in history some eight hundred years before.

2 | The Origins and Emergence of the Nabataeans

PETER J. PARR

FROM AT LEAST AS EARLY AS the second century BC until the beginning of the second century AD a large part of what is now southern Jordan and Israel, together with the northwest corner of Saudi Arabia, was ruled from the city of Petra by a succession of kings who called themselves kings of the Nabatu (*Nbṭw*), a name that contemporary Greek historians translated as Ναβαταίοι and we as Nabataeans. Archaeological evidence indicates that these people lived in numerous towns and villages throughout this region, gaining a livelihood from the exploitation of the land, which they terraced and irrigated to support a thriving agriculture, and also—and perhaps primarily—from international trade, especially in aromatics from South Arabia, which they helped to convey to Egypt and the Levant. By the beginning of the second century BC, they were carving inscriptions in a distinct form of the Aramaic language and script, while their autonomous coinage—a sure sign of political maturity and sophistication—was first minted about a century later. The capital itself, Petra (called by themselves Reqem), which had been settled already in the third century BC, was important enough in 129 BC to have been visited by an ambassador from Priene in distant Asia Minor. The earliest evidence for the rock-hewn monuments which are the most famous remains of Petra comes from the first decade of the first century BC. Although much remains uncertain about the chronology of the city's urban development, it must have been during the following years that it gradually assumed much of the appearance it presents today, and there is no reason to question the description given of it by the Greek author Strabo (*Geography,* 16.4.21-26) toward the end of the century as a magnificent, wealthy, cosmopolitan city inhabited by people who took great pride in their wealth and possessions and appreciated to the full the benefits of urban civilisation.

10. Camel caravan, oasis of Madā'in Ṣāliḥ (ancient Hegra), Saudi Arabia.

Yet barely three centuries before, at the end of the fourth century BC, the ancestors of these people had been described by another Greek writer, Hieronymus of Cardia, in very different terms. Hieronymus—whose account, unfortunately, is known only from a summary in the *Universal History* (2.48-49; 19.94-100) of Diodorus Siculus, compiled three centuries later—had probably taken part in raids against the Nabataeans[1] instigated by Antigonus Monophthalmus in 312 BC, when the Macedonian army had twice attacked their stronghold, "a certain rock (πέτρα)," which for obvious reasons is generally identified with the later Nabataean capital of Petra.[2] He had also served the same king as governor of the Dead Sea region, and his account of the Nabataeans has thus generally been accepted as being based on firsthand knowledge. The Ναβαταίοι, he tells us, were an Arab people living in "the eastern parts" of a region which he locates between Syria and Egypt. They were entirely nomadic, wandering with their flocks of sheep and camels through a countryside which was "partly desert, partly waterless, though a small section [was] fruitful," but resorting from time to time to brigandage and raiding their neighbors. They eschewed agriculture and permanent settlements of houses, which they judged made them more likely to be subjugated by others. Their diet consisted of meat and such edible wild plants as they could find, and they drank milk and a concoction of wild honey and water, totally avoiding wine. Anyone found contravening these customs could be punished by death. Unlike other nomadic tribes in the region they were reported to be skilled in the construction of underground cisterns, which enabled them, uniquely, to retreat far into the desert with their flocks in times of danger. They were also unlike other tribes in respect of their exceptional wealth, owing to the fact that "not a few of them" traded in the valuable aromatics, incense and myrrh, which they obtained from that part of Arabia "which is called Fortunate"—that is, the south. They also exported the asphalt thrown up from the Dead Sea. It can be assumed that some of them, at least, were literate in Aramaic, the lingua franca of the day, since, although Hieronymus does not explicitly say so, he does report that in 312 BC they wrote to the Greeks "in Syrian letters" when they tried to persuade the enemy to leave them in peace. Their negotiations with the Greek army makes it clear that, despite their wealth, they were not attracted by sedentary civilization, preferring to retain the freedom and independence which they believed only a nomadic existence could guarantee.[3]

Hieronymus's account is the essential, in fact the only, starting point for any investigation into what may be called the proto-history of the Nabataeans, and it is unfortunate that legitimate doubts can be entertained regarding its reliability, despite its apparent immediacy. It has been argued that it reads in many respects very like the stereotypical portrait of the nomad, sometimes laudatory, sometimes disparaging, often found in ancient literature, for example in the Old Testament with respect to the Rekabites, and it has also been pointed out that neither Hieronymus himself nor Diodorus were the most careful or critical of historians, judging from what is known about other episodes in their writings.[4] In view of these observations, as well as on grounds of sheer common sense, it would be unwise to take every comment made by Hieronymus at face value. It might thus be wondered whether he did not exaggerate, for the sake of a good story, their aversion to settled life or the uniqueness of their water-conservation methods, and caution should certainly be used in accepting such things as his estimate of their numbers ("hardly more than 10,000"). Yet the fact that Hieronymus refers also to other nomadic groups who, unlike the Nabataeans, did cultivate the soil and, apart from their lack of permanent dwellings, lived "like Syrians," suggests that he was attempting to give an honestly balanced and not simply a conventionalized picture of the situation. The details he records concerning the Dead Sea bitumen have also been shown to be substantially correct.[5] There is thus no strong reason to doubt the essential accuracy of his account, which accords passably well with what is known of northern Arabian nomads from somewhat earlier sources, particularly representations on Neo-Assyrian reliefs.

There is, then, a general consensus that by the end of the fourth century BC the Nabataeans were present as nomadic pastoralists and traders in the country on both sides of the Wadi Araba south of the Dead Sea and in northwest Arabia, which, a few centuries later, was to become the heartland of their nation-state. However, whether this was their original homeland or whether they had migrated here from elsewhere, and if so when, are matters on which much has been written, despite—or perhaps because of—the lack of evidence. Several points are relevant. To begin with, if we are to believe Hieronymus's statement that the Nabataeans were already engaged in trading in bitumen from the Dead Sea, some period of time must be allowed for their occupation of the region to have become established by the end of the fourth century BC, although how long a time can only be conjectured. It is also clear from later evidence concerning Nabataean religion that over the course of time they developed a particular attachment to the region, since one of their principal deities, if not actually the head of their pantheon, was Dushara (= "The One of Shara"), who (it is generally assumed) took his name from the Jebel esh-Shara, the limestone plateau which overlooks the Petra basin from the east (fig. 11).[6] But again, it is impossible to tell how long this territorial attachment would have taken to form. A clue has been sought in Herodotus (*Histories,* III, 8), who, when visiting Egypt in the mid-fifth century BC and reporting what he had been told of the religion of the (presumably neighboring) "Arabians," writes that their female deity was called Alilat. This is undoubtedly a Greek rendering of al-Ilat "The Goddess," and it has often been suggested that, since the use of the prefixed definite article *al-* is a feature of Nabataean Arabic, distinguishing it from other north-Arabian dialects which use the suffix *-han*, Herodotus's fifth-century Arabs should already be identified as Nabataeans or at least as proto-Nabataeans.[7] But Herodotus does not mention Dushara; he reports that the Arabs worshipped only two deities, and that the male was named Orotalt. This might imply that Herodotus's Arabs were not Nabataeans, or that if they were, they had not been present in the region of the Jebel esh-Shara long enough for them to establish any particular association with it and its god. Supporting this view is the fact that the name of the Arab male deity recorded by Herodotus, Orotalt, is probably a Greek form of Ruḍa, a deity well known from elsewhere in northern Arabia but never mentioned in the Nabataean inscriptions; although, in answer to this and to confuse matters further, it has also been argued that Orotalt and Dushara were in fact one and the same deity, the former being the "personal" name and the latter simply an anonymous descriptive title which eventually replaced it.[8] Axel Knauf may well be justified in calling Herodotus's Arabs "Proto-Nabataeans," but the evidence is by no means conclusive.

The same may be said of the search for Nabataean origins further afield, away from their later heartland south of the Dead Sea. Since Hieronymus's description of them as Arabs

11. Jebel esh-Shara (western edge of the Jordanian limestone plateau) overlooking Petra.

has been borne out to the satisfaction of most authorities by the evidence of their personal names, this search has been directed mainly towards the Arabian Peninsula. There is nothing inherently impossible about the migration of Arab tribes over long distances within the peninsula and beyond, there being much information from more recent times to prove that this happened. However, in the case of the Nabataeans, convincing evidence is lacking. Some early writers, such as Nelson Glueck,[9] assumed that both the skills in water conservation which were attributed to them already in the fourth century BC and their later well-known proficiency in art and architecture must have been learned in south Arabia, where urban civilization had flourished for many centuries, and that their ultimate origins must therefore be sought in this direction. Yet there is in fact little if anything in the "classic" Nabataean material culture of the second century BC onwards which has specifically south Arabian characteristics; it is primarily and obviously of Hellenistic-Roman inspiration, and what is not can easily be accounted for by later Nabataean commercial and thus cultural contact with the centers of ancient oriental civilizations in Mesopotamia, Egypt, and Syria. As for water conservation, it is now known that this was practiced in the north of the Arabian Peninsula before the emergence of the Nabataeans, as we shall see. Neither is there anything in the religion or language of the Nabataeans to suggest direct south Arabian influence; none of the major south Arabian deities are found in the Nabataean pantheon, while there are basic features of the Arabic dialect spoken by the Nabataeans, such as the use of the prefixed definite article *al-* already mentioned, which make it quite unlike the Arabic of the kingdoms of the Yemen.

Attempts to find a Nabataean "original homeland" in the northeast corner of the peninsula, near the coast of the Arabian Gulf, have been also unconvincing. J. Milik,[10] for instance, has located there a place called Saʿbu (*Sʿbw*), which, on the grounds that in a Palmyrene inscription a "god of Sa bu" is termed "the Fortune God of the Nabataeans," he claims must have been an original Nabataean cult center. However, his argument for locating the site in northeastern Arabia rests upon a reading of certain passages in Strabo and Ptolemy which, as David Graf has pointed out,[11] involves too many textual emendations and gratuitous assumptions to be persuasive. Graf himself, however, has recently stated that the Nabataean homeland "was in the region of northeastern Arabia adjacent to the Persian Gulf"[12] and (slightly differently) that "the Mesopotamian region is where the search for Nabataean origins must begin." His discussion is complex, but his main argument seems to be that Nabataean proper names, although Arabic, are spelled in accordance with the rules of early Aramaic orthography, the use of the nominative suffix *-w* (*-u*, as in Nabatu) being the prime example. Recalling that the Neo-Assyrian annals of the eighth and seventh centuries BC refer to Aramaean and Arab tribes living side-by-side in southern Mesopotamia, he concludes that there is at least a "possibility that the Arabic dialect used by the Nabataeans crystallized during the period of imperial Aramaic and in the Syrian-Mesopotamian region." It was therefore "along [the east-west] Trans-Arabian route that the Nabataeans must have originally migrated from Mesopotamia to their new western homeland at Petra."[13] He is thus inclined to support the old theory that the Nabataeans (Nabatu) are to be identified with the Nabayati of the Assyrian records and the Nebaioth of the Old Testament, although he recognizes that this is controversial.[14] Few philological specialists would agree with Graf's interpretations. J. Healey, for example, writes that although the "most distinctive type of [Nabataean] name with final *-w* (*-u* or *-o*) is somewhat enigmatic... [it] is neither an Arabic nor an Aramaean feature,"[15] while M. Macdonald avers that "the *-u* and *-i* case endings are never found in Aramaic of any period."[16] As for the identity of Nabataeans and Nabayati/Nebaioth, this theory is now almost universally rejected on the grounds that Nabaṭu is spelled with an emphatic ṭ and Nabayati/Nebaioth is not, while Nabayati/Nebaioth has an additional vowel *y* that Nabaṭu lacks.[17] It must be concluded that, despite the imaginative efforts of Milik and Graf, there is as little hard evidence for seeing an original Nabataean homeland near the eastern end of the Fertile Crescent as there is for locating it in the south of the peninsula.

This preoccupation with ultimate Nabataean origins has been unfortunate as well as abortive, since it has diverted attention from two much more profound and interesting questions concerning their early history, namely, why and how the nomads of Hieronymus became the urbanites of Strabo. The answers to these questions must surely lie in the southern Levant and in northwestern Arabia, since it is safe to assume that, whatever distant homeland, if any, the Nabataeans may have had, the processes of sedentarization and urbanization they experienced must have taken place in the region which was to become the core of their realm. But before addressing these questions we should consider the geography of the area, especially those aspects which might have had a bearing on the subject.

Broadly speaking the region can be divided into two very different zones, the limestone uplands of southern Jordan and the northern Negev on the one hand, and the igneous and sandstone mountains of northwestern Arabia (the Hejaz) and Sinai to the south (figs. 13, 14); it is tempting to see in this diversity the factual basis of the distinctions made by

Above: **12.** Village and cultivation on the western scarp of the Jordanian plateau.

13. View of the Hisma (the beginning of the sandstone region) from the southern scarp of the Jordanian plateau.

Hieronymus in his description, quoted above, of the Nabataean countryside.[18] Although much of the limestone region consists of inhospitable stony desert, the highest parts receive up to 500 mm (20 in) annual rainfall, sufficient to supply numerous perennial springs, particularly along the western edge of the Jordan plateau, where the mountains are broken by wadis draining into the Dead Sea–Araba rift and where, with sufficient moisture, the limestone weathers into a rich fertile soil admirably suited for the cultivation of cereals, fruits, and vegetables, if only on a small scale. In contrast, the rugged sandstones and crystalline rocks of the Hejaz and Sinai, interspersed with sand dunes and gravel plains and often overlaid with lava flows, give rise to spectacular scenery but make communications difficult and produce little in the way of cultivable soils. The little precipitation that falls—generally less than 100 mm (4 in) a year—is mostly lost through flash floods, the waters of which can only be utilized at the mouths of the tortuous wadis which spill out onto the narrow coastal plain of the Red Sea and the Gulf of Aqaba or into the depressions and broader valleys of the interior, where they are trapped by the sandy and clayey alluvial deposits and can be reached by wells and *qanats* or by diversion dams. These two different environments give rise to two different patterns of settlement. On the more fertile western edge of the Jordanian plateau (fig. 12), and in the northern Negev a network of small interdependent communities—towns, villages, and farmsteads—can flourish under favorable political conditions, while even the drier stony desert has sufficient steppe vegetation in the winter months to make it attractive to pastoralists. In the Hejaz and Sinai, on the other hand, communities of any permanent nature are restricted to a few coastal or inland oases, irregularly distributed and relatively isolated one from the other, and devoid of any supporting hinterland of smaller settlements.[19] The camel nomad can gain a living here, of course, as in the limestone country, and pastoralism is one of the things which unites the populations and economies of the two zones, as is the fact that both are strategically placed athwart the trade routes from south Arabia to the Mediterranean coastlands. They thus have much in common; yet the fact remains that whereas Sinai and the Hejaz are primarily the home of the camel nomad, the limestone uplands are more the home of the peasant.

During the centuries immediately preceding Hieronymus's visit to the area these environmentally different zones had experienced different, though related, histories. Following a long period of abandonment, southern Jordan and the northern Negev had been gradually resettled during the early part of the first millennium BC, and—although the chronology is much disputed—it seems likely that by the end of the ninth century, a nation-state—the kingdom of Edom—had been established east of the Wadi Araba.[20] At the same time the Negev was coming increasingly under the control of the kingdom of Judah. Following the westward expansion of the Assyrian empire in the mid-eighth century BC Edom lost some of its independence and became to some degree a vassal state, though whether there was actually an Assyrian administrative and military presence on the ground is uncertain. Certainly the region profited from the political stability which the proximity of Assyria brought, and the economy—based on farming, the Arabian trade, and the exploitation of the Araba copper mines—flourished. Edomite tribute flowed into the imperial treasury, and the population must have grown, since it was probably at this time that the Edomites began to spread westwards across the Araba and settle in the Negev. However, the replacement of the Assyrian empire by that of the Babylonians in the final years of the seventh century BC signaled an end to this fortunate state of affairs. The fall of the kingdom of Judah to Nebuchadnezzar in 587 BC was followed five years later by that of Edom's northern neighbor, Moab, and although Edom itself survived another generation, it too was destroyed in 552 BC by his successor Nabonidus. The devastation caused by the Babylonian armies in southern Jordan may not have been as catastrophic as had been predicted by the Old Testament prophets, and some few centers of population seem to have survived at places such as Tawilan, overlooking Petra, and Tell el-Kheleifeh, at the head of the Gulf of Aqaba, throughout the sixth and perhaps into the fifth century BC. Those Edomites who had settled west of the Araba, in the towns of southern Judah, also probably survived. Nevertheless, the evidence from extensive archaeological surveys leaves little room to doubt that these were the exceptions, and that there must have been considerable economic collapse throughout Edom as a result of the Babylonian action.[21] The population did not disappear overnight, of course, and many of the inhabitants may well have adopted pastoralism and remained; some may even have migrated to neighboring regions, such as Judah or into Arabia.[22] But whatever the details, it is clear that during the time when the region south of the Dead Sea was nominally part of the Persian empire, between 539 BC and 332 BC, it was largely devoid of sedentary occupation.

The history of the Hejaz at this time seems to have been very different from that of Edom.[23] For the ninth–seventh centuries BC, the period of the establishment and flourishing of the Edomite kingdom, there is as yet no archaeological or literary evidence to indicate permanent settlement in northern Arabia. The Assyrians were certainly active in the region, and their annals record both the diplomatic contacts and the military campaigns which were deemed necessary to control the inhabitants and secure the payment of tribute. The reliefs to which reference has already been made relate to these episodes, but it is noteworthy that none of them show the Arabs as anything other than nomads, pasturing their sheep, tending their camels, managing caravans, and living in tents. In the light of this it is not surprising to find that, although tribal centers, groups, and leaders are mentioned in the texts, nowhere is there any indication of agricultural activities or sedentary occupation, let alone urbanization. Judging from the Assyrian evidence, the inhabitants of northern Arabia in the earlier part of the first millennium BC were very much as Hieronymous was to describe the Nabataeans a few centuries later, and it is, of course, partly owing to this similarity that the false identification of the Nabataeans with the Assyria Nabayati, referred to above, once seemed so convincing.

Following the destruction of Edom in 552 BC Nabonidus continued his campaign into Arabia, and it is now that we get our first indication that conditions there were changing. The Babylonian king is reported to have attacked a number of centers, including Tayma and Dedan (modern al-'Ula) (fig. 15), two of the most fertile oases in the region. The ruler of Tayma was killed, and the wording of the text perhaps implies that there already was some sort of settlement there. If not, there was soon to be, for Nabonidus claims to have fortified the site and embellished it, notably with a palace comparable to that of Babylon itself. He then proceeded to settle there, and for ten years Tayma was effectively the seat of government of the Babylonian empire.[24] Unfortunately nothing more is known for certain of the Babylonian town of Tayma from either the literary or archaeological sources; it is particularly disappointing that no part of the extensive defensive walls which surround the oasis today can securely be attributed to Nabonidus. That it continued as an important urban center throughout the sixth and fifth centuries BC, when northern Arabia was at least to some degree under the control of Persian governors, is clear. Recent excavations have uncovered buildings, including a shrine, dated to this period, and—although proof of this is presently lacking—it is probable that parts of the defensive walls and of the irrigated field systems which surround the site are contemporary (unless, indeed, they owe their existence to Nabonidus). Most important are the epigraphic finds from the fifth or early fourth century BC, including two stelae with dedicatory texts in Imperial Aramaic, in which both Mesopotamian and Egyptian names occur, associated with religious sculpture displaying a similar cosmopolitan mixture of iconographic detail.

A slightly more complete account, based on the many short inscriptions inscribed on the rocks surrounding the site, can be given of the history of Dedan, situated in one of the most fertile valleys of the Hejaz. It was probably already a flourishing caravan center when Nabonidus attacked it, since the references in the books of Isaiah and Ezekiel to its trading links with Tyre, on the distant coast of Phoenicia, date to around this time. Its status under the Babylonian empire is unknown, but following the latter's demise in 539 BC it seems likely that an independent Dedanite kingdom emerged. In the middle of the fifth century BC a governor of Dedan is mentioned, though whether a governor acting on behalf of the Persian rulers or on that of a more local king (perhaps that of Tayma) is unclear. But by about 400 BC another independent—or semi-independent—kingdom, called in the inscriptions that of Lihyan, had formed, and it was under its aegis that a colony of Minaean merchants from south Arabia made its appearance in the oasis, bringing with it the worship of Wadd, the Minaean national god, as well as other elements of South Arabian culture. Minaean traders were also active at this time in Egypt, and it is reasonable to suppose that the two groups, those in northwestern Arabia and those in the Nile valley, were in contact with one another across the Red Sea. Relations between the two regions certainly seem to have existed a lttle later, following the fall of the Persian Empire in 332 BC and its replacement in Egypt by the Greek Ptolemaic dynasty. Ptolemy II is known to have promoted the Red Sea trade at the beginning of the third century BC, and there are strong hints of Egyptian political and cultural influence at Dedan. Statuary of obvious Egyptian inspiration has been found there and it is possible that the name "Tulmay" borne by two of the Lihyanite kings is a form of the Greek dynastic name. The Egyptian rulers may well have wanted to support the Lihyanite rulers of Dedan, in the face of the rising power of the Nabataeans, just beginning to occupy Petra, on the same trade route further north.

When Hieronymus encountered the Nabataeans towards the end of the fourth century BC, therefore, the situation he found would have been as follows. The country around "The Rock" (whether that was indeed Petra or a comparable stronghold east or west of the Araba) would have been devoid of settled communities, although descendants of the Edomites might well have still been pasturing their flocks, and if there had been any intermarriage there might well have been Edomite blood flowing in Nabataean veins. Whether any element of Edomite culture survived strongly enough to have influenced the Nabataean nomads is, however, extremely doubtful. It is true that the name of the Edomite national deity, Qaws, is found in Nabataean texts, and it is often argued that this implies direct Edomite-Nabataean contact,[25] but the name is probably of Arabian origin and his veneration wider than just in Edom, and the Nabataeans may well have encountered him in

14. Sandstone mountains in the Hejaz, northwestern Arabia.

below: **15.** Oasis of al-ʿUla (ancient Dedan), northwestern Arabia.

Arabia.[26] It is also noticeable that no trace of the Edomite dialect of the seventh–sixth centuries BC (a close relative of the contemporary Hebrew) is found in the Nabataean language, and the same must be said of Edomite and Nabataean material culture—nothing links them. Much stronger evidence must be adduced before it is possible to claim that Edomite influence on the Nabataeans was anything other than minimal.[27]

Things were different in the south. In the course of controlling their caravans and tending their flocks the Nabataeans would perforce have spent much of their time amongst the barren mountains and deserts of the Hejaz, but they must also have visited on business the cosmopolitan trading centers of Tayma and Dedan (and possibly others of which nothing yet is known)[28] which, as we have seen, were established towns, with defensive walls, public buildings, monumental sculpture and inscriptions, and (probably) irrigation technology. The Nabataeans must also have been acquainted with the royal houses and political organization of these towns, and would have had contact with the foreign merchants who resided there. The "caravan cities" of Tayma and Dedan and the small kingdoms that surrounded them must have played a large part in the Nabataeans' lives, and it certainly cannot be supposed that their negative attitude towards sedentary "civilization," as reported by Hieronymus, was based on ignorance.

What made them change their minds and, within a few generations, follow the example of their Taymanite, Dedanite, and Lihyanite predecessors, succumbing to the attractions of urban life and dynastic government? Although in the absence of written sources it is unlikely that we shall ever know the full answer, certain things can safely be said. First is the somewhat paradoxical fact that nomadic pastoral communities often exhibit a considerable degree of social cohesion and, indeed, political centralization, necessary for regulating pasturage rights and avoiding conflicts with neighbors.[29] These tendencies would have certainly been enhanced in the case of the "not a few" Nabataeans engaged in the organization of trade. Hieronymus's words hint at social and wealth stratification in Nabataean society, and the existence of the "rock" where they left their possessions for safety suggests that already by the late fourth century BC they had laid claim to a specific "national" center. A stronghold was presumably initially required as protection from local dangers, but the role it played in the events of 312 BC indicates another, and more important, factor in the formation of the Nabataean state. In the late fourth century the Nabataeans faced actual or potential external threat from two directions. The first, that of the Macedonians, was repulsed, but must have made the Nabataeans aware that conditions to the north of their territory were changing, and that the vacuum left by the destruction of the kingdoms of Edom and Judah, never adequately filled by the Persian administration, was now coming to an end as the emerging Hellenistic states sought to pursue their ambitions in the region, amongst which, of course, would be to bring the Arabian trade under their control. But the political scene had changed in the south also, following the establishment of Greek rule in Egypt, and the potential threat from this direction became a reality in 278 BC, when Ptolemy II raided the Nabataeans east of the Gulf of Aqaba in retaliation for their plundering of Egyptian shipping. Such threats must have made the Nabataeans aware of their vulnerability, and could only have encouraged the tendency towards greater centralization of leadership and the emergence of a political and military elite, most likely the members of one particularly able and ambitious family. But at the same time the stability which the new Hellenistic order brought to the eastern Mediterranean region encouraged trade and so increased Nabataean wealth. Not only the protection but also the utilization of that burgeoning wealth would have exercised Nabataean minds, and what more natural than that they should have begun to invest it in those things which previously they had held in contempt?

Seen in an Arabian perspective the settlement of the once-nomadic Nabataeans is just one more example of a process which had been characteristic of the region over the previous centuries; Petra was as normal an Arabian phenomenon as was Tayma and Dedan. But it also obviously became something very different from Tayma and Dedan, and this for two reasons. The first is its location. Petra lies on the very edge of Arabia, just below the escarpment of the limestone plateau which the Arab geographers called the "brow of Syria." As already mentioned, the escarpment is fertile compared with the Hejaz, and well suited to agriculture, and probably well before the beginning of the Christian Era the Nabataeans had established farming villages all over what is now southern Jordan and the Negev, repopulating the abandoned kingdom of Edom. They were thus no longer dependent upon the incense trade or the products of pastoralism; economically they had moved away from their Arabian background and become Levantine. And the second reason relates to time. Between the time when Tayma and Dedan were settled and Petra was settled, the Near East had become Hellenized. The Taymanites, the Dedanites, and the Lihyanites had absorbed and adopted foreign fashions, but they were the fashions of Mesopotamia and south Arabia. When, in the first century BC, the Nabataeans looked outside the confines of Petra for inspiration for the material culture that they now desired and could afford, it was above all in the Hellenized world that they found what they needed.

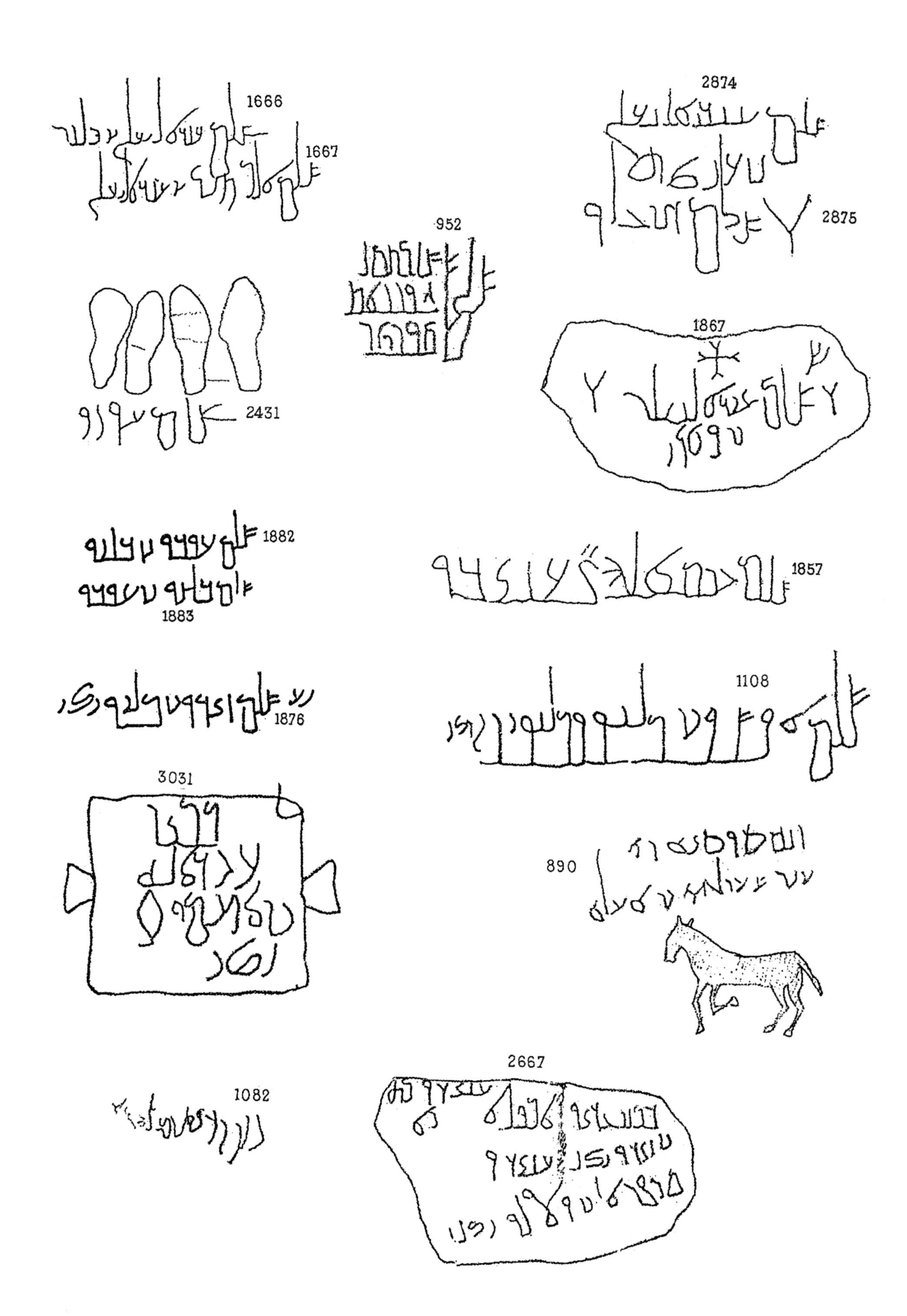
1666
1667
2874
2875
952
1867
2431
1882
1883
1857
1876
1108
3031
890
1082
2667

3 | Languages, Scripts, and the Uses of Writing among the Nabataeans

M.C.A. MACDONALD

SOMETIME IN THE MID-SIXTH CENTURY AD, an Alexandrian merchant, known to history as Cosmas Indicopleustes, was traveling through the Sinai Peninsula when he noticed that many of the rocks were covered with writing, in a script which he took to be Hebrew (fig 16).[1] These inscriptions excited his curiosity, and after copying some and having them "translated"—alas rather inaccurately—he decided that they must be graffiti carved by the Children of Israel during their forty years in the Wilderness. From this, he reasoned that the script must be the God-given primeval alphabet in which the Israelites had received the Ten Commandments on Mount Sinai and from which, he thought, all other alphabets were derived. He would have been surprised to learn that these inscriptions were in fact no more than three or four centuries old when he saw them and that their authors were not the Israelites of the Exodus but, for the most part, the pagan inhabitants of the Sinai in the Roman period. However, unlike many later writers, he was at least correct in identifying the texts as graffiti.

Although innumerable travelers and pilgrims in the Sinai must have noticed these inscriptions in subsequent centuries, it was more than a thousand years before they are mentioned again in surviving records, this time in the works of seventeenth-century European travelers. From then on, there were numerous speculations as to who had written them and what they might say but, though many copies were published, the script remains undeciphered and unidentified.

It was only in 1818 that the English traveler W. J. Bankes made the first copy of an inscription at Petra, in southern Jordan. With great perceptiveness, he immediately connected the script of this beautiful monumental text (fig. 17) with that of the roughly pecked graffiti in the Sinai (fig. 16) which he had seen and copied three years earlier, and suggested that both were the work of the Nabataeans.[2]

16. Graffiti from Sinai in the "Nabataean" script. All numbers refer to the texts in CIS 2.

Unfortunately, Bankes never published his copy of the Petra inscription nor his speculations about it and so it was not until 1840 that the connection between the Nabataeans and the graffiti in the Sinai was finally suggested in print.[3] This was the work of the brilliant young German scholar E. E. F. Beer, who produced a virtually complete decipherment of the script and an extraordinarily accurate analysis of the content and background of the texts. To the shame of the scholarly community of his day, "he died of starvation and neglect, just as [his monograph] had acquired celebrity enough to procure him aid too late."[4]

It was not until twenty years later that M. A. Levy, following the publication of new texts, was able to show palaeographical connections between the script of the graffiti in the Sinai, and the scripts used in texts at Petra and the Aramaic inscriptions of the Hauran (southern Syria).[5] Then, in the 1880s, Charles Doughty returned from a journey in northwest Arabia with many copies of inscriptions, some of which were immediately recognized as being in a script similar to those which were by this time known as "Nabataean."[6]

Since then, almost 6,000 texts on stone in similar scripts have been found in Arabia, Jordan, and Syria, as well as in the Negev, in the Sinai, in Egypt,[7] and as far away as the Greek islands and southern Italy.[8] In addition, several papyri bearing Nabataean writing by both scribes and non-scribes, have been found in caves near the Dead Sea.[9] Finally, a few fragments of plaster bearing writing in ink or paint have been excavated,[10] as well as a handful of informal texts written in ink on potsherds or pebbles.[11]

Unfortunately, this large body of writing represents a very narrow range of content. For example, we have no Nabataean literary, philosophical, or scholarly texts; no codes of laws, religious liturgies or scriptures, no historical annals, administrative

17

18

20

19

17. The inscription on the Turkmaniyah Tomb, Petra, thought to be mid-first century AD. See fig. 38.5.

18. The earliest inscription so far found in Petra. A dedication by Aṣlaḥ son of Aṣlaḥ, dated to the first year of Obodat I, c. 96/95 BC. See fig. 38.4.

19. A fragment of a Nabataean inscription from Petra dated to year 18 of Aretas IV [= 10 AD] commemorating the construction of buildings at Petra by a commander of cavalry "for the life of" King Aretas, his queen, Hagarū, and their children. Department of Antiquities, Amman, Jordan.

20. Signature ("May Aṣlaḥ be safe and sound") carved on a rock-face on the route between the Deir plateau and the small High Place at Jabal Qarūn, Petra (cf. Lindner 1986, 98 and 100).

21

22

21–22. Scripts used by some of the Nabataeans' neighbors.

21. A Hismaic inscription from the Wadi Ramm area, with a prayer to Dūsharā. "O Dūsharā. [grant] good fortune to ʾAjad" (See King 1990, no. KJC 405.)

22. A Safaitic inscription by a Nabataean. "By Munʿīm son of Arsʾ-Manawat son of Abgar son of ʾAʿtil, the Nabataean" (See Macdonald, Al Muʾazzin, and Nehmé 1996, 444-449, no. B1).

archives, business letters or accounts; and most of what we know of the history, way-of-life, and commercial activities of the Nabataeans comes, not from their own writings but from relatively brief descriptions by Greek and Roman authors.

The label "Nabataean" is nowadays applied to a number of related forms of the Aramaic script, found in texts spread over a wide area of the Near East and beyond. It is convenient to use this label but it is important to remember two things. Firstly, these varieties of the Aramaic script have been grouped together and called "Nabataean" by modern scholars, and we do not know whether those who used them in antiquity would have seen the same connections between them, or whether they called all, or any, of them "Nabataean."

Secondly, we should not assume that all those who wrote or commissioned a text in what *we* call the "Nabataean language and script" thought of themselves as ethnically or politically "Nabataean," any more than someone who writes in the language we call "English" is necessarily "English" by nationality. This is vividly illustrated in several of the papyri just mentioned, where some members of a Jewish community in the Nabataean kingdom wrote in Nabataean and others in Jewish Palestinian Aramaic. Conversely, there is an inscription in the Palmyrene language and script, commissioned by a man who specifies that he was a Nabataean but who happened to be working in the area of Palmyra. [12] Other Nabataeans, out in the desert east of the Hauran, wrote graffiti in the language and script of the local nomads (fig. 22). [13] Thus, when someone wrote a document or commissioned an inscription, the language and script they used would depend more on where they had been brought up, or where they happened to be at the time, than on their ethnic or political affiliations.

In view of this, and of the fact that the "Nabataean" language and script were used, often extensively, in geographical areas which did not form part of the kingdom (e.g., the Sinai and Egypt) and at periods after it ceased to exist (e.g., in the Hauran, Arabia, and the Sinai), it seems wise when discussing the inscriptions and their language and script to distinguish between, on the one hand, the "Nabataean cultural area" and, on the other, political entities such as "Nabataea" or the "Nabataean kingdom."

THE USES OF WRITING

Social, political, and environmental conditions differed from region to region of the Nabataean cultural area and this is reflected in the ways in which writing was used in each. This means that Nabataean written documents do not form a coherent, homogeneous corpus and it is misleading to assume that a feature in a text from one area is typical of "Nabataean" as a whole. Like everything else, a document is much better understood when seen within its context. In this chapter I shall therefore describe not only the various types of Nabataean texts which have survived but examine what they can tell us about the use of written languages in each region of the cultural area.

Over 90 percent of the surviving Nabataean inscriptions are "signatures." These texts consist of the name of the author with usually that of his father and sometimes a longer genealogy. Occasionally other members of his family (e.g., brothers, sons, daughters, etc.) are included. This "signature" can appear alone but, more often, it is preceded, followed, or enclosed by conventional words of blessing such as

šlm "may he be safe and sound,"[14]
dkyr "may he be remembered,"
bryk "may he be blessed,"
b-ṭb "in well-being," etc.

Thus, for example, *šlm* N *br* N *b-ṭb* "May N son of N be safe and sound in well-being."

Petra In Petra, these signatures (fig. 20) make up approximately 82 percent of the known written documents.[15] In the past, they have been regarded simply as graffiti and dismissed as uninformative and of little interest. However, in an important study of the geographical distribution of the inscriptions in Petra, Laïla Nehmé has recently pointed out that large numbers of the signatures are grouped at particular sites. Among these are five small sanctuaries, such as that of Obodas the god at An-Nmeir, which alone has 132 of these texts, and other meeting places of the *thiasoi*, or "dining-clubs" associated with religious or funerary cults. These meeting places are only found in certain parts of Petra and are usually associated with Strabo's statement that the Nabataeans "prepare common meals together in groups of thirteen persons, and have two singing-girls for each banquet."[16] These signatures, which are rarely found elsewhere in Petra such as the great high-places of sacrifice or the city center, seem to have been intended to commemorate the authors' participation in these ritual banquets.[17]

Of the monumental inscriptions at Petra, the largest group is funerary, though this represents surprisingly few texts given the large numbers of tombs there. Moreover, of these, only the Latin epitaph of the Roman governor, Sextius Florentinus,[18] and the Greek epitaph of a Roman soldier,[19] were carved on the *exterior* of tombs and both these date from after the Roman Annexation in 106 AD and so may reflect a practice different from the local Nabataean one. These are also practically the only true epitaphs in Petra.[20] The only Nabataean text which could be called an epitaph reads

> this is the *nefesh* of Petraios son of Threptos and he is honored because he had been at Raqmu [the Semitic name for Petra]. He died at Jerash and his master, Taymu, buried him there.[21]

A *nefesh* is a memorial which usually took the form of an elongated pyramid on a base which could be carved on the interior or exterior walls of a tomb, or could be engraved or carved in relief on a rock-face, as a simple memorial independent of a tomb. The inscriptions on these usually say simply "*nefesh* of so-and-so." Other grave markers were engraved on the rock inside the tomb near the loculus where the body was placed, or on a stone used to close the loculus, or were painted on the plaster which covered the interior walls of the tomb. However, those found so far give no more than the name, patronym, and occasionally profession or title of the deceased.

In Hegra (modern Madāʾin Ṣāliḥ), the Nabataean city in northwest Arabia, a number of tombs have inscriptions on the façades. These are not epitaphs but copies or summaries of the title deeds to the property (see below under ***Hegra***). There is only one text of this type at Petra, the elegant five-line inscription on the façade of the so-called Turkmaniyah tomb (fig. 17).[22] Although in some ways it is similar in content to the Hegra texts, there are significant differences, most notably that it does not mention the owner of the tomb (compare the Hegra tomb inscription quoted below). It has been suggested that the tomb was carved by a property developer, possibly working on behalf of a temple or religious corporation, and that the names of the eventual owner and occupants were to be inserted in the original deeds, written on papyrus, which were probably lodged at a temple.[23]

Scholars have long tried to explain why there are so few monumental inscriptions carved directly onto the façades of tombs at Petra, but none of the explanations which have been proposed is particularly convincing. It should be remembered that the only Nabataean inscriptions on the exteriors of the tombs at Hegra or Petra are, without exception, deeds of real estate *not* epitaphs, grave-markers, or memorials. Hegra has yet to be comprehensively explored, but at Petra, the commonest surviving commemoration of the dead is on a *nefesh* memorial, while grave-markers in both Hegra and Petra are found *inside* the tombs near the loculus, not on the exterior.

Thus, it may simply be that there was a difference in legal practice between Hegra and Petra in this matter. It is possible that, at Petra, the deposition of a deed of ownership in a temple was deemed sufficient protection for the owner(s) of the tomb and it was not felt necessary to carve a "private property" notice on the monument itself. Or it may simply be that the Petrans were less litigious than the population of Hegra. The Greek philosopher Athenodorus of Tarsus, who had lived in Petra, noted that it was only foreigners living there who initiated law-suits "both with one another and with the natives. None of the natives prosecuted one another, and they in every way kept peace with one another."[24] This, possibly idealized, view seems to reflect a general reluctance to go to law among the Petrans, which is in marked contrast to the impression presented by the tomb inscriptions at Hegra.

Of the small number of Nabataean inscriptions of a religious nature at Petra, most are simple dedications or identifications of cult statues, baetyls[25] or niches.[26] However, fragments of what appears to be a decree listing religious obligations and penalties, found in the Temple of the Winged Lions at Petra, hint at a much more sophisticated use of monumental writing in the service of temple and cult, though, alas, we have at present no other evidence for this.[27]

In Petra, as in all parts of the Nabataean realm, there are only a handful of Nabataean honorific inscriptions, all of them referring to kings.[28] This is in marked contrast to Palmyra, for instance, where the great men of the city were regularly honored with statues or busts. In Sīʿ, too, which was in an area of the Hauran that was not under Nabataean rule, statues were erected to public benefactors (see below). We can only guess at the reasons for this apparent difference in practice, but both Palmyra and Sīʿ were far more heavily Hellenized than Petra, while in Palmyra, at least, the key civic institutions were modeled on those of a Greek city. Interestingly, the situation in Petra seems to have changed in the period after the Roman annexation in 106 AD, when inscriptions in Greek and Latin honoring individuals begin to appear, albeit in very small numbers.[29]

On the present evidence, it seems that within the Nabataean realm, and especially at Petra, a living individual could only be commemorated in an inscription, "obliquely" by stating that he had erected or dedicated a cult image or structure to a deity "for the life of" the king, and often other members of the royal family. This practice is documented from the earliest inscription so far found in Petra (fig. 18), which reads

> This is the chamber and the cistern which Aṣlaḥ son of Aṣlaḥ made ... for Dushara, the god of Mankatū [or Manbatū] [30] for the life of Obodat [I], king of Nabatū, son of Aretas king of Nabatū, year 1 (?)

and continues right up to the end of the first century AD when an inscription was set up to "the god of [...]lū ... for the life of Rabbel [II]" and his family.[31] An elegantly carved example, alas broken, is illustrated in fig. 19. Apart from semi-honorific dedications of this sort, there are very few Nabataean inscriptions at Petra which record the construction or cutting out of buildings, though one is the so-called Bab al-Siq Nabataean–Greek bilingual inscription which records that a certain ʿAbd-Mankū made the tomb for himself and his descendants in perpetuity.[32]

Thus, as might be expected, Petra, the principal city of the Nabataean realm, has examples of most types of inscription, both public and private, but they have survived in meager quantities. Whereas at Petra just under 1,100 inscriptions in Nabataean, Greek, and Latin have been discovered, of which 82 percent are simple signatures, at Palmyra, if one excludes the inscribed *tesserae* (small tokens), there are more than 2,100 inscriptions, in Palmyrene, Greek, and Latin, of which the vast majority are public texts, such as official pronouncements, honorific or commemorative inscriptions, and hardly any are signatures. Moreover, while in Palmyra large numbers of inscriptions adorned the city center in Petra the equivalent area has provided less than 1 percent of a much smaller total.

Individual Nabataean funerary inscriptions, dedications, and signatures have been found in other parts of Transjordan.[33] However, only in Wadi Ramm is there a concentration of Nabataean inscriptions of different sorts.

Ramm Southeast of Petra the land continues to rise until you come to the edge of a great escarpment. From here, the land falls away several hundred meters to the Hisma desert from which multicolored mountains stick up like islands in a sea of sand which stretches from southern Jordan down into northwest Saudi Arabia. In the Nabataean period, this was home to tribes of camel-breeding nomads, some of whom were in close contact with the Nabataeans since they gave their children names such as Taym-ʿObodat or ʿAbd-Ḥarethat, that is "servant" or "worshipper" of the Nabataean kings Obodas and Aretas. These nomads were literate and left thousands of graffiti on the rocks and cliff-faces of the region, not in Nabataean but in a language and alphabet of their own called "Hismaic" (fig. 21), though a few were able to write their names in both scripts.

This region is one of the few places in the Nabataean cultural area where we can glimpse what must have been an

23

24

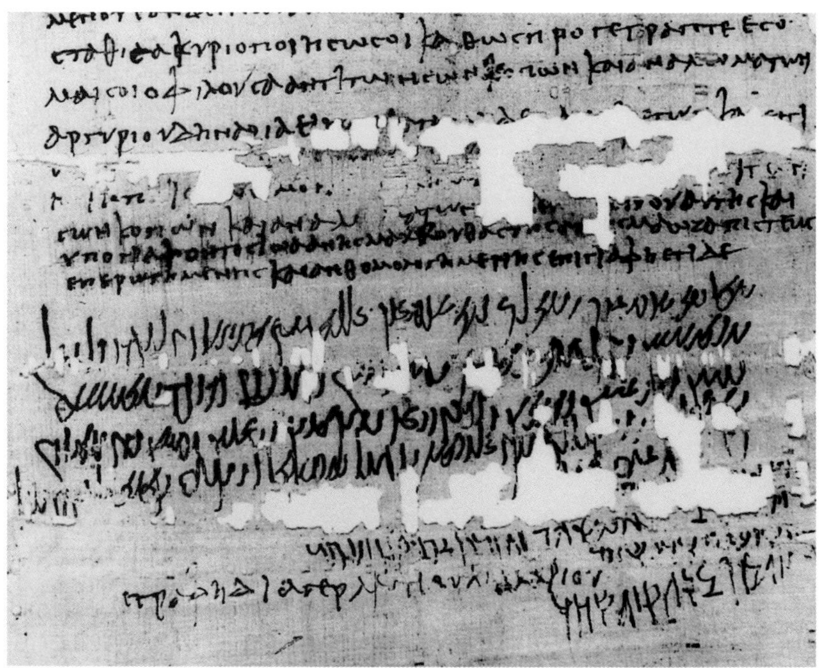

25

26

23–26. Nabataean handwriting. Compare the hands of experienced scribes on plaster (23) and on papyrus (24), with those of literate laymen on papyrus (25) and on a pebble (26).

23. Dedication to the goddess Allat written in ink on plaster in her temple at Ramm, southern Jordan. Dated to year 40+ (?) either of Aretas IV [= between 33 and 40 AD] or of the Roman Province of Arabia [= between 146 and 154 AD]. See fig. 38.14. (See Savignac and Horsfield 1935, pl. X.)

24. Part of a papyrus from Naḥal Ḥever, *P. Starcky* = *P. Yadin* 36, written in Nabataean, showing the script of a professional scribe. Dated to year 20 (?) of Malichus II [= between 58 and 67 AD]. (See Starcky 1954, pl. I and Yardeni 2001)

25. Part of a papyrus from Naḥal Ḥever, *P. Yadin* 22 [130 AD], showing (1) part of the Greek text, (2) the 5-line witness statement in Nabataean, in the hand of a literate layman with a Jewish name (Yoḥana son of Makhoutha), see fig. 38.16, followed by signatures in Jewish Palestinian Aramaic (3 and 5) and Greek (4). (See Lewis, Yadin, and Greenfield) 1989, Pl. 27.

26. A list of names written in Nabataean in ink on a pebble from Nessana in the Negev. 1.'Klybw br Mnḥlw 2. Mḥlmw br Bny 3. ʿbdʾlgʾ br-h 4. Mwtnw br ʿbdʿbdt 5. Zydʾlbʿly br Lhw 6. —— br ʿlyw. (See Rosenthal 1962, pl. XXXIV, 1).

almost universal phenomenon: the symbiosis and interaction of the Nabataeans with neighboring peoples using other languages and scripts. The Hisma, whose mountains contain many springs, has been a favorite route from Arabia to the Levant for millennia and so seems to have been a rather cosmopolitan place in which merchants, nomads, soldiers, and pilgrims traveled, mixed, and sometimes left graffiti. As well as thousands of Hismaic and tens of Nabataean inscriptions, there is a fragment in Latin, and small numbers of texts in Greek, Minaic (from south Arabia), Dadanitic (from nortwest Arabia), Thamudic B, C, and D (by nomads from central Arabia),[34] and early Arabic, as well as thousands of rock drawings from many periods.

One of the valleys in this desert is Wadi Ramm[35] which has many springs, some of which were regarded as holy places in antiquity. One of these is today called Ain Shallalah, and here we find the signatures and prayers of worshippers of the goddess Allat, as well as the baetyls of several other deities carved on the same cliff-face and identified in accompanying inscriptions. At this sanctuary there was also a small building on which was placed a dedication,[36] presumably to Allat (the divine name is lost), "who is at Iram," "for the life of" the last Nabataean king, Rabbel II, and at least seven members of his family, a type of text familiar from Petra. Interestingly, this is the only formal Nabataean inscription so far found in Ramm.

In the shadow of Jabal Ramm itself there was a temple to Allat. Here a fragmentary dedication to the goddess in Nabataean was written in ink on the plaster of the interior walls together with signatures in Greek and Nabataean (fig. 23).[37] A stone re-used in the building bears a graffito in the Hismaic language and script by a man who took part in the construction of the temple.[38]

On the opposite side of Wadi Ramm, at a place today called Khashm Judaydah, near the entrance to a small building which may have been another sanctuary of Allat, three signatures were carved into the rock, two by a *kahin* (i.e., "soothsayer, diviner") of the goddess, and the third by a certain Ḥayyān "in the presence of Allat the goddess who is at Iram for ever."[39]

Ramm and its environs seem therefore to have been an area where the settled Nabataeans and their nomadic neighbors joined in the worship of Allat and probably in many other activities. It is important because it provides more evidence than any other region of the Nabataean cultural area for interaction between the Nabataeans and their neighbors, though it should be recognized that even here the evidence is very meager. The inscriptions reveal the cosmopolitan atmosphere of the area not only in the range of their languages and scripts but in their religious content. While only one Nabataean text mentioning Dushara has yet been found here, there are numerous prayers to him in Hismaic. The Nabataean baetyls and their inscriptions are dedicated to deities from all over the Nabataean kingdom. Thus, besides Allat "who is at Iram," there is Allat "who is at Bosra," al-Kutba "who is at Gaʾya" (modern Wadi Musa, outside Petra), al-ʿUzza and the "lord of the temple," whose worship is found throughout the Nabataean cultural area and beyond, and Baal-Shamin, the lord of Heaven, whose principal cult-sites were in Syria.

Hegra and Arabia Hegra rivals Petra in the range, if not the number, of its inscriptions. There are many more monumental texts than at Petra, but they are almost all of one particular type: legal documents proclaiming property rights. The property in question is always one of the elaborately carved tombs cut into the rock-face that resemble those at Petra. Thus, although they are often known as "tomb inscriptions," it is important to recognize that they are in no way epitaphs. An example may make this clear (fig. 27).

> This is the tomb that Kamkam daughter of Waʾilat daughter of Ḥaramū, and Kulaybat her daughter, made for themselves and their descendants. In the month of Ṭebet, the ninth year of Ḥaretat king of Nabatū, lover of his people. And may Dushara and his Mōtab, and Allat of ʿAmnad, and Manōtū and her Qaysha curse anyone who sells this tomb or who buys it or gives it in pledge or makes a gift of it or removes from it body or limb or who buries in it anyone other than Kamkam and her daughter and their descendants. And whoever does not act according to what is written above shall be liable to Dushara and Hubalū and to Manōtū in the sum of 5 shamads and to the priest for a fine of a thousand Hegratite selaʿs, except that whoever produces in his hand a document from the hand of Kamkam or Kulaybat her daughter, regarding this tomb, that document shall be valid.[40]

These texts have many interesting features. Firstly, in contrast to the situation at Petra, they are carved directly onto the façades of the tombs, usually within a frame that is in relief (e.g., fig. 27). Secondly, when one examines them closely they are often rather carelessly laid out, with lines running over onto the frame (e.g., the last line on fig. 27). In addition, the masons have very often added their signatures at the bottom of the text, on the bottom of the frame, or immediately under it (see fig. 27). However, most of this is more or less invisible without binoculars since the inscriptions are usually positioned too high to be read with any ease from ground level. Given that they are detailed and complex legal documents, one might have expected them to be placed in a position where they could easily be read. As noted above, one inscrip-

27. Arabia. The earliest dated inscription [1 BC/AD] on the facade of a tomb at Hegra (H 16). Note that the last line of the text is carved on the bottom of the frame and below it is the mason's signature, "Wahb-ʾallāhī son of ʿAbd-ʿObodat made [it]." See fig. 38.6. (See Healey 1993, 154-162).

tion refers to a copy of the text which was deposited in one of the temples[41] and it may be that this was the version used for reference, while the one inscribed on the tomb was intended to have a more talismanic than practical function.

None of these texts mentions the achievements of the dead or displays any grief for him or her, for they were probably carved before any of the prospective occupants of the tomb had died. Only in three cases does a second text, inside the tomb, refer to the deceased. From this it seems clear that tombs at Hegra were considered to be pieces of real estate that were either commissioned by a family, or carved by a developer as a speculation, and could be purchased, transferred by gift, leased, or mortgaged. There are even sections of cliff on which no tomb has been carved, which seem to have been reserved by an individual.[42]

This situation is paralleled at the neighboring oasis of Dedan, twenty kilometers away, where inscriptions in the local language and script, Dadanitic, record the construction and taking possession of tombs—or sections of cliff-face preparatory to the carving of tombs—using the same word for assuming ownership of a piece of real estate, *ʾḥd* in Nabataean, *ʾḫḏ* in Dadanitic.[43]

There are no epitaphs at Hegra. The emphasis is always on tombs as *property*, in marked contrast to the simple statements that so-and-so made a tomb for himself and/or another, which are found occasionally at other places in Arabia,[44] once in Petra,[45] and are fairly common in the Hauran (see below). Only one inscription at Hegra is of this sort,[46] and that is *inside* a tomb which has a property inscription on the façade.

There are also some simple prayers, and a handful of dedications and identifications of niches and baetyls, but the vast majority of the Nabataean inscriptions of Hegra are property-inscriptions and signatures.

Unfortunately, it is not yet possible to subject the inscriptions of Hegra to the same meticulous analysis that Nehmé has provided for Petra, but preliminary indications suggest that the distribution of signatures in the two cities may well be similar. In addition, however, at Hegra, though interestingly not at Petra, we also have the signatures of some of the masons who carved the great rock-cut tombs in the first century AD.[47] One of these can be seen below the frame round the tomb inscription on fig. 27.

The Nabataeans were also established at other centers in northwest Arabia, for instance at Dedan just south of Hegra, where many inscriptions have been found,[48] and Dūmā (modern al-Jawf) where they seem to have had a military presence.[49] They also left large numbers of graffiti, mainly signatures, on the rocks along the tracks between the various oases of the area.[50] The most southerly Nabataean inscription so far found is northeast of Najran near the border between Saudi Arabia and Yemen.[51]

Hauran Of all the regions within the Nabataean cultural area, the Hauran is epigraphically the most complex. Our knowledge of the chronological and geographical limits of Nabataean rule there is very sketchy, but it seems to have been at best intermittent and localized. At the same time, at least one "native" form of the Aramaic script seems to have been in use in the Hauran in parallel with the Nabataean script from Petra (see below, under ***Script***).

Moreover, only about 180 inscriptions in the local and the Nabataean versions of the Aramaic script have been published from the whole of the Hauran, with an unknown number of additional texts—probably little more than 100—found but still awaiting publication.[52] We therefore have about the same number of Aramaic inscriptions from the whole region of the Hauran as from the single city of Hegra, and this is only about a quarter of the total from Petra.

The inscriptions found in the Hauran are very different in content and purpose from those of Petra and Arabia. Firstly, no groups of signatures have been found here. This may partly be due to topography, for in areas such as the Hauran, as also in the Negev, where buildings were constructed from blocks of stone rather than carved out of the rock, lists of members of *thiasoi*, if they existed, were probably written on perishable materials which have not survived, such as plaster (as at Ramm), papyrus, or wood.

By contrast, it seems to have been common in the Hauran for sculptors and masons to carve their names in prominent places on their work and there are a number of such signatures on reliefs and sections of architectural decoration, a practice which does not seem to be found at Petra, though the masons' signatures on the Hegra tomb inscriptions provide a parallel. Thus, the base of a sculpture of an eagle bears the text carved in relief "this is the eagle which Rabbū son of Ḥanīpū, the mason, made."[53] The pedestals of statues have the artists' signatures along the bottom, while on the arch of a niche another artist has signed his work in a crude *tabula ansata*, this time in Greek: "Tauēlos son of Rabbos son of Socheros made [it]."[54] On the lintel of a mausoleum shown on fig. 28, the mason's "signature" is as prominent as the name of the deceased (see the translation below).

Although in every case the signature of the artisan is carved in a prominent position on the object, with the exception of the last, it is seldom an integral part of the composition. Usually, it is squeezed into an area of unused space or carved on the frame or base, and, to our eyes, often mars the effect of the sculpture. This practice is comparable to that of the masons who left their signatures on or below the tomb inscriptions at Hegra, but those would have been less obvious from ground level. A closer parallel is with the funerary and religious sculptures at Palmyra, where the inscriptions giving the name of the deceased or the dedicant are again often squeezed into unused spaces between the figures in an apparently haphazard manner.

These artisans' signatures and a handful of graffiti in the desert,[55] and very occasionally elsewhere,[56] seem to be the only texts of this type found so far in the Hauran, in stark contrast with all other regions of the cultural area.

Another distinctive feature is that a large proportion of the Nabataean and other Aramaic inscriptions in the Hauran are grave markers. The normal custom seems to have been to set up simple gravestones with just the name of the deceased and his or her patronym (e.g., fig. 29), though there are some more elaborate texts, occasionally on stelae, but more often on lintels, probably intended for the doorways of stone-built mausolea (e.g., fig. 28).[57] However, even these latter simply record the name of the occupant of the tomb and, sometimes, who built it and/or a date.[58] Thus, for instance, the lintel from Sīʿ mentioned above (fig. 28), which is in Greek and the local Aramaic script, rather than Nabataean, reads:

> [Greek] The monument of Tanenos son of Annēlos
> [Aramaic] For Ṭaninū son of Ḥannʾel [is] the funerary monument [*npšʾ*]
> Ḥūrū son of ʿUbayshat [was] the mason.

As will be described below, the Hauran was a region in which several languages were used. Greek and Aramaic were the principal ones spoken and written in the settled areas, but the nomads in the desert east and southeast of the Hauran spoke, and at this period wrote, a different language, using an Ancient North Arabian script that today is known as Safaitic (fig. 22). The contact between these nomads and the population of the Hauran is symbolized by a handful of Safaitic-Greek and Safaitic-Nabataean bilingual inscriptions and by a cave-tomb not far from the Roman fort at Deir al-Kahf (northeastern Jordan). There, a Nabataean inscription was carved around three of the four walls explaining that the tomb was built by Khulayf son of Awshū for himself and his brothers, while on each sarcophagus the deceased's name and patronym were written in Safaitic.[59]

Of all the regions in the Nabataean cultural area, the Hauran has the largest concentration of inscriptions recording the construction of sacred buildings and the dedication of

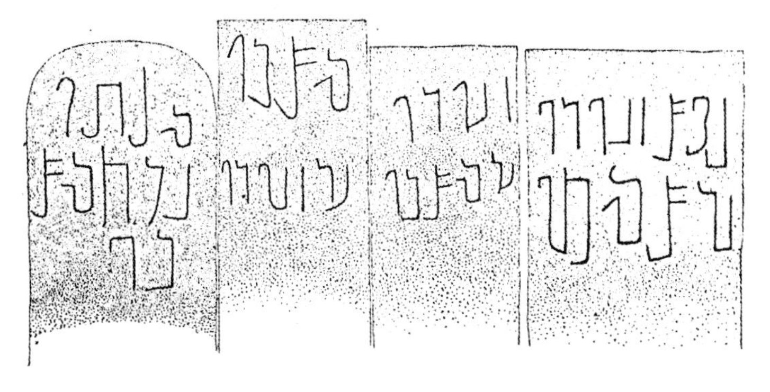

28–29. Aramaic inscriptions from the Hauran.

28. Lintel, probably of a mausoleum, with an inscription in Greek and Hauran Aramaic "For Ṭaninū son of Ḥannʾel [is] the funerary monument. Ḥūrū son of ʿUbayshat [was] the mason." (Photograph of a squeeze. See Littmann 1914, 84, no. 105).

29. Gravestones with the names of four members of one family from Umm al-Jimāl in the Hauran. The one with the rounded top commemorates a woman. (See Littmann 1914, 52, nos. 60-63).

30

31

32

30–33. Nabataean and local Aramaic inscriptions from the Hauran.

30. Nabataean inscription on an altar from Bosra, dated to year 11 of Malichus I [= 47 BC]. (CIS 2, no. 174. Musée du Louvre, A.O. 4990.

31. Aramaic inscription on the pedestal of a statue at Sīʿ, dated to year 33 of Philip the Tetrarch [= 29/30 AD]. (LPNab 101, Suweidah Museum no. 158.

32. Aramaic inscription from Hebron recording the construction of a gateway, dated to year seven of the Roman emperor Claudius (= 47 AD). (CIS 2, no. 170. Musée du Louvre, A.O. 4992).

33. Nabataean inscription from Ṣalkhad, dated to year 17 of Malichus II [= 57 AD] recording the construction and repair of the temple of Allat at Ṣalkhad. (Compare the script of this text with that of fig. 36). (CIS 2, no. 182. Suweidah Museum no. 377).

33

altars and sacred objects. They are found in Greek, Nabataean, and Hauran Aramaic and in some cases are bilingual.

While, in Petra, the only traces of statues seem to have been those of kings, in those parts of the Hauran outside Nabataean control, such as Sīʿ, statues of non-royal individuals were erected. Thus, the pedestal shown on fig. 31 bears the inscription

> In the year 33 of our lord Philip [the Tetrarch], Witrū son of Bard and Qaṣiyū son of Shuday, and Ḥannʾel son of Mashakʾel, and Munaʿ son of Garmū, made this pedestal (?) of the statue of Galishū son of Banatū.[60]

As usual in the Hauran, the mason has signed his work, this time along the bottom of the object.

Thus, the Aramaic epigraphy of the Hauran consists almost entirely of formal, i.e., monumental, inscriptions, the very few simple signatures being mainly those of artisans "signing" their work. In this it is in marked contrast with the rest of the Nabataean cultural area, where signatures vastly outnumber formal texts. The epigraphy of the Hauran is also unique in the range of subject matter and the variety of objects that bear inscriptions. Finally, it is one of only two regions where Nabataean coexisted in close proximity to a different form of the Aramaic script, the other being the southern end of the Dead Sea, to which we will turn next.

The Southern Dead Sea Valley In the late first and early second centuries AD, Maḥōza at the southern end of the Dead Sea, was a prosperous settlement with large numbers of date palms. It was part of the Nabataean kingdom until the annexation by Rome in 106 AD, after which it became part of the Roman Province of Arabia. As well as the gentile population, it also had a thriving Jewish community, at least until the Second Jewish Revolt (132–135 AD) led by Simon Bar Kokhba, when some of its members took refuge in a cave in the Naḥal Ḥever, on the western side of the Dead Sea. Among them were two women, one called Babatha and the other called Salome Komaïse. Each of them took with her a bundle of legal documents on papyrus relating to property and family matters,[61] and others from the community probably did the same. It seems that they died before they could return to their homes and the documents remained in the cave until their discovery there in 1961.

The majority of these papyri were written in Greek, but some are in Jewish Palestinian Aramaic [JPA] and others are in Nabataean (e.g., fig. 24).[62] A number of the Greek documents also bear the signatures and statements of witnesses in Greek and/or Nabataean and/or JPA (e.g., fig. 25).[63]

As might be expected, legal documents written before the annexation were couched in Nabataean and those composed under Roman rule were generally written in Greek, though there is at least one exception to this, *P. Yadin* no. 6, which apparently dates to 119 AD.[64] The continued use of Nabataean in official documents more than ten years after the annexation is extremely interesting.

It is significant that in most of the papyri written in Nabataean the people involved, both as principals and witnesses, are all Jews. Similarly, in the signatures and statements of witnesses on many of the Greek papyri, some witnesses wrote in JPA and others in Nabataean. Some of those who wrote in Nabataean have Jewish names and are very closely involved with the Jewish family of Babatha.[65] Thus the division does not seem to be between Jews writing in JPA and gentiles using Nabataean. Members of the Jewish community in the same village appear to have used both, and this suggests that, while some were locals and wrote in the Nabataean dialect of Aramaic and the Nabataean form of the Aramaic script,[66] others may have moved to the Nabataean kingdom relatively recently (perhaps after the Romans crushed the First Jewish Revolt in 70 AD) bringing with them the dialect and form of the Aramaic script used in Judaea (i.e., JPA).

The Negev Our knowledge of the Nabataean epigraphy of the Negev is still very patchy. Although large numbers of informal inscriptions on the rocks of the desert have been reported, [67] only a handful have been published.[68] Similarly, many of the inscriptions found during the excavations of the Nabataean sites there apparently remain unpublished,[69] and those that have appeared are almost all fragmentary. On the other hand, the site of Nessana has produced some of the very few Nabataean texts in ink (e.g., fig. 26),[70] in a script comparable, but not identical, to that used in the signatures and witness statements in Nabataean on the Greek and Nabataean papyri from the Dead Sea area. From northwest of Beer-Sheba has come an incantation text of about 100 BC written in ink on a pebble in a pre-Nabataean script (fig. 38.3), and from Khalaṣa/Elusa, an inscribed stela dated to the mid-second century BC and mentioning "Ḥa[r]etat king of Nabatū," which is probably in another pre-Nabataean Aramaic script of the Negev (fig. 38.2).[71]

Apart from these, almost all the published Nabataean inscriptions from the Negev, most of which are fragments, come from the ruins of Oboda/Avdat and its environs. Among them are parts of two well-carved texts on fragments of marble, one of which apparently mentions three of the sons of Aretas IV.[72] There are also three interesting and enigmatic religious inscriptions on large stone troughs found in and around Oboda, the most complete of which refers to "Dushara the god of Gaʾya."[73]

Even more extraordinary, however, is a six-line inscription on a rock at ʿĒn ʿAvdat, not far from the city of Oboda, which was the cult center of the deified Nabataean king Obodas I.[74] The text was written ("in his own hand") by a certain Garm-ʾallahī son of Taym-ʾallahī and records that he set up a statue before Obodas the god. He then includes two lines of Old Arabic verse[75] (written in the Nabataean script), in praise of Obodas, which may have been part of a liturgy used in the worship of the god.[76]

All this amounts to approximately twenty-five published Nabataean inscriptions, most of which are fragments. There are far more texts in Greek, though all those that are dated come from the period after the Annexation.[77] It is difficult to explain this apparent dearth of Nabataean inscriptions in a region which was of vital economic importance to the Nabataeans and which contained a number of cities including the cult center of the deified Obodas.

The Sinai By contrast, the Sinai Peninsula, another region crossed by important trade-routes, has produced more Nabataean inscriptions than any other part of the cultural area. Almost 4,000 have been recorded so far,[78] but they are all graffiti (fig. 16) and not a single monumental Nabataean inscription has yet been found there. The handful of dated texts all seem to refer to the second and third centuries AD, the earliest apparently being forty-five years after the end of the Nabataean state. However, there is no way of telling how long before and/or after this period they were being written. At one end of the chronological scale there is nothing in the content of the inscriptions to connect the people who wrote them specifically with the Nabataeans, and at the other, although a number of Nabataean and Greek graffiti in the Sinai are accompanied by crosses,[79] none of the Nabataean texts contains any reference to Christianity.

As might be expected, the graffiti of the Sinai are in a wide range of styles (fig. 16). A few are enclosed in a rough *tabula ansata*,[80] others are very carefully, almost elegantly, carved,[81] yet others are so messy that they are barely legible.[82] Some may well have been the work of travelers or pilgrims, but the huge numbers of inscriptions, the limited range of names they contain, the fact that the same person seems often to have written several different texts,[83] and the peculiarities and relative homogeneity of the script (see below under ***Script***), all suggest that the vast majority were carved by the local population of desert herdsmen and cultivators of the oases. In this they would be comparable to the Safaitic and Hismaic graffiti of the generally nomadic neighbors of the Nabataeans in other regions.[84]

The presence of huge numbers of Nabataean graffiti but a total absence of Nabataean monumental inscriptions makes the Sinai one of the most curious and intriguing regions of the cultural area. If, indeed, the vast majority of the texts are by the indigenous population and date to a period after the end of the Nabataean kingdom, we should be particularly careful about identifying their authors as "Nabataeans" and drawing conclusions about Nabataean language or culture as a whole from features specific to these texts, though this has been a common practice among scholars in the past. By the beginning of the second century AD, the political and commercial activities of the Nabataeans had made their script *the* prestige Semitic writing system throughout the whole region south of the Hauran, with the exception of Palestine, as far as the area of Sabaean cultural hegemony in the southern half of the Arabian Peninsula. Thus, whatever their ethnic origins, if members of the population of the Sinai were going to learn to write at this period, the Nabataean alphabet was the most obvious, perhaps the only, one to choose.[85]

Egypt Fewer than one hundred Nabataean graffiti have also been found in eastern Egypt, mainly on well-established trade routes, in the eastern Delta, and between the Red Sea and the Nile.[86] Most have been published from extremely bad hand copies and their content is often uncertain,[87] so it is not clear how closely related they are to the texts of the Sinai.

However, the site of Tell el-Shuqafiyeh in the southeastern Delta has produced two monumental inscriptions of great importance. One is a dedication to the goddess al-Kutba,[88] dated to "year 4 of Ptolemy the king," that is either 77 BC (Ptolemy XIII) or 48 BC (Ptolemy XIV). The second is the dedication of a sanctuary "to Dushara the god who is at Daphne [?]" (identified as modern Tell el-Defenneh, in the eastern Delta),[89] which is dated to "year 18 of Queen Cleopatra, which is year 26 of Malichus king of the Nabataeans" and year 2 of an unidentified person or institution named *ʾṭlḥ*. This is a reference to the famous Cleopatra and the date is equivalent to 34 BC.[90] These dedications of the first century BC suggest an established Nabataean presence and religious infrastructure in the eastern Delta at an early period, a situation in marked contrast to that which we find in the Sinai.

It will be clear from this brief survey that the term "Nabataean inscriptions" does not refer to a homogeneous group of texts, but to a wide range of documents that vary in both form and purpose from one region of the Nabataean cultural area to another. To take just one example, we have seen how signatures were used in one way in Petra and Hegra and quite another in the Hauran, and yet another in the Sinai. Similarly, while most of the texts in Petra and Hegra can probably be ascribed to people who were subjects of the Nabataean king, in the Hauran the texts reflect a complex, frequently changing, political situation that does not interlock neatly with the equally complex relationships of the different varieties of the Aramaic script in use there. Thus, the inscriptions cannot be treated as a single, uniform source for "the Nabataeans." Instead, a regional approach is vital to an understanding both of the documents themselves and of what they can (and cannot) tell us about the Nabataeans and their neighbors.

LANGUAGE

The Nabataeans lived in a region of many languages and scripts and their commercial activities would have brought them into contact with others from further afield. In southern Jordan, they might possibly have encountered the vestiges of Edomite and would almost certainly have found one or more dialects of Aramaic. By the first century AD, at the latest, they were certainly in close touch with people speaking and writing the Ancient North Arabian[91] dialect Hismaic (fig. 21) in the sand desert of southern Jordan and northwest Arabia, of which Wadi Ramm is a part. They were also in contact with speakers of Old Arabic,[92] and the Nabataean kings would certainly have had some subjects for whom this was their first language, though, as will be seen below, it is at present impossible to know whether this was true of the majority.

In the Hauran, they would have come into contact with Greek, with Aramaic, and with Safaitic, another Ancient North Arabian language, spoken and written by the nomads in the deserts which stretch away to the east and the southeast (see fig. 22). In northwest Arabia, they would have encountered Old Arabic and several dialects of Ancient North Arabian.[93] Aramaic was also written there, but it is not certain

35

36

34

34–36. Nabataean and local Aramaic inscriptions from the Hauran. Inscriptions from the reign of Rabbel II. Note the sharp differences in the script among these three almost contemporary texts.

34. Dedication on an altar from Imtān, dated to year 23 of Rabbel II [= 93/94 AD]. RES 83. (Facsimile from Cantineau 1930-1932, 2, 22).

35. Part of the inscription on a hexagonal altar at Dmeir, dated to 405 of the Seleucid era and 24 of Rabbel II [= 94 AD]. The script is very close to that of Petra. See fig. 38.12. (CIS 2, no. 161. Musée du Louvre, A. O. 3025).

36. Inscription recording the reconstruction of the temple of Allat at Ṣalkhad in year 25 of Rabbel II (= 95 AD). Compare the very square script, closer to the Hauran type than to that of Petra, with the much more Nabataean script of fig. 33 from the same temple and by members of the same family, 40 years earlier. See fig. 38.11. (CIS 2, nos. 184+183 = Milik 1958, 227-231, no. 1. Suweidah Museum nos. 374 and 375).

whether it was spoken. In the Dead Sea Valley, the Nabataeans would have heard the Jewish Palestinian dialect of Aramaic and possibly Hebrew. In the Negev, they would have found Old Arabic, and probably one or more dialects of Ancient North Arabian, since for centuries people from the Arabian Peninsula had been settling along the trade route across the Negev to Gaza, which was the major Mediterranean outlet for the frankincense trade. Other groups from the peninsula seem to have settled in large numbers in the Sinai and eastern Egypt, so Old Arabic was almost certainly spoken there too, along with Greek, Aramaic, and Egyptian.[94] Even when they were still nomadic, the Nabataeans seem to have been heavily involved in the frankincense trade from south Arabia to the Levant[95] and so would also have come into contact with the south Arabian languages of the Sabaeans and the Minaeans.

In this polyglot environment, many Nabataeans must have been capable of speaking and writing several languages and it is not surprising that we find occasional bilingual texts. The most common combination is Nabataean-Aramaic and Greek, which represented the two languages of international prestige in this part of the Near East during the Hellenistic and Roman periods and, understandably, these are all formal inscriptions.[96] However, a few bilingual Nabataean/Hismaic and Nabataean/Safaitic graffiti have also been found.[97] On many of the Greek legal documents from the Dead Sea area (see above), some witnesses signed their names and made their witness statements in Greek, some in Nabataean, and some in Jewish Palestinian Aramaic (e.g., fig. 25). Finally, at the great city of Qaryat al-Faw, in central Arabia, on the northwest edge of the Empty Quarter, a bilingual inscription has been found in Nabataean and the local language of prestige, Sabaic.[98]

Aramaic, which originated in Syria, later spread to Mesopotamia, the southern Levant, and northern Arabia. In many of these places it was used as a vehicular language enabling people whose mother tongues were mutually incomprehensible to communicate and so was much used in administration and commerce. Because of this, in about 500 BC, the Achaemenid king Darius I made Aramaic the administrative language of the western part of his empire and, as a result, it came to be spoken and written from Egypt to Mesopotamia. There were already many spoken dialects of Aramaic in different regions and new ones no doubt developed over time, but throughout the Achaemenid empire, the written language and script maintained an extraordinary homogeneity, no doubt under the influence of the imperial chancellery.

However, with the conquests of Alexander the Great at the end of the fourth century BC, Greek became the new official language, and, without the unifying force of the Achaemenid chancellery, the local spoken Aramaic dialects began to intrude more and more into the written language.

It is often said that "the Nabataeans" used Aramaic simply as a literary language and *spoke* a dialect of Old Arabic in daily life, but this idea is based on several false assumptions. For a start, one has to decide whom exactly one means by "the Nabataeans" in this context. It is unwise to generalize about the population of a kingdom spread over a wide and polyglot area. The Nabataean kings would almost certainly have had some subjects who spoke Old Arabic or dialects of Ancient North Arabian, particularly in northwest Arabia and probably in the Negev. Equally, elsewhere in the kingdom there were people who wrote, and almost certainly spoke, Greek or Jewish Palestinian Aramaic, and there seems no reason to suppose that among all these languages there were not also people who spoke the Nabataean dialect of Aramaic.

In the past, it has usually been assumed that most of the personal names found in Nabataean inscriptions are linguistically Arabic.[99] The real and supposed Arabic etymologies of these names have then been used as an argument that the "native language" of the Nabataeans must have been Arabic.[100] But, of course, the etymological language of a personal name does not mean that its bearer speaks that language.[101] For instance, etymologically, the names Sarah and Alexander are respectively Hebrew and Macedonian Greek, but it would be absurd to assume that these are the native languages of everyone called Sarah and Alexander today. Personal names can "travel" and, within a particular community, names very often come from several different linguistic traditions.[102] This is especially true of mixed and cosmopolitan societies heavily involved in trade, such as that of the Nabataeans, or of areas on trade-routes such as the Sinai. Thus, while it is possible, even likely, that some Nabataeans with "Arabic names" spoke Old Arabic, we cannot deduce this simply from their names. This is well illustrated in the few Nabataean graffiti in the Sinai that contain more than just names and stock phrases. In these, the language is clearly Aramaic, despite the fact that the authors of these texts and their relations have names that are etymologically Arabic.[103]

When one removes the personal names from the equation, the visible Arabic influence on the Nabataean language is seen to be extraordinarily small. There are remarkably few loan-words which can definitely be said to come from Arabic[104] and all but two of these are found exclusively in texts from northwest Arabia. This is exactly where one would expect to find *external* Arabic influence.[105] These words appear with Aramaic grammatical endings and there is little evidence of Arabic influence on the morphology of words or on syntax,[106] which are the clearest indications of a writer thinking in one language while writing another.[107]

Even in Arabia, we have only one example of a text apparently composed by an Arabic-speaker with only a limited grasp of Aramaic. It is a funerary inscription at Hegra and was carved in 267 AD, i.e., 162 years after the end of the Nabataean kingdom. It contains a mixture of Aramaic and Arabic words, misplaced endings, Arabic syntax, and stock Aramaic expressions.[108] A comparison of this with true Nabataean texts from Arabia and elsewhere in the cultural area shows just how consistent is the Aramaic of the latter.[109]

On the other hand, we need to remember that the texts of monumental inscriptions were almost certainly composed by professional scribes, while Nabataean "signatures" and graffiti consist mainly of names and stock expressions. So the available evidence is unlikely to tell us what language a person who wrote or commissioned a Nabataean inscription *spoke* in any part of the cultural area, at any period.

37. The Old Arabic inscription in the Nabataean script from al-Namārah, east of the Hauran. Dated to year 223 [of the era of Province of Arabia? = 328 AD]. See fig. 38.13. (See Bordreuil et al. 1997. Musée du Louvre A.O. 4083).

Nabataean-Aramaic continued to be used as a *written* language long after the kingdom was replaced by the Roman Province of Arabia, in 106 AD: it simply became dissociated from a political entity. Certainly in the Hauran, but possibly also in the Nabataean heartland of southern Jordan and the Negev, Greek may already have been well established by the time it became the official language of administration in the new Province of Arabia.

However, as time passes, we begin to glimpse another language being used in the same area. The first tiny fragments of hard evidence for the use of Old Arabic in the former Nabataean cultural area begin to appear. In the Negev, there is the inscription from ʿĒn ʿAvdat with its two lines of Arabic verse written in the Nabataean script,[110] while at al-Namarah, east of the Hauran, an epitaph, composed in Old Arabic written in the Nabataean script (fig. 37);[111] was set up to commemorate a certain Imruʾ-l-qays, who called himself "king of all the Arabs." In the late fourth century, the Palestinian monk Epiphanius (d. 403 AD) recorded that the people of Petra used Arabic in the liturgical worship of Dushara;[112] and, by the early sixth century, the Greek papyri recently found in a church in Petra show that many of the fields and orchards in the vicinity of the city and even some buildings in Petra itself had Arabic names.[113] Frustratingly, however, we know so little about the demography of the region at this period, that it is impossible to say whether this was a recent or a long-standing situation.

Ironically, it is in Arabia that the Nabataean-Aramaic language seems to have been preserved for longest. For, while Greek became the official language in the heartland of the former kingdom, it seems not to have penetrated to any great extent into its southernmost extension. Here, the Ancient North Arabian languages used by the settled populations (Taymanitic and Dadanitic) ceased to be written and seem to have disappeared well before the early second century AD, no doubt leaving Old Arabic as the predominant spoken language and Nabataean-Aramaic as the only local written language of prestige.[114]

Thus, sixty years after the Annexation, in the late 160s AD, a small temple in the Classical style was erected at a remote spot in northwest Arabia, called Rawwafah. The temple was for the worship of the local god *ʾlh*, venerated by the Arab tribe of Thamūd,[115] some of whom may have been formed into an auxiliary unit of the Roman army.[116] A classical temple to the local god was a symbol of the inclusion of the tribe in the Roman cultural and political sphere. Around the outside of the building was carved a long dedication (nominally by the members of this unit) to the Roman emperors Marcus Aurelius and Lucius Verus, in Greek for the Roman side and in Nabataean as the local written language (fig. 38.7).[117] It is not known whether the tribesmen of Thamūd, in whose name and for whose benefit the inscriptions were set up, were able to read either language.

A century later, at Hegra, the funerary inscription described above was composed in a mixture of Nabataean-Aramaic and Old Arabic. Down the right side of the text, a brief summary was inscribed in the Thamudic D script,[118] and so this one inscription brings together three languages and two scripts. Yet almost a century later than this, in 356 AD, again in Hegra, an inscription was carved in perfect Nabataean-Aramaic to commemorate the wife of the ruler (*ryšʾ*) of the city (fig. 38.8).[119] This is the latest dated inscription in the Nabataean-Aramaic language to have been discovered so far, and is more than two centuries later than anything further north, where the Nabataean script seems already to have been appropriated to express the Old Arabic language.

SCRIPT

The surviving inscriptions, papyri, and ostraca in the Nabataean script must represent only a tiny and random selection of what once was written. Moreover, the circumstances in which each text was produced may well have influenced how it was written in ways that we can rarely even guess at. It is therefore risky to draw detailed palaeographical conclusions from the differences between one text and another, particularly when they are on different surfaces (stone, papyrus, plaster, potsherd, etc.). Here, I shall simply suggest some of the processes by which the different ways of writing Nabataean, as represented in the surviving documents, could have developed.[120]

Even as nomads, the Nabataeans were clearly entrepreneurs, and would probably have needed written documents in their business activities. Given that shortly after the Macedonian conquest they were already famous for the wealth they had accumulated from this trade,[121] their involvement must certainly have begun under the Achaemenid empire when Aramaic would have been the natural, indeed the only realistic, choice. The form of the script they adopted was presumably that used in southern Jordan. The earliest reference to writing in connection with the Nabataeans occurs at the end of the fourth century, when they were in that area and still nomadic. The Greek historian Hieronymus of Cardia, who took part in the events, says that after Antigonus the One-eyed, one of Alexander's successors, had sent an army to attack them, the Nabataeans wrote him "a letter in Syrian characters,"[122] a phrase which can only refer to the Aramaic script.

The form of the Aramaic alphabet used by the Nabataeans is distinctive but seems to belong to a continuum of local developments which stretch from the Hauran, through Transjordan and the Negev (figs. 38.2, 38.3) to the Sinai, Egypt, and northwest Arabia. In all these regions individual versions of the Aramaic letter-forms probably grew up in the centuries following the end of the Achaemenid empire, though alas very few documents have survived.

In the Aramaic scripts used under the Achaemenid empire (fig. 38.1) each letter was written separately. This was true both of texts carved in stone and of those written in ink.[123] Yet, even in the earliest Nabataean inscriptions at Petra (e.g., figs. 18, 38.4), some of the letters are joined by ligatures.[124] There are relatively few of these in the earliest texts but as time goes on they steadily increase and they occur equally in inscribed formal texts and in the carved signatures of individuals.[125]

Ligatures normally develop when one is writing in ink, to save the writer having to lift the pen between each letter.[126] They have no practical use on stone, require more work from the mason, and reduce the clarity of the text for the reader. Thus their presence in the earliest Nabataean inscriptions at Petra, and their increasing use in later texts, suggest that this form of the Aramaic script originally developed for writing in ink and that it continued to be employed in this way parallel with its use in inscriptions.

We are fortunate in having some Nabataean texts on papyrus, and these, like the monumental inscriptions, are official documents written by professional scribes (e.g., figs. 24, 38.15). The script in these, and in the dipinti from Ramm (e.g., figs. 23, 38.14), is recognizably the same as that of the monumental inscriptions of Petra and Hegra, but more compressed. This compression allows more text to be fitted into each line and is easy to achieve when writing in ink, but it often results in the distortion of letter shapes and so is another factor in the development of the script. It is, however, much more difficult to compress the text when carving on stone—even the relatively soft sandstone of Petra or Hegra—and it is anyway usually unnecessary and undesirable in a public inscription.[127]

Thus, the Aramaic script of Petra, which was then carried to other regions of the Nabataean cultural area, must have been used primarily for writing in ink and it was in this medium that it developed and changed. When transferred to stone, at least for monumental inscriptions, a somewhat more "calligraphic" version was used, in which greater care was taken in shaping and spacing the letters, with the occasional inclusion of archaisms for aesthetic purposes or for emphasis.[128] There were not, therefore, two separate Nabataean scripts—a lapidary and a cursive—but a single script, whose development, through writing in ink, can be traced only

38. Script table showing some varieties of the Nabataean and Hauran Aramaic scripts. Note this table is not intended to suggest a linear development of the script.

An * above a letter in the table indicates that this form is found at the end of a word in this text. In some cases, this is a special "final form" of the letter, in others it is identical to the forms in other positions, and in yet other cases, there are too few examples in the text to be sure. Those forms not marked with an * occur in initial or medial positions.

The vertical positions of the letters relative those of the other letters in the same line reflect their arrangement within the text.

Where space permits, all the significantly different forms of each letter in each text are shown, to illustrate the lack of consistency in letter shapes even within monument inscriptions.

Key to the script table:

1. Imperial Aramaic: The Tayma Stelae 5th/4th century BC (CIS ii, 113, Musée du Louvre A.O. 1505).

2. A pre-Nabataean local script of the Negev used on stone in an inscription from Elusa in the Negev, 3rd/2nd century BC (?) (Cowley 1914–1915).

3. A pre-Nabataean local script of the Negev c. 100 BC (?), used for a text written in ink on a pebble (Naveh 1979).

4. The earliest inscription so far found in Petra c. 96/95 BC. See fig. 18. Note that the form of k marked with a "?" is often read as a b, though k seems the more likely reading.

5. The Turkmaniyah inscription in Petra, c. mid-first century AD. See fig. 17.

6. The earliest dated inscription from the façade of a tomb at Hegra, Arabia, 1 BC/AD. See fig. 27.

7. The Nabataean part of the bilingual inscription at Rawwāfah, Arabia (between 167 and 169 AD). (See Milik 1971). Note the cross-stroke on the stem of the r to distinguish it from d (see Macdonald 1995, 96, n. 15).

8. The latest text in the Nabataean script. An epitaph from Hegra dated to 357 AD. (Stiehl 1970). Note the diacritical dot over the d to distinguish it from r, even though the two letters by now have distinct forms.

9. The second inscription from Tell el-Shuqafiyeh, Egypt, 34 BC (Jones et al. 1988, Fiema and Jones 1990). Note that the unusual forms of medial of n and medial p marked with "?" occur in a place name which has been tentatively read as Dpnʾ "Daphne."

10. The local Aramaic script of the Hauran in an inscription from Sīʿ dated to year 308 of the Seleucid era = 5 BC (Littmann 1904, 90ff, no. 2).

11. The local Aramaic script of the Hauran in an inscription from Ṣalkhad dated to year 25 of Rabbel II [= 95 AD]. See fig. 36. There is one example of k in final position in this text but its form is not sufficiently clear on the photographs available to me for it to be included in the table.

12. The inscription on a hexagonal altar at Dmeir, southern Syria, dated to 405 of the Seleucid era and 24 of Rabbel II [= 94 AD]. See fig. 35. The script is very close to that of Petra.

13. The epitaph in Old Arabic written in the Nabataean script at al-Namārah, east of the Hauran and dated to 328 AD. See fig. 37.

14. A text painted on plaster at Ramm. See fig. 23.

15. Nabataean script used by a professional scribe, 97/98 AD . *P. Yadin* 3 recto (Yadin et al. 2002, Pl. 24).

16. Nabataean script used by a literate layman, 130 AD. *P. Yadin.* 22, see fig. 25. Note that the s is marked with a "?" because the only (possible) example in the text is damaged.

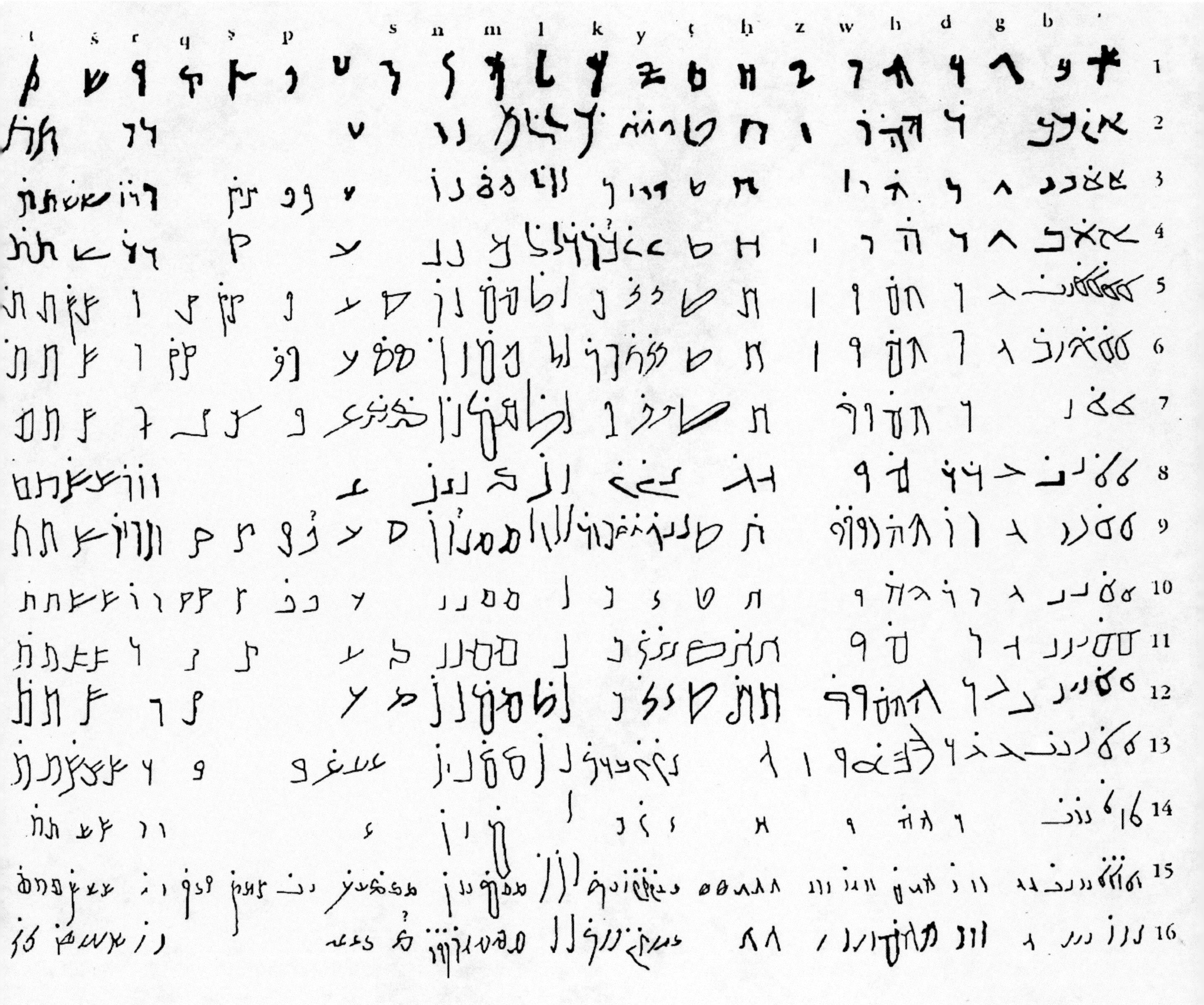

t š r q ṣ p s n m l k y ṭ ḥ z w h d g b ʾ

1
2
3
4
5
6
7
8
9
10
11
12
13
14
15
16

imperfectly through the occasional "snap-shots" of various stages of its evolution provided by the inscriptions.

The form of the script used by literate people who were not scribes was much less conservative, and developed letter-forms and ligatures which reflect a preference for ease and speed of writing over clarity.[129] The shapes of many letters became drastically different from those used by the scribes and masons, and a number of letters became indistinguishable from each other. Examples of this sort of handwriting can be seen on figs. 25–26, 38.16.

The only examples from Petra are written in ink on a handful of fragmentary sherds and, in one case, on the outside of a pot that was probably complete at the time.[130] The script is remarkably similar to that on the pebbles and ostraca found at Nessana (e.g., fig. 26) and is not far removed from that of the signatures and witness statements in the Naḥal Ḥever papyri (e.g., figs. 25, 38.6).

When people who were not scribes carved their names on rock, either at, or on the way to, a sanctuary (e.g, fig. 20) or simply as a graffito (e.g., fig. 16), they used approximations to the "calligraphic" form of the script, just as graffiti in the West are almost always written in capitals rather than lower-case letters. This was probably the result not only of a desire for clarity, in view of the permanence and public position of the text, but also of the extra time and effort involved in carving on rock, as opposed to writing in ink where speed and ease are more often determining factors. It also means that those who were literate but not necessarily professional writers must have carried in their minds the ideal forms of each letter (not simply the shapes they assumed on papyrus), even if their attempts to reproduce these were not always successful.

As the Nabataean kingdom expanded, the "Petra script" spread to other parts of the region where it encountered other, indigenous, forms of the Aramaic script. As mentioned above, the mid-second century BC inscription at Elusa/Khalaṣa in the Negev (fig. 38.2) is in a local variety of the Aramaic alphabet.[131] But, all the later Aramaic formal inscriptions so far found in the Negev are "Nabataean," i.e., they are in a script very close to that of the inscriptions of Petra. However, the corpus of texts from the Negev is so tiny that no conclusions can be drawn from this.

As noted above, only part of the Hauran was ruled by the Nabataeans for any length of time and many of the Aramaic inscriptions of the region are in local forms of the Aramaic script rather than in Nabataean.[132] In these local forms, in contrast to the Petra script, there is a marked tendency to keep the letters separate, and ligatures are relatively rare. Virtually all the letters are of the same height, with only the *lamedh* rising slightly above the others to distinguish it from the *nūn*, and none descending below the rest. Special final forms of letters, which in the Petra script and that of the papyri usually continue below the line, are therefore rare (e.g., figs. 28, 29, 31, 33, 36, 38.10, 38.11). Several letters have shapes which, though recognizably similar to their Nabataean counterparts are distinct from them, e.g., the squat, square or triangular *ʾaleph* (figs. 38.10, 38.11), a *mēm* usually closed on the left side in all positions (figs. 38.10, 38.11), and in some texts the *hē* with an open base even in final position (fig. 38.10), etc.

The type of script used in any particular text was almost certainly the result, not of political considerations, but of the background of the particular scribe. Those brought up in the Hauran would have used the local script, regardless of whether they found themselves subjects of the Nabataean king,[133] the Herodian rulers,[134] the Romans, or others.[135] Similarly, a scribe who came from Petra to the Hauran, and any pupils he may have trained there, would have used the Petra form of the script, or approximations to it.

A study of the inscriptions on pages 46 and 48 will illustrate this (see also 38.10-12). The inscription on figure 31 comes from an area outside Nabataean control. It is in the Hauran script and is dated by a regnal year of Philip the Tetrarch. Contrast its script with those of 30 and 33, from within the Nabataean kingdom. These are dated respectively by regnal years of the Nabataean kings Malichus I (47 BC) and, a century later, Malichus II (57 AD), and the script of both is much closer to that of Petra inscriptions at these respective dates.

On the other hand, figs. 34–36 show three almost contemporary inscriptions, dated respectively to years 23, 24, and 25 of Rabbel II (93-95 AD). Text 34, whose script is very similar to that of Petra, comes from Imtan which was almost certainly within the Nabataean kingdom. Here, although the letter shapes are similar to those of Petra (including the use of special final forms), the more or less uniform height of the letters suggests local influence. Contrast this with 36 (see also fig. 38.11), which also comes from within the Nabataean kingdom and is dated by a regnal year of a Nabataean king, but whose script is clearly the local Hauran Aramaic. Finally, 35 (see also fig. 38.12), whose script is indistinguishable from that of Petra and shows no local Hauran features, comes from Dmeir, some 40 km northeast of Damascus and apparently well outside the Nabataean kingdom. It is dated by both the Seleucid era and a regnal year of Rabbel II.

But perhaps the most telling comparison is between fig. 33 and 36 (see also fig. 38.11). Both texts are from the temple of Allat at Ṣalkhad, which was within the Nabataean kingdom, and they were almost certainly commissioned by members of the same family. The inscription shown on fig. 33 is dated to year 17 of Malichus II (57 AD) and is written in a close approximation to the Petra script. That on fig. 36 is dated forty years later, to year 25 of Rabbel II (95 AD) and is in the local Hauran script. Thus, even in that part of the Hauran that was under Nabataean control, both scripts were used by monument masons in the same town, for texts on the same temple, commissioned by members of the same family. Moreover, far from the Nabataean replacing the local form, it is the earlier text that is in Nabataean, and the later one—carved in the reign of Rabbel II and only a few kilometers from his capital at Bosra—that is in the Hauran script.

Thus, in the Hauran, the Petra script seems not to have "dominated" the local forms[136] but to have co-existed with them. Indeed, there are texts which seem to show elements of both, such as that on fig. 32 (47 AD), where the letter-forms are close to those of Petra, but most of the letters are written separately, as in the Hauran scripts rather than joined as in the Petra-script of this period.[137]

It will be clear from this that in the Hauran, as elsewhere, it is important not to regard script as a vehicle of political expression and that such terms as "national scripts"[138] can therefore be misleading. We have already seen that the use of Jewish Palestinian Aramaic or Nabataean in the Jewish communities of the Dead Sea Valley was not dependent on the ethnic or religious community to which the user belonged, but more on the region from which they came (though the two might, of course, coincide). Equally, in the Hauran, the use of these only subtly different forms of the Aramaic alphabet must surely have been a matter of background and train-

39. A fragment of a Greek-Nabataean bilingual inscription found at Jerash (Gerasa of the Decapolis), on the slopes below the the present museum. Both texts are too badly damaged to allow a coherent interpretation, but two kings, Aretas (IV?) and Rabbel (II?), are mentioned in the Nabataean section. If this is correct, it would place the inscription in the late first century AD. Department of Antiquities, Amman, Jordan.

ing, not of politics and ethnicity. Only very rarely was a script used to make a political point as, for example, when the Jewish leader Bar Kokhba replaced Aramaic with the revived ancient Hebrew script in his official documents.

As one might expect, the graffiti of the Sinai are in a multitude of different handwritings, and yet, taken as a whole, there is a surprising homogeneity about the script (see fig. 16). Of course, there are some bizarre and exceptional letter-forms and there are plenty of examples of individuals playing with the inscriptions they wrote, adding decorative flourishes or drawing a line along the bottom of the text joining all (or most of) the letters.[139] Yet, despite these oddities, in the vast majority of texts the forms of the individual letters and their relationships to each other are remarkably constant, given that some inscriptions were the work of travelers or pilgrims but most were probably written by the local nomads and cultivators.

It is instructive to compare the graffiti of the Sinai with the Safaitic graffiti in the desert east of the Hauran. The script of the latter is also remarkably homogeneous, despite the long period (approximately 400 years) over which they appear to have been written and the huge numbers of texts involved. They represent the different "handwritings" of innumerable individuals, but there seems to be relatively little development in the script. One possible reason for this is that it was used *only* for carving graffiti on rocks and not generally for writing in ink, where the very speed and flexibility of the medium produces change. With a script which is well adapted for use on stone and which is used for nothing else, there is no particular stimulus to alter the shapes of the letters or their relationship to each other. Thus, instead of a development of letter-forms in the Safaitic and Hismaic scripts and the Nabataean of the graffiti in the Sinai, we find the occasional playful additions, as described above. While interesting in themselves and not without significance, these should not be confused with palaeographical developments.

In the various oases of northwest Arabia, forms of the Aramaic script were in use from at least the fifth century BC, and there are inscriptions at Tayma (fig. 38.1), Dedan, and Hegra in approximations to Imperial Aramaic, and at Taymaʾ in local developments of the script (cf., for example, the votive inscription from Tayma, Louvre A.O. 26599).[140] However, with the Nabataean development of Hegra, the northwest Arabian Aramaic scripts seem to have been swamped by the Nabataean form. Eventually, the native Ancient North Arabian Dadanitic script disappeared (the Taymanitic had apparently long since died out), and Nabataean was left as the only "local" written language, hence its use at Rawwafah (fig. 38.7).

This dominance of the Nabataean script in Arabia continued until at least the mid-fourth century AD (fig. 38.8).[141] But by this time, further north, it was already being used to write the Arabic language. The epitaph at al-Namarah for Imruʾ-l-qays "king of all the Arabs" (figs. 37, 38.13), is dated to 328 AD and although by no means the earliest example of Old Arabic written in a borrowed script, it is the first which seems to make a political statement associating the use of the Arabic language with a sense of being "Arab."[142]

Unfortunately, there are no inscriptions in the Nabataean script dated later than the mid-fourth century AD, while the first inscriptions in what is recognizably the Arabic script do not appear until the early sixth century.[143] So, while it is generally accepted that the Arabic script developed out of the Nabataean, we cannot follow the processes of this development in any detail. The fact that the Namarah epitaph and all the pre-Islamic inscriptions in the Arabic script have been found in Syria suggests that the development may have taken place there, rather than in Arabia, where the association of the Aramaic language with the Nabataean script seems to have lasted much longer.[144] But this could equally well be an accident of discovery.

Although what has survived of the Nabataeans' own writings is relatively meager, their legacy has been incalculable. In their heyday their alphabet was used more widely than any other of the late Aramaic scripts and it continued to be so long after the demise of their kingdom, eventually to be rivaled only by Syriac in the extent of its use. Centuries after the other achievements of the Nabataeans had been forgotten, a late form of their script was given new life when it was used as the vehicle for recording the Revelation of Islam and was spread with the Muslim conquests from the Atlantic to the Far East, becoming the script for a large number of different languages and developing new and often very beautiful forms.

4 | The Nabataean Gods and Their Sanctuaries

FAWZI ZAYADINE

The Ancestral God IN THE ANCIENT NEAR EAST, THE gods were attached to a site, usually a high mountain. This fact is well attested in the treaty between Mursilis, King of Hatti and Duppi-Tessub, King of Amurru around 1350 BC, where the storm gods and their mountains are invoked.[1] Similarly, in Phoenicia, the main god was known as Baal Saphon. Saphon may be identified with the mountain Jabal Al-Aqra' in northern Syria, famous to the Greeks under the name of Mount Cassius. The pantheon of Central and north Arabia was no exception to this tradition: in the oasis of Tayma, the main god Salm was identified as Salm Mahram or Salm Hgm, both being place-names.[2] According to a few inscriptions, the ancestral god of the Nabataeans was identified as *'lh Ṣ'b*, the god of 'Ṣa'b. The most significant dedication was found at Palmyra[3]: "Made by Wahballat, son of Abammart, to the god of Sa'bu who is called the fortune of the Nabataeans, for his life (and the life) of his son."[4] A second inscription to the same god was found by G. Dalman at the foot of Jabal al-Khubtha at Petra and a third one at Jabal Ethlib, near Hegra/Madā'in Ṣāliḥ. Using the geographical indications provided by Ptolemy in the second century AD, J. T. Milik[5] succeeded in locating the area of Sa'b at the high Plateau of Mutayr, to the east-southeast of Kuwait. This is an area difficult to live in. Nevertheless, if the Nabataean tribes originated from northeast Arabia, from the oasis of al-Hufuf,[6] they might have brought with them the cult of their ancestral god of Sa'b. It is noteworthy that Strabo records in *Geography* 16.4.21: "The first people who dwell in Arabia Felix are the Nabataeans and the Saaboi." This is indeed the best transcription in Greek of the guttural *'ain* and the evidence of the Sa'bean presence together with the Nabataeans in Arabia. Recently an eleven-line dedication in the so-called Thadmudic E script to *'lh Ṣa'b* has been found in the Madaba district. [6b]

Qaws and the Edomite Heritage With their sedentarization and acculturation, the Nabataean tribes adopted the gods of Edom, the country of southern Jordan where they first settled. They worshipped the Edomite god Qaws on the rugged .summit of Tannur, opposite the extinct crater of Dhikr et-Tannur. Qaws is identified in the Nabataean inscription as "the god of Ḥarawa," meaning "burnt." This was probably a reference to the volcanic mountain opposite Khirbet et-Tannur. The cultic statue represented Qaws seated on a throne that was protected by a bull and an eagle. As the god of rain and storms, he brandished the thunderbolt, his attribute (fig. 1). His consort was Atargatis, the goddess of springs and vegetation. She was seated by the side of the god on a throne flanked by two lions. This cultic statue is now lost and only fragments of her statue remain (including a portion of the goddess's skirt, her left foot, and the corresponding lion-throne support). In the tympanon of the outer temenos of Khirbet et-Tannur, however, the goddess is represented in high relief among intricate scrolls and fruits (figs. 4, 41).[7]

At Ascalon, on the Palestinian coast, Atargatis was identified with Derketo, whose temple was prosperous in the first century BC. According to Diodorus of Sicily (*Hist. Lib.* II, 4.2–3), Derketo fell in love with a Syrian youth and conceived a daughter by him, Semiramis. Tortured by shame, the goddess of Ascalon killed her lover, abandoned her daughter in the desert, and threw herself in a lake where she was turned into a creature half-fish and half-woman.[8] The panel of Khirbet et-Tannur in the Jordan Archeological Museum represents a veiled goddess with long plaited hair emerging from a rosette and crowned by two fish (p. 183, fig. 192). Judith McKenzie now identifies this panel as a representation of Pisces and the panel in the Cincinnati Art Museum with ears of wheat as Virgo (see p. 191 in this volume). But this interpretation does not exclude their identification with Atargatis-Derketo.

The cult of Atargatis was famous in Manbidj/Hierapolis in northern Syria and was described in invaluable detail by Lucian of Samosate in *De Dea Syria*.[9]

Left: **40.** Sandstone cult statue of Qaws. Altar platform, Khirbet et-Tannur. h: 1.15 m. Cincinnati Art Museum, 1939.224.

Above: **41.** Limestone tympanon panel with the bust of Atargatis, Khirbet et-Tannur. Department of Antiquities, Amman, Jordan.

Dushara, the Main God It is believed that the name of the main Nabataean god derived from the mountains of al-Sharāh which enclose the site of Petra. Dushara would mean "The Lord of Sharāh." His name is written with a long *aleph* in Nabataean.

According to the Muslim authors, Dhu al-Sharā (with *aleph maqsura*) is the name of two mountains in Najd and in Tuhama, the latter being famous for a great number of lions. Dushara is also the god of the tribe of al-Ḥārith ibn Mubashsher, a sub-tribe of the Azd. There is, between Saudi Arabia and Yemen, a mountain range known as Sarāt al-Azd.[10]

In Yaqut,[11] Dhu al-Sharā is also the idol of the Bani Daws of the Azd tribe. They have consecrated to him a temenos (*hima*) where a waterfall was gushing out.

In two inscriptions from the Negev and from Dumat al-Jandal in Wadi as-Sarhan, Dushara is venerated as the god of Gaia, the modern village of Wadi Musa, which served as an important caravan station at the eastern entrance of Petra.[12] In the inscription of Turkmaniyah, the main god of the Nabataeans is designated as "the god of our Lord," the king,[13] and on other dedications of the Hauran and Hegra, Dushara is identified with the god of Rabbel II.[14] He is to be considered, in this case, as the dynastic deity.

An altar from Umm al-Jimal, an important station in northern Jordan, was inscribed in Greek and Nabataean with a dedication to Dushara A'ra. On the dedication of Imtan in the Hauran, dated 93 AD, under Rabbel II, he is "the god of our Lord who dwells in Bosra;"[15] *A'ra* is the elative form of *ghry*, meaning "to sprinkle with blood." This is a reference to the custom of spraying the baetyl of the gods with the blood of victims.

Since Dushara was the supreme god of the Nabataeans, he was the equivalent of Zeus; this fact is evident from the dedication to Zeus-Dusares, inscribed in the port of Miletos by Syllaeus, Minister of Obodas III (30-9 BC).[16] An altar discovered at Petra is dedicated in Greek to "The saint god who hears (prayers), Dusares (?)."[17]

In the Roman period, Dusares was identified with Dionysus, the god of wine in Greek mythology. The coin of Bosra under Commodus (176-192 AD) represents the bust of the emperor on the obverse and, on the reverse, a young god

42. Medallion and baetyl of Dusares-Dionysus. High Place, Petra.

with long curly hair identified as "Dusares of Bosra." The Byzantine author Hesychius (c. fifth century AD) confirms this identification when he notes "Dusares is Dionysus of the Nabataeans."[18]

On the way to the High Place in Petra, after the Lion Fountain, a baetyl carved in a niche is surmounted by a medallion representing a god crowned with a vegetal scroll (fig. 42). This is probably Dusares-Dionysus.

When Epiphanius, a Palestinian monk from Beit Jibrin (Eleutheropolis) near Hebron, wrote his *Panarion* against heresies in the fourth century AD, paganism was still alive at Petra. He asserts that the Nabataeans "sing hymns in Arabic to the Virgin and call her Chaamou, that is Kore or rather virgin and to her newborn Dusares." But this reference is considered by G. Bowersock[19] to be a Christian interpretation by Epiphanius, since Kore-Persephone was not described as a virgin in Greek mythology. However, the conviction that Dusares, like Jesus Christ, was born of a virgin is conceivable in the religious context of that period, and Chaamou is most probably a corruption of Aramaic *'almou*, meaning "virgin."

Al-Kutba and Hermes-Mercury Al-Kutba was identified for the first time by J. Strugnell,[20] at the spring-sanctuary of Ain ash-Shalaleh in Wadi Ramm (Iram): two baetyls are carved side by side at the foot of Jabal Ramm and are identified by Nabataean inscriptions: *'LKTB' DY BGY', 'L ʿUZZA*, that is "al-Kutba who is in Gaia, al-ʿUzza." Both baetyls are carved with relief schematic eyes in the form of stars, separated by a rectangular band, a type of eye-idol common in Arabia.

Morphologically, al-Kutba derives from Arabic *KTB*, written in the elative form and meaning: "the great He scribe."[21] The masculine gender of the god is evidenced by the dedication of Wadi as-Siyyagh at Petra: *QDM 'LKTB' 'LH' DNH*: "In front of al-Kutba, this very god."[22]

As a scribal god, al-Kutba is to be equated with Egyptian Thot, Assyrian Nabu, Palmyrene Arṣu, and Arabian Ruḍa. He corresponds to the Graeco-Roman Hermes-Mercury, the patron of divination, travel, trade, music, and the evening star. The association of al-Kutba and al-ʿUzza alludes, no doubt, to the two gods as evening and morning stars.

It was probably the Nabataean caravaneers who brought the cult of al-Kutba to the Arabian Nome of Egypt in the Lower Delta, called in the Roman period "*Nea Arabia*."[23] The two sites of Tell ash-Shuqafieh in the eastern Delta and Qasrawit in the northern Sinai yielded epigraphic and archaeological testimonies of the god's veneration: at the first site, the Nabataean dedication[24] is addressed to al-Kutba "who is at *'awytw*." This site was correctly identified with Qasr Gheit, or Qasrawet, in the northern Sinai, on the caravan road from Jabal Maghara to al-'Arish (Rhinocolura) and Gaza. Two temples were excavated at Qasrawet by E. D. Oren.[25] In the western temple, dated to the first century BC, an altar was dedicated to al-Kutba by Ḥawyrw, son of Faram.

So far, no temple dedicated to al-Kutba or his equivalent Hermes-Mercury has been identified at Petra, or elsewhere. But this sanctuary should exist, considering the large number of sculptures representing the Greco-Roman god that were discovered at Petra (fig. 43), Khirbet et-Tannur, and Khirbet edh-Dharih.

Shay' al-Qaum, the Protector of the Tribe Shay' al-Qaum is a god venerated by the Bedouin tribes of the Ledja in the Hauran,[26] and mainly at Tell Ghariyeh.[27] He is also mentioned in two inscriptions of Hegra.[28] At Palmyra, a Nabataean horseman from the garrison of 'Anat on the Euphrates offered two altars to "Shay' al-Qaum, the god who drinks no wine."[29] The interdiction to drink wine was common in nomadic societies, as it was with the Nabataeans before their full sedentarization (Diodorus of Sicily, *Geography* XIX, 94, 3).

It is noteworthy in this respect that a nomadic clan of the sixth century BC in Judaea, the Rechabites, were ordered by their ancestor Jonadab, son of Rechab: "You must never drink wine, neither you nor your sons; nor must you build houses, sow seeds, plant vineyards, or own property; but you must live in tents all your lives. . ." (*Jeremiah* 35: 6-7). It is possible, in this case, that the nomadic style of life attributed by Diodorus to the Nabataeans is but a literary topos, borrowed from other Bedouin societies. In fact, Rhodian jar handles of the third century BC were found in the house complex of ez-Zantur at

43. Limestone winged head of Hermes-Mercury, Area of Temenos Gate, Petra. h: 55 cm. Department of Antiquities, Amman, Jordan.

44. Limestone panel with head of Dushara-Dionysus. Area of Temenos Gate, Petra. h: 36 cm. Department of Antiquities, Amman, Jordan.

Petra.[30] On the other hand, there is no mention of Shay' al-Qaum at Petra, probably because of the widespread cults of Dionysos in the city (above and fig. 44)

The Three Goddesses: Allat, al-ᶜUzza and Manāt Allat, whose name is the contraction of Arabic *al-Ilahat*, was widely venerated from South Arabia to Palmyra in the north. Herodotus (*Histories* III, 8, 10) connected her cult with that of Orotalt or Ruḍa in the Arabian Nome of Egypt. The Arabian tribes introduced the cult of Allat in the Hauran as early as the first century BC. At Salkhad, the temple of the goddess was founded by Rawhu, son of Qussay.[31] She also possessed a temple at Bosra as can be deduced from the inscription of Ain ash-Shallaleh in Wadi Iram, under the baetyl of the goddess.[32] There is no mention of Allat in the inscriptions of Petra, but she is represented as Athena on a pilaster panel in the temenos of Qasr al-Bint.[33] The temple of Allat was discovered at Palmyra by M. Gawlikowski[34] together with a unique cultic statue. Beside her role as a war deity, Allat assumes the attributes of Atargatis as the goddess of springs, as indicated by a Greek Roman inscription of Raha in the Hauran.[35]

Under the name of Attarsamain or Ashtart, al-ᶜUzza was venerated at Adumatu (al-Jauf in Wadi as-Sarhan) as early as the seventh century BC, under the Assyrian king Assurbanipal.[36] She appears in the Lihyanite inscriptions of Dedan (fourth–third century BC) as *'Uzzay* or *han 'Uzzay*.[37] The cult of the goddess spread in the Nabataean kingdom at Petra, Wadi Iram, in the Hauran, the Negev, and the Sinai.[38] At Petra, a dedication is engraved in Wadi as-Siyyagh to al-ᶜUzza by Hana'at, her servant.[39] In the sanctuary of Sadd al-Maᶜjen, at the end of Wadi al-Muzlem, the dedication was inscribed by 'Abdalga, servant of al-ᶜUzza. Two other dedications are recorded on the stairway leading to the high place of Khubtha, recently restored by the Department of Antiquities.[40] It is likely that this mountain was consecrated to al-ᶜUzza, who was the patroness of the Nabataean capital together with Dushara.

Al-ᶜUzza was identified with the Greco-Roman Aphrodite, according to a dedication found on the island of Kos in the

Aegean Sea and probably left by Syllaeus on his way to Rome in 9 BC.[41] Her cult was alive until the third century AD at Qasr al-Bint, according to a Greek fragmentary inscription.[42] As late as the tenth century AD, the abjuration texts of the Greek church considered al-ʿUzza-Aphrodite as the goddess of Mecca, but these texts have no historical grounds because we know from al-Kalbi[43] that the Prophet Mohammed ordered Khalid ibn al-Walid to destroy her sanctuary in Wadi Ḥurad (above), on the year of the conquest of Mecca (Jan. 630 AD). We hear no more of her cult in Arabia after that date.

Manāt, the goddess of human destiny, corresponds to the Greco-Roman Nemesis. She is mentioned eight times in the

45. Isis of Sadd al-Mreriyyeh. Wadi as-Siyyagh, Petra.

funerary inscriptions of Hegra, in most cases, immediately after Dhu-Shara, as warrantor of tomb deeds.[44] In two inscriptions she is invoked with her "*Qaysa*" that is the measuring rod or cubit. In another,[45] it is stated that a copy of the deed is deposited in "*bayt qaysa*," the "house of measure." This was probably a shrine or an official building where the archives were deposited.

At Tayma, in northeastern Arabia, an Aramaic dedication on a limestone basin qualifies Manāt as the "goddess of goddesses," i.e., "the greater goddess." The basin is dated to the third century BC.[46] At Palmyra, she is mentioned in the first century BC in the temple of Bêl and possessed a sanctuary on Jabal Muntar, where she was venerated by the Bene 'Ajrud, together with the god Baal Hamon. In a significant Palmyrene inscription discovered in the temple of Arṣu and dated 63 AD, Manāt is worshipped under the name Qismaya, together with Arṣu and the "daughters of the god."[47] The attribution of daughters to the god is attested in a Qatabanite inscription of Tumna' (Ḥajar Kahlān) in Yemen.[48] The same tradition was also followed at Mecca, where the Quraysh performed the "ṭawāf" (circumambulation) around the Ka'ba chanting: "By Allat, al-ʿUzza and Manāt, the third of the triad."[49] This tradition was opposed by Quran LIII, 20–21: "Have you considered Allat, al-'Uzza and Manāt, the third of the triad? Is he to have daughters and you sons? This is indeed an unfair partition". In 630 AD, Prophet Mohammed dispatched 'Ali ibn Abi Ṭāleb, who destroyed the idol of Manåt. He brought back all of her treasures including two swords. They were the attributes of justice and punishment.

In the Roman East, the cult of Manāt-Nemesis was very popular and Seyrig listed fifteen cities from Antioch to Gerasa where the deity was worshipped. She appears draped and veiled, holding the measuring rod, with the wheel as a symbol of the changing fate, while a griffin is represented at her feet.[50] On some reliefs, she practices the rite of aversion by moving away the collar of her tunic to spit into her breast.[51]

Isis in Petra The great Egyptian goddess who patronized life and death was considered in the ancient religious texts of the Pyramids as the sister-wife of Osiris and the mother of Horus. She borrowed the ancient crown of Hathor, consisting of the solar disc, flanked by two horns and surmounted by the two feathers of falcon.[52] Her cult spread in the Mediterranean basin during the Ptolemaic period. Ptolemy I in the fourth century BC called upon two experts: Manetho, an Egyptian, and Timotheus, a Greek, to systematize the cult of Isis.[53] The Greek interpretation of the Isis myth prevailed. As early as the fifth century BC, she was assimilated by Herodotus (*Histories* II, 59) to Demeter, and corn ears were added to her

46. Seated Isis of the Wadi ad-Dalaw, on the way to Jebel Harun.

47. Terracotta figurine of mourning Isis, discovered in the potter's kiln at Zurrabeh, Petra. h: 5.5 cm. Department of Antiquities, Amman, Jordan.

crown. It was through Alexandria that the worship and iconography of Isis penetrated into Petra: In the Oxyrhynchos papyri,[54] Petra is mentioned as a worship place of the deity in line 90, where she is qualified as *Soteira*. Several iconographic and epigraphic documents confirm the well-rooted cult of Isis in the city. On the most renowned monument, the Treasury, Isis is depicted as Tyche standing on a podium at the center of the tholos. She holds in her left hand the cornucopia and in the right, the cup of sacrifice. Her attributes, the solar disk flanked by two horns and corn ears, appear on the acroterion of the lower pediment (p. 195, fig. 207). The Alexandrian origin of this relief is confirmed by the representation of the goddess on the Alexandrian *oinochoai* of Berenike, wife of Ptolemy III (246-222 BC). The dating of the mid-first century BC is generally accepted. From that period, another relief of Sadd al-Mreriyyeh, a tributary of Wadi as-Siyyagh, represents Isis seated on a throne and draped in a long mantle, with a conical cap over the head (fig. 45). A phallus-like baetyl is carved in a nearby niche. A similar seated figure of Isis in a better state of preservation is carved in a niche in Wadi ad-Daluw, a tributary of Wadi Waghit, on the way to Egypt by Naqab ar-Ruba'i, through Jabal Harun. The goddess rests her feet on a molded stool and is dressed in the long mantle that is adorned by the Isis knot (fig. 46). Several pottery figurines found at the pottery kilns of Zurrabah represent a seated Isis resting on her right arm, her head crowned with the *basileion* (fig. 47). This is the type of mourning Isis, borrowed from the iconography of Demeter, who was afflicted by the kidnapping of her daughter, Persephone.[55]

In Roman Egypt and Greece, Isis was assimilated with Aphrodite.[56] The same phenomenon most probably happened at Petra: The many representations of Isis suggest that the Egyptian goddess was at home in the Nabataean capital. In the so-called Winged Lions Temple on the northern bank of Wadi Musa, the American Expedition of the University of Utah unearthed a statuette of black-green schist, representing a priest carrying a figure of the mummiform god Osiris.[57] This artifact is dated by the inscription to the end of the seventh or beginning of the sixth century BC, to the pharaoh Psamtik I. The cult of Osiris at Petra cannot be demonstrated, but his consort, Isis, enjoyed wide veneration in the city. After hesitating on the goddess of the Winged Lions Temple, P. Hammond[58] finally admitted her possible identification with Isis (see pp. 224–27 in this volume). However, he assumed that the Egyptian goddess was assimilated with Allat (who is not mentioned in the inscriptions of Petra); it is more logical to assume that she was assimilated with al-ʿUzza-Aphrodite.

Other Nabataean Gods The pre-Islamic Arab tribes venerated Ilah or Ilahy, and a confederation of Thamudic tribes worshipped him in a temple at Rawwafa in the second century AD.[59] At Mecca, the name al-Ilah ("the god") was contracted into Allah. According to the Arab chroniclers, the Quraysh worshipped Allah, but 'Amr ibn Luhayy (c. fourth century AD) introduced idols from Moab into Mecca and associated them with Allah. Among them was the god Hubal, described by al-Kalbi[60] as a carnelian-red statue, missing the right arm. He was placed in the Ka'ba with seven divination arrows.

Baal Shamin, the god of heaven and storms, was venerated in the late Bronze Age at Byblos and Ugarit. In the second century BC, Antiochus IV imposed his cult on the Hellenized cities of the Decapolis and the Jerusalem temple under the name of Zeus Olympios.[61] The cult of Baal Shamin was popular in the Nabataean Hauran, and a temple was dedicated to him at Sīʿ, in Jabal al-Druze, in 33/32 BC. The worship of the god penetrated into Petra and Wadi Iram probably under the influence of the Hauran and the cities of the Decapolis. Baal Shamin is commemorated in the chapel of al-Madras at the eastern entrance of Petra. Allah was also known to the pagan Arabs, but Islam proclaimed His absolute unicity. Like the Christians, the Nabataeans believed in the virgin birth of Dusares with the difference, however, that Christianity believed in the redemption of mankind by the birth and death of Jesus Christ.

5 | Nabataean Trade

DAVID F. GRAF AND STEVEN E. SIDEBOTHAM

The earliest classical literary reference to the Nabataeans depicts them as transporters of frankincense and myrrh to the ports of the eastern Mediterranean and of bitumen from the Dead Sea probably to Egypt (Hieronymus of Cardia in the fourth century BC preserved in Diodorus Siculus, *Bibliotheca Historica* 19.94.4-5, and 10). By the early Roman era, the Nabataean role as traders and conveyors of spices and incense was dominant. Although this commercial activity is amply reflected in ancient Greek and Latin literary sources, the documentation and details remain obscure and the Nabataean epigraphic and archaeological records are mystifyingly silent about their involvement in this international trade. What is known is preserved in a variety of sources from the Hellenistic and early Roman imperial era. Ancient authors provide only a sketchy outline about the commercial routes, the items involved in the trade, and Nabataean commerce with the wider Mediterranean world. Clearly, participation in this "international" commerce was of major economic importance to the Nabataeans (see map, p. 66).

The Nabataean emergence and involvement in this trade is just as murky. From their earliest homeland probably somewhere in the northeastern Arabian Peninsula,[1] the Nabataeans appear to have migrated across the major north Arabian trade route linking Mesopotamia and Egypt. In the early Hellenistic era, the geographer Eratosthenes indicates that Heroonpolis (modern Tell el-Maskhuta), located in Wadi Tumilat in the eastern Egyptian Delta, was connected to a trade route through the territory of the Nabataeans via Petra to Babylon on the Euphrates and to the Persian Gulf (in Strabo, *Geography* 16.4.2 [767]). This placed the Nabataeans strategically in a situation where they could take part in the flourishing aromatics trade with south Arabia by controlling the northern part of the incense route. Frankincense and myrrh were the monopoly of Hadramawt and Qataban in southern Arabia, where the incenses were produced and then bartered to neighboring merchants who transported the aromatics north to the Mediterranean world (Strabo, *Geography* 16.4.4 [768]; Pliny, *Natural History*. 6.54; 12.54 and 63). During the Persian and Hellenistic periods, the south Arabian kingdom of the Minaeans was the primary transporter of these aromatics to the Mediterranean, establishing a north Arabian mercantile colony at Dedan (al-ʿUla) in the Hejaz, and distribution centers throughout the Levant (Diodorus Siculus 3.42.5, Strabo, *Geography* 16.4.18 [776]), including Syria, north Arabia, Palestine, and Egypt.[2] Initially, the Nabataeans were merely middlemen in this flourishing trade (Strabo, *Geography* 16.4.18 [776]; cf. Diodorus Siculus 19.94.5), but by 100 BC, the Minaean kingdom collapsed and the Nabataeans replaced them as the primary transporters of south Arabian incense to the Mediterranean world (fig. 48).

By this time, the Nabataean capital at Petra had already achieved an international reputation as a prominent emporium. This is reflected in the honors received in 129 BC by Moschion son of Kydimos, an ambassador from Priene, whose diplomatic missions in the eastern Mediterranean included visits to Alexandria and "Petra in Arabia."[3] From the more distant Far East, the Han Chinese dynasty expedition led by Chang Ch'ien to Bactria in the west in 126 BC appears to have also picked up information about the commercial importance of Petra. His description of the far west mentions *Li-kan* (var. *Li-chien*). The name was initially taken to be the transcription of the ancient name of Petra, *Rekem*, but later sinologists preferred to view the term as a corrupt abbreviation for Ptolemaic Alexandria in Egypt. This proposal, however, ignores the fact that the initial *a* sound (Chinese Han *wu* = Western a) is present in the transcription of the cities named Alexandria in Asia that appear in the same records (*Wu-ch'ih-san* and *Wu-i-shan-li*). Nor is the middle *s* sound present in *Li-Kan*. As a result, the original proposal that *Li-kan* refers to Petra seems correct.[4] In addition, other Chinese

Nabataean Trade

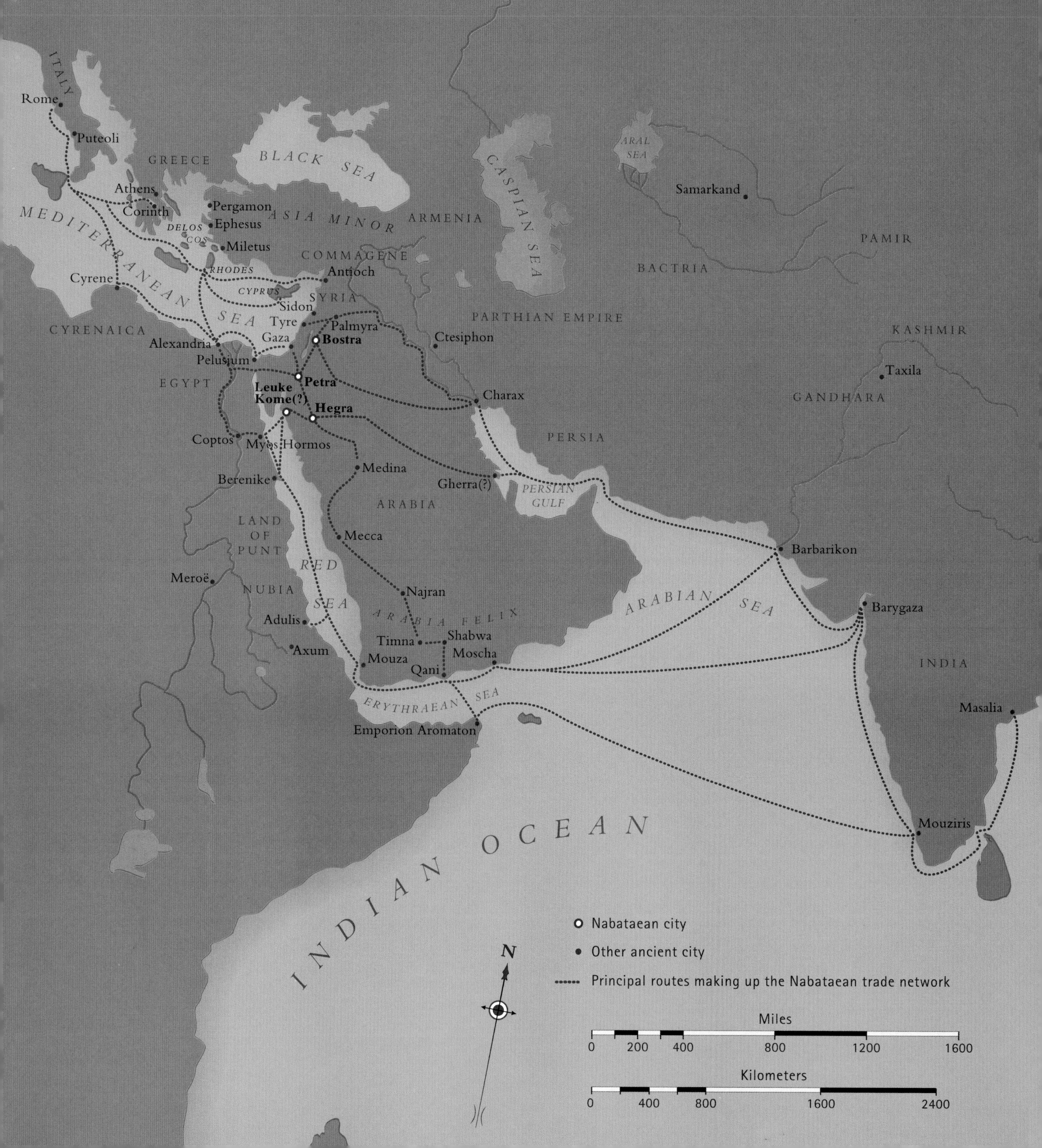

ITALY
Rome
Puteoli
GREECE
Athens
Corinth
MEDITERRANEAN SEA
DELOS
COS
RHODES
CYPRUS
BLACK SEA
Pergamon
Ephesus
Miletus
ASIA MINOR
ARMENIA
CASPIAN SEA
ARAL SEA
Samarkand
PAMIR
BACTRIA
COMMAGENE
Antioch
SYRIA
Sidon
Tyre
Palmyra
Bostra
Gaza
Cyrene
CYRENAICA
Alexandria
Pelusium
EGYPT
Petra
Leuke Kome(?)
Hegra
PARTHIAN EMPIRE
Ctesiphon
Charax
KASHMIR
Taxila
GANDHARA
PERSIA
Coptos
Myos Hormos
Berenike
Medina
Gherra(?)
PERSIAN GULF
ARABIA
LAND OF PUNT
Mecca
RED SEA
Meroë
NUBIA
Najran
Barbarikon
ARABIAN SEA
Barygaza
ARABIA FELIX
Adulis
Axum
Timna
Shabwa
Moscha
Mouza
Qani
INDIA
ERYTHRAEAN SEA
Emporion Aromaton
Masalia
Mouziris
INDIAN OCEAN

○ Nabataean city
● Other ancient city
······ Principal routes making up the Nabataean trade network

N

Miles
0 200 400 800 1200 1600

Kilometers
0 400 800 1600 2400

sources at the time mention a place in the far west named *Wu-tan*, whose characters literally mean "dark cinnabar."[5] This seems to be another Chinese reference to Petra, recalling Dean Burgon's famous poem about the "rose red city half as old as Time."

Trade Routes By the first century BC the Nabataeans dominated the overland caravan trade between their territory and that of southern Arabia (Arabia Felix), replacing merchants from the south Arabian kingdom of Minaea as the principal middlemen. In the early Roman imperial era, they were transporting aromatics from Petra to Rhinocoura on the Mediterranean coast of north Sinai (Strabo, *Geography* 16.4.24 [781]), and traveling from Petra eastward across Arabia via Dumata al-Jandal (modern al-Jawf) to southern Mesopotamia and Charax on the Tigris (Pliny, *Natural History* 6.145–146). According to Pliny the Younger, writing in the second half of the first century AD (*Natural History* 12.32.64), caravans coming from the town of Thomna in south Arabia traveled overland to Gaza on the Mediterranean coast in 65 stages each with a halt for camels, and at a cost of 688 denarii for a single camel load by the time it reached the Mediterranean ports (12.32.65). This high cost was due, in large part, to tolls and extortion/protection payments made to various tribes through whose territory the caravans passed. No ancient author discusses the times of year when the long-distance caravans bore the frankincense and myrrh northward to Petra, but these would have been dictated to some extent by the seasons when these gum resins were harvested.[6] The local and regional caravan traffic would, of course, have been conducted year round.

In the middle of the first century AD, freight from south Arabia was also shipped through the Red Sea to the port of Leuke Kome and, thence, overland to Petra, according to the *Periplus Maris Erythraei* (19), an anonymously authored mid-first-century AD sailor's and entrepreneur's handbook of ports, products and sailing conditions in the Red Sea and Indian Ocean.[7] The harbor-emporium at Leuke Kome was prominent enough to be discussed earlier by Strabo (*Geography* 16.4.23–24 [780–781]). This mainly maritime route undoubtedly minimized costs and was more efficient than the overland routes.[8] Goods transported by sea from south Arabia to Berenike took only thirty days (Pliny, *Natural History* 6.26.104); the onward journey to Leuke Kome would have added only a few extra days of travel. This movement of cargo by sea would have been faster than by overland caravan and would have avoided the high overland transportation costs.

Although the location of Leuke Kome is still a matter of debate, the most likely candidate for the site appears to be the region of Kuraybah-'Aynunah on the northwest coast of

48. Limestone incense burner/altar inscribed for Alexandros Amrou, Khirbet et-Tannur. h: 55 cm. Department of Antiquities, Amman, Jordan.

Saudi Arabia across from the Sinai near the Straits of Tiran.[9] Although the *Periplus* reports that none of the ships which put in at Leuke Kome were large, its harbor received enough traffic that a tax collector with a garrison was stationed there to ensure that the state received its share of revenues from the commerce, *viz.* a 25 percent *ad valorem* tax. That merchants and shippers could afford to pay this tax and that the government or tax farmers felt they could collect such an amount from those engaged in this commerce is some measure of the huge profits realized from this trade. There has been debate as to the "nationality" of the tax-collecting official and the garrison. Some suggest they were Nabataean,[10] since the Nabataeans adopted Greek and Roman terms for their officials. But, more recently, it has been contended that this tax collector and the troops supporting him were Roman.[11]

The possible commercial connections of the Nabataean settlement at Aila (Aqaba) at the northern end of the Gulf of Aqaba with Red Sea trade have yet to be determined, but recent excavations suggest it was thriving in the first century AD.[12] Nevertheless, given their relative locations, sailing conditions, and prevailing winds, Leuke Kome would have been the preferred emporium as it would have been easier to reach from southerly areas of the Red Sea than the more northerly port of Aila.[13] Aila appeared as an emporium from the Hellenistic era (Strabo. *Geography* 16.4.4. [768]), but it was in Roman times that it first became important as a major seaport.[14] Nevertheless, Jerome (*De Situ* col. 907), writing in the fourth century AD, was the first to refer to Aila as a major maritime emporium and its status in that capacity seems to have grown thereafter (Cosmas Indikopleustes, *Christian Topography* 2.6.72; Antonius of Placentia, *Itinera* 1899: 192).[15]

Earlier evidence of Nabataean maritime activity is also limited. In the Hellenistic period, the Nabataeans engaged in piratical practices on the Red Sea (Diodorus Siculus, *Bibliotheca Historica* 3.43.4–5; Strabo, *Geography* 16.4.18 [777]) which one or more of the Ptolemaic kings in neighboring Egypt actively suppressed.[16] Whether these were genuine piratical activities or merely clashes resulting from commercial maritime competition between Nabataean and Ptolemaic merchants and their governments is uncertain.[17] Whatever the case, thereafter the Nabataeans seem to have enjoyed more harmonious relations with the Ptolemies, with Ptolemaic commanders even occasionally leading Nabataean troops (Josephus, *BJ* 1.19.2 [367])[18]. Perhaps this was part of the arrangement which was the result of cessation of hostilities between Nabataea and Ptolemaic Egypt in the Red Sea, but any such policy was short-lived, precipitated by Cleopatra's aggressive activities against Nabataea. As a result, the Nabataeans burned Cleopatra's beached ships after the battle of Actium in 31 BC (Plutarch, *Antony* 69.3; Dio Cassius 51.7.1). If the Nabataeans maintained a navy, at least in part to protect maritime commercial activities through the Nabataean Red Sea ports, it has failed to leave any impression in literary or documentary evidence; whereas the Nabataean army is abundantly attested. After the annexation of the kingdom in 106 AD, a substantial number of these detachments became official Roman auxiliary units.[19] At least part of this force must have formerly been utilized in protecting Nabataean trade.

Of course, the security of caravans was a constant concern for the Nabataeans, as well as other merchants in the Near East.[20] At the advent of Islam, such long-distance caravans numbered from 1,000 to 2,500 camels, a virtual "army" (cf. Strabo, *Geography* 16.4.23 [781]). The organization of this large mass of men and animals by the Nabataeans remains unknown, but inscriptions from Palmyra provide some insight as to how another ancient Near Eastern trading state organized its caravans at the time.[21] The Palmyrene commander of a military escort for caravans was known as the "strategos" (*'strtg'*), who accompanied the "leader of the caravan" (*rb šyrt*), and the "members of the caravan" (*bny šyrt*). Wealthy merchants organized the whole enterprise.[22] Nabataean parallels to this terminology and organization are few. The term for "caravan" (*šyrt*) appears possible only once, and in a doubtful context.[23] *Strategoi*, on the other hand, appear throughout the Nabataean realm, but are concentrated at Hegra in the Hejaz, with several in northern Transjordan, and at Sidon and Dmeir just east of Damascus,[24] the latter suggesting at least a similar role in escorting caravans. Finally, the Nabataean god Shai' al-Qaum, the "escort of people," was known as the protector of the army and the caravans.[25]

The great prosperity resulting from this extensive trade is evident in the opulence of the royal capital at Petra in southern Jordan, with its large temples, tombs, and other public buildings,[26] and the equally impressive tombs at Hegra.[27] But perhaps the best visual testament to the importance of the caravan trade to the city's prosperity can be seen in the Siq, the narrow passageway through the mountains which connected the city to the outside world (p. 10, fig. 2). Along the south side of the Siq, close to where it debouches into the city, excavations in 1997 brought to light the remains of a large (approximately 1.3 times life-size) relief carved into the rock which depicts camels carrying merchandise (fig. 49). There are also men leading the camels. The sculptures are older than the hydraulic system behind them. The hydraulic system was built at the same time as the elaborate paved road, probably in the mid to last quarter of the first century BC. Carved probably in the early first century BC,[28] this relief of camels and their drivers reflects the importance of trade to the kingdom. The excavators suggest that these reliefs were dedicated by wealthy Nabataean merchants and believe they have located a similar relief with accompanying inscription dedicated by Nabataean entrepreneurs in the storerooms of the Naples Museum.[29]

By the late first century BC, the Nabataeans controlled a vast kingdom that included areas of southern Syria, Transjordan, the Negev of Palestine, the Sinai Peninsula, and northwestern Saudi Arabia.[30] It remains difficult to determine the exact limits or frontiers of their kingdom,[31] but from the

49. Sandstone relief with camel caravan. Siq, Petra.

north to the south it encompassed the regions south of Damascus in the Hauran of southern Syria to Hegra in northwestern Saudi Arabia. From the east, it extended from Dumat al-Jandal in the Wadi Sirhan in northern Saudi Arabia to the eastern Delta of Egypt in the west. Of course, its burgeoning trade connections extended far beyond these regions to the Persian Gulf, southern Arabia, Egypt, and even the central Mediterranean. The precise itineraries used by caravans along the overland trade route remain rather obscure and conjectural,[32] but some of the nodal points can be postulated from archaeological and epigraphic finds.

Across their vast territory, the Nabataeans established by the first century AD a number of important cities, trading posts, and caravan centers to sustain the vital trade routes connecting Petra with the prosperous kingdoms of south Arabia, the thriving cities in the Levant, and the major ports on the eastern Mediterranean. From Petra, routes led northwards to the Decapolis region, the major Syrian urban center of Damascus, and the Levantine coastal ports. Routes also linked various centers in the Negev (e.g., Oboda/'Avdat, Nessana/Awj al-Hafir, Elusa/Khalasa/Halutza, and Mamsis/Kurnub), Sinai, and Egypt.[33] Less well known are stations of greater or lesser size and importance linking the Nabataean heartland to its emporia on its periphery and even well beyond its political borders. As a result of archaeological surveys and excavations at a number of these locations, the extent of the Nabataean transit trade can be better visualized. Examination of the southern, eastern, and western peripheries of the Nabataean kingdom yields just such evidence.

Southern Arabia It is doubtful that Nabataean political and military power extended beyond the Hijaz, but their economic impact and presence throughout the Arabian Peninsula is well attested. Excavations at Qaryat al-Faw in southwestern Saudi Arabia have yielded Nabataean sherds dating from the first century BC to the fourth century AD, as well as a Nabataean graffito.[34] Nabataean coins from the reigns of Malichus I (34/32 BC) and Aretas IV (5/4 BC) as well as a few Nabataean sherds have appeared at Thaj in northeastern Saudi Arabia near the Persian Gulf.[35] Other Nabataean sherds have been discovered at scattered sites in Arabia including Oman,[36] the island of Garrayn off the coast of 'Asir,[37] Najran,[38] Marib in Saba,[39] and Qana on the Hadramawt coast.[40] In sum, the finds extend from southwest Yemen to the head of the Persian Gulf, where the emporium at Gerrha (Thaj?)was connected to a route leading to Qaryat al-Faw and the flourishing aromatic trade in southern Arabia.

In contrast, the epigraphic evidence for Nabataean activity in southern Arabia is minimal. A Sabaean (south Arabian) inscription records the name of a Nabataean—Taim'obodat—who resided in southern Arabia sometime in the first century BC or first century AD.[41] Several other south Arabian texts from Najran refer to an attack by the "Nabataeans" on a camp in the vicinity and their defeat.[42] The events and date remain obscure. More recently, a Nabataean inscription was found at Jebel al-Qara, twelve and one-half miles northwest of Hima in southern Arabia that is dated to the seventeenth year of the reign probably of Rabbel II, i.e. 88 AD.[43] Neither text specifies their occupation or activity, but it is likely that their presence in the region is associated with the incense trade. That the epigraphic evidence for Nabataean presence in southern Arabia is so minimal perhaps is not so surprising as other Arab middlemen may have been primarily engaged in the trade in this quarter, not Nabataeans. Nabataean presence in commercially related contexts in other areas of the Indian Ocean basin is unknown.

Hejaz Nabataean settlements in the northern Hejaz were abundant, and extended as far as Ha'il on the edge of the southern Nefud Desert in northern Saudi Arabia.[44] The main Nabataean caravan center in the northern Hejaz was at Hegra, where they were firmly in control of the area by the reign of King Aretas IV early in the first century AD.[45] Archaeological investigations have revealed little of the dynamics of this entrepôt on the southern fringes of Nabataea.[46] The prosperity of the settlement can best be gleaned from the impressive remains of the rock-cut tombs and the rich harvest of epitaphs for their occupants: the texts begin in 1 BC/AD with the latest dated to 74/75 AD.[47] Much of this epigraphic evidence relates to the presence of high-ranking military officers at the site in the mid-first century AD,[48] whose function, at least in part, must have been to protect Nabataean commerce along the caravan routes linking Petra to south Arabia. Others have suggested that its military strategic importance must be considered just as important as any commercial interests,[49] perhaps countering Arab raids against caravans.[50]

North Arabia In the lower region of the Wadi al-Sirhan, 300 miles east of Petra, the oasis of Dumat al-Jandal was the royal seat of the Qedarites and a series of north Arabian queens in the Neo-Assyria era. Adummatu, as it was known at the time, was the focus of Neo-Assyrian and Babylonian attacks ostensibly to seize lucrative centers of the incense trade, which was just having an impact on the Mesopotamian world. This effort even led the Babylonian king Nabonidis into the Hejaz where he resided at Tayma and seized the important caravan cities from Dedan (modern Al-'Ula) to Yathrib (modern Medina) for a decade.[51] It is, therefore, not surprising later to find the presence of a Nabataean official at the oasis entitled "the head of the camp" (*rb mšryt'*) and that he and his brother (also present) were members of one of the high-ranking military families at Hegra in the Hejaz.[52] After the annexation of the Nabataean kingdom, Roman military detachments of the Third Cyrenaica legion based at Bosra served both at al-Jawf and Hegra, with supporting auxiliary units.[53] This pattern from Neo-Assyrian to the Roman era seems clear: the control of the important nexus points on the vital trade routes was a desideratum. The Nabataean presence at these oases is best understood in this same context.

North Sinai Tracking the Nabataean routes across the northern Sinai remains difficult,[54] but Pliny informs us that the port cities along the north Sinai coast of the Mediterranean were connected by a route that passed through the territory of the Arab tribe named the Autaei (*Natural History* 6.166-167). This area has been identified with the Nabataean temple complex and settlement of Qasrawet in northwestern Sinai roughly nineteen miles southwest of Pelusium in the extremity of the northeast Delta, where Hellenistic sherds (including imported amphorae from Rhodes, Kos, and Knidos, and Megarian bowls) and a Nabataean lamp and inscription attest its commercial relations with the coastal regions and the culture of Petra.[55] One of the two Nabataean inscriptions from nearby Tell el-Shuqafiya in the Suez region (dating to 77 and 35 BC) seems to mention the site[56] and a Greek ostracon found at Qasrawet referring to a route connecting the *kastron* with Egypt[57] suggests that this was, indeed, Pliny's *Castrum Autaei*. The settlement appears to be the main Nabataean commercial center in the northern Sinai that linked the trade network of the Egyptian Delta with Petra.[58] Several thousand Nabataean graffiti in southern Sinai were once connected with a trade route, but this no longer seems the most feasible explanation for their presence.[59] Although most of them probably date to the period after the annexation of the Nabataean kingdom, at least one Nabataean graffito mentions a military official (Abdharetat, a *hipparch* or cavalry officer).[60] The Nabataeans certainly had a significant presence in the Sinai for an extended period as their temples and numerous graffiti throughout the peninsula indicate,[61] even if that presence remains enigmatic.

The Mediterranean Even before the Roman annexation of Nabataea in 106 AD, inscriptions in Latin, Greek, and Nabataean record the presence of Nabataean merchants and political envoys throughout the Mediterranean. These include the ports in the Levant and Aegean areas at such places as Gaza, Sidon, Beirut, Salamis in Cyprus, Rhodes, Kos, Miletos, Priene, Delos, Rhene Island near Delos, Tinos, and Athens.[62] Farther west they appear in the major Italian port of Puteoli near Naples, where a cult to Dushara/Dusares, the royal dynastic Nabataean deity, existed.[63] The Nabataeans are also attested to at Ostia, the port of Rome, as well as at Rome itself.[64]

TRADE ITEMS

The commerce that flowed across this vast network of trade routes must have been substantial, but archaeological evidence in the form of physical remains of objects involved in this traffic is scarce. Most of our knowledge for the merchandise traded derives from ancient literary sources. The most important commodities in the trade from southern Arabia to Nabataea and beyond to the Mediterranean were frankincense and myrrh[65] and the classical literary sources are replete with references to the importance and cost of these gum resins.[66] Other commodities which might have made the long caravan journey transiting through southern Arabia to the Mediterranean via Petra were pearls, cinnabar, cardamom, gum, and styptic. These contacts and those of the Persian Gulf also brought the Nabataeans in touch with the spices of India and silk from China (fig. 50; p. 219, figs. 236, 37).

As primarily middlemen, the Nabataeans also procured and manufactured objects for their own use and, to a limited extent, for re-export. These items of commercial value came from Sinai in the first century AD, especially copper and iron, which suggest a more highly settled/urbanized Nabataean population by that date.[67] Nabataean graffiti found near the amethyst mines at Abu Diyeiba, close to Wadi Safaga adjacent to the Red Sea coast of Egypt and the discovery of large quantities of unworked amethyst and amethyst beads at Petra, indicate that bead manufacturing using semi-precious stones imported from Egypt took place at the Nabataean capital.[68]

It is difficult to ascertain what commodities the caravans received in exchange from the Mediterranean ports to return back to Petra or used in payment to south Arabia for purchasing aromatics. Finds in south Arabia of Mediterranean-made glass, ceramics (undoubtedly for transport of commodities such as wine), bronze objects (statues and statuettes), and Roman coins offer a few clues, but not all of these goods were transported by overland caravans. Indeed, the relatively low cost of the mass-produced glass and ceramics of heavy weight like jars of wine (*Periplus Maris Erythraei* 28) would, most likely, have been transported to southern Arabia by sea.

50. Ivory handle with female figure, probably from south Asia. Temple of the Winged Lions, Petra. l: 16 cm. Department of Antiquities, Amman, Jordan.

Strabo also indicates that certain items were not imported from other countries because they were readily available within Nabataea. These included gold and silver, as well as "*most* of the aromatics" (*Geography* 16.4.26 [784]). This neglected statement suggests that the Nabataeans could have exported from their own kingdom a number of valuable items normally associated with south Arabia. Each of these items deserves attention. The items mentioned recall the treasures of the wise men deposited at the Bethlehem manager: gifts of "gold, frankincense and myrrh" (Matthew 2.11). The earliest known interpretation of these Magi was that they represented Arabs (Justin, Tertullian), and perhaps Nabataeans.[69] The references to precious metals also recall the famous "gold mines of Midian" popularized by Sir Richard Burton, and the legend is justified by finds of several dozen small deposits of gold scattered across the northern Hejaz, with associated settlements that seem to have been engaged in mining.[70]

The Nabataean reputation for gold and silver also has literary support. At a banquet in 17 AD, the Nabataean king Aretas IV offered "massive gold crowns" to Germanicus and Agrippina, and "lighter" ones to Piso and others who were present (Tacitus, *Annals* 2.57). There are some suggestions of a goldsmith industry in Nabataea in finds of jewelry at Mampsis and Avdat (Oboda) in the Negev.[71] The Macedonian army in the fourth century BC seized booty that included "five hundred talents of silver" (Diodorus Siculus 19.95.3), and the attack of the Syrian governor Scaurus was warded off by payment of 300 talents in 62 BC (Josephus *AJ* 14.80-81; *BJ* 1.159).

The identity of the specific types of aromatics produced within Nabataea can also be traced. The resin perfume known as Ladanum (*L. cistaceae*) is characterized as exclusively produced by the Nabataeans, who combed it from the beards of their goats (Pliny, *Natural History* 12.73; cf. Herodotus 3.112). By the first century AD, there were other varieties of this incense that competed with that from Arabia (Dioscorides, *Materia Medica* I.97/128), but its importance as a native good is important. The gummy substance of bdellium used in perfumery, pharmacy, and in making incense was procured from India, Persia, and Arabia (Pliny, *Natural History* 12.35; cf. *Periplus Maris Erythraei* 37, 39, and 48), but these varieties (known as *Commiphora mukul*) lack the sweet smell associated with bdellium.[72] The dark variety from Petra (Dioscorides, *Materia Medica* 1.67/80) may perhaps have been this type, for it remained important as an aromatic into late antiquity. Finally, the spice known as "sweet rush" (*L. juncus odoratus*) or "camel grass" was common throughout the Middle East, but also associated with Nabataea (Pliny, *Natural History* 12.104; Dioscorides, *Materia Medica* 1.17/16). These aromatics seem to be the most likely ones that Strabo indicates were indigenous to Nabataea.

Relations with Rome and the West The importance of the Kingdom of Nabataea came to Rome's attention early during the first century BC. Pompey's eastern expansion and annexation of Syria in 63 BC brought him in contact with Nabataea.[73] As a client kingdom of Rome, cordial relations existed with Julius Caesar, but soured with Antony and Cleopatra. After the Battle of Actium in 31 BC, the Nabataeans supported Augustus. In a famous episode in 26/25 BC, the Nabataean King Obodas III sent 1,000 troops and his vizier Syllaeus to assist the Roman commander Aelius Gallus—under orders from the emperor Augustus—in his expedition against Arabia Felix (Strabo, *Geography* 16.4.22-24; *Res Gestae* 5.26; Pliny, *Natural History* 6.32.160-162; Josephus *AJ* 15.3.17; Dio Cassius 53.29.3-8). This campaign was certainly commercially motivated[74] and the inclusion of a sizeable Nabataean contingent suggests that that Arab state anticipated substantial economic benefits from the expedition. It was certainly perceived as a positive enterprise from the Roman perspective.[75] Afterwards, there may have been an aborted attempt at annexation of Nabataea by Rome during the reign of Tiberius (14-37 AD)—perhaps as part of an overall plan, which may have included repair and refurbishment of Egypt's Red Sea ports and roads joining them to the Nile—to increase Roman participation in the lucrative Red Sea–Indian Ocean trade.[76]

The enlargement and construction of various Egyptian Red Sea ports following the Roman annexation of Egypt in 30 BC dramatically increased the flow of commerce via Roman Egypt between the Mediterranean basin on the one hand and the Red Sea and Indian Ocean littorals on the other. Since transport by sea was substantially cheaper than shipment overland throughout antiquity,[77] some have argued that the opening of these emporia had an adverse effect on the overland caravan route from south Arabia to Nabataea and the Nabataean entrepreneurs who profited from it.[78] The impact on Nabataea, however, is difficult to determine. What is clear is that Hegra reached its zenith after these developments and archaeological evidence from Petra suggests that the overland caravan routes in Arabia continued to prosper.[79] It seems more likely that the demand for aromatics and other exotic items was so great that the newly constructed and enlarged Egyptian Red Sea ports of the early Roman period merely complemented the flourishing trans-Arabian caravan trade conducted by the Nabataeans.[80]

The rise of Palmyra as a caravan city in Syria during the early Roman imperial period was also previously thought to have diminished the importance of Petra and its caravan routes across the Arabian Peninsula. But long-distance caravans across Arabia are still mentioned by Pliny in the third quarter of the first century AD and the ships carrying frankincense, myrrh, and other high-cost merchandise between southern Arabia and Nabataea are still mentioned in the *Periplus Maris Erythraei* in the mid-first century AD. What is just as important is the silence in the *Periplus* about any role of Palmyra in the commerce in the Persian Gulf or India at the time, while mentioning the flourishing trade in Nabataea of the mid-first century AD. Excavations at Nabataean centers in Humayma, the Negev cities, and Bosra in Syria suggest that they were prospering in the first century AD, precisely when Hegra was flourishing as a caravan center. A constant flow of internal local and regional overland caravan traffic was necessary for maintaining these settlements along the caravan routes.

Finally, some have considered the annexation of the Nabataean kingdom in 106 AD as marking the eclipse of Petra and the incense trade. Whatever the motivations were for annexation, securing the trade routes in Nabataean territory and in adjacent regions does not seem to have been the priority; Rome would have seized the kingdom earlier if that were the case. Petra received as early as 114 AD the honorific title of *metropolis*, the epithet of *Hadriane* in 130, and the status of *colonia* by the third century, even before Bosra. Petra was the regional center of government assizes in the Hadrianic era and the burial place of T. Aninius Sextius Florentinus, governor of Arabia between 127 and 130. If the capital maintained its administrative and political importance, the establishment of the *via nova Traiana* connecting it with Aila on the Red Sea and Bosra ensured its economic significance.[81] Petra and other Nabataean centers even maintained their native traditions into late antiquity.[82]

Rome's annexation of Nabataea may have resulted in a shift in the commercial patterns forced by its loss of autonomy. A few Nabataeans were active in the commerce of Ptolemaic Egypt,[83] but after Rome's annexation of Egypt in 30 BC their number significantly increased. The Red Sea–Indian Ocean commerce dramatically changed from the way it had been conducted via Egypt under the Ptolemies. Under the Romans, the tight state control of the Ptolemies was replaced by trade dominated by private entrepreneurs, some with military and government connections. The Nabataeans were especially active in Egypt after the Roman annexation in 30 BC. Over eighty inscriptions, mainly graffiti, have been found in the Eastern Desert between the Nile and the Red Sea coast, attesting their presence in that region,[84] most likely in trade-related contexts. One inscription even records Palmyrene-Nabataean commercial relations in Egypt.[85] Other Nabataean graffiti have been found in the vicinity of the early Roman Red Sea port of Quseir al-Qadim,[86] along the road thence to Coptos[87] and some Nabataean ostraca have recently come to light at Wakalat al-Zerqa (ancient Maximianon), one of the ancient stations on the route joining Quseir al-Qadim to Coptos.[88] Previously graffiti were known at a rock shelter on the route between Coptos and the large Red Sea port of Berenike.[89] While these texts, for the most part, do not specify the activities of their authors, a commercially-related function is likely.[90]

In addition, fragments of Nabataean fine-ware pottery dated between the late first century BC and second century AD have been recovered in excavations at two of the ancient Egyptian Red Sea ports: Quseir al-Qadim[91] and Berenike.[92] Whether this slight ceramic evidence indicates Nabataean presence at these emporia or merely the passage of some of their pottery through those ports is difficult to determine. The numerous Nabataean graffiti found along the routes joining the Nile to the Red Sea ports suggest, however, at least an ephemeral presence of Nabataean entrepreneurs at the Egyptian Red Sea emporia.

It is difficult to determine how much of the Nabataean trade was conducted in a laissez-faire economic environment free of Nabataean government control and how much of the commerce was, in fact, state sponsored or at least protected by the Nabataean or Roman military. That commerce was a critical component of the Nabataean royal economy in the first century BC and first century AD suggests that some degree of Nabataean government regulation and protection may have existed. Still lacking is a better understanding of Nabataean commerce from the documentary evidence; this is relatively plentiful for the caravan trade of Palmyra. It can only be hoped that future exploration of the Nabataean realm and beyond will produce such evidence.

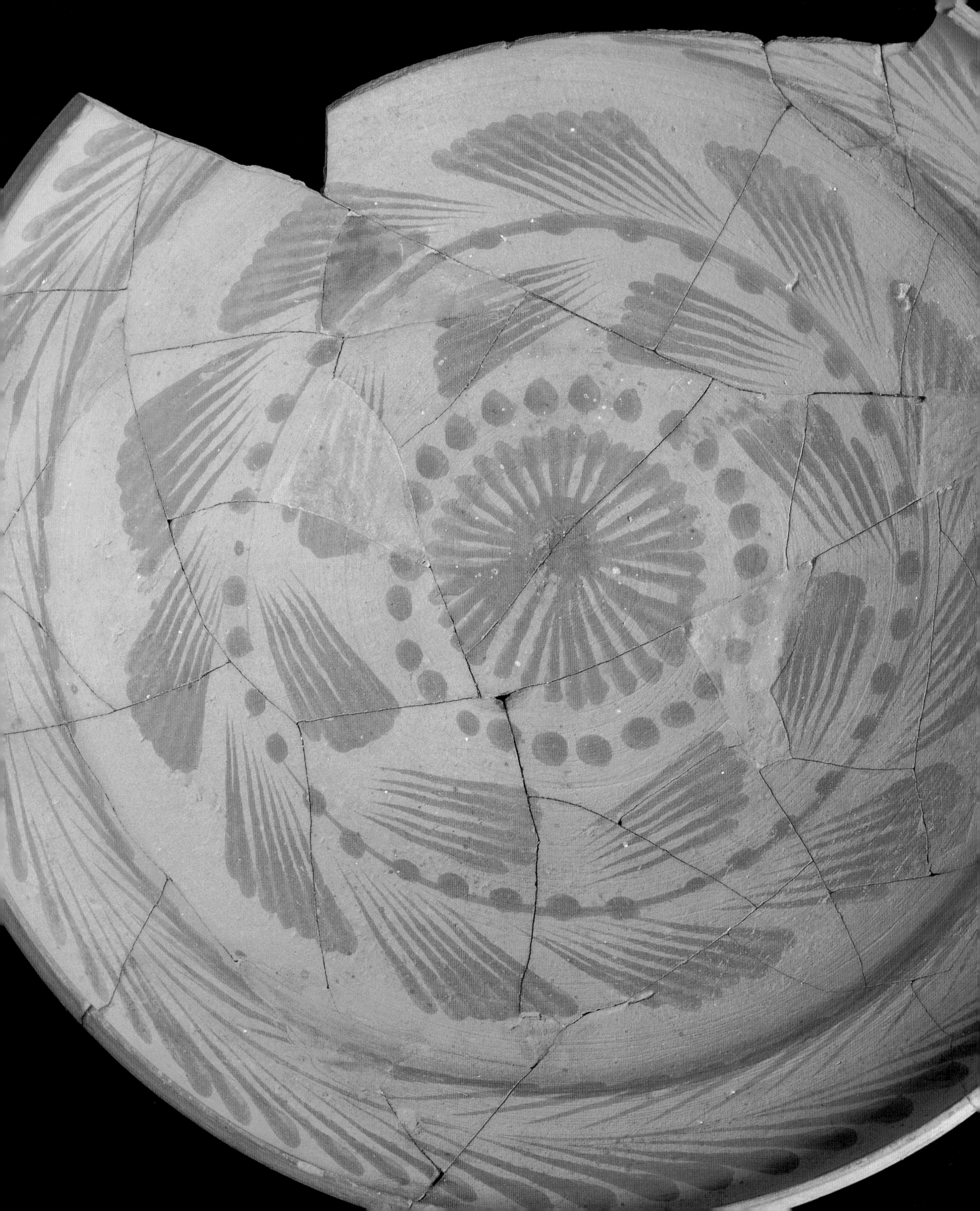

6 | Nabataean Pottery

STEPHAN G. SCHMID

POTTERY USUALLY IS FOUND in abundance at archaeological sites from the late Neolithic period onward. It therefore can be used as a major tool in order to establish chronologies and it can help in understanding about inter-cultural exchanges, import and export mechanisms, and trade in general.

In the case of the Nabataeans the situation is, as we shall see below, somewhat special. The characteristic thin-walled pottery, mostly open forms like plates and shallow bowls, sometimes painted, was first mentioned and described by G. Dalman in the year 1908, although he did not connect it with the Nabataeans. But already Dalman observed that in Petra pottery belongs to the richest archaeological remains, readily covering the surface. The identification of that pottery as Nabataean goes back to the year 1929, when G. and A. Horsfield excavated in Petra and found important quantities of this earthenware.[1]

Although almost a century passed since the first description of Nabataean pottery, it took quite a long time to establish a valuable typology and chronology of it. This may be due to the fact that the fascination of its fine painted decoration challenged most people toward a stylistic analysis without considering the stratigraphic background of regular excavations in the first place. Indeed, the painting of Nabataean plates and bowls is exceptional, most of all because it occurs at a time, i.e., the late Hellenistic and Early Roman periods, when most pottery in the Mediterranean and the Near East was no longer painted, but stamped or molded, if decorated at all. This development is connected to economic aspects leading toward a larger and more rapid, i.e., industrial, production of the more important pottery categories, like Hellenistic moldmade bowls or Roman *terra sigillata*. In order to place Nabataean pottery in this general picture we shall have a brief look at the forms and chronology of the more characteristic types of the fine ware.[2]

In its first stage, Nabataean fine-ware pottery truly follows the shapes of Hellenistic pottery, as commonly attested in the Eastern Mediterranean and the Middle East. The open forms are gently rounded, either showing inverted or out-turned rims (fig. 52.1–4). They further show a common thickness of about 4 mm. It is important to mention that, although these open forms cover about 75 percent or even more of the pottery found on Nabataean sites, there are contemporary closed vessels like the amphora (fig. 52.5) already from this first phase on. Quite special is the painting of some of the open forms, showing rather thick red lines on the inner side of the vessel, usually occurring in pairs and crossing each other at the bottom of the vessel (fig. 53).

A further characteristic is the often-occurring red slip covering the surface of the bright orange-red clay. This red slip, too, points distinctively toward the late Hellenistic background of this pottery. In the Middle East fine wares used to show a mainly red surface from the Iron Age at the latest. With Alexander the Great's conquests of these regions not only the shapes but also the black surface of Greek pottery was brought to the East. In the following centuries the forms of Greek pottery remained but the surface turned again toward the traditional red.[3] It was precisely this development that led, toward the end of the second century BC, to the creation of Eastern *terra sigillata* A (henceforth referred to as ESA), one of the most helpful chronological tools in Near Eastern archaeology: The shapes of the earlier series are purely (Greek) Hellenistic forms with a characteristic red surface slip.

As ESA was produced—most probably in Syria—for exportation throughout the Eastern Mediterranean, it became a valuable instrument for dating less common pottery types like Nabataean fine ware.[4] As the pottery from Petra and other Nabataean sites described above is found together with the earlier shapes of ESA, we may conclude that Nabataean pottery production started around 100 BC. This may seem a serious problem at first glance, since the Nabataeans are

51. Painted bowl of Phase 2c (c. 1–20 AD)

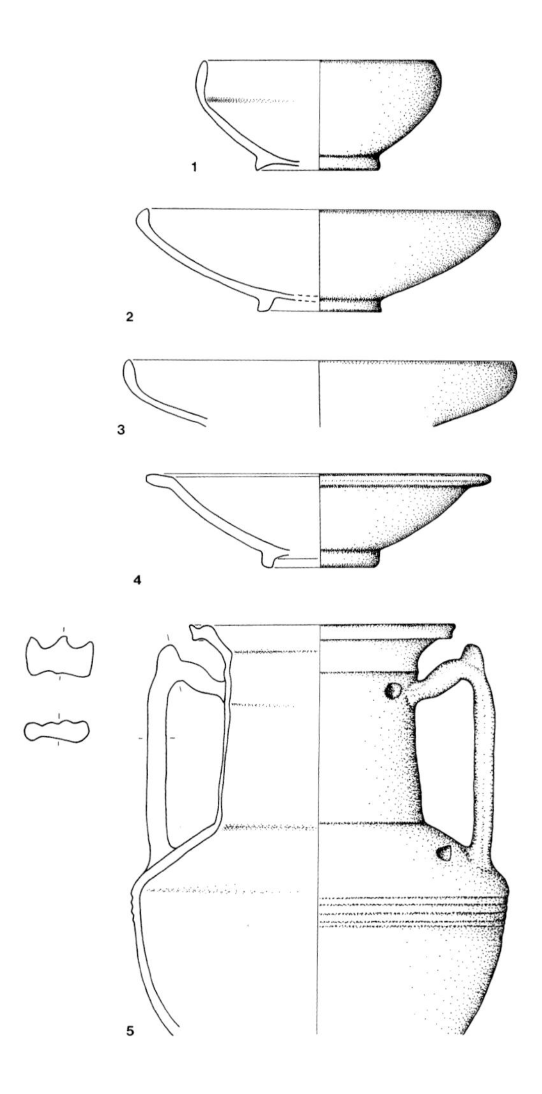

52. Plain pottery of Phase 1 (c. 100–50 BC).

documented historically by 312 BC and, from the outset, are associated with central and southern Jordan (see Chapter 2). We must therefore explain why the Nabataeans produced no pottery for two hundred years and then suddenly began adopting late Hellenistic tablewares. As a matter of fact, this archaeological enigma extends beyond just the pottery, since it counts for the entire culture of this people. In fact, there are no material remains (firmly) associated with the Nabataeans that can be dated before the late second century BC. As odd as this seems, there is a logical explanation. The first account of the Nabataeans by Diodorus of Sicily describes them as a nomadic tribe, without a permanent base, that met but once a year at a specific place in order to conduct trade and other business (*Universal History* 19.94.1; 19.95.2ff.). As nomads, the Nabataeans would not have required a highly developed material culture and would (in all likelihood) have produced non-permanent craftwork like textiles and wooden tools—characteristic nomadic products. Toward the end of the second century BC, however, circumstances changed considerably in the Near East. The Seleucid empire was weak and, on its periphery, several smaller kingdoms arose, like the Hasmoneans in Judea. It must have been during this time that the Nabataeans settled down to a more permanent base, at least at Petra and its surroundings. This change in lifestyle was probably related to economic factors: with a permanent base the Nabataeans could more fully participate in international long-distance trade, for instance, shipping spices from Arabia to the Mediterranean (see Chapter 5). Proof of the economic basis of this change—from nomadic to settled lifestyle—may be found in the fact that, along with their first pottery, the Nabataeans began producing their first coins, which were strongly influenced by Hellenistic prototypes too.[5]

As for the function of Nabataean pottery, it had been theorized that it was used mainly for cultic purposes, such as offerings to the gods. However, this interpretation seems to have been erroneously based on a misunderstanding of the historical sources and on the fact that Nabataean private architecture has only recently begun to be investigated, with the result that the pottery itself had no context into which to be placed.[6] The composition of the pottery types found together already in the first phase, that is, a large quantity of plates and open bowls and a small quantity of amphorae and other closed vessels (fig. 52.1–5), makes clear that it covers the normal needs of an ancient household. It should be mentioned that, in antiquity, the most common drinking vessels were not, as nowadays, forms like beakers or cups but rather flat bowls. Therefore, the plates of Nabataean pottery must have been used for eating, the bowls for drinking, and the closed vessels for serving and storage purposes. To this spectrum should be added the coarse-ware pottery that was used for cooking and storage purposes.

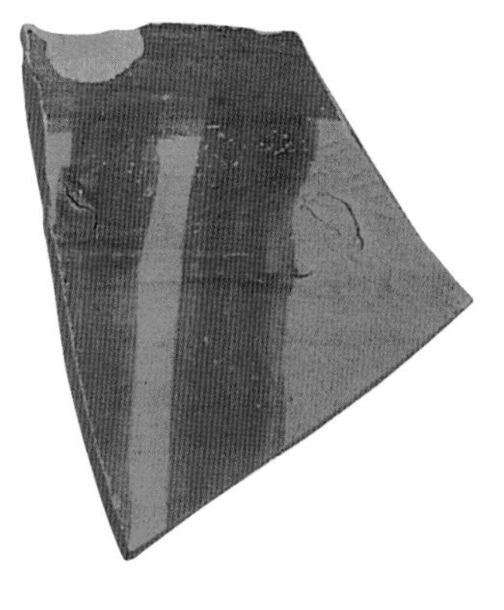

53. Painted pottery of Phase 1 (c. 100–50 BC).

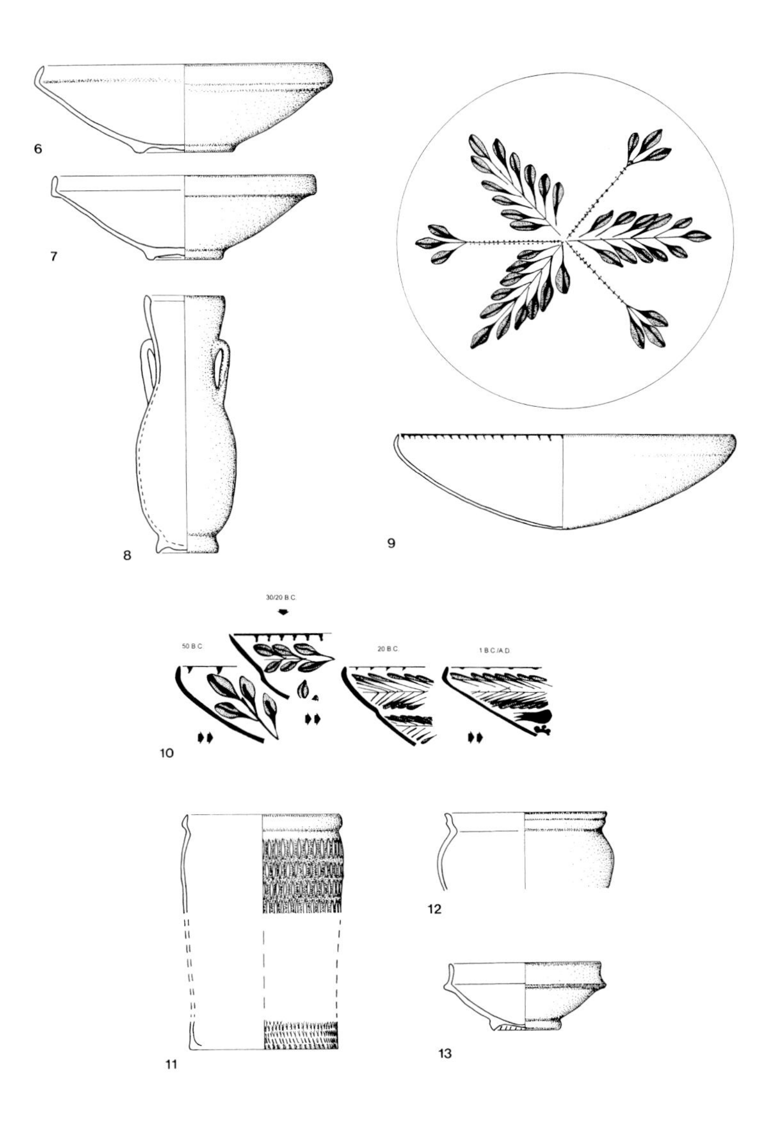

54.6–13. Plain and painted pottery of Phase 2 (c. 50 BC–20 AD).

Although the Nabataeans were known as smart traders between East and West, it seems they did not participate in the industrialization of the goods they transported, i.e., the refinement and packing of spices. First of all, the ancient sources refer only to the commercial role of the Nabataeans as traders.[7] Second, during the first century BC *unguentaria*, vessel types for unguents and perfumes of oil base, are completely lacking from the Nabataean pottery repertoire. There are occasionally imported specimens coming from Asia Minor, according to their grayish clay and the painted red stripes.[8]

As we have seen, the beginning of the first phase of Nabataean fine ware can be dated around 100 BC. During the first half of the first century BC this pottery continues to be produced without major changes. Around 50 BC new forms and motifs of decoration are introduced, consequently called Phase 2. As in the first phase, the main shapes are plates and open bowls (fig. 54.6, 7). Their forms could be called developed variants of their forerunners, being finer and thinner (around 2 to 3 mm). Further, there is a tendency toward sharper forms, which are not so smoothly rounded as in phase 1. Here too, some types of closed vessels, such as fig. 54.8, go together with huge quantities of flatter shapes, thus offering all the necessary categories of vessels for daily life.

The most remarkable change is clearly observed in the painted decoration of the flat bowls, presumably the drinking vessels. The main type of this category is a flat, rounded bowl without any standing device such as a base or foot (figs. 54.9; 56). As there are almost no finds of stands reported, these vessels were most probably held continuously in the hand, a typical characteristic of drinking vessels in antiquity. The use of these bowls as drinking cups is further supported by the fact that they have some close parallels in Near Eastern metal vessels, both for their forms and for their floral decoration.[9] The painting consists of simple floral motifs, fleshy leaves, or groups of leaves forming limbs in red color, the same as the surface slip so prominent in Phase 1 (which now occurs but rarely) (figs. 55, 56).

Nabataean pottery is decorated almost exclusively with floral motifs. There are, however, some very rare exceptions to this rule. It is during Phase 2a (c. 50–25 BC) that we witness two different variants of representations of human or human-like figures. The first example is the relief-decorated lower part of a handle of a jug (fig. 58), showing the very naturalistic face of a bearded silen. Such applied masks are very common in late Hellenistic or early Roman Imperial pottery and, more specifically, in luxury bronze and silver vessels.[10] While the prototype or form for the molded face on our jug may have been imported from the Mediterranean, the vessel itself is clearly a local product. Another very special example is the fragment with a bearded youthful face painted in polychrome technique (fig. 57). This fragment belongs to one of the very characteristic bowls such as in fig. 56. Such polychrome painting was applied after firing and the vessel therefore had a purely decorative character. The shape and the orientation of the youth's torso seem to indicate that he is not standing or sitting upright but rather reclining on a *kline*, a typical pose for participants in drinking parties, or *symposia*. This is a unique case in which we have a direct indication for the use of such vessels; moreover, the pink band around the youth's head most probably is a wreath, another typical characteristic of drinkers in ancient iconography.

After roughly one generation, i.e., around 25 BC, an additional step appears in the walls of these drinking bowls, reflecting influence from Mesopotamia and Iran, where such forms had already been produced for many centuries.[11] With the introduction of the new shape, the decorative patterns

55. Painted pottery of Phase 2a (c. 50–25 BC).
56. Painted bowl of Phase 2a (c. 50–25 BC).

57. Polychrome painted sherd with face of a youth, Phase 2a (c. 50–25 BC).
58. Lower part of handle decorated with silen's mask, Phase 2a (c. 50–25 BC).

also change, becoming finer and oriented concentrically (fig. 59) rather than radially as before, or displaying fine floral patterns of diverse orientation. However, after roughly one quarter of a century, this foreign element disappears again from the repertoire of Nabataean pottery. The detailed evolution of the main shapes of Nabataean painted bowls in the second half of the first century BC can be seen on (fig. 54.10).

Around the turn of the millennium, further remarkable developments can be observed. The major unpainted shapes become still finer although they basically follow the same line of evolution described above. The main painted types appear again without the step in the wall (fig. 54.10, far right), but they become finer too, with a bigger diameter and a completely new painted style. Now, in the first two or three decades of the first century AD, the entire inner body of the vessel is almost completely covered with small patterns, consisting of "eyes" (small circles with inscribed dots), small floral elements, points, and others (cf. fig. 51). The color of the painted decoration, too, has changed from the previously strong red to something rather violet or brownish. Good comparisons for the shape and, especially, for the decorative patterns can be found in late Hellenistic and early Roman glassware.[12] As in the case of the Near Eastern metal bowls mentioned above, this is another typical category of luxury vessel, commonly used for drinking. As both of these categories—metal bowls and glass vessels—are rather uncommon in Nabataean sites and may have been the privilege of only a few rich people, in all likelihood the numerous comparably shaped

59. Painted bowl of Phase 2b (c. 25–1 BC).
60. Painted bowl of Phase 3a (c. 20–75 AD)

61.14–26. Plain, stamped, and rouletted pottery of Phase 3 (c. 20–100 AD).

ceramic vessels were taking over their function for the needs of the common people.

It is also during Phase 2 (c. 50 BC to c. 20 AD) that a stronger Roman influence can be traced in Nabataean pottery production for the first time. Several local products have good parallels in Roman thin-walled pottery or even in Italian *sigillata* wares (fig. 54.11–13).[13] Therefore, the Nabataeans were quite sensitive to international fashions in the field of pottery production. On the other hand, we may see reflections of historical events in the adoption of these specific pottery forms too. It is precisely during this period, beginning with the campaign of Pompey the Great in Syria in 63 BC and the conquest of Egypt by Octavian (later Augustus) in 30 BC, that Rome exerted a much stronger influence in the wider region. Suddenly, the Nabataeans had become rivals of the Romans in the long-distance trade on the Arabian Peninsula, as is vividly illustrated by Aelius Gallus's campaign to South Arabia, which was said by Roman propaganda to have been sabotaged by the Nabataeans (see Chapter 1, p. 22).[14]

Around 20 AD the next important stage in the evolution of Nabataean fine-ware pottery occurs, initiating Phase 3. In general terms, all the forms become even finer, reaching a peak of an average thickness of about 1 to 2 mm. The main shapes of the plain pottery are now very sharp, cut bowls and plates with a characteristic vertical rim (fig. 61.14, 15). In Phase 3, lasting to the very beginning of the second century AD, not only the essential shapes of closed vessels are represented to form a kind of "service," but there is also a very rich

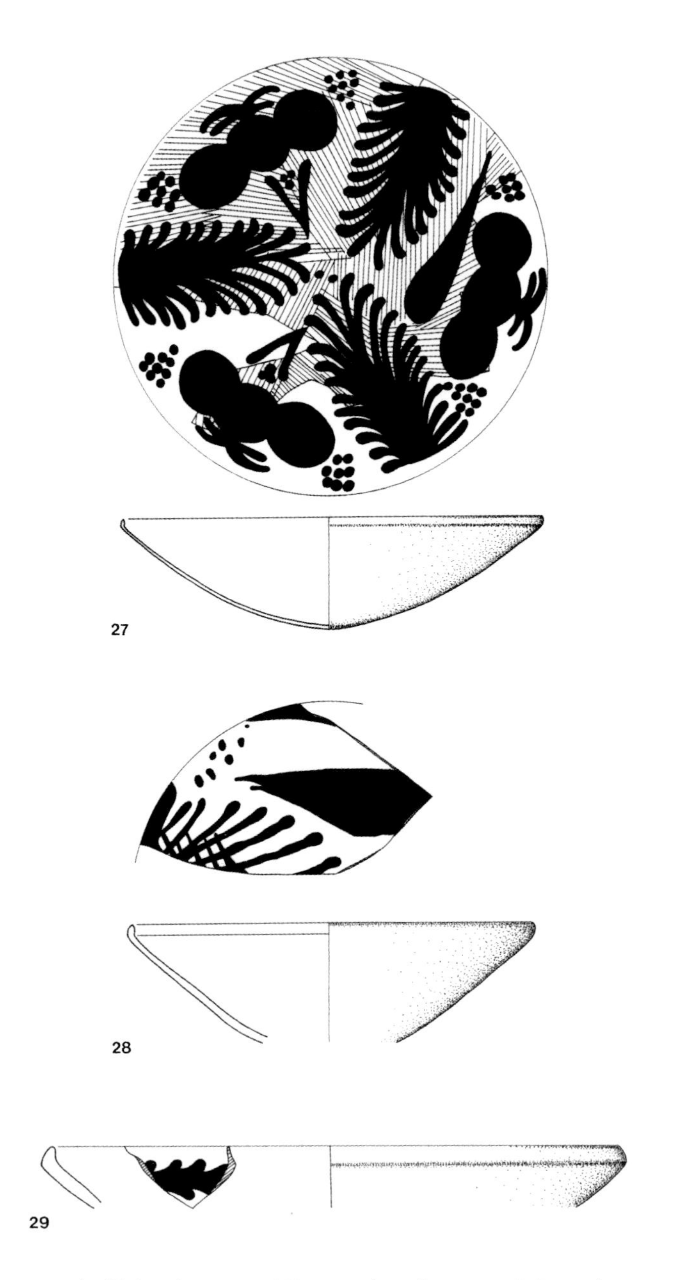

62.27–29. [27]Painted pottery of Phase 3b (c. 70/80–100 AD). [28, 29] Painted pottery of the 2nd and 3rd centuries AD.

63. Painted bowl of Phase 3b (c. 70/80–100 AD)

variation of many different forms of small flasks, juglets, *amphoriskoi,* and other vessels (fig. 16.16–26).

The most detailed development can be traced in the main types of the painted drinking bowls. At the beginning of Phase 3 there are still traces of the decorative patterns as in the later phase of the previous Phase 2. We can still observe the same tendency to cover the entire vessel's body with small decorative elements, some of them evoking naturalistic floral patterns (fig. 64). The distinctive new elements are the forms: the most important type is a very flat bowl, usually without foot or ring base, with a small degenerated rim (fig. 62.27). This basic type will remain the most important form in Nabataean painted pottery for about a century.

Around 70/80 AD a new sub-phase occurs within Phase 3. The main types of pottery are basically the same, but the painting changes entirely. The new style consists of decorative elements ranging from dark brown to black in color; larger in size, they are more sparsely distributed, leaving considerable free space between them. Alongside a few simple and abstract floral patterns there is a predominance of geometric motifs, set against a background consisting of fine lines (figs. 62.27; 63). It is a very striking fact that this notable change from naturalistic and small-scale decoration to more strongly abstract and ornamental painting coincides almost precisely with the assumption of the Nabataean throne by Rabbel II (70 AD), "the one who renewed his people." It has been assumed by historical and archaeological analysis that, within his reign there occurred a strong shift/tendency away from western (Hellenistic and Roman) elements toward a more traditional Arabic expression in Nabataean art and culture.[15] This was probably related to attempts to liberate the Nabataean kingdom from the increasing control of the Roman empire, and to stem the loss of economic power. Because of its fine chronological differentiation, Nabataean pottery provides one of the clearest indications that, indeed, major changes occurred in the Nabataean world around 70 AD. Similar phenomena can be observed in other media that are less precisely datable, such as the richly decorated tomb façades of Petra, and the evolving relief decoration of Nabataean temples, such as the Qasr al-Bint at Petra (dated to the late first century BC) as compared with that of Khirbet et-Tannur (assignable to the second half of the first century AD).

Another characteristic feature of Nabataean fine ware, especially in the second half of the first century AD, is the variety of small, fine cups and beakers with stamped, incised, and rouletted decoration, as represented on (fig. 61.18–26).[16] During the first century AD the Nabataeans started producing their own unguent containers (fig. 61.17), which display the basic Roman form of that vessel type, including a few formal changes during the century. Although there was no longer a need to import such unguents from the Mediterranean, as in the first century BC (cf. above), the output of local *unguentaria* never reaches the quantities of other contemporaneous forms, like the main type (figs. 61.14, 15; 62.27). During this period, it would therefore appear that the Nabataeans concentrated exclusively on trading and not on the refining of spices from Arabia and the Far East.[17]

Around 100 AD we can observe the next evolutionary stage in Nabataean pottery (Phase 3c). The shapes remain rather the same, although, as we can observe, they become somewhat carelessly formed. The decoration supports this picture: on the whole, the motifs are similar, but not as carefully applied to the body as before; moreover, the fine lines forming the background disappear about this time. As for the chronology, excavations at Petra and other Nabataean sites now reveal evidence of a violent destruction. The rich, datable material, such as Eastern *terra sigillata* vessels and coins of Rabbel II, points to a date of destruction at the very beginning of the second century AD, which is perhaps related to the annexation of the Nabataean kingdom by the Roman army in 106 AD (see Chapter 1, pp. 22–23) or to a devastating hypothetical earthquake a few years later.[18] However, the layers attributed to this destruction already contained some pottery of the careless style (described above), which must therefore have been introduced shortly before. To this phase belongs one particular specimen of Nabataean fine ware. It is one of the typical flat bowls painted not only with ornamental decoration but with a rather complex figural scene with humans, quadrupeds, and birds (fig. 65). If we compare the painting of this bowl, with its rather clumsy drawings of animals and human beings, with the very naturalistic representation of the silen's head from Phase 2a (fig. 58) or the bearded face from the same phase (fig. 57), we see that the same stylistic development that can be observed in other categories of Nabataean material culture has good parallels within their pottery, too.

Under Roman rule the typical variety of Nabataean pottery continued to be produced, easily recognizable by its characteristic painting and familiar forms (fig. 62.28, 29). In closed contexts this pottery occurs until the very end of the fourth and even the beginning of the fifth century AD or later.[19]

A major difference with the ceramic development previously described is that no new elements are added to the (once innovative) Nabataean pottery tradition after the Roman take-over. The patterns of painting and the basic shapes of the plates and bowls remain the same as in the late first century AD, and are simply more degenerated. The painted bowl (fig. 62.28) could be described as a successor to the more sophisticated specimens of the later first century AD (fig. 62.27); the same is true for the unpainted forms. It would seem that, with the loss of their political independence, the Nabataeans also lost their innovative spirit, at least in the field of pottery production.

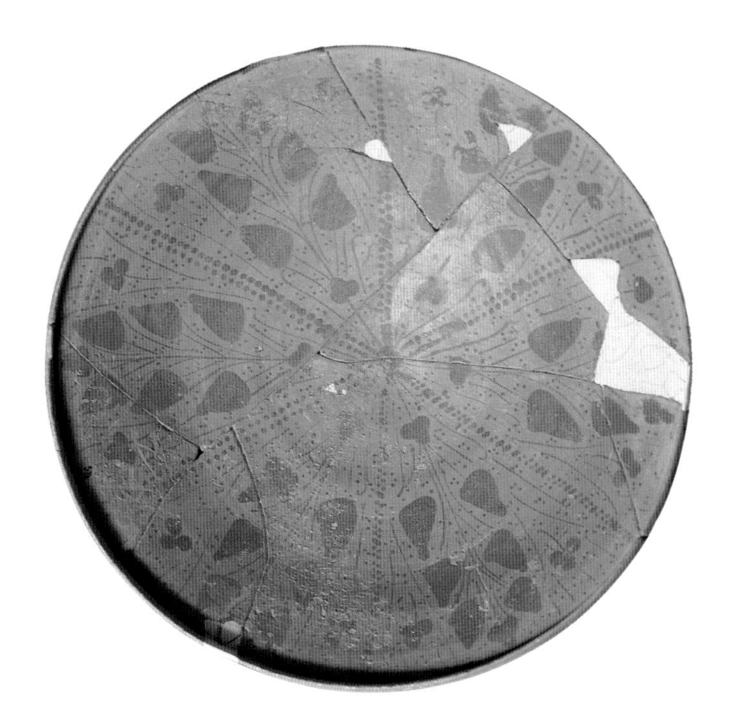

64. Painted bowl of Phase 3a (c. 20–70/80 AD).

65. Fragments of figural painted bowl of Phase 3c (c. 100–106 AD).

7 | Dharih and Tannur, Sanctuaries of Central Nabataea

FRANÇOIS VILLENEUVE AND ZEIDOUN AL-MUHEISEN

Introduction THE NABATAEAN SETTLEMENT PATTERN, both during the period of the Nabataean kingdom until 106 AD and, later, during the Roman period, seems to have been different from what we know elsewhere in relatively fertile areas of the Near East in the Hellenistic and Roman periods. Elsewhere, as in Palestine, in most parts of Hauran in southern Syria, and in the limestone regions of northern Syria, we find networks of numerous small, medium, or large villages, small cities, and a few larger urban centers. On the contrary, within the Nabataean population area, especially in the central part of the kingdom, i.e., in Transjordan around Petra and to the north of that city, villages—even small ones—were apparently uncommon: aside from a few cities like Petra or Rabbathmoba and a few possible towns or large villages, like Dhat Ras or Zo'ara, there was a very dense network of scattered hamlets, isolated farms, and individual buildings (such as caravansaries), indicating small areas of cultivation. That figure did not appear after the first archaeological surveys dedicated to southern Transjordan—Nelson Glueck's surveys in the 1930s and 1940s,[1] the results of which seemed to indicate a village-type organization—but was clearly established by the much more detailed and accurate surveys carried out at the end of the twentieth century.[2]

This raises the question of what and where were the local centers of sedentary, semi-nomadic, and nomadic life in most areas of the relatively fertile part of Nabataea. It now seems probable, according to the archaeological excavations and surveys, that *sanctuaries*, both isolated and associated with small, dependent villages, played the role of local or even regional centers. This role occurred quite clearly at least at the early stages of sedentary settlements, i.e., until the first century AD, but probably still at the end of the Nabataean kingdom period and within Roman Provincia Arabia. Archaeology reveals that most sanctuaries were located along the main caravan roads, especially the north-south roads between Hegra, Petra, and Madaba (and, eventually, Bosra). Thus, they probably served both as halts for caravans and travelers and as easily accessible centers for periodic pilgrimages. Moreover, we may observe that dwellings developed around some of these sanctuaries, such as at Dhiban, north of Wadi Mujib.

2. Sanctuaries: Centers of Life and Travel in the Nabataean Countryside This observation is documented by a few ancient literary texts, and, more extensively, by archaeology. In his *Jewish Antiquities,* Flavius Josephus tells of Herod's travels from Jerusalem in 40 BC—southeastward to Petra, then westward towards Alexandria, and eventually, to Rome. Obliged to flee Jerusalem by the Parthian occupation and by his Jewish enemies, Herod first established his relatives and his small army in Masada, then tried to find financial and political help outside his country. His first move was towards Petra, seeking assistance from the Nabataean king Malichos, who was apparently indebted to Herod's father, Antipatros. But he was promptly stopped on his way from Masada to Petra, inside Nabataean territory, by Nabataean envoys who told him to leave, obviously fearful of the Parthians. "Then, thinking it wise to depart, Herod set off very cautiously towards Egypt. He halted in a sanctuary, where he had earlier left many of his company, and, on the following day, he arrived in Rhinocolura"[3] (a harbor in the northern Sinai). Thus, it is obvious that this Nabataean sanctuary, located somewhere among Masada, Petra, and Rhinocolura, was a usual place for a halt and might accommodate at least a small troop.

On the other hand, Josephus's narrative, despite some difficulties (such as the unusually short travel time to Rhinocolura through northern Negev), is detailed enough to situate this enigmatic sanctuary, in general terms. It lies on the shortest road from Masada to Petra, since Herod was in a hurry and since he had already passed through the sanctuary before being met by the Nabataean envoys and later returning to the same sanctuary. The shortest road runs first from Masada

66. Aerial view of Khirbet edh-Dharih temple under excavation, 1996.

to the southern end of the Dead Sea (probable site of the border between Judaean and Nabataean territories), then either continues southward through Wadi Arabah, then directly eastward to Petra; or briefly eastward through Wadi al-Hasa, then southward to Petra through the ancient "King's Highway." As no Nabataean sanctuary is known in Wadi Arabah or in the precipitous area between Wadi Arabah and Petra, the second way is more probable; thus, the sanctuary mentioned by Josephus must have been situated somewhere on the "King's Highway" south of Wadi al-Hasa. Thus, the two sanctuaries documented by archaeology in that region, Khirbet et-Tannur and Khirbet edh-Dharih, are possible candidates. Until now, the excavations at Dharih have not revealed any serious remains or strata dating back to the first century BC. The first architectural phase at Tannur, however, has been tentatively dated to this century (even to around 100 BC, although nothing is actually certain before 8/7 BC). Moreover, the steep, commanding position of Tannur would have fit the needs of Herod and his companions during their dangerous flight.

Whatever the truth of this hypothesis, the sanctuaries of Dharih and Tannur are not isolated examples of important sanctuaries and halting-places for troops or caravans along main roads. A few other Nabataean or Nabataean-Roman sites distant from such roads and identified by early explorers as "sanctuaries," are certainly doubtful as such, e.g., Thawaneh, southeast of Dharih, or Muhay, east of the southern Moabite plateau, and most of the real Nabataean sanctuaries known today are clearly located on ancient caravan roads, either in the northern Negev and northern Sinai (Oboda, Qasr Gheit), or along the "King's Highway" in central Transjordan (Dhat Ras and Dhiban in Moab, previously mentioned) or on the routes from Petra towards Hijaz (Ramm/Iram, Ruwwafah). Moreover, some of these cultic places, it appears, were initially small, isolated temples or shrines, or simply sacred places, which then developed into larger sanctuaries and, sometimes, into small dependent villages and associated halt-facilities. This was perhaps the case at Dhiban, Dhat Ras, Ramm, Qasr Gheit, and quite probably at Dharih. This evolution, unfortunately, is not well documented in Nabataea by ancient texts, either epigraphic or literary; in other areas of the Near East, however, we may cite clear examples, such as Baetocaecae in the coastal mountains of Syria, celebrated, through its festivals and fairs, from the Hellenistic period onwards, or Sia in southern Syria (near the Nabataean border), a mountain sanctuary provided with a medium-size village and center of a pilgrimage, frequented even by the "Safaitic" nomads of the eastern steppe. The Nabataean *panegureis* (the Greek word for a combined religious festival and commercial fair) attended by people from distant places in Nabataea are documented, at least, by a famous inscription in the Siq of Petra. Thus, the case study of Dharih and Tannur, well documented by archaeology of the twentieth century, informs us not only about Nabataean religion, but about Nabataean culture in general.

3. The Two Sanctuaries of the Wadi al-Laaban: Geography and Archaeology The distance between Dharih and Tannur is only a one-and-a-half hour walk (7 km). The distance between them and Petra (located 70 km to the south in a straight line, a little more, following the "King's Highway," which very probably coincides roughly with the Nabataean caravan road) is a three-day walk. Between them and Petra, no sanctuary of significance is known to exist (although a small temple was partly discovered in the village of Gharandal, between Petra and Tafileh). Why two important sanctuaries so close together while there is nothing comparable to the south? The reasons are several. First, Dharih and Tannur were built at the very northern limit of ancient Edom. Tannur has a commanding position over—and Dharih is not far away from—the natural border, Wadi al-Hasa (ancient Zered) between the Edomite hills or mountains (*al Jibal*, Hellenistic *Gobolitis*) to the south and the high Moabite plateau to the north. That earlier border between the Iron Age kingdoms of Edom and Moab was no longer a political boundary within the Nabataean kingdom and later Roman Arabia, but the natural frontier formed by the canyon of al-Hasa is very impressive. Going through it takes long hours of walking or riding, and it was still possibly in Nabataean and Roman times a kind of ethnic or administrative border. Second, within the entire limestone region, there is in the immediate neighborhood of Tannur and Dharih a sole, massive volcano of black basalt on the northern bank of al-Hasa: Jabal al-Hammah, or Jabal al-Laaban (marked in red, fig. 67). Scholars of the mid-twentieth century, like Starcky and Broome,[4] correctly observed that the dark mass of this volcano may have strongly impressed the religious imagination of the Nabataeans; whether there was a cult of the god (Jabal al-) Laaban at Dharih or Tannur is, however, highly uncertain. Third, the hot springs of Burbaitah, also located near Tannur to the west and still famous today, were perhaps another reason to have cults in both places; the association between thermal springs and religion is well known in antiquity in general. Fourth, in the middle of an arid environment (the low altitude in the valley of al-Hasa does not allow annual precipitation above 150 mm), both sanctuaries are close to watering places and small, fertile areas: due to ancient irrigation (clearly evidenced around Dharih), the small oasis of Ainah on the northern bank of al-Hasa and the bottom of Wadi al-Laaban down from Dharih (both in green on fig. 67) provided food, together with water furnished by the three perennial springs around Dharih, to the

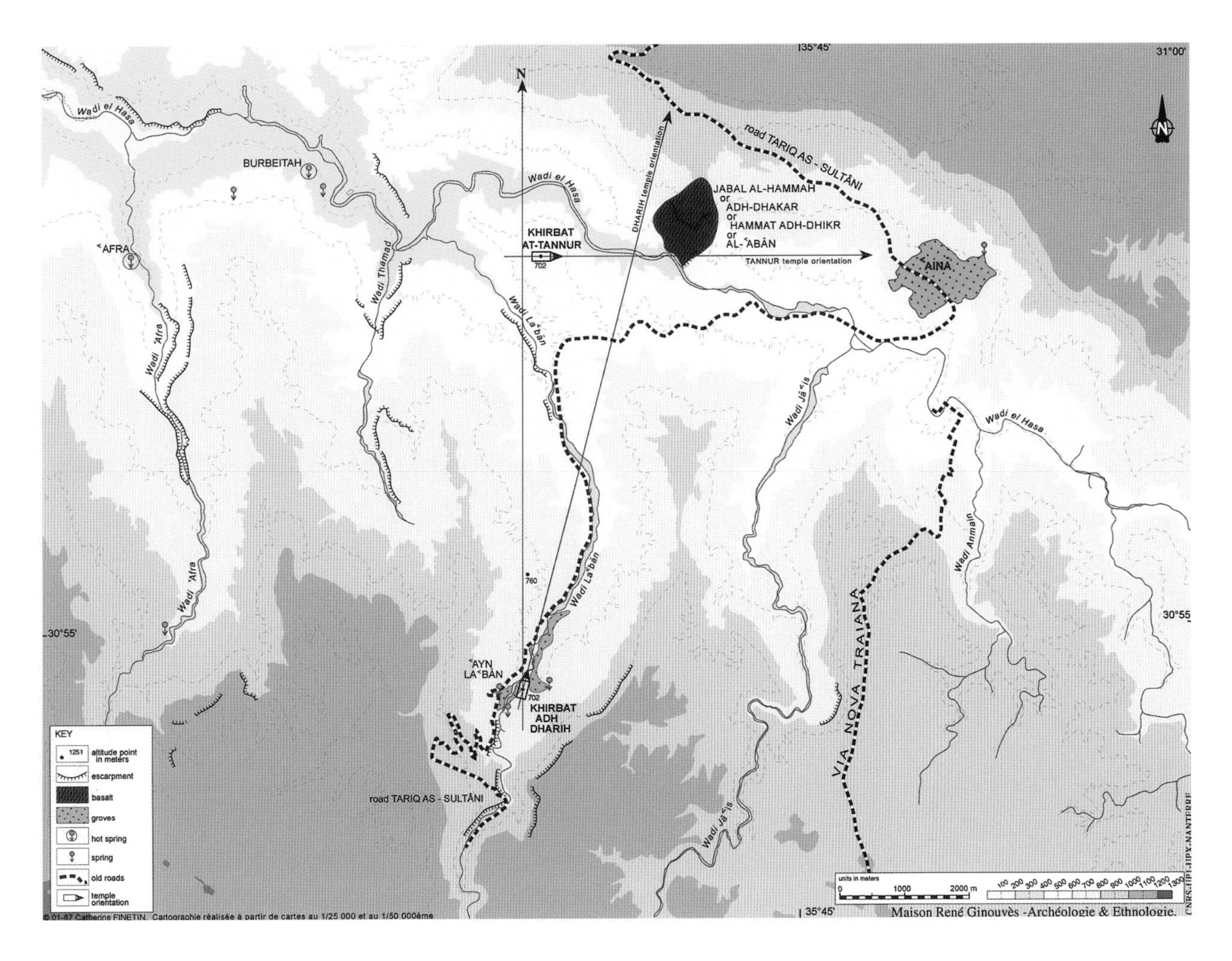

67. Archaeological map of the area of Khirbet edh-Dharih and Khirbet et-Tannur, near Wadi al-Hasa, central Jordan.

sanctuaries, their pilgrims and travelers, and later to the inhabitants of the small village at Dharih. Last, but not least, the valley of Wadi al-Laaban, the wider southern tributary of al-Hasa, was clearly the easiest way to travel through that region. Thus, it is almost certain that the main Nabataean thoroughfare of trade and travel from Petra northwards (here possibly identical with the Iron Age "King's Highway") passed through it; in any case it was the itinerary of the Ottoman road called "Tariq as-Sultani" (see fig. 67), which was very slightly modified for the current main road. Moreover, the military road built just after the Roman annexation in the early second century AD was established just a few kilometers to the east, on the plateau, for strategic reasons (fig. 67: *Via nova traiana*). Thus, the area of Dharih and Tannur was an ideal place for religious, or more practical, halts.

Though their altitudes are exactly identical, the positions of Dharih and Tannur in the Laaban valley are quite different from each other. Dharih, though not in the *wadi* bed, is at the bottom of the valley, just at the outlet of gorges, and is built on easy slopes and partially artificial terraces; it lies in the middle of three springs and controls a vast territory of irrigated plantations (with many small, ancient hamlets) and of dry-farming fields on the sides of the valley: a place marked by water and fertility. It is easily accessible today by a small, asphalted road, and was accessed in antiquity by a pathway diverging from the main road and crossing the Laaban south of the sanctuary. All this accounts for a very long occupational history at different periods and, consequently, a poor state of preservation for the Nabataean remains before excavations. Tannur was built on the very top of a steep and narrow, rocky, isolated hill commanding the confluence of Wadi Laaban and Wadi al-Hasa. From there, the landscape towards the east and west is magnificent, but the place was (and still is) only ascended by a painful half-hour walk. Tannur was an ideal place for occasional short pilgrimages, but clearly not for permanent life; water, in particular, was absent completely. For these reasons, Tannur was occupied, throughout history, only during the Nabataean and Roman periods, and just very slightly in the succeeding Byzantine era.

Although both sites were discovered at the same time, in the nineteenth century, the impressive location and abundant visible remains of Tannur led to its early and complete

68. Façade of *môtab* of Khirbet edh-Dharih temple, before the 2001 season of excavations. The steps in the foreground are of Umayyad date.

excavation in 1937. The work, undertaken by the Department of Antiquities, Palestine, and the American School of Oriental Research, Jerusalem, was directed by Nelson Glueck in a campaign lasting only seven weeks. After excavations, a large portion of the most interesting sculptures and architectural fragments was transferred to museums in the United States and Jordan (Cincinnati Art Museum and Amman Citadel Museum). After sixty-five years of abandonment and unsupervised visits, almost nothing remains now at Tannur except for the natural site. Consequently, there is little left in a controlled archaeological setting. Glueck published only very short and allusive reports in the years following the excavations.[5] It was only in 1965 that a synthesis of the excavations was produced, integrating the finds at Tannur with many other discoveries and brilliant, but doubtful, ideas of the author.[6] Many of Glueck's hypotheses, among them the main dedication of the sanctuary to Hadad and Atargatis, were promptly criticized and sometimes corrected by Starky.[7] However, it was not until the end of the twentieth century that specialists carefully reexamined the sculptures in the Amman and Cincinnati Museums, the traces on the site, and Glueck's publications and field notes, and provided a much clearer idea of the whole sanctuary.[8]

Dharih was less visible and more difficult to excavate, being covered by huge heaps of stones and earth. The situation discouraged archaeologists, until excavations (and later restorations) were undertaken in 1984 with a French and Jordanian team from Yarmouk University and the French Institute for Archaeology in the Near East (IFAPO). The program is scheduled to end in 2004, after thirteen seasons (probably twenty months on the whole) of excavations. Preliminary reports,[9] and now the first final report,[10] are available. Though the site at Dharih is much larger than Tannur, the reader may notice that excavations at Dharih were conducted more slowly, according to more modern standards of field archaeology. Thus, the picture now obtained for the sanctuary at Dharih, though not yet complete, may be confidently used to gain a more accurate idea of the sanctuary at Tannur.[11]

It is quite probable, however, that some pieces of the puzzle will be missing forever, due to the lack of literary texts dealing with those places (even Josephus's text alluded to above, if related to our area, does not give any ancient name for the sanctuary visited by Herod) as well as of epigraphical texts found on the sites. The epigraphic evidence at Tannur is very scant—just a few dedicatory inscriptions in Nabataean; at Dharih it is almost nonexistent until the Byzantine period. We may perhaps always be ignorant of the ancient names of both sites. *Tannur*, "the oven" in Arabic, is probably a modern place-name, simply relating to the shape of the hill. The meaning of *Dharih*, as locally pronounced and written (Arabic *dhal* as first letter), is obscure and controversial. A fifth-century Greek document of the Negev gives the place-name "Ellebana"[12] (cf. al Laaban) for a garrison somewhere in the area, but unfortunately nothing is known through archaeology at Dharih and Tannur in the fifth century. Our ideas about the sanctuaries, their public, and even their deities, depend mostly on archaeology.

4. Similar Sanctuaries, Complementary Sites In addition to their close proximity, many elements of both sites document their strong mutual relationship. Their phases of occupation and enlargement are very close (see *infra* § 5). The layouts of both sanctuaries exhibit striking similarities (see figs. 71 and p. 172, fig. 175 and *infra* §§ 6–7). The style of the stonecutting and of the architectural decoration (see J. McKenzie in this volume) is identical, especially in the main phase of both sites. Accordingly, it is generally agreed that the architects and teams of carvers who worked at Tannur and Dharih were the same.

Moreover, one of the few Nabataean inscriptions found at Tannur, dated 8/7 BC and deriving from an unknown monument of the sanctuary, reads as follows: "... built by Natir'el son of Zayd'el, head of Ain Laaban, for the life of Haritat, king of the Nabataeans, who loves his people, and for the life of Huldu his wife, in the year 2" (of the reign).[13] Ain Laaban, the spring of Laaban, is traditionally the name of one of the three springs surrounding Dharih, and was surely the same in antiquity. Thus, Natir'el, a prominent person at Tannur, had responsibility for one of the springs of Dharih. We may hypothesize that he actually lived at Dharih, the main settlement center in the area, and was a member of one of the leading families there, associated with the sanctuary.

There are also notable differences between Dharih and Tannur. The main one concerns their context. At Tannur, there is absolutely nothing except for the sanctuary, which was totally isolated. There are no dwellings, only one cistern on the slopes of the hill. At Dharih, there is, in addition to the sanctuary, a complete village, including its necropolis and remains of its fields and water channels. Dharih was a permanent place of residence for a community; Tannur was only a site for temporary cult activity. A second difference is that of size. Not only is Dharih a much larger site (measuring over 500 by 200 meters, for the buildings only: see fig. 69), but its sanctuary (totaling at least 160 m x 45 m, with a minimum of two temenos courtyards) is considerably larger than the sanctuary at Tannur, which measures only 48 m x 40 m with only one temenos. The latter actually could not have been larger (without the aid of huge terracing works), due to the size of the summit on which it is located.

We may thus conclude that Tannur, a small, isolated, sacred high place, was a dependence of the chief residence, Dharih, and its large sanctuary. This seems to be confirmed by the spatial relationship between both sites (see fig. 67). Despite their vicinity and identical altitudes (702 m), it is impossible to see one from the other, due to intervening hills (of 760 m in height). Logically, then, both temples are not oriented towards each other. In fact, their orientations are completely different. Glueck noticed that the Tannur temple is aligned almost exactly west (1°30' north).[14] (We checked that orientation, which is aligned even more accurately towards west.) Thus, it is almost certain that the pilgrimages to Tannur were enacted in relation to sunrise (temple gates to the east) or sunset, and took place perhaps only at the equinoxes, with essential phases of the cult at sunrise, at midnight, or at sunset. This fact is hardly surprising, considering the abundance of astral symbols in the sculpture of Tannur (see pp. 186–91 in this volume). The Dharih temple is oriented north, 13°38' east. This unusual orientation, of course, does not exclude a special celebration on some day in February, when sunrise and sunset are on the line perpendicular to the axis of the temple (there are also astral symbols at Dharih, see below), but we may guess that the orientation of the temple and of the whole sanctuary complex was guided mainly by the natural features of the ground at the spot. Incidentally, it may be observed that neither sanctuary is oriented towards the Jabal Laaban volcano.

Thus, we may conclude that Tannur was *not* an earlier and more important cultic high place associated with this mysterious volcano; otherwise, the Dharih temple would have been situated somewhere in visual contact with Tannur and oriented towards it or at least toward the volcano. Rather, it seems reasonable to suppose that the earlier sanctuary was at Dharih, the main halting-place and cultivated oasis in the area, and that the inhabitants or leading families at Dharih later erected a secondary sanctuary at Tannur for astral cults at equinoxes. This seems to be supported by the Natir'el inscription mentioned above.

5. Chronology The actual chronology at both sites partially confirms this idea. The shortest history is that of Tannur. Three building phases were recognized there, each associated with one of the three stages of the progressively enlarged "altar" or "altar platform" in the inner enclosure. Glueck[15] proposed to date the first phase around 100 BC, the second, at

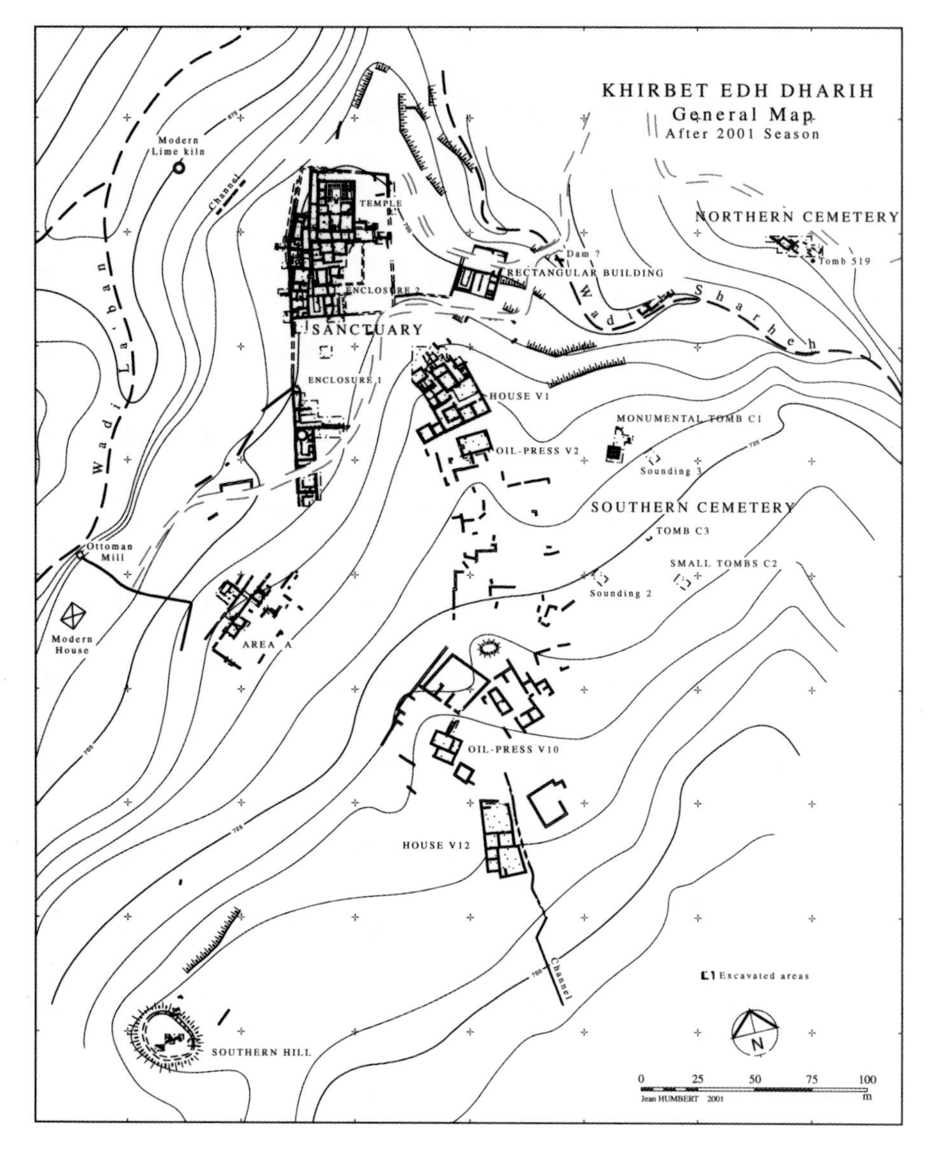

69. General plan of the site of Khirbet edh-Dharih.

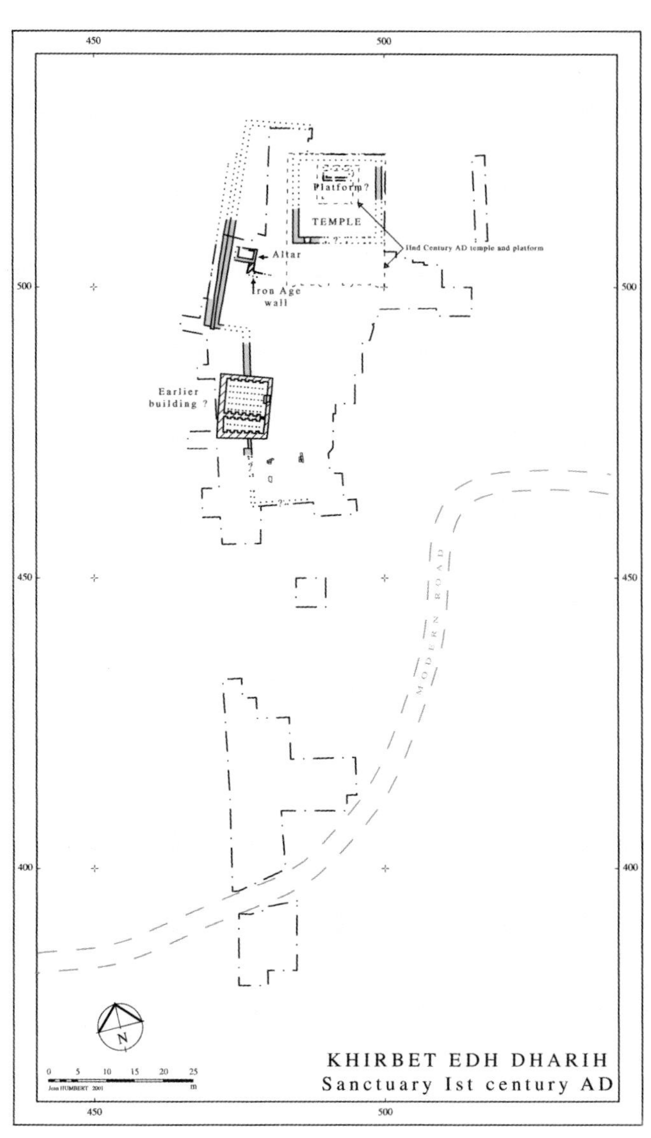

70. Plan of the sanctuary of Khirbet edh-Dharih, Phase 1, probably 1st century AD.

the end of the first century BC, and the third, at the beginning of the second century AD. J. McKenzie[16] assigns the first phase to the time of the Natir'el inscription (8/7 BC), an interesting idea, notwithstanding that the unlocated monument dedicated by that inscription may well have been preceded by various elements of the sanctuary, including the first "altar" itself. Convincingly, McKenzie corrects Glueck's picture for the second phase, which she dates to the late first or early second century AD, and we agree with her. She tentatively proposes a dating in the third century AD for Phase 3. Subsequently, the whole sanctuary was destroyed and abandoned—at a date that we think to be in the mid-fourth century, probably during the famous earthquake of 363, which destroyed Petra. Later, Tannur was only slightly reused by dwellers, apparently in the Byzantine period.

As expected, the history of the occupation of the fertile spot at Dharih was much longer and more complicated. The site or its surroundings were inhabited during the Neolithic and Early Bronze Age periods, then again in the Edomite period, during the Iron Age (c. seventh-sixth centuries BC). Excavations revealed at least one house of that period, and the earlier wall discovered beneath the sanctuary (see fig. 70) dates back to that phase. But it is, of course, impossible to say if that wall was already part of an early sanctuary, or part of some dwellings. Subsequently, there seems to have been a complete abandonment of Dharih until the first century AD; this is not certain, however, since the deeper strata beneath the central part of the sanctuary, especially below the temple, have not yet been reached. Thus, there is at present no factual evidence at Dharih that a portion of the Nabataean sanctuary or village antecedes the date of 8/7 BC provided at Tannur by the Natir'el inscription. However, in the first century AD

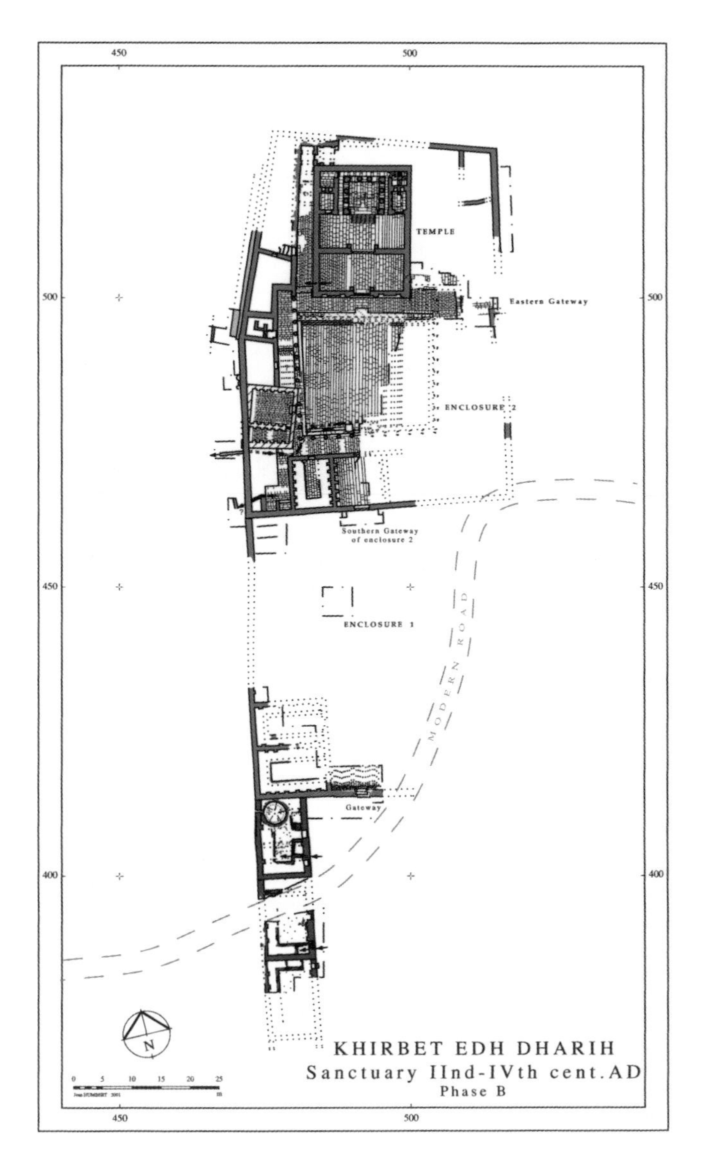

71. Plan of the sanctuary of Khirbet edh-Dharih, Phase 2b, late 2nd to mid-4th century AD.

72. Plan of the sanctuary of Khirbet edh-Dharih, Phase 3, 6th–7th century AD

there is clear evidence of a Nabataean settlement, with both a small sanctuary (Phase 1, see fig. 70) and elements of the village, at least an oil press (see fig. 69:V10). A decisive evolution took place at the turn of the first and second centuries or slightly later. In the cemetery, a monumental tomb was erected shortly after 110 AD[17] (see fig. 69, tomb C1). Just prior (perhaps at the end of the first century AD), the small sanctuary of phase 1 was mainly destroyed to be incorporated within the much larger temple of Phase 2 (see fig. 71). Work probably started with the temple itself (early second century?), then continued until at least the decade of 150 AD for the temenos enclosures. Unfortunately, the archaeological chronology is not accurate enough at the moment to say if this enlargement started before or after the Roman annexation in 106 AD. During and after the second century, modifications to the sanctuary continued to occur: small changes in the temple, the addition of rooms outside the southern entrance of the temenos (late second–early third century), and a remodeling of that southern area (quickly abandoned) in the third century. The newly discovered buildings (area A on fig. 69) on the sacred way to the sanctuary apparently date back to these late phases as well. From the late first/early second century AD until the mid-fourth century, the houses and oil presses of the village and the tombs of the necropolis also grew and became more numerous. But the whole site was rocked by the earthquake in 363 AD and immediately abandoned, including the sanctuary.

Nevertheless, later reoccupations were numerous and important at Dharih, but all of them ignored the Nabataean and Roman village and concentrated inside the perimeter of the northern temenos of the sanctuary. The first reoccupation took place during the late Byzantine and early Umayyad

73. Aerial view of Khirbet edh-Dharih sanctuary, 2001.

periods (see fig. 72), making extensive reuse of the Nabataean and Roman stones for building new walls; interestingly, at that time, part of the Nabataean temple was reused as a small church. But it is impossible to say if the Christians of that period were still descendants of the Nabataeans. That use of Dharih lasted until the early Abbassid period. After another abandonment, poor dwellers settled again within the ancient sanctuary around the sixteenth century. All this "recent" history of Dharih explains the difficulty of the excavation of the earlier, Nabataean and Roman, remains, and the uncertainties and gaps in the reconstruction of the main sanctuary.

6. Dharih: A Large Caravan Sanctuary and Its Village and Cemetery The general plan of Dharih (fig. 69) shows the different elements of the site before its first destruction in 363 AD: the sanctuary (largely excavated), with its temple to the north, on partly artificial terraces above the bed of Wadi Laaban; a village of about twenty buildings (four excavated), on the slopes overlooking to the southeast; and a cemetery to the east of the village and sanctuary. Lastly, there are a few individual buildings: one large "rectangular building" east of the sanctuary; and two structures to the south of the sanctuary, along a processional way leading to it.

The village consists of ordinary small-size peasant houses and oil presses. House V1, the one closest to the sanctuary, is much larger than the others, and much more luxurious; it has an interior paved courtyard, reception rooms, even a bath with hypocaust. It is clearly the house of the most prominent family of Dharih. It also possesses an external paved courtyard facing towards the temple, with traces of a fine stairway descending towards an eastern side gateway of the temenos. A baetyl was found among the debris in that courtyard. Thus, the leading family of Dharih, who lived in that house, had strong connections with the sanctuary and with its religious worship. We would assume that it was the local family of the resident priests.

The cemetery, as well, consists of a large series of poor- or medium-quality individual pit- or, occasionally, collective shaft-tombs, contrasting with the monumental tomb C1[18] (cf. above), built shortly after 110 AD and used until 363. The underground part of that tomb housed six shafts of five tombs each, totaling thirty graves: it is highly probable that it was the monument of the leading priestly family that lived in House V1. Some golden objects from the tomb document the wealth of that family, which employed Nabataean funerary practices (leather shrouds). Moreover, the whole monument was built above the sarcophagus of the first dead buried in the monument, whose grave was sealed by the walls of the building. We consider this person as the "ancestor" of the group, which then used that funerary monument until the fourth century.

Considering the typical and similar features of the village and the cemetery, we conclude that Dharih and its surroundings, inhabited by ordinary Nabataean peasants, were dominated by a unique leading family, which was probably in charge of the sanctuary there and of the temple at Tannur. Going further, it is licit to imagine that this family was that of Natir'el, the head of the Laaban spring who dedicated a monument at Tannur in 8/7 BC. In other words, the anonymous "ancestor" buried in the sarcophagus of tomb C1 at Dharih after 110 AD could have Natir'el as his "ancestor."

Two additional buildings or groups at the site are of interest. Immediately to the east of the northern enclosure of the sanctuary, outside of it, is a large, massive, well-built, two storied rectangular building measuring 23 m x 19 m. The first floor, partly underground, has a large, three-benched dining room (triclinium), a central hall with pillars, and small storerooms; the destroyed second floor had elements of architectural and stuccoed decoration, plus a small altar. The building being only half excavated at the moment, and having no known parallel elsewhere, its interpretation is difficult. Due to the proximity of the sanctuary, its contemporaneity with it, the easy access to and from it through the eastern gateway of the temenos and (due to its position outside the village) the presence of the triclinium and the storerooms, the possibility of an inn for pilgrims and travelers may be considered. The other group is the newly and partly excavated "area A," located to the very south of the site, along the unpaved processional way towards the sanctuary. It developed between the end of the first and the third century and was in use until the 363 AD earthquake. East of the way, and opening onto it through a central porch, extends a large rectangular structure (30 m x 22 m). It has a large rectangular courtyard flanked by rows of rooms on three sides. Small, nicely paved shops with stone basins were later added to the north and east, along the way. The whole may well be a caravansary. West of the sacred way, the long and complicated A2 building, with paved rooms, has a good chance of having been a thermal complex, since a huge number of ceramic hot-air pipes are found there. Thus, the access to the area of the sanctuary was probably provided both with a khan and with public baths.

Let us come to the sanctuary. The sanctuary precinct of Phase 1 (see fig. 70) had a unique irregular enclosure, the surrounding wall of which was then reused, north and northwest, for the later enclosure; it housed a small temple, probably 15 m square, the pavement of which was found 70 cm beneath the later temple pavement; the façade was probably provided with three gates and the temple had a kind of small massif or platform inside. The orientation is exactly the same as that of the later temple. In addition, there was a small, off-centered altar, outside the temple to the west. We do not know the reason for the decision to destroy this Phase 1 sanctuary and to incorporate it (as was usual in the Semitic world rather than to destroy it completely) inside a much larger one.

The sanctuary of Phase 2, although built over several decades (with two main phases, 2a and 2b (see fig. 71 for 2b, probably situated during the late second century), was conceived as a whole, as evidenced by the homogenous orientation of the entire complex (both temple and temenos) and by the simultaneous construction (between 150 and 160 AD) of the two enclosures. There are certainly some irregularities in the layout, but this is only due to the pre-existing buildings and to features of the ground. Only the external rooms to the southwest of enclosure 1 (south) were added later—but not after the end of the second century—beside slight modifications elsewhere. The whole picture is clear, south to north, following the progression towards the temple: first, a row of side-rooms, just before the entrance, southwest of that entrance; then, two large, almost rectangular, enclosures (1 and 2, south and north), and finally, a rectangular temple (17 m x 23 m) in the back of enclosure 2 (figs. 71, 73). It is not uncommon in the Near East to find several *temene*, or courtyards, as a consequence of a probable segregation of the worshippers (possibly women in enclosure 1, men in enclosure 2). The axiality of the courtyards and the temple also evokes a sacred progression. As already mentioned, enclosure 2 is provided with a side gateway to the east (perhaps an exit for the pilgrims, or a communication with the main house and the possible inn.) To that eastern gateway corresponds an eastern, right side-door of the vestibule of the temple (blocked at the end of the second century; see fig. 71). The same detail exists at the temple or "inner enclosure" of Tannur (see p. 172, fig. 175), on the left (southern) side. It probably represents a special access and exit for priests, even when the gate of the main façade was closed, before and after celebrations.

Situated just before the entrance to the whole sanctuary, to the southwest, are (from the late second century onwards) at least three large rectangular rooms, which form a row. It is still impossible to say if they had symmetrical counterparts to the southeast or not, and if they were or were not included within a preliminary enclosure, or temenos. They were, at first, each provided with a central door and a smaller side-door, thus serving probably as cloakrooms, with worshippers, usually clothed, entering by the side-room and exiting without shoes and in special clothes through the central door. Subsequently, all these rooms were transformed into cultic triclinia, the side-rooms being blocked. Around 260 AD, these triclinia were dismantled and transformed into a temporary working area, where dumps of a potter's workshop and architectural blocks under processing (evidencing an aborted, new enlargement of the sanctuary) were found. The area was then quickly abandoned and ceased to function as part of the sanctuary.

One entered enclosure 1 through a very narrow gate. This first enclosure was an oblong, paved courtyard, flanked west and (probably) east by rows of large cultic triclinia. A few elements of decoration testify to the existence of small, completely destroyed, cultic monuments. The access to enclosure 2 was through a much wider gate, which opened towards a roofed porch. From there, two flights of steps enabled descent within a paved, nearly square courtyard. Draining of rain water from this courtyard was ensured by a complex system: an open-air drain along the southern limit of the courtyard (the same exists at the "outside enclosure" at Tannur), which collected water either into a large underground sewer or into a decanting vat, and then into an underground cistern below the southeastern corner of the courtyard. That courtyard was framed by two steps and by a columned portico on three sides: a device which allowed worshippers to be seated around the court, as in the al-Madhbah cultic high-place at Petra. The sacrificial altar, not yet discovered, was thus situated in the as-yet-unexcavated portion of the courtyard in the southeast corner, as at Tannur—off center and to the right of the courtyard after the entrance. Additionally, a few, small cultic monuments and altars, some of them added to the first layout, were present in that northern enclosure. Behind the porticos, the side-rooms cannot all be interpreted, but they had varied layouts and functions. On the southern and western sides are: a large triclinium; an adjoining open-air space provided with a drain (possibly a kitchen for the preparation of the meats of sacrificed animals); an off-axis complex (actually earlier than the second century) consisting of a large square room and a small, adjacent, oblong room (a building for the priests in charge?); a room which is completely obliterated by a later, Byzantine oil press; and a staircase leading to the terraces above the porticos and rooms. Lastly, west of the temple, a paved open-air corridor covers a long narrow underground room, which is connected to another running along the northern side of the temple. From the corridor, a short stairway descended westward, providing access to a large gamma-shaped room of unknown function, situated above the first-century AD altar destroyed in that century. In that area, strong differences of height and irregularities in plan are explained by the original ground topography and by the contact between the enclosure wall of the Phase 1 and Phase 2 sanctuaries. The remaining areas of that northern enclosure, mainly in the eastern half, are not yet excavated.

The temple consists of an open-air vestibule to the south and an almost square complex to the north. From the vestibule one faces an interior façade, which was adorned with stuccoed niches; in the middle of that façade is a very wide gate situated towards the rear square part of the temple, almost identical in dimensions to the former temple. This complex is formed by a cella, richly adorned with architectural painted stuccos, and by a square cultic platform (built over two crypts) surrounded by a narrow corridor and flanked east and west by four small angle rooms, one of them enclosing a staircase leading to the terrace-roof. The room to the south of the staircase has an additional crypt under it.

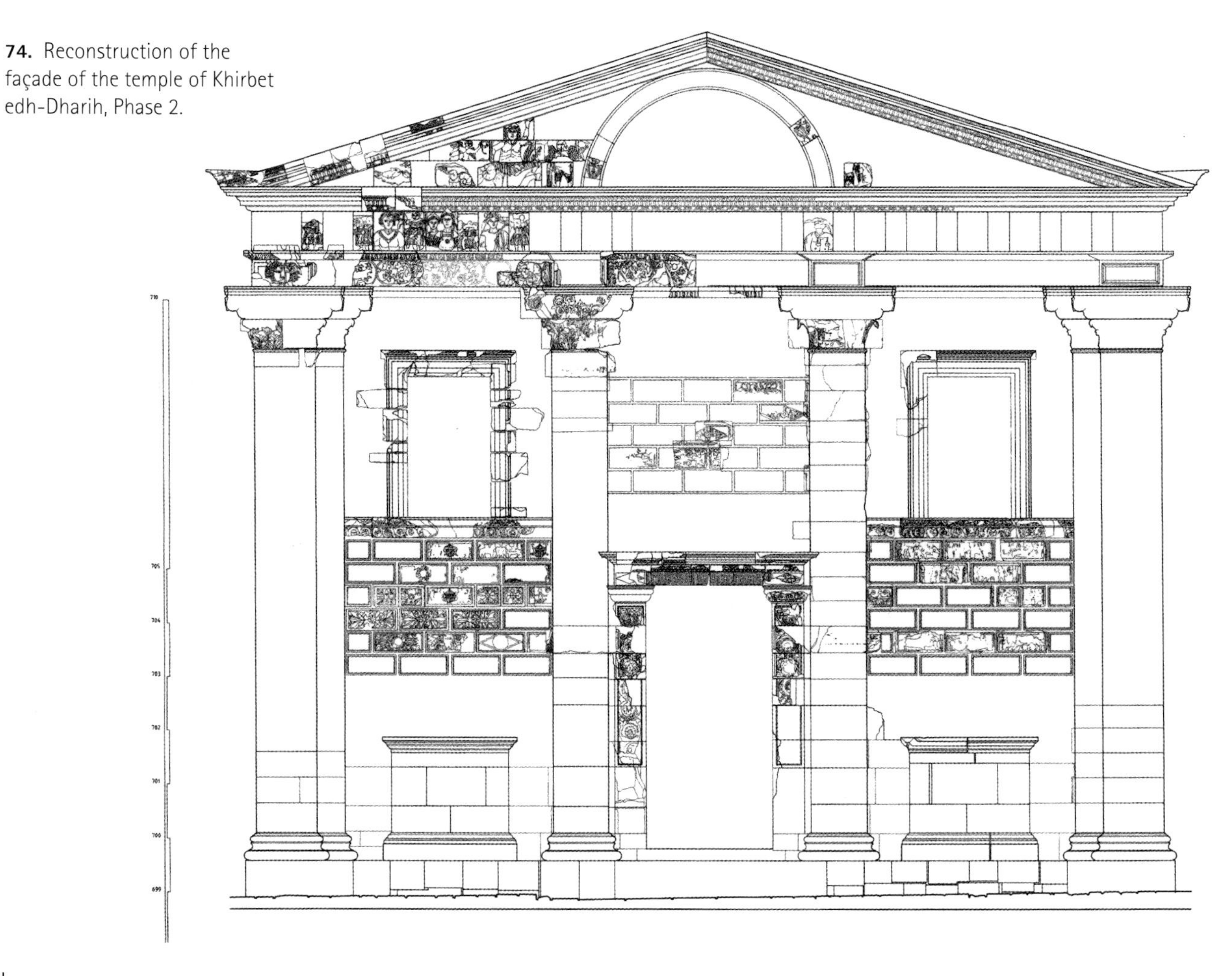

74. Reconstruction of the façade of the temple of Khirbet edh-Dharih, Phase 2.

75. Relief-decorated southwestern corner pilaster of perimeter wall surrounding the corridor around the *môtab*, Khirbet edh-Dharih.

76. Taurus panel from Zodiac limestone frieze. Khirbet edh-Dharih temple façade. h: 83.6 cm. Department of Antiquities, Amman, Jordan.

77. Cancer panel from Zodiac limestone frieze. Khirbet edh-Dharih temple façade. h: 74.0 cm. Department of Antiquities, Amman, Jordan.

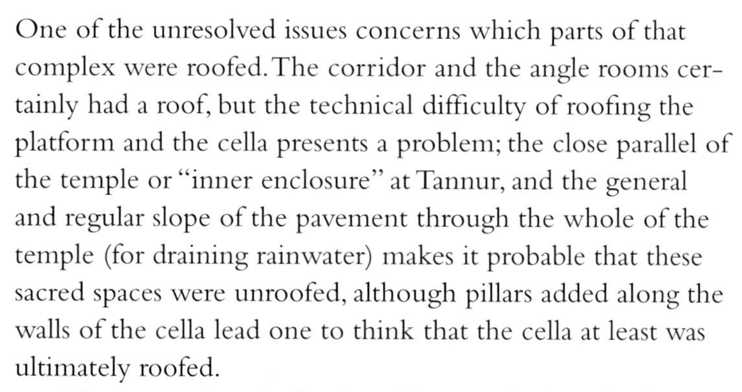

One of the unresolved issues concerns which parts of that complex were roofed. The corridor and the angle rooms certainly had a roof, but the technical difficulty of roofing the platform and the cella presents a problem; the close parallel of the temple or "inner enclosure" at Tannur, and the general and regular slope of the pavement through the whole of the temple (for draining rainwater) makes it probable that these sacred spaces were unroofed, although pillars added along the walls of the cella lead one to think that the cella at least was ultimately roofed.

The external, main façade of the temple (i.e., the façade of the vestibule, see fig. 74) was 15 meters high. It must be understood, like the façade of the "inner enclosure" at Tannur (fig. 180), as the "projection" on a unique wall of the façade of a distyle *in antis* monument with Corinthian capitals, but it presents a strong architectonic originality. This consists of: two protruding pedestals at the base, right and left of the door, each bearing possibly a feline; two large windows high in the façade; and a pediment with a semicircular tympanum. The whole is exuberantly decorated by sculptures in relief: right and left of the door and above it as well were decorative panels consisting of frames bearing religious motifs, among which the animated figures were defaced in late antiquity (during the eighth century) by religious iconoclasm. Among them, one may distinguish shields, winged or vegetal thunderbolts, lidded metallic craters borne by winged figures; and many mythological scenes, but also a triad with standards (either Roman military *signa* with the Capitoline triad or religious *semeia* of oriental deities) and even a Roman she-wolf, treated in an extremely provincial way. Above a foliated architrave populated with animals, with Medusa heads at the angles, stands a high-relief frieze with alternating figures of the Zodiac and winged Victories (fig. 79), who crown these figures. The anthropomorphic busts discovered consist, from left to right, of Taurus (fig. 76), the Gemini (fig. 78), Cancer (fig. 77), Libra (fig. 81), and a fragment of a cuirassed Sagittarius; the others are terribly worn or missing. The triangular pediment (fig. 80) presents, to the left and right of an arch of

78. Gemini panel from Zodiac limestone frieze. Khirbet edh-Dharih temple façade. h: 94.9 cm. Department of Antiquities, Amman, Jordan.

79. Nike panel from Zodiac limestone frieze. Khirbet edh-Dharih temple façade. h: 95.0 cm. Department of Antiquities, Amman, Jordan

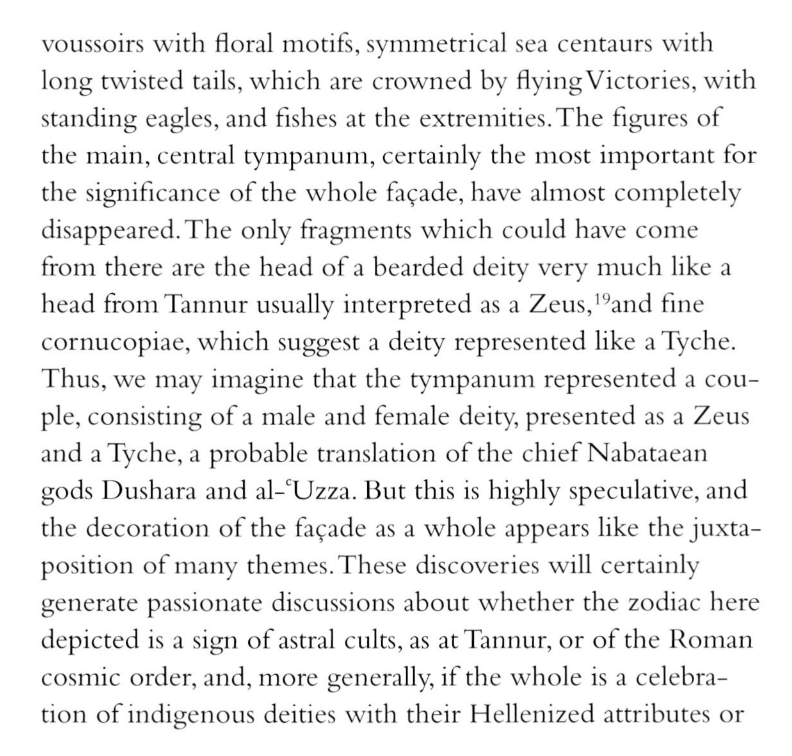
voussoirs with floral motifs, symmetrical sea centaurs with long twisted tails, which are crowned by flying Victories, with standing eagles, and fishes at the extremities. The figures of the main, central tympanum, certainly the most important for the significance of the whole façade, have almost completely disappeared. The only fragments which could have come from there are the head of a bearded deity very much like a head from Tannur usually interpreted as a Zeus,[19] and fine cornucopiae, which suggest a deity represented like a Tyche. Thus, we may imagine that the tympanum represented a couple, consisting of a male and female deity, presented as a Zeus and a Tyche, a probable translation of the chief Nabataean gods Dushara and al-ʿUzza. But this is highly speculative, and the decoration of the façade as a whole appears like the juxtaposition of many themes. These discoveries will certainly generate passionate discussions about whether the zodiac here depicted is a sign of astral cults, as at Tannur, or of the Roman cosmic order, and, more generally, if the whole is a celebration of indigenous deities with their Hellenized attributes or of the new Roman order. The question is complicated by the fact that we will probably never know if the Dharih temple was built before or after 106 AD. We would suggest temporarily that the date is slightly later than the Roman annexation and that the iconography of Dharih is a clever, diplomatic, maybe ambivalent, combination of the Greek-influenced Nabataean religion and a spectacular, professed allegiance to Roman power. The Roman she-wolf has hooves, which seems to be derisive, if it is not an indication of the artist's clumsiness.

Within the temple, the essential element is the square (7 m x 7 m) platform (height 1.40 m; figs. 66, 68, 82). The access to it on its façade, in the late second century phase (see figs. 71, 82), was through a wide, wooden stairway (earlier through small stone stairways positioned inside the platform façade itself). The platform was surmounted on three sides by a columned baldachin, itself surmounted by a richly decorated entablature, again including figures of Victories and deities. That platform is the *môtab* or *môtbâ*, the name given by inscriptions of Petra and Hegra[20] to the seat of the deities, thus

80

81

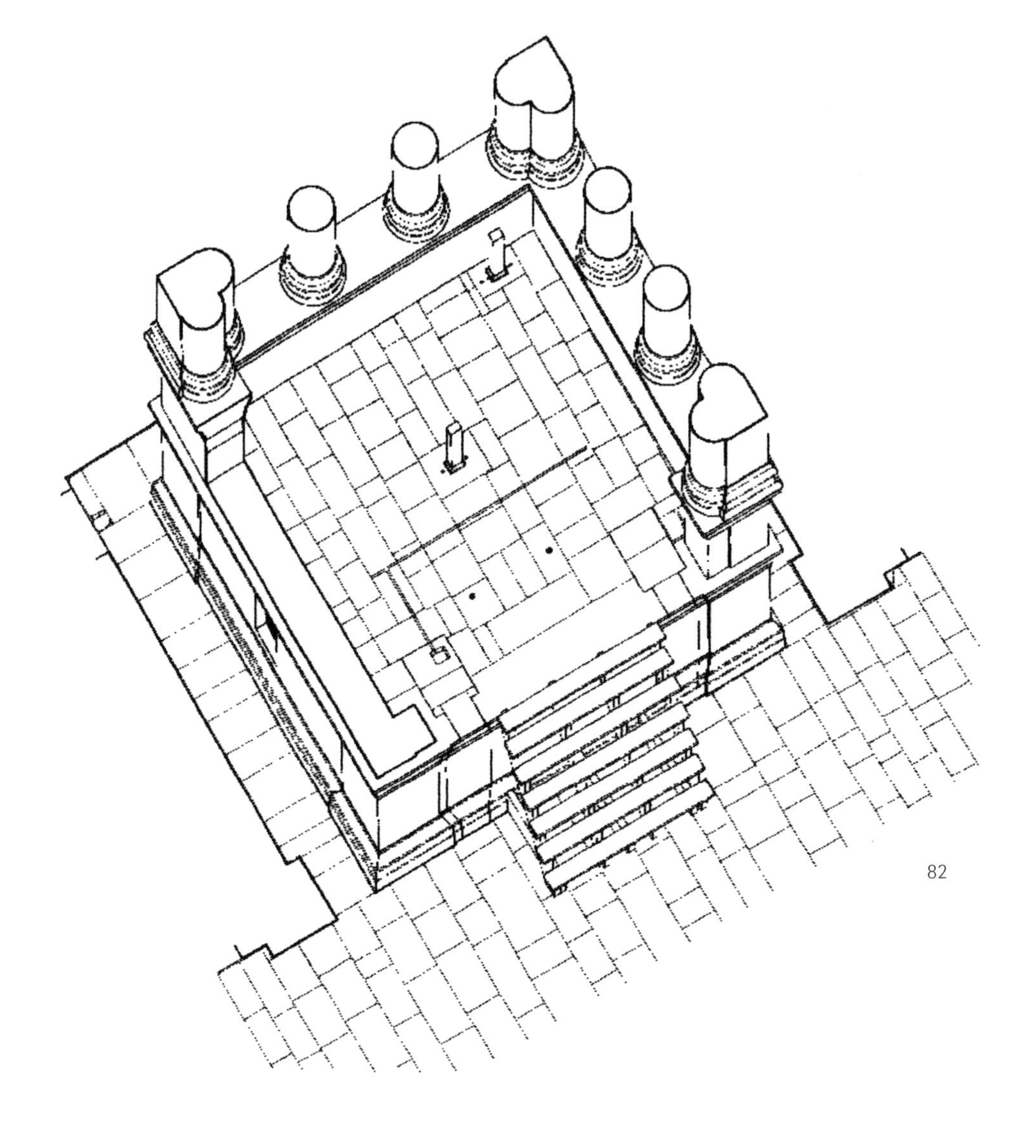

82

80. Pediment, left (west) part of Dharih temple façade. Department of Antiquities, Amman, Jordan.

81. Libra panel from Zodiac limestone frieze. Khirbet edh-Dharih temple façade. h: 74.9 cm. Department of Antiquities, Amman, Jordan.

82. Cultic platform inside Khirbet edh-Dharih temple, Phase 2b, with rectangular fixtures holes for baetyls and small circular holes for the exit of blood sacrifice into vats beneath. Axonometric reconstruction.

the base of their sacred standing stones, or baetyls. The paved surface of the *môtab* shows (see fig. 82) three mortises, diagonally disposed, one of which is at the center of the platform: these are rectangular holes for fixing removable baetyls. Beside two of these mortises, one may notice, left and right, two small exit-holes for the flow of blood[21] from sacrificed animals, which was poured by the priests on the baetyls, towards vats placed beneath the paved surface of the *môtab*. The whole thing could be veiled and unveiled, due to a metallic balustrade in front of the platform. The narrow corridor surrounding the *môtab* gives access to the angle rooms, including the staircase leading to the terrace-roof, where the baetyls might have been transported up for theophanies. It also gives access to the symmetrical crypts under the *môtab*. A third crypt, accessible through a trap door, is located under the oblong small room to the northeast of the cella, a room whose religious function was important, according to its stuccoed decoration. A fourth-century Greek text of the Christian author Epiphanius, dealing with pagan cults at Alexandria, Petra, and Elusa in the Negev, reveals that these crypts were the deposit areas for baetyls, from which they were taken for a procession: "When they have concluded their nightlong vigil, torchbearers descend into an underground shrine after cock-crow and bring up a wooden image" (this detail refers apparently to Alexandria) "(...) And they carry the image itself seven times around the innermost shrine with flutes, tambourines and hymns, hold a feast, and take it back down to its place underground."[22]

However the debate over the iconography of the façade and interior walls of the Dharih temple may ultimately be resolved, it is thus clear that its architecture was conceived for a totally Semitic cult of the baetyls. The *môtab* inside the temple was probably not the only place at Dharih to erect and worship these standing stones: a kind of stepped pedestal against the northern wall of House V 1, near the place where a baetyl was uncovered, was perhaps another *môtab*; within the pavement of enclosure 2, at least one trace of a rectangular mortise sided by two small circular holes survives. There is a possibility that the so-called offering-boxes discovered by Glueck at three places within the pavement of the temenos at Tannur[23] were actually vats below mortises for baetyls.

7. The High-Place Sanctuary at Tannur Our analysis of Tannur will be quite a bit shorter, since the site, restricted to an isolated sanctuary, is much smaller, and since many of its elements have already been discussed in our Dharih analysis or are presented in Chapter 15 in this volume. Moreover, as a result of Glueck's very rapid excavations, of his elliptic first reports[24] and rather imaginative and eclectic final publication,[25] and of the poor state of preservation of the site and its ruins, it is impossible to give a secure analysis of many elements, as concerns stratigraphy, chronology, and even certain architectural reconstructions. It is perhaps only through continuation of the courageous study of Glueck's archive, initiated by J. McKenzie, M.-J. Roche, and L. Tholbecq, that our understanding of certain details may still grow. This presentation is based mainly (apart from our own personal knowledge of the site) on McKenzie's enlightening, recent review of the sanctuary.[26]

Except for an adjoining cistern on the steep slopes of its narrow summit and for a few traces of stonecutting for the sacred pathway leading to it, Tannur is only a sanctuary. Indeed, the lack of water resources and the singularity of its remote cistern provide the clearest evidence that the sanctuary was used only for short periods—during the equinox pilgrimages.

A first glance at the general plan of the temple (p. 172, fig. 175) shows that Tannur, in its second and third phases, belongs to the type of sanctuary with an interlocking plan (like "Russian dolls"): enclosures within each other, and eventually, at the main spot, a small, highly sacred building or kiosk, called an "altar" or "altar platform." Very famous examples of that general concept are known in the ancient Levant, among them, the Zeus sanctuary in Damascus and the Temple of Jerusalem, where the public (women, gentiles, Jews, priests) was admitted into the different enclosures and the central place—the "Holy of Holies"—is inaccessible to anybody. As for Dharih, if we eliminate the southern enclosure and some sophisticated details inside the temple proper, its basic structure is exactly the same as that of Tannur: an outer enclosure, an inner enclosure or temple, and a small building or platform.

By observing only its ground plan, one could get the impression that Tannur is actually a very simple example of a temple inside a temenos, with a kind of *adyton* within the temple proper. In order to correct this false impression, one should review figure 176, p. 173, an axonometric presentation of the entire complex which, although more dubious in its details, is much more representative of the whole. There, one realizes that within the temenos there is no "temple" in the usual sense of the term, but an inner enclosure (ca. 10 m x 10 m) surrounding an inner shrine that is actually a platform.

Let us now examine the three components of the Tannur complex, starting from the entrance in the east: the outside enclosure, the inside enclosure, and the inner platform. Before entering the temenos we find, on the right (at the northeast angle of the complex) a triclinium. This recalls the three-or-more (left-hand) side-rooms before the entrance of the Dharih temenos, which were also triclinia during a part of their history. In both cases, we may suppose that these dining rooms were used for cultic meals either by individuals who were not allowed to enter the temenos or by those who had not yet performed the purificatory rituals necessary for entry.

The outer enclosure is roughly square, measuring 33 m in length by 35 m in width. The large northwest angle room, possibly an addition to the complex, exceeds these measurements. This enclosure consists mainly of a well-paved courtyard (called "forecourt" by J. McKenzie), framed north and south by columned porticos. Notwithstanding the lack of a third portico along the wall on the entrance side, this courtyard is strikingly similar to that of enclosure 2 at Dharih, with steps around the courtyard (probably used as seats by the worshippers during the cultic performances), a water drain in the pavement, traces of small monuments including burning altars (possibly incense altars or altars for the burning of meats), and various rooms, including triclinia on both sides of the courtyard behind the porticos (in contrast to three sides at Dharih). The square base of a sacrificial altar, where animals were killed, is clearly visible in the northeastern corner of the courtyard, allowing free access from the main gate to the door of the inner enclosure. We have seen that the main altar at Dharih must have been in the same position. Thus, the main (and most important) difference between the two sanctuaries is the use of a single temenos at Tannur, which contrasts with the two-or-more successive enclosures at Dharih. This obviously is not only a matter of size: if we recall the meaning of the different enclosures at the Temple of Jerusalem (one specifically for women, others for men), and if we remember that Tannur was probably used for short pilgrimages or festivals only, one may suppose that the worshippers who partook of the ceremonies at Dharih only within the (southern) enclosure 1 *did not* take part in the Tannur rituals. A trivial, but perhaps correct, idea is that women did not come to Tannur.

Due to the complete excavations at Tannur, the rooms on both sides of the courtyard are all known (unlike the ones at Dharih), even though their relative chronology and their history are not certain. The two northeastern rooms are clearly roofed triclinia, paralleled by the triclinium known at Dharih along the western half of the southern side of enclosure 2. On the southern side at Tannur, the very long and narrow room has traces of benches in its western part: it should have been another triclinium, or more probably several triclinia, if, as noted by Glueck and McKenzie,[27] it was partitioned in several adjacent rooms. Nothing is known (as in Dharih for the northwestern rooms in similar relative position) of the function of the two small rooms in the southwest angle. The large protruding room in the northwestern angle, which probably accommodated a stairway accessing the roof on its eastern side, was clearly not a triclinium. One or both of these rooms (at the southwest and northwest) may have served as enclosures for the priests in charge.

The "inner enclosure," according to McKenzie's terminology, which could be classified as "open-air temple" as well, is formed by a highly decorated wall surrounding a small paved courtyard, in the middle of which stood the shrine or platform. As established by McKenzie, it was built in Tannur's second phase, in the late first or early second century AD, contemporary with the beginning of the second and main phase at Dharih.[28] Although the evidence is lacking, it is probable that such an enclosure existed in the sanctuary's first phase. Despite one's initial impression in comparing Tannur (pp. 172–73, figs. 175, 176) with the more sophisticated Dharih temple (fig. 71), the similarities between the two complexes are strong. To begin with, the rear part of the phase 2 temple at Dharih (and the whole of the phase 1 temple) has a square layout, identical (although larger) to that of Tannur, allowing the possibility of ritual processions around the inner shrine or platform. The Tannur temple was unroofed: we have seen that parts of Dharih temple were as well, surely in the vestibule, and possibly in the cella and platform. Both temples are provided with a side-door (later blocked in both cases) in the front part of the temple—on the right side at Dharih, and on the left at Tannur. These may be interpreted either as service doors for the priests (thus indicating at Tannur that angle-rooms 12 and 13 of the outer enclosure were priestly enclosures) or as an exit for a portion of the worshippers, if they were allowed to enter the temple. The similarities are worth noticing as well, if we consider the façades of both temples (fig. 74, height 15 m, and fig. 180,[29] height 10 m), although the decoration of the Tannur façade seems to have been less abundant than at Dharih. The structure is clearly the same, with engaged half-columns on both sides of the door and engaged quarter-columns and pilasters at the angles, an entablature decorated with reliefs, and a pediment. The only structural difference would have been the presence at Tannur, above the pediment, of an attic surmounted by an Egyptian cornice. However, in our opinion, the existence of such an attic is quite doubtful since the only existing evidence—two blocks of Egyptian cornice—could actually come, not from the façade, but from the crowning of the side-walls of the temple, as at Dharih. Unique to the Tannur façade is the so-called Atargatis Tympanum (p. 15, fig. 4), which more probably depicts the main Nabataean goddess, al-ʿUzza. Its position is discussed. Glueck placed it above the main entablature of the façade, but not within a pediment, which he had not recognized. McKenzie's reconstruction places it immediately above the door, where its measurements, with the *acroteria*, actually fit. But they would fit within the pediment as well, with the eagle *acroterium* of the tympanum serving also as the *acroterium* of the pediment, if the pediment was "broken" at its summit, as was customary in Nabataean architecture. Thus, we suggest that the "Atargatis" panel was actually inserted within the pediment. This solution has two advantages: it does not leave the pediment empty, which would be unusual in Nabataean architecture; it would have a good parallel at Dharih, where the tympanum in the pediment is surrounded by an arch, as the "Atargatis panel" is. As for the other sculpted decoration of the Tannur façade, we may notice that the main frieze is formed, as in Dharih, by reliefs depicting alternating busts of deities and figures of standing Victories (who crown the deity beside them). L. Tholbecq,[30] who discovered this similarity with the Dharih frieze, suggests convincingly that the busts actually represented the seven planets.

Since conclusion of the excavations, Khirbet et-Tannur's central interior shrine or platform (pp. 172–74, figs. 175, 176, 178) has correctly formed the basis for the three-phase chronology of the sanctuary. The first platform, which was very small (1.5 m square; height 1.75 m [suggested, but uncertain]), was twice enlarged. After the first enlargement (2 m square, height 2.61 m), it resembled a cultic niche, one furnished with a stairway providing access to its top. The niche façade (p. 174, figs. 178, 179) was adorned with a crude cult image depicting two seated deities, one bearded male divinity bearing a thunderbolt (thus a Nabataean equivalent to Zeus, better identified as the main god Dushara than the Syrian Hadad), and a female deity completely destroyed except for one of her feet, and a lion-throne support with adjoining lower garment. We would suggest that this quite archaic image was reused from the Phase 1 (late first century BC?) monument. Lastly, within Phase 3 (which we hesitate to date as late as the third century, as J. McKenzie does), the shrine was once more enlarged (3.5 m square, height 3 to 4 m), still provided with steps but also with a small recess in its back (a recess which may be compared to the one present at Dharih within the angle staircase of the temple: a cupboard for utensils of the cult). The baroque and exuberant decoration of the façade includes on the side pilasters a clear representation of the zodiac, in two rows, with Virgo (referred to by Glueck as the "Grain goddess") at the bottom left and Pisces (Glueck's "Dolphin goddess") at the bottom right (pp. 182–83). We have seen above that standing Victories were present in the decoration of the area of the platform of Dharih, suggesting also there the presence of a zodiac decoration as here, but not on pilasters.

The main problem with the Tannur shrine and platform is its function. It is clear that it was a cultic niche, at least in periods 2 and 3 (in contrast to the Dharih platform), and an elevated platform, at least in both these periods, due to the presence of stairways. It has always been referred to as an altar, or more accurately, as an altar platform. This is an intuitive idea, which apparently fits well with the location: it is evocative to imagine the smoke of burning offerings, rising in the air from this platform towards the sky of Tannur hill, clearly visible from everywhere in the area. But there are difficulties. First, the only evidence for an altar on the platform is the presence of burnt grains and bones within the debris, filling, or pavements in and around the platform area. This does not clearly indicate the existence of offerings and certainly does not indicate sacrifices. Second, no remains or fragments of an altar or altars were found there, which is, at least, strange. Third, the presence of an altar—at least sacrificial—inside an ancient temple, especially a Semitic one, would have been quite surprising. Considering the evidence at Dharih, we would like to suggest that the Tannur platform was a *môtab*, a monumental elevated base for baetyls–which does not exclude, of course, offerings, perhaps incense fumigations in front of the baetyls. Fragments of baetyls and of mortises for fixing them would have more easily been missed by the excavators than fragments of altars. Nevertheless, it is clear that the general aspect of the Tannur *môtab* differed greatly from the one at Dharih: It was smaller, much higher, and not provided with a baldaquin. It did not look like a kiosk, but like a niche.

One important difference remains between the temples at Dharih and Tannur: unlike Dharih, the Tannur temple did not possess crypts. If our interpretation of the crypts at Dharih as sacred underground spaces for storing the baetyls outside of religious performances is correct, this means that there were no baetyls permanently kept at Tannur. One should conclude that the baetyls were *brought* to Tannur (likely from Dharih) during the equinox pilgrimages, a tradition of transporting the idols well known in ancient Arabic religions, and, more broadly, in many religions.

8. Still Mysterious Places Completely excavated Tannur and largely excavated Dharih are, at the moment, the best-known Nabataean sites and sanctuaries, archaeologically. Their general significance and chronology and their mutual relationship is clear, as analyzed above. In both sanctuaries, the number of triclinia (at least four at Tannur, and at least seven at Dharih, including the one in the "rectangular building," and more, probably, to be discovered), is surprisingly high for a relatively small population center like Dharih and for an isolated high-place like Tannur.

Such a concentration testifies to the role that these cult places played as caravan and pilgrimage sanctuaries of regional or even national significance. The emergence of both sanctuaries, initially as very small cultic places in the first century BC and early first century AD, coincides with and probably contributed to the beginning of the sedentarization of the Nabataeans in the countryside. Their climax, in the second and third centuries, is also the climax of the Nabataean population within Roman Arabia. The social organization of that population may be confidently deduced from the evidence at Dharih—with a main priestly family dominating a community of peasants. The complete abandonment of both sanctuaries after the middle of the fourth century is not solely a consequence of the earthquake in 363 AD: this occurred in a period of decline of pagan cults.

But these places remain mysterious in many aspects. A number of mysteries, merely technical, have already been mentioned; but two main ones remain. The first concerns the deities. The primary female deity depicted within the tympanum at Tannur may be the Nabataean al-ʿUzza (p.15, fig. 4); she is possibly present in the "reconstructed" female cult image of the Tannur platform (figs. 179, 193, 195), which once accompanied a bearded god with a thunderbolt—a possible Dushara (fig. 40). But in that case, why is she alone in the tympanum, while associated with Dushara in the cult image? Is the male god at Tannur only the companion of the main, female, deity of the sanctuary? At Dharih, the situation is worse, since the tympanum of the temple façade has almost disappeared: our proposal to see the face of Dushara and the *cornucopiae* of Tyche/al-ʿUzza, (thus possibly the same pair as at Tannur), is only tentative. Due to the paucity of inscriptions at Tannur, their absence at Dharih, and the difficulty of interpreting a native religious iconography that is both ambivalent and Greek-influenced, it is impossible to identify the main gods of the Dharih and Tannur sanctuaries with certainty. The only explicit evidence, at Tannur, is that of a cult of Qaws (fig. 196). But this is obviously not the main inscription of the sanctuary, and Starcky's hypothesis,[31] that the primary cult of this late Nabataean and Roman sanctuary was devoted to a very old Edomite deity, seems doubtful. More likely, Qawsmilk, the worshipper of Qaws at Tannur, would have been one of many adherents who used the sacral place at Tannur to mark his personal devotion to the god of his family or clan, apparently of Edomite origin. This was quite natural within the completely polytheistic context of such sanctuaries, a polytheism also evidenced by the richness of religious evocations on the sculptures of both places (the Tyche at Tannur, the Victories, the thunderbolts throughout, the sea-centaurs and eagles in the pediment at Dharih, etc.). Among them, the contextual significance of the zodiac images is impressive: at Dharih, on the frieze of the temple façade and quite probably on the decoration around the *môtab*; and at Tannur, on the frieze of the temple façade, on the pilasters of the platform façade, and on the famous relief of a Victory bearing a Tyche (Virgo? Nabataean al-ʿUzza?) encircled by a zodiac (figs. 197–99). The astral significance of these zodiacal motifs has long been underlined, but what is their contextual implication? Such images remain unparalleled within the Nabataean realm (except for a Roman-period oil lamp discovered at Petra in the Temple of the Winged Lions (fig. 246). Do they mean that astral ceremonies were actually performed at Tannur and Dharih, as probably indicated by the precise east-west orientation of Tannur? Were they mainly decorative and fashionable, as everywhere in the Roman Empire since Augustus? Are they cosmic symbols of the reigning Roman authority? This last question raises the yet unsolved problem of the exact date of the beginning of "Phase 2" at Dharih and Tannur: did it start slightly before or slightly after the Roman annexation of 106 AD ?

According to the scant evidence at Dharih concerning this second problem, as suggested above, we prefer the latter hypothesis. As a rough, working hypothesis, we would propose the following explanation for the incomprehensible absence of inscriptions at the large (Phase 2 and later) sanctuaries at Dharih and Tannur and on the monumental tomb at Dharih. The theory is that the leading (and priestly) family of Dharih and Tannur was, by circumstance, forced into silence and, as a result, was not inclined to promulgate itself (and consequently its deities) through dedicatory or cultic inscriptions. Why such a silence? Indeed, we do not know what happened to the leading Nabataean clans of Petra (including the king's family) after the Roman annexation. Nothing in the Petra texts indicates that they continued to be active and dominant at Petra. We believe that these princes may have chosen, or were forced, to exile themselves to their native countryside, where they owned estates. The Dharih family would have been one of them. Still wealthy, it would have chosen, settling at the site shortly after 106 AD, to enlarge and embellish the traditional sanctuaries there with the intention of formally honoring their Roman host with certain images (some perhaps ironic) on the façade of Dharih (and possibly at Tannur). However, as exiles and subjects, they chose not to leave a permanent record of themselves through the use of stone inscriptions. The "ancestor" buried (without any exterior sign of wealth, unlike the other dead within the same tomb) in the monumental tomb at Dharih would have been not only the descendant of the local chief Natir'el, head of the Laaban spring, but also the head of this recently exiled Nabataean princely family. But, obviously, this is only a suggestion.

8 | The Negev and the Nabataeans

AVRAHAM NEGEV

The Nabataean Negev occupied a central place in the Nabataean realm. Situated between Arabia and Edom and east of the Sinai Peninsula, it formed part of the original nucleus of the kingdom. The Nabataean Negev enters the state of Nabataean history at the end of the fourth century, at the time when Antigonos Monophtalmos marched to Egypt in 312 BC. At Gaza he hears of the fabulous riches of the Nabataeans, from which he decided to benefit.[1]

The only possible way to reach the Nabataean kingdom, Antigonos's target, was to cross the Plain of Beersheba. For him the end of the inhabited land (the *Oikumene* mentioned in the text) may have been the area of Arad, where there was a strong tower in the Hellenistic era, and a *limes* fortress in the Roman period.[2] From the region of Arad Antigonos and his army made incursions into the waterless country. To obtain sheep and goats the Macedonians must have gone as far south as Oboda, where they would have learned of the skill of the Nabataeans in procuring water.

There remains the matter of a certain "rock" (in Greek, *petra*) on which the Nabataeans deposited their property. Most scholars believe that this is the Petra that was to become the capital of the Nabataean kingdom.[3] If we are to believe the distance to "*petra*" as given by the Greek writer Hieronymus (as preserved in the *Histories* of Diodorus), it could hardly have been the actual site of Petra, but may have been a rock fortress in the southwestern corner of the Dead Sea. I have suggested that the early "*petra*" was at "En Boqeq," where a Herodian pharmaceutical and cosmetics production center existed in Roman times and a fort in the late Roman period.[4] Above the Herodian site there rises a Masada-type summit, where I have proposed to locate Hieronymus' Nabataean rock. As this rock is steep only on the eastern side facing the Dead Sea, it is a more likely candidate than Mezad Zohar.[5] After the Macedonians' campaign, Hieronymus, the historian, was placed in charge of the exploitation of the asphalt from the Dead Sea. Taking into account that the main object of Antigonos was to conquer Egypt, I doubt whether he ever reached the Edomite Nabataean region.

The Nabataeans possessed the central Negev in two stages. In the initial, early fourth-century stage the triangle consisted of Elusa in the north, Nessana bordering Sinai, and Oboda on the east. There were no permanent structures at this time, and the Nabataeans lived in tents. After the reconquest of the Negev by the middle of the first century BC, the three settlements of the later triangle were founded. These were Rehovot between Elusa and Nessana, Sobata between Nessana and Oboda, and Mampsis, northeast of Oboda.

Elusa (el Khalasa in Arabic, Haluza in Hebrew). Situated closest to Judea and the harbor of Gaza, Elusa is located in the heart of sand dunes. It was surveyed by scholars in the nineteenth and early twentieth centuries.[6] In the Late Roman period Elusa figures quite frequently in the letters of Libanius, a pupil of Zenobius, the famous teacher of rhetoric, a native of Elusa. The general opinion is that Elusa was totally destroyed.[7] In 1979 a church was excavated.[8] Around the city cemeteries were discerned. The existence of a well-preserved city buried in the sands is thus certain. The earliest known Nabataean inscription was found at Elusa.

Nessana (Auja el Hafir, Nitzana). Situated on the border of the Sinai, Nessana has suffered greatly from wars in modern times. Its ancient name was determined with the discovery of the Nessana papyri.[9] Nessana was surveyed and excavated in the 1930s by the Anglo-American Colt Expedition. It consists of a lower city, much destroyed, and an acropolis, of which parts were excavated.[10] Stamped wine jar handles of the Hellenistic period were found in unstratified contexts, and plentiful sherds pertain to Nabataean and Early Roman times.

Numerous documents were discovered at Nessana. Inscriptions on stone consist of epitaphs and Christian religious formulae. Other written material consists of a cache of literary papyri,[11] which may have comprised the curriculum of the local school. Much more numerous are the non-literary papyri, which contain abundant information on all aspects of the economy and social life of the town.[12] Of interest is the large number of personal names, from which it is clear that the Nabataeans, the original ethnic element, constituted an important part of the town's population until the end of its existence in the Early Arabic period.[13]

Oboda (Abdeh, Avdat). Oboda, frequently mentioned in historical sources, was mistakenly identified by early scholars.[14] The importance of the archeological work done at Oboda lies in the vivid picture of a large Nabataean caravan station on the major trade route leading from northern Arabia and Petra to the Mediterranean. A few sherds of the Hellenistic period came from crevices in the rock and others derived from a dump and the remains of a hearth of an encampment. This evidences the occupation of Oboda in the Hellenistic period, most probably by Nabataeans. This is the Early Nabataean Period.

The most prosperous phase of Oboda was in the Middle Nabataean Period, around the middle of the first century BC. According to Greek sources, Oboda was named after a Nabataean king who was buried at Oboda and venerated there. A temple excavated in 1989 was probably dedicated to him.[15] The construction of the temple dates to about the middle of the first century BC; it belongs to the type of "southern" Nabataean temple, continuing the old Canaanite variety. Like the temple of Qasr al-Bint, it consists of an *ulam* (*pronaos*), *hechal* (*naos*), and *debir* (holy of holies). A unique feature of the *debir* is its division into two rooms, occupying two-thirds and one-third of the space, the former possibly housing two gods and the latter, the abode of a single god, perhaps the deified king Obodas. One of the temple's gates and column drums were transferred in the Byzantine period from the temple to the nearby Christian church.

The building of this temple took place when the acropolis was a hill covered with natural rocks. The rather small temple was built close to its slope. Probably at the beginning of the reign of Obodas III, the great builder of Nabataean temples, the preparation of the terrain and the construction of other temples on the acropolis began.[16] Very little of these temples remain. One, whose identification is based on Nabataean[17] and Greek inscriptions,[18] existed as late as the end of the third century AD, a very short time before the arrival of Christianity. Among the decorated stonework found on the acropolis of Oboda, one fact stands out: the almost total absence of human or animal motifs. This forms a complete contrast with the stone decoration of the sanctuary of Khirbet et-Tannur.[19]

The Economy of Oboda. In addition to their religious functions, the temples of Oboda provided financial services, operating as banks. Besides serving as a way station, where caravans could halt and replenish their supplies of water, there is much evidence that Oboda was also an important center for the production of food. From the air, rectangular structures made of fieldstones are visible all over the hill of Oboda. When I examined the terrain I found that large boulders had been removed and sherds of the first century BC/AD covered the ground. In all probability these were enclosures for the breeding of camels, sheep, and goats. Animals were the most important source of food, supplying meat, milk and milk products, wool for garments and tents, and skins for transporting water. The meat was mostly consumed in a dried state. At a few places on the acropolis of Oboda were discovered large quantities of saltpeter, a necessary substance for curing meat. Potassium brought from the Dead Sea, processed with animal or human urine, constituted the conserving agent. Necessary ingredients for seasoning the meat and milk products were brought by Nabataean traders from elsewhere in the East.

A small number of installations were used for a completely different purpose. These I saw for the first time in 1990, when I flew above one of them in a helicopter. It was a large perfect circle with low walls. Being convinced that this was a water reservoir, I asked the pilot to land. When he did, I examined it and found that the circle contained only dust and not a single stone. The pole standing in the center, which was supplied by my imagination, explained it all. This was a unique Nabataean horse-training ground. We could not date the installation without excavating it. Examining the surroundings of this circle, we found traces of several others.

Caravan Protection. In the northern part of the hill at Oboda early visitors already observed a large military camp, which the French scholars identified as Roman. On several occasions I conducted excavations on it. It is a square (100 x 100 m), protected by square corner and middle towers. It is divided by two main streets into four quarters, with barracks in each. The main southern gate of the camp was built of smooth ashlars.[20]

Pottery Production. Oboda of the first centuries BC and AD was a city of solidly built temples. On the other hand, the inhabitants, except for those quartered in the military camps, lived in tents. It is the quality of the pottery produced at Oboda that testifies to the standard of living there. The potter's workshop, situated east of the city, is a rather small installation.[21] The local Nabataean potter was an importer of pottery from all corners of the Roman world, from as far west as England, and as far east as the Crimea.[22] Almost none of the types of pottery represented at Petra is missing from the

83. Aerial view of Mampsis, southwestern corner of town, looking east, 1990. On the right, Early Byzantine South Church; on the left, Late Nabataean Palace with adjacent tower and court.

Oboda repertoire. Only a very wealthy society could have afforded the use of pottery of such quality and quantity.

Agriculture at Oboda. By the middle of the first century AD the Nabataeans began to lose control of the spice trade, and agriculture started to take its place. In three locations at Oboda there were discovered inscriptions engraved on one or more faces of large stone objects, which I identified as libation altars.[23] The first word of some of these inscriptions I read as *sichra*, meaning dam in Aramaic. The other words specify that in a certain religious festival a solemn feast was held, commemorating the construction of something, in which a religious brotherhood took part. This "something" is apparently the construction of dams and the inauguration of agriculture. Two of the three pairs of "stone objects" were found in the middle of agricultural farms, which is an entirely new phenomenon in Nabataean life. Some of these inscriptions contain the king's title: "In the year 18 (in some cases 'in the year 28') of King Rabbel, who brought life and deliverance to his people." I have suggested that King Rabbel II earned this title for the introduction of agriculture. The entire region of Oboda, to a distance of several kilometers from the city, is covered with terraced fields, but at present a distinction between the Nabataean and Late Roman/Byzantine periods cannot be made.

Nabataean agriculture occurred mainly in the period when the kingdom was transformed into a Roman province. At Oboda there is ample proof that no internal changes took place during the first decades of *Provincia Arabia*.[24] Construction of temples continued during the second century AD, and the deified King Obodas was venerated until as late as 294 AD.[25] Christianity arrived at Oboda around the middle of the fourth century, and the transition between paganism and the new religion must have been a stormy one, as one may gather from the construction of the North Church on the site of the temple. Christianity brought an entirely new cultural life to Oboda, as is evidenced by the building of two churches, which retained very few of the former qualities of Nabataean architecture.

Mampsis (Kurnub, the Arabic name, probably a name of Nabataean origin. Mamshit, an entirely new Hebrew name). Together with Rehovot and Sobata, Mampsis belongs to the later Nabataean triangle, formed at the end of the first century BC. Far from Oboda and from any other major Nabataean site, its task was to keep watch on the road from Petra, coming up from the Araba. Although the hills to the east and south of the town are higher and climatically superior, the planners of Mampsis preferred a much lower and less ventilated elevation. The sole reason for this was the availability of drinking water. There are no springs in the region, and the only way to procure water was by the construction of dams in the wadis. Nahal Mamshit, a slow-running stream, was crossed by three dams, with a combined capacity of some 10,000 cubic meters; there was a smaller dam to the east of the settlement. Calculation shows that this supply was adequate for the town. From the dams water was drawn to cisterns in the houses, streets, and squares, and into a reservoir located in the town.

Many early travelers visited Mampsis, which was considered a totally ruined site.[26] I excavated there in 1965–1967. The outstanding feature of Mampsis is its architecture from different periods; from the beginning there came to light buildings of exquisite quality.[27] It seemed to me unlikely that this building tradition originated at Mampsis, and I waited for the discovery of similar buildings in the larger towns of the Negev, or elsewhere in the Nabataean kingdom. No such buildings, however, were found. It was only during my work at Mampsis in 1990, a short while before my retirement, that I came closer to the solution of this problem.

Town planning of Mampsis. Most buildings visible today at Mampsis are solid structures of the Late Nabataean Period (fig. 83). However, between these there crop up older buildings of the Middle Nabataean Period. A striking feature is that the buildings of earlier times were constructed of rather large blocks of hammer-dressed stone, while in the later period the larger blocks were replaced by smaller stones, smoothly dressed and sometimes with smooth margins. This rule applies until the cessation of Nabataean construction at the end of the third century AD.

The two large buildings XXI and XXII,[28] to which we returned in 1990, are situated outside of the town limits of Mampsis. At first we believed that they were part of the city fortifications, in which were stationed Roman soldiers; however, their civilian nature was soon apparent. What were they then? I shall first refer to some of the other buildings that we excavated at the site.

Building I. [29] This building, of which the exterior walls and the interior door frames are of ashlars, contains a *liwan*, a library, an installation to keep water cool, a baking and cooking oven, a "refrigerator," a washroom, elaborately constructed living quarters, a *gamma* device and an elaborately constructed staircase tower for reaching upper floors. It has a rather small court, and consequently the cisterns were excavated in the square outside the building. The building extended over 1,000 square meters. We identified it as a palace, though no comparisons for this building were found.

Building II.[30] A tower, consisting of three rooms and a staircase room, is preserved almost intact. A cistern covered by a barrel vault is under the pavement of the court. Other rooms include a kitchen and a guest suite. This was probably a watchtower and the station for the local police force.

Building XI.[31] Half of this structure, which is south of Building II, is occupied by a church. A vestibule leads into a court with a small cistern. On the east is a staircase of a different type from others at Mampsis. A magnificently built stable occupies the corner of the building, and a room nearby might have served as a house shrine. Other rooms were either incorporated in the church or destroyed. The building extended over 600 square meters, and is the smallest excavated at Mampsis.

Building XII.[32] Situated in the eastern half of the town, this building occupies an area of 1,600 square meters. A paved vestibule leads into the house. At the entrance is a guardroom. Next is a large guest room with a separate washroom. In a staircase the hoard of 10,500 silver coins of the second and early third centuries AD was discovered. Further east is an entrance, with classic Nabataean capitals, to an inner court containing a *gamma* device, serving two staircase-towers. From the court one enters two wings of rooms. On the south is a vestibule leading into a strongroom; the inner court and the vestibule were decorated by frescoes. At the eastern end of the large court there is a *gamma* device consisting of freestanding columns with Nabataean capitals. This leads into an elaborately planned water closet and to a large stable of the type of Building XI.

Building VII.[33] The public reservoir, well built of drafted stones, is covered with thick water-resistant plaster. It is provided with a settling tank for filling with water, and a flight of stairs for periodic cleaning. It was roofed by arches resting on heavy piers.

Building V.[34] The bathhouse, of Roman style, includes a *frigidarium*, *tepidarium*, and *caldarium*. In order to conserve heat, the caldarium and tepidarium were built deep in the ground. The installation seems to have saved water by the extensive use of steam. Water came from the nearby reservoir.

Buildings XXII-XXIII.[35] When we first excavated the buildings of the Late Nabataean Period described above, we believed that this architectural style originated in some other Nabataean center. As nothing similar was revealed, we came to the conclusion that this high-quality architecture developed in a school at Mampsis. Why at Mampsis? Economically Mampsis was the weakest link in the Nabataean chain of the Negev. However, the presence of a Nabataean station in this part of the region was essential. In order to encourage the settlers of Mampsis, the Nabataean authorities installed there a school of architecture.

Building XXIII.[36] This building, earlier in date than the above, occupies an area of about 30 x 30 m. It is entered from the east through a spacious vestibule, leading into a large court. There are two rooms and an oblong hall on the south. Apart from the door frames and arches, the whole building is made of rather large hammer-dressed blocks of stone. Because of its architecture, and the pottery thrown out of the building when it was prepared for later use, we dated it to the Middle Nabataean Period, e.g., to the first century AD.

Building XXII.[37] Much larger and more elaborately planned, this building measures 45 x 35 m, covering an area of some 1,600 square meters. It is built of smooth ashlars outside and of squared blocks of stone inside, except for ashlar doorframes. The building is entered through a spacious Vestibule on the southeast, adjoined by two offices and guardrooms. A large hall, whose roof was supported by four columns, occupies the rest of the southern wing. The distances between the columns and the lateral walls are too large to be roofed by stone slabs, and the roofing must have been wooden beams. The only sources of wood were the forests of Syria and Lebanon; segments of beams of Syrian Black Pine and Lebanese Cedar were found at Oboda and Mampsis.

In the eastern wing of the house there are eight rooms of equal size, entered from the court. In the opposite western wing are one hall and four smaller rooms. The northern hall, 35 m long, is outstanding. Three wide doors lead from the spacious court into the hall. Nine arches, resting on heavy piers, span its whole length. When one looks out from the wide doors, the feeling of empty space is not interrupted, since none of the piers was placed opposite an opening.

This is not a military installation, as we originally believed. With the exception of the staircase tower, all the splendor of Mampsis private architecture is present. In all likelihood, it was a technical school where the art of planning and building was taught. Similarly, in the earlier, smaller school (building XXIII), instruction in the building of temples took place. When the construction of private buildings began in the late first century AD, the larger school was founded. No two private buildings at Mampsis are alike, and it is possible that these were planned and built by teachers and master-builders of the school.

This is also likely from the standpoint of economics. With the decline of the spice trade, the small town was looking for new sources of income. These were horse breeding, and probably also the school of architecture, which expanded at the beginning of the second century AD.

The influence of the Mampsis school of architecture was long-standing; both of the churches in Mampsis were of excellent construction.[38] It seems that this resulted from the fact that the school closed during the economic crisis in the Roman world. The builders of the churches during the mid-fourth century AD used the deserted building as a quarry for the new structures. A series of pilasters adorns the long walls of the East Church. This type of decoration is already rare in the fourth century. In the case of Mampsis the piers were simply transferred from the earlier Nabataean building to the later church. The wooden roof of the East Church was probably also taken from the hall of arches in Building XXII.

From the fourth–fifth centuries AD onward, the stumps of the walls of these two buildings apparently served as bases for the tents of the militia stationed at Mampsis.[39]

The Cemeteries of Mampsis.[40] The Nabataean cemetery was in use from the end of the first century BC (Middle Nabataean Period) to about the end of the third century AD (Late Nabataean Period and post-Nabataean). There were discovered about twenty-five tombs, tables for serving funerary meals, and remains of the funerary meals. Burial was with or without wooden coffins, and either primary or secondary.[41] Burial in the form of stepped pyramids was also found. Women's tombs contained much gold jewelry.[42] In one tomb was found a large number of seal impressions of cities in Arabia.[43]

In another part of the town a cremation cemetery of the Roman army was discovered.[44] The presence of Romans in the Nabataean Negev at the time of the annexation was previously unknown.[45] This is the only known cemetery of its type in Arabia. The third cemetery at Mampsis is of the Byzantine period.

Nabataean life at Mampsis and in the Negev in general comprises about half of the life of the settlement, which continued in the Late Roman and Byzantine periods. The history of the towns of Rehovot-in-the-Negev,[46] and Sobata[47] in the Nabataean periods has been little investigated. These two sites complete the later triangle in the history of the Nabataeans in the Negev.

9 | Nabataeans on the Dead Sea Littoral

KONSTANTINOS D. POLITIS AND HERO GRANGER-TAYLOR

THE ANCIENT HISTORIANS DIODORUS, Strabo, and Josephus described a Nabataean community living by the Dead Sea that flourished by trading in the rich natural resources of the area such as bitumen, salt, balsam, and sulphur. Several archaeological sites which have clear evidence of such Nabataean communities include the large fortress of Umm al Tawabeen and the urban center at Khirbet Sheikh 'Isa in the Ghor es-Safi, the cave sanctuary and cemetery at Deir 'Ain 'Abata, the forts at the mouths of the Wadis Numeira and 'Isal, the farmstead at Beliedah in the mouth of the Wadi Kerak and the cemetery of Khirbet Qazone in the Ghor al-Mazra'a (fig. 84).

Khirbet Qazone Excavations Khirbet Qazone has over 3,500 shaft graves, most of which were recently looted. A rescue excavation mounted at this site in 1996 and 1997 by the Jordanian Department of Antiquities and the British Museum unearthed twenty-three burials.[1] Each of the graves had a single burial and there was no evidence of re-internment. Most of the graves were dug into the soft soil, undercut to the east and covered by adobe brick slabs. At least two were constructed of stone cists. Men, women, and children alike were laid to rest with their heads placed to the south side of the grave (fig. 85). Although the graves were constructed in a similar manner to those found at Khirbet Qumran on the northwest side of the Dead Sea, there was no other evidence to indicate that these belonged to an Essene community. It is plausible to suggest that these burials belonged to the Nabataean residents of Mahoza in the Zoar region, as mentioned in the Babatha papyri from the Cave of Letters.[2]

The dry conditions of the soil into which the burial shafts at Khirbet Qazone were cut and the nearly airtight construction of the graves desiccated many of the bodies, resulting in the survival of skin, hair, and even internal organs. Some of these bodies were wrapped in leather and textile material. The leather hides were made specifically into shrouds that were stitched together, decorated, and sometimes painted in red (fig. 86). The textiles, on the other hand, consisted mostly of reused Greco-Roman style mantles and tunics (figs. 89, 91). One of the best-preserved bodies, which was confiscated from an antiquities dealer in 1997, is now in the Yarmuk University, Irbid, Jordan. The "mummy," as it is erroneously named, is actually the body of an adult male wrapped in remnants of three to four textiles, at least one of which is a tunic.[3]

Although local tomb robbers claimed to have found jewelry, glass vessels, small wooden boxes, and papyri in the graves at Khirbet Qazone, only a few of the burials which were legally excavated contained any such grave goods. Adornments found included iron bracelets, copper and silver torcs and earrings, gold earrings and bracelets, beads, and a very worn scarab. A wooden staff, a pair of sandals, and a laurel wreath were discovered in the grave of an adult male.

Surface collections made at Khirbet Qazone yielded more metalwork as well as pottery and glass fragments belonging to the first to second century AD. Broken pottery

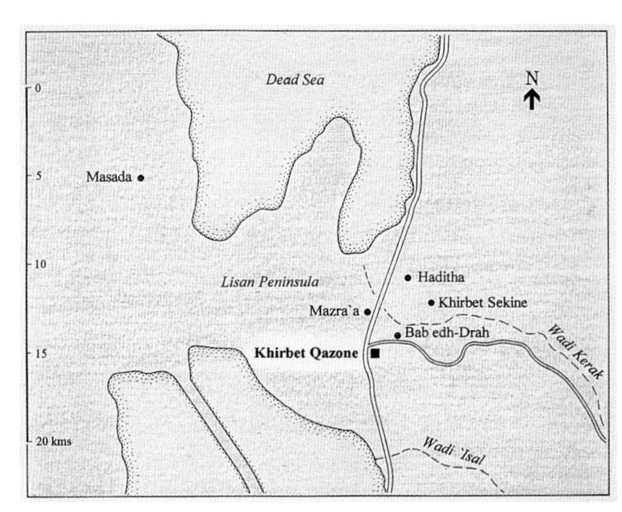

84. Location map of Khirbet Qazone.

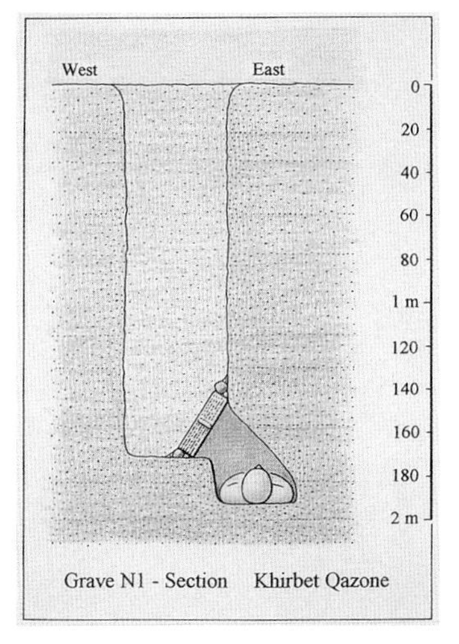

85. Section of grave at Khirbet Qazone, which was characteristically undercut to the east and covered by adobe bricks.

86. Leather shroud from grave at Khirbet Qazone.

bowls, plates, and drinking vessels scattered around the cemetery may be interpreted as remnants of funerary meals, a common Nabataean practice.[4]

Four "Dushara" baetyls and/or *nefesh* stelae (fig. 88), recovered from looted tombs, are similar to ones found at Petra.[5] One adobe brick had a Dushara sign engraved on it. One funerary stele was inscribed in Greek, reading: "Afseni the pretty one" (fig. 87). The use of the Greek language in Nabataea during the first through third centuries AD was not unusual, as it was the lingua franca of the eastern Roman Empire. Two Greek papyri found by tomb robbers at Khirbet Qazone mention Nabataean names and refer to land ownership (currently in the Shlomo Moussaieff collection).[6]

To the north, in the ashy deposits of the medieval Islamic town in Mazra'a by the Wadi Kerak, earlier surveys had revealed pottery sherds dating to the first through third centuries AD. This may have been the location of the settlement site related to the Khirbet Qazone cemetery. Regional investigations indicate the possibility that cemeteries and settlements of a similar period were situated at Khirbet Sekine and Haditha (fig. 84). In 1998 a new cemetery was discovered by Politis at Feifa, which had identical burial structures and textile fragments to those at Khirbet Qazone.[7]

The Textiles The textiles of Khirbet Qazone form an important addition to the corpus of excavated textiles from the Roman period. Coming from burials rather than from middens, a commoner source, they survive relatively complete and are of particular interest for the history of dress. At the same time they provide valuable information about contemporary burial practices.

The textiles appear to date from the second to third centuries AD. They compare most closely with textiles from the Cave of Letters, a Jewish site on the western side of the Dead Sea, with finds dating from about 130–135 AD (including many semi-complete garments[8]), and with discoveries at Dura

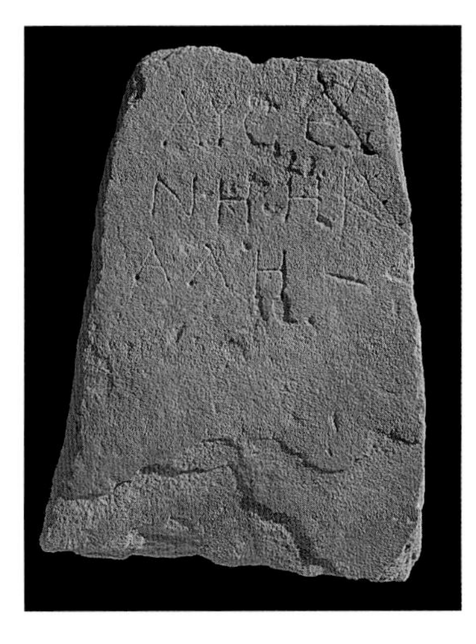

87. Funerary stele inscribed in Greek. Khirbet Qazone. Department of Antiquities, Ghor es-Safi.

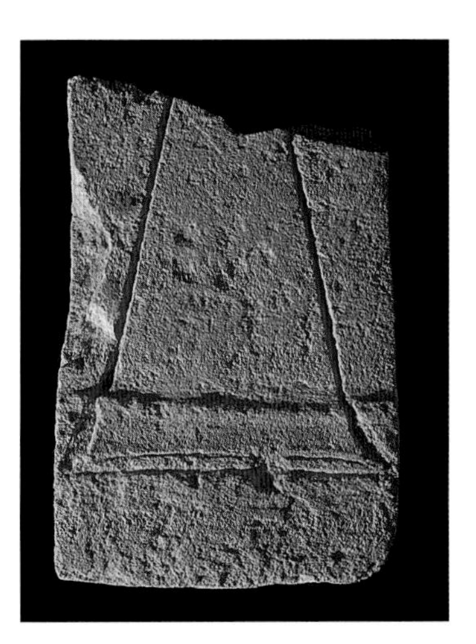

88. "Dushara" baetyl/*nefesh* stele. Khirbet Qazone. Department of Antiquities, Ghor es-Safi.

Europos, a Roman garrison town on the Euphrates, where textiles of the first half of the third century AD have been found in burials and in middens.[9]

The majority of textiles discovered at Khirbet Qazone are pieces of clothing made of wool, in a range of qualities. The remains of at least ten different wool tunics have been recovered (four are baby- or child-sized) as well as fragments of five different wool mantles. The tunics are of the Roman *tunica* type with a purple-colored stripe or *clavus* running down from either side of the neck opening and, with one exception, are sleeveless (fig. 89). The ground of the tunics is usually undyed cream but, in two cases, it is apricot-colored. The mantles are of the rectangular Greek type (*himation*, or *pallium* in Latin), undyed or, in one case, bright red, and decorated with four symmetrically placed purple-colored motifs, gamma-shaped in the case of women's mantles.

The combination of wool tunic and rectangular wool mantle can be described as Greco-Roman, but this term disguises the universality of a style of dress, which by this date had become standard among the peoples of the eastern

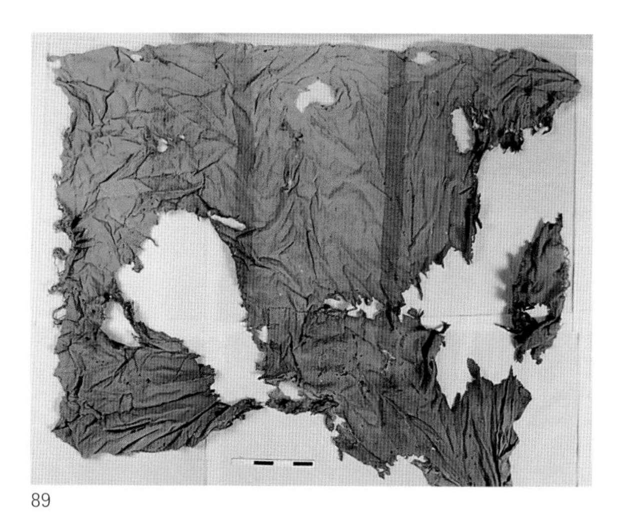
89

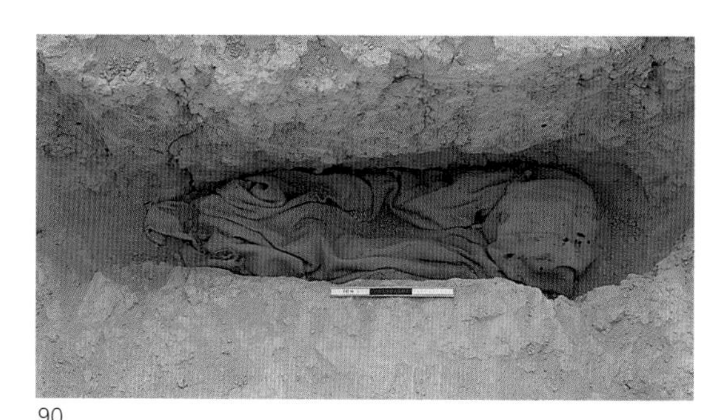
90

91

89. Wool tunic, tex. 23, from burial A1 at Khirbet Qazone. Department of Antiquities, Amman, Jordan.

90. Burial A1 with wool textile wrapped around body. Khirbet Qazone.

91. Fragments of a large [wool?] fringed scarf, Tex. 13. Khirbet Qazone. Department of Antiquities, Amman, Jordan.

Mediterranean. Judging by finds from Masada it had been adopted by the Judaean Jews by the first century AD and it must have been carried into Nabataea in the early second century AD with the Romans, if not at an earlier date. Represented many times in stone portraiture, this style is recorded most clearly in the painted "Fayum portraits" of Greco-Egyptian men and women.

Other pieces of wool clothing include an almost complete, large fringed red wool scarf (fig. 91), fragments of five more scarves (pink, yellow, and undyed) and possible linen loincloths (undyed).

Linen is relatively poorly represented at the site, but a fragmentary baby's tunic is of linen, as is the outer shroud of burial I1. One child's tunic is of cotton but its shape is constructed vertically, unlike the Roman-style tunics where the warp runs horizontally. This may record an older Near Eastern style of linen tunic.

The majority of the textiles from Khirbet Qazone show signs of having been well used before burial and many are patched and repaired. Most of the pieces of clothing were used in the burials as anonymous wrappings; for example, in burial A1, where one-half of an adult woman's tunic was used to wrap a baby's body (figs. 89, 90). The finds from Khirbet Qazone also include, in addition to the two leather shrouds (from burials H1 and H2), perhaps the first example from the Roman period of a "dedicated" textile-shroud: in burial I1, the outer wrapping (above a child's sleeved tunic, the red sash, and an adult's mantle) was an unused and undecorated fringed linen textile, which must have been bought or made for this purpose. A long wool cloth without any identifying clothing features may also have been made as a shroud.

Three of the intact burials contained remnants of another textile-related feature: a "hat" or "chin strap" made from a combination of wool felt rove of combed wool fiber. (Such roves were normally made when preparing wool for spinning.) The roves had been tied around the deceased's chin probably in order to keep the jaw from dropping.

In the course of recent archaeological fieldwork around the southeastern shore of the Dead Sea, a number of sites belonging to the first to third centuries AD which are Nabataean in character have come to light. At Khirbet Qazone this character was demonstrated by the presence of typical painted pottery and jewelry, and, more importantly by four "Dushara" baetyls and/or *nefesh* stelae. Other finds such as the laurel wreath, wooden staff, and textiles are generally characteristic of the entire Greco-Roman period. The exceptionally good preservation of these organic materials, as well as the human bodies themselves, give us a unique picture of the life of ordinary Nabataeans living on the Dead Sea littoral.

10 | The Nabataeans at Bosra and in Southern Syria

JEAN-MARIE DENTZER

The Historical Setting The preeminent place occupied by Bosra in the Nabataean realm, attested by a few historical documents, has been confirmed by excavations of the last ten years.[1] The advance of the Nabataeans to the north, toward the middle of the second century BC at the latest, may be understood in context with the difficulties of regional control experienced by the Seleucids.[2] A sporadic Nabataean presence, either of individuals or tribes, is attested in the north of the Transjordan in the Papyrus of Zenon[3] by the middle of the third century BC. Nabataean authority, in any event, exerted itself over the south of the Hauran during the period when Aretas III had been summoned to rule over Damascus, between 84 and 72 BC.[4] It has been accepted that the Nabataean dynasty had made Bosra into a second capital during the course of the first century AD, even though Petra had not lost its preeminent position.[5] One may imagine a rebalancing of the Nabataean realm in both a geographic and economic sense. This effort sought, by developing the agricultural resources of the territory, to make up for the decline in revenue from the caravan trade, which was progressively diverted by Rome to Alexandria by the maritime route.[6] The agricultural wealth of the Hauran, at any rate, gives sense to the urban development of Bosra.

Remains of the City in the Nabataean Era From an archaeological point of view, while some vestiges of the Bronze Age are known, in particular the city's rampart,[7] no construction of the Iron Age has yet been uncovered at Bosra. Nor has any archaeological trace of the "Hellenistic" city evoked by the Book of Maccabees (I *Macc.* 5.24) been identified, with the exception of a few sherds.

92. Nabataean stylobate and enclosure wall under the level of the Byzantine Cathedral (end of fifth century). Bosra, Syria.

The Nabataean city is now emerging from the shadows. Its extension was not limited, as has sometimes been supposed, to its eastern "Nabataean" quarter. The largest part of what was to become its urban space had already been occupied; Nabataean pottery has been found in an area extending from the western periphery of the city (excavations by the American University of Beirut and alongside the "Naumachie") up to the Nabataean arch and building discovered under the "new cathedral." Ceramic material is likewise present beneath the Church of Saints Sergius Bacchus and Leontius and in all the excavations in the center of the city (Southern Baths and the area recently discovered to the east, Nymphaeum, Cryptoporticus), where strata beneath the Roman levels have been attained.[8]

The East Quarter Recent excavations have shown that the Nabataeans had realized an urbanization program of great scope at Bosra, clearly revealed by the plan of the Nabataean arch (fig. 93) and a monumental construction to the east of it.[9] This arch, the façade of which is associated with the general tradition of Roman monumental arches, was completed to the east by two pillars decorated with Nabataean half-columns and set at a different orientation (at an angle of 29 degrees). These two constructions form a single unit: they are linked with carefully constructed walls pierced by two large doors. To the west, the arch proper has been conceived as a monumental conclusion of the street that constitutes the principal east-west axis of the city; in its turn, the eastern façade of this complex apparently serves as a passage toward another monumental area commanded by a different orientation. However, the broken axis of this architectural program corresponds to the divergent orientations that dominate the two parts of the city, west and east. The hinge device thus created had the function of masking the rupture in the urban organization, on the one hand, and, of glorifying a monumental program, on the other. The ceramic material discovered allows the arch to be dated to between the middle and the end of the first century AD. This large-scale program of urbanization was the work of the Nabataean dynasty, which had tried clearly to mark its imprint by the use of decoration, the most characteristic element of which was the "horned capital."

The extension of excavations further to the east has revealed, under the great cathedral-church, a vast porticoed court, which dates to the same period as the two pillars with Nabataean half-columns (fig. 92). It is oriented precisely as the eastern façade of these pillars and should be situated along the same axis. The comparisons with the great sanctuaries of the Roman Near East suggest its interpretation as a temenos, or "sacred enclosure," which one is tempted to attribute to Dusares, dynastic god of the Nabataeans. Next to that of Allat, his cult is well attested in the region—during the second half of the first century AD—by a number of inscriptions dedicated to Dusares, "god of the ruler who is at Bosra."[10] Inscriptions with this form designate the Nabataean king Rabbel II. These indications suggest that the Nabataeans had created a new city quarter, which was developed around one or more monuments of particular importance, both religious and political.

In contrast to the rest of the city, which was not oriented on a strict grid, the new city district appears to have been developed on a geometric plan, as a new urban foundation. In effect, one recognizes, both in the recently excavated porticoed courtyard and in the totality of the city quarter, a module close to 35 meters which should correspond to a multiple of the cubit or of the phileterian foot.[11]

The Center of the City The program of urbanization undoubtedly extended to the central part of the city without modifying its fundamental structure. It had marked the major east-west axis, very likely adopting, straightening and monumentalizing a preexisting artery. The Southern Baths area and the district extending eastward, where digging was recently carried out by the Directorate of Antiquities at Bosra, were both densely populated in the last quarter of the first century BC, probably as dwelling areas. Around the central crossroads near the so-called Nymphaeum and the "Kalybe," we find in some buildings evidence of a consistent system of directions.[12] These traces seem to result from an attempted organization of the city center on a more geometrical pattern, in the last years of the Nabataean kingdom. Such a project seems to have been discarded after the Roman Province of Arabia was created.[13]

Lost Monuments Characteristic elements of Nabataean architectural decoration—horned capitals (with a rare example of a Nabataean ionic capital with known parallels at Petra), fragments of entablatures with beveled moldings and, especially, Doric friezes associated with horned capitals in a composite order characteristic of the end of the Hellenistic period—have been found chiefly in the eastern quarter but also in the center of the city.[14] Like the Nabataean inscriptions, these fragments, of differing scale, attest to the presence of buildings of diverse type over much of the city. Capitals of small dimensions mark the vestiges of porticoes and houses of the Nabataean period. In particular, one can imagine the presence of a Nabataean temple in proximity to the major crossroads of the principal east-west and north-south axes, as apparently confirmed by a Nabataean inscription found nearby, which evokes a cult and priests.[15] Up to the fourth century AD this building limited the extension of the Southern Baths in this direction.

The Nabataeans in Southern Syria The northern boundary of the Nabataean kingdom has been identified about ten kilometers to the north of Bosra, where another political and cultural area in the same basalt-based geographic regional context begins. This area, which probably was attached to the Aramaean domain of Damascus had, from the first century BC, been entrusted by Rome to client princes, such as Herod and the two Agrippas, between episodes of direct Roman administration. The very original art that is expressed in the architecture and sculpture around the sanctuary of Sīᶜ and Suweiida has been defined wrongly as Nabataean. It is, in fact, connected with the traditions of inland Syria, which stand apart from the more direct Hellenization of the coastal zone.[16] In this perspective, the presence of Nabataean horned capitals in a small temple that dominates the third courtyard of the sanctuary of Sīᶜ should be emphasized.[17] As at Bosra, it may be interpreted as a mark of the Nabataean dynasty. This monument of common rectangular plan, which clearly dates to the second half of the first century AD and was restored by H. C. Butler, with a roof of basalt flagstones resting on arches in the local style, has nothing in common with the different variants of Nabataean temples. The presence of these Nabataean horned capitals signifies that the Nabataean dynasty, like the Roman authorities and the Herodian princes, had tried to mark its presence in this regional sanctuary, which was frequented not only by agriculturalists from the area but by nomads of the steppes beyond the Jebel al'Arab, as attested by the so-called Safaitic inscriptions.[18]

End of Nabataean Presence at Bosra The programs of Nabataean construction may have developed up to about 100 AD. There is no reason to think that they were continued later in the second century.

In Nabataean ceramics the characteristic forms of the second century AD are practically absent at Bosra. The fine painted Nabataean pottery seems not to have been imported anymore in southern Syria after the creation of the Roman province of Arabia. From this time, relations with the ancient center of the Nabataean realm clearly slacken and Bosra now enters into a network involving the Roman provinces.

93. Nabataean Gate: East façade. Bosra, Syria.

11 | Petra: The First-Comers

NORMAN N. LEWIS

J. L. Burckhardt was the first European in modern times to reach Wadi Musa and to identify the ruins there as those of the ancient Petra. W. J. Bankes was the first person to make drawings of the ruins and to transcribe inscriptions there. Summary accounts of the journeys of Burckhardt in 1812 and of Bankes and his companions in 1818 are given below.

BORN AT LAUSANNE IN SWITZERLAND in 1784, Johann Ludwig Burckhardt came to London in 1806 looking for worthwhile employment beyond the frontiers of Napoleonic Europe.[1] In 1808 he offered his services as an explorer to the Association for Promoting the Discovery of the Interior Parts of Africa and was accepted. It was agreed that he should spend two years in Syria preparatory to proceeding to Cairo, where he would hope to join a caravan going to the Fezzan and from there endeavor to penetrate "the interior countries" of western Africa.

Burckhardt reached Syria in September 1809 and established himself in Aleppo, where he studied and practiced his Arabic intensively and from which he made exploratory journeys to various parts of Syria. His objective was to become so adept in the language and so habituated to the dress, manners, and customs of the country as to be able to pass as a Syrian Arab. He knew that if he could manage this he would have little to fear when he arrived in Egypt and traveled further afield; his manner of speech would differ from that of the people around him, but not perceptibly more than that of any Syrian. There would be little likelihood of his being thought a European.

He found that two years was too short a time for him to achieve his objective but by the middle of 1812 he felt ready to undertake the great journey to Cairo. He decided to travel due south from Damascus, east of the Jordan and the Dead Sea and still further south until he reached the latitude of Cairo, where he would turn west directly toward the city. He left Damascus on June 18, traveling as a Syrian countryman in humble circumstances, wearing very ordinary clothes (which were gradually reduced to rags as he traveled) and carrying no baggage. At first he rode a mare but sold it later, went for a time on foot, and did the last stages on camelback. At times in the next three months he suffered great hardships and sometimes experienced moments of tension when people wondered who he was and what he was doing.

One such moment came when, being within a day's march of Wadi Musa and having heard of the "antiquities" there, he decided to try to get there. He knew that to make a detour out of mere curiosity would arouse suspicion. He therefore pretended that he had made a vow to sacrifice a goat in honor of Haroun (Aaron), whose tomb, a famous place of pilgrimage, was near the valley in which the ruins were situated. "By this stratagem," he wrote, "I thought that I should have the means of seeing the valley on my way to the tomb." The "stratagem" succeeded; he hired a guide to take him to the tomb (paying him with a pair of old horseshoes) and they started out towards the ruins carrying a goat and a water-skin. At this point in his account of the journey Burckhardt interrupts the narrative to say that he regretted that he could not give a very complete account of the antiquities, explaining why as follows: "I knew very well the character of the people around me; I was without protection in the midst of a desert where no traveller had ever before been seen; and a close examination of these works of the infidels, as they are called, would have excited suspicions that I was a magician in search of treasures; I should at least have been detained and prevented from prosecuting my journey to Egypt, and in all probability should have been stripped of the little money which I possessed and what was infinitely more valuable to me, of my journal book."

He and his guide walked under the high arch that at that time spanned the gorge through the Siq and eventually came to the Khazneh, which made the same "extraordinary impression" on him as it would on countless future visitors. They

94. W. J. Bankes, "Approach to Petra." Bankes's party passing under the arch at the beginning of the Siq. (The arch collapsed and fell in 1895.)

95. W. J. Bankes, drawing of the first glimpse of the Khazneh beyond the end of the Siq.

went on, past the theater, to the center of the ancient city and the "stately edifice" now usually known as the Qasr al-Bint. Despite the fears that he expressed in the passage quoted above, he behaved in a way which he knew was unwise; he went inside the Khazneh, made estimates of its dimensions, and drew a little plan of it. After that he entered several of the tombs and cannot have been surprised that, when he turned aside as if to look more closely at the Qasr al-Bint, his guide exclaimed: "I see clearly now that you are an infidel, who has some particular business amongst the ruins of your forefathers; but depend on it that we shall not suffer you to take out a single para of all the treasures hidden therein." Burckhardt replied that it was mere curiosity which led him to look at the ruins and that he had no other reason to come there than to sacrifice to Haroun, but the guide was not easily persuaded and Burckhardt took no further risks.

They climbed towards Aaron's tomb and were in sight of it when the sun set. They could go no further, and at a spot where heaps of stones showed that other sacrifices had been made Burckhardt killed the goat as the guide repeated the customary formulae. They dressed the best part of the flesh for their supper and then slept, returning in the morning by the way they had come.

Burckhardt's description of the ruins was indeed very short, as he had said it would be, but he had seen enough to allow him to suggest that the ruins were "very probably" those of the ancient Petra. With characteristic modesty he added that he must "leave to the decision of Greek scholars" whether or not he had "discovered the remains of the capital of Arabia Petraea."

A few days later he joined a little camel caravan bound for Cairo, which was reached after ten days of forced marches. Burckhardt entered the city before sunrise on September 4 and "thus concluded my journey, by the blessing of God." In the next five years he accomplished a series of tremendous journeys in Egypt, Nubia, and Arabia but was never able to reach the Fezzan, his original goal. He died of dysentery in Cairo on October 15, 1817.

It would be difficult to imagine a greater contrast between the manner of Burckhardt's approach to Petra and that of the next European visitors who arrived six years later. W. J. Bankes, T. Legh, C. L. Irby, and J. Mangles were young

96. W. J. Bankes, drawing of the front of the Khazneh.

97. W. J. Bankes, drawing of unidentified tomb, perhaps Brünnow's 813.

98. W. J. Bankes, "Petra, ground plan of gt. Tomb or Temple." Plan of the interior of the Khazneh. Measurements in feet and inches.

Englishmen who made no secret of their identity. They were well mounted, well armed, well provided with "small gold coins," attended by servants and guides—and, in the last stages of the journey to Petra, were accompanied by a cavalcade of Bedouin horsemen. They were all seasoned travelers and Bankes had himself spent almost three years in the Near East investigating the remains of antiquity. He was a scholarly man, a good draftsman, and something of an artist and, wherever he went, he drew sketches and plans of what he saw. He possessed a phenomenal aptitude for copying inscriptions in whatever language or script they were written.

Bankes had heard from Burckhardt about his journey to Petra and "had long meditated" an attempt to get there himself. He made a first attempt with Irby and Mangles in March 1818, hoping to follow Burckhardt's route east of the Dead Sea. This bid failed but they decided to try again, starting in Jerusalem on May 6, traveling southward to Hebron and then around the southern extremity of the Dead Sea to reach Kerak, where they hoped to find guides to Petra. While they were making preparations in Jerusalem they were joined by five other men, notably Giovanni Finati, Bankes's right-hand man during his Egyptian travels, and Thomas Legh, who had just completed his epic ride from Moscow. These accessions to their strength gave them confidence and helped them in their dealings with some of the key men they met on the journey.

The first of these was Yusuf Majali, the "Lord of Kerak," who undertook to accompany them throughout. The second was Muhammad Abu Rashid, a young Bedouin sheikh, locally renowned and respected, to whose tent Yusuf took them. Abu Rashid readily agreed to take them to Wadi Musa but was immediately and vehemently opposed by another guest of his who was in the tent at the time. This was Abu Zaitun, the sheikh of Wadi Musa, who swore that he would never allow the travelers to enter his territory. The more vociferously he declared his opposition, however, the more determined Abu Rashid became, vowing that he would get them there by force if necessary. This was the beginning of five days of argument and negotiation carried on at first as Abu Rashid with the travelers and Abu Zeitun with his followers moved toward Wadi Musa and afterwards camped within sight of it. Tribal war appeared imminent but after a series of conferences, "peace was proclaimed" and the travelers were told that they could visit the ruins under the protection of Abu Rashid.

This they did, starting early in the morning of May 24. Bankes made sketches and copied inscriptions as they went, and subsequently, with the help of his companions, wrote a 10,000-word description of the ruins that contains a great deal of perceptive comment.[2] One of the first of Bankes's sketches shows the party passing under the arch at the beginning of the Siq (fig. 94), while another attempts to capture the marvelous first glimpse of the Khazneh bathed in early morning light and framed by the towering cliff of the Siq (fig. 95). That sketch hardly did justice to the subject but once out of the Siq and in the open area facing the great temple, Bankes settled down to produce a careful drawing of the whole façade (fig. 96). This was, as Finati wrote, "a work of many hours" and even then it was not finished in every detail. It is, however, a beautiful and accurate representation of its subject. Unlike several of his successors Bankes made no attempt to "restore" the original appearance of the defaced representations of human and other figures on the façade, and a comparison of the drawing with the façade as it is today (or with photographs taken at any time in the last hundred years) shows that the carving has suffered relatively little damage from weathering or other causes since 1818. We are fortunate that the drawing has survived; Irby and Mangles tell us that it was later purloined by an Arab, but that "after some days' negotiation [Bankes] was allowed to purchase it back again." Bankes also sketched one of the side entrances to the temple and he or his friends produced an excellent plan, with measurements, of the interior (fig. 98).

Of Bankes's numerous sketches of individual tombs figure 97 is the most precisely drawn. Another view depicted the assemblage of great tombs at the foot of the eastern cliff, seen from the vicinity of the Temenos Gate. Bankes and his friends examined one of these, the one now known as the Urn Tomb, and noted the changes which had been made to the main chamber to adapt it for use as a church. Bankes could only pick out a few words of the inscription in the chamber but these were enough for him to conclude that it "proves the establishment of Christianity at Petra." The words he could read included the reference to "the most holy bishop," from which he deduced that the inscription commemorated the consecration of the church. (If he had been able to read the whole text he would have seen that he was correct; the church or cathedral was consecrated in 446-47 AD).

Bankes's most remarkable achievement in Petra was his transcription of "a long inscription in some strange character which it was a great labour for my master to copy," as a sympathetic Finati put it. The inscription, in Nabataean script, is on the front of a tomb in Wadi Turkmaniyah at the northern edge of the ruins. It must have been a difficult task for Bankes, quite apart from the fact that he did not know the script of the language in which the inscription is written. The five long lines are cut in the rock more than twenty feet above the ground, and below it the lower face of the tomb has fallen away, leaving a vast gaping hole; Bankes could not have climbed up to the inscription. Fortunately, as he observed, the letters, though not deeply incised, are cut "with much neatness and precision and are in a state of wonderful preservation owing to the shelter which they receive from the projection of the corniches and to the Eastern aspect."

Despite the difficulties, Bankes produced what Michael Macdonald has described as "an extraordinarily accurate" copy of this, the longest and most informative inscription in Petra. Furthermore, he realized that the letters of the inscription were "exactly similar to those scratched upon the rocks in the Wadi Makutub and about the foot of Mt. Sinai," some of which he had copied two-and-a-half years earlier (and which he and Burckhardt had discussed in correspondence). Bankes went on to suggest that this script might be the "Syriac character" in which, according to Diordorus Siculus, the Nabataeans wrote a letter to Antigonus the One-eyed (a former general of Alexander the Great and would-be successor to his empire) at the end of the fourth century BC. In all of this Bankes was far ahead of his time; unfortunately, his copy of the inscription remained unknown and the first reading and translation of the text, not published until 1896, was from a less accurate copy made some thirty years after his visit to Petra. (A further discussion of Bankes's copy of the text and related matters by M.C.A. Macdonald and the present writer is now in preparation.)

Bankes and his companions had accomplished a great deal (they had even climbed up to Aaron's tomb, which Burckhardt had been unable to reach) and they wanted to do more, but the two days which Abu Rashid had agreed to allow them amongst the ruins were now ended and at daybreak on May 26 they left Petra to return with him to his camp. Yusuf Majali was waiting there to take them back to Kerak and eventually to the vicinity of Amman, where they parted company with him. After a brief visit to Jerash they crossed the Jordan and ended their journey at Acre on June 25, 1818.

Bankes returned to England in 1820. He was expected to publish accounts of his explorations and discoveries and he evidently intended to do so. He started by having lithographs made of inscriptions copied in Syria and Egypt but he gradually tired of the work and eventually abandoned it. In 1841 he was arrested for "indecently exposing himself" (a euphemism of the period for homosexual activity); rather than face trial with possible dire consequences, he fled to Italy, where he spent the rest of his life. His drawings, copies of inscriptions, journals, correspondence, and notes were left and almost forgotten in his house, Kingston Lacy in the County of Dorset. In 1981, however, Mr. Ralph Bankes bequeathed Kingston Lacy to the National Trust, and some years later the trust made the collection available to interested enquirers.

99. From a sketch by Léon de Laborde, hand-colored lithograph by Courtin with figures by V. Adam, *Triumphal Arch in Ruins (Petra)*, 22.7 x 30.6 cm; from *Voyage de L'Arabie Pétrée*, 1830. Cincinnati Art Museum.

12 | The Real and the Ideal: Petra in the Minds and Eyes of Nineteenth-Century British and American Artist-Travelers

BRIONY LLEWELLYN

FRANCIS STEWART, Lord Castlereagh, visited Petra in 1842 and from Jerusalem shortly afterwards wrote ecstatically to his stepmother, third Marchioness of Londonderry:

> I did not write by last post, because I did not dare to say what was pending. However now that the thing is done I don't feel any reason for silence. I have been to Petra.... You will see by my pufferage in my journal the impression which Petra made upon me. I think it more extraordinary, & more lovely than any place I ever saw. Unlike anything else and perfectly matchless. Fancy oleanders thirty feet high, covered so thickly with blossom that you can hardly see that they have green leaves. The blossom is rose colour, and I think more brilliant than any rhododendron that ever was seen. And then picture to yourself them growing among temples and tombs, in complete desolation and amid the silence of death. I never can forget the savage beauty of that place.[1]

An earlier visitor, John Lloyd Stephens, who in 1836 had become the first American traveler to reach Petra, wrote even more effusively of the extraordinary impression that the site had made:

> Turning back from the theatre, the whole area of the city burst upon the sight at once, filled with crumbling masses of rock & stone, the ruined habitation of a people long since perished from the face of the earth, and encompassed on every side by high ranges of mountains. I had just completed one of the most interesting days of my life, for the singular character of the city, and the uncommon beauty of its ruins, its great antiquity, the prophetic denunciations of whose truth it was the witness, its loss for more than a thousand years to the civilised world, its very existence being known only to the wandering Arab, the difficulty of reaching it, and the hurried and dangerous manner in which I had reached it, gave a thrilling and almost fearful interest to the time and place, of which I feel it utterly impossible to convey any idea.[2]

These two descriptions are typical of the kind of response elicited by the remote and long-lost ancient city of Petra in the mid-nineteenth century and, in part, they reveal why Petra exerted such a deep fascination over Western visitors at this time. During the course of the nineteenth century many travelers of different nationalities and from different walks of life wrote accounts of their experiences. In the space available here it is possible to focus on only a few of these travelers, particularly some of those who produced visual images of the spectacular ruins and scenery at the site. Constraints of space also mean that only artists who drew or painted at Petra, and not the photographers who traveled there during the latter half of the nineteenth century, will be discussed. In order to set the work of these artists in the context of their time and culture, some of the factors that conditioned their response, and the extent to which their own circumstances affected the images that they produced, will be examined.

What images did the name Petra conjure up in the minds of educated men and women with the means and determination to travel beyond the well-trodden paths of Europe? What did they know of it before they went, and why did they endure considerable discomfort, expense, and danger to achieve their goal of experiencing it for themselves? What did they expect to find there? Was it sublime scenery, was it classical architecture to rival Greece and Rome, was it a religious experience to uplift their souls? When they reached their object how did they react? Did the site measure up to their expectations? Did each traveler respond individually or was he or she influenced by those who had preceded them? Did they see it merely as a spectacular array of monuments carved out of the rock or was their vision conditioned by the innate prejudices that they had brought with them from their Western culture? How did the artists who traveled there depict what they saw? What subjects did they choose and how did they perceive them? How did their own prejudices and expectations affect the images that they produced?

100. From a sketch by Linant de Bellefonds, hand-colored lithograph by Deroi with figures by V. Adam, *Tomb opposite the Theatre*, 22.4 x 33.0 cm; from *Voyage de L'Arabie Pétrée*, 1830. Cincinnati Art Museum.

The story of Petra's rediscovery in 1812 by Johann Ludwig Burckhardt is well known.[3] News of his achievement reached Europe long before his journal was published in 1822 and inspired a group of British travelers to make an expedition there in 1818. One of these was the wealthy owner of Kingston Lacy in Dorset, William Bankes, who became the first Westerner to succeed in drawing some of Petra's antiquities; but although two of his companions, Captains Irby and Mangles, later published an account of the journey, his sketches were not reproduced.[4]

It was not until some fifteen years later that the next Europeans reached Petra: an intrepid pair of Frenchmen, Léon de Laborde and L.M.A. Linant de Bellefonds. Léon de Laborde had arrived in Cairo in 1827. After accompanying his father on a tour of the Near East, he was determined to find his way to Petra and by good fortune met Linant de Bellefonds, whose greater experience of travel and thorough knowledge of the region and its people was vital to the organization and success of the expedition. After several months of careful preparations, the two men crossed the Sinai peninsula to Aqaba and, from there, entered Petra from the south. Their anticipation was keen: "We set out the next morning for the mysterious valley of Petra, that destination to which all my hopes had been directed for nearly two years," wrote Laborde.[5] Both competent draftsmen, they succeeded in spending several days in Petra examining and drawing some of the monuments from different angles. They also reached ed-Deir, the first Europeans to do so, for Burckhardt had not known about it and Bankes and his party had only glimpsed it through a telescope.

It would be superfluous here to give a detailed account of their discoveries or an analysis of the drawings that each of them made, as this has been excellently covered elsewhere.[6] It is useful to reiterate, though, how extensive and methodical these drawings were and, through their publication, how important they were for the creation of an image of Petra that endured for several decades. Before leaving Cairo the two men had agreed that, after a year, each could publish separate accounts of their travels. However, Linant was too occupied with engineering projects for his patron Muhammad Ali, Viceroy of Egypt, to publish his; but some of his drawings, duly acknowledged, appeared alongside Laborde's in the latter's lavish folio volume, *Voyage de L'Arabie Pétrée*, published in France in 1830 (figs. 99, 100). The volume contained twenty plates, and the publication of so many hitherto entirely unknown images of the monuments in Petra was, as Madame Linant de Bellefonds has written, "truly a revelation to the educated public of the times."[7] It was immediately successful and became the touchstone that determined how the next generation of European travelers envisaged Petra. The text was translated into English and a smaller and cheaper volume with reduced plates was published in London in 1836.[8] Perhaps as a result, a large number of Western travelers who visited Petra in subsequent decades were British and American.

For Linant and Laborde and for the many Western travelers who followed in their footsteps during the nineteenth century, the image of Petra carried meanings seldom uppermost in the minds of tourists today. Petra was not so much a great city built on the successful commercial activities of the Nabataean kingdom during the first century BC, but, first and foremost, the land of Edom, the subject of terrifying biblical prophesies. The one most often quoted in travelers' accounts is Jeremiah 49: 16–17:

> Thy terribleness hath deceived thee, and the pride of thine heart, O thou that dwellest in the clefts of the rock, that holdest the height of the hill: though thou shouldest make thy nest as high as the eagle, I will bring thee down from thence, saith the Lord. Also Edom shall be a desolation: every one that goeth by it shall be astonished, and shall hiss at all the plagues thereof.

The apparent fulfillment of the prophecy in the deserted city with its crumbling monuments created a romantic image that was augmented rather than dispelled by tales of hostile Bedouin who exacted exorbitant fees for a safe passage through the ruins. Nor were the powerful visions of desolation and destruction familiar to them through passages in Jeremiah, Isaiah, and other books of the Old Testament modified by Laborde's and Linant's detailed views of the architectural remains at Petra. Thereafter travelers carried with them in their mind's eye both sets of images.

Most travelers had come to the region usually described as the Holy Land in order to locate places that they had encountered through the Scriptures. Lord Lindsay, who visited Petra in 1837, later wrote: "Throughout the Holy Land we tried every spot pointed out as the scene of Scriptural events by the words of the Bible, the only safe guide-book in this land of ignorance and superstition, where a locality has been assigned to every incident recorded in it. . ."[9]

A year earlier, John Lloyd Stevens had traveled through Sinai intending to go straight to Gaza, but nearing Aqaba: "Petra the rock of Edom, the excavated city was uppermost in my mind." At the last minute he changed his mind and diverted his entourage towards Petra. When he arrived there, although aware of the danger that the local Arabs posed, he saw them as Biblical characters: "Read of the patriarchs in the Bible, and it is the best description you can have of pastoral life in the East at the present day."[10] Two years later, Edward Robinson, the American theologian, traveled in the area in an attempt to locate, in a scientific manner, the sites of biblical history. His publication was titled *Biblical Researches in Palestine, Mount Sinai and Arabia Petraea* (1841). For him Petra was a city of the dead, as foretold by the prophets:

> Around us were the desolations of ages; the dwelling and edifices of the ancient city crumbled and strewed in the dust: the mausolea of the dead in all their pristine beauty and freshness but long since rifled, and the ashes of their tenants scattered to the winds. Well might there be the stillness of death, for it was the grave itself, a city of the dead, by which we were surrounded.[11]

At the same time, he marveled at the strange beauty of the architecture and the varied color of the rocks. As he explored the ruins he used the publications of Laborde and other previous travelers as guides, but he had no hesitation in disagreeing with them when his own observations conflicted with theirs.

The increase in the number of visitors to Petra and the Near East in general in the late 1830s was no coincidence. The mechanics of travel were becoming easier and there was relative political stability in the region through the extension to Syria of the authority of Muhammad Ali of Egypt. Several pioneering explorers had published accounts of their travels. The middle-class church-going public was now aware that it was possible, if time and money allowed, to visit real places that had seemed to belong only in the ancient world.

In 1836 an immensely successful publication both exploited and reinforced this interest. *Landscape Illustrations of the Bible* contained engravings of biblical sites by Edward and William Finden after watercolors by well-known artists such as Turner, Clarkson Stanfield, Harding, and Roberts, who had not then visited the area but who based their compositions on sketches by artists and travelers who had. Four of these illustrations were of Petra from initial sketches by Bankes (one) and Laborde (three; fig. 101).[12] Two of the latter were worked up for illustration by Roberts, who by then had achieved recognition as a topographical artist of English, Scottish, and European views. His involvement with this publication was one of the factors that prompted his decision to visit the Near East in 1838. He had long held this ambition and, encouraged by the success that his views of Spain had brought him, he now felt that he had the talent to match and even surpass in scope and accuracy the illustrations in publications like *Landscape Illustrations* and Laborde's *Voyage de L'Arabie Pétrée*.[13]

Arriving in Egypt in September 1838, Roberts first sailed up the Nile as far as Abu Simbel, stopping on the return journey to sketch the antiquities. In Cairo he drew the streets and mosques and met other English and French residents and

left: **101.** After David Roberts, from a sketch by Léon de Laborde, engraved by Edward Finden, *Ruins of Selah (Petra). Temple Excavated out of the Rock*, engraving, from W. and E. Finden, *Landscape Illustrations of the Bible*, 1836.

opposite **102.** David Roberts, *Petra [Al Khasne]*, pencil, watercolor and bodycolor, 54 x 34 cm; on the verso, *Studies of Architectural Details at Petra*; signed and erroneously dated *D Roberts 1838*, inscribed and dated *Petra March 7th 1839*. The preliminary watercolor for the version published as a lithograph in *Holy Land*, 1849, vol. III [pl. 92]. Private collection.

travelers, including Linant who showed him his drawings of Petra. Reports of plague in Jerusalem nearly caused him to abandon his plan of continuing on to Syria, but eventually, persuaded by Mr. Pell, another seasoned traveler who wanted to accompany him, he made up his mind to go:

> . . . I have settled my proceeding to Syria by the way of Mount Sinai and Petra to Hebron and Jerusalem—it will be a long and fatiguing journey to say nothing of the expense. . . I am in excellent health and care nothing for fatigue or, as far as I am myself concerned, for danger but there are those at home who do. Well, I have no doubt all will end well—then for home with one of the richest folios that ever left the East. It is worth the hazard.[14]

Pragmatic Scot that he was, his attitude was rather less idealistic than that of many of his contemporaries. He traveled with the specific intention of gathering material for subjects that would bring him fame and fortune on his return.

Roberts and his party reached Petra on March 6, 1839:

> We encamped in the centre of this extraordinary city or rather the remains of it. Situated in the midst of mountains and though surrounded by the desert abounding in every vegetable production the difficulty of access to it is so great that the curse seems still to hang over it.[15]

He had wondered whether Petra would be worth the considerable trouble of getting there and, despite the eulogies of previous writers, had not expected to be much surprised by it, but, as he explored, his astonishment grew:

> I am more and more bewildered with the extent of this extraordinary city; not only the city which must be two miles in extent by nearly the same in breadth, but every ravine has been inhabited, even to the tops of the mountains. The valley itself has been filled with temples, public buildings, triumphal arches and bridges, all of which are laid prostrate with the exception of one triumphal arch & one temple and of this the portico has fallen. The stream still flows through it as heretofore and the shrubs & wild flowers spring up in the wildest luxuriance; every spot and crevice of the rock is covered with them, and they perfume the air with the most delicious fragrance. Those of the buildings (or rather excavations in the rock) which remain are rent and worn away by time, with the exception of the Khasné or treasury which seems to owe its preservation to the narrowness of the defile, and the deep recess in which it is situated.[16]

In the five days that he spent among the ruins, he made sketches for watercolors that constituted the most extensive and detailed visual survey of Petra since Laborde's. These and his other Holy Land views were published as lithographs in 1842 and received an enthusiastic response from the critics.[17] Predictably, the commentaries emphasized the biblical associations of their subject matter, as this *Literary Gazette* extract exemplifies: "Not a spot but is embalmed in sacred history, or immortalised in connexion with succeeding changes, which impart the deepest historical interest to objects of striking pictorial grandeur or beauty."[18]

The critics referred to the "moral grandeur" and "religious

awe" that informed his work and his treatment of these sacred subjects was described as "grand and solemn" and characterized by "variety and excellence."[19] Certainly such adjectives could be applied to the thirteen views of Petra, for never before had the ancient city received such pictorially striking and diverse treatment. In each view, using his skills as a stage-scene painter on a large scale, Roberts maximizes the dramatic potential of his chosen subject, emphasizing the height, mass, and extent of the rocks by taking a low or a high viewpoint or creating a wide-angled view in order to incorporate more of the ruins into the composition than might have been possible from a single spot.

Sometimes he added or changed architectural features. The central pediment of the Khazneh, for example, was never adorned with an eagle, as he shows; nor was the statue of Isis above half naked but fully dressed (fig. 102). Curiously, Laborde had interpreted these details in the same way.[20] Was Roberts copying Laborde, or was this merely a result of similar expectations, so that they both added what their knowledge of classical architecture conditioned them to see? In general, Roberts's views of Petra are very different from Laborde's and Linant's. He was determined to outdo and improve on theirs. Whereas Laborde and Linant chose, in addition to the main monuments, to depict a number of the smaller tombs, valuable from an archaeological point of view, Roberts realized that these would seem repetitive for a general audience and focused on the spectacular ruins and vast expanses of soaring rocks and plunging ravines. The French views are notable for their detailed portrayal of a variety of different monuments at Petra; Roberts uses the ruins as the focus of a pictorially satisfying whole, prescribed by the requirements of British topographical tradition. Nevertheless, Laborde provided a base for Roberts to work from and even some visual ideas: for example, both Laborde's and Roberts's views of the Eastern Cliffs include camels moving towards the ruins.[21]

In most of Roberts's compositions groups of Bedouin Arabs are introduced in order to add narrative interest and to act as a device both to lead the eye towards the main architectural feature and to create a foil to the architectural mass of natural and carved rock. Like the architecture, the figures are manipulated. They are deliberately posed and too elaborately dressed for their status as nomadic shepherds, who, in any case, were hostile to foreigners, as Roberts and his party had discovered when they had arrived and been allowed to camp in the city only after tense negotiations and heavy payment; later they were robbed the night before they departed. Despite this he was allowed to wander about the city, sketchbook in hand, virtually unmolested.

In one view—*Conference at Wady Moosa*—a group of Arabs assumes greater importance than usual, dominating the composition, in which a tomb is merely sketched in behind (fig. 103). The scene recalls an event described at length in the text accompanying the lithograph but not, curiously enough, in the original diary.[22] In general, though, figures play a subsidiary though important role in what are essentially created compositions supplying what Roberts's public expected: "grandeur and animation: the grandeur belonging to the buildings and the animation, to the groups of natives in the foreground."[23] It would not have entered either the artist's or his public's heads to inquire how the people lived in such strange surroundings or to ponder what effect the increasing influx of foreign visitors might have on them. To do so raises interesting questions, but imposes a late twentieth/early twenty-first-century approach on mid-nineteenth-century attitudes.

How Roberts's pictorial construction evolved may be observed through the existence of several of the watercolors on which the lithographs of Petra were based: for example, *Entrance to Petra* (fig. 104).[24] In one case at least—*El Deir*—both the watercolor worked up from his on-the-spot sketch and the watercolor made at home in England specifically for the lithographer, have survived (figs. 105, 106).[25] In each, slight changes create subtle but significant shifts in emphasis. While there, not content with the cramped view of ed-Deir that Laborde had shown, Roberts had climbed to a rock opposite, on which lay the remains of a temple, so that he could encompass both the huge structure of the so-called monastery against the massive rocks and the extensive view beyond. In the later watercolor he has shifted his vantage point slightly to the left to show more of the column bases and to open out the view of the city below. Other details are clarified and the figures regrouped. The ruins gain definition and the whole conveys a greater sense of space but the effect is more contrived—a quality less valued today than in the 1840s.

Conscious manipulation of the subject to suit contemporary picturesque convention also characterizes the work of another successful British topographical artist of the 1840s—William Bartlett. An indefatigable traveler who explored Britain, Europe, North America, and the Near East in search of interesting subjects, he described himself as one of "a flying corps of light-armed skirmishers, who, going lightly over the ground, busy themselves chiefly with its picturesque aspect; who aim at giving lively impressions of actual sights."[26] He wrote and illustrated numerous travel books, several on the Near East. His visit to Petra, from Sinai, in 1845—his third to

103. David Roberts, *Conference at Wady Moosa [Petra]*, pencil, watercolor and bodycolor, 24.1 x 34.6 cm.; signed David Roberts. R.A., inscribed and dated *Petra. March 6th 1839*, inscribed *Conference at Wady Moosa*. Published as a lithograph in *Holy Land*, 1849, vol. III [pl.101]. Private collection.

104. David Roberts, *Entrance to Petra*, pencil, watercolor and bodycolor, 53.4 x 33.1 cm.; inscribed and dated *Entrance to Petra March 10th 1839*, signed David Roberts. Published as a lithograph in *Holy Land*, 1849, vol. III [pl. 98]. Cecil Higgins Art Gallery, Bedford, England.

105. David Roberts, *El Deir, Petra*, pencil, watercolor and body-color, 23.5 x 33.3 cm; signed and dated *David Roberts. 1839*, inscribed and dated *El Deir, Petra March 8th 1839*. The preliminary watercolor for the version published as a lithograph in *Holy Land*, 1849, vol.II [pl. 90]. Private collection.

106. David Roberts, *El Deir, Petra*, pencil, watercolor and body-color, 34.5 x 50 cm.; inscribed, dated and signed *El Deir. Petra / March 8th 1839. /* David Roberts. Published as a lithograph in *Holy Land*, 1849, vol. II [pl. 90].

107. William Bartlett, *Principal Range of Tombs, Petra*, pencil, ink, watercolor and bodycolor, 22.3 x 35.9 cm; inscribed *Petra* and with note, and, on the verso, *Principal Range of Tombs, 1845–48.* Engraved by J. Cousen for W. Bartlett, *Forty Days in the Desert*, 1848 (facing p.134). The Victoria and Albert Museum, London (Searight Collection).

Syria—resulted in his publication, *Forty Days in the Desert on the Track of the Israelites* (1848). Self-evidently the title reveals the framework that circumscribed Bartlett's entire visit: the reliance, yet again, on the Bible, to bring meaning to the site. It was only through the Bible that Bartlett and his contemporaries could relate to so strange and remote a place. For them the reality of Petra was its manifestation of the fulfillment of the biblical prophesies. These illusions did not however prevent Bartlett from carrying out a thorough and detailed survey of the ruins. He acknowledged the value of Laborde's and Linant's drawings and of Robinson's text, but oddly makes no reference to Roberts's *Holy Land*, even though the Petra lithographs had been published in late 1842. This was the year that Bartlett himself visited Jerusalem and subsequently produced his own illustrated book, *Walks about the City and Environs of Jerusalem* (1844). It seems inconceivable that he would not have been aware of Roberts's grandiose production. Perhaps it was professional rivalry that prompted him to ignore it, or a determination to create a very different set of images. Certainly his seven engravings of Petra bear no resemblance to Roberts's views: they are small-scale, pictorially dramatic vignettes, usually built around a formula: architectural ruin framed by rocks, with foreground enlivened by figures to introduce movement and narrative interest, and foliage to soften the harsh terrain and enhance the romantic effect.

More relevant are the engravings in *Landscape Illustrations of the Bible*, from which Bartlett appears to have derived much in form and impact.[27] Both *The Khasné* and *The Ravine* are similar to the plates of these subjects in *Landscape Illustrations*, themselves based on Laborde's compositions. Bartlett's *Principal Range of Tombs* may also derive from Laborde's view of the southern tombs (fig. 107). For this engraving, the watercolor that Bartlett would have worked up from his on-the-spot sketch has survived. Apart from the color—predominantly blue and brown washes—and some variation in the figures, characteristically outlined in black ink, this differs only in a few details from the engraving. More original is his plate of *El Deir*, where the building is looked up to from a low view-point across a chasm; in the foreground, vultures add an eerie touch and remind the viewer of Isaiah's desolate prophecy: chapter 34, verse 15: "... there shall the vultures also be gathered, every one with her mate."

Clearly Bartlett carried with him to Petra much cultural baggage: the Bible, Laborde, the Finden engravings, picturesque convention, and the romantic response of previous writers. Yet in the details of his experiences during the visit—how, for example, his Arab escort tried to shoot some gazelle from the summit of Mount Hor, and how, in order to avoid the extortionate levy demanded by the local tribe, he entered the city by an unexpected route—he brings to his account his own very practical character.[28] Bartlett's book was immensely popular when it was published in 1848, and, by the time he died six years later, had already reached a fourth edition.

Roberts and Bartlett were two successful professional artists whose publications ensured that their images of Petra became familiar to the general public during the 1840s. Two other, less established artists who traveled there in the same decade, were not so well known—Antonio Schranz and Lady Louisa Tenison.

Antonio Schranz, a member of a German family of artists, was a professional journeyman artist based in Malta, who accompanied European travelers around the Mediterranean making topographical views.[29] He accompanied Lord Castlereagh on his tour of Egypt and the Holy Land in 1842, producing approximately two hundred drawings (fig. 108), only ten of which were published in the Irish peer's *Journey to Damascus through Egypt, Nubia, Arabia Petraea, Palestine, and Syria* (1847). Schranz, like other artists of his kind, seems to have been regarded by Castlereagh as a camera would be today: a means of making visual records of the places he had visited, which could later be mounted and kept in albums for inspection by family and friends rather than a wider public.[30]

Working for a private patron, Schranz was free from the constraints of public demands. Current notions of the sublime and the picturesque conditioned public taste, and these elements were looked for in topographical views. Artists like Bartlett and Roberts, who had to rely on public favor for a living could not afford to ignore such expectations and, indeed, successfully exploited them. Schranz's approach to his subject was less self-conscious and more spontaneous. He was not an artist of particular originality, nor of special technical skill. Generally, he chose standard viewpoints and used accepted conventions: foreground interest consisting of foliage or groups of figures help to focus the eye on the main subject—a ruin, or group of ruins—in the middle ground; behind this, rocks or mountains close in the view or gradually fade away into a misty distance. He did not exaggerate elements

108. Antonio Schranz, *Petra Tombs*, 1841–42, watercolor on paper, 34.0 x 50.4 cm; folio page inscribed in pencil *Petra Tombs*, ref. D/24b, vol. 5. The National Trust, Lyme Park.

of the composition to increase dramatic impact, as did Roberts and Bartlett, but formed what he saw into less sophisticated and simpler compositions.

Schranz's reactions to Petra are not recorded, and Castlereagh does not mention his name either in surviving letters home or in his published narrative, other than to acknowledge his work in the preface. His watercolors of Petra do not reveal any greater sense of excitement than those of other places that he recorded. By contrast, Castlereagh's account is exceptionally effusive. Describing the Khazneh, he enthused:

> No description will ever do justice to it—no pencil can ever portray the brilliancy of the colouring; but in its bed of flowers, buried in the heart of the mountain gorge, and hiding its beauties in the chasms of a precipice, it stands alone in the catalogue of earth's riches, perhaps the loveliest creation of man, not less perfect, though different in form or colouring, than the blossoms which nature has scattered round its base. [31]

109. Lady Louisa Tenison, *Entrance to Petra*, pencil with white bodycolor, 44.0 x 28.5 cm; inscribed on verso in pencil: *Entrance to Petra / April 10, 1843.* Cincinnati Art Museum.

Inside, he noted several previous travelers' graffiti, but records only one name—Charlotte Rowley, "on the sandstone of Petra's fairy temple. This was an English flower not misplaced among the bright ones that encompass it."[32] Charlotte Rowley had visited Petra in 1836, on honeymoon with her husband, Richard, brother William Shipley-Conwy, and a friend, Mr. Seymer, as part of a long and remarkable tour of Egypt, the Sudan, and Palestine. She may well have been the first Western woman to reach Petra.[33]

Conditions of travel in the Near East, particularly to so remote a place as Petra, were extremely arduous, as many writers testify. Often their thoughts turned to home, but they were prevented from turning back by the excitement of venturing into places that they had known of since childhood but that few westerners had actually seen. "I am weary unto death, sick of this wandering life of endless discomfort," wrote Castlereagh to his stepmother. Perhaps to dampen any thoughts she might have had of accompanying him, even though he knew that Charlotte Rowley had traveled there, he maintained that she would have found the conditions impossible:

> No woman could go through these countries without sinking under the labour & fatigue, putting the heat out of the question, the bad food and the weakening effects of the climate. There is no moving about, from place to place without endless difficulty and worry. No English servant could stay with you or go through the work. You would have to serve them.[34]

The year after Castlereagh's visit, however, another intrepid and talented lady visited Petra, also with her husband, and also as part of a longer tour of Egypt and the Holy Land. This was Lady Louisa Tenison, daughter of the first Earl of Lichfield and, since 1838, wife of Edward King Tenison, of Kilronan Castle, County Roscommon, Ireland. The trip seems to have whetted her appetite for further travel—though not so far afield—for she and her family spent two years in Spain, 1850-52, and in 1864 made a tour through Europe to Italy. As well as possessing adequate sketching abilities, she, with her husband, became a keen amateur photographer, and they acquired one of the few licences from William Henry Fox Talbot, originator of the paper negative. In her later years she was renowned for her outspokenness.[35] All the more of a pity it is, therefore, that no personal correspondence or journals from the Near Eastern trip have yet come to light. Many of her drawings of the places she visited have survived, including three of Petra (fig. 109). After she returned, thirty of these, accompanied by brief descriptions, were published in 1846 in a portfolio of lithographs entitled *Sketches in the East*. As an artist she was competent but unremarkable. She displayed no great vitality or technical dexterity, but recorded what she saw with reasonable accuracy and delicacy. For publication, the lithographers, Dickenson & Sons, found it necessary to adapt and "improve" her compositions to suit picturesque convention. In *Entrance to Petra*, for example, figures and a camel have been added to draw the eye inwards, the path has been opened out and the vegetation softened into bushes that would be more recognizable in an English country garden[36].

Tourism in the Near East was now gathering momentum. In 1847, Harriet Martineau, already one of the most highly regarded women writers of her day, visited Petra as part of a large group. She was no artist, but in her book, *Eastern Life Present and Past*, published in 1848, she paints pictures with words instead of colors. This is not the place for a detailed analysis of her book, but the response to Petra of so intelligent and individual a woman should not be overlooked. Her account is an unusual mix of convention and originality. She expressed the usual biblical sentiments, believing herself to be among the haunts of Esau and his tribe and of the children of Ishmael, and she used Laborde and Robinson as points of reference, if only, at times, to assert their inaccuracy. But her acute observation of the flora and fauna, her sympathetic attitude towards the local Bedouin, her readiness to question her predecessors' opinions, and her vivid descriptions that reveal her own excitement and involvement with her surroundings, are all significantly different from previous accounts.

In criticizing the architectural style of the Khazneh: "Its position is wonderfully fine; and its material and preservation very striking: but it is inconceivable how any one can praise its architecture," she was not unique, since Austin Henry Layard had also been disappointed, but she was certainly in the minority. How many other writers described the Khazneh as standing "in a cupboard" or likened the Siq with its "strip of sky" above, to "being drawn up out of a coal-pit." She was fortunate to witness a violent storm that produced a rushing torrent of water along the wadi and brought in the Arabs from all around. From being an arid ravine, home only to the dead, the city was now alive: "I had seen Petra populous once more." Next day she left Petra to "its mists and mysterious quietude" having experienced "the most romantic vision of the travels of my life."[37] Her response reveals her sensitivity to the romanticism of Petra, but lacks the sentimentality of many other writers. Such individuality did not find an artistic parallel until eleven years later, in the work of Edward Lear.

Landscape artist, humorous illustrator, nonsense writer, intrepid traveler and much else, Lear visited Petra in April 1858.[38] His visit there was one of the highlights of his two-month sojourn in Palestine, made "for the sake of paintings which may convey pleasure & knowledge to others."[39] Twice in the previous decade he had intended to visit Palestine, but although on both occasions he had got as far as Egypt, he had been prevented from continuing, first by ill health, and second, when he should have accompanied William Holman Hunt, by lack of finance. Now, the sale of a painting of Corfu and commissions for two Holy Land subjects had made the venture feasible.

He had arrived in Jerusalem just before Easter but was overcome by the noise and crowds there, and decided to move on to Petra via Bethlehem and Hebron. He reached the ancient city on April 13 and, although he had read the accounts of Edward Robinson and other previous travelers, he was still unprepared for "one of the great marvels of the world." "I had expected a great deal," he wrote in a letter to his sister Ann,

> but was overwhelmed with extra surprise & admiration at the truly beautiful & astonishing scenes. The whole valley is a great ruin—temples—foundations—arches—palaces—in inconceivable quantity & confusion; & on 2 sides of the valley are great cliffs, all cut into millions of tombs—magnificent temples with pillars,—theatres etc. so that the whole place is like magic; & when I add that every crevice is full of Oleander & white Broom, & alive with doves, gazelles, & partridges—you may suppose my delight was great. All the cliffs are of a wonderful colour—like ham in stripes; & parts are salmon colour.[40]

So vivid an expression of his wonderment at Petra is typical of this idiosyncratic writer and artist. His more extensive account, in his journal, of his experiences there, is remarkable for the depth of his emotional response to the scenery and its associations and the lack of the clichéd biblical references that characterize many earlier writers. He felt "the loneliness in the very midst of scenes so plainly telling of a past glory and a race of days long gone" but also saw with a painter's eye "the vivid contrast of the countless fragments of ruin, basement, foundation, wall, and scattered stone, with the bright green of the vegetation and the rainbow hues of rock and cliff" and wrote with a poet's pen of "a magical condensation of beauty and wonder" and "the star-bright flitting of the wild dove and rock-partridge through the oleander-gloom."[41] He felt powerless to render "the visible witchery of wild nature and human toil" or to reproduce "the dead silence and strange feeling of solitude which are among the chief characteristics of this enchanted region," but he was determined to try, and the sketches that he made of various aspects of the city

110. Edward Lear, *Petra*, oil on canvas, 69.7 x 115.5 cm; signed with monogram and dated 1859. Private collection.

successfully convey some of the unique qualities of Petra that he describes. The scattered remains of temples and tombs hewn out of the reddish-colored rocks and overgrown with lush green vegetation, for example, are the distinguishing features of two drawings of the eastern cliffs from different viewpoints, and both convey the emptiness and decay that Lear had so strongly felt (fig. 111).[42]

Lear's sense of the poetry in the landscape of Petra is in marked contrast to the prosaic but more dramatic renderings of David Roberts, with their more detailed articulation of the architecture within their surroundings. It was perhaps inevitable that, many years later, Lear should choose to redraw the most poetic of his Petra compositions for his series of illustrations to Tennyson's poems, depicting the line, "Rose blossoms in a hot ravine" from *Daisy* (fig. 112).[43]

Lear's prime purpose at Petra, however, was to collect material for oil paintings, for at this stage in his career he still aspired to gain recognition as a serious landscape painter, rather than as a mere topographical draughtsman. In the year after his return from Palestine he worked on two oils of Petra, one of the eastern cliffs (fig. 110), the other of the theater,[44] based on sketches he had made on the spot—the sketch for the latter (apparently not extant) his last before he and his Corfiot manservant, Giorgio, were surrounded and set upon by hordes of quarreling Bedouin, all demanding further payment. No hint of the harassment he endured appears in either painting; he has eliminated the present-day figures that occur in some of his sketches and instead imparts his sense of "the loneliness of this bygone world, where on every side are tokens of older greatness."[45] Lear's painting of the theater vividly illustrates his graphic description in his journal:

> The pile of vast rocks before me was dark purple and awful in the shadows of the morning, and the perpendicular walls of the wild rent of the Sik were indescribably grand, closed almost at their roots, but reflecting bright sky and white clouds in the stream which bursts through them amid thickets of oleander and broom and rushed onward below the semicircle of the ancient theatre cut into the living rock below me.[46]

In conveying both his own emotional response to the site and his consciousness of its past history, as well as the intensity with which he depicts light, color and form, Lear was emulating the ideology of his Pre-Raphaelite friend and mentor, William Holman Hunt, with whom he had worked in England in 1852, and whose recent paintings of Egyptian and Holy Land subjects he would have seen in England.[47] In addition he had visited the studio exhibition of Thomas Seddon in 1855 which included several Near Eastern watercolors as well as the oil *The Valley of Jehoshaphat*, which had been praised by Ruskin as being the first representatives of a "truly historic

111. Edward Lear, *Petra, 13 April 1858,* watercolor and sepia ink over graphite on white paper, Edward Lear, Landscape drawings. Edward Lear Drawings and Manuscripts, Petra (36), NII.L12 [859], Department of Printing and Graphic Arts, Houghton Library, Harvard College Library.

112. Edward Lear, *Petra,* black and brown pen and ink over black chalk, with grey wash and white chalk highlight, 34 x 54 cm. (sheet size); inscribed 21 [crossed out in pencil] *rosy blossom in hot ravine,* and with further notes; numbered *(172)* within ruled margin, and outside *162, 172* [both crossed out] and *177.* Illustration for "Rose blossoms in a hot ravine," from Tennyson's *Daisy.* Eton College Library, Windsor, Berkshire.

113. Frederic Edwin Church, *Preparatory sketch for El Khasné*, Petra, Jordan, February, 1868, brush and oil paint on paper laminate, 32.6 x 50.8 cm. Cooper Hewitt National Design Museum, Smithsonian Institution. Gift of Louis P. Church, 1917-4-485-a.

landscape art."[48] The intense vision that informs the mountainous and rocky landscapes of other Pre-Raphaelite followers such as John Brett and J.W. Inchbold may also have inspired Lear's own interpretation of equally imposing scenery.

The last nineteenth-century artist of stature whose visit to Petra produced an impressive legacy was Frederic Edwin Church, the highly acclaimed American landscape painter of wild and remote scenery.[49] Ten years after Lear, in February 1868, Church spent two and a half days at Petra, with two companions and, despite threats from the native Bedouin, and several showers of rain, he managed to make several sketches (some using oil colors), and to describe his experiences in his diary, without being subjected to the indignities that Lear and other travelers had suffered. Like his predecessors, Church was fully conscious of the biblical associations of the site, but while there his attention was focused primarily on the sublimity of the scenery, and his response to its exotic splendor is remarkable for its powerful imagery. He describes the "beauty of color" of the ravine, "ribboned with graded stripes, cross-barred with other tints, and worn by time into fantastic honeycombed forms" and later, as they climbed up to ed-Deir, "every turn disclosed new scenes—the most terrific chasms I have yet seen, the most ragged rocks. We looked down abysses awful in their profundity, and we looked up to cliffs that shut out the light of day."[50]

For him the Khazneh, "of a beautiful rich reddish salmon color," "cut in the face of a tremendous precipice," was the single most magnificent sight: "It is wonderful to see so lovely and luminous a color blazing out of black stern frightful rocks, to behold the beautiful temple rich in sculptured ornament shining as if by its own internal light."[51] This "self-illuminating"[52] quality is the most striking feature of the only major oil painting that resulted from Church's visit to Petra (figs. 113, 114). *El Khasné Petra*, first exhibited in 1874, has been comprehensively documented elsewhere, and its significance and the acclaim it received assessed.[53] Precedents for the frontal composition—a lithograph after David Roberts and an engraving after William Bartlett—were likewise detected,[54] but it is also interesting to note that the view of the façade of the Khazneh, glimpsed through the overhanging rocks of the Siq, had appeared thirty-eight years before as the frontispiece to *Landscape Illustrations of the Bible*.[55] Further, it is salient that this engraving, in its turn, was based on a sketch, made eighteen years before by William Bankes, which was the very first visual image of Petra to be executed.[56] The wheel had come full circle.

114. Frederic Edwin Church, *El Khasné*, oil on canvas, by April 1874, 153.7 x 127.6 cm; inscribed in oil paint, lower right: *F. E. Church/-74*. Olana State Historic Site, New York State Office of Parks and Recreation and Historic Preservation, OL.1981.10A.

13 | The Rock-Cut Architecture of Petra

ROBERT WENNING

FROM THE VERY BEGINNING up until the present, the rock-cut façades have been the most impressive and most characteristic monuments of Petra. Numerous covers of books and journals illustrate either the famous Khazneh or the façade of ed-Deir. The travelers of the nineteenth century have left a series of wonderful descriptions and drawings of these façades. The earliest of them, the Khazneh drawn by William John Bankes in 1833, has only just been published—in 1997 (see p. 114, fig. 96).[1]

The first thorough treatment of the façades—a detailed catalogue, description, and analysis—was given by Brünnow and von Domaszewski who, in 1904, recorded 619 rock-cut tombs and even more rock-cut rooms used for dwelling or cultic activities. Their numbering system for these monuments remains standard today. A new thorough study was done by Judith McKenzie in 1990.[2] Rock-cut façades are found not only at tombs but also at triclinia. A triclinium is a room with large benches on three sides on which to lie down to have a meal. Many of the triclinia are connected with nearby tombs, while others are used by associations of particular deities. The tombs are distributed all around the city of Petra, partly at the foot of the hills towards the city and partly in the adjoining wadis.[3] The first tomb to be seen by the visitor is the Khazneh in the Siq of Petra. It is a dramatic moment for everybody—every time.

Typology Von Domaszewski established the first terminology and typology of the rock-cut tomb façades at Petra.[4] His study relates to the upper part of the façades, though the doorway may vary separately. Scholars have followed him with slight changes.

The *Crowstep Tomb* (fig. 116) is characterized by either one row of crowsteps with a torus below them or two rows of crowsteps, the lower row framed by tori. Von Domaszewski called the type the *Pylon Tomb*, but this refers too directly to Egyptian monuments and is more related to the shape than the decor. Others called the type *Assyrian*, because of the crowsteps which are known from ancient Near Eastern art. But this decoration was quite common in the Hellenistic East and the Nabataeans probably got their prototypes from such a context.[5] Mostly the façades are plain. Often they are somewhat inclined towards the rock face. Some of these tombs are carved from the rock on three sides or even as freestanding monuments, or towers. The few cubes among the tower tombs form a type of their own: the *Cube Tomb* (fig. 117). This type again combines Near Eastern traditions with Hellenistic art, a feature especially characteristic of the tombs in the Kidron valley at Jerusalem.

The doorway is plain, but sometimes has framing and a pediment as well. There is an interesting peculiarity: many of these tombs show a groove above the entrance. It has been suggested that this groove was carved to accept either an inset stone cornice or a wooden plaque recording the name of the tomb's owner. The triangular shape of some of the grooves and the evidence of traces of a stone slab in at least one example point to the first explanation.

The *Step Tomb* (fig. 118) exhibits two sets of five more monumental steps arranged in mirror image with the lowest step in the center. This upper part can be called an "attic" and is about one-third of the height of the lower façade. Below, there is a large cavetto cornice, a torus, and a fascia. These tombs are sometimes referred to as the "cavetto" type. These kinds of steps are known from Assyrian and Achaemenid art, while the cavetto is an Egyptian feature that was introduced to Phoenicia in the Persian Period. Different from the Egyptian shape, the Nabataean (and the Phoenician) cavetto is cut as a quadrant. That means a reduction of the vivid Egyptian form into a geometric ornament.[6]

The Step Tombs can be subdivided into the *Proto-Hegr*

115. Obelisk Tomb (Br. 35) and, below, the Triclinium (Br. 34), Petra.

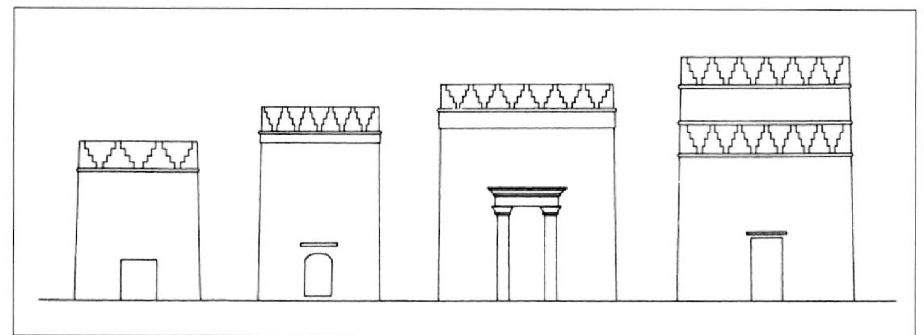
116 Crowstep Tomb.

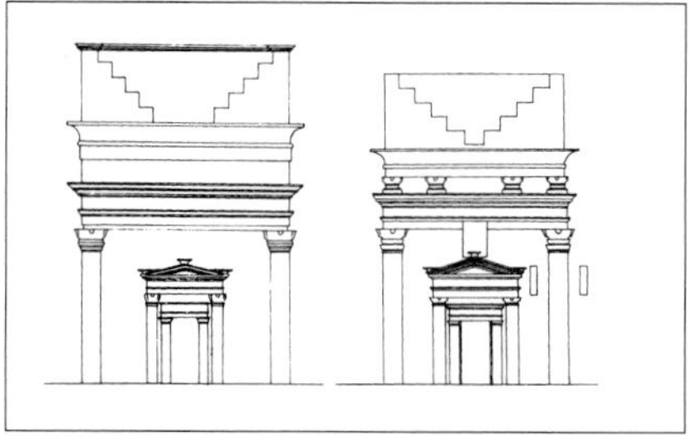
119 Proto-Hegr (left) and Hegr (right) Tombs.

117 Cube Tomb.

120 Gable Tomb.

116–122. The main types of Nabataean rock-cut façades at Petra:

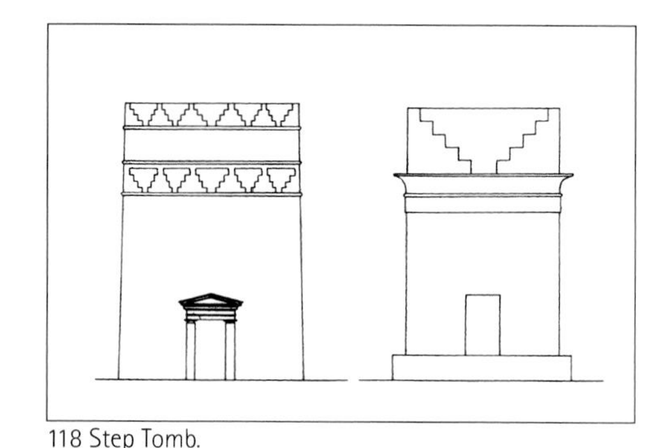
118 Step Tomb.

121 Arch Tomb.

Tomb (fig. 119 left), where pilasters are added to support the cornice, and the *Hegr Tomb* (fig. 119 right), which features a second "attic" with four dwarf pilasters below the cavetto cornice and above a classical entablature. Some tombs have half-columns instead of the pilasters and quarter-columns added to them. Pilasters and columns are crowned by the typical Nabataean capital ("*Hörnerkapitell*") (fig. 123), a blocked-out form of a capital. This is not to be understood as being unfinished, but, rather, as a reduction and abstraction of the Hellenistic Corinthian capital. It is debated whether these capitals may have had plaster or painting; there is evidence for stucco and painting on at least some of the façades.[7]

Among these tombs are very richly decorated examples, especially as concerns the gateway, where framings and entablature are often found doubled. Tomb Br. 649 shows a frieze of masks and armor between the dwarf pilasters. Such friezes are well known elsewhere in the Hellenistic world.[8]

The *Arch Tomb* (fig. 121) is characterized by an arch supported by pilasters. The doorways take up that feature again either with another arch or with a classical entablature, or are plain.

The *Gable Tomb* (fig. 120) is decorated with a pediment supported by pilasters.

The *Temple Tomb* (fig. 122) is a more elaborate version of the *Gable Tomb* with a pediment or a broken pediment, but with arched elements sometimes included. Some of the tombs are rather broad, with more than a pair of pilasters and more than one doorway; others are two-storied. Usually quarter-columns are added to the pilasters. On a few façades there are sculptures, some figural decoration, or a Doric frieze. The Hellenistic influence is strong for this group and demonstrates that the Petra necropolis was not an isolated phenomenon[9]. The

122. Temple Tomb, so-called Corinthian Tomb (Br. 776) with Palace Tomb at left, Petra.

attribution of these tombs as provincial by von Domaszewski is not correct; therefore they should not be called "*Roman*." Most of the famous tombs belong to this group.

Some façades have never been finished and remain in various stages of completion (fig. 124). From them we learn that a façade was cut out of a steep rock face from the top down. All of the façades are completely rock-cut with the exception of the Palace Tomb (Br. 765) (fig. 134), where parts of the upper story are built free-standing. This tomb is exceptional in having more than two stories (which in themselves are a rare feature at Petra.) It is believed that the upper order of the Palace Tomb illustrates a separate element of architecture situated behind the entrance building, which is restricted to the lower order.

In all of the rock-cut tombs at Petra there is always a single doorway leading into a burial chamber (fig. 127). Although the Palace Tomb and the Corinthian Tomb seem to have four entrances, each opens into a separate chamber. Often the chambers are enormous in size, and are nicely cut and smoothed. Niches (*loculi*) for burial are cut into the rear and lateral walls of the chamber. The more elaborate, richly decorated tombs are equipped with a few broad loculi (decorated partly with framings or arches (*arcosolia*)) which are often situated high up on the wall; other tombs have tall loculi cut as long boxes.[10] There are graves in the floor of some burial chambers as well. A few façades have loculi cut into them; the one at the Urn Tomb seems to be closed with a relief depicting a portrait of the deceased, perhaps a king. (fig. 125) (cf. the well-known Palmyrene relief slabs). The large hall of the Khazneh opens onto three burial chambers without loculi. Here and in some other tombs burials in sarcophagi have thus been postulated.

123

124

124. Unfinished tomb (Br. 396), Petra.

125

126

upper left: **123.** Nabataean Capital from tomb (Br. 825), Petra.

above: **125.** Loculus slab with portrait bust in the façade. Urn Tomb (Br. 772), Petra.

right: **126.** Tomb of Sextius Florentinus (Br. 763), Petra.

Dating The typology and the position of tombs of particular types led von Domaszewski to assume that there was a chronological development from plain to richly decorated and classical types at Petra. He dated the tombs from the sixth century BC to the third century AD. Today we know that this classification does not work and that the different types can be contemporaneous. Their chronological range may, rather, be limited between the second century BC and the second century AD. It must be considered that Petra's rock-cut tomb façades reflect a great economic and political power that dissipated when the Nabataean kingdom was transformed into the *provincia Arabia* under Roman rule in 106 AD. Beside these large tombs there are innumerable shaft tombs and simple graves.

During the last hundred years a number of attempts have been made to associate various tombs with particular Nabataean kings. None could be proven. It is only reasonable to attribute the Khazneh and the large "Royal Tombs" at the slope of Jebel el-Khubthah (pp. 2–3) to the Nabataean kings; however, one can only speculate about the particular occupant to which a tomb belongs. The dating and classification of Petra's tomb façades has remained the primary interest of researchers up until now. Nevertheless, the results have been rather meager.

There is other evidence for dating besides the typology and the distribution of the rock-cut tombs. Not all of this evidence has contributed much to a closer dating, as can be shown below.

Tomb Br. 763 (fig. 126) is the burial chamber of the Roman governor of Arabia, T. Aninius Sextius Florentinus, as we are told by the Latin inscription on the frieze. He died in 128/9 AD; thus we should have a specific date. But some scholars have suggested that Florentinus had reused an older tomb.[11] Most scholars do not accept the re-dating, but, based upon stylistic analysis, this hypothesis deserves more consideration. As long as the date cannot be established by other criteria we should avoid using tomb Br. 763 as the cornerstone for the dating of other façades.

Opposite the Obelisk Tomb (Br. 35) (fig. 115) there is a Nabataean-Greek bilingual inscription written high on the face of the rock (fig. 128). In Nabataean: "*'Abdmanku son of 'Akayus son of Shullay son of 'Utayhu . . . built this burial-monument (for himself) and his descendants and their descendants for ever (in the year . . .) of Maliku, during his lifetime.*" And shortened in a Greek version: "*Abdomanchos son of Achaios has made the (funeral) monument for himself and his sons.*"[12] The inscription is to be dated to the reign of the Nabataean king Malichus II (40–70 AD) following the stylistic classification of tomb Br. 35.[13] But does it really relate to tomb Br. 35 on the opposite site of the wadi—or to triclinium Br. 34 below that tomb? The terminology of the dedication is not clear at all. It seems to indicate a burial place or, following the Greek, a burial monument. There is no monument in the rock of the inscription except for a cave below and a monument which itself has remained unfinished or is lost today.[14] People should thus be cautious about associating the Obelisk Tomb with this inscription and using that dating for further classification of façades.

The only funerary monument at Petra with a long inscription on its façade is the Turkmaniyah Tomb (Br. 633; p. 38, fig. 17). Different from the situation at Hegra (Madāʾin Ṣāliḥ), a frontier city and great marketplace with a mixed population, there seems to have been no need at Petra to write the ownership and regulations of use on the tomb

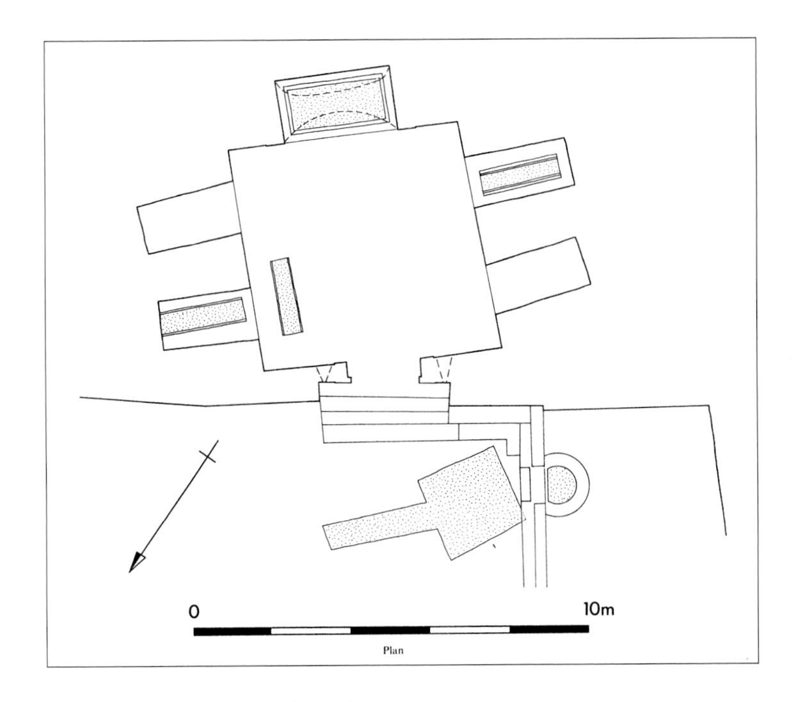

127. Plan of Obelisk Tomb (Br. 35), Petra.

façades. Nevertheless, we learn from this inscription that there was an office or an archive that housed written documents. We may assume that among the tribal population of Petra it was well-known to whom each tomb belonged or that everything was controlled at best by that office.[15] This important inscription reads:

> This tomb and the large burial-chamber within it and the small burial-chamber beyond it, in which are burial-places, niche-arrangements, and the enclosure in front of them and the porticos and rooms within it and the gardens(?) and the triclinium(?) and the wells of water and the cisterns(?) and walls(?) and all the rest of the property which is in these places are sacred and dedicated to Dushara, the god of our lord, and his sacred throne and all the gods, (as) in the documents of consecration according to their contents. And it is the responsibility of Dushara and his

128. Greek-Nabataean bilingual inscription opposite the Obelisk Tomb (Br. 35), Petra.

opposite:
130. The Theater, Petra.

throne and all the gods that it should be done as in these documents of consecration and nothing of all that is in them shall be changed or removed and none shall be buried in this tomb except whoever has written for him an authorization for burial in these documents of consecration for ever.[16]

It is interesting to note that there is no name of the owners and no date given in the inscription, which would have been expected. Therefore it might be that the inscription was placed on the façade to indicate the rights of the (known) owner, but is an extract from the document of consecration, which was still the only legal document. Considering its palaeography, the inscription and the tomb can be dated to the latter part of the first century AD, but there is no possibility for a closer dating.

Evidently there were inscribed closing slabs at the loculi within the tombs, which indicated the burial places of the deceased; fragments of such slabs are found in tomb Br. 813.[17] One of the inscriptions reads: "'*Unaishu, the brother of Shaqilat the queen of the Nabataeans, son...*," others give elements of dating formulae with names of the dynasty (Aretas, Malichus, Shaqilat). Clearly, tomb Br. 813 (fig. 129) was owned by high-ranking officials of the royal court, but was not a "Royal tomb." We knew that Shaqilat II reigned 70/71–75/76 AD, when the elected king, Rabbel II, was still too young to assume the throne. 'Unaishu had been her *epitropos*, an adminis-

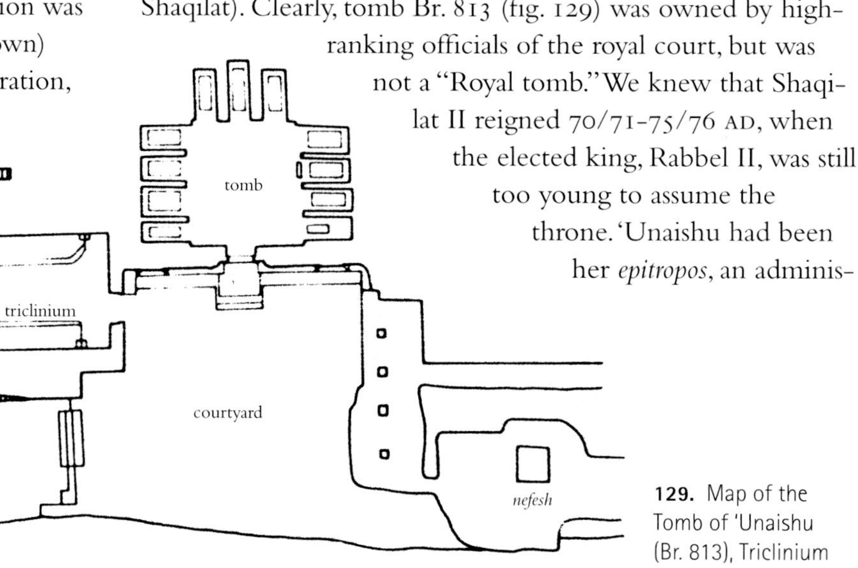

129. Map of the Tomb of 'Unaishu (Br. 813), Triclinium (Br. 812) and other installations, Petra.

trator, probably the head of government. This would give us an indication when the tomb was in use. It does fit with the dates of the finds from the tomb (see below). It might be that ʻUnaishu was the owner of the tomb, therefore providing a close dating for the monument, but this cannot be proven. As the tomb could have been constructed earlier it cannot be used as the starting point for the dating of other façades. The tomb façade belongs to the Hegr Tomb type with elaborate classical doorway; it is connected with a triclinium (Br. 812), porticos, a *nefesh*, a cistern, and other installations, which can illuminate the complex indicated in the Turkmaniyah inscription (fig. 17). There are a few other tombs with a yard and porticos.

With the exception of a few burial places, all of the rock-cut tombs at Petra were found completely robbed. From tomb Br. 813 and its yard sherds of pottery, coins, and jewelry were reported. The sherds may be classified mainly as Phase 3b—from the end of the first century AD,[18] a date that fits with the coins of Rabbel II, from 101/02 AD. In Hegr Tomb Br. 64 B, located opposite the Khazneh, F. Zayadine excavated some loculi with datable finds: an inscribed slab of a woman, slabs with a *nefesh*-sign, lamps, and a bowl, all assignable to the late first or second century AD.[19] The tomb continued to be in use until the Byzantine period. The finds do not establish when the tomb was constructed, but illustrate burial customs.[20]

When the great theater was cut into the slope of the outcropping with the High Place, a few rock-cut tombs were

destroyed. Dark holes attesting to the remains of rock-cut chambers still survive in the plain rock face behind the upper seating (figs. 130, 135). Following Phillip C. Hammond, who dates the construction of the theatre to the reign of Aretas IV (9 BC–40 AD),[21] these tombs have been understood to predate the Augustean period. That might be the case, but there are a few objections: Hammond has no clear stratigraphy for the earliest phase of the theater. Based upon a palaeographic analysis of the masons' marks, a date later in the first century AD would fit better.[22] Furthermore, the theater follows Vitruvian "canon," more or less, but only when the upper of the three sections of the *cavea* is excluded. The height of the *cavea* should correspond with the height of the *scenae frons*, and that corresponds with the second section of seating. Indeed, the rows of that upper section seem to be cut more roughly. It cannot be excluded that this section is a later enlargement of the *cavea* during the second century AD. The destroyed tombs might be from the Hellenistic period, but they are not unambiguously dated by the theater.

The oldest dated Nabataean inscription can be found in the triclinium (Br. 21) of a sanctuary, which was built by Aslah for Dushara in 96/95 BC (p. 38, fig. 18). From this complex we learn that nicely cut large halls were carved as early as the beginning of the first century BC. But this triclinium is not decorated by a façade.

After the publication of the eighty-two rock-cut tomb façades at Hegra by Jaussen and Savignac, thirty-one of which are dated by inscription between 1 BC/AD and 74/75 AD, these monuments have greatly influenced the discussion of the Petra tombs.[23] Indeed, the tombs from both sites are closely related. Nevertheless, the façades at Hegra show various peculiarities. That the earliest examples have closer connections with the rock-cut tombs at Petra is not surprising.[24] Artists from Petra appear to have been sent there to cut the façades. The knowledge of the job remained in the hands of a few families of stone-cutters who developed workshops at Hegra. Their traditions and stylistic features and the instructions of the tomb owners may explain why we have almost

131. Ed-Deir (Br. 462), a monumental triclinium, Petra.

132. Interior of Urn Tomb (Br. 772), Petra. The burial chamber was later converted into a church.

133. Interior of Triclinium (Br. 235) opposite the Tomb of the Statues, Petra.

no similar tombs at both sites. There is no Gable Tomb or Temple Tomb at Hegra. When the types are associated with their inscribed dates it becomes clear that the suggested developmental sequence of tombs, from simple to elaborate, is not at fault. Rather, tomb ownership seems to have been crucial for the arrangement of types and features. When the first tombs were cut at Hegra, of course, there was already a long tradition of such façades at Petra. Therefore, it should come as no surprise that the oldest tomb at Hegra—tomb B 6 from 1 BC/AD—is of the Step Tomb type with elaborate doorway with pediment and figural acroteria. On the other hand, tombs of the Crowstep Tomb type are as late as 72 AD (E 14, E 16).

The most Hellenistic façade at Petra is that of the Khazneh (fig. 201; see Chapter 16). It is so closely related to Alexandrian palace and tomb architecture (and even iconography) that it is believed to have been worked by Alexandrian artists. As has been observed by many scholars, the second style of Pompeian wall-painting (fig. 209) reflects the same Alexandrian tradition as the façades at Petra.[25] The Khazneh became the prototype for all other Hellenistic façades at Petra, although not all Hellenistic features of that façade were later adopted by the Nabataeans. Unlike most other tomb façades the Khazneh has Corinthian capitals (Type 1 and 2 floral capitals), and these can be compared with capitals of the temples at Petra and other buildings. Accepting that the Qasr al-Bint is to be dated to the last quarter of the first century BC, the Khazneh capitals cannot be much older because of their affinity with the capitals of that temple, as was shown already in 1932 by K. Ronczewski. The Khazneh can be dated to the third quarter of the first century BC.[26]

There is still room for further studies on the capitals and other architectural elements at Petra, which must go beyond matters of typology. Such an approach seems to be promising.[27] Judith McKenzie[28] has demonstrated its importance by her discussion of architectural moldings. She also observed changes by a development of single features as well as the general appearance of tomb façades. Among other things, McKenzie noted a simplification of architectural details in the younger façades.[29] The chances for new research seem to have improved, since we can now date Nabataean pottery very precisely and have stratigraphic evidence for dating Nabataean architecture, as well as a rich corpus of architectural elements from the Roman Near East. There are many architectural fragments from both Petra and other sites known from surveys and excavations that still await a thorough study, which is very much needed. At the very least, Nabataean rock-cut architecture must be placed in the much larger context of Hellenistic traditions in the Near East. Clearly, the Nabataeans participated within the monuments of the surrounding cultures, selecting different elements (not only Alexandrian ones), and integrating them, in the face of classical rules, into a new style marked by the intelligent integration of foreign forms into its own traditions, ideas, and taste.

Owners and Cult Rock-cut tombs with façades are

known from Petra and Hegra and are imitated at two sites in Midian (el-Bad', ed-Disa), but at no other site settled by the Nabataeans. To explain this phenomenon we can only speculate. The monuments clearly represent family tombs of an upper class. When we assume that Petra was the tribal seat, where the Nabataean tribal upper class chose to have its family tombs (and clan sanctuaries), this explains the evidence at Petra. As for Hegra, we have to assume that a group of Nabataean nobility moved to that site (or remained at Hegra, in an area where the tribe may, in fact, have originated) and performed their duties for the king and the tribe. This group settled permanently at the site (as did the stone-cutters), but was eager to show the same presentation of status and wealth as other tribal members at Petra. It is possible to show up particular features in the representation of the Hegra façades, such as the inscriptions and the figurative art.[30]

In contrast to Hegra, the tomb occupants at Petra remain unknown to us. Probably Nabataeans living outside Petra buried their dead here too. The few inscriptions at Petra, the costs and prestige of the elaborate façades, especially of the Temple Tombs,[31] may allow us to associate these precious monuments with Nabataean kings and other dynastic members; the "Gable" and "Step" tombs, with leading families of the tribe and other nobilities; and the large group of "Crow-step" and "Arch" tombs, with other less prosperous members of the tribe.[32] The large number of rock-cut tombs seems to indicate that almost all members of the tribe had been able to have their own tomb. We can suggest that the richer owners, as patrons, allowed their clients to be buried in their tombs or in nearby graves. Assuming these considerations about the owners are correct, it is interesting to note that Hellenistic influence on the façades increased within the upper ranks of the social groupings.[33] At the same time, the forms of the façades move towards simplification, as demonstrated by Judith McKenzie.

As for figural decoration, the Khazneh, with its complex funerary program, remains the exception. The cuirassed statue and the two adjoining sculptures on the Tomb of Statues (which hardly constitutes the tomb of, nor depicts, a Roman soldier) (fig. 153) appear to correspond to the figures of Isis and the Dioscuri from the Khazneh, and could represent deities rather than the tomb owners.[34] The Urn Tomb and the Obelisk Tomb, on the other hand, appear to show reliefs of the owners.[35] All other figural elements are reduced to decoration: busts of Tychai and other genii, Medusa and other masks, armor, urns, and metopes, as well as lions (which appear as guardians on triclinium Br. 452). The snake monument Br. 302 is funerary in character.

On both sides of the Khazneh façade there are rows of small holes, which have been understood as supports for scaffolding erected during formulation of the façade. Even smaller holes at the bays on both sides of the doorway are connected either with attached inscriptions, garlands, and crowns, or votive gifts. Such holes may often be observed.[36] On the threshold of or near the tomb entrance are semicircular cavities for libations to the dead (fig. 205).

On the walls of some tombs, both outside and inside, or at the loculi, are incised depictions of a *nefesh* (fig. 154), a sign or monument drawn in remembrance of a person. A monumental *nefesh* can be found on tomb Br. 813; four of them crown the Obelisk Tomb. A great deal of evidence concerning cults of the dead remains to be researched at Petra and other Nabataean sites.[37] The notice in Strabo (*Geography* XVI 4, 26) that the Nabataeans buried their kings beside dung-heaps seems to confuse the Semitic term for tomb (*qbr*) with the Greek word for dung (*kopros*).

Ed-Deir (fig. 131) is neither a monastery nor a tomb but a monumental cella or biclinium with a cultic podium (*môtab*) at the back.[38] Judging from its composition and stylistic features, the façade seems to be rather late in the Nabataean rock-cut architectural sequence. The most Hellenistic triclinium is Br. 235 (situated opposite the Tomb of the Statues), with its walls decorated by fifteen architectural niches with fluted columns (fig. 133). The marvelous colors of the room are the result of weathering. Originally, the walls had been plastered and painted in a different way. These triclinia formed centers for cultic associations (*marzeah*).

To Preserve a Heritage Through the Byzantine period the tombs at Petra continued in use as burial places, or were used for other purposes. The Urn Tomb, for example, was converted into a church by Bishop Jason in 446/47 AD (fig. 132). Until a few years ago the B'dul-Bedouins used the tombs for dwellings or as cowsheds. Although recently resettled, they remain a viable presence at the site, offering tourists cokes, tea, postcards, fine Nabataean sherds, and unbelievable "antiques" made in India.

The surfaces of the tomb façades at Petra are badly weathered, the dramatic result of an ongoing process of destruction; the silky colors we so much appreciate are but the result of erosion. Vandalism is a new phenomenon in the Petra area. The Petra National Trust is actively engaged in preserving the monuments and the site. In 1994, the Conservation and Restoration Center in Petra (CARCIP) was established, where Jordanian experts are trained by German colleagues so that they will be able to continue work by themselves. One of the first façades to be treated was Br. 825.[39]

134. The Palace Tomb (Br. 765), Petra.

14 | The Petra Survey Project

LAÏLA NEHMÉ

PETRA HAS BEEN EXPLORED for almost two centuries by dozens of travelers and archaeologists. They criss-crossed its wadis, cliffs, and mountains, marveling at its beauty and trying to get to know those who had inhabited it between the fourth century BC and the sixth or seventh century AD, that is Taymū, Waʾilū, ʿAbdū, Wahbʾallahī, Saʿdʾallahī and all the other Nabataeans whose names appear in the inscriptions less frequently than these equivalents of John or Bill. Since 1929 it has also been excavated by archaeologists from a number of different countries: Jordan, England, France, Germany, Switzerland, the United States, etc. Thanks to their combined efforts, large sections of Petra's history, especially from the Roman and Byzantine periods, have come to light. My purpose here is not to deplore, once again, the lack of chronological markers which (despite this dynamic archaeological activity) still hamper our understanding of the site, but to insist on the role that a proper archaeological map can play both in our knowledge of the history, development, and spatial organization of the Nabataean capital and in the preservation of this heritage site, which is listed among the world's finest jewels by UNESCO.

For example, it has recently been demonstrated that erosion damages those façades which look west and east far more than those which face south, and that those which look north are the least affected.[1] With a map and a catalogue, it will be possible to establish the list of those archaeologically significant monuments which face east or west, so that suitable action can be taken for their preservation. It is also obvious that a map is needed to set up a proper policy for the management of tourism, which would meet the expectations of both the tourists and the Department of Antiquities.

135. East part of the Great Theater and theater necropolis, Petra.

MAP-MAKING IN PETRA, A HISTORICAL ACCOUNT

The first attempts at map-making in Petra coincide with the earliest exploration of the Nabataean capital. However, from sketches of the landscape made by more or less talented draftsmen to photogrammetric restitutions of aerial photographs, cartography has unfortunately always followed, rather than accompanied, archaeological activity in Petra.[2] It is true that the making of an archaeological and topographical map has always been listed among the main concerns of the archaeologists and authorities in charge of the site, and several attempts have been made to produce one. Unfortunately, none of them has been completely satisfactory and it is hoped that the present project, when published, will fill a gap felt by most of those who undertake research on Petra.

Sketch Maps, 1812–1921 The Swiss traveler J.-L. Burckhardt, who visited the site on August 22, 1812, was not only the first Westerner[3] to identify it with Petra, the lost city of the Nabataeans mentioned in the ancient sources, but was also the first person to draw a rough plan of the ruins that he saw (fig.137).[4] This plan shows his itinerary from the Siq to Jabal Hārūn and gives the position of the main monuments: the Khazneh, the Theater, Qasr al-Bint, Zibb Firʿawn and the mausoleum of Aaron. In a small note next to his plan, the Deir ("Monastery"), which was found a few years after his visit to Petra but before his book was published (in 1822), is said to be somewhere to the northwest of the site. The course of Wadi Musa is represented by a line and the rock-cut tombs along the Jibāl Madhbaḥ, Khubthah, and Umm al-Biyarah by small black rectangles. The rest of the site is not represented. In 1823, C. L. Irby and J. Mangles, the two British naval officers who had accompanied W. J. Bankes on his visit to the site (see N. Lewis in this volume), published a second sketch map in the account of their travels (fig.138).[5] The only improvement on Burckhardt's plan is that it shows the "Track which leads out," that is, probably the modern track leading to the

136. General view of Petra from the northeast.

central basin of Petra from the northeast. The ancient caravan track, which crosses Mghār an-Naṣārah and which is still visible today, lies further south, closer to the "High perpendicular cliffs" marked D on their map. The stream shown is the Wadi Abū ʿUllayqah followed, in an east-west direction, by the Wadi aṣ-Ṣiyyagh. Although still very schematic, the map published by Léon de Laborde in 1830[6] is the first to give a relatively good idea of both the topography and the city ruins lying on the banks of Wadi Musa. The main wadis are represented and the position of about fifteen monuments is given.

No real progress was made during the second half of the nineteenth century, but in 1904, R. E. Brünnow and A. von Domaszewski published their monumental work *Die Provincia Arabia*, which contained eighteen detailed and impressively accurate maps of the site, together with a catalogue of 851 monuments, each of which was positioned on one of the maps with almost total accuracy (fig. 139).[7] All but two of these are at a scale of 1:3,333 and show the reliefs, the wadis, and the monuments, each of which is identified by a number in the catalogue. They are extraordinarily good and make it easy to find any monument mentioned in the text. Their only fault is the fanciful toponymy which the authors have given to some geographical entities, such as *Kegelberg* (Rās al-Maghārīq), *Akropolisberg* (Al-Ḥabīs) or *Zweites Nordwestwadi* (wadi Mʿayṣrah al-Gharbiyyah). A few years later, in 1907/8, A. Musil and G. Dalman[8] each published a map of Petra, at scales of 1:20,000 and roughly 1:18,000 respectively. Although they are less detailed than Brünnow and Domaszewski's maps and it is much more difficult to identify monuments on them (as the present author can testify!), they are more accurate and contain much more information than any of the previous general maps of the site as a whole, especially as regards toponymy (fig. 140). Dalman, who was particularly interested in sanctuaries, niches, rock-cut chambers, cisterns, and all structures other than tombs, also included in his works[9] more than two hundred sketches of monuments, or groups of

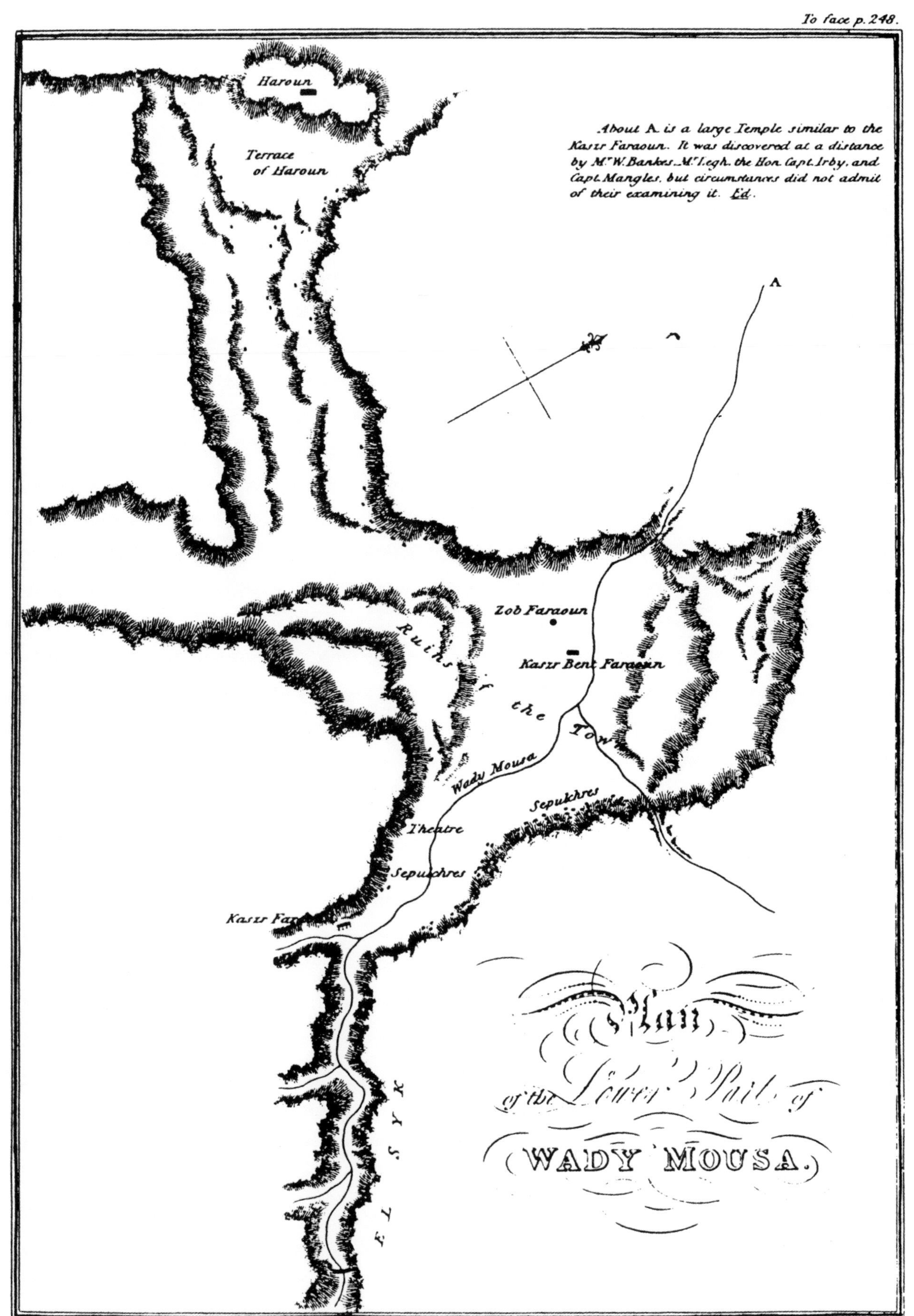

137. J. L. Burckhardt's map of Petra, 1822.

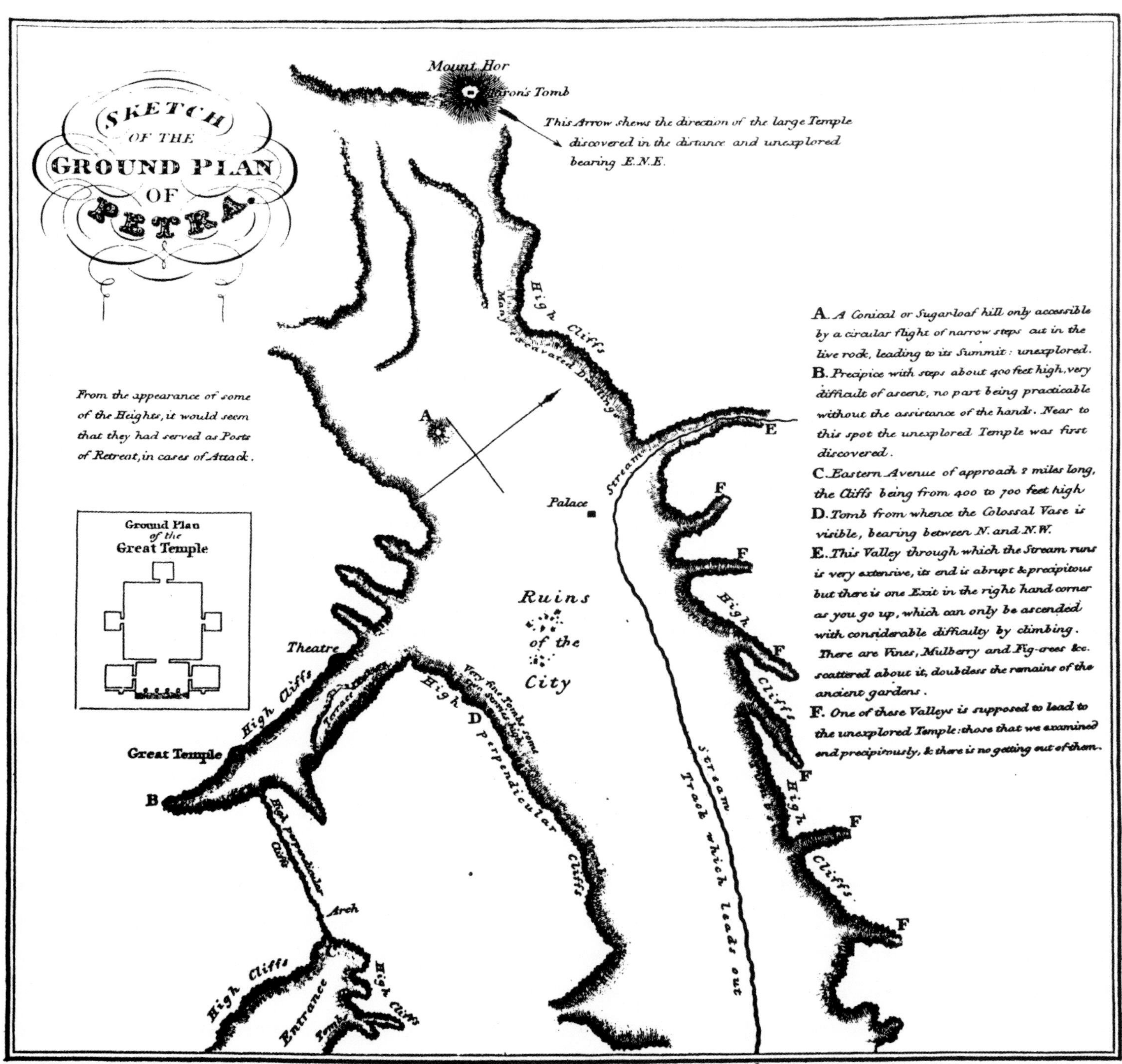

138. Irby and Mangles's map of Petra, 1823.

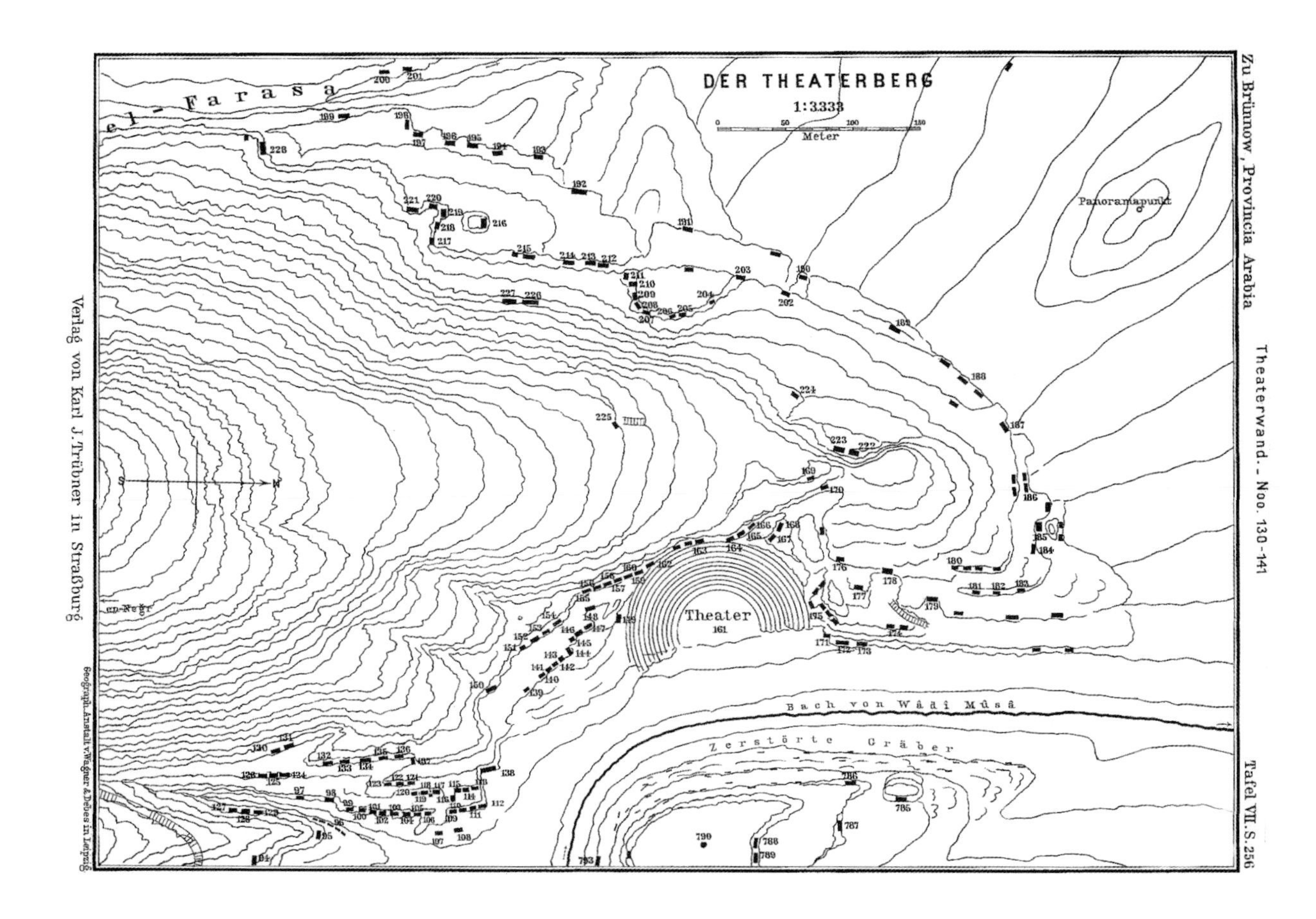

139. One of Brünnow and Domaszewski's maps of Petra: the Theater area, 1904.

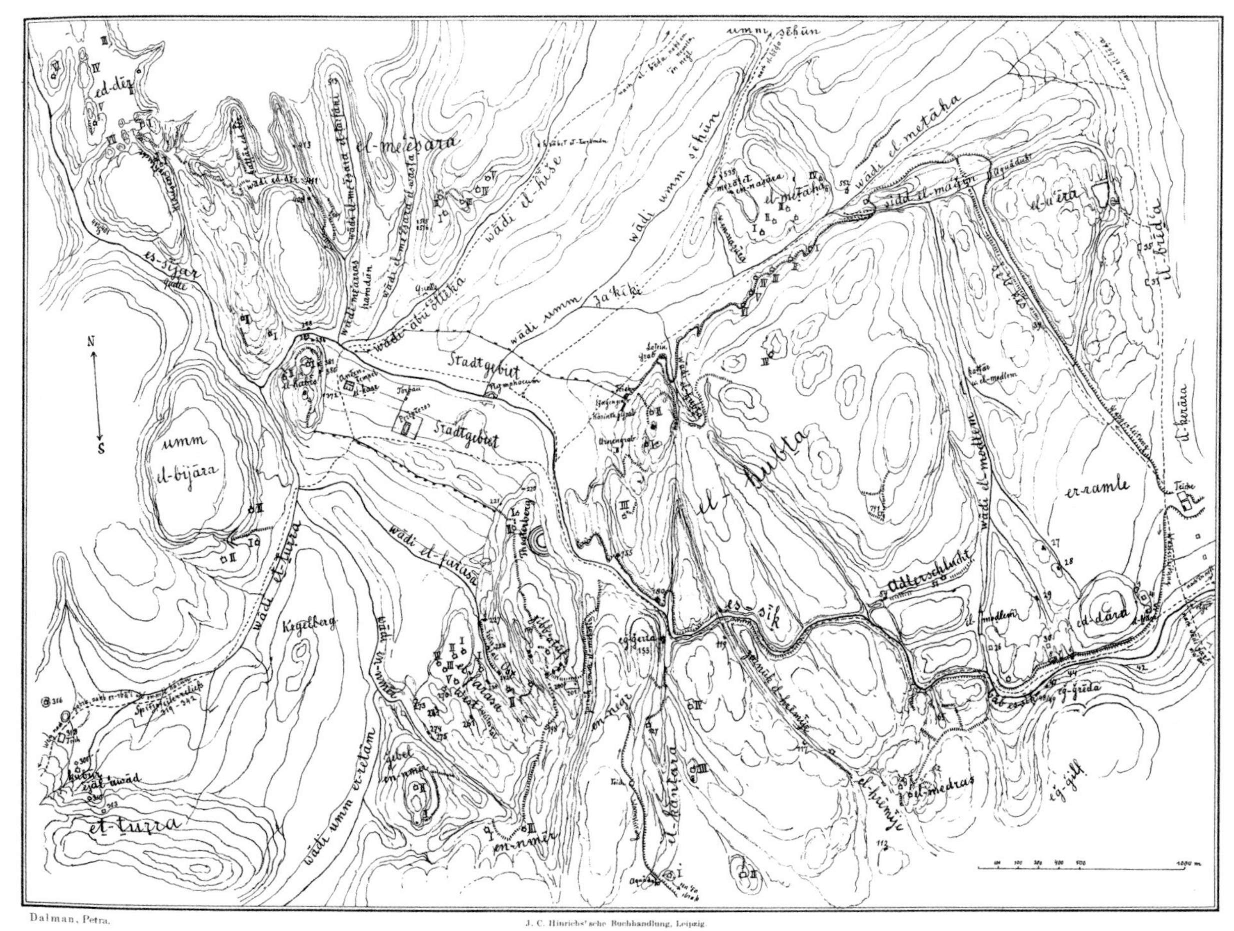

140. Dalman's map of Petra, 1908.

monuments, which are an invaluable and unequalled source of information. One should, however, bear in mind that all these maps respect neither exact proportions nor distances and that they cannot be used to take measurements.

During the first World War, the ruins of the city center, from the Nymphaeum to the Qasr al-Bint, were surveyed by a German team directed by Th. Wiegand, who produced a plan of the freestanding monuments lying immediately north and south of Wadi Musa, together with a detailed description of each of them.[10] Since this was done before any of these had been excavated, it obviously contains some inaccuracies. However, it very usefully complements the earlier maps that were restricted to the monuments carved in the rock.

"Scientific" Maps, 1923–1975 The first aerial photographs of Petra were made by the Royal Air Force in 1923 at the instigation of Sir Alexander Kennedy. They were then

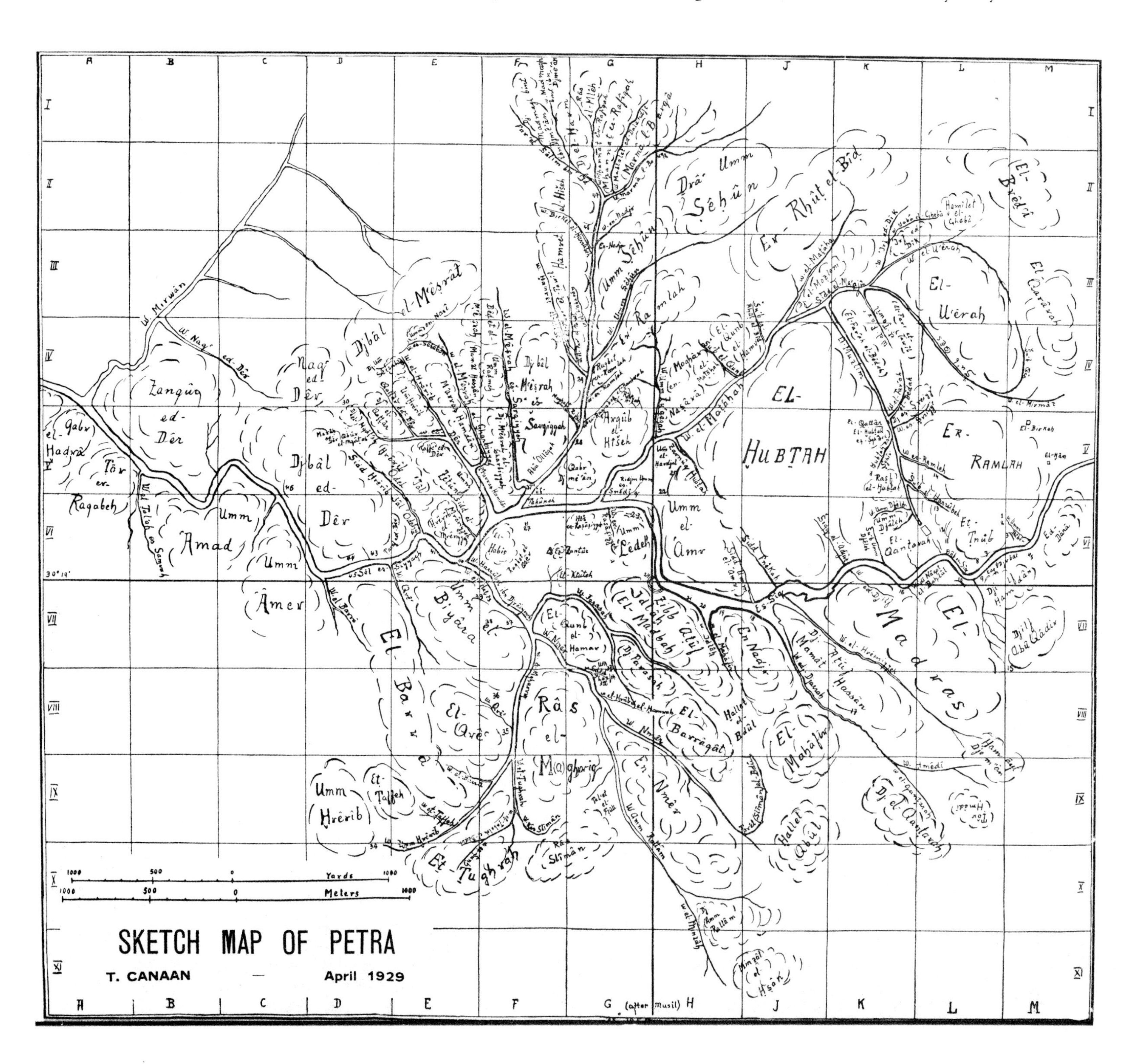

used to produce a map of Petra and its surroundings covering the area between Wadi Namalah, north of Baya, and the latitude of Jabal Hārūn.[11] Although this map is certainly more reliable than its predecessors, its usefulness is reduced by the total absence of contour lines—only hydrography is shown—and the large scale, approximately 1:29,000.

For the sake of completeness, one should mention the map at roughly 1:19,000, made by T. Canaan, who was a member of the Horsfield expedition (fig. 141).[12] It is accompanied by a detailed "Comparative list of place-names," and both map and list are extremely valuable working tools in studying the toponymy of Petra (fig. p.154).

In 1953, at the request of the Jordanian government, the British firm Hunting Aero Survey carried out an aerial survey of the site, producing a series of photographs at 1:25,000. Twelve years later, the British archaeological mission directed by P. J. Parr was allowed to use them to produce a new topographical map of Petra. The task was entrusted to the Department of Photogrammetry and Topography of University College, London, and resulted in the publication of a map, at 1:2,500, of the central basin of Petra covering an area of four square kilometers, with contour lines at ten-meter intervals.[13] The positions of the main monuments were checked by a ground survey carried out in 1968.[14] Despite the ratio of one-to-ten between the scale of the photographs and that of the map and the absence of proper ground control, this document is accurate and has been used by archaeologists to locate excavations and surveys.[15]

The New Archaeological Map The idea of a new map of Petra, using aerial coverage at a larger scale than 1:25,000, was first discussed in 1973 by Maurice Gory of the Institut Géographique National de France (IGN) and the inspectors of the Department of Antiquities of Jordan.[16] In February 1974, thanks to a grant from the French Ministry of Foreign Affairs, the IGN made an aerial survey of Petra at a height of approximately 1,500 m, which resulted in two series of 197 24-x-24-cm, black-and-white and color aerial photographs at a scale of 1:10,000.[17] They cover an area of 320 square kilometers including the National Park of Petra[18] and its surroundings. The series of photographs is divided into eleven strips that have a longitudinal overlap of between 60 percent and 80 percent and an overlap from one strip to another of between 5 percent and 40 percent. Such a large overlap—the norm is between 5 percent and 20 percent—was necessary because of the depth of the wadis. Unfortunately, these photographs have one major disadvantage: they were taken in February and so contain large areas of shade in the steep-sided parts of the relief, which makes them difficult to interpret. A second series of aerial photographs was therefore taken by the IGN for the Royal Jordanian Geographic Center (RJGC) in the spring of 1981.[19] This shows very little shade and is perfect for photo-interpretation.

141. Canaan's map of Petra, 1929.

The photographs covering the area with the greatest density of archaeological remains, that is almost eighty square kilometers, were prepared for stereoscopic viewing[20] and a ground survey was undertaken in October and November of 1974 by M. Gory, F. Zayadine, J. Starcky, and J. T. Milik. They traversed all the wadis and mountains of Petra, locating the monuments recorded by Brünnow and Domaszewski, finding dozens of others, asking systematically for the place-names, and recording about one thousand inscriptions, mainly Nabataean, two-thirds of which are still unpublished. The triangulations needed for the development of a photoplan were made by a team of the IGN. Two years later, M. Gory said: "this international cooperation will bear fruit only if the two other planned projects, which justify this initial effort, are carried out: the 1:10,000 photoplan and the 1:2,000 archaeological map."[21]

The photoplan was completed by the IGN in 1977 but the map was never finished.[22] In 1983, the RJGC produced a series of cartographic documents which include a map in eight sheets at 1:5,000, with contour lines at five-meter intervals (only one of which, no. 5, was published in three colors); a planimetric map at 1:10,000, which is the reduction of sheets 3 to 6; and finally a planimetric and orographic map at 1:2,500 of the center of Petra (2.5 square kilometers). Unfortunately, none of these documents is usable in its present form because of the numerous mistakes and major gaps which occurred between the planimetry and orography.

One should also note the existence of a map of the central part of Petra, in four sheets at 1:1,000, which covers the area between the Theater and Qasr al-Bint, extending 400 m north and 700 m south of Wadi Musa, with contour lines at one-meter intervals. This was made by a Spanish team, using aerial photographs taken in 1978 over various regions of Jordan: Amman, Irbid, Kerak, Petra, Aqaba, the Desert Castles, and Mafraq.[23]

In 1988, the RJGC published the first topographic and archaeological map of the whole of Petra.[24] The stereoscopic realization, using the 1981 IGN aerial coverage, had been drawn in the RJGC workshops in 1985–1986 by René Saupin, who was at that time an IGN expert seconded to Amman. On a single sheet, it covers the area from Zurrabah to the Deir plateau and from beyond the Turkmaniyah tomb to the southern part of Jabal an-Nmayr. The position of the monuments (which represent only a fraction of those in Brünnow and Domaszewski's catalogue) is, however, not always exact and

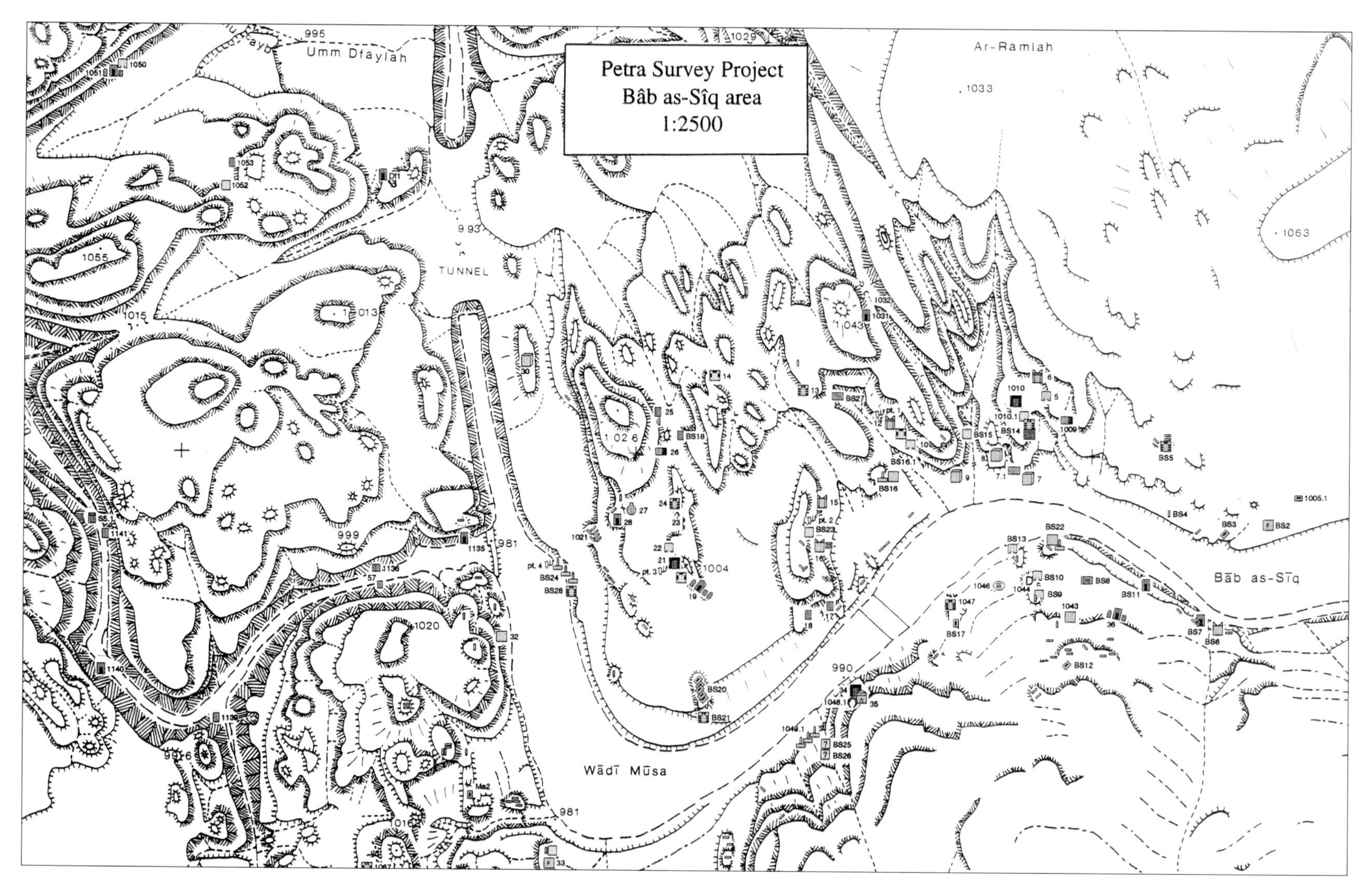

142. Section of Petra Survey Project's map, 1999.

orography is shown only in the lower right corner of the map. It has been used as a basis for the new atlas of Petra, which will include thirteen sheets at 1:2,000 for Petra proper and two at 1:5,000 for the Bayḍā area north of Petra (fig. 142).[25] These new maps have been made through a stereoscopic reinterpretation of the 1974 aerial photographs with the help of several ground surveys. Because of Petra's very unusual type of relief and the main objective of the map—to make it possible to locate and refind every monument—priority was not given to planimetry but to the representation of rocks and hillsides, the main components of the Petra landscape.

Six ground surveys, made between 1988 and 1997 by members of the Equipe de Recherche Associée no. 20 [26] of the Centre National de la Recherche Scientifique (CNRS), complemented the data collected by the IGN mission in 1974. All the monuments were located and described and most of them were photographed. This included *every* visible monument, even the less impressive ones, such as simple rock-cut chambers, not just those in Brünnow and Domaszewski's catalogue. When relevant, the monuments seen during these surveys were identified with those recorded by other archaeologists.[27] The Brünnow and Dalman numbers were retained, the monuments published by the latter, but not the former, being preceded by a "1." All the data collected were then entered on a relational database which includes a complete bibliography on Petra, and the Nabataean, Greek, Latin, and Thamudic inscriptions found there and recorded by J. T. Milik and J. Starcky.

THE RESULTS

The Petra database contains at present 3,197 monuments, the smallest of which is a niche containing a 3-x-6-cm baetyl (Dalman no. 850f) while the largest is the Palace Tomb, 49 x 46 m (Brünnow no. 765). Among these, 894 were recorded by Brünnow, 698 by Dalman and, of these, 230 were recorded by both.[28] Thus, 1,592 monuments, representing almost half of

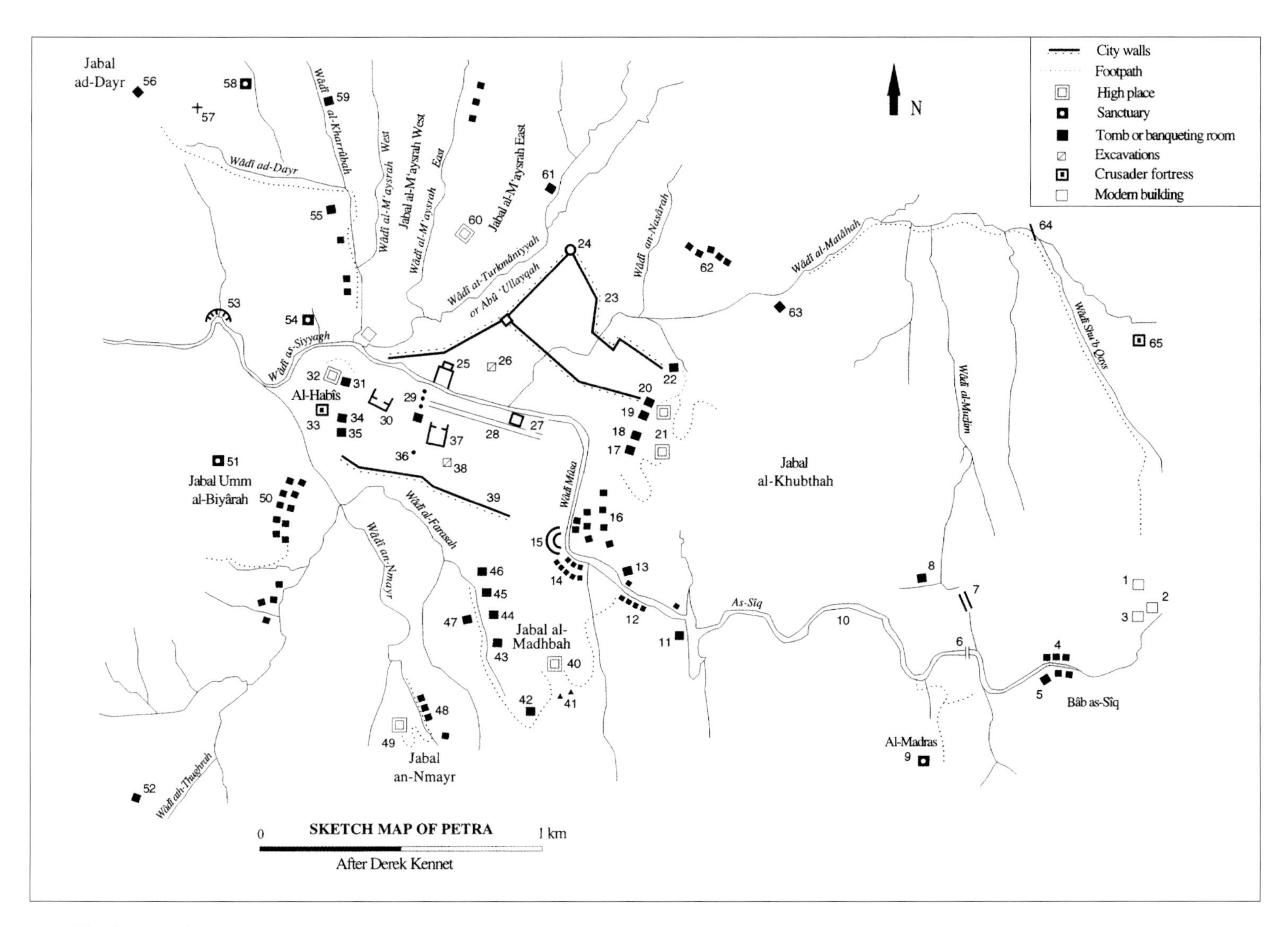

143. Sketch map of Petra.

Key to sketch map of Petra

Numbers preceded by [1] are Dalman nos.
Numbers preceded by a letter are new.

1. Forum Hotel
2. Visitors' Centre
3. Rest House
4. "Sahrîj" tombs, nos. 7-9
5. Obelisk tomb, nos. 34-35
6. Dam, no.29
7. Tunnel, no. 31
8. Eagle niche, no. [1]051
9. Al-Madras sanctuaries
10. The Sîq
11. The Khaznah, no. 62
12. Tomb no. 67
13. Unayshû tomb, no. 813
14. Theater necropolis
15. Theater, no. 161
16. Al-Khubthah necropolis
17. Urn tomb, no. 772
18. Silk tomb, no. 770
19. Corinthian tomb, no. 766
20. Palace tomb, no. 765
21. Al-Khubthah high place, nos. [1]762, [1]769
22. Tomb of Sextius Florentinus, no. 763
23. Nabataean city wall (discontinuous)
24. Conway tower, no. AH13.1
25. Temple of the Winged Lions, no. 422
26. Petra Church (Ridge Church above north), no. QJ1
27. Nymphaeum, no. 416.1
28. Colonnaded Street, no. 404
29. Temenos gate, no. 406
30. Qasr al-Bint, no. 403
31. Museum, no. 400
32. Al-Habîs high place, no. [1]379
33. Al-Habîs fortress, no. [1]371
34. Unfinished tomb, no. 396
35. Columbarium, no. 395
36. Zibb Fir'awn, no. 409
37. Great Temple, no. 410
38. Az-Zantûr excavations, no. Z1
39. Southern city wall
40. Al-Madhbah high place, no. 85.1
41. Al-Madhbah obelisks, nos. 89-90
42. Lion fountain, no. [1]254
43. Garden temple, no. 244
44. Triclinium of the Roman soldier, no. 235
45. Renaissance tomb, no. 229
46. Tomb with the broken pediment, no. 228
47. Tomb of the Roman soldier, no. 239
48. Wâdî an-Nmayr tombs
49. Jabal an-Nmayr high place, no. [1]285
50. Umm al-Biyârah necropolis
51. Umm al-Biyârah sanctuary, no. Byh6
52. Snake monument, no. 302
53. Wâdî as-Siyyagh quarries
54. Isis sanctuary, no. Sy40.1
55. Lions triclinium, no. 452
56. Ad-Dayr, no. 462
57. Christian hermitage, no. 460
58. Qattâr ad-Dayr sanctuary, nos. [1]430-[1]440
59. Urn biclinium, no. 455
60. Al-M'aysrah sanctuaries (or houses), no. [1]527, etc.
61. Qabr at-Turkmân, no. 633
62. Mughr an-Nasarah necropolis
63. Dorotheos house, no. 717
64. Aqueduct
65. Al-Wu'ayrah fortress, no. 851

144

145

146

147

148

149

144. Funerary chamber, no. M227 (al-M'aysrah East), Petra.

145. Domestic chamber, no. Khb137 (foot of al-Khubthah), Petra.

146. Tomb with two rows of crowsteps, no. 581, Petra.

147. Tomb with two half-crowsteps, no. 567, Petra.

148. Cist tomb, no. H 15.1 (Al-Habîs), Petra. Notice the cups for the offerings.

149. The so-called Obodas Chapel, now proved to be a triclinium (no. 290). Petra.

150

151

152

153

154

155

150. Proto-Hegr tomb, no. 472, Petra. Note the pilasters flanking the façade.

151. Hegr tomb, no. 559, Petra. Note the double architrave separated by an attic.

152. Arch tomb, no. 587, Petra.

153. Hellenized tomb, no. 239, Petra.

154. *Nefesh*, no. B125 (Sîq Umm al-'Aldah), Petra.

155. *Môtab*, no. [1] 694, Petra.

156

157

158

159

160

161

156. Altar of sacrifice, no. 85.1, Petra.

157. Small group of niches, no. Byh6 (Umm al-Biyārah), Petra.

158. Niche with more than one baetyl, no. 60.10, Petra.

159. Cistern installed in a cave, no. M 267 (Al-Mʾayṣrah West), Petra.

160. Piriform cistern, no. F38.2 (Al-Farasah West), Petra.

161. Altar in relief, no. [1]251, Petra.

162

163

164

165

162. Roofed triclinium, no. 704, Petra.

163. Open-air triclinium, no. [1]379, Petra.

164. Open-air *stibadium*, no. Ma4 (Al-Madras), Petra.

165. Simple roofed cistern, no. M78 (Al-Mʾayṣrah West), Petra.

the database, had already been recorded by the end of the first decade of the twentieth century. Among the others, 1,376 are new monuments which have neither been published nor, as far as the author is aware, been mentioned in an unpublished work, whereas 229 have been recorded by other archaeologists since Brünnow and Dalman's works. As might be expected, the most prolific of these archaeologists are those who wrote their doctoral dissertations on certain categories of monuments, such as M.-J. Roche in 1985 on the niches and other small cultic monuments,[29] Z. al-Muheisen in 1986 on the cisterns and other hydraulic and agricultural installations,[30] and D. Tarrier in 1988 on triclinia and other types of banqueting rooms.[31] The other archaeologists who either discovered, described or excavated monuments which had not been seen by the early German explorers are: G. & A. Horsfield and M. Lindner[32] (about 30 monuments each); F. Zayadine (14 monuments); P. J. Parr (9 monuments); J. T. Milik and J. Starcky (6 monuments each); I. Browning and Th. Wiegand (4 monuments each); Patricia and Pierre Bikai, N. I. Khairy, B. Kolb,[33] W. H. Morton, and M. Murray (3 monuments each); P. C. Hammond[34] and J. P. Zeitler (2 monuments each). To these can be added Kh. ʿAmr, C.-M. Bennett, H. Merklein, F. Pflüger (1 monument each). Finally, one should not forget P. C. Hammond and M. S. Joukowsky who, although they have excavated monuments previously numbered by Brünnow, have revealed so much more of the Temple of the Winged Lions and the Great Temple respectively, that these can be considered as new discoveries (see Chapters 18 and 19).

The Monuments of Petra The 3,197 monuments of Petra can be subdivided as follows: 1179 rock-cut chambers, 628 monumental tombs, 516 small religious monuments, 188 cisterns, 118 banqueting rooms, 101 shaft tombs, twenty-two wine presses, thirty-four *nefesh*, groups of *nefesh* or niches including a *nefesh*, and seven temples or possible temples.

These represent a total of 2793 monuments. The remaining 404 are divided into numerous categories, each of which comprises a small number of monuments: aqueduct, arch, basin, water channel, caravanserai, church, dam, fort, fountain, gaming-board, wash-basin (forty-three), niches prepared to receive the springer of an arch (eighteen), obelisk, offering cup, quarry, reliefs, artificial rock platform, rock engraving, shelter, staircase, steps to place offerings, track, unidentified building, etc. Finally, there are at least 730 cist or shaft tombs, most of which have been identified only on the aerial photographs and there are certainly many more still to be discovered.

It should always be borne in mind that the figures given above refer only to those monuments that have been given a number in the Petra database. Thus, for instance, there are more *môtabs* in Petra than the three that were recorded as independant monuments by Brünnow or Dalman (*môtabs* can be part of another monument).

Among the 1,179 chambers (figs. 144, 145, 149): 235 are identified as funerary (including ten doubtful cases), because they contain any form of *loculus* or cist-tomb; 550 are identified as domestic (including eighty-four doubtful cases), either because they do not contain any particular installation or because they contain cupboardlike structures; thirty-four are identified as places of worship (including eight doubtful cases), because they contain at least one baetyl, altar, or other religious feature.[34a] Finally, the function of 360 monuments is undetermined because they are too full of sand or debris of various sorts for any internal installation to be seen.

Among the 628 monumental tombs (figs. 146–48, 150–53): ten are either completely detached from the rock or detached on all sides except the back,[35] fifty-nine (including six doubtful cases) have two halves of crowsteps facing each other, 144 (including eight doubtful cases) have one row of crowsteps, 106 (including ten doubtful cases) have two rows of crowsteps, five have either one or two rows of crowsteps (they are badly preserved), seventy (including five doubtful cases) are of the "Proto-Hegra" type, seventy-two (including five doubtful cases) are of the "Hegra" type, forty-six (including two doubtful cases) are of the "arched" type, twenty-eight (including two doubtful cases) are of the "Hellenized" type, seventy-two (including sixteen that might not even be tomb façades) are undetermined, three have a double opening system, that is a shaft and a door, and one is of the obelisk type. The remaining eighteen are façades without any decoration (nine), destroyed tombs (one group), unfinished tombs (seven), and a *colombarium* (one).

Among the 516 small religious monuments (figs. 154–58, 161): three are *môtabs*; twenty-two are either altars of sacrifice, horn altars (either in relief or engraved), or altars without horns; fifteen are independent baetyls; eight are independent groups of two to six baetyls; four are large groups of niches; thirty-one are small groups of niches (roughly from one to ten); 412 are niches which can be subdivided as follows: 234 are empty, 141 contain one baetyl, twenty-seven contain more than one baetyl, three contain a sculpted figure, two contain an altar, one contains another niche, and four are undetermined.

Among the 188 cisterns (figs. 159–60, 165): thirty-one are piriform cisterns; thirty-seven are installed in a cave; sixty are simple cisterns (of which thirty-four are unroofed and twenty are roofed, while the roofing system, if any, is invisible in six of them); twenty-seven are reservoirs with an area of more than forty-eight square meters (of which twenty-two are unroofed and five are roofed); seven are installed behind a dam; seventeen are subterranean; six are of an undetermined type; and in three cases it is doubtful whether they are cisterns.

Finally, among the 118 banqueting rooms (figs. 162–64): six are rooms without benches, the interpretation of which is uncertain; one is simply an open-air bench; five are rooms with one bench; sixteen (including one doubtful case) are roofed triclinia (banqueting places with three benches); forty (including one doubtful case) are open-air triclinia; sixteen (including two doubtful cases) are roofed biclinia (banqueting places with two benches); twelve are open-air biclinia; eighteen are open-air *stibadia* (banqueting places which have the form of a horseshoe); two are roofed *stibadia*; and the purpose of two is unknown. These rooms had one of the following functions: funerary, in which case a meal was shared to honor a deceased person; religious, in which case it was made in honor either of a god or a deified king; or domestic when it was used as such by the inhabitants of a rock-cut house. It is often difficult to identify the exact function of a particular example because of the almost total absence of inscriptions. Thus, only six rooms contain either a dedication or a group of inscriptions, the latter being the signatures of the members of the symposium who met there. Similarly, conclusions drawn from the archaeological context or from the characteristics of the room plan, presence of windows, niches, etc., are very uncertain. It is possible that about forty rooms may have had a religious, twenty-seven a funerary, and twenty-six a domestic function, while the purpose of the others is undetermined.

It has long been assumed that the distribution of the rock-cut monuments on the hills and mountains that surround the monumental center of the city is chaotic and completely unplanned. For instance, the necropoli are *apparently* mixed up with sanctuaries and dwellings. The recording and mapping of all the visible monuments, whether previously

166. End of the processional way leading to the Khubthah High Place, Petra.

known or not, combined with the chronological data given by the inscriptions (when dated), by the stylistic analysis of some of the tombs, and by the excavations, allow us to establish schematically the spatial organization of the site and possibly the main stages of its development in the course of the millennium during which it was inhabited—roughly from the fourth century BC to the sixth–seventh centuries AD.

The Urban Space of Petra The spatial organization of Petra is determined mainly by the distribution of four categories of monuments: cisterns and water-channels, tombs, sanctuaries of all types, and dwellings. To these can be added the crucial question of the two successive lines of city-walls: one discontinuous dating to the Nabataean period, and one continuous from a much later date, possibly the third century AD.

Although at first sight it appears that there are tombs everywhere, a close examination of the archaeological map shows that this is not actually true (fig. 143). There are, in fact, concentrations of tombs in areas that merit the title necropoli. This is clearly the case with the Theater massif, the Wadi Farasah, Rās al-Māgharīq (between Farasah and an-Nmayr), the Umm al-Biyarah cliff, the lower part of Wadi ed-Deir, the two Mᶜayṣrah ridges, Mghār an-Naṣārah, Mghār al-Maṭāḥah and the Khubthah cliff. Most of these lie outside the artificial line drawn by the segments of the early city walls, as described by P. Parr and F. Zayadine.[36] The same, of course, is also true of the two other area in which tombs have been recorded, Bāb as-Sīq and ath-Thughrah. Moreover, these two areas are separated from the city itself, respectively by the Siq and by a section of the caravan track which leaves Petra from the southwest. The two necropoli which, in the Nabataean period, can be considered as lying within the city are those of the Theater and the Khubthah. During the construction of the Theater, some tomb façades were destroyed and only the back walls of their funerary chambers remain as evidence of their existence (figs. 130, 135). As the theater was built some time during the first half of the first century AD,[37] the necropolis was necessarily started earlier. Moreover, although it has been demonstrated that the chronology based on the typology of the Petra façades is groundless,[38] it is still worth noting that most tombs in this necropolis are of the simplest types, façades with one or two rows of crowsteps. It is possible that this necropolis was begun before the limits of the urban space were fixed by the fortifications, i.e., before the first century BC, and that by the time the city developed and the theater was built, at least some of it was abandoned. The Khubthah necropolis should be subdivided into two different sections: north, from the Palace Tomb to the Urn Tomb, and south, from beyond the Urn Tomb to the last tomb recorded by Brünnow and Domaszewski in Petra, no. 831, which is located about 200 m west of the Khazneh. The very few chronological markers available for this necropolis point to its being used during the first or second half of the first century AD. The presence of the northern part of this necropolis could be explained by its exceptional character: All these monumental and elaborate, so-called Royal Tombs, probably belonged to very wealthy notables in Petra who could insist on building their tombs in an area bordering the city (pp. 2–3). This hypothesis is based on the rule which the Nabataeans appear to have followed when they had their tombs built: the monuments had to be seen and the most expensive sites were probably those which looked toward the city and which were visible from a long way away. On the other hand the southern part of this necropolis could perfectly well be considered as lying outside the limits of the inhabited city.

There are about 680 religious monuments in Petra. These include all sorts of niches or groups of niches, baetyls, altars, *môtabs*, etc., to which can be added the rock-cut chambers considered as places of worship, those banqueting places which have a religious function (some of which belong to high places), and the temples. The distribution of these monuments on the site is the result of several factors, such as the topography, the typology of the monuments, the deities to which they were dedicated, and the worshipers who frequented them. The combination of these factors with the analysis of the archaeological map (fig. 143) shows, however, that the real clue to the understanding of the religious space of the Nabataean capital is to be found in a double opposition between a *public* and a *private* space on the one hand, and an *individual* and a *collective* space on the other.

The first type of religious space is public and collective. It consists of both the high places and the temples, the building and the managing of which required the intervention of either the municipal or the royal authorities. There are very few of them in Petra and they certainly attracted worshipers from all over the site. Whether or not the same deities were worshiped in each of these public sanctuaries is still debated and the question will not be answered until new discoveries are made. This type of religious space is thus composed of a center—containing the main temples—from which a series of processional ways radiate towards the high places installed on almost every mountain surrounding the lower city.

The second type of space is private and collective and can be divided into three subcategories:

1. one shared by people living in the same area and including both domestic places of worship and high places installed on terraces of medium altitude;
2. one shared by people worshipping the same deity who could come from various quarters of the site. It is usually

167. Nabataean dwellings in the Wadi aṣ-Ṣiyyagh, Petra.

made up of groups of niches, like the Isis sanctuaries of the Wadi aṣ-Ṣiyyagh and the Wadi Waqīt—the latter located a few kilometers southwest of Petra proper;

3. one shared by people belonging to the same social group such as slaves, women, or persons practicing the same profession, for which we have epigraphic evidence in the form of the signatures of members of symposia carved on the walls of the cave or triclinium in which they met.

The third and last type of space is private and individual and includes what has been defined earlier as "small religious monuments," most of which are carved along processional ways leading to more important sanctuaries or among large groups of niches. In the latter case, each niche may have been the offering of a single individual. This would explain the large variety in their forms, size, and internal decoration.

Excavations by the University of Basel on the Zanṭūr hill south of Wadi Musa have revealed several houses which were inhabited in both the Nabataean and the Roman (i.e., post-106 AD) periods.[39] These excavations have confirmed, if this were needed,[40] that the lower city of Petra contained domestic quarters as well as public and religious buildings. It is highly probable that the majority of the numerous walls which cover the surface of the slopes north and south of Wadi Musa belong to dwellings awaiting excavation. However, these freestanding houses represent only one part of the domestic areas of Petra, and it is not yet clear what proportion of the total it forms. The other parts are located in areas

168. Canalization and dwellings along the Khubthah ridge, Petra.

closer to the cliffs and slopes, where the houses consisted of one or more rock-cut chambers.[41] From the archaeological map it appears that at least three areas were reserved exclusively for dwellings: the west side of al-Ḥabīs, the Wadi aṣ-Ṣiyyagh (fig. 167), and both banks of the lower part of the Wadi ed-Deir. It is probable that it was in these areas, which are situated close to the lower city and could make use of the Ṣiyyagh spring, that the city first expanded. In other parts, such as the Jibal Mᶜayṣrah, the area lying between the Conway Tower and the lower city (ᶜArqūb al-Hīshah), the southern part of Mghār an-Naṣārah, the southwestern part of Jabal al-Khubthah, the northern end of the Theater mount and the northern part of Rās al-Maghārīq, the dwellings are sometimes mixed with tombs. This may represent an extension of the domestic parts of the city into places where tombs had already been installed. Finally, two areas which are not directly in contact with the city proper, the Deir plateau and the northeastern part of the Khubthah cliff, contain almost no tombs (the tomb of the Roman governor, Sextius Florentinus, marks the limit between the domestic quarters, to the north, and the Khubthah necropolis, to the south of it).

In a region where the average annual rainfall is 150 mm, a city of the importance of Petra, with several thousand permanent inhabitants, could not survive without sophisticated and well-maintained water catchment systems. Three such systems were used in combination in order to collect and store as much water as possible to supply the population through the dry season, which is from April to October. The first, which certainly would have required the intervention of the public authorities, used the springs which rise a few kilometers away from the site: Ain Musa to the east (which in modern times produces 500 m3 per day), Ain Brāq to the south (which in modern times produces 20 m3 per day), and Ain Dabdabah to the north (which in modern times produces 60 m3 per day).[42] Thanks to their position at the foot of the limestone plateau, and therefore at a much higher level than Petra itself, and to the presence of sandstone massifs between them and the lower city, their water could easily be conveyed in rock-cut channels to the central basin of Petra. Ain Musa was first channeled to the area of ar-Ramlah, where the water was stored in two large open-air cisterns, and from there through the Wadi Shuᶜb Qays and along the Jabal Khubthah ridge (fig. 168) to the large rock-cut cistern which lies near the Palace Tomb. On the way, it filled several cisterns belonging to dwellings or associated with sanctuaries. Ain Musa also supplied the channels which run along both sides of the Siq, the destination of which has not yet been determined precisely. The cistern at the Palace Tomb was presumably used as a water tower from which the water was redistributed via a network of channels which still need to be traced. The same is probably true of some of the large cisterns of Wadi Farasah, which receive water from the Brāq spring.[43] The Nymphaeum, the possible baths, and the water channels, which have recently come to light during the excavations of the Great Temple,[44] point to the use of some cisterns as water towers in which large quantities of water were stored in order to maintain the level of running water.

The second drainage system is based on the idea that the rain water running on the surface of the rock can be collected in order to fill up a cistern. The rock is thus covered with many incised channels that collect the water over an area the size of which gets larger as the cistern gets bigger. Petra contains dozens of such drainage systems, some of which are still used today by the Bedouin for watering their animals. Their size and importance varies considerably and the larger ones may have been set up and used by more than one family.

The third drainage system and probably the easiest to set up is based on the direct use of the springs which rise inside Petra. These are the Wadi aṣ-Ṣiyyagh and the Wadi Abū ᶜUllayqah springs, both of which have a low flow rate. It is almost certain that those who lived within a radius of a few hundred meters around them came daily to the spring to fill up containers. This would explain the fact that only two cisterns have been found in the Ṣiyyagh area.

The combination of the water-catchment systems established by the city authorities, single families or groups of families, and individuals, gave the inhabitants of Petra, with a minimum of effort, the invaluable luxury of having at their disposal enough water to support pools and gardens.[45]

It is possible to draw a brief and schematic provisional chronology of the development of Petra. We know from the excavations undertaken by P. J. Parr along the colonnaded street that this area was occupied by dwellings from the third to the first centuries BC.[46] There is unfortunately no way of knowing whether or not this occupation was contemporary with the use of the Umm al-Biyārah plateau as a refuge, as reported by Diodorus of Sicily *à propos* of the events which took place at the end of the fourth century BC (*Universal History* XIX, 95, 1–2). During this first period, the tombs were located in the immediate surroundings of the lower city, as is attested by the tomb excavated at the foot of the Khubthah ridge by the Naturhistorische Gesellschaft and by the Department of Antiquities of Jordan[47] and by the numerous cist and shaft tombs cut into the southern part of the Jibal Mᶜayṣrah. During the first century BC, these dwellings were abandoned and an unpaved street was constructed instead. It is probable that this corresponds to the eighteen-meter-wide sand-and-gravel track discovered during the American Center for Oriental Research's excavations around the staircase leading to the Upper Market.[48] As early as the first century BC, the domestic areas extended towards the Wadi aṣ-Ṣiyyagh, al-Ḥabīs and the lower part of the Wadi ed-Deir. They then began to extend to areas previously reserved for tombs, which were consequently abandoned. This is particularly clear in the Wadi ed-Deir and on the Mᶜayṣrah ridges where the spread of the dwellings meant that tombs had to be built further away. This development of the domestic areas of the city continued during the first century AD, which saw the construction of most public buildings. Nor did it end with the Roman annexation of the Nabataean kingdom in 106 AD. Recent excavations and research show that, although it was not the capital of the new *Arabia Provincia*, Petra continued to play an important role both as a political and an urban center.

15 | Carvings in the Desert: The Sculpture of Petra and Khirbet et-Tannur

JUDITH S. MCKENZIE

THE INSPIRATION FOR THIS EXHIBITION arose from the fact that the largest collection of Nabataean sculpture outside Jordan is the architectural sculpture in Cincinnati from the sanctuary at Khirbet et-Tannur, situated on the Kings Highway about seventy kilometers north of Petra. It was excavated in 1937 by Nelson Glueck in conjunction with the Department of Antiquities of Transjordan. In 1939 about half of the pieces were brought back to Cincinnati, where Glueck later became president of the Hebrew Union College. The remainder is in the Jordan Archaeological Museum in Amman, or at the site.

In this chapter we will consider how most of the pieces fitted together in their original setting, and what they meant to the Nabataeans. However, we begin by examining the sculpture from the city of Petra, the capital of the Nabataeans, to provide some context for the richness of the sculptural decoration of this hilltop sanctuary.

THE SCULPTURE AT PETRA

Excavations at Petra during the second half of the twentieth century have revealed it to be far more than a rock-cut necropolis. Rather, it had the same facilities as other classical (Hellenistic and Roman) cities of the living, with tombs carved at its margins. It not only had classical buildings, such as a colonnaded main street, a theater, a baths-building, and a fountain house, but it also had sculpture to adorn these monuments. Like the architecture, this sculpture reflected a combination of local and imported features. Made in a variety of materials, it had the diversity of subject matter and functions which would be expected in such a city.

We will first consider the sculpture from buildings, before looking at the freestanding statues. The main group of sculpture is carved in relief on the monuments, such as the Khazneh, belonging to so-called Group A.[1] This is the earliest group of major monuments at Petra, dating to about the time of Christ and possibly earlier. On the freestanding monuments in this group the sculpture is carved from fine local limestone.[2] These include the Qasr al-Bint (see Chapter 17), the temple at the end of Petra's Colonnaded Street, on which busts of gods, such as the sun god Helios, were used on the metopes of the Doric frieze (fig. 169). Hellenistic influence is visible in the details of it, such as the pronounced frown. The limestone blocks in Group A were carved locally at the site itself, as obviously was the Khazneh. The sculpture on the Khazneh is the subject of a separate essay in this volume (see Chapter 16), and thus will not be discussed here in detail.

An important group of sculptural fragments from architecture is the so-called 1967 Group of Sculpture (named after the year of its publication), which was found near the present Temenos Gate.[3] It was apparently carved for one, or more, earlier buildings on this site, or nearby. This group is important, as it provides information about the variety of subject matter used for Nabataean figured sculpture, as well as an indication of where, on an otherwise lost building or buildings, it was used. It included a number of panels, such as the bust of a veiled woman (fig. 170), as well as gods or goddesses, such as Hermes (Mercury), Athena, Ares (Mars), and Dionysus (fig. 44).[4] These panels, which had frames around them, could have been used on a main entablature, as seen on the Urn Tomb at Petra, where there is a rock-cut panel containing a bust above each of the main pilasters or engaged columns (fig. 125).[5] The corner block with Hermes and Athena on each face is most likely to have come from an entablature. The single panels could, alternatively, have been panels on pilasters, as later used on the Temenos Gate.[6]

Blocks with armor carved on them also survive from the 1967 Group including cuirasses (body armor; fig. 171),

169. Limestone bust of the sun god Helios from the metope of a Doric frieze. Qasr al-Bint, Petra. h: 50 cm. Department of Antiquities, Amman, Jordan.

opposite:
170. Limestone bust of a woman with veil. Area of Temenos Gate, Petra. h: 48 cm. Department of Antiquities, Amman, Jordan.

171. Limestone relief with head of Medusa with the edge of a cuirass. Petra. h: 34 cm. Department of Antiquities, Amman, Jordan.

helmets, shields, and a distinctive Parthian axe .[7] These could have come from an armor frieze like the rock-cut one on Tomb 649, the "Tomb with the Armour."[8] Friezes and panels depicting armor were often used in other cities on monuments, such as triumphal arches.

A large oval shield with a central Medusa head is carved on the front of a half pediment from the 1967 Group. It features Aphrodite (Venus) with a small Cupid (Eros) on the side, and Herakles (Hercules) with his club on the corner.[9] This half pediment would have been one of a pair forming a broken pediment projecting from the face of the lost building, in a similar arrangement to the rock-cut example on the Tomb of the Broken Pediment.[10]

Besides deities and weapons, the sculptures in the 1967 Group also depict more sophisticated subjects, such as the Muses, the classical goddesses who inspired poets and philosophers. One of these Muses holds a dramatic mask of a bearded old man from Greek comedy, but the details of it are rather generalized (fig. 172).[11] There are also other masks carved in fine limestone at Petra, as well as those on the top frieze of the Khazneh (figs. 206–08). The slave mask (now destroyed) on a fine limestone capital that was found near the baths-building is close to the standard masks used on stage, suggesting that it was carved by a sculptor with a firsthand acquaintance with the theater. This is important, as the stone was carved locally. It could have been fashioned by an imported craftsman, perhaps from Alexandria.[12] Alternatively, as stage masks are relatively rare in sculpture in other cities of

172. Limestone bust of a Muse (Melpomene) holding a theater mask. Area of Temenos Gate, Petra. h: 41 cm. Department of Antiquities, Amman, Jordan.

the Near East, their occurrence in Petra could reflect the performance of Greek plays in the theater there (fig. 130).[13]

The sophisticated subject matter for sculpture on buildings is also observed in the Nabataean sculpture of the northernmost Nabataean territory, the Hauran in Syria. This is exemplified by a lintel from Soueïda, now in the Musée du Louvre in Paris, which depicts the famous classical story of the Judgment of Paris (fig. 200). The goddesses Aphrodite, Athena, and Hera asked Paris to choose among them, and they were brought to him by Hermes (Mercury). In this version Zeus has been added to the figures usually depicted in the scene. The participants are arranged in order of importance on a couch (*kline*), with their names given above, in Greek: Paris, Hermes (Mercury), Aphrodite (Venus), Athena, Hera, and Zeus (Jupiter). This lintel is dated to the second century AD.[14] The sculpture of the towns of the Hauran, and the city of Bosra, was carved in the local dark basalt—a very hard stone. Consequently, it has a simpler style that reflects the difficulty of carving it, rather than a lack of sophistication.[15] The subject of the scene on the lintel suggests that perhaps the Nabataeans were acquainted with the story which it depicts.

Petra was also decorated with freestanding sculptures made of imported marble, like any other city of the Mediterranean world in the first and second centuries AD. These included statues of the gods, such as Herakles (Hercules) with his lion skin, found in the theater,[16] and a naked torso of Aphrodite (Venus) (fig. 173).[17] The statue of Herakles was probably erected in a niche in the stage building (the *scenae frons*) of the theater, along with other statues, as occurred in theaters in other cities and towns. The fountain house (*nymphaeum*) on the colonnaded street probably also had similar statues decorating it.

The Nabataean kingdom, of which Petra was the capital, became part of the Roman empire in 106 AD. Its continued importance was reflected in the fact that the Roman governor of the Roman province of Arabia was buried there in about 129 AD. Portrait statues of the imperial family were erected in Petra. This is indicated by the recently discovered, more than life-sized, head of Aelius Caesar, the father of the Roman emperor Lucius Verus (161–169 AD; p. 23, fig. 8).[18] It was carved of imported marble, and reflects the continued affluence of Petra during the second century AD.

Evidence of other portrait sculpture also survives from Petra from the first through third centuries AD. This includes a torso of a man in the traditional Roman attire of a toga, which is carved in marble and of a conventional type also used elsewhere.[19] Another marble example is a standard body

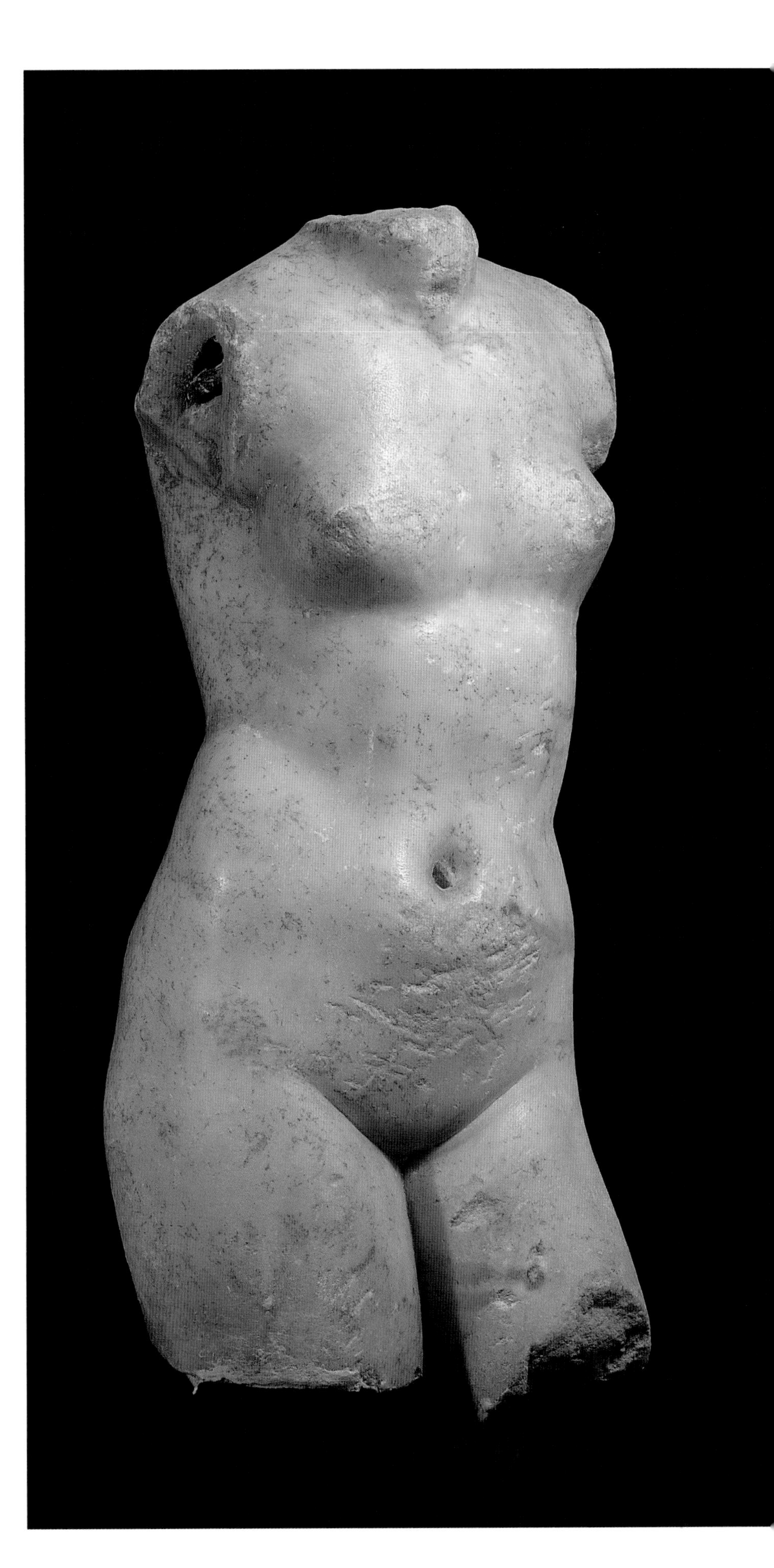

173. Marble torso of Venus/Aphrodite from the Theater, Petra. h: 63.5 cm. Department of Antiquities, Amman, Jordan.

of a woman, wearing a cloak, to which the portrait head would have been attached.[20]

Some of the figures and busts carved in relief on the tomb façades were possibly portraits, which are depicted in the conventional classical dress of a toga or cuirass. These include the soldier wearing a cuirass on the Tomb of the Roman Soldier (fig. 153),[21] the bust in a toga in the central panel inset in the Urn Tomb (fig. 124),[22] and possibly the draped figure on the Obelisk Tomb.[23] Portrait busts are very common on the tombs at Palmyra in Syria,[24] unlike at Petra. They appear there about the middle of the first century AD, about the same time that mummy portraits become common in Egypt.[25] Thus, each place has a local solution to a similar idea, which is a reflection of Roman influence.

Other materials were also used for sculpture at Petra, in addition to limestone, marble, and sandstone. A less-than-life-size bronze figure of a woman in a short tunic was found in Wadi aṣ-Ṣiyyagh, and dated to the second century AD.[26] It was possibly the goddess Artemis, and the running pose suggests it would have been used for decoration (for example, in a garden), rather than as a cult statue.

Sculptures of imported stone include a small statuette of the Egyptian god Osiris from Athribis in Egypt. It is carved in Egyptian style in fine black-green schist.[27] A small classical bust of the Egyptian goddess Isis is made of alabaster, which would have been imported to Petra (fig. 174).[28] Traces of paint survive on her eyes. She is identified as Isis by the distinctive knot in her drapery, between her breasts.

Larger rock-cut representations of Isis were also carved in Petra. On the Khazneh Isis is apparently depicted holding a horn of plenty or cornucopia (fig. 207). Her identity is indicated by the acroterion below her, which bears the solar disk and horns from her crown.[29] The ears of wheat on it refer to the *kore* version of Isis, alluding to her relationship to Persephone and Demeter.

The depiction of the solar disk and horns of Isis crowning Huldu, wife of King Aretas IV, of 5–1 BC suggests that she was deified (like King Obodas). This raises the question whether the Khazneh was a temple-tomb rather than either only a temple or a tomb.[30]

By contrast, Isis is also depicted as a rectangular stone block, or "eye idol," on which she is identified by the solar disk and horns in the center of the wreath.[31] There are many other representations of gods and goddesses as stone blocks at Petra and other Nabataean sites.[32] Atargatis of Hierapolis-Membidj is also depicted as a rock-cut eye idol at Petra, identified by the inscription carved beside her.[33] An eye idol was found in the Temple of the Winged Lions at Petra with an inscription on it mentioning a goddess, but without indicating which one (fig. 246).[34] Consequently, it is sometimes suggested that the Nabataeans only worshipped their gods in this aniconic, or non-human form. However, anthropomorphic cult statues of Isis seated are carved at Petra in the rock face in Wadi aṣ-Ṣiyyagh,[35] and Wadi Abu Ollequa (figs. 45, 46).[36]

The iconographic bilingualism reflected in these representations of Isis, in local and classical form, is also observed at Petra in the heads depicted on some of the tombs with a protective, or apotropaic, function. The weathered bust of the gorgon Medusa is depicted in the segmental pediment of the Tomb of Sextius Florentinus, the Roman governor of Arabia (fig. 126).[37] Classical heads of Medusa are carved at either end of the entablature of the Lion Triclinium,[38] but on Tomb 649 (the "Tomb with the Armor") the head of Humbaba is used in the equivalent position.[39] Humbaba is the Near Eastern equivalent of Medusa. In the Gilgamesh epic Humbaba is the hideous-faced demon whose head was cut off by Gilgamesh and Enkidu. In classical mythology Medusa is the gorgon who was similarly killed by Perseus.[40] Humbaba's head is also depicted at the southern Nabataean site of Madā'in Ṣaliḥ in Saudi Arabia in place of Medusa's head on some tombs, especially in the pediment.[41] This suggests that the Nabataeans knew the relationship between the Near Eastern monster, Humbaba, and the classical equivalent, Medusa.

Similarly, in Alexandria, in a parallel Egyptian and classical scene on a tomb painting we see the apotropaic use of the Egyptian god Bes, with Medusa in the equivalent position below. The decorative schema of these tomb paintings of the late first century AD has classical scenes of Persephone's journey to the underworld depicted below the equivalent Egyptian scenes of the death and resurrection of Osiris.[42]

Thus, the bilingual use of both local and classical iconography was not unique to the Nabataeans. Rather, they kept their local culture, religion, and identity, while at the same time making judicious use of some features from outside. This was not a blind assimilation of classical culture, but a very sophisticated and selective use of it. It is within this context that we will now consider the sculpture of the sanctuary at Khirbet et-Tannur.

RECONSTRUCTION OF THE SANCTUARY AT KHIRBET ET-TANNUR

The sanctuary at Khirbet et-Tannur was approached by a stepped path to the top of the hill (Jebel et-Tannur) on which it stands, above the Wadi el-Hasa. This is the deep gorge which divides biblical Moab to the north from the territory of the

174. Alabaster bust of Isis. Ez-Zantur, Petra. h: 9.5 cm. Department of Antiquities, Amman, Jordan.

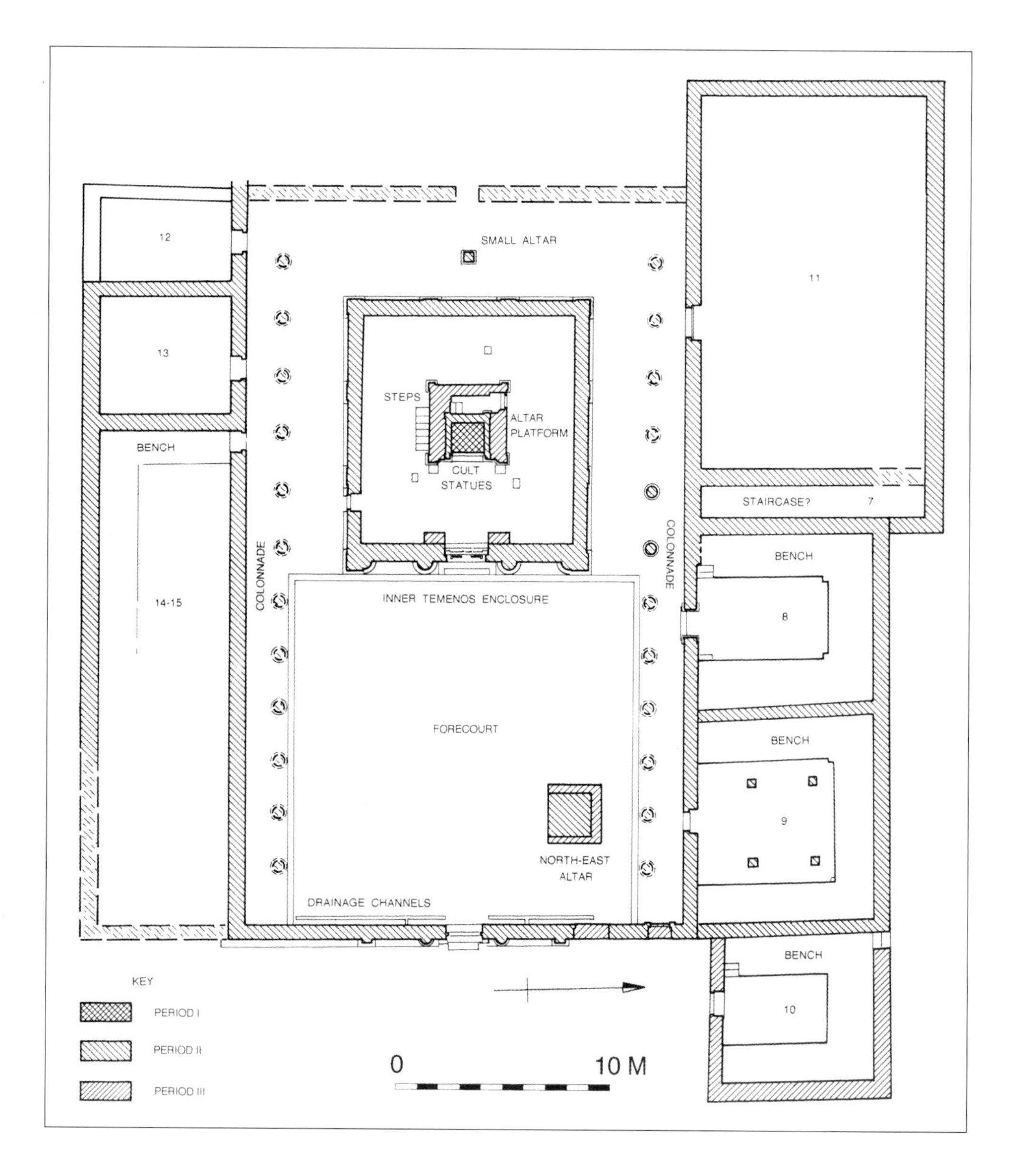

175. Plan of temple complex, Khirbet et-Tannur.

Edomites, the predecessors of the Nabataeans. There is no archaeological evidence of a village beside the sanctuary, indicating its sole function was religious, and suggesting it was a pilgrimage site. The temple complex consisted of a rectangular paved court with a walled enclosure around the altar platform, and rooms along both sides of the court (figs. 175, 76).

The earliest phase (Period I) of the sanctuary consisted of a simple altar. The area around this altar was later paved; then, in the main period of construction of the temple, Period II, a layer was built around three sides of the altar with ornate decoration at the front, and steps at the back (west) side of it. In Period III a further decorated layer was added to this altar, forming a monumental altar platform, with a staircase beginning on the left (south) side of it, for access to the top. The so-called inner temenos enclosure was built in Period II to enclose the altar. The paving on either side of the court around this enclosure does not go as far as the sidewalls of the court. Rather, there was a colonnade along either side of this court, which must have supported a roof covering the beaten earth floor. This colonnade continued along either side of the court in front of the inner temenos enclosure.[43] The center of this court was open because on the eastern side of it inside the front wall, there are drainage channels for rain water. The front of this court was decorated with plain pilasters and engaged columns.

In 1937 the draughtsman, Carl Pape, measured the architectural pieces and moldings in the site. The architect Clarence S. Fisher[44] used these for the architectural reconstruction drawings that were published after his death by Glueck in *Deities and Dolphins* in 1965, nearly three decades after the excavation. There was some confusion of the attribution of the surviving architecture to each of the main periods, resulting in

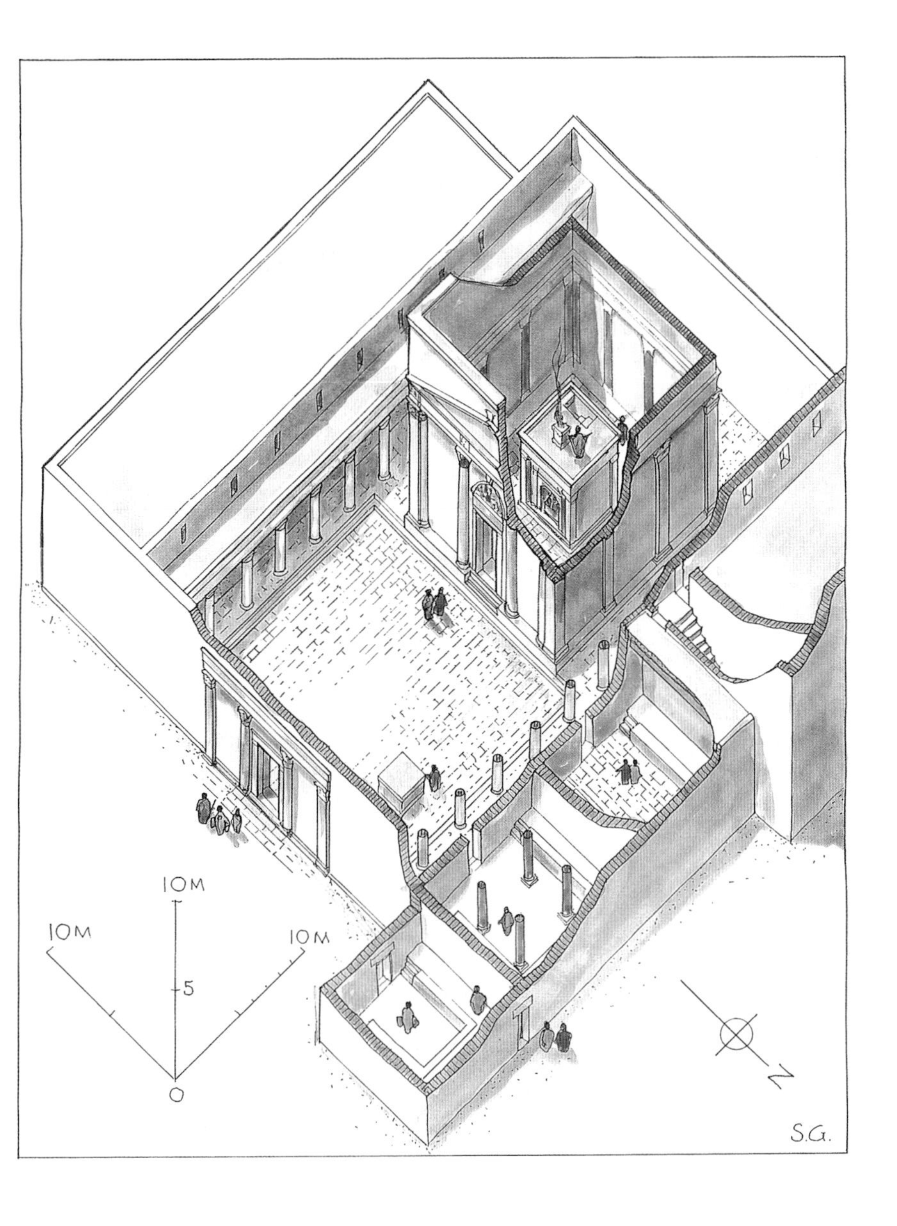

176. Axonometric drawing of temple complex, Khirbet et-Tannur.

some problems with their reconstructions. Recent reexamination of the evidence at the site, and the published record, has resulted in the preparation of the reconstructions reproduced here, which are more consistent with the evidence.[45] These have been confirmed by the records and photographs from Glueck's excavations in the ASOR Nelson Glueck Archive in the Semitic Museum, Harvard University.[46]

As Periods II and III of the altar platform were clearly built one after the other, and each has a distinct style of decoration, they provide important information about the relative chronology and development of the sculpture at Khirbet et-Tannur. Thus, it is necessary to give a brief description of how the main pieces fit together, before discussing what they indicate about the development of Nabataean sculpture. Once this architectural context has been established, it also provides information about the function and meaning of the sculpture.

177. Base of Period II and III altar in situ after excavations, 1937, Khirbet et-Tannur.

178. Reconstructed limestone façade of Period II altar niche, Khirbet et-Tannur. h: 2.54 m. w (at base): 2.36 m. Cincinnati Art Museum, 1939.223.

179. Elevation of Period II altar, Khirbet et-Tannur.

Period II Altar and Inner Temenos Enclosure The Attic base and pilaster up to the lowest block of the floral frieze of the south pilaster of the Period II altar were found in situ (fig. 177).[47] Consequently, it is possible to reconstruct these pilasters with the joining blocks, which formed a niche with the segmental arch, and frieze blocks (fig. 178). The florals on these pilasters and frieze have the same flowers and details. As the capitals from Period II of the altar were not found, those indicated in the reconstruction are hypothetical (fig. 179).[48] The cult statues which this niche framed are discussed below.

The plinth of the inner temenos enclosure survived, indicating the front of it had engaged columns at the center, and quarter columns and pilasters at the corners, and pilasters on the sides and back. These side and back pilasters supported plain Type 1 Nabataean capitals, which are the Nabataean blocked-out version of the floral capitals used on the façade.[49] Fragments of the floral capitals of the façade columns were found fallen in front of it.[50] They had flowers with identical details to those on the friezes of the Period II altar (fig. 178), confirming the attribution of the inner temenos enclosure to Period II. Some blocks of the cornice of the entablature, which these capitals supported, were also found.[51] The corner blocks of the frieze of this entablature have framed panels with busts of gods in them. The north one has a Tyche (Fortune) with a figure with a horn of plenty (cornucopia) at right angles to it,[52] and the south one, Zeus-Hadad (Jupiter) with a Tyche (Fortune) around the corner.[53] The framed bust with a lyre[54] would also have been placed over one of the half columns, in an arrangement similar to that seen on the main entablature of the Urn Tomb at Petra.[55] The relief busts of Helios (fig. 181), Kronos (Saturn), and Zeus-Hadad belong to the frieze of the entablature of the inner temenos enclosure. These busts would have alternated with the series of winged Victories (Nikes) (figs. 180, 183).[56] This is indicated by the main frieze of the temple at Khirbet edh-Dharih, about 7 km south of Khirbet et-Tannur, on which busts of the personifications of the signs of the zodiac alternated with winged Victories (figs. 76–79, 81).[57] The main entablature of the inner temenos enclosure at Khirbet et-Tannur had a pediment above it of which the top block survives at the site,[58] as also occurred on the temple at Khirbet edh-Dharih (figs. 74, 80).

There was an Egyptian cavetto cornice crowning the wall

of the inner temple enclosure.[59] No other details have been added to the upper part (or attic) of the reconstruction, as the pieces have not survived (fig. 180).

The so-called Atargatis panel—the semicircular panel depicting the bust of a veiled goddess surrounded by florals—which was found in the fall of the façade, was placed above the doorway (p. 15, fig. 4).[60] It had a simple cornice around it with an acroterion at either end. Above the panel there was an acroterion with an eagle carved on the front face of it, rather than supported by it as would be expected. The style of the florals on the Atargatis panel is identical to that of the capitals of the façade and on the Period II altar (fig. 178), confirming the attribution of the panel to Period II. Other blocks that apparently belong to Period II include a head with Parthian features,[61] lion's-head architectural ornaments that have similar eyes to the busts, and an eagle wrestling with a serpent (fig. 186).

180. Elevation of façade of inner temple enclosure, Period II, Khirbet et-Tannur.

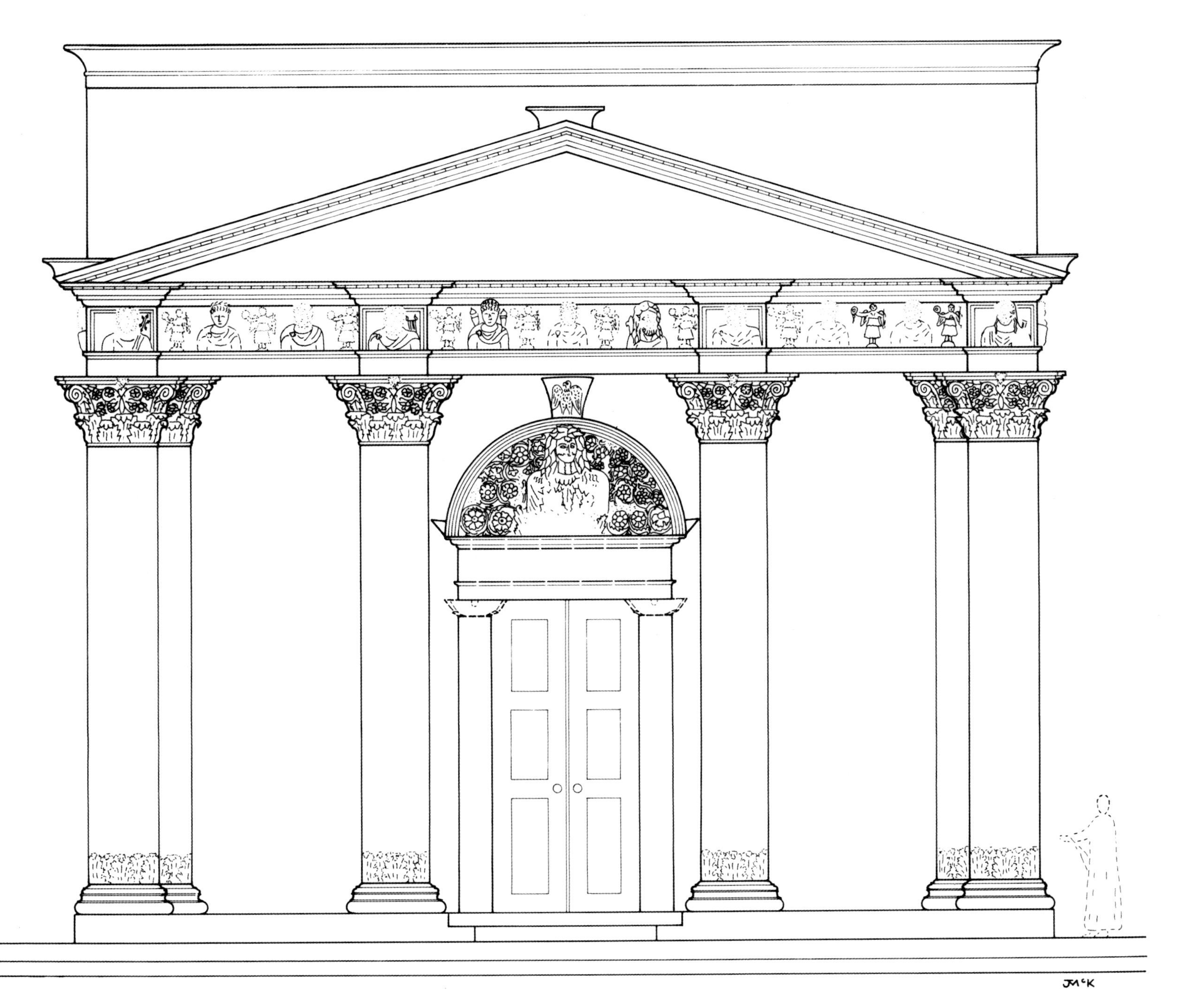

181. Limestone bust of the sun god Helios from main frieze of inner temple enclosure, Period II, Khirbet et-Tannur. h: 55 cm. Cincinnati Art Museum, 1939.225.

182. Limestone bust of Zeus (Jupiter) from main frieze of inner temple enclosure, Period II, Khirbet et-Tannur. h: 53 cm. Cincinnati Art Museum, 1939.213.

183. Limestone relief of a winged Victory (Nike) standing on a globe, Khirbet et-Tannur. h: 54.5 cm. Cincinnati Art Museum, 1939.226.

184. Fragmentary limestone wreathed head, Period II, Khirbet et-Tannur. h: 19.4 cm. Cincinnati Art Museum, 1939.231.

182

184

183

185. Limestone head from a relief sculpture of standing eagle. Area of Temenos Gate, Petra. Department of Antiquities, Amman. Jordan.

186. Limestone sculpture of eagle wrestling with a serpent, Period II, Khirbet et-Tannur. h: 46.1 cm. Cincinnati Art Museum, 1939.222.

187. Limestone pseudo-Doric frieze block with male busts wearing helmets, Period III, Khirbet et-Tannur. h: 26 cm. Department of Antiquities, Amman, Jordan.

Period III As indicated, the Period III altar platform was built around the Period II altar on three sides, leaving the sculptural decoration of Period II still visible at the front (fig. 188). The bases of the Period III corner pilasters and quarter columns were found in situ (fig. 177) so that it was possible to reconstruct them reliably with the joining pieces. These pilasters had a series of busts in medallions decorating them, with the "grain goddess" on the viewer's lower left (fig. 191) and the "fish goddess" on the lower right (fig. 192). The heads of the busts above them have been knocked off.[62] The quarter columns beside these pilasters are decorated with a grape vine rising from a basket of acanthus leaves. The blocks between these quarter columns and the Period II pilasters are decorated with an alternating leaf pattern.[63] Fragments of a floral capital of these pilasters survive.[64] A frieze block with vine decoration is the correct size to have come from the entablature that they would have supported.[65] As the cornice and architrave which would have been used with it have not survived, hypothetical ones are depicted in the reconstruction (fig. 188).

There are two other sets of blocks which may be attributed to Period III, based on stylistic details on them, but whose original location within the building is not clear. The first set belonged to two niches which were framed by pilasters decorated with florals, with a quarter column on the inner side of each. They supported floral capitals with a head in place of the boss on the abacus (fig. 189). Glueck suggested that these blocks formed a small altar placed on the altar platform, but this is not certain.[66]

The second set of pieces which apparently belongs to Period III is the pair of pseudo-Doric frieze blocks from two other niches. In place of the triglyphs, which are typical of a Doric frieze, they have narrow panels with a single groove giving them two vertical bands instead of the conventional three. The busts in the panels at either end of one of these blocks are female,[67] while on the other they are wearing helmets (fig. 187). The details of these busts, such as the faces and carving of the drapery, are close to the busts on the pilasters of the Period III altar platform, and so place them in Period III. In their reconstruction Glueck and Fisher placed these two blocks on the inner temenos enclosure façade. However, as this façade was built in Period II, they would have had to have been inserted into it as part of a later repair, if they did come from it.[68] The details of the hair and flat, stepped drapery on another male bust indicate that it also belonged to Period III (fig. 190).

188. Elevation of Period III altar platform, Khirbet et-Tannur.

190. Limestone fragment of a male bust wearing a wreath, Period III, Khirbet et-Tannur. h: 21.4 cm. Cincinnati Art Museum, 1939.235, 282.

189. Detail of female head on limestone pilaster capital from a niche of Period III, Khirbet et-Tannur. h: 35.4 cm. Cincinnati Art Museum, 1939.250a.

191. Limestone bust of Virgo ("grain goddess"), Period III altar platform, Khirbet et-Tannur. h: 27 cm. Cincinnati Art Museum, 1939.227.

192. Limestone bust of personification of Pisces ("fish goddess"), Period III altar platform, Khirbet et-Tannur. h: 27 cm. Department of Antiquities, Amman, Jordan.

CHRONOLOGY AND ARTISTIC INFLUENCES

As mentioned, Periods II and III at Khirbet et-Tannur provide two distinct phases of the sculpture, with two distinctive styles. The style of Period II is more naturalistic than Period III, which is more stylized. This is most obvious in the drapery, which in Period III is treated as a series of flat stepped surfaces (fig. 191), whereas in Period II it was more naturalistic with gradually contoured folds (fig. 181). Similarly, in Period II the locks of hair are treated as diminishing strands (p. 15, fig. 4), whereas in Period III they are simpler (figs. 191, 192).

The forerunners of the naturalistic style of Period II are seen at Petra in Group A. For example, the furrowed brow of the Helios bust of Period II at Khirbet et-Tannur with the frontal head (fig. 181) can be compared with the one from the Qasr al-Bint at Petra (fig. 169). The latter is more sophisticated, with the head carved in three-quarter view. This difference is also seen in the flowers of Period II at Khirbet et-Tannur on the "Atargatis panel," which are derived from those of Group A at Petra. The latter are more finely carved, often in three-quarter view,[69] whereas those at Khirbet et-Tannur are always depicted either flat or fully frontal (fig. 178; p. 15, fig. 4).

The monument at Petra which is closest to Period II at Khirbet et-Tannur is the Temenos Gate, which has related details such as cornices and flowers.[70] However, the sculpture on the temple at Khirbet edh-Dharih was carved by the same workmen as that of Period II at Khirbet et-Tannur, because the details are so close. These include features such as the moldings, capitals, lions' heads, winged Victories (figs. 183 and 79) and relief busts (figs. 181 and 76).

Consequently, the date of Period II at Khirbet et-Tannur is about the same as the construction of the temple at Khirbet edh-Dharih, and both close in date to the Temenos Gate at Petra.[71] At present, this phase of Khirbet edh-Dharih, which is the subject of scientific excavations by the French, is thought to date to the second half of the first century or first half of the second century AD.[72] Thus, the Period II sculpture at Khirbet et-Tannur reflects developments in Nabataean sculpture occurring elsewhere, nearby at Khirbet edh-Dharih and further away at Petra. These also show continuity of influence of Hellenistic sculpture.

The increasingly simplified and repetitive style of Period III might, at first, be thought to be merely a local simplification with time. However, it in fact reflects stylistic developments which occur elsewhere, although the details are local. This continued assimilation of influences from outside indicates the continuity of a wider artistic awareness. The treatment of the faces in Period III is distinctive, with large eyes, on which the eyebrows join the nose at an acute angle, and a short nose which does not protrude much below the lower eyelid (figs. 191, 192). The enlarged eyes and more frontal treatment of Period III are observed in the second century AD in Syria: in the Hauran, at Palmyra, and at Dura Europos.[73] They also occur in the Late Antique or so-called Coptic sculpture of Egypt,[74] as do other details, such as the simplification of the drapery and hair.

In Period III the flowers and leaves in the friezes are stylized and arranged repetitively so that they fill all the background space of the frieze.[75] This reflects a general trend of such patterns in the East, as observed in Syria[76] and Egypt.[77] This *horror vacui* later becomes characteristic of Islamic art, and is seen in the carved decoration of the façade from the Umayyad palace at Mschatta near Amman, now in Berlin.[78] The conceptual forerunner of this phenomenon is observed in the relief decoration filling the flat areas between the pilasters on the Period III altar platform at Khirbet et-Tannur (fig. 188) and on the temple at Khirbet edh-Dharih (fig. 75). In addition, on the latter the conventions of classical architecture begin to break down, with the Medusa head (in a panel which would traditionally go in the frieze) being placed on the architrave.

Thus, rather than reflecting the local style of a backwater, both of the main periods at Khirbet et-Tannur reflect contemporary developments elsewhere, both in Nabataea and further afield. In the light of this we will now consider the influences on the function and meaning of these sculptures.

193. Sandstone lion throne support and lower garment of cult statue of Atargatis, Period III, Khirbet et-Tannur. h: c. 45 cm. Cincinnati Art Museum, 1939.218a, 278.

194. Limestone beardless head of a youth, Period III, Khirbet et-Tannur. h: 20 cm. Department of Antiquities, Amman, Jordan.

MEANING OF THE SCULPTURE ON THE KHIRBET ET-TANNUR SANCTUARY

The iconography of the sculpture on the sanctuary at Khirbet et-Tannur was examined by Glueck after its discovery,[79] and later by Starcky.[80] In *Deities and Dolphins* Glueck gives a detailed discussion of over 300 pages, with illustrations of comparative examples from across the Mediterranean.[81] Concentration will be placed here on the interpretation of the sculpture, as indicated by its architectural context. We will begin with the cult statues, then consider the busts on the architecture, and finally examine the enigmatic zodiac.

Cult Statues and Decorative Busts of Period II The male cult statue was found by Glueck leaning against the front of the altar platform to the left of the niche which framed it.[82] This statue has the form of Hadad, the Syrian god of heaven, rain, and fertility (p. 58, fig. 40),[83] identified by the bulls on either side of him, and the thunderbolt he is holding. The statue has other Eastern features, such as the twisted torque with lions' heads around his neck. Because some of his features, such as the style of his head, are very similar to that used for the Greek god Zeus, Glueck called him Zeus-Hadad.[84] Zeus is the Greek equivalent of the main Roman male deity, Jupiter, while Baal Shamin ("Lord of Heaven") was a title of Hadad.[85] Unlike the architectural sculpture at the site, which is of local limestone, this cult statue (h. 1.15 m) is carved from sandstone, as are the fragments of a lion of similar size to the bulls on the throne of the cult statue (fig. 193). These fragments would have belonged to the throne of the statue of his consort Atargatis. The remainder of her cult statue has not survived, except for her foot and a lower portion of her garment, but a smaller version of her seated figure did, with a torque around her neck like the statue of Hadad (fig. 195). She is about half the size of the cult statue of Zeus-Hadad, and gives an indication of how her larger cult statue would have looked (fig. 179). These sandstone statues were contemporary with Phase II of the altar, indicating it was built to function as both an altar and a compressed cella.[86]

At the time of their discovery Glueck noted the similarity of the cult statues and sanctuary to those at Hierapolis described by Lucian in the second century AD in *The Syrian Goddess (De dea Syria)*. Lucian's description is worth repeating:

> "The temple faces the rising sun.... A large platform rises above the ground to a height of 12 feet and on this the temple rests....
>
> In the interior, the temple is not a single unit, for a second chamber has been made in it. The entry ramp to it is also short. It is not furnished with doors, but in the front is completely open. All enter the large part of the temple, but into the chamber only priests go... In this chamber are set statues of gods. One is Hera and the other is Zeus, whom, however they call by another name. Both are of gold and both are seated, but lions support Hera, while the god sits on bulls.
>
> The statue of Zeus certainly looks like Zeus in every respect: his head, clothes, throne. Nor will you, even if you want to, liken him to anyone else.
>
> As one looks at Hera, however, she presents many different forms. On the whole, she is certainly Hera, but she also has something of Athena, Aphrodite, Selene, Rhea, Artemis, Nemesis and the Fates. In one hand she holds a sceptre, in the other a spindle. On her head she bears rays and a tower and she wears a girdle with which they adorn only celestial Aphrodite."[87]

Similarly, the cult statues at Khirbet et-Tannur have the iconographical features of classical and Syrian deities, but they are used to represent local Nabataean divinities. The only inscription from Khirbet et-Tannur mentioning a deity is written in Nabataean, but it mentions the Edomite god Qaws (fig. 196).[88] Qaws was the equivalent of the Arab Quzah, god of the sky, who could have been worshiped in the form of Zeus-Hadad. The form of Zeus-Hadad and Atargatis was used at Khirbet et-Tannur to represent the main Nabataean god Dushara and his spouse (who was al-ᶜUzza in Petra and Allat elsewhere).[89]

This cult statue of Dushara (in the form of Zeus-Hadad) is important not only because it is the only complete cult statue found in a Nabataean temple, and nearly in its original position, but also because it is anthropomorphic. As mentioned, it is often assumed that the Nabataeans used only the nonfigured forms of rectangular stone blocks as cult statues. However, other major Nabataean temples apparently also had anthropomorphic cult statues, such as the Qasr al-Bint in Petra and the temple in Wadi Ramm.[90]

In addition to using anthropomorphic forms for cult statues, the Nabataeans also used busts of gods for decoration, as in the temple at Khirbet edh-Dharih, where busts of male personifications of the zodiac decorated the main entablature (figs. 76–78, 81). Panels with busts of deities also decorated the entablature of the inner temenos enclosure at Khirbet et-Tannur. These included Zeus (Jupiter) on the far left and a Tyche (Fortune) on the far right. Other busts from the entablature include the sun god Helios (fig. 181), Kronos (Saturn), and apparently another depiction of Zeus (Jupiter) (fig. 182). Glueck observed that these busts included some of the deities related to the seven planets,[91] an identification that Laurent Tholbecq has now confirmed.[92]

The Khirbet et-Tannur Zodiac The zodiac Tyche, which belongs to Period II, was originally built into a wall, but it is not

195. Limestone statue of Atargatis, Period II, Khirbet et-Tannur. h: 40 cm. Department of Antiquities, Amman, Jordan.

196. Limestone stele with Nabataean inscription mentioning the Edomite god Qaws, Khirbet et-Tannur. h: 38.1 cm. Cincinnati Art Museum, 1939.268.

known where in the complex. This zodiac is unusual for two reasons: because of the order in which the symbols are represented, and because the signs are a mixture of symbols and personifications (fig. 198).[93] These reflect the Nabataeans' sophisticated use of classical iconography for their own purposes.

Usually, when the signs of the zodiac are depicted in a circle they run round it continuously, either in a counterclockwise direction or clockwise, although the month positioned at the top of the circle can vary. However, on the Khirbet et-Tannur zodiac the symbols begin from the top (with March) and run counterclockwise down the left-hand side for the first half of the year; then from September, they return to the top of the circle and run down the right-hand side for the other half of the year. Glueck suggested that this change of direction was to indicate the two halves of the Nabataean calendar: the New Year beginning with spring, and the second half with autumn.[94] It is notable that the sanctuary is oriented due east, so that on the spring and autumn equinoxes the first rays of the rising sun would penetrate the maximum distance into the sanctuary.[95] The small altar on the west was possibly also used on these days, when the sun would have set in alignment with it. Attention may be drawn to Egyptian coffins from the first and second centuries AD, which have the zodiac symbols depicted in a combination of the clockwise and counterclockwise directions.[96]

The signs used on the Khirbet et-Tannur zodiac are

197. Limestone supporting figure of winged Victory (Nike). h: 75 cm. Department of Antiquities, Amman, Jordan.

opposite: **198.** Limestone disk with Tyche (Fortune) framed by zodiac. h: 44.1 cm. Cincinnati Art Museum, 1939.233.

199. Completed statue of winged Victory (Nike) supporting disk with Tyche (Fortune) framed by a zodiac. Original Tyche disk; plaster cast of Nike figure.

unusual because they are a mixture of symbols and busts (fig. 198). The conventional Roman signs and their order can be seen on a sculpture in Rome,[97] in which the symbols run counterclockwise: beginning at the top with the ram for Aries, followed by a bull for Taurus, twins for Gemini, a crab for Cancer, a lion for Leo, the figure of Virgo, the figure of Libra holding scales, a scorpion for Scorpio, a centaur with bow drawn for Sagittarius, a goat (sometimes a goat with a fish's tail) for Capricorn, a water-bearer pouring water for Aquarius, and two fish (facing in opposite directions) for Pisces. These same symbols are also used later in synagogue mosaics, such as the one at Hammat-Tiberias[98] and the simplified version at Beth Alpha.[99]

On the Khirbet et-Tannur zodiac (fig. 198), some of the animal symbols are used, such as the bull, crab, and the lion. The fish face in the same direction as on Egyptian examples,[100] rather than in opposite directions as on Roman ones. They notably also face in the same direction as the lamp with zodiacal symbols found in the excavation of the Temple of the Winged Lions at Petra (fig. 248).[101] On the Khirbet et-Tannur Zodiac, the scorpion, although damaged, is rather similar to the crab. The small size of the panels results in the figures being represented as busts, instead of full-length figures. These include the twins (with pointed helmets, indicating they are probably Castor and Pollux), Virgo with a damaged ear of wheat, Libra with scales above, Sagittarius with an arrow or spear, and the water-carrier pouring water. An unusual feature is the replacement of two of the animals with busts: the ram of Aries and the goat of Capricorn.

Dots have been carefully carved in relief in the background of some of the panels. There are two in Aries, and one in each of Gemini, Leo, and Capricorn. Some panels have no dots, and in the remainder the backgrounds have not survived intact. It is possible that these dots represent planets or stars.

The Khirbet et-Tannur zodiac disk is supported by a winged Victory (Nike), with the bust of a Tyche (Fortune) at the center of the disk (fig. 199). Winged Victories are depicted elsewhere supporting disks containing the bust of a Tyche (Fortune).[102] Some of these other winged Victories are depicted standing on a globe,[103] like some of those at Khirbet et-Tannur (fig. 183). On the aforementioned example in Rome, the zodiac is supported by Atlas in an arrangement similar to the Khirbet et-Tannur sculpture, but with a full-length figure of Jupiter seated at its center. On the Khirbet et-Tannur example there is only space for a bust, and it is of a Tyche (Fortune)(fig. 198). However, she has the crescent moon on her right, as depicted at the center of the mosaic at Beth Shan, which dislays the seasons around its circle.[104]

On the synagogue mosaics the sun god Helios is shown at the center of the zodiac. These zodiacs have the conventional Roman symbols, with those at Beth Alpha and Hammat-Tiberias running counterclockwise, and those at Na'aran[105] running clockwise. Zodiacs were used in temples in many places throughout the Roman realm. However, it is in these synagogue pavements that we see the local continuity of these symbols for the celestial bodies marking the passage of time.

Decorative Busts of Period III When additional decoration was added to the altar platform in Period III, six busts were carved on the pilasters on either side of it. The lowest one on each side has survived intact. The one on the left, the "grain goddess," depicts a goddess with ears of wheat under her veil (fig. 191). The bust on the right, the "fish goddess" or "dolphin goddess," has two fish on her head (fig. 192). These are fish, not simplified dolphins, as they clearly have fish tails.[106] These two busts have traditionally been identified as representing two aspects of Atargatis, in her role as goddess of fertility and as Atargatis-Derketo of Ascalon, who took the form of a fish.[107] However, the keys to the identity of these busts are provided by the unusual order of the symbols on the Khirbet et-Tannur zodiac, and the new discoveries from Khirbet edh-Dharih where, as mentioned, the temple frieze had busts of personified symbols of the zodiac.[108] If we apply the order of the symbols on the Khirbet et-Tannur zodiac to the panels with busts on the Period III altar platform we would expect Virgo with an ear of wheat on the lower left and Pisces on the lower right, where we in fact find them. Thus, the "grain goddess" represents Virgo, and the famous "fish goddess," the personification of Pisces.

Traces of paint were found on the sculptures, so when we visualize the altar platform decoration we need to remember that they would have been brightly colored, not the pale limestone we see today (fig. 188).

From Petra a diverse range of sculpture survives, which served a variety of purposes. Figured sculpture was used to represent both deities and mortals. Portrait sculpture included funerary reliefs of the deceased, and freestanding statues of prominent citizens and the imperial family. Representations of gods and goddesses include decorative busts and cult statues. They are depicted in classical figured form, and also represented as simple stone blocks, or "eye idols." Sculpture was also used on tombs for protective, apotropaic, purposes, as well as decoration. The iconography of these sculptures was chosen by the Nabataeans from a variety of sources reflecting local influences and needs, as well as trends in the wider cultural milieu to which they belonged. The sophistication and rich variety of sculpture results from the Nabataeans' selective use of classical features while at the same time keeping their own distinctive culture and religion.[109]

200. Basalt lintel with participants in the Judgement of Paris. Soueïda, Syria. Musée du Louvre, Paris. A.O. 11077.

16 | The Khazneh

ANDREW STEWART

No visitor to Petra can forget the Khazneh (figs. 201, 203-06). First, the long, dusty walk down the Outer Siq; then the rising anticipation as the rose-red cliffs close in; and finally the breathtaking glimpse of columns, sculptures, and gables as the exit draws near. From Frederic Edwin Church's *El Khasné, Petra* (fig. 114) through George Lucas's *Indiana Jones and the Last Crusade*, this majestic façade has captivated the Western imagination for a century and a half.[1]

In Arabic "khazneh" means "treasury": hence the monument's sadly battered condition. For centuries the local Bedouin believed that an evil Pharaoh's fabulous treasure was hidden in its central rotunda, and tried to liberate it by gunfire. Others objected to its graven images—its wealth of figural sculpture—which they systematically defaced.[2] Yet the Khazneh is neither a treasury nor (as some still maintain) a temple.[3] It is a tomb. It looks like a tomb; is laid out like a tomb; is embellished like a tomb; is furnished with arrangements for tomb-cult (fig. 205); two Nabataean tomb-obelisks rise from its upper pavilions (fig. 201)[4]; a typically Nabataean funerary triclinium is to be found opposite it, across the Siq; and all its friends and neighbors are tombs.

The partisans of treasury and temple have forgotten that for all its uniqueness and beauty, Petra is laid out like a conventional Greco-Roman city. Like Athens or Rome it has a central inhabited area; a High Place; and a city of the dead: *polis*, *akropolis*, and *nekropolis*. As usual in the Greco-Roman world, the latter occupies the city's approaches—the gorges that link it to the outside world. The Khazneh, dramatically located at the heart of the foremost of these approaches, declares itself to be the tomb of tombs, the final resting-place of someone who was both a major player in the city's history and an extraordinarily sophisticated connoisseur as well.

Unfortunately, the Khazneh is uninscribed and no papyri or other texts identify its owner. Yet it was surely the last resting place of a king. Its stunning location apart, the rosettes that prominently embellish the podium of its upper story (figs. 201, 203) were a traditional symbol of Near Eastern royalty, and the eagles that crown it were adopted by the neighboring Ptolemaic kings of Egypt (330-322 BC) as their badge. On Ptolemaic and Nabataean royal coins they are standard reverse devices to the king's own head.[5]

No documentation also means no secure date. Conjectures on this score range from the early first century BC to after the Roman annexation of 106 AD.[6] Strongly indebted to the architecture of Ptolemaic Alexandria, the Khazneh is often ascribed to Alexandrian masons. Its location in this prime spot, which surely would have been snapped up early in the city's life as a royal capital, could even suggest that it was the first of Petra's monumental colonnaded tombs. The

201. The Khazneh, Petra. (A. Stewart)

202. The Propylon or Gateway to the sanctuary of Athena Polias Nikephoros at Pergamon, c. 180 BC.

3:2 ratio of the heights of its two stories, which it shares with the Palace Tomb (fig. 134), was favored by Pergamene architects of the second century BC (fig. 202) and their imitators (Alexandrians included?). In early Roman times, however, this scheme largely gave way to the 1:1 ratio of Petra's Corinthian Tomb and ed-Deir. Furthermore, the Khazneh's Corinthian capitals (figs. 203, 204, 206–08) are best paralleled in the architecture of Augustan Rome (31 BC–14 AD).[7]

Finally, there is the compactness and coherence of the Khazneh's façade (fig. 201); its strong adherence to a single frontal plane; its dominant central axis; its relatively discreet employment of setbacks and voids; its amazingly delicate detailing; and its obvious influence upon other Petran monuments such as the Corinthian Tomb and ed-Deir (figs. 122, 131). All this suggests that it predates the long, sprawling façade of the Palace tomb; the complex, pleonastic Corinthian Tomb; and ed-Deir with its much looser syntax; more emphatic setbacks and voids; disconnected flanking piers in the upper story; and far heavier detailing. In short, the Khazneh is still in touch with classical Greek architecture. It represents the first act of the Hellenistic-Roman baroque, not its later ones, and certainly not its finale.

So of the two current favorites for the Khazneh's patron and eventual occupant—Aretas III Philhellen (reigned c. 85-62 BC) and Aretas IV Philopatris (reigned 9 BC-40 AD)—the second looks like the better candidate. True, Aretas III conquered Damascus; thereby became the first Nabataean to rule Greeks; and programmatically adopted the title of "Philhellen." Yet Aretas IV was responsible for Petra's first extensive program of urbanization, perhaps including its foremost temple, the Qasr al-Bint, and its Roman-style theater. An alternative opinion makes the Khazneh a *heroon* dedicated to the deified King Obodas I (reigned c. 96–85 BC) by Huldu, his descendant and Aretas IV's first wife, but this may raise more problems than it solves.[8]

A Closer Look The Khazneh's rock-cut, two-storied façade (fig. 201) is 24.9 m wide and a breathtaking 38.77 m (127 ft.) high. Its lower story opens onto a shallow vestibule with two side chambers and a stairway that leads to a larger, central one. Both stories and the vestibule are embellished in the Corinthian order and are elaborately decked out with figural sculpture and with animal, vegetable, and other motifs.

The lower story consists of a four-columned, pedimented portico flanked by shallow recesses and two side columns. In each recess, a pedestal supports a life-size, high-relief sculpture of a cloaked, bare-chested man and his horse. These are surely the Dioscuri—the divine twins, Castor and Pollux. The column-capitals (figs. 203, 204) are decorated with poppies and a hanging pine cone at top center. Above the columns, the frieze (fig. 203) bears carinated, high-handled drinking cups or *kantharoi* flanked by griffins and interspersed with spiraling vine-tendrils; a head (now defaced) sits above each corner column. The pediment carries another now-defaced head at center, flanked by more tendrils laden with fruit. Five *akroteria* crown the ensemble (fig. 203). Above the apex of the pediment, tendrils flanked by horns and ears of wheat curl around Isis's sun opposite: **203.** View of the upper story from below. The Khazneh, Petra.

204. Corner capital and entablature of the lower story. The Khazneh, Petra.

205. Offering basin at the entrance to the tomb-chamber. The Khazneh, Petra.

206. Pavilion on upper story, left side. The Khazneh, Petra.

207. Tholos on the upper story. The Khazneh, Petra.

208. Pavilion on upper story, right side. The Khazneh, Petra.

204

205

disk; upon its corners grow more flower-laden tendrils; and upon the consoles over the side columns stride winged felines.

The portico, as mentioned earlier, leads to a vestibule and a set of three rooms. At 11 x 12.5 m square and 10 m high, the central one is huge; the other two are about two-thirds this size. Holes behind the rooms' thresholds for door jambs and bolts show that they were guarded by heavy wooden doors or even bronze ones. The threshold of the central chamber has a basin for libations and a drain cut into it (fig. 205); this drain leads to a pit or *bothros* at the right of the stair. This arrangement smacks strongly of Greek-style mortuary ritual, in which wine was poured into the ground for the ever-thirsty dead during the funeral and at specified intervals thereafter.

The vestibule and doorways are framed by Corinthian pilasters. The capitals of those of the vestibule carry now-defaced heads, and the door frames are further embellished with

206

207

208

ivy, grape, and laurel. Above the lintels of the two side doors sit two sphinxes.[9] The central room has a large niche in its back wall and a smaller one in each side wall, presumably for sarcophagi. Suggestively, our prime candidate, King Aretas IV, had two wives: Huldu, who died in 15/16 AD; and Shaqilat, who replaced her in 18/19 and died in 40 AD, the same year as he.

To return to the exterior, above and behind the portico an attic crowned by thirty-two rosettes and a cornice stretches the full width of the façade and supports the upper story (fig. 203). There, a central rotunda or *tholos* with a conical roof terminates in a massive Corinthian capital and a much-battered stone urn (fig. 201). On each side of this rotunda, a recessed Corinthian colonnade furnishes a link with two projecting pavilions capped by half pediments (figs. 206, 208). Each of this story's nine bays carries high-relief sculpture.

At the front of the rotunda stands a heavily draped woman with a kind of crown on her head, holding a cornucopia in the crook of her left arm and a much-battered object in her lowered right hand (fig. 207). We shall return to her shortly.

On the sides of the rotunda and the fronts and sides of the pavilions dance six women, probably Amazons (figs. 206–08). Dressed in flying cloaks and short, fluttering tunics or *chitoniskoi* that leave one breast bare, they brandish double-bladed axes above their heads. Those at the front (fig. 206, 208) do so with the right hand only, allowing each to carry a flattish, rectangular object, presumably a shield, at waist-level with the left. A feline is still visible on the right-hand one, carved in low relief.

Finally, two very different figures occupy the recesses between the rotunda and the pavilions (fig. 207). Winged and dressed in full-length chitons, they must be Victories or *Nikai*. The left-hand one perhaps stands behind an altar and offers a libation from a dish or *patera* in her right hand.

The friezes of the upper story (figs. 206–08) are as lavishly embellished as their counterparts below. Garlands of laurel, grapes, vine-leaves, pinecones, poppies, pomegranates, and ivy hang between now-defaced heads, some of which are bearded and wear long fillets in their hair that flutter out to either side. Above, four eagles serve as akroteria to the side pavilions, and behind them rise two huge funerary obelisks that disappear grandly and mysteriously into the overhanging cliff (figs. 201, 203).

The Architecture Speaks . . . In our world architectural form is no longer closely aligned with genre and function. Yet everyone still instinctively reads a skyscraper as *the* symbol of corporate America ("for *this* business, the sky's the limit"), and a steeple as signaling the worship of a nobler god. In the ancient world, the link between form and function was more strictly observed, with the result that at first encounter buildings often spoke volumes. And in the ancient Near East, a magnificent tomb constructed in one's prime was among the most eloquent architectural statements one could make.

So what message does the Khazneh send? Although we know little about Nabataean eschatology, the façade's distinctive form and iconography allow us to make some inferences. Purely Greek in style apart from its two crowning obelisks, and dramatically located at the chief point of entry to the city, it signals that its builder and future occupant is steeped in Hellenism, accepting *and promoting* the world's then-dominant culture. Although a non-Greek and thus technically a "barbarian," he is thoroughly civilized: a worthy leader of his people in a Hellenized world and thus good to do business with. Everyone would have got the point.

But there is more, for the Khazneh's façade looks like a Greco-Roman sanctuary seen in bird's-eye view (cf. fig. 209).[10] Since this kind of stacked perspective where "up" equals "back" had been standard both in Greece and in the Near East for centuries, to read the Khazneh thus would have been instinctive for any visitor. The lower story would represent the sanctuary's entrance or *propylon*, and the upper one (fig. 203) its temple and

209. Roman wall painting from Boscoreale, Italy: Sanctuary scene, c. 50 BC. The Metropolitan Museum of Art, New York, MMA 03.14.13.

a framing, P-shaped colonnade or *stoa*. Invented in the third century BC, this temple-stoa combination soon achieved widespread popularity, and is frequently illustrated in first-century Roman painting (fig. 209). At Petra, the recently discovered Great Temple, built in the last quarter of the first century BC and so roughly contemporary with the Khazneh, is of this type.[11]

Yet none of this allows us to resurrect the old identification of the Khazneh as *itself* a temple. (All else apart, no one in the ancient world ever built a two-story temple.) Nor does it show that whoever was buried here was actually deified during his lifetime. The Nabataeans did not consider their kings divine, and Greeks and Romans would never have stooped to worship a "barbarian" princeling. Yet none of them would have had a problem with honoring a great benefactor *like* a god, especially after his death, and many would have been comfortable with actual post-mortem deification. For as Aristotle had famously remarked three centuries earlier, "the constituent parts of honor are sacrifices, memorials in verse or prose, gifts of honor, sanctuaries, front-row seating at public events, tombs, statues, board at state expense" and so on (*Rhetoric* 1. 5. 9, 1361 a28–b2).[12] Notice how the philosopher makes no fundamental distinction between honors allowed to gods and those allowed to men. For since a man's achievements determined the honors he deserved, if he gave his community something that only gods could normally give, then he deserved godlike honors. For this reason, the Greeks had long honored their kings, both alive and dead, with cult. The Nabataeans had deified their own King Obodas I after he died destroying the Seleucid army at Cana in 85 BC. And the emperor Augustus had been widely worshiped as a god during his lifetime and was formally deified by the Senate after his death in 14 AD. As we have seen, at least one scholar would like to identify the Khazneh itself as Obodas's *heroon*.[13]

So as a *representation* of a temple, the Khazneh announces that its patron is worthy of such a dwelling; that he deserves to live like a god in paradise after his death; and that in all probability he will do just that. These ideas need not have been explicitly articulated during the king's lifetime or even after it. For the beauty of this kind of visual symbolism (especially when no inscription names or eulogizes the deceased) is that it allows a decent ambiguity to prevail.

. . . And the Sculpture Answers What of the Khazneh's sculptural program? As noted above, it was designed to speak primarily to Greeks and Romans. Local Nabataeans could in theory have read their own theology and mythology into it, but since their own convictions and visual traditions were strongly aniconic, only the cosmopolitan elite would have had the incentive and visual vocabulary to do so.[14]

Yet everyone could relate to the laurel, grapes, poppies, vine-leaves, pinecones, pomegranates, ivy, wheat, and miscellaneous other fruits and flowers of the capitals, consoles, friezes, pediments, and akroteria (figs. 203, 204, 206–08). For not only did they signal life's renewal after death, but the vines, pinecones, and drinking-cups added a decidedly Dionysiac and festive touch, recalling the ubiquitous funerary triclinia of the Petra necropolis itself. In the East, the vine-clad frieze of the so-called Alexander Sarcophagus (fig. 210), carved three centuries earlier for King Abdalonymos of Sidon (died c. 310 BC), offers an excellent precedent.[15]

210. So-called Alexander Sarcophagus from Sidon, c. 320 BC. Archaeological Museum, Istanbul, Inv. 370.

The rosettes, as remarked earlier, were traditional royal symbols. So too were the guardian eagles, griffins, and felines (lions and panthers), which also appear on the Alexander Sarcophagus (fig. 210). (The eagles—only the stumps of their wings survive—lined its roof-ridge; the griffins flank its central akroteria; and the lions guard the corners of its pediments.) Furthermore, the eagle had the added distinction of being both Zeus/Jupiter's favorite bird—the king of the skies—and the one whose form he took to carry Ganymede off to Olympos. His Nabataean equivalent, Dushara, was even identified with Dionysus and sometimes also with Osiris, the Egyptian god of the dead. Dushara's own mother-cum-consort, al-ʿUzza, equated with Aphrodite and perhaps also Isis, might also be glimpsed in the Isis-disk and horns that crown the pediment (fig. 203).[16]

The disembodied heads are more problematic, being uniformly defaced, but if the bearded ones are Gorgons, these too were traditional apotropaic symbols and protective talismans. Whoever the others were, they must also have spoken first and foremost to Westerners, not locals. The latter, however, could easily have taken them for one or more of their own goddesses, such as al-ʿUzza or Allat—local equivalents of the Atargatis heads that alternate with the eagles on the Alexander Sarcophagus's roof (fig. 210).

This brings us to the figural sculpture proper, where any Westerner would immediately have recognized the two dismounted riders that flank the entrance (fig. 201) as the Dioscuri, Castor and Pollux. These divine twins, one mortal and one immortal, protected travelers on sea and land; accompanied the dead on their journey to the other world; and were much venerated in both Greek and Roman cult. Here at Petra they both ministered to the tomb's occupant and greeted the tired and dusty traveler arriving from the desert—like the camels and their drivers carved on the Siq's left-hand wall as one approaches the Khazneh (p. 69, fig. 49). For the visitor's first glimpse of the tomb's façade is precisely of the right-hand twin, heading west into the city, who turns toward him as he emerges from the Siq.

The figures in the upper story are just as potent. Although early scholars identified the pirouetting, bare-breasted, shield-holding, axe-wielding young women (figs. 203, 206, 208) as Furies or *Erinyes*, images of these discovered in the interim are quite different. Instead, they are surely Amazons. Led by their queen, Myrina, the Libyan branch of this legendary tribe of female warriors had allegedly invaded Egypt, allied with Isis's son Horus, invaded Arabia, and swept through Syria and Turkey all the way to the Aegean. Exotic, bellicose, and invincible, they now guard the tomb from all comers.[17] Meanwhile, in the background (fig. 207), the winged Victories announce success for this enterprise; for the Khazneh's patron and eventual occupant; and for the Nabataean state as a whole.

The woman at center with the cornucopia (fig. 207) is the most controversial of all. She is often identified as Isis, or as a composite Isis-Demeter or Isis-Tyche. Figures of loss and grief *par excellence*, both Isis and Demeter had blighted the earth with perpetual winter: Isis in mourning for her brother and consort Osiris, murdered by Seth; and Demeter for her daughter Persephone, ravished by Hades. But after the two were resurrected, the goddesses joyfully lifted the spell, and so became venerated patrons of life, rebirth, and fertility. Hence, presumably, the cornucopia—an important Nabataean royal symbol. On the coinage, it alternates with the eagle as the preferred reverse motif to the king's head.[18]

In support, scholars have pointed to the emblems of Isis, the sun disk and horns, that crown the pediment below this figure (fig. 203); a photograph of 1897 (when she was in somewhat better condition) showing Isis's trademark U-shaped drapery folds apparently gathered into what looks like a (badly damaged) knot below her throat; Isis's title "Savior of Petra" in a second-century AD Egyptian papyrus; and a coin portrait of Huldu, Aretas IV's first wife, wearing an Isis-crown.[19]

These proposals all have their drawbacks. Isis-Demeter in particular seems a non-starter since Demeter is otherwise unknown in the Nabataean kingdom and outside it never carries a cornucopia at all. Nor can our figure's headdress be Demeter's stumpy, lunate *stephane* and obligatory veil or Isis's high *basileion* (a horned sun disk topped by feathers and/or corn-ears). Medium-sized and resembling a flowerpot, it must be a *polos*, *kalathos*, or *modius*. The first is an Eastern-style crown and the others are basketlike fertility symbols. They are often hard to tell apart, especially when damaged—as here.

Furthermore, Petra's rare images of Isis are always seated and empty-handed (figs. 45, 46); usually she bows her head and cradles it in her right hand, mourning her murdered consort Osiris. Outside Petra she carries a cornucopia only when syncretized with Tyche/Fortuna and holding a steering-oar in her right hand. Yet a steering-oar would be somewhat *de trop* in the desert, and early travelers saw this object very differently, as an offering-dish or *phiale* or a branch or sprig of some kind.

But even so, a combination of Isis-knot, *polos/modius*, and cornucopia would readily identify the bearer as Isis-Tyche—the divine creator, life-giver, protector, deliverer, and Queen of the Universe all rolled into one—whether she carried an oar or *basileion* or not.[20] Standing before her *tholos* and just above the entrance to the tomb-chamber (figs. 201, 203, 204), she would announce that she has delegated "her" Amazons to guard the tomb's royal occupants; that she herself especially favors and protects them; that through them she has signally enhanced Petra's fortunes; and even that they and Nabataean good fortune are indivisible. Once again, these messages are neither mutually exclusive nor spelled out in explicit detail, but left for the discerning spectator to infer.

Looking Forward Justly renowned as Petra's crown jewel, the Khazneh is the most graceful and sophisticated monumental tomb of the Hellenized East. Beside it, the tombs of other Hellenized non-Greek rulers like Simon Maccabee (c. 140 BC) and Antiochos I of Kommagene (c. 40 BC) seem bombastic and coarse.[21] At Petra, it started a tradition of royal and elite monuments among which the Palace Tomb, Corinthian Tomb, and ed-Deir are the most impressive.

Yet the vast majority of Petra's tombs, an astonishing 94 percent, continued to adhere to the native architectural idiom, and an even more amazing 99 percent rejected the Khazneh's figural embellishment.[22] Happy to profit from the Westerner in any way they could, but jealous of their desert heritage, fiercely independent, and resolutely aniconic, the Nabataeans by and large turned their backs on it. So for all the Khazneh's cosmopolitan sophistication, taken in context it actually betrays its patron's idiosyncrasy and his subjects' stubborn independence.

17 | The Qasr al-Bint of Petra

FRANÇOIS LARCHÉ AND FAWZI ZAYADINE

INTRODUCTION AND CHRONOLOGY

FAWZI ZAYADINE

An Introduction to the Temple The Nabataean temple known today as the Qasr al-Bint (from the Arabic *Qasr Bint Fir'aoun* ("Castle of the Daughter of the Pharaoh"), dominates a large paved temenos (c. 180 x 100 m), at the end of Petra's Colonnaded Street. The only built monument still extant (with walls standing to a height of 23 m), it is remarkably situated at the convergence of the main caravan roads leading to the city's center (fig. 211). The tetrastyle vestibule of the temple faces north to the sacrificial altar. This rectangular platform, which measures 10.80 m x 12 m x 2.25 m high, is approached by two flights of steps: the first flight of fifteen steps, which was supported by a vault, leads to a landing, while the second flight of six steps is only of small size and terminates at the top of the altar. The whole monument was revetted with white marble.

A monumental stairway of twenty-seven marble steps, divided in two flights by a landing, provides access to the Qasr al-Bint's vestibule, which was originally framed by four columns *in antis,* now largely gone (fig. 221). The northwest column is the only one to preserve four drums, and no single complete capital has ever been found. The vestibule was originally paved with white marble slabs: this pavement had long ago been previously stripped out and replaced, in its western part, by irregular sandstone flags.

The main gateway to the cella of the Qasr al-Bint (5.65 m wide) is spanned by a lofty arch, access to which was reduced in width to 1.70 m in a later period. A ramp about 1.80 m high, which employed reused column drums, architectural fragments, and marble slabs from the temple, was built in front of the gateway, probably in the Medieval period, to allow the removal of building blocks for the construction of the Crusader castle of al-Habis, called al-Aswît at that time.[1]

In plan, the temple's main hall, or cella, is almost square (27.90 m x 27.62 m) and is set on a podium. Three compartments occupy the rear part of the cella; the middle compartment—the sanctuary's "holy-of-holies"—contained a platform, 1.40 m high, which is accessible by two flights of seven steps located at each corner. This platform originally housed the sacred standing stone, or baetyl, a block 4 feet high (120 cm) by 2 feet wide (60 cm). It was set, according to a Byzantine lexicon, on a base revetted with gold.[2] During excavations of the room, the upper part of a miniature sandstone baetyl of the eye-idol type was found on the floor of the central platform (fig. 212). At Wadi Iram (Ramm), located south of Petra, the baetyls at the spring-sanctuary of Ain al-Shallaleh are identified by Nabataean inscriptions as the goddesses al-ᶜUzza and al-Kutba of Gaia, modern Wadi Musa, at the eastern entrance of Petra (see essay on Nabataean religion by Zayadine in this volume). Al-ᶜUzza is equated with the Greek goddess Aphrodite, as confirmed by an inscription from the island of Cos in the Aegean; a Greek dedication to Aphrodite, dateable to the third century AD, was found in the cella of the Qasr al-Bint.[3] The archives of Babatha, a Jewish woman who lived on the eastern shore of the Dead Sea at the time of the Bar Kochba Revolt in the second century AD, prove that official documents were stored in the temple of Aphrodite.[4] Another Greek inscription from the sanctuary's eastern compartment reveals that Zeus Hypsistos ("Heavenly Zeus"), the equivalent of the Syrian Baal Shamin ("Lord of Heavens"), was also worshipped in the temple.

The two compartments flanking the Qasr al-Bint's central platform had balcony terraces that were supported by two columns *in antis* and were reached by a stairway concealed in walls 3 and 4. In the southeastern compartment [I], the tumble averaged 2.90 m in height and contained a layer of ash about 20 cm thick. This burnt layer resulted, no doubt, from the collapse of the terrace lodged in the south wall, which was originally supported by wooden beams. When the tumble was excavated, seven irregular cists, built with reused stones and marble fragments from small column shafts, were

uncovered in front of the southeastern compartment. Marble stands (fig. 213) decorated with lion heads were included in the cists; these probably supported benches for the meeting of the sacred associations: the *symposia* of thirteen members reported by Strabo (*Geography* 16.4.26). It is remarkable that the floor of this compartment was paved with marble slabs that were inscribed, in some cases, with Greek letters, and had walls that were revetted with a marble dado to a height of 0.70 m. The southwestern compartment is still obstructed by heavy tumble, but the marble step at the entrance was exposed. It is engraved with grooves for the fixing of a balustrade.

The Chronology of the Qasr al-Bint The chronology of the Qasr al-Bint was the subject of contradictory opinions by the various specialists who originally worked at the site. In their early report on the temple, P. J. Parr and G. R. H. Wright dated the monument to the Antonine period, or mid-second century AD. The discovery of an inscription of Aretas IV (9 BC –40 AD) on the benches added to the sanctuary's temenos wall, however, led Parr to revise his earlier dating, and conclude "that the Qasr was constructed no later than the early years of the first century AD, with a generation or so before being more likely."[5]

In a recent review of McKenzie's *The Architecture of Petra*, Parr seems to have distanced himself from his previous opinion, stating that "there was and still is no certain stratigraphic or physical connection between the temenos wall and the

opposite: **211.** General view of the Qasr al-Bint, Petra, looking southwest.

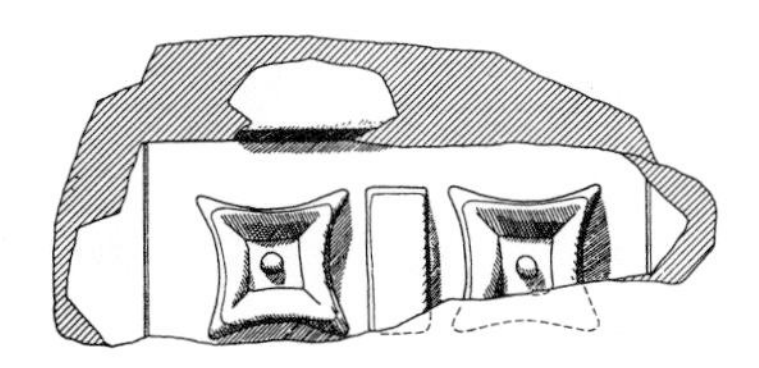

212. Upper part of an eye-idol, discovered on the central platform of the cella. Qasr al-Bint, Petra. Petra Museum.

213. Marble Lion Stand found in the southeast compartment of the Qasr al-Bint, Petra. Petra Museum.

214. The stucco decoration on the south wall of the Qasr al-Bint, Petra.

existing [temple]."[6] However, he observed "that the temenos wall changes direction at a point some 5 m from the Qasr, and then runs southwards, more or less parallel to the flank of the temple." This change of direction makes sense if an important monument existed prior to the temple's construction. On the other hand, a preliminary analysis of the pottery associated with the building of the temple is assigned by him to the early style, dating "from c. 60 BC to c. 25 AD."[7] Yet, Parr is puzzled by the difference between the "design and build of the eastern benches," which are constructed of well-dressed stones, and those of the western row, which are "more-poorly built."[8] His remark that the dedication of the statue of Aretas IV was not the only one in the temenos wall is correct: A marble slab bearing a dedication to Maliku II and his wife Shaqilat (40–70 AD) was found near the arched gate.[9] In my excavation of the southeastern angle of the temenos wall, another dedication to Aretas IV was recovered.[10]

It should be concluded, in this case, that the benches and royal statues were added to the temenos wall at various periods and that the difference in workmanship between the eastern and western benches should not come as any surprise.

Because of its finely dressed blocks the temenos wall is earlier than the benches added to its northern face. The chronology of the Qasr al-Bint can be summarized as follows:

1. An earlier monument, probably a sacred platform, existed before the construction of the Qasr al-Bint. This can be proved by a sounding made in the northeastern angle of the temenos precinct, which brought to light a platform under the temple stairway, the foundation of which contained several reused, well-dressed ashlar blocks originally coated with stucco. This earlier monument, however, could not have been important enough to merit such a magnificent temenos wall.
2. The Qasr al-Bint and the temenos wall, as already noticed by Parr,[11] belong to the same architectural program.
3. As J. McKenzie established, both the Khazneh and the Qasr al-Bint belong to group A, the *terminus ante quem* [date] for which is the early first century BC.[12] Thus, Parr was correct in assuming that the sanctuary was built at least one generation before the dedication of the statue of Aretas IV.
4. Based upon an analysis of the stucco decoration, the sculptures, and the architectural techniques, it is plausible to assign the foundation of the Qasr al-Bint to the reign of the Nabataean king Obodas III (28–9 BC). The final completion of the monument, especially the stucco decoration, however, may be attributed to the early years of Aretas IV (9 BC–40 AD). A subsequent Roman phase, extending from Petra's annexation by Trajan in 106 AD to the late third century AD, is well attested by coins, inscriptions and pottery retrieved from the temple's vestibule and the cella. Recently, a Greek dedication to Marcus Aurelius and Lucius Verus (162–169 AD) was discovered in the excavations of the *exedra* of the Qasr al-Bint, which terminates the sanctuary's temenos wall to the northwest.
5. At the end of the third century AD, the Qasr al-Bint was vandalized and intentionally burned prior to the earthquake of May 19th, 353 AD. This destruction most likely occurred at the time of the Palmyrene revolt (268–272 AD).
6. A Byzantine tomb of the fourth century AD was found outside the temple, along the south wall.
7. Excavation of the Qasr al-Bint's marble stairway revealed evidence for a casual occupation of the sanctuary in the Medieval period, during the twelfth century AD. It was at this time that the ramp which blocked the monumental gateway was probably prepared to remove ashlar stones for the construction of the Crusader castle on al-Habis.

215. The brick decoration of Trajan's Market in Rome.

216. East face of wall 2. Qasr al-Bint, Petra.

The Temple and its Decorative Program It is indeed a surprise for modern visitors to Petra, who marvel at its colorful "[rose-red] rock façades," to learn that the city's monuments and rock-cut tombs were originally covered with colored stucco. As for the Qasr al-Bint, H. Kohl was the first specialist to observe that the "stucco decoration is the most precious element of the whole construction."[13] In 1979, the temple was equipped with wooden scaffoldings in an effort to protect it from serious earth tremors. (An earthquake occurred much later, in 1993, and did not affect Petra.) The scaffoldings thus erected enable architect François Larché to make careful drawings of all of the temple's stucco hole affixes. This patient technical effort resulted in the reconstruction of the entire scheme of stucco decoration which revetted the inner and outer walls of the temple, as summarized (fig. 214) by F. Larché.

The architectural stucco decoration of the Qasr al-Bint can be compared to the brick decoration of Trajan's market in Rome (fig. 215), which, as was suggested, was covered with stucco.[14] Traditionally, it is believed that the architect of Trajan's Market was Apollodoros of Damascus. Lyttleton[15] assumes "that he [Apollodoros] exported this motif to Rome, rather than the example in Petra is a provincial imitation of the architecture of the capital." Even though the tradition of the involvement of Apollodoros in Trajan's Forum cannot be ascertained, it at least points to the strong Oriental influence of Roman decorative techniques, especially from Alexandria. A large amount of architectural stucco was collected in the baths situated south of the monumental gateway of Qasr al-Bint temenos. The dentilled cornices and the painted egg-and-dart motif painted in ochre and black are comparable to the decorative stucco technique of the Alexandrian necropolis.[16] In Palestine, the decorative stucco discovered in the bathhouse of Herod's Palace at Masada is the best parallel to the Petra decoration system.[17] In Rome, the House of Sallust and the vault of the villa near the Farnesina,[18] dated around 10 BC, preserve similar architectural stucco. As outlined above, the Qasr al-Bint temple can be assigned to the second half of the first century BC.

ARCHITECTURAL STUDY OF THE QASR AL-BINT

FRANÇOIS LARCHÉ

The Access Laid on a nearly square podium, this tetrastyle temple *in antis* rises 23 meters above a paved temenos (fig. 220). Located at the convergence of the city's access roads, it is set at the end of the main axis, which terminates at the Temenos Gate.[1] A monumental stairway[2] built against its northern façade constitutes the only access to the vestibule. Its twenty-seven white marble steps (each 16 cm high) are divided into two flights by a landing; the eight steps of the second flight are embedded between six pedestals supporting the bases of four columns and two pilasters. The bases of the sidewalls

217. The southeast corner: wall 2, wall 3. Qasr al-Bint, Petra.

218. The composite entablature crowning the east face of wall 2. Qasr al-Bint, Petra.

219. The southwest corner: west face of wall 4 and south face of wall 3. Qasr al-Bint, Petra.

were faced with marble, as is evident by the dado which remains in place. Along the first step, a drain surmounted by a gutter facilitated the collection of rainwater.

The Podium and its Portico The podium supporting the Qasr al-Bint extends the outer walls of this monument by 3.7 meters in all directions but the north (fig. 221).[3] Its own retaining wall, which is four meters high, does not project beyond the line of the northern face. The eastern sidewall of the stairway, which is inset 39 centimeters from the podium's eastern face, hides the podium's return against the corner pilaster.

The presence of column drums, 69 centimeters in diameter, as well as fragments of Corinthian capitals, bases, and cornices, permit the reconstruction of a low portico, the ceiling beams of which fitted into recesses prepared above the eastern wall's second corbelled course 8.12 meters above the podium. To the south and west, beams could very well have rested upon the corbel without being embedded into walls 3 and 4.

The Decoration under the Portico Between the large corner pilasters, the first three courses form a plinth. On the next two are carved frames spaced seven centimeters apart. The fourth course consists of large, smooth, undecorated stretchers (1.60 x 1.60 m) separated by narrow piles of four courses. These stretchers are framed by a molding carved on the blocks surrounding them. The third course bore the lower part of the frame and the fifth course, the upper part. A row of pedestals is set above. Each pedestal, set plumb with the frame below, has the same width and is similarly spaced at seven-centimeter intervals. The southern wall is decorated with thirteen frames and pedestals, while the eastern and western ones show only eleven. At the northern end the twelfth and thirteenth frames are replaced by a smooth surface—the stuccoed decoration of which has disappeared—which probably marked the northern limit of the low portico.

On the next five courses, a row of twin pilasters, 2.2 meters in height, were stuccoed on the three walls. The last stuccoed pilaster to the north is plumb with the edge of the last pedestal and, thus, of the last frame. The capitals have lost their Corinthian decoration. The entablature is formed of a smooth band capped with a dentil cornice stuccoed on a sandstone corbel. This carved molding also continues on the two corner pilasters of the southern wall. Plumb with each small stuccoed pilaster, the cornice forms a projection together with the band which is no longer smooth but decorated with a framed bust.

On the rear of the Qasr al-Bint's inner sanctum, or *adyton*, these pilasters give way to a representation of a hexastyle kiosk with six fluted half-columns capped with Corinthian capitals. Their architrave is decorated above the intercolumniation with a foliated scroll, while, plumb with each column, its projection shows a human face with loose hair. The middle architrave has been suppressed to give way to a rectangular niche. Between the half-columns, the frieze is decorated with a cupid holding two garlands and, plumb with each column, with a stuccoed projection representing a framed human face. The middle frieze is decorated with two square frames bearing a starry decoration in stucco. The cornice, projecting plumb with the half-columns, is capped with two half-pediments above the side-columns and with a surbased arch above the middle columns. The arch's tympanum and the half-pediments retain traces of foliated scrolls. Above this entablature, the six half-columns are continued by pilasters supporting a dentil cornice, which is level with the cornice capping the twin pilasters but decorated with a different molding. The panels between the half-columns are pierced with numerous binding-holes for stucco, which permit restoration of a pedestal in their lower part. Above, scattered holes served to fix stuccoed decoration, probably depicting human faces rather than easily recognizable

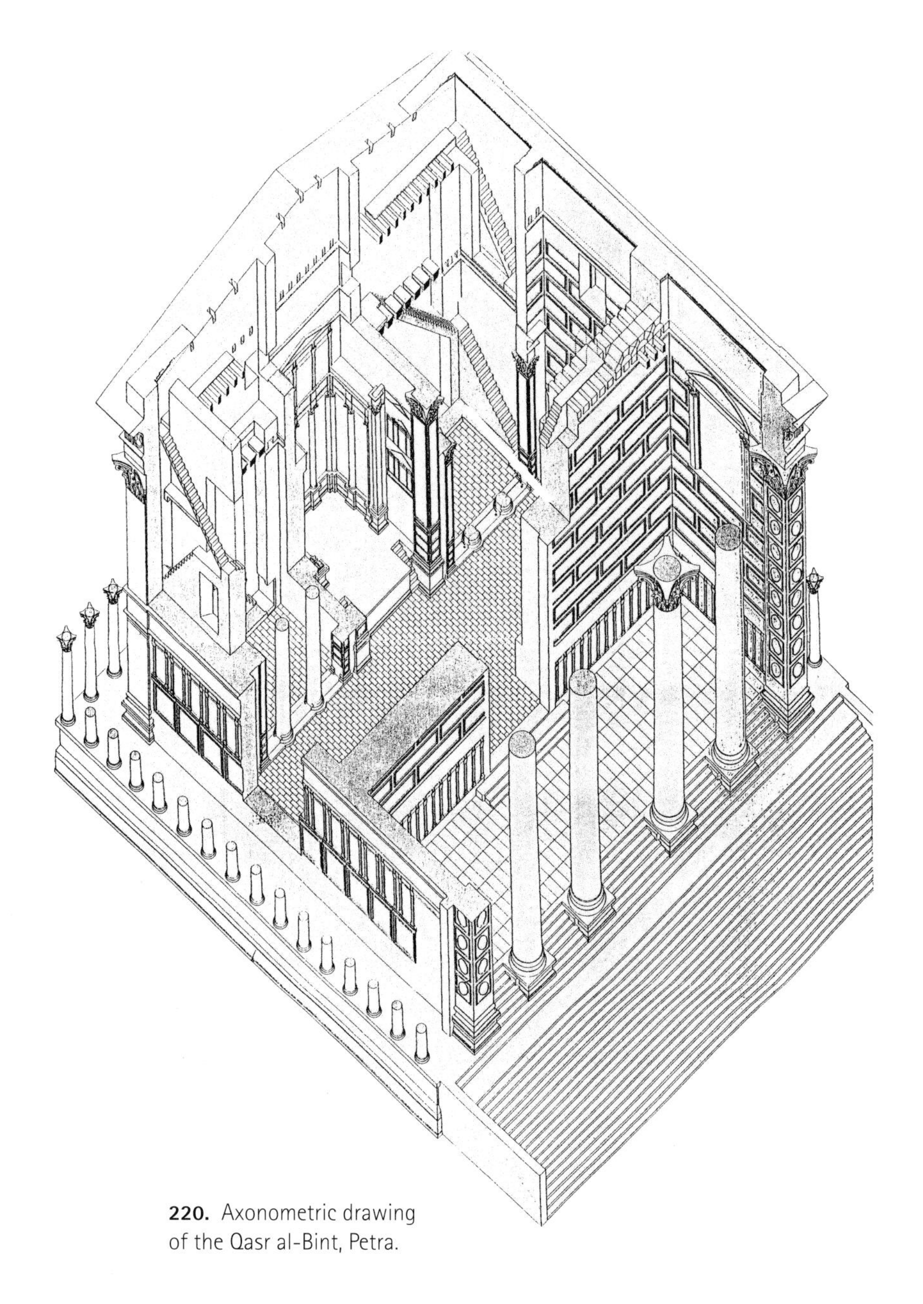

220. Axonometric drawing of the Qasr al-Bint, Petra.

geometrical and floral patterns. As no binding-holes exist at the place of the missing pilasters, the slight thickness of these pilasters suggests that holes were used only to fix protruding stuccoes like those representing human faces.

Above this stuccoed decoration, a register of two courses capped with a second corbel has retained neither stuccoed traces nor binding-holes. One block with a protruding boss, set above the stuccoed kiosk, excludes the restoration proposed by H. Kohl.

The Facings above the Portico Above the portico of the Qasr al-Bint, the wall facings were covered with a smooth, painted coating. The middle of the southern wall, particularly thin at the back of the *adyton*, has been strengthened with a large relieving arch (figs. 217–219).

The temple architecture is emphasized by four corner pilasters, whose bases are set on the podium and whose Corinthian capitals are carved on four courses composed of small blocks of that peculiar yellow sandstone used by Nabataean stone carvers (fig. 220). They support a composite entablature capped with a pediment on the northern and southern sides and showing a projection plumb with each pilaster (fig. 218). The architrave carved on three courses is decorated with two fasciae surmounted by a molding. The Doric frieze rests on the architrave by means of wooden battens set along the outer facing. Triglyphs are formed outward with three courses of headers, while metopes show a contrary disposition: the inner headers are covered with an outer facing. This yellow sandstone facing is carved with medallions showing an irregularly alternating decoration: some are composed of five to six elements of a rosette radiating from a blossom; others assemble four units around a disk decorated with a bust. The strongly protruding cornice is carved on four courses of headers. Two fallen blocks from the southwest and northeast corners show the foot of a pediment which would have crowned the northern and southern sides. The cornice is topped by three courses whose weight counterbalances the cornice projection. The inner facing of the last course is grooved with slots into which the tiles of the roof's lower part fit. The whole system formed a gutter conducting rainwater toward an as yet unidentified sinkhole.

The Northern Façade The Qasr al-Bint's northern façade, which marks the temple's entrance, is composed of four columns *in antis* capped with Corinthian capitals (figs. 220–22). These, in turn, are surmounted by a composite entablature supporting a monumental pediment. The two corner pilasters are stuccoed on their three faces with superimposed frames enclosing, alternatively, a medallion or an octagon. They frame the four columns separating the monumental stairway from the vestibule. Few monolithic drums are still in place. However, the presence of numerous half-drums with the same diameter, fallen within the vestibule, suggests that the upper part of the shaft was made of two coupled half-drums alternating with monolithic ones. Square mortises cut into the shaft form parallel lines, which were used to attach stuccoed frames identical to those decorating the corner pilasters.

Each column is set on a pedestal embedded between the last six steps of the monumental stairway. The lower part of the marble revetment of the eastern pedestal is still in place. Numerous marble fragments permit restoration of molding on the upper part. Complete on its northern face, the pedestal is partially hidden by steps on the sides, which are grooved with slots to allow the fitting of a railing. No southern face exists, since the base of the column is directly set onto the vestibule pavement.

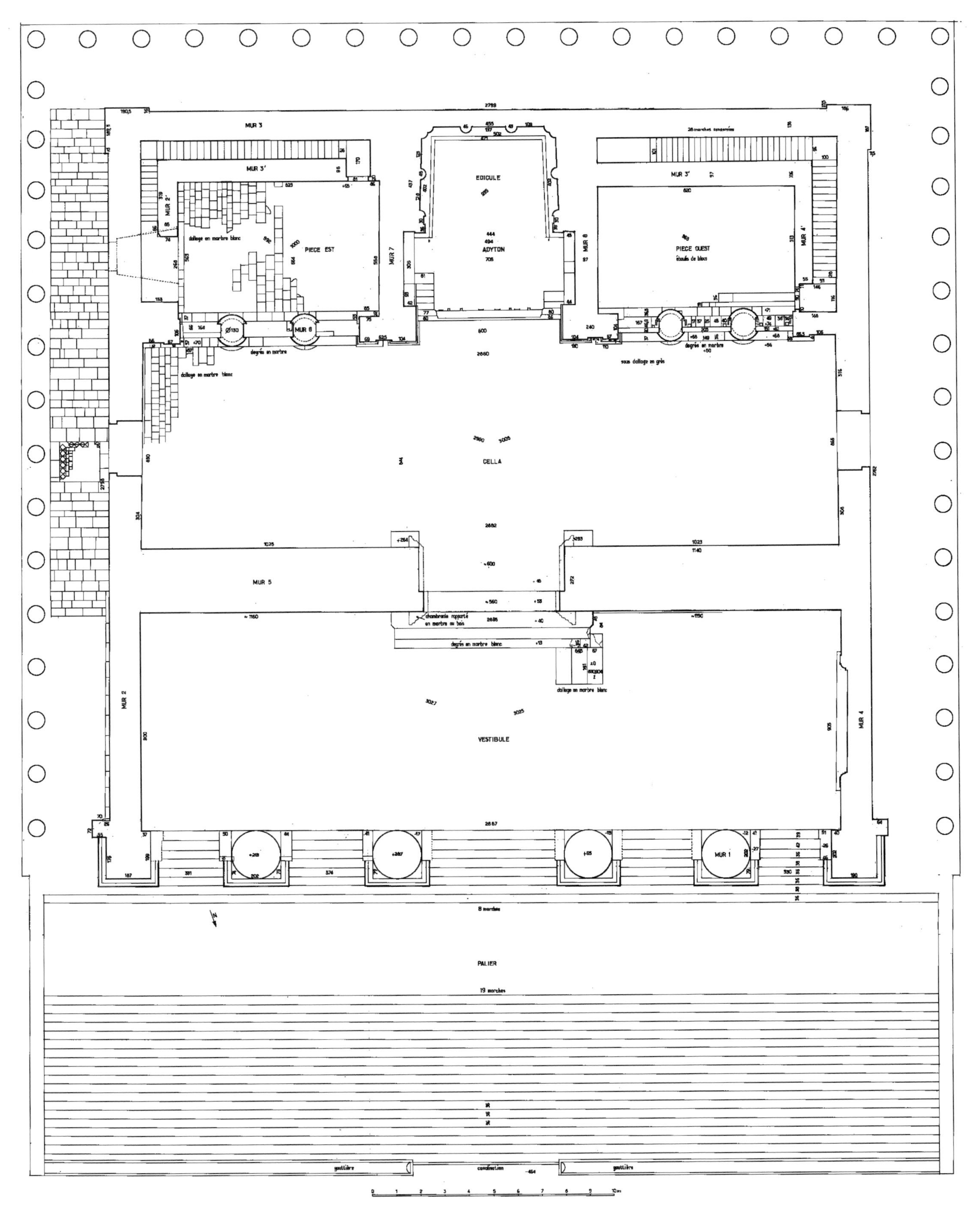

221. Plan of the Qasr al-Bint, Petra.

222. North face of wall 1 restored. Qasr al-Bint, Petra.

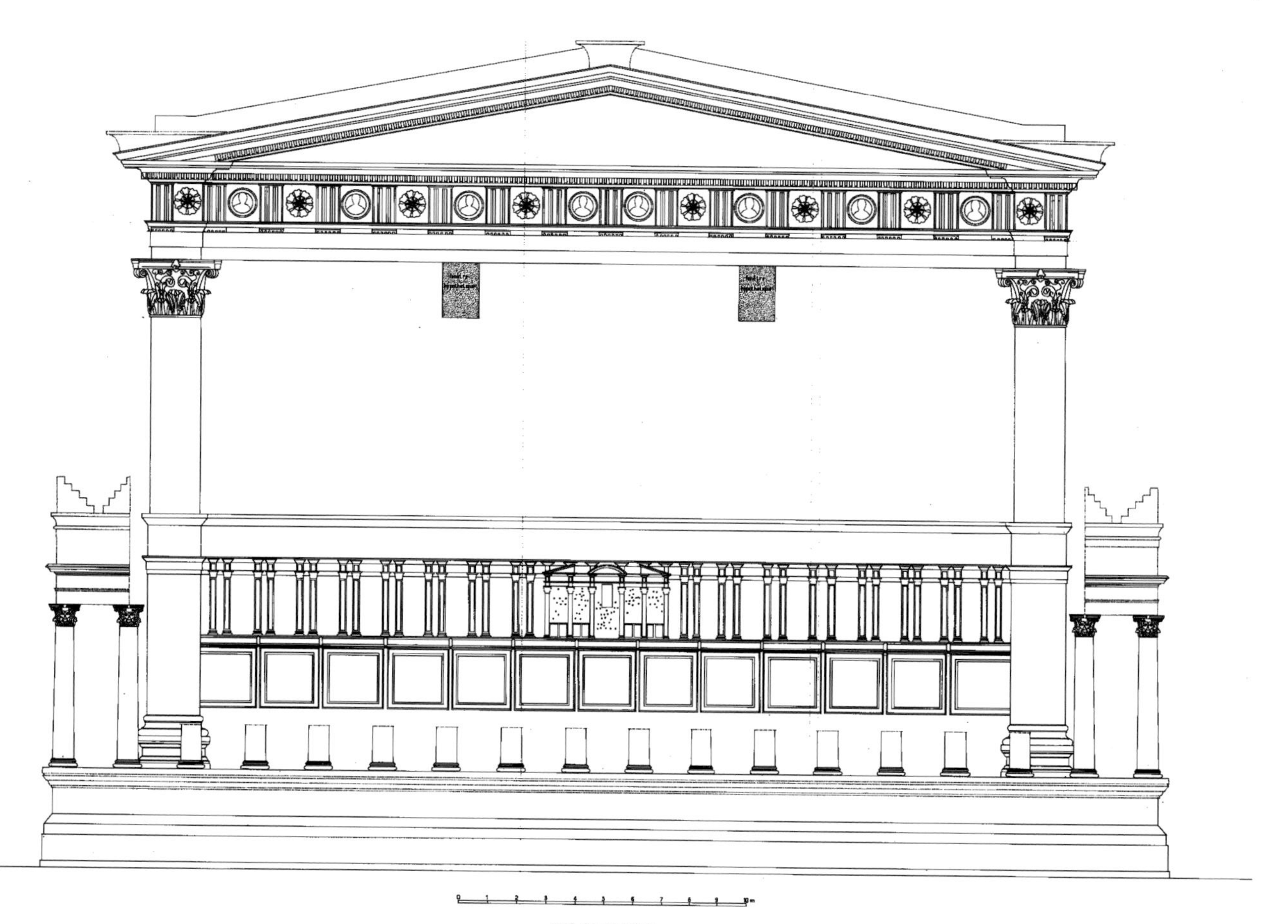

223. South face of wall 3 restored. Qasr al-Bint, Petra.

The first drum possesses no base molding but presents a slight protuberance at the pedestal level. Although none has been found, it is likely that segments of molded marble, set on the pedestal, have been applied around the first drum. An identical system is still visible in the Temple of the Winged Lions.

The spacing of the four columns is not equal and diminishes from the center to the sides. These irregular intervals complicate the restoration of the frieze. No fragments of capital, architrave, or frieze were identified, although numerous pieces of the cornice were stored around the altar.

The breaking-strength of Petra sandstone is insufficient to allow for long architraves to span the intercolumniation. As no architrave of a tougher stone has been discovered, it is likely that the technique used to span the large gate linking the vestibule to the cella, as well as to cover the colonnade of the side-rooms, had been used here, too: architraves composed of wooden beams or joggled sandstone blocks joined in a flat arch. Five arches made of sandstone voussoirs (on the extrados of which the cornice rested) could have been built between the capitals to replace the bearing function of the architraves and to support the pediment weight. A carved or stuccoed wooden revetment, hiding this succession of arches, would then have given the appearance of the entablature of the other walls. The restoration of a pediment is the most orthodox, although the kiosk stuccoed under the portico of the southern wall might reflect an image of the northern façade.

The Vestibule The four columns *in antis* of the Qasr al-Bint's façade form the northern side of the temple's vestibule (fig. 222). Its two small eastern and western sides are blind, while its southern long one is pierced with a monumental gate opening onto the cella.

The southwest corner of the Qasr al-Bint's vestibule is well preserved up to the corbelled course. Its small west side is distinguished from the east by a large niche set 9.75 meters above the pavement (figs. 211, 221, 227). It is framed by a surround, each jamb of which is carved with a pilaster coupled to a quarter-column and topped with a capital. The missing entablature could have been composed of an architrave capped with a surbase arch. The rear of the niche preserves traces of decoration: below, a smooth coating of stucco is separated from the higher part by a timber framing. The courses above the framing are pierced with numerous binding-holes whose horizontal alignments do not permit restoration of the decoration.

The highly damaged jambs of the monumental gate show no projection of the surround. The holes binding the stuccoed decoration extend to within fifty centimeters of the gate reveals; the poor condition of these holes does not allow one to verify whether they extended as far as the reveals. However, this interval of fifty centimeters, now devoid of evidence, is insufficient to have allowed for the carving of a surround proportional to the gate dimensions. Only the hypothesis of a marble covering, applied to the reveals with a 50-centimeter return on the facing of wall 5, allows for the restoration of a molding wide enough for a surround of suitable height.

A course of corbelling crowns the vestibule walls and underlines the ceiling beams. Above this course, wall 5 is preserved on five courses, the first three of which form a row of nineteen cases. Each case is framed by two square blocks set on the corbel and linked by an arch of five voussoirs. In the middle of each case, a third square block, also set on the corbel, supports a half-drum-shaped block which is embedded under the arch and which covers two small niches (25 cm in length and 47 cm in height) cut on each side of the square block on which it is set. Some retain an impression and charred fragments of a wooden beam in the filling mortar. Thirty-eight beams linked the northern façade to wall 5, nine meters distant (figs. 220, 224). The vaulted cases supporting the weight of the upper courses and roof prevented the beam's embedded end from being crushed. Thirty-eight identical niches would have existed in the northern façade's entablature to receive the other ends of the beams.

White marble pavement of thin slabs covered a sandstone pavement which is still in place. Two white marble steps permitted ascent from the vestibule to the threshold of the monumental gate. A marble plinth, still in place west of the gate, was applied against the lower part of the wall, as indicated by a horizontal line of binding-holes containing traces of metallic bolts.

Above, holes were used to fix stuccoes probably representing a row of simple pilasters capped with an entablature, as underneath the roofed portico. Higher up, the better preserved stuccoes are located in the southeast corner of the vestibule. Horizontally aligned holes extending to a stucco fragment of dentil cornice permit continuation of this cornice along the three walls of the vestibule.

Higher up, at a height of eleven meters, large binding-holes are aligned in eighteen horizontal lines and four vertical ones. In the southwest corner, the fragments of frame moldings that are covering these holes are the remains of nine rows of long horizontal frames set in staggered rows and spaced out at intervals of thirty centimeters. In the corners are superposed, in turn, either the vertical molding terminating a complete frame or the folding of a frame whose two halves follow the corner of the wall. These corner frames are supported by small caryatids perched on a kind of stem. The interiors of the frame are pierced with numerous stucco binding-holes on which one fragment of a drapery is still visible. Their repetitive layout suggests groups of figures. The only comparable example known is the façade of the temple at Khirbet edh-Dharih, where long horizontal frames laid in staggered rows are carved in limestone. Their inner frame is decorated with mythological scenes alternating with geometrical and floral patterns[4] (see Chapter 7).

On either side of the monumental gate, the superposed frames were alternatively complete or half-severed. These half frames would have abutted the lost marble reveal. On the short west side, the large niche interrupts the staggered layout of the frames, which are terminated either by their vertical molding or by the niche.

Finally, under the corbelled course underlining the ceiling beams, the space crowning the walls of the vestibule is pierced by numerous binding-holes which were used to hang large, stuccoed, foliated scrolls.

The Monumental Gate Separating the vestibule from the cella (fig. 211), the wall containing the monumental gate of the Qasr al-Bint is much thicker than the sanctuary's outer walls. The position of the lintel shows that its ends were embedded 80 centimeters above each jamb. Sandstone could not be used to cover a seven-meter span. As no fragment of a lintel carved in a harder stone has been found, it is possible to restore it in wood or joggled sandstone blocks combined in a flat arch.

The split arch relieving this lintel of the weight of the upper part, and therefore of the roof, is still in place towards the cella. It rests on two springers that not only rest on the lintel but are partly embedded in the courses. Sixteen voussoirs supported by these two springers form an arch, whose top is tangential to the corbelled course underlining the ceiling beams.

On each side, the space within the split arch contains two narrow stairways descending from the level of the beams to that of the lost lintel. They are perhaps linked to the double-door operation. In the cella, two low walls extending the lower part of the jambs could have been used as abutment for this double door.

The Cella After climbing three white marble steps, the topmost of which serves as the gate threshold, the visitor reaches the cella of the Qasr al-Bint. Its pavement, preserved in places, is made of thin, white marble slabs set on a sandstone pavement. The base of the walls was covered by a gray marble plinth, whose single surviving fragment is still visible in the southeast corner.

The cella is lit by two windows situated in the axis of the short sides under the corbelled course underlining the ceiling beams (figs. 226, 227). A shutter was installed, since a tread is carved in the reveals. The absence of vertical lines of binding-holes for stucco along the reveals shows that no vertical molded frame was provided. The wall thickness suggests that their lost lintels were made of two adjoining blocks: outwardly the lintel was molded as an architrave, while inwardly the inward counter-lintel belonged to the corbelled course.

As in the vestibule, thirty-eight wooden beams supporting the ceiling were embedded in cases built in walls 5 and 6, which are situated 8.44 meters apart from each other (fig. 225). In wall 5, their structure visible above the corbel is less elaborate than that of the vaulted cases previously described in the vestibule. Each case is delineated below by the corbelled course, on each side by a square block, and above by a kind of lintel covering a pair of cases. In wall 6, the tearing out of the first eastern beam is evidenced in the preserved mortar. The corbelling on the short sides is capped by two thin courses (B) applied against the frieze headers and molded like a wooden beam. Over the cases, the upper courses present two openings covered by an arch. These two openings, which do not cross the wall, provide access to two stairways descending to the lintel over the gate.

Plotting of the binding-holes makes it possible to restore a decoration very similar to that of the vestibule. At a height of 1.5 meters above the pavement, a horizontal line of holes marks the bottom of the stuccoed decoration above the plinth. Above, a new horizontal line of holes prevents restoration of a row of pilasters like the one in the vestibule. Finally, at a height of 4.4 meters above the pavement, circular patterns of holes surrounding smaller ones suggest the presence of busts. Four medallions, each decorated with a bust, can be restored on each of the short sides (figs. 226, 227), while five medallions are visible on either side of the gate. Between medallions, holes form unidentified symmetrical figures. A dentil cornice, set under the frames of the vestibule, does not seem to have existed in the cella. Over the remainder of the elevation of the Qasr al-Bint's cella walls, binding-holes permit restoration of the system of long frames in staggered rows. As in the vestibule, the binding-holes of the frames extend too near the gate reveals to allow for a door frame carved in sandstone. The marble revetment proposed as a door frame in the vestibule (fig. 224) may also have existed in the cella. The facing of the gate's relieving arch and its surrounding courses are pierced with binding-holes revealing that a stuccoed decoration extended above the gate (fig. 225). The placement of these holes permits the restoration of four medallions, each decorated with a bust and surrounded by unidentified, possibly winged, symmetrical figures.

The cella of the Qasr al-Bint opens onto the sanctuary's central *adyton* by means of a wide passage built between two corner pilasters (figs. 220, 225, 228), and onto its two side rooms by way of two columns *in antis*, whose intact capitals and cornices make it possible to measure its height. Numerous blocks pierced with binding-holes, fallen within the cella, can belong only to the upper part of wall 6, where, on each side of the passage, they formed the courses between the

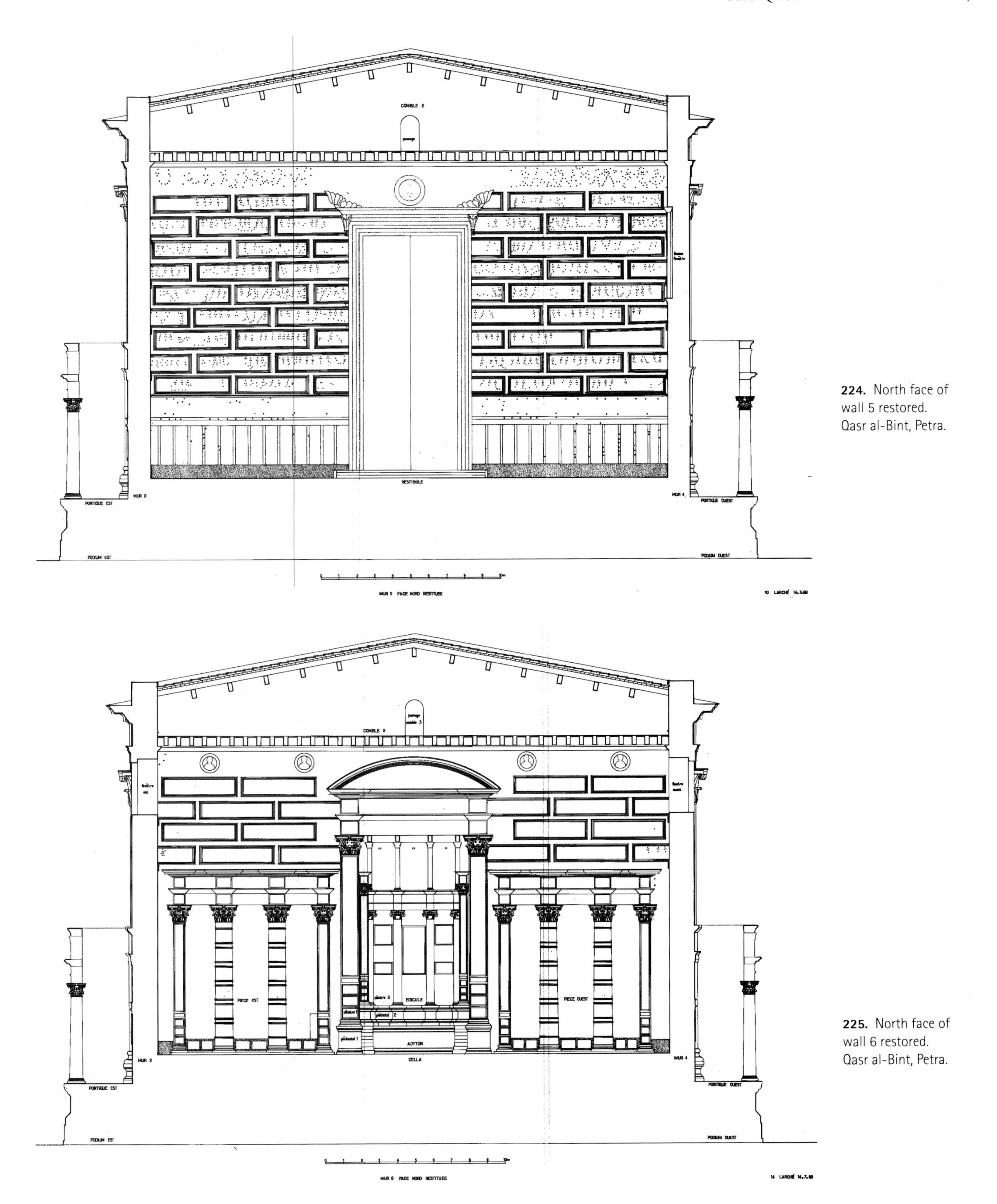

224. North face of wall 5 restored. Qasr al-Bint, Petra.

225. North face of wall 6 restored. Qasr al-Bint, Petra.

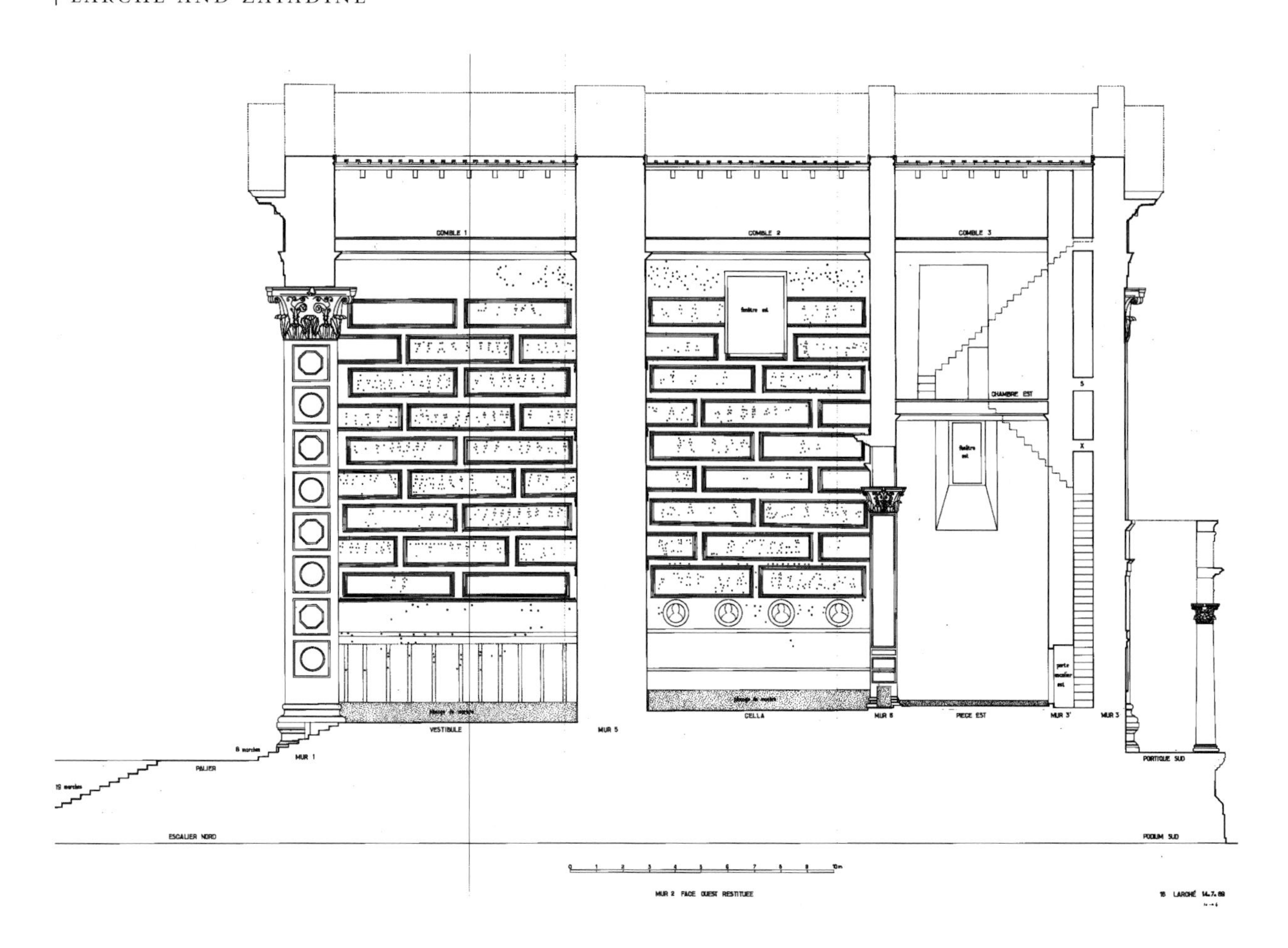

226. West face of wall 2 restored. Qasr al-Bint, Petra.

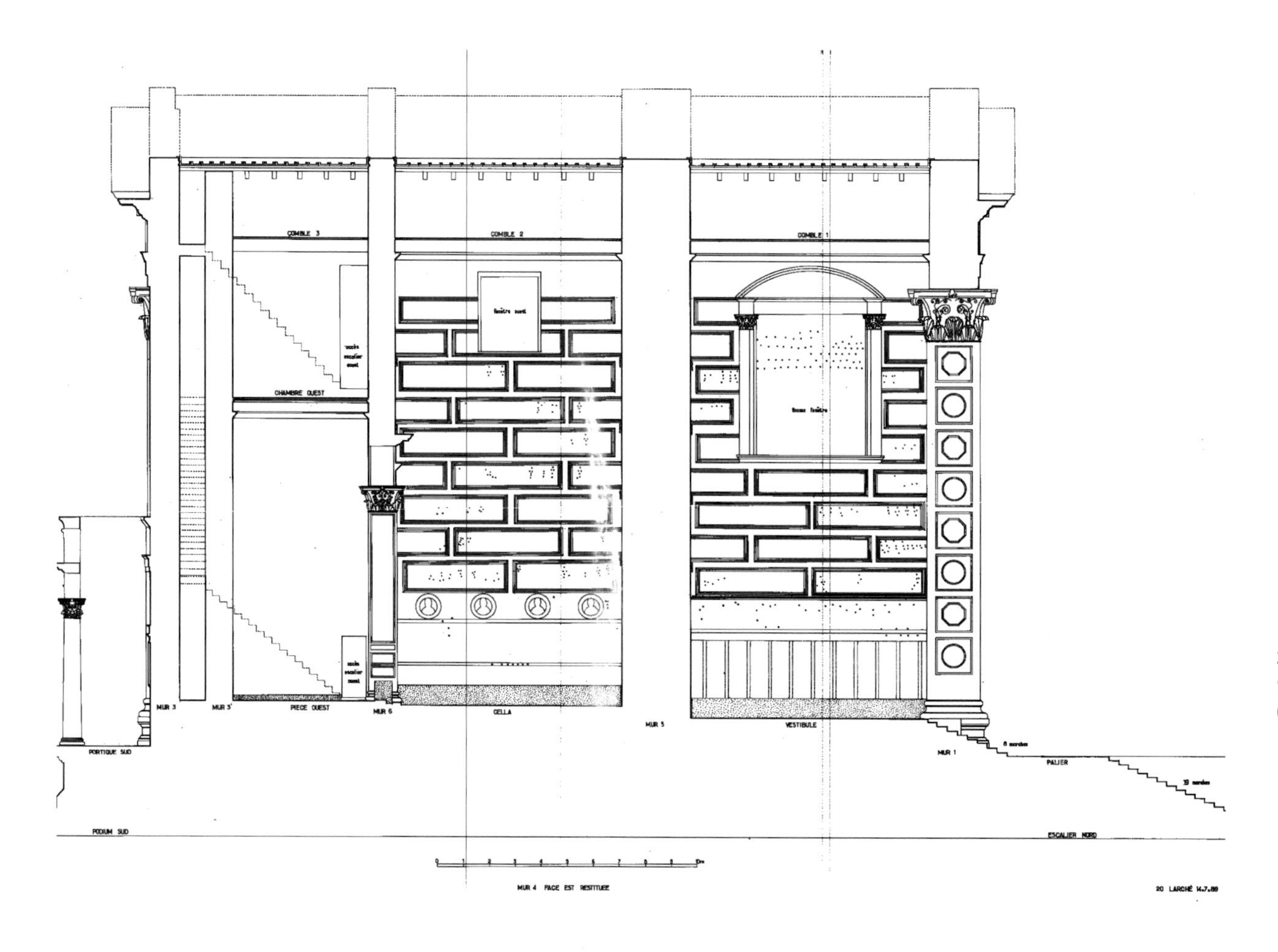

227. East face of wall 4 restored. Qasr al-Bint, Petra.

cornice of both colonnades and the corbelled course underlining the ceiling. These courses, partly preserved in the corners, show binding-holes delineating frames continued from those of the sidewalls. The traces of these frames probably continued in staggered rows on both sides of the central *adyton*. As no element of the balconies restored by H. Kohl has been identified, they cannot have existed. Numerous fragments of gilded stucco were found during the excavation of the cella.

The Adyton Since no trace of central columns has been discovered, the two high pilasters must have framed a six-meter-wide passage. Each pilaster rests on a pedestal (1) cut into the first three courses (K), which should have received a marble, molded revetment. The base of the pilaster, which was probably carved in an added marble block, rested on pedestal 1. Its eroded capital is carved in the two last courses, which are made of yellow sandstone. No element of the entablature has been identified; nevertheless, since the span between the pilasters matches the width of the monumental gate, a similar lintel can be proposed: an architrave—either in wood or in assembled, joggled sandstone blocks gathered in a flat arch—relieved of the weight of the roof by a true arch made of stone voussoirs. The space between this architrave and the true arch could have been decorated towards the cella, with a composite entablature capped by a depressed arch, and towards the *adyton*, by the continuation of foliated scrolls crowning the kiosk walls.

In the passage, the pavement of the cella projects ninety centimeters between the high pilasters before abutting two preserved sandstone steps. The upper one is blocked in the direction of the *adyton* by two ashlars behind which rises a filling of stones and mortar. Its side facing the cella is pierced with four small mortises and four large notches in which a marble, molded revetment could be set so as to shape a pedestal identical to the one supporting the pilasters. On each side, along the wall of the *adyton*, is a narrow stairway of seven sandstone steps formerly covered with marble. These two narrow stairways provide access to the elevated holy-of-holies, the inner sanctum of the temple (fig. 228).

The rear of the *adyton* in the Qasr al-Bint is occupied by a kiosk decorated with an applied order and framed by two raised anta pilasters (figs. 220, 221, 225). Its baetyl, or sacred standing stone, was set on a pavement of which only the bedding (consisting of a stone-and-mortar filling) remains. This kiosk is set on a podium (M) divided into two steps comprising the lower part of its three sidewalls. The lower step marks the position of a pavement set level with the top of pedestal 1, previously described. At the rear of the kiosk, the upper step covers the lower courses of wall 3, which becomes narrower above this level. This step is pierced with mortises similar to those described on the base of pedestal 1.

228. View from the cella towards the *adyton*. Qasr al-Bint, Petra.

Above this stepped podium, two courses (N) form the plinth of the three walls of the kiosk. They are engraved vertically every forty centimeters. These engravings, in the same way as the mortises of the upper step of the *adyton*, received a marble revetment probably decorated with the same molding as pedestal 1. On the three sides of the kiosk, this pedestal 1 supported the bases of the applied order as well as those of the anta pilasters. The restoration proposes a projection of the molding of pedestal 2 plumb with each base.

In the back of the *adyton* (fig. 228), two half-columns are applied between two quarter-columns. The wall behind the three panels that these half-columns delineate is very thin. On the sides, the middle half-column is framed by two quarter-columns. The whole system doubles the thickness of the side walls 7 and 8. Their fitted marble bases rested on pedestal 2. There, the shafts and panels of the columns have been intentionally hammered and only square mortises regularly carved along the drums make it possible to assert that a stuccoed decoration was applied. Their entablature is made of three courses corresponding to architrave, frieze, and cornice, but its stuccoed molding has been lost. Finally course O caps the cornice. Slight cuts carved on its top surface could have supported wooden beams.

The narrow space separating the sidewalls and the two pilasters framing the kiosk was decorated with stucco held in three superposed square mortises. Both pilaster bases should be a marble revetment resting on pedestal 2. Their capitals are carved in two courses, the first of which continues the kiosk cornice. Their entablature, which survives on two courses in the corners, has not retained its decoration.

The stuccoed decoration of the sidewalls continues right around the kiosk. On the back wall above the kiosk, a tetrastyle construction supports a pediment, while on the side walls in front of the kiosk, two other superposed constructions, also tetrastyle, are surmounted by pediments. Large foliated scrolls stuccoed between these constructions and a dentil cornice applied to the sandstone corbel unfolded on the three walls. The corbel does not mark the ceiling level, for stucco traces are visible above. The ceiling of the *adyton* of the Qasr al-Bint should have been at the level of those of the vestibule and cella.

A similar system of two superposed podiums, surmounted by a kiosk accessed by two narrow stairways, is known from the temple of Khirbet edh-Dharih (see figs. 71, 73, 82).

The Side Rooms On each side of the *adyton*, the cella of the Qasr al-Bint communicates with a side room by a colonnade made of two columns *in antis*, whose entablature supported the upper part of wall 6 (figs. 220, 221). Their first drums are set on the cella's sandstone pavement. The side rooms' two white marble steps are set between the columns and pilasters. The lower step, located 12 centimeters higher than the cella floor, protrudes beyond each column and extends into the cella; made of two white marble blocks joined and carved in a circular arc, its top surface is prepared to receive a marble base applied against the first drum. The upper step, which stands 6 centimeters higher than the former, is embedded between the columns and pilasters. This difference in level obliges us to restore two half-bases added at two different heights: the lower one, facing towards the cella, at a height of 12 centimeters above its pavement, and the upper one, facing towards the side room, at 6 centimeters higher. A balustrade embedded between these half-bases would hide this anomaly. A vertical notch, carved into the lower part of the pilasters and on each side of the corresponding parts of the columns, would receive the balustrade uprights. Horizontal lines of mortises cut into the drums would support a stuccoed decoration similar to that on the pilasters of the northern façade. At the lower part of the walls, binding-holes lined up 15 centimeters above the pavement would have helped to fix a marble plinth. Thin white marble slabs cover the sandstone pavement of the side rooms.

The pilasters have retained fragments of their stuccoed decoration. Their protruding lower part was covered with a marble base. The angle cornice intact in the cella's southwest corner ensures a two-meter height for the entablature capping the colonnades of the side rooms. The pilaster capital supports two superposed blocks: the lower one is set back from the pilaster projection on wall 6, while the upper one is shaped as an arch springer. Their depth is slightly less than that of the pilaster. On each side, a thin vertical slot dug into the side walls contains fragments of charred wood retained in mortar. Found on both sides of the columns, numerous voussoirs and joggled stones have the same depth as the pilasters (1.06 meters). Traces of stucco prove that they were set in the decorated part of wall 6. Laid in a flat arch, the joggled stones rested on the capital's upper bed and against the block supporting the springer. Voussoirs formed three arches resting on these springers, thus relieving the flat arches of the weight of the upper part of wall 6. The architrave and frieze would have been carved on wooden planks embedded in the thin side slots and set against the flat and round arches.

Eleven meters above the pavement, a corbelled course caps the three walls of the side rooms. In the back wall, this course is surmounted by nine transverse openings delineated by headers with cut upper angles. Within the openings, the mortar retains impressions of wooden beams which were embedded there. Symmetrical openings must have existed in wall 6 for their other ends. The corbelled course of the sidewalls is topped with a course whose height equaled that of the openings and whose molding gave the illusion of a beam embedded in the sidewalls. Excavation of the side rooms showed a thick layer of ash containing charred wooden fragments under the heap of blocks fallen from the upper story. This layer corresponds to the charred beams that had fallen directly from the ceiling.

The eastern room alone is lit by a window opened in the middle of its eastern wall (figs. 220, 226). Its split lintel was composed externally of a wooden or stone element supporting the upper part of wall 2; internally, a counter lintel continued the corbelled course underlining the ceiling and supported the landing of a wide opening (Q), which, offset northwards, opened into the eastern upper room. No binding-holes exist, but numerous stucco traces are visible everywhere. As has already been seen under the roofed portico, stuccoed decoration could be applied without binding holes.

The Upper Eastern Room To the right of the rear wall 3 of the eastern room, a door without surrounds opens onto a stairway with steps that are not embedded in the wall facings but are set on a filling (figs. 220, 226). Along the length of this room, wall 3 has been split to install a first flight of 28 steps which ascends to a landing constructed in the southeast corner. After turning northwards at a right angle, a second flight of 11 steps, built into the thickness of wall 2, emerges onto a large landing which leads by a wide opening (Q) to the floor of the upper room. Three of its walls, which are well preserved, show no traces of decoration, while the fourth wall (6) is entirely destroyed. A high opening (R), plumb with the door of the stairway, leads to a landing (S) made of five sandstone slabs. Located inside split wall 3, this landing covers part of the stairway's first flight. Externally, above landing S, wall 3 is preserved to a height of three courses (T). Between the outside entablature and the top of these courses, a window may be restored facing the opening (R), which admitted light to both the stairway and the upper room. Another row of five slabs (X) set plumb with landing S three courses beneath the corbel, defines an inaccessible niche opening onto the stairway. Slabs S and X function as ties, both bracing part of wall 3.

Inside the thickness of wall 2, the stairway's second flight is covered with five slabs (Y) supporting an ashlar filling which held a flight of ten steps ascending southwards. As the highest step is 90 centimeters below the ceiling level of the upper room, three steps leading to the attic level are clearly missing. The lowest of the ten steps is located three meters above the level of opening Q and therefore of the eastern room. These steps would have been continued inside opening Q by a wooden stairway, which permitted descent to the level of the upper room.

The Upper Western Room Contrary to the situation in the eastern room, where construction of the stairway within the side wall was hampered by a window, a door without surrounds opens onto a stairway set inside the split wall 4 in the western room (figs. 220, 227). A first flight of steps goes up to a landing built in the southwest corner. After turning eastwards at a right angle, a second flight set inside the split back wall gives access to a landing running into the west room through opening R. Contrary to the eastern stairway, which is set on ashlar masonry, the steps of the second flight are laid within the two parts of wall 3 which they bind.

The walls of the western room are badly preserved. Nevertheless, as with the eastern one, it is possible to restore, under the outer entablature, a window which faces opening R and which lights both the stairway and the western room. Two courses above the corbel and plumb with the stairway door, the wall is pierced with an opening which provides access to stairway Z built inside the split wall 4. Seven steps, which remain in place, are set on a masonry filling, which itself is set on slabs forming the ceiling of the stairway's first flight. About fifteen steps of this second flight ascending to the attic level are missing.

The Roof A series of attics has been set inside the space between the roof and the ceiling of the vestibule, cella, *adyton,* and upper rooms of the Qasr al-Bint. Above the vestibule and cella, the attic level is determined by the top of the orifices in which the ceiling beams were embedded. All courses still in place above this level show a reddened and cracked surface, while all those located below are in good shape. The cause of this change in appearance is the blaze which destroyed the woodwork of the roof and ceilings. The level of the attic covering both the upper rooms and the central *adyton* is not so clearly marked, because the upper part of the walls had collapsed. In the west, three steps are missing in the stairway leading to the attic covering the cella and vestibule.

Hundreds of tile fragments have been found inside the temple. Set on woodwork, a two-slope roof had its ridge centered on both pediments surmounting the north and south façades. The roof's woodwork rested upon cross-walls which demarcated three independent attics. These walls stood slightly higher than the level of the tiles, as shown by the grooved blocks in which the gutter tiles were embedded. Fallen blocks bearing slots parallel or sloping in relation to their beds have been discovered in the cella and the vestibule. Fragments of tiles are still embedded in these slots. Identical blocks remain in place in the upper parts. Along the four cross-walls and at the bottom of the slope along both longitudinal walls, a double fitting of tiles in the sandstone ensured that the roof was waterproof.

Rainwater, thus channeled towards the bottom of the slope by the last course of the outer walls, which served as gutter, could have been conducted to the top of the cornice, three courses below, or directly to the ground through an as yet undiscovered pipe built in the wall.[5]

18 | The Great Temple

MARTHA SHARP JOUKOWSKY

When visiting Petra, one is immediately thrust into a magical theatrical set on a dramatic natural site, an awe-inspiring crystallization of natural beauty and magic. Petra is the unique artistic creation of Nabataean will. Two thousand years ago, its imaginative rulers ordered a great city to be built. Employing thousands of masons, the Nabataeans carved out the city on a scale, and of a character, unmatched in the ancient world. It may well be that they regarded Petra and its setting as a special gift from their gods, believing that it was shaped by the supernatural and that it held a holy meaning. Before then, nothing had existed on the site but a geologic miracle, a dramatic, rocky ravine. It is the combination of natural wonder and human intervention that enthralls us today.

In the first century BC, Petra awaited the dramas for which it would serve as a setting. With a paucity of written records, it is archaeologists who must bring life to those who built and lived at Petra. This is the intrigue of archaeology: Every shred of information rewards us with excitement.

The Great Temple Site The Great Temple represents one of the major archaeological and architectural components of Petra.[1] Located in the central city to the south of the Colonnaded Street and southeast of the Temenos Gate, this precinct of 7,560 square meters is composed of a Propylaeum (monumental entranceway) and a Lower Temenos with monumental east and west Stairways, which in turn lead to the Upper Temenos—the sacred enclosure for the Temple proper (fig. 230).

The Great Temple is sited on the north edge of the el-Katute slope, rising to an elevation of 930 meters above sea level. Its northern border parallels the Colonnaded Street, and its south, the ridge. Walls extend along its east perimeter, delimiting it from the "Lower Market" and on the northwest from the "baths." Its two great terraces overlook the Colonnaded Street and the Wadi Musa to its north, the Qasr al-Bint to its west, and the Lower Market to its east. The site topography can be divided into three sectors: the Propylaeum, the Lower Temenos, which is eight meters higher than the Colonnaded Street, and the Upper Temenos and the temple, which rise some five meters above the Lower Temenos (fig. 229).

This precinct was first explored by R. E. Brünnow and A. von Domaszewski in the 1890s; but it was W. Bachmann, in his 1921 revision of the Petra city plan, who postulated the existence of a "Great Temple." While no standing structures were revealed before the recent excavations, the site was littered with architectural fragments, including column drums and richly carved capitals, probably toppled by one of the earthquakes that rocked the site. Given the promise of the Great Temple and its importance in understanding Petra's architectural and intercultural history, it is remarkable that its precinct remained unexcavated until 1993, when Brown University investigations began under the auspices of the Department of Antiquities of the Hashemite Kingdom of Jordan.

The Propylaeum The stairs of the Propylaeum (monumental entranceway) leading up to the precinct from the Colonnaded Street measure 17.66 meters in length (fig. 230). They were reconstructed several times. Positioned at an oblique angle, these stairs were modified when the Colonnaded Street was constructed later than 76 AD, and they were reconstructed after the building of the Great Temple. These impressions were verified in 1998 by the discovery of an earlier arched walkway overbuilt by the later stair treads. Here in the West Propylaeum is a shrine of Nabataean double aniconic baetyls (idols) discovered by our team in 2000.

The Lower Temenos The Nabataean penchant for formal symmetry in architecture is revealed by the discovery, in the Lower Temenos, of east and west triple colonnades adorned with more than 120 columns with Asian elephant-headed capitals—60 flanking each side of the Lower Temenos, in addition to those across the Propylaeum façade (figs. 229, 230, 234, 236, 237). These colonnades lead into elegantly buttressed,

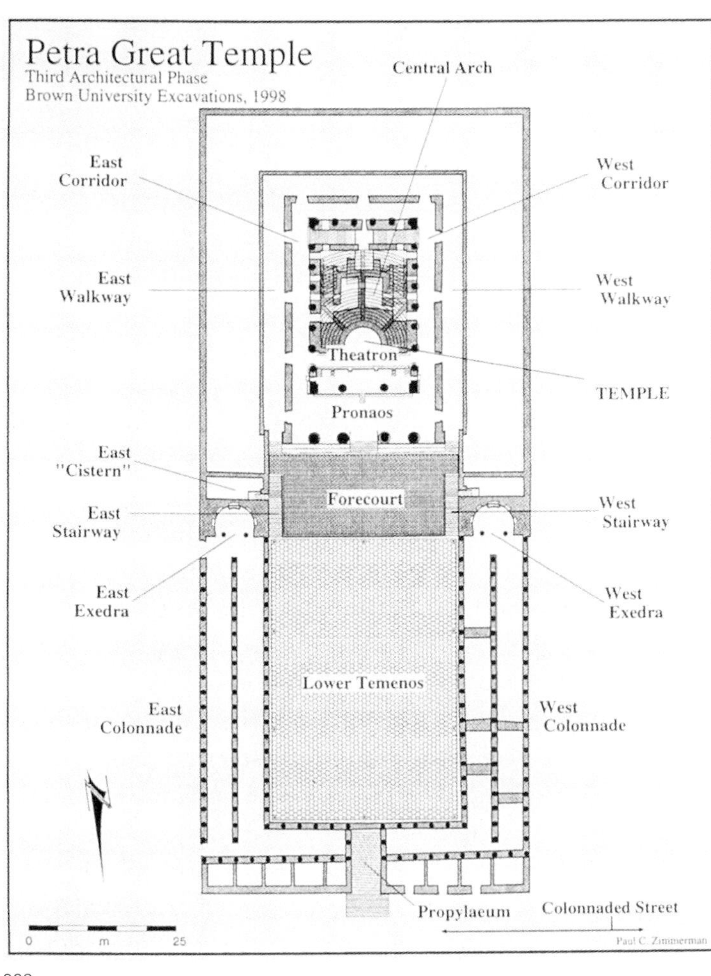

229

230

231

229. Plan of the Great Temple excavations, 1998, Petra.

230. "Cistern" in the Upper Temenos behind the East Exedra, 1998. Great Temple, Petra.

231. Aerial view of the Great Temple Precinct, 2002, Petra.

semi-circular exedrae to the east and west. The east exedra is appointed with interior benches and a central podium, which may have served for the placement of statuary. Like the west exedra, this semi-circular structure is preserved to a height of 6.8 meters, is 12.4 meters in exterior width, and is 5.4 meters in depth from the double entry columns to its rear wall. These exedrae provide a grand vista over the Lower Temenos.

One of the most significant discoveries of the Brown University expedition is the monumental stairways leading from the Lower Temenos to the Upper Temenos (fig. 233). Measuring some 10 meters in length (north/south) by 2.23 meters in width (east/west), they are found to bond with the exedrae and the orthostat retaining wall, which extends 32.7 meters east/west across the Lower Temenos.

The Upper Temenos The completely excavated Upper Temenos provides the surround for the Great Temple. Fully revealed behind the east exedra is an arched cistern partially cut into the bedrock, measuring 11.0 m east/west by 3.15 m north/south by 1.70 m in depth. Recovered here is a rich repertoire of early second-century Nabataean painted and plain wares, a plethora of exquisitely painted plaster (including two with partial Nabataean inscriptions) and a Nabataean-inscribed bronze plaque (fig. 239). In the south passageeway the relief of a sword deity can be seen carved into the rear wall, and here there is an extensive north/south channel leading from another massive underground cistern with a volume of 327,000 liters.

232. Subterranean canalization system. Great Temple, Petra.

In the temple forecourt, small hexagonal pavers are positioned above an extensive subterranean canalization system (figs. 231, 232). Now, through excavation and ground-penetrating radar, the system has been traced through the precinct, from the rear of the temple to the forecourt, under the Lower Temenos, to the Propylaeum, where there may be another cistern—as yet undiscovered.

The Great Temple The Great Temple is tetrastyle *in antis* (with four front columns). These porch columns are red-, yellow-, and white-stuccoed, which, at a height of approximately 15 to 16 meters, must have had a dramatic impact when set against their sandstone brown and rose-red environment. If we add to the columns what would have been the superstructure, including the entablature (i.e., the architrave, frieze, and cornice) and the pediment, we arrive at a hypothetical height for this colossal edifice of approximately 19 to 20 meters.

Measuring 35.5 meters in width and some 42.5 meters in length, the Great Temple rests on a forecourt of small hexagonal pavers; a stairway approaches the entry (*pronaos*), which in turn leads into side corridors that access a theater (*theatron*) of 565 to 620 seats. The *pronaos* entry is marked by two columns that are the same diameter as those at the temple entrance but are larger than the eight flanking the walls or those of the Temple rear, which measure 1.10 to 1.20 meters. Supporting the structure's rear corners are two massive, heart-shaped columns.

In the interior are end walls (*antae*) resting on finely carved Attic bases. From these antae extend inter-columnar casemate walls with arches and windows. On the ground floor at the rear is a large, central vaulted arch, excavated to a depth of 5.25 meters. Cut into bedrock, and measuring 8.52 meters by 3.32 meters, its floor is composed of the canalization system with an additional series of bedrock-cut channels (figs. 229, 231). Flanking this central arch are two sets of twin-vaulted stairways (north/south and east/west, measuring 7 meters in length by 2.2 meters in width), which lead up to paved platforms built over the arch. From the ground floor, these access the second story from the temple corridors and exit. Parallel with the north/south stairways are vaulted chambers. Additionally, the temple is equipped with exterior paved walkways east and west, where sculpted facial fragments and fine deeply carved architectural elements have been recovered.

The Theatron Structure An apsidal structure with tiers of seating in the form of a theater was discovered in 1997 (p. 24, fig. 9). Facing north were five extant courses of carefully hewn, limestone seats, with two stairways (*scalaria*) in the seating area (*cavea*). This *cavea* was above a 1.5 meter-high apsidal plastered wall. Below the lowest tier was a paved horizontal passageway (*diazoma*) on the lower cavea wall, measuring 1.5 meters in width and set with alternating white and dark red sandstone pavers. Unquestionably, the auditorium was central to the structure, and it dominated the monument's interior.

The second to fifth tiers of *cavea* seats were of white sandstone ashlars, divided into four wedge-shaped sections (*cunei*). Based on the excavated evidence, we can predict that the *cavea* was divided by three staircases—with one in the center and two on either side. Although the collapse of the columns and the inter-columnar walls scarred the structure, further evidence for the seating was found to continue up to its rear, which in antiquity extended over the vaulted substructures of the east and west stairways and over the vaulted east and west chambers, as well as over the central arch. Although the upper portions of the theater are either in poor condition or are completely missing, we project that there may have been as many as 20 original tiers, with a *diazoma* bisecting the *cavea* between the tenth and the eleventh row. A conservative estimate of the seating capacity would be a minimum of 565 and a maximum of 620 persons.

The orchestra area is too restricted and small for any large assembly but may have been used for dramatic presentations, simple religious rituals, and ceremonies. The projected diameter of the orchestra is approximately 6.3 meters; the estimated diameter of the outermost seats is 33.2 meters. The floor of the orchestra is paved with rectilinear sandstones placed longitudinally, north/south, and perpendicular to the center of the *cavea*. Unfortunately, the damage to this floor is appreciable—perhaps in our future excavations of the remaining part of the structure the design may become better delineated.

We identified a raised platform (*pulpitum*) between the *pronaos* columns which was later added to the theater. Constructed of four courses of ashlars, its curb is set just above the orchestra floor. In the wall facing the *cavea* are two small staircases, and in the center is an oval niche. A paved walkway of some three meters in width lies between this stage-like structure or platform—either the *pulpitum* or the stage building (*scaenae frons*)—and the orchestra. To the east and west of this walkway are thresholds, 3 meters in length by 0.30 meter in width, with deeply cut, squared, hollow cavities in its upper surface. Because quantities of metal were found, it is probable that these cavities supported a gate or door with metal fittings.

233. Side gallery with stairway. Great Temple, Petra.

The interior of the Great Temple is highly decorated. The corridor walls are frescoed with red-, yellow-, green,- and blue-painted stucco. Columns covered with vestiges of red, white, and yellow stucco serve as decorative idioms. Recovered are many well preserved, worked, decorative stucco fragments, with egg-and-tongue and egg-and-dart motifs, vegetal elements, and painted cornice fragments. Two massive stucco lion heads must have guarded this rear entry. Several limestone acanthus capital fragments still have traces of gold leaf adhering to their surfaces.

234. View of colonnaded portico, Lower Temenos. Great Temple, Petra.

Basic Design—Flow Pattern Given the plan for this building, we found the flow patterns to be extraordinarily well planned and efficient (fig. 235). Access was from the Lower Temenos, up the east or west stairways, to the east or west walkways, and from the walkways into the east or west corridors. Alternatively, access might also have been through the front entrance. A visitor or ceremonial participant was obliged either to turn to the right or left into the corridors. The major route was observed to be from the corridors through the arched doorways to one set of stairways. Once these stairs had been mounted, access to the *cavea* was directed to the paved platforms at the top of these stairs, which accessed twin small flights of steps that provided access into the *cavea* at the middle *diazoma*.

Discussion Interpreting this large public edifice is at the heart of the archaeological process. The Great Temple stands alone above a large colonnaded Lower Temenos among thousands of architectural fragments, including Asian elephant-headed capitals. The temple itself is embellished with floral Nabataean capitals, and this well-preserved building is also

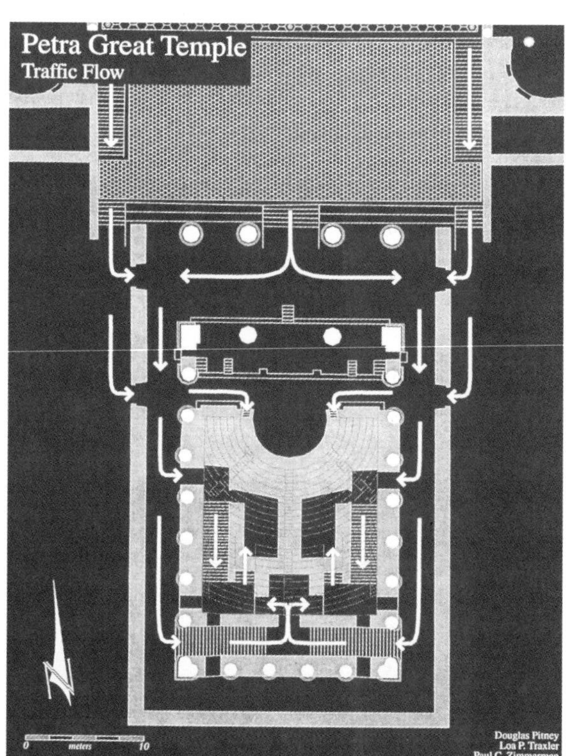

235. Flow pattern in the Great Temple, Petra.

236. Fragmentary limestone elephant-headed capital. Great Temple, Petra.

237. Limestone elephant-headed terminal from capital. Great Temple, Petra.

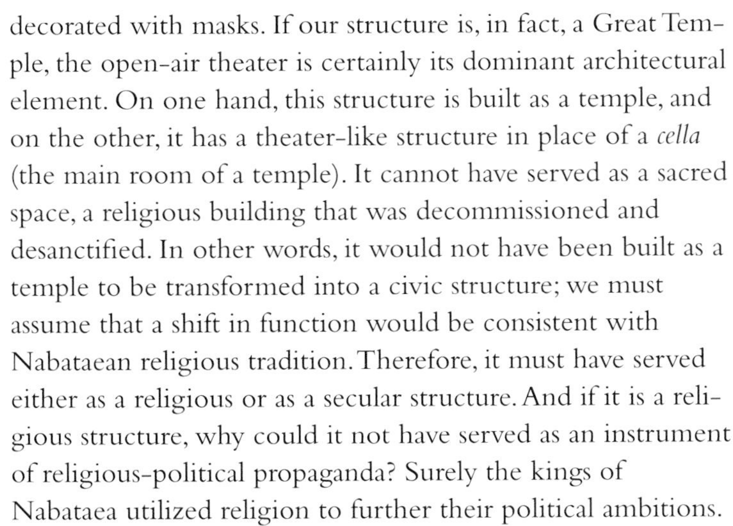

decorated with masks. If our structure is, in fact, a Great Temple, the open-air theater is certainly its dominant architectural element. On one hand, this structure is built as a temple, and on the other, it has a theater-like structure in place of a *cella* (the main room of a temple). It cannot have served as a sacred space, a religious building that was decommissioned and desanctified. In other words, it would not have been built as a temple to be transformed into a civic structure; we must assume that a shift in function would be consistent with Nabataean religious tradition. Therefore, it must have served either as a religious or as a secular structure. And if it is a religious structure, why could it not have served as an instrument of religious-political propaganda? Surely the kings of Nabataea utilized religion to further their political ambitions.

It is clear that Nabataean creativity, their lack of preconceived ideas, and their unusual architectural borrowings from the classical world could have led them to utilize the Great Temple either for ritual or administrative purposes. Although this theater-like structure must have served as the central focus for the Great Temple after it was rebuilt, its function has yet to be determined; it remains enigmatic. In future seasons we will test several hypotheses to explain and understand this building: 1) it was a temple or a theater-temple, or 2) it served as the civic center for Petra in the Nabataean and Nabataean-Roman periods. In the latter capacity it functioned as either: a) a *bouleuterion* (council chamber), where the *boule* (city council) met or as a *comitium* or *curia,* a Roman political meeting place; b) an odeum or small concert hall, or c) a law court, council chamber, audience hall, or meeting hall.

Now it is possible that this is a civic structure—perhaps it is where the Nabataean "popular assembly" held their meetings. Perhaps the Great Temple was built as a *bouleuterion*? We must be mindful of the Latin Imperial inscription, studied by Stephen V. Tracy and dated between 112 and 114 AD, found in the rear west vaulted chamber on the floor (fig. 238). And we should not forget the multiple references to the *boule* at Petra in the Babatha Archives discovered by Yigael Yadin from the *Cave of the Letters.*[2] The Great Temple's location adjacent to the Temenos Gate and the most sacred Qasr al-Bint is not accidental. It must be considered of paramount importance in relation to the central Petra city plan. A Great Temple or a *bouleuterion*-odeum should be accessible to the citizens and provide a gathering place where the decisions of the day could be announced and discussed by the populace. So, was it a center of worship where events of a ritual nature were performed, or was it the location of the highest court? Or did this structure serve

238. Latin inscription. Great Temple, Petra.

239. Bronze plaque with Nabataean inscription 98-M-2. Great Temple, Petra.

240. Fresco of a man's face 98-S-65. Great Temple, Petra. The iris of the eye is pale blue.

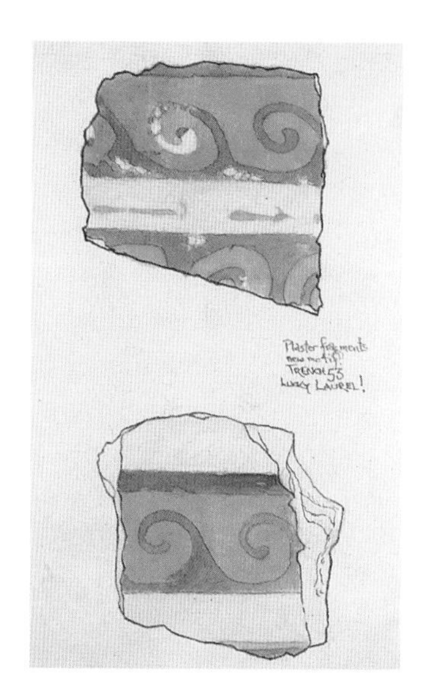

241. Fragments of painted stucco. Great Temple, Petra.

perhaps even multiple civic and religious functions? Even if we restrict the functional interpretation of the precinct, we are still left with a number of compelling questions. If it is a temple, what deity was worshipped there? And if it served as a civic center, what was its intended use: *bouleuterion* or odeum? How does this precinct relate to the urban fabric of the city itself? While the function of this structure remains obscure, it surely presents a significant architectural component of Petra. We seek scholarly discussion of these issues.

Highly informative is our artifact record, however few clues it offers as to the function of this structure. After ten excavation seasons, the catalogue register includes 539 coins, several inscriptions, including two in Nabataean, several fragments in Greek, and an Imperial Latin inscription (fig. 238). Exquisitely painted stucco fragments abound—including one with a partial human face (figs. 240, 241). Over 400 elephant-head fragments are included in our database of architectural fragments, which now numbers over 10,000 elements; this inventory includes fragments of elaborate floral friezes and acanthus-laden limestone capitals. Among the 325,575 fragments of pottery, glass, bone, and metal that have been classified are 500 lamp fragments as well as complete Nabataean bowls, small cups, juglets, unguentaria, cooking pots, and figurines.

Site Deposition Analysis—Interpretation of Construction Phases and Use Based on site deposition, our annual excavations tentatively have determined the general sequence or phases of the Great Temple's construction, collapse, and abandonment. These phases may be modified through subsequent excavations, but at present they are used as the backbone for the archaeological evidence.

The earliest phase is reserved for the preparation of the site and represents the construction of the Temple precinct. The major Nabataean goal was to position a building of importance in central Petra and to orient it toward the city's main thoroughfare. The dramatic backdrop of the Al-Katute provides a perfect siting—12 meters of bedrock are chiseled away, and multiple east/west terrace walls and impressive cisterns and canalization systems are constructed. Built into the site is a three-tiered precinct with an imposing temple structure set on a terrace platform. The temple is designed with eight interior bichrome, plastered columns on each of its flanks and six columns at the rear. These columns are embellished with red and yellow plaster above which is a white, ridged, cable-fluted plaster, and they are decorated with deeply carved limestone capitals with fine floral, sculptural decoration. Side corridors are decorated in the second style of Pompeiian wall painting dated to the first century BC. To protect both the wall and column plaster, roofing probably extended from the side columns to the corridor walls. The evidence suggests that this architecture belongs to the last quarter of the first century BC, during the reign of either King Malichus I (62–30 BC) or Obodas II (30–9 BC), or perhaps both.

In a later building phase, there is a new, monumental rebuilding program—an architectural metamorphosis is launched. The architects wanted to make a strong statement, and they might have drawn their inspiration for the precinct perhaps from Alexandria, which at that time epitomized the architecture of a great city. It is obvious that the rulers of Petra took pride in the embellishment of the area—providing for its functional demands with a sense of spatial logic. This new precinct had to emanate a sense of power befitting Nabataean wealth. To begin with, there had to be a grand access to the precinct. To achieve this, subterranean cryptoporticoes were constructed, above which were set an elegant columnar propylaeum and triple colonnades with elephant-headed capitals. The architects ably conceptualized the Lower Temenos as a symmetrical, formal presence that purposefully emphasized the Great Temple. This set in motion a completely new series of challenges that made the design of the Lower Temenos radically different from what it had been before. This may have provided the impetus for a scheme that would involve precise planning for the complete remodeling of the Lower Temenos. The architects approached all aspects of the Lower Temenos design simultaneously—from the laying out of the stairways and the exedrae, to the enhancing of the area with triple colonnades. In short, they reconfigured the area, creating a vast architectural foreground for the Great Temple. The lateral staircases had to have accompanying luxurious exedrae and other appurtenances to complete the finished look of the ensemble. Another massive east/west retaining wall had to be built on the same line as the twin lateral stairways and the exedrae, which delimited the Lower Temenos on its south. This Lower Temenos plaza was then embellished with a sweeping, white, limestone hexagonal pavement, which tied all the elements together and gave them the feeling of association. These architectural components were all interconnected features that boldly defined the area's spacious importance.

The temple continues to crown the composition of space, and the edifice we know today emerges. The exterior is enlarged with exterior walkways on its flanks. In the interior, there is the careful construction of inter-columnar walls (walls with arched doorways and windows between the columns; these casemate walls are still preserved to a seven-meter height). The major reconfiguration of the Temple interior is also modified—its core is reconstructed as a theater-like structure, open to the sky. The heart of the Temple is now the theater, and the architects expertly blend its proportions with the earlier architectural phases. Additionally, multiple sets of new stairs are installed in the Temple rear: these access the lateral corridors with adjacent east and west vaulted chambers and lead to the Temple walkway exits. It is suggested that these modifications took place sometime in the first or early second centuries AD. This renovation we have placed sometime near the end of the reign of Aretas IV (c. 40/44 AD) or that of Malichus II (40/44–70 AD) and possibly that of Rabbel II (70–106 AD). But questions persist: what was the transition between the earlier Nabataean structure and that which we know as the Great

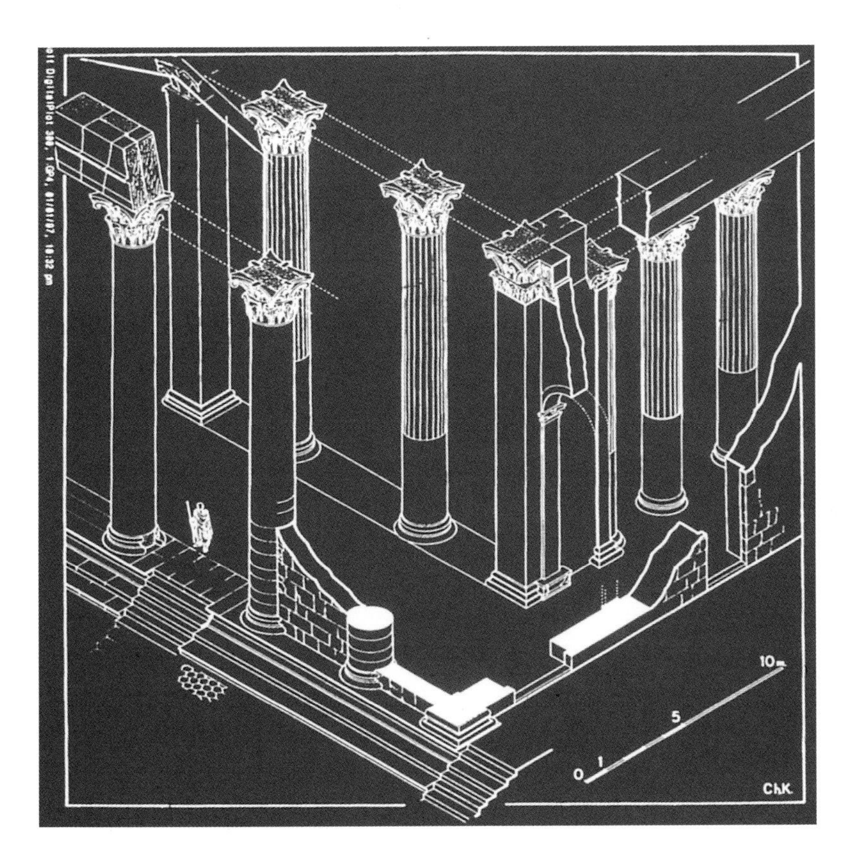

242. Phase I Great Temple reconstruction.

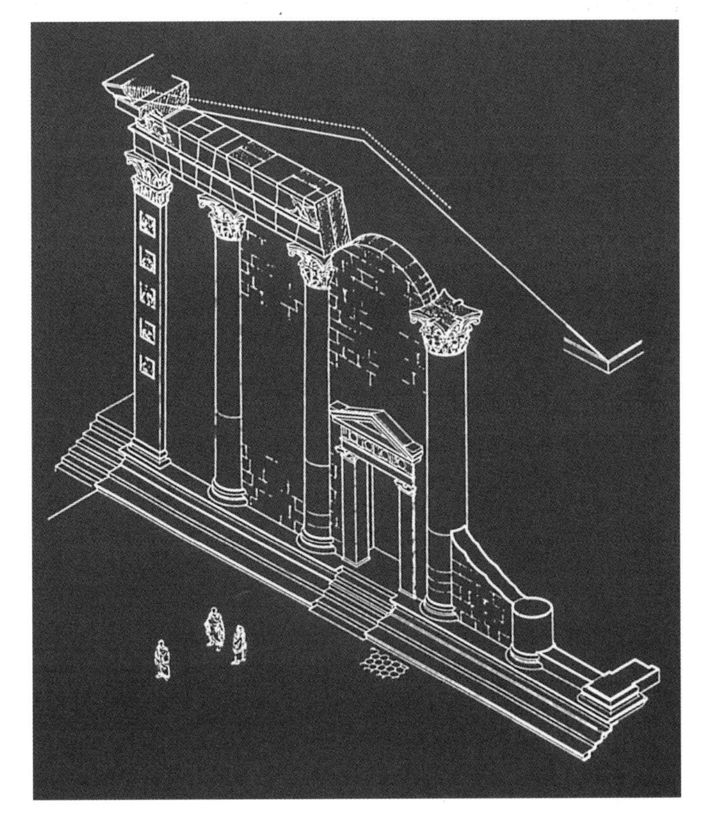

243. Phase II Great Temple reconstruction.

Temple? Why was the transition from one type of installation to another so swift—less than 100 or so years?

We have identified the following phase as Nabataean-Roman. Serving as a buffer state against the desert tribes, Nabataea retained its independence but paid taxes to Rome. Completely subsumed by the Romans under the Emperor Trajan in 106 AD, Petra and Nabataea then became part of the Roman province known as *Arabia Petraea*. Under Roman rule, Roman classical monuments abounded, many with Nabataean overtones. When Petra entered into the second-century "Roman" world, we assume the Great Temple was recycled by Nabataean-Roman architects. The precinct continued to serve as one of the principal monuments of the city. And if there were post-106 AD alterations, these are not yet evident from the archaeological record.

As we know, Petra continued to flourish during the Roman period, with a monumental arch spanning the Siq and tomb structures either carved out of the living rock or built freestanding. There is no reason why the Great Temple should not have continued to serve as a principal monument of the city. The fragmented Latin imperial inscription (if we assume it is in some way associated with this building) attests to its importance and one of its last uses. The evidence suggests that the Great Temple continued to serve the people of Petra until some point in the late third or early fourth centuries AD. There was then a major collapse and abandonment of the structure. The following phase was represented by the accumulation of fill.

By 313 AD, Christianity had become the state-recognized religion of the Roman Empire. In 330 AD, the Emperor Constantine established the Eastern Roman Empire, with its capital at Constantinople. Although the earthquake of 363 AD destroyed half of the city, it is generally accepted that Petra retained its urban vitality into late antiquity, when it became the seat of a Byzantine bishopric. As a result of this earthquake, at least part of the temple precinct collapsed onto accumulated fill. Up to this point, although we have no evidence to suggest that the Great Temple continued to function, there was domestic reuse of the temple precinct. The latest phase represents the modern reuse of the site. Although, thankfully, the major portion of the Great Temple crumbled under its massive collapse, Bedouin farming activities had taken place in the Lower Temenos.

As excavations continue, it must be borne in mind that this interpretation is ongoing and may be revised in light of future excavation. There are few sealed deposits, and much more has yet to be explored before we can understand the archaeological deposition of these remains. Our understanding of the site has been difficult, not because of the lack of dateable materials, but because of the mixture, within archaeological contexts, of artifact stylistics ranging in date from the first century BC to the early fifth century AD. We posit that the Great Temple precinct was in use for approximately 500 years.

The existence of a Great Temple is now an established fact. Our discoveries over the past ten campaigns are enabling scholars and the public at large to study and visit this great edifice. It is my intention to reveal more of the precinct's architectural layout, but also to better understand its function, phasing, and how it is woven into the fabric of its Nabataean, Nabataean-Roman, and Byzantine urban environment.

The wealth and importance of Petra as the Nabataean capital had to be made clear to both her subjects and those powers with whom she interacted. In the heart of the city, the Great Temple must have been impressive. Visitors today are stunned as they enter the complex from the Propylaeum and cross the great open expanse of the Lower Temenos—they are at once involved in a great architectural experience. The drama of the Nabataean planning is evident—there are exciting vistas of the exedrae, the extraordinary double staircases, the seemingly limitless rows of columns, and the remarkable façade of the Great Temple itself. The fabulous architectural decoration of the elephant-headed capitals, set against the monumental architecture of the Lower Temenos and the impact of the Temple structure with its deeply sculpted, elaborate floral capitals, demonstrates power and wealth. The overall construct of the precinct, directed by royal patronage, clearly is a response to the needs of the Nabataean court and its administration. Although we have shed new light on urban Petra, the implications of the Great Temple are opening further questions about the site and the city. The reappraisal of the Great Temple architecture chronologically and stratigraphically is enhancing our understanding of the socio-political and religious culture of Nabataean Petra.

19 | The Temple of the Winged Lions

PHILIP C. HAMMOND

HALFWAY UP THE SLOPE of the northern hill of the city center of ancient Petra are the partially excavated ruins of a building covered by over 1,300 years of drifted sands. These are the remains of a temple dedicated to the supreme goddess of the Nabataeans, who settled in Petra sometime around the sixth century BC and eventually urbanized a barren valley.[1]

In 1973, an intrepid group of students conducted the first major electronically instrumented survey to be done in Jordan.[2] A month's work identified over thirty sites for potential excavation. Two were chosen, and one turned out to be a temple, which, because of winged feline capitals found around the altar, became popularly known as the Temple of the Winged Lions.

Excavation at the temple site, which began in 1974, has continued up to the present time, uncovering not only a temple, but a complex of support buildings as well (fig. 244). The temple is a model of any classical temple structure of the period, but what is most unique are the surrounding residential and work rooms, which apparently not only provided for the upkeep of the temple, but also provided for housing of the temple personnel, pilgrims awaiting initiation into its rites, metal and oil fabrication areas, servicing facilities, and even for the production of religious artifacts for visiting tourists!

The temple itself is a rectangular combination of cella, or *naos* (the actual worship area) and *pronaos* (the entry porch of the building) (fig. 245). Half-columns line the interior walls, with freestanding ones separating the floor space into two bays on each side. A roughly square elevated altar platform is off-set toward the rear. Two stairways lead up to the top of the altar platform, once barred by iron gates. The top of the platform was decorated with simple mosaic patterns in marble. A storage cabinet was built into the rear wall of the platform, probably to house necessary religious paraphernalia for worship services. Altogether, the temple proper is relatively small, with the actual worship area only measuring about 300 square meters, less the space taken up by the columns and the altar platform. However, this amount of interior space was quite adequate for the type of religious activities for which the temple was designed. The entry porch is likewise relatively small, made even more so by gigantic columns supporting the porch roof.

The interior of the temple was lavishly decorated with plaster painted in reds, yellows, greens, white, and black designs, with a variety of cornices and moldings setting off recessed niches along the walls. In those recesses were, originally, fresco scenes reminiscent of the "mystery scenes" on the walls of Pompeii, which may have been the source of the decorative inspiration. Somewhat later, in the history of the building and the political leadership of the Nabataean monarchy, the interior of the temple was remodeled. It appears that an iconoclastic, or at least a conservative, emphasis resulted in the fresco panels being over-painted with plain colors and the columns to be re-done with applied floral patterns. The floor of the interior was paved with varicolored marble and had marble baseboard tiles along the base of the walls.

Because the structure was demolished by an earthquake, much of the decoration and all of the plan have been preserved for archaeological—and cultural—analysis. Because of the preservation of material remains, the destruction has permitted an extraordinary look at Nabataean life, not only religious, but also technological, artistic, and commercial.

Likewise, the earthquake which destroyed the temple was of such a magnitude throughout the area, from well above Jerusalem all the way south to Petra, that it was documented by a contemporary observer. The letter states that the massive destruction took place on "Monday at the third hour, and partly at the ninth hour of the night on 19 Iyyar of the Year 674 of the Kingdom of Alexander the Great"[3]—i.e. on Monday, May 19, 363 AD. Hence, an exact date, to the year, month, day, and hour of the destruction has been preserved. This is

244. The Temple of the Winged Lions, Petra. General view after excavations.

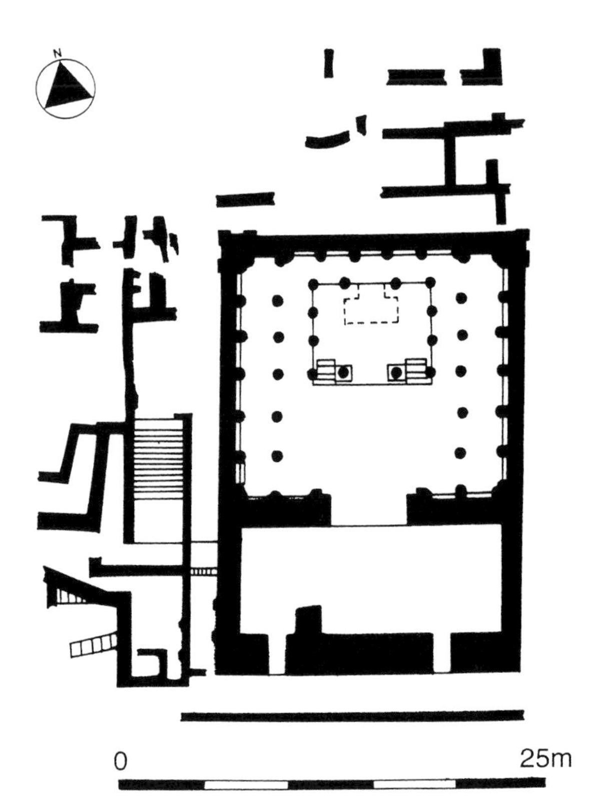

245. Plan of the Temple and its annexes. In a fashion typical of a Nabataean sanctuary, its ground plan consists of a shallow portico, a square cella, and a central platform altar, or *môtab*.

therefore one of the most closely documented chronologies ever possible! The result is that not only the destruction itself, but a mass of artifacts found on floors immediately below the destruction debris, can also be dated.

Still further, in the course of the use of the building, when a remodeling took place, original dedicatory inscriptions, carved on marble slabs, were removed, probably to "erase" the credit given to the original builder.[4] Here, again, a precise date was given—"On the fourth day of Ab (15 August/15 September), the thirty-seventh year of Aretas, king of the Nabataeans, who loves his people." The "king who loves his people," as his coins attested, was Aretas IV, who ruled from 9 BC to 40 AD. His thirty-seventh year was 27/28 AD. Seldom are archaeologists granted such precise dates.

The methodology employed in the excavation also increased the precision of the results. Over 2,000 "stratigraphic units" were identified over the entire temple complex. These "units" are actually the levels, or strata, laid down in the use and disuse of the building through time. Each represents an "event" in the history of the site. When these are brought together into "phases," both the archaeological and the cultural history can be reconstructed. Sixty-eight such phases emerged in the analysis, laying out the life of the area from the building of the temple, through its use and destruction, up to modern times. Twenty-seven of these phases preceded the earthquake destruction in 363 AD.

One mystery concerning the temple was its attribution—to whom was it dedicated? During the 1975 season an "eye idol" plaque was discovered, which showed a stylized face and an inscription along its base reading: "... the goddess of... son of...." (fig. 246) This indicated that the temple was dedicated to a goddess. But, unfortunately, the name of the goddess had been on another part of the plaque, which had broken off and had been lost. This has resulted in discussion among scholars as to which of the two probable female deities the temple was indeed dedicated to! The author urges that it was a goddess named Allat, while others hold out for the one named al-ʿUzza. In either case, the goddess of the temple was the supreme female one for the Nabataeans, confronting the temple to their chief male deity, Dushara, which is situated just across the wadi, called in popular folklore today "Qasr Bint Faroun" ("Palace of the Daughter of the Pharaoh").

On the basis of the type of temple, the altar platform, the decoration, and other features, it appears that the temple involved the kind of religious practices associated with the Egyptian goddess Isis. Other suggestions of Isis are also found

246. Limestone stele ("eye idol"), "Goddess of Hayyan." Temple of the Winged Lions, Petra. Department of Antiquities, Amman, Jordan.

247. Bronze bust of Serapis or Dushara. Temple of the Winged Lions, Petra. Department of Antiquities, Amman, Jordan.

at Petra (see pp. 63, 170). For the Nabataeans to have chosen a "foreign" goddess as their chief goddess would have been very unusual, but, by the time the temple was built, the cult of Isis had traveled throughout the Roman Empire. The Nabataeans, who were notorious for borrowing everything from architecture to technology, apparently merely borrowed the attributes of the Egyptian goddess for their own goddess.[5] This fits well into the "mystery cult" appearance of the Temple, along with an unusual decoration that appeared there, as well as in other Nabataean temples—the dolphin. Dolphin images have been discovered at a major temple at a site called Khirbet et-Tannur in the north, at a small temple in Wadi Ramm in southern Jordan, and as far away as a site in the Egyptian Delta called Tell es-Shuquafiya. It was something of a problem, for a long time, to understand why a desert culture should be so interested in dolphins. One excavator even suggested that the desert was like the sea, hence the motif was quite understandable. However, that was grasping at straws and not a real answer. If the Nabataeans simply adopted the attributes of Isis, but not the goddess herself, the answer is quite simple—Isis was, along with all her other titles, Mistress of the Sea, and even had a chariot pulled by dolphins! Other indications of the Nabataean connection with Isis also appeared at Khirbet et-Tannur, where the goddess had a "vegetation" aspect, along with one connected to the zodiac, which also made her Mistress of the Heavens (see pp. 181–191). The meaning of the "eye-idol" plaque, mentioned above, is also clear, on the same basis, since that particular type of plaque appears in southern Arabia on funerary stele, again connecting the goddess of the Temple with Isis as Mistress of the Underworld. Even the feline capitals on the columns of the temple's altar platform fit into the same scenario, since Isis is often seen with felines borrowed from the attributes of even earlier Middle Eastern goddesses.

The workshop areas of the temple complex were unique, also, since no other excavated Nabataean temple ever had similar facilities.[6] In the "Painters' Workshop," a large collection of ceramic vessels was found, containing pigments, mixed paints, and binding agents. Some of the vessels were also unique finds, especially large funnels, but most of them were the usual cups and bowls common on Nabataean sites.

The "Metal Workshop" produced items in bronze, and, especially, in iron. Adjacent to it were all sorts of hooks and hangers, very possibly used for hanging up meats and poultry. Throughout the temple itself, hundreds of iron nails were recovered, which were used to "key" the rough undercoat of cement plaster to the interior walls. Also found in great numbers were small copper tacks, used to hold the final coats of plaster on the undercoats. Whether both items were also fabricated on the site, or were imported, cannot be determined, but facilities existed, in any case, for local production. Lead items were also found in the Temple, probably serving as hangers for a curtain, or veil, around the altar platform and could easily have been made in the "Metal Workshop." This workshop is also important, in that the plastered ceiling fell directly upon a paved floor and was preserved. The plaster still had imbedded in it fragments of the reeds which had been used in the roofing and the marks of the string which had bound them together. This technique is recorded in the architectural works of the period and is seen here for the first time.

Another recovered item in metal was the bronze bust of a deity, probably for export (fig. 247). However, this piece may also reveal that not all of the temple's workshop products were strictly honest. The bust had been hollow-cast in bronze, with a separate base. Next to both was a large piece of lead. On the basis of known tax lists, such items were probably sold by weight in bronze—not lead! Other bronze items recovered on the site included a beautiful bronze lamp with a lion-head decoration; a winged figure, possibly a harpy; and small affixes.

One side room of the complex appears to have been devoted to the making of small portable altars, with the face of the deity on one side. Since a similar example, with no adjoining workshop, is known from elsewhere, these were undoubtedly sold to pilgrims as souvenirs of their visit to the temple.

Near the front of the building was an "Oil Processing Workshop," complete with a large grinding mill, similar to the ones used for grains, along with a ceramic trough to assist in conveying the oil to jars. Most interesting, here, was a well-worn stone facing the mill, obviously the seat for the overseer of the work. The gender of this person became clear when her spindle whorl was also found next to the seat. She could while away the time spent watching the milling being done by spinning yarn for future weaving.

In another side room, a "Marble Workshop" was found. It was among over a thousand pieces of discarded marble piled up there awaiting cutting for reuse that the dedication plaques noted above were discovered. Important, also, was the fact that the pieces showed the various steps the masons carried out in the production of marble tiles, by marking, cutting, and finishing.

With the numerous workshops within the complex, the temple could probably have sustained itself financially without difficulty. It also appears, however, that there may have been even other sources of funds. All around the altar platform, and within a subterranean room outside, were small well sculpted human heads. Their variety suggests that they may represent donors to the temple, since they do not represent the faces of any known gods, goddesses, emperors, kings, nor any other persons known from contemporary art works, or from coins. In addition to those, tucked within the floral decorations of the capitals of columns, a number of floral pieces cast in plaster were found, some almost complete and with painting still partially visible on the surface. No parallel for these exists, either, and they, also, may represent recognition of smaller donations made to the temple and its goddess. Both may have served like the bronze plaques, or windows, donated to churches still today.

The "mystery cult" appearance of the temple was mentioned above. This feeling was fostered by a number of aspects associated with the main worship center of the building. First of all, the size of that area was too restricted, when the bay columns are taken into consideration, for a large congregation of worshippers, indicating that a small number of people were accommodated at any one time. No apparent window spaces seem probable in the recovered wall architecture, but a lamp chain was recovered, indicating that mode of interior lighting, adding to the "mystery" atmosphere. Lead fixtures found around the altar platform suggest that the altar was curtained, or veiled, in the manner described for the temples of Isis in contemporary literature. No altar-based idol of the goddess was recovered, suggesting a portable one, again cited in contemporary reports of the Isis cult. Since the altar was elevated and access closed by iron gates, access was prohibited to non-priestly worshippers. One of the recovered fresco fragments, in a wall niche, shows a scene reminiscent of a similar "initiation" scene from Pompeii. Finally, the "liwan," or apartment complex at the southern edge of the temple, again reflects known Isis-related practice in which initiates were housed close to the temple while going through the long initiation process.

In spite of the fact that the interior of the temple was relatively barren of artifacts, the surrounding rooms of the complex were rich in recovered materials. Pottery sherds, the most common finds on any Middle Eastern site, were recovered in massive amounts. Most of them were from common household vessels and a great number of them were complete enough to reconstruct most of the original vessel, at least by drawing.

Entire pottery vessels were also recovered, including the hoard from the "Painters' Workshop." One amazingly complete piece had been saved from destruction when a stone from the wall fell at an angle over it. It was a small juglet, probably used for eye paint, resting in a clam shell, with a copper tool for applying it still intact. Cups, bowls, water jars, cooking pots, pitchers, jugs, juglets, and similar everyday vessels represented the majority of those found in complete, or almost complete shape. One pottery form, however, was of the strictly commercial variety, the "unguentarium." These were small, round, long necked juglets designed to contain unguents, perfumes, and similar luxury items for which the Nabataeans were famous. Bringing ingredients from southern Arabia and other sources, they were conveyed to Petra for processing and reshipping to the western Roman world in a variety of sizes of the unguentaria. Most important, of course, were frankincense and myrrh, used throughout the Mediterranean area for funerary and religious purposes. The Nabataeans had early cornered the sources and the markets of these two items and had become rich from their sales.

Miscellaneous metal artifacts were recovered, as noted above in the discussion of the "Metal Workshop," but these generally suffered from the effects of almost two thousand years of weathering. Hundreds of corroded nails and tiny tacks were found, but most of them were badly deteriorated. Actually, one of the strata of the interior of the temple had been colored green from the disintegration of the small copper tacks used in the plastering. Bronze and lead suffered less from time, with the former being able to be cleaned to its original state. Of more than passing interest was the recovery of a few iron keys and the remains of a door lock. The precise meaning of the latter cannot be verified, but it may suggest either the need for security for some temple valuables, or the securing of slaves used in work around the site.

Coins varied in the degree of preservation, but a great number could be read and their dates assigned. In this regard, Nabataean coins were easiest to identify, since the name of the king and queen appeared on the reverse and generally even a single letter permitted identification of the reign, if not the actual year in which the coin had been minted. Recovered Nabataean coins were all in bronze, or copper, and no silver, or gold, issues were found. Likewise, most Roman coins on the site were in the same metals, although a single silver coin of Trajan was recovered, virtually in mint condition!

Small finds were recovered in great numbers. Lamps, especially, were discovered virtually every day, both imported and local types (fig. 248). Many of the imported ones, coming from Roman markets, were broken, but often the top, or "discus" was preserved, showing gladiatorial, religious, and other typical decorative scenes used in that period. A number of Nabataean molded figurines were also found, including a seated deity type, horse and camel examples, and even a monkey head. Beads occurred in quite some numbers, as did cowrie shells sacred to Venus, quite appropriate to the goddess of the temple. Glass fragments were also all over the complex, with only one glass bowl being preserved enough to be completely reconstructed.

Some late ostraca (short messages written on pottery sherds) were also recovered and were of major importance, even when the complete message could not be read. The Nabataean writing appearing on them represented not the form used on stone inscriptions, nor the earlier more cursive type, but a transition into a flowing script, which would, in later times, become the Arabic script that we know today.

Since the site has been stratigraphically dug and the beginning and end dates are assured, it will be possible to date the ceramic and other materials recovered in excavation with much greater accuracy than has been possible at Petra before. The recovered coins also assist in filling in dates between the absolute ones.

The contributions of the excavations, spanning over a quarter of a century, include not only the archaeological finds and the precise chronology, but also the ability to derive cultural information from the recovered materials, as well. This should really be the end sought in archaeological excavations, not finds, nor statistics, but data that assist in reconstructing the culture of the people and the processes, through time, which made that culture possible.

The cultural contributions of the excavations at the temple include, first of all, considerable information regarding at least one glimpse of Nabataean religion. Other than the admonition against misuse inscribed over the doorway of the Turkmaniyah Tomb at Petra, and a few inscriptions mention-

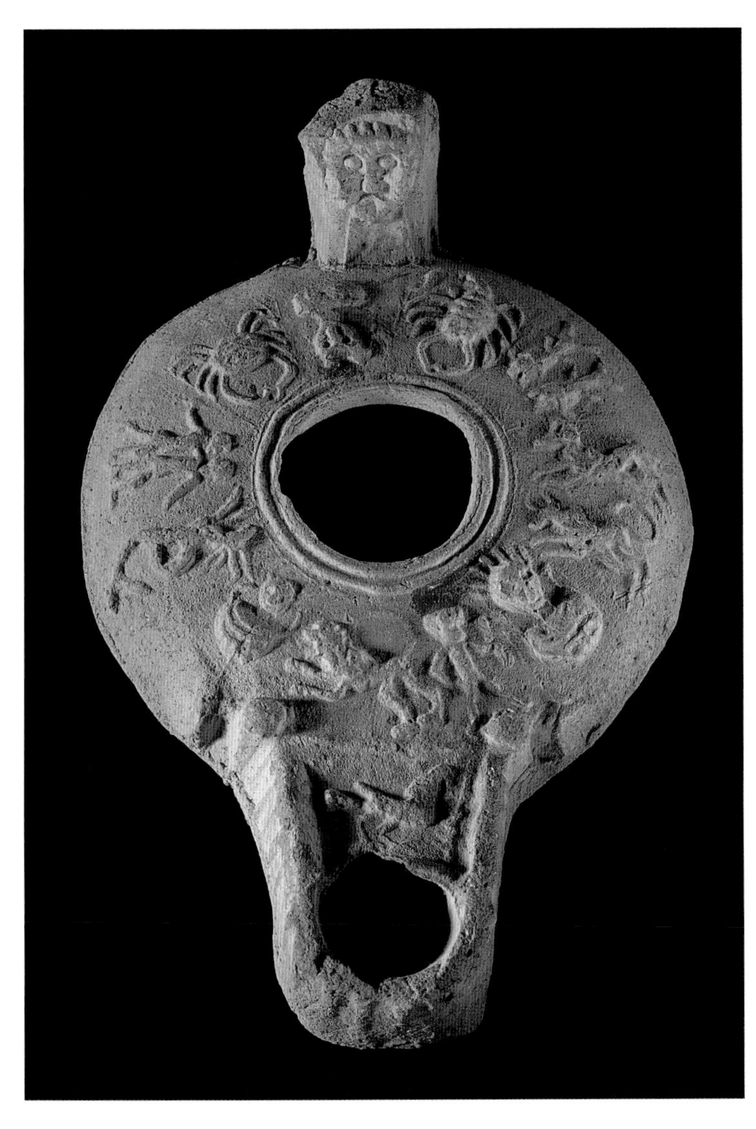

248. Terracotta lamp with signs of zodiac. Temple of the Winged Lions, Petra. diam: 12.3 cm. Department of Antiquities, Amman, Jordan.

ing Nabataean deities, very little is known concerning that aspect of the life of the people. Thus, finding a virtually intact altar platform, fresco decorations, the general layout of the temple complex, the fact of the adoption of a foreign model for a native goddess, the answer to why a desert people held dolphins in so much esteem, and the explanation of certain features of the finds at the temple at et-Tannur, among other things, all represent new data, formerly unknown.

Nabataean commerce and economics also were aspects verified, or seen for the first time in non-documentary, or non-inscriptional, form. The presence of imported luxury ceramic materials, well after the Roman annexation of the city, put to rest the long-held view that Nabataean economic levels declined as a result of that annexation. The funerary fragment brought from Athribis in Egypt was the first artifact to verify the trade line through Wadi Tumilat in the Delta, along with blue pigment raw materials and some faience fragments. Likewise, a Far Eastern "dancing girl" on an ivory wand (p. 71, fig. 50) accomplished the same thing in regard to the trade lines in that direction. Continued occurrence of the small unguentaria bottles also pointed to a continuance of "middleman" activities, which had long been the source of the considerable wealth of the Nabataeans.

Likewise of major importance was the vast amount of architectural data preserved by the earthquake destruction. The method by which plastering was done on ashlar blocks, the fact that the plastering covered not-very-well-dressed stone work on the interior of the building, the chemical formulae for the paints and plasters, the lavish use of iron, copper, and lead fixtures, and other aspects of both actual construction and decoration methods, all contributed more specific information to that which has previously been recovered at Petra and elsewhere regarding Nabataean architecture and architectural technology.

The evolution of Nabataean script into Arabic has long rested upon a very few late inscriptions. The recovery of graffiti among the sherds of Nabataean pottery now furnishes both the direction of the evolution and a firm date for the examples.

Political trends and political maneuvering also appeared in the recovered materials. In a remodeling phase, not long after the temple had actually been in use, the dedicatory inscriptions of King Aretas IV, the original builder of the temple, were removed and cast into the dump heap of marble fragments for re-cutting for other purposes, as noted above. The interior of the temple was then redone in a most conservative manner, by replastering over the original frescos and simply painting the panels without any human scenes. The time frame of the phase appears to reflect the reign of Aretas's successor, Malichus, known for his conservatism in other areas as well. Deviously, what appeared to be necessary refurbishing of the temple painting got rid of both the dedications to a renowned predecessor and the unacceptable frescoes!

Finally, and perhaps of equal interest, the Nabataeans' habit of borrowing, from wherever they traveled in the Roman Empire, was again amply illustrated in many facets of the Temple Complex as a whole. It was possibly this rather unique feature of the culture which assisted in both the material and cultural rise of the people well beyond what might have been expected from a group of pastoral nomads who had made the long trek from the Arabian Peninsula northward following herds of sheep and goats!

20 | Petra—From Tent to Mansion: Living on the Terraces of Ez-Zantur

BERNHARD KOLB

EVER SINCE ARCHAEOLOGICAL RESEARCH in Petra began, the focus has been on the carved rock façades of the so-called royal tombs on the one hand, and on the public area on the other. The investigation of the urban residential areas, however, started only very recently.[1]

Since 1988, under the patronage of the Swiss-Liechtenstein Foundation for Archaeological Research Abroad (SLFA), Basel University has been investigating Nabataean private architecture on the terraces EZ I, III, and IV to the north and south of ez-Zantur (EZ)—a rocky crest in the south above the Colonnaded Street (figs. 249, 251).[2] From 1988 to 1994, important discoveries were made regarding the history of habitation, house construction, and urbanization in Petra—particularly on terrace EZ I: a sequence in residential history became discernible from layers of a tent camp dating from the early first century BC, to the first stone-built construction in the late first century BC, and that of a large dwelling of the first century AD, which spread across the whole terrace. This sequence is consistent with the general development of Nabataean culture, a civilization that reached its peak in the first half of the first century AD.[3] After the destruction of the aforementioned Nabataean dwelling by a fire in the early second century AD,[4] terrace EZ I remained abandoned until the early fourth century AD, when two small houses were erected from the rubble of the preceding building.

Since 1996 the author has led the excavation of a Nabataean mansion from the early first century AD on terrace EZ IV, which exceeds the construction on EZ I with regard to size as well as decoration.

EZ I: Testimonies to the Transition from Nomadic to Settled Life Two ancient written sources provide the crucial dates as to the Nabataean transition from nomadic to settled life. Diodorus (*Universal History* 19, 94, 2–5), who reported Antigonos Monophthalmos's unsuccessful attempts to conquer Petra in 312 BC—relying on the description of the eyewitness Hieronymus of Cardia—described the Nabataeans as nomads facing a death penalty for constructing houses. For the first century BC we know from Athenodoros's description of Petra, as quoted in Strabo (*Geography,* 16, 4, 21), that Petra was a thriving town with houses and gardens. Thus the transition to settled life of at least a part of the Nabataeans was completed between the third century, at the earliest, and the first century BC.

A deep sounding on EZ I in the area of room II (figs. 250, 252) disclosed a sequence of alternating sterile strata and strata containing settlement waste, which were identified as testimonies to seasonal settlement activity.[5] These strata, green in color and highly compressed, bore small finds, allowing dating between the early and the latter part of the first century BC. The significant change to a settled lifestyle must have happened

249. Aerial view of the ez-Zantur area with the sites EZ I-IV, Petra.

250

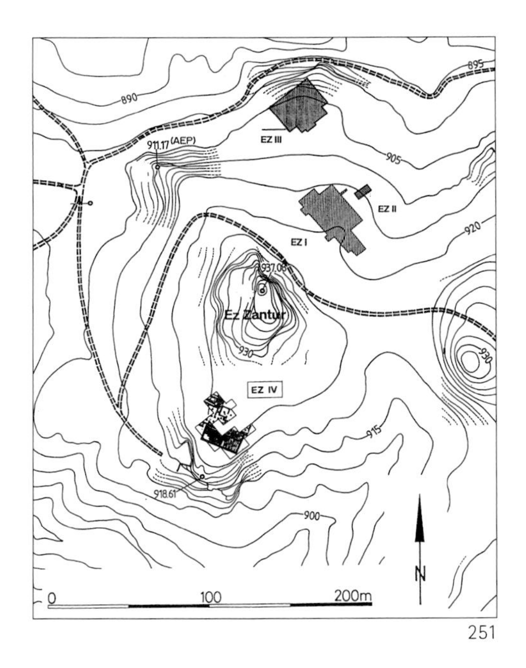

251

252

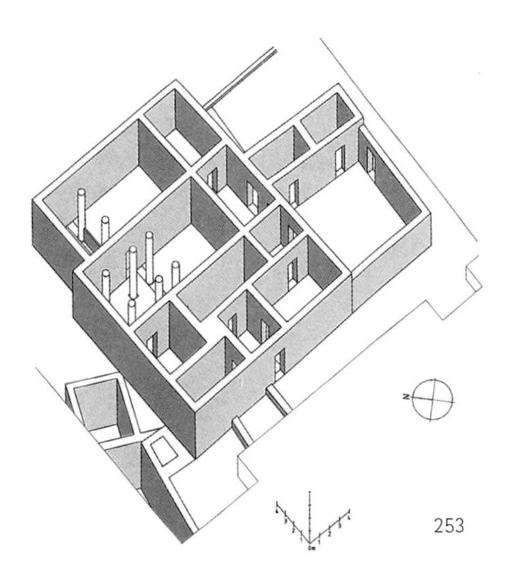

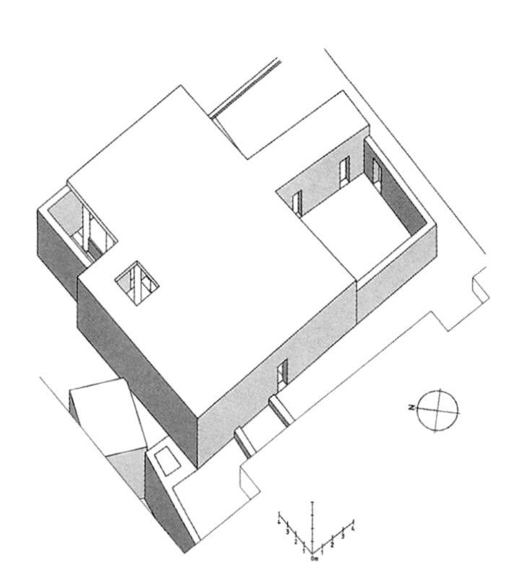

253

250. Aerial view of terrace EZ I from the north-west. Ez-Zantur, Petra.

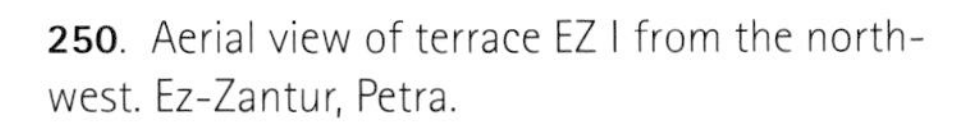

251. Topographical plan of the ez-Zantur area with the sites EZ I-IV, Petra.

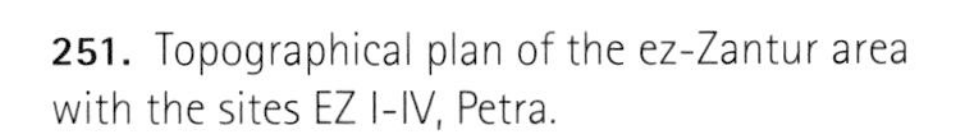

252. Schematic plan of Nabataean house, EZ I (first century AD). Ez-Zantur, Petra.

253. Isometric reconstruction of Nabataean house, EZ I (first century AD). Ez-Zantur, Petra.

gradually. It is probable that the erection of the first stone structure on the terrace took place in the first century BC, next to the tent camp. Of this structure, merely the foundations of two oblong walls have been preserved, which do not allow any further assumptions about size and ground plan.

EZ I: The Nabataean Dwelling of the First Century AD In the early part of the first century AD, a generously proportioned house, measuring about 30 x 30 m, was erected on top of the earlier structure (figs. 250, 252, 253). Its masonry was built from local sandstone and limestone. As far as could be ascertained, the floors of all rooms were paved with stone slabs. There is no evidence that roof tiles had been used; thus it can be presumed that this building was covered with the usual flat roofs, as has been the tradition in Levantine architecture to this day. After a period of reconstruction, the house burnt down in the early second century AD, and the remaining structures were plundered, re-used, and built over by later residents in the fourth century. Despite this, the ground plan of the house could be reconstructed to a large extent. It consisted of two different areas: that in the northwest (rooms I–VII) being used for presentational purposes, while that in the southeast (rooms VI, VIII–XI, XVII–XX, XXII) served as private living and working quarters. The stately part included the reception rooms II and IV,[6] which originally contained polychrome linear wall paintings and were provided with air and light by room I and by the small peristyle III. The two columns between the airwell I and room II, as well as the columns of the peristyle, were crowned by Corinthian capitals in the local style.

The peristyle, the Corinthian capitals, and the fragments of the former wall decorations make clear that, from the first century AD at the latest, the Nabataeans were familiar with the Greco-Roman standards of house planning. In contrast to the social rooms, no indications of "Hellenization" could be found in the living and working area: The small, sturdy private tract with its large paved courtyard XXII form a unit, which seems to be rooted in the Oriental tradition.

Although the current state of research does not yet allow definitive conclusions, a juxtaposition of innovation and tradition can be ascertained in Petra's urbanism. The "hippodamic" layout of the civic center along the Colonnaded Street displays the typical elements of a Greco-Roman town plan. In the residential areas, which were located further up the slopes, however, such uniform housing blocks, as are common in the Hellenistic towns of Marisa and Dor,[7] for instance, were absent. On the basis of current knowledge, the houses of Petra were built onto the many steps of a naturally terraced landscape, which were not connected by any structural axes, and tended to convey the image of a petrified camp site rather than that of the residential area of a Greco-Roman town.

EZ I: Houses 1 and 2 of the Fourth and Fifth Century AD and the End of the Settlement In the early fourth century, two new houses were built on the ruins of the above-mentioned Nabataean dwelling (figs. 254, 255).[8] The walls of northwestern rooms I–III and V of the preceding Nabataean dwelling that were not to be part of the new buildings, were dismantled, and ashlars, paving slabs, and column drums as well as capitals were re-used as building material.

House I includes rooms 2–4, 6 and 10, and House II, rooms 5, 7–9, and 27–28. Room I seems to have been used as a separate living unit, independent of House I. Between the dwellings, detached from the actual building complex, stood baking house 26 with two ovens for bread production. The isolated position of this facility and that of adjacent room 29 can be explained by the fire risk that such a building implies, and by the communal use by the residents of both houses. In rural villages of Jordan such communally used baking houses on the periphery of a residential area have persisted to this day.

The strong influence that the preceding Nabataean building had on the small Late Roman Houses I and II could be distinctly noted in the ground plans. A successful compromise was found by adapting the then-existing structures to the new requirements. The rooms IV (2), XVIII (3), VIII/X (7), and XI (9) were kept more or less unchanged and were integrated into the new building plan. The paved courtyard area XXII of the generous Nabataean ground plan was the most obvious part to alter (cf. figs. 252, 254). This open zone was newly structured by separating walls, and the original peripheral courtyard became the central point of the later dwellings. In House II this restructuring is particularly easy to observe.

Although the two houses formed part of one polygonal block, they were two clearly separate units. The entry to House I was in the northwest, while that of House II was in the southeast of the terrace. On the basis of the finds and findings, both houses can be rated as non-commercial, residential buildings.

The living and working areas had no windows to the outside, but they were open towards the courtyards, which supplied the rooms with air and light (fig. 255 right). In the eastern corner of courtyard 8 (House II) a twin-flight staircase is preserved, originally leading up to a gallery. This L-shaped gallery, which was made of wood and supported by an arch (still traceable), provided access to rooms 9 and 27 on the upper floor. The staircase of House I was located next to the main door in the annex-like expansion 10 of corridor 6. The first flight of steps was constructed of stone, while the second flight must have been a wooden construction leading to the upper floor of room 2.

In House II, the characteristic L-shaped gallery in courtyard 8 is reminiscent of a feature found in Mampsis (House Va) as early as the first century AD.[9] Further parallels to house construction in the Negev zone are outlined in papyrus 22 from Nessana: a certificate apportioning inheritance dating from the year 566.[10] This papyrus documents that dwellings in the Negev settlements commonly consisted of two floors and a central courtyard, and also that the rooms upstairs were used as bedrooms, with doors opening onto a balcony above the courtyard. The reconstruction of House II interpreted the upper floor area in exactly this way. The correspondence between the residential buildings of the first and the sixth century AD, as outlined, confirms that this building tradition for residential homes covered the aforementioned Negev area as well as the southern Transjordan, including Petra.[11]

The builders of ez-Zantur competently combined the existing Nabataean structures with the basic ideas of traditional house construction of that time. Various walls lead to the southwest, away from the housing complex, indicating that Houses I and II formed part of a larger coherent quarter that expanded across the top terrace, reaching up to the rocky crest of ez-Zantur. There were, therefore, no dramatic changes in the townscape of Petra's private quarters between the first and fifth century AD.

Three hoards of coins were uncovered within the Late Roman structures, attesting to the fact that some of the rooms were completely destroyed by the earthquake disaster of the year 363.[12] About ten years later, the greater part of the rooms were reused up until the houses' final destruction in the early fifth century—probably by the earthquake in the year 419.[13]

EZ IV: The Nabataean Mansion of the First Century AD

In summer 1996 we started investigating the structures on the oblong terrace EZ IV just south of ez-Zantur[14] (figs. 249, 251). During the past three excavation campaigns, most of the southern rooms belonging to a wealthy Nabataean mansion of the first century AD were exposed, which probably—as with the house of the first century AD on EZ I—extended across the whole terrace (fig. 256).[15]

The building stretches across the entire east-west extension of 25 m of the narrow southern spur of the terrace, and consists of the three rooms 6, 7, and 17, which were originally decorated with wall paintings and decorative stucco.[16] The central vestibule or exedra 7 is flanked in the east and west by the two stately rooms: 6 and 17. Room 6 is connected to exedra 7 by an open passageway (c. 1.8 m wide) and two lateral doors (each ca. 0.8 m wide) while room 17 contained only a single but wider access (c. 2.4 m wide), which related to the axially opposed passageway leading to room 6. The floors in rooms 6 and 7 are paved with sandstone flags, while the floor

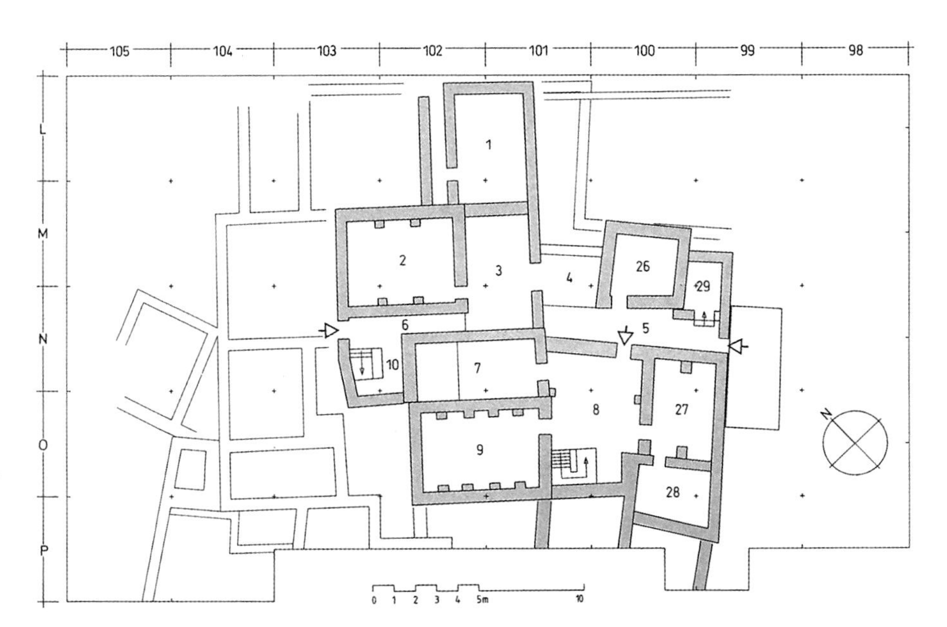

254. Schematic plan of Houses I and II, EZ I (fourth century AD). Ez-Zantur, Petra.

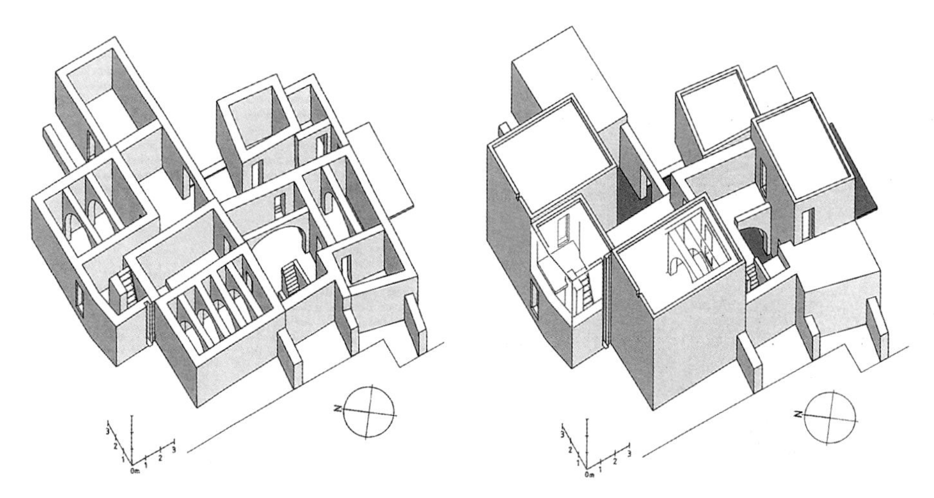

255. Isometric reconstruction of Houses I and II, EZ I (fourth century AD). Ez-Zantur, Petra.

of room 17 was originally decorated with a sumptuous *opus-sectile* pavement.[17] A double row of arches between walls L, N, and H supported the floor, most of which is now lost.[18]

Figure 6 implies that the north side of exedra 7 was arranged as a distylos *in antis*. The intercolumniations were closed off with doors, as the marks left by doors scraping on the pavement indicate. The resulting façade-like northern face of room 7 must be viewed in conjunction with pilaster Z (grid square 90/AO): A courtyard-like room, it is assumed, lay to the north of exedra 7.

The stately area of the house is believed, according to current thinking, to have been rounded off by room 1, c. 4 x 5 m, which is decorated with the extraordinary wall paintings discussed below. Room 1, like room 17, was furnished with an *opus-sectile* pavement, which was plundered in subsequent

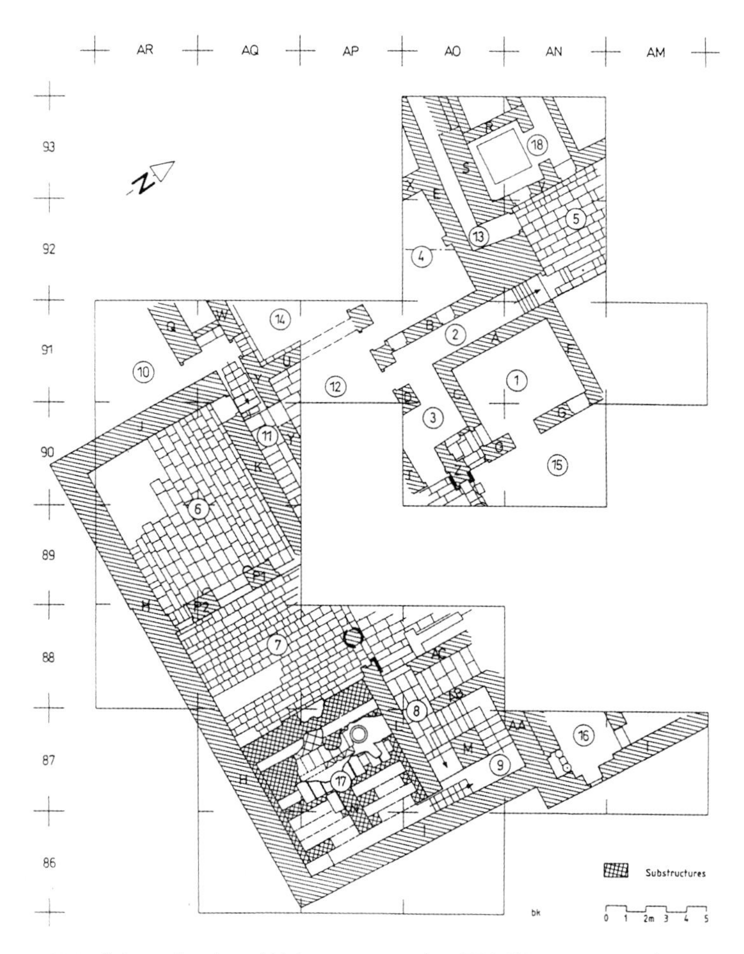

256. Schematic plan of Nabataean mansion, EZ IV (first century AD), after 1998 season. Ez-Zantur, Petra

times. The rooms around courtyard 5 in the west and room 16 in the east were far smaller and simpler with regard to decoration. These rooms probably formed part of the domestic area or the servants' quarters.

Dating The sherds of painted Nabataean pottery from the mortar bedding of the *opus-sectile* pavements in rooms 1, 10, and 17, and from the rough coat of rendering plaster on the walls, all belong to the decorative phase 3A, and define a *terminus post quem* of 20 AD for the building.[19] However, it cannot be ruled out completely that the floor paving as well as the remaining fragments of rendering plaster belong to a later reconstructional phase. The homogeneity of the ceramic material would imply that a major renovation of the interior furnishing took place in the first century AD without obvious structural changes to the building. From our point of view though, this scenario seems quite unlikely. There is no question about the time of the last use of the building: Small finds of the fourth century AD were found on the floors of several rooms, sealed under deposits of fragmented decorative materials from the walls. On the basis of dated coins, the end of occupation of the site and the building's final destruction can be set during the earthquake of 363 AD.[20]

Notes on Rooms 6, 7, and 17 There are only very few examples in the greater region comparable to this characteristic three-room group, which consists of a central exedra with two flanking rooms. The rooms 458 and 521 in the early Herodian core of the Western Palace at Masada, dating from the thirties BC, offer an astonishing parallel to rooms 6 and 7 on EZ IV, although the two flanking rooms were not symmetrically arranged, with a reception room on only one side of the exedra 521.[21] The reception and banquet room 458, as with room 6, had one central and two side entrances. Further, it is remarkable that the ground plans of the two exedrae 521 and 7 were almost identical, and that both opened to the north onto a courtyard with a distylos *in antis*. Symmetrical suites of three rooms were a crucial element of Macedonian palace architecture from the late fourth century BC onwards,[22] echoed in the three-room suite of the Late Hellenistic Palazzo delle Colonne in Ptolemais/Cyrenaica.[23] The Palazzo plays a key role as a geographical and chronological link between the Macedonian architecture of the fourth century BC and Palestinian buildings of the first century BC/AD. Although there are still only a few buildings of this type to refer to, it is assumed that the three-room suite had its firm place in Ptolemaic architecture of North Africa, and that the Herodian palaces, as well as the building on EZ IV, depended on Ptolemaic models.

Wall Decoration in Hellenistic Masonry Style The use of decorative stucco and wall paintings in temples, tomb façades, and residential buildings in Petra is well attested. The German Heinrich Kohl was the first scholar to publish a comprehensive study of the stucco decoration in Petra in his 1910 book on the Qasr al-Bint temple.[24] This work remained basic until the publication of a seminal article on decorative stucco at Petra by Fawzi Zayadine.[25]

The fragmented decoration carried out in the so-called Masonry Style[26] on EZ IV is important, because it is dated with a *terminus post quem* of 20 AD; the décor therefore offers the opportunity to reassess the dating of other comparable decoration in Petra. On walls A and C in rooms 2 and 3 large surfaces of stuccoed Masonry-Style wall decoration are preserved (figs. 257, 258). On wall C the following scheme of decoration can be reconstructed: above a shallow, black plinth, of c. 35 cm in height, there are panels or orthostats of roughly 70 x 140 cm, separated by incised lines. The orthostats are alternately colored in red and yellow and have white drafts, which are also separated by incisions. The string-course above, roughly 20 cm high, displays the same color scheme and is followed by the remains of two bottom courses of isodomic masonry. The yellow panels of the stuccoed string-course headers on wall A preserve a fine marbling (fig. 258).

A very similar decoration remains in the staircase of the so-called baths, located directly to the south of Petra's Temenos Gate.[27] There are close parallels, not only in the system of decoration but also in the color scheme employed: The orthostats are painted in the same shades of alternating red and yellow and have the same white drafts. As to dating, it seems reasonable to suggest that the two almost identical decorations are contemporary. It is assumed, as outlined above, that the building on EZ IV was not erected before 20 AD. The decoration of the staircase of the "baths" has recently been discussed by the expert A. Barbet, who, on the basis of stylistic arguments, dated it to the turn of the second/first century BC.[28] The striking difference of more than 100 years between the suggested dates demonstrates clearly how difficult it is to date Masonry-Style decorations in general, and in the Nabataean metropolis of Petra, with its numerous undated monuments in particular.

257. Masonry-Style decoration of wall C, Nabataean mansion, Room 3, EZ IV. Ez-Zantur, Petra.

258. Detail of Masonry-Style decoration on wall A, Nabataean mansion, Room 2, EZ IV. Ez-Zantur, Petra.

The obvious persistence of the Masonry Style was certainly not a purely Petraean phenomenon. The remains of decoration found in the Herodian palaces, as well as the residential houses of the so-called Herodian Quarter in Jerusalem, clearly reveal that this type of decoration enjoyed an above-average life span in the Middle East.[29] A similar anachronistic tendency in Nabataean interior decoration is found on EZ IV in conjunction with the architectural paintings in room 1.

Illusionistic Architectural Wall Paintings in Room 1 The rather small room 1, measuring 5 x 4 m, was originally decorated on all four walls with illusionistic architectural paintings. The murals on walls A and C remain in very good condition (fig. 260). On wall C the paintings are in situ to a length of c. 2.9 m, while those on the adjacent wall A are preserved to a length of c. 1.8 m.

The paintings depict architectural façades on a background of yellowish imitation alabaster. The façades are framed by broad pilasters at the sides and spanned by a narrow blue-green epistyle. Both pilasters are divided into squares that are painted with two-dimensional motifs. The pilaster in the wall corner C/A delineates a scheme of alternating red diamonds on a white background and white diamonds on a red background. The pilaster at the other end of wall C is decorated in the same color scheme with a sequence of quadrilobes of four diagonally placed peltae and discs.[30] The bottom edges of the paintings are mostly lost, apart from some fragments which remain in situ on wall G, and give evidence that the painted façades were not intended to stand on painted socles, but to reach down to floor level. Above the painted decoration running round the interior of the room up to a height of just around 1.5 m, there is a system of stuccoed architecture in the Masonry Style. The pilaster motif—painted in the main zone of wall corner A/C—continues as stucco in the upper zone (fig. 260).

The central symmetric architectural compositions develop from a closed background of yellowish imitation alabaster: from the broadly arranged façade on wall C a central pavilion with a segmental pediment flanked by two pavilions seem to project towards the viewer. The front columns of the pavilions reproduce red imitation marble on a white background, contrasting the rear blue-gray columns and the crowning dark brown Corinthian capitals.[31] Above the capitals there is a red-marbled epistyle, headed by a red-brown frieze, dentils on a white background, and the red-marbled geison and sima. The side pavilions are decorated by disc-shaped *acroteria* with *gorgoneia*.[32]

The pavilion's backdrop is decorated with a conspicuous variety of polychrome geometrical patterns, which are plainly borrowed from the repertoire of *opus-sectile* and mosaic motifs (figs. 259, 260).[33]

259. Detail showing painted *opus-sectile* motifs on wall C, Nabataean mansion, Room 1, EZ IV. Ez-Zantur, Petra.

Stylistic Classification In the course of the first century BC, illusionistic representation of architectural façades became the main characteristic of the Roman (p. 196, fig. 209) Second Pompeian Style.[34] The frescoes on EZ IV are closely related to architectural paintings of the Augustan period—such as those in room 5 in the house of Augustus on the Palatine, dated soon after 31 BC.[35] The linking elements are the tripartite façade, within the classicistic rigidity of the architectural interpretation, with details less vivid, as was still the case in the middle of the first century BC.[36] Further comparable components are the somewhat elongated and fragile architecture and the relatively flat framework, consisting of corner pilasters and a narrow architrave. But there are also notable differences: The frescoes in Augustus's house account for the entire wall surface, as is usual in Roman wall painting, but is not the case on EZ IV.

A clear wall-piercing perspective is observable, achieved chiefly by the vista through the dominant central *aedicula* and by the openings above the lateral screen-walls. The illusionistic painting on EZ IV, in contrast, is composed against a solid background and seems to project forwards.

The architectural painting on EZ IV is restricted to the lower part of the wall in a striking way; this, however, is not the only such case in Petra. This particularity seems to be repeated in a cave in Wadi Siyyagh.[37] The wall paintings there are very flat—i.e., without illusionistic effects—consisting of a row of closed doors, set into a subordinate architectural system of supports and an epistyle. As F. Zayadine remarked, the paintings in Wadi Siyyagh belong not to the Roman but rather to the Hellenistic tradition of Ptolemaic Egypt.[38] Firstly the door-row motif, within a subordinate architectural frame, is closely related to the architecture of the Hellenistic *hypogaea* of Alexandria.[39] Secondly, the two-dimensional interpretation of the architectural theme must be assessed in conjunction with Ptolemaic tomb painting, whose tendency to flatness is regarded as one of its main characteristics by R. Gordon.[40] In Judea, there are also a few examples of architectural painting in the second Pompeian Style.[41] The fragments, relevant in this case, are situated in the northwest corner of room 5 in the Herodian Palatial Mansion in Jerusalem.[42] The remains of small *aediculae* are framed by an architectural system, consisting of pilaster and epistyle. The epistyle ran, as on EZ IV, approximately at eye level—i.e., here too, the architectural painting seems to have been restricted to the lower part of the wall only. One is tempted to interpret the limitation of these Hellenistic and Roman-inspired paintings to a narrow zone of the lower wall as a regional peculiarity, but this remains conjectural since the evidence is too slight.

As mentioned above, the architectural façades of EZ IV were painted onto a background of imitation alabaster. Forerunners or models for imitation alabaster may have included monuments like the Hellenistic alabaster tomb in Alexandria, which was built from polished monolithic alabaster slabs.[43] In

Alexandria there are also early examples of painted imitation alabaster, e.g. in tomb 3 of Mustapha Pasha from the second half of the third century BC,[44] and in tombs 2 and 3 of the Anfushi necropolis from the third–second century BC.[45] It therefore seems reasonable to seek the models for the inconspicuous handling of the background of the architectural paintings in room 1 in Ptolemaic Egypt. This seems also to be true in the case of the flatly painted decoration of the pilaster squares on wall C. They have a direct forerunner in Petra's monumental architecture in the form of the stuccoed panel decoration on the *antae* of the Qasr al-Bint (*terminus ante*: late first century BC), which is again linked to Alexandrian prototypes. Comparable features are the painted pilasters of the *aediculae* in the above-mentioned *hypogaeum* 2 at Anfushi.[46]

In conclusion, it can be said that, on the one hand, both the architecture of the mansion on EZ IV and certain details of its interior room decoration relate closely to Macedonian-inspired Ptolemaic Alexandria. On the other hand, a clearly Roman component is present in the illusionistic wall painting of room 1. The details of the wall paintings referred to reveal, however, that their Roman forerunners were freely interpreted, with the inclusion of Alexandrian elements. The limitation of the painted zone to the lower half of the wall, in combination with a system of decoration in the Masonry Style, gives the paintings in room 1 a new and un-Roman aspect. The anachronistic tendencies one is confronted with on EZ IV, specifically the use of the Hellenistic Masonry Style and the adaptation of Augustan architectural painting in the first century AD, are especially striking.

260. Architectural paintings on walls C and A, Nabataean mansion, EZ IV. Ez-Zantur, Petra.

21 | The Byzantine Church at Petra

ZBIGNIEW T. FIEMA

The *Byzantine Period in Petra* While the cultural history of Nabataean Petra is a relatively well-researched and documented subject, few scholarly analyses have been devoted to the Byzantine period (fourth–early seventh century AD) in Petra. The historical information concerning the city during that period is meager. As the result of the extensive but poorly understood administrative changes throughout the fourth century AD, a new Byzantine province of *Palaestina Salutaris/Tertia* was created, which included southern Jordan, southern Israel, and probably the Sinai, with Petra as the capital city.[1] The growing power of Christianity almost overnight changed the status of the neighboring Palestine from a minor troublesome province to *terra sancta*,[2] but these fundamental changes and the associated building construction prosperity do not seem to have significantly affected Petra and southern Jordan. This area possessed few places worth pilgrimage and donation by pious travelers. In fact, the progress of Christianity in Petra was slow and uneven. The persecutions of Christians in Petra are reported during the reign of Emperor Diocletian (284–305 AD). The Church historian Eusebius, while noting the construction of churches in Petra in the fourth century, also mentioned the existence of pagan superstitions there,[3] and Epiphanius described curious practices of mixed pagan idolatry and Christian elements.[4] Sozomen, the Church historian, noted that during the reign of Theodosius I, many pagans still zealously supported and protected their temples in Petra.[5] The apocryphic story of the monk Bar Sauma suggests that even in the early fifth century, pagan temples and priests still flourished in Petra. Upon the monk's call to abandon pagan practices and temples, the inhabitants of Petra closed city gates against him. Only a divine intervention—a miraculous rain in the city suffering long drought—changed their attitude and led to the conversion of the pagan priests.[6]

261. Aerial photo of the Petra Church.

Initially, Petra remained under the ecclesiastical jurisdiction of the Patriarchate of Antioch and the Metropolitan See of Bosra. However, following the Fourth Ecumenical Council of Chalcedon (451 AD),[7] Petra was transferred to the newly established Patriarchate of Jerusalem, and elevated to the status of a metropolitan see, as one of three metropolitan bishoprics of *Tres Palaestinae*. Bishops from Petra are attested at Church Councils in 347 AD (Sardica), 359 (Seleucia), 362 (Alexandria), and 536 (Jerusalem).[8] During the reigns of Anastasius (491–518 AD) and Justin I (518–527 AD), Petra had acquired a less than honorable status as a place of banishment. The exilees to Petra included common criminals,[9] and the ecclesiastics who advocated a form of Christian faith, which differed from that followed by the reigning emperors. Among the exiled ecclesiastics were Flavian II, the Nestorian patriarch of Antioch,[10] and Mare, the Monophysite bishop of Amida.[11] John of Ephesus observed that Mare and his associates were banished to "a hard and distant place of exile at Petra."[12]

Compared with the Nabataean-Roman periods, the archaeological information concerning the Byzantine period is still relatively limited. On May 19, 363, Petra was seriously affected by a catastrophic earthquake, as documented in *Harvard Syriac 99*.[13] Substantial destruction has been observed in the area of the Colonnaded Street, and also among civic and domestic structures in the city center, some of which were not reconstructed. Entire areas of the city were only partially cleared from ruins, while others were abandoned following that destruction.[14] Despite recent discoveries, the church-construction activities, so well attested in other regions of the Byzantine East, are still poorly documented at Petra.[15] The monumental Urn Tomb of the Nabataean period was converted into a cathedral church on June 24, 446 AD, during the episcopate of Bishop Jason (p. 141, fig. 132).[16] The ed-Deir ("monastery") monument was probably also involved in Christian practices, as painted crosses are still visible on its back wall. The area nearby preserves hermitage and monastic cells, also decorated with crosses. The Mount of Aaron (Jebel Haroun) a few miles to the southwest of Petra possessed a church on its top, which later on was replaced by an Islamic shrine. On the small plateau directly below the summit, remains of a large architectural complex are preserved. This presumably monastic–pilgrimage establishment included a large basilican church and a chapel, as recent excavations indicate.[17]

Description of the Church Complex In light of the scant archaeological and historical information concerning Byzantine Petra, the discovery of the spectacular Byzantine church excavated between 1992 and 1996 is of utmost importance.[18] The project was funded by a grant from the United States Agency for International Development (USAID), organized by the American Center of Oriental Research (ACOR) in Amman, and supported by the Ministry of Tourism and Antiquities of Jordan. The goal of the Petra Church Project was to enhance tourism in Petra by excavating the church, conserving the building and mosaics, and constructing a protective shelter over the church. All these goals were accomplished by 1998. The director of the project, Kenneth W. Russell, who had identified the church in 1990, died tragically in May 1992, just as the excavation was to begin. Pierre M. Bikai, ACOR Director, then became the overall project director, while Zbigniew T. Fiema and Robert Schick of ACOR, and Khairieh 'Amr of the Department of Antiquities of Jordan co-directed the fieldwork during the first phase of excavations (1992–93). During the 1993–96 seasons, Fiema was solely in charge of the fieldwork.

The following description generally outlines the *extant* appearance of the church complex and its components (figs. 261, 277). The modifications to which the church complex was subjected throughout its existence, are presented in the phasing section. The representative parallels with churches from neighboring regions quoted here concentrate on these from the Negev region in southern Israel, where, due to long-standing cultural and economic ties with southern Jordan, and the similarity in environmental conditions, Byzantine churches are the most comparable in terms of the development and the architectural features with the Petra church.[19]

The Petra church site is located on a ridge north of the Colonnaded Street. A few hundred meters north is the Ridge church, also recently excavated.[20] The Petra church is a standard basilica divided into three longitudinal spaces (nave and side aisles) by two east-west rows of eight columns each (fig. 261). At the east end of the aisles are semicircular apses, while the nave ends in a larger semicircular apse. As in the Negev, the apses in the Petra church are in a horseshoe form,[21] rather than semicircle, although less pronounced than in the Negev. The ground plan of the basilica is very harmonious. The church is internally c. 23.21 m long and c. 15.35 m wide. The ratio of the inner length to the inner width (save the apses) is exactly 3:2. The ratio of the nave width to the aisle width is 2:1. The walls of the church, some preserved to a height of three meters, are built with sandstone ashlar facing, rubble fill, and ash or mud mortar. Interior faces display extensively preserved white plaster. Many of the ashlar blocks are dressed in the typical Nabataean fashion displaying tightly spaced diagonal chisel-marks. These blocks, as well as some column capitals were obviously reused from earlier and already abandoned buildings in Petra. The pitched roof structure of the basilica was the standard type with a framework of wooden beams and a clerestory over the nave.

The *bema*,[22] in the front of the central apse, is raised two steps above the aisles and nave, and it projects westward into the nave as far as the second set of columns from the east (figs. 261, 262). Originally, the *bema* was enclosed by marble panels all along the west side, except for the central, stepped entranceway. Along the north and south sides of the *bema*, walls four courses high were constructed between the first and second columns, while between the easternmost columns and the east church wall were marble panels and steps leading up from the side aisles. Contrary to its usual position in the Byzantine churches in northern and central Jordan, but following the known examples from Israel and especially from the Negev, the *ambo* (pulpit) at the Petra church is located at the northwestern edge of the chancel platform.[23] The only other churches in southern Jordan, which display the same arrangement are the church at Deir Ain Abata,[24] and the Lower Church at Humeima.[25] The steps up from the *bema* and their foundation are still in place, but the marble hexagonal base, colonettes, platform, and panels were badly broken up, and most pieces removed from the church in antiquity.

The central apse contains a portion of four curved rows of a *synthronon*—a semicircular installation which originally consisted of five gradually superimposed steps (fig. 262). This installation is well-evidenced in other Byzantine churches in Palestine and Jordan,[26] but as opposed to a more common one-to-three tier type, the *synthronon* in Petra belongs to a multi-tiered type better attested for the sixth century.[27] The whole upper central section, which would have had a bishop's throne, is missing. Ostensibly, the function of a *synthronon* was to accommodate the clergy during ceremonies.[28] More probably, the semi-rings of the *synthronon* served only to ascend the bishop's throne. The clergy might have used the top tier for seating, as well as lightweight or portable benches presumably situated on the north and south sides of the *bema*. The location of the main altar—whether at the central apse's chord[29] or nearby—remains unknown. Concentrations of

262. The central apse including the *synthronon*. The Petra Church.

263. General view of the atrium. The Petra Church.

264. The baptismal font. The Petra Church.

charred beams against and along the north and south walls of the church suggest the existence of wooden benches, a feature well known from Palestinian churches.[30] This suggestion is also supported by the wall plaster, which breaks off at a uniform height of c. 0.45 m above the floor, indicating the original position of the benches.

In addition to the church proper, the ecclesiastical complex uncovered during the excavations includes the atrium, a fully enclosed colonnaded courtyard located directly west of the church, the baptistery farther west, and rooms adjacent to the church and the atrium on their northern sides (fig. 277). The atrium (fig. 263) has the almost square, standard open-air form with a flagstone pavement, surrounded on all sides by a portico with four columns on each side. In the center of the atrium, a large masonry-constructed cistern had been dug in.[31] The cistern is associated with the settling tank through which rainwater from the roof of the portico was chanelled into the cistern. The church's visitors would first enter the atrium then proceed to the church through three doors located in its western wall, which correspond to the tripartite division of the interior (figs. 261, 277). The central door is wider than the aisle doors, and it has door-jambs decorated with finely carved shallow reliefs which most probably represent personifications of Greco-Roman deities. The entry into the church could also be effected by means of two doors in the north wall of the church. These entrances, however, would most probably serve the ecclesiastics.

Directly west of the atrium is the baptismal complex which consists of Rooms IX, X, and XI (fig. 277). The baptistery, located in Room X, is the first installation of this kind known from southern Jordan and one of the best preserved in the entire Syro-Palestine. The font belongs to the cruciform type, which is usually built in masonry and generally earlier in date than the monolithic fonts. Also, the cruciform type is rather common in southern Palestine, especially in the Negev,[32] while in Jordan this type is unknown north of the Madaba-Mt. Nebo area.[33] The dimensions and the depth of the Petra font parallel those of the largest fonts in the region.

265. Nabataean limestone niche frame. The Petra Church. Department of Antiquities, Amman, Jordan.

The archaeological dating of the early phase of the church complex—mid-to-later fifth century AD—makes the baptistery in Petra the earliest known structure of this kind in Jordan.[34]

The cruciform baptismal font is sunk in a large, almost square platform made of stones and paved with marble slabs, located in the eastern half of Room X (fig. 265). The basin of the font is accessible by steps in each of the cross's arms, which lead down to the bottom. No traces of a drain system have been found; the water must have been brought in buckets and afterwards drawn away by hand. Close to the southwest corner is a large stone jar fully integrated with the platform. Such small basins or containers are also known from other baptisteries, being more common in association with cruciform fonts.[35] It was suggested that these auxiliary basins served in the baptism of infants,[36] especially in areas where water was scarce,[37] but these could equally have served for extra water supply/storage. Four limestone columns are situated in the corners of the platform. The columns must have supported a *ciborium* (canopy) over the font. Fragments of capitals and arches marked with crosses, which connected the capitals, were found inside the room. The closest parallel for the baptistry at Petra comes from the East Church in Mampsis (Kurnub) in the Negev, where a cruciform baptismal font is sunk inside the area marked by four columns and a quadrangular frame which connected them. The Mampsis baptistry is dated to the early fifth century AD.[38] A parallel from Jordan, although without a canopy or additional small basin, is provided by a poorly preserved and obviously modified installation in the Church of Bishop Sergius at Umm ar-Rasas.[39] The type and construction manner of the baptistery installation at Petra again confirm close affinities with the Negev region. The cruciform fonts are known from the East Church at Mampsis, the North Church at Oboda/'Avdat, and the North and South Churches at Sobata/Shivta; the first two are masonry-built.[40]

The design of the baptismal complex of the Petra church perfectly suits the requirements of the processional rite associated with the baptism, and reflects the symbolism of the baptismal liturgy, as known from ancient sources.[41] Particularly suitable is the arrangement of the baptistery room with rooms on either side of it, and a straight passage between all. Considering the extant furnishing, Room XI could be defined as a *catechumeneum*—the starting point of rite—and Room IX as *consignatorium*—where the rite ended.[42] With a lower level of the floor in Room X vs. the adjacent ones, the procession would have to *descend* into its interior and then *ascend* the space of the following room, regardless of the movement direction. This obviously intentional effect resembles the baptismal rite of immersion, and ascension to the membership in the church's community. At a later time, the door leading to Room XI had been expertly blocked. Thus, while before the blocking, the font in Room X designated a focal point in a straight-line itinerary, afterwards, it would have become a final point from which the procession had to retrace its steps.

Room XI, which adjoins the baptistery on its southern side, features two cupboards and a marble shelf in the south wall. An elaborate frame in Nabataean style[43] that originally fit a niche or an *aedicula*, probably on the upper (second) floor of the room, was found in the stone tumble inside this room (fig. 265). The frame is undoubtedly reused, perhaps from a private house or a shrine, and should be dated to the Nabataean period. The elements of the frame included the cornice with dentils, the triglyph and metope frieze, and two engaged half-columns with Nabataean capitals. The architrave was missing. All were made of greenish limestone, originally painted with red trim and later decorated with a lime wash.

The architectural entities on the northern side of the basilica and the atrium include (from the east to west): Room I (= Scroll Room); Room II, Courtyard III, and Rooms IV, V, VI, VII, and VIII (fig. 277). The first three spaces existed

before the church complex was built. Room I, the ceiling of which was supported by three arches, contained the remains of the burnt archive of papyrus documents, discussed in a separate chapter of this volume. Barrel vaulting was utilized as a ceiling of Room II. Both rooms had a second floor. These rooms might have served as the storage for liturgical paraphernalia or other church-related objects. The function of other rooms could not be determined, but the size and location of Room VI would make it a good candidate for a chapel. The pavement of all these entities included large sand or limestone slabs and occasional marble.

Mosaic Floors The nave, *bema*, and the central apse were paved with a pavement in *opus-sectile* style—a geometric design made of small and large marble and purple sandstone slabs. This pavement was mostly stolen. The north and south aisles are paved with mosaic floors.[44] In addition to stone tesserae (mosaic cubes), glass tesserae, some of which are gold-plated, were used in both aisles, as well as red-fired ceramic tesserae. The mosaic in the north aisle, c. 22.6 m x 3 m, features rows of circular medallions formed by vine scrolls—called "inhabited scrolls." This particular design, which consists of animal, human, and inanimate object representations inside the medallions, is also known from classical Hellenistic and Roman art (fig. 266).[45] Each of the three vertical rows contains 28 medallions. The central vertical row of medallions

266. General view of the mosaic floor from the north aisle. The Petra Church.

267. Panel with camel carrying tree from the north aisle. The Petra Church.

268. General view of the mosaic floor from the south aisle. The Petra Church.

depicts containers such as amphorae, vases, goblets, baskets, kraters, as well as trees, fruit, compositions (bird in a cage, a fish head on a plate), and animals or birds (dog, camel, eagle). The medallions located on either side of each central medallion contain a bird, animal, or human, always in pairs, and with each pair representing a male and female of the same species (except for the humans). The largest group of representations includes common animals such as the donkey or camel, predatory beasts such as lions, bears, and leopards, and exotic species including giraffes and elephants. The three human pairs include a shepherd and a man with an amphora, separated by a dog; two camel drivers separated by a camel carrying a tree trunk (fig. 267); and a black man and a man with a plate, separated by a pyxis. The background outside the medallions is yellow, while white marble cubes are used as background within the medallions. Comparison of this mosaic with other Palestinian examples reveals the high artistic value of the majority of the representations at Petra. The figures of humans and animals are very realistic, and their proportions dexterously met. The analogies point to the Gaza school as the inspiration for Petra mosaics in terms of both the composition of scenes and the figures themselves, although the probable influence of the Madaba mosaic school is also to be noted.[46]

The south aisle measures 23.2 m x 3.3 m, and it features a mosaic floor with a variety of anthropo- and zoomorphic (human- and animal-form) representations in rows of medal-

269

270

269. Personification of spring from the south aisle. The Petra Church.

270. Personification of summer from the south aisle. The Petra Church.

opposite:
271. Okeanos (Ocean) mosaic panel from the south aisle. The Petra Church.

272. Panel with fisherman from the south aisle. The Petra Church.

lions (figs. 268, 274). The central row of rectangular medallions contains the personified images of the Four Seasons (figs. 269, 270), Ocean, Earth, and Wisdom, which undoubtedly draw upon Classical models. Flanking the central row are square and circular medallions depicting fish, birds, and animals. Although the iconographical themes of the central row are well known throughout the Near East, the representations at Petra clearly testify to the special sensibility of the client to Greco-Roman culture. Of interest is the representation of Okeanos (Ocean; fig. 271). The maritime deities, such as Neptune/Poseidon are well known in the iconography of the Roman period. The parallel examples include Antioch, where this particular motif generally enjoyed considerable popularity, and Roman North Africa, where Okeanos is often associated with an oar, warship, and dolphin. The mosaics with sea monsters, boats, fishermen (fig. 272) and even personifications of the sea enjoyed tremendous popularity in Palestine during the sixth and seventh centuries. The personifications in the southern aisle, which after all have clearly pagan implications in Hellenistic and Roman culture must have become in the Byzantine period something like rhetorical figures, rather than actual bearers of old religious ideas. The floor appears to be the work of a local team of mosaicists influenced by the Classical patterns available in an artistic center such as Gaza or Caesarea Maritima, where ancient culture was deeply rooted.[47]

The style of the Petra mosaics, which is characterized by the departure from the Roman narrative convention in favor of a geometrized composition, enters the sixth-century history of Byzantine art, which features the so-called Justinian Renaissance lasting from the beginning of the century. As these mosaics exemplify the changes that Byzantine mosaics were undergoing with respect to the Roman patterns, they equally represent tradition and innovation in Byzantine art. The earlier illusionism has largely been abandoned, the figures have become more flat and two-dimensional, although an attempt at three-dimensionality of some animals is continued by showing all four legs, additionally emphasized by shading (fig. 274).[48]

The floor mosaics constitute but a part of the church decoration's iconographic program. Discovered fragments of wall mosaics clearly testify to the fact that the semidomes over the apses of the church at Petra, as well as the clerestory walls over the nave, were decorated by wall mosaics, obviously

271

272

rich in design and gilding (fig. 273). The overwhelming majority of tesserae are glass-made (some gilded) although some marble cubes were also used. While the restoration of hundreds of mosaic chunks and the study of the designs are still in progress, the wall mosaics of the Petra church must have resembled the mosaics decorating the apse of the Basilica of St. Catherine on the Sinai, which date to the same period.

The Ecclesiastical Phases The Byzantine church site represents, in fact, a microcosm of the urban history of Petra, from the Nabataean through the Roman and Byzantine periods, until the Early Islamic period.[49] The site was inhabited at least 400 years before the church was constructed. In contrast to the date proposed in the early reports, the fully reviewed archaeological data suggest now that the early church complex came into existence in the mid-to later fifth century AD. Generally, two major phases—early and late—of ecclesiastical occupation can be distinguished at the site. In the early phase, the complex included a basilican church with the narthex (entrance porch), the forecourt following the narthex, and the baptismal rooms. In addition, rooms and spaces situated on the north side, mentioned above, were also incorporated. The basilica was then a mono-apsidal church with two lateral rooms (*pastophoria*) located on each side of the central apse. The decoration of the church proper consisted of the mosaic with anthropomorphic representations in two-thirds of the south aisle, and an unknown pavement in the north aisle. The nave's floor was probably paved with the combined shale-marble slabs. A slightly raised (?) sanctuary area was flanked by abstract-designed mosaics.

In addition to archaeological indicators, the fifth century date for this development is also supported from the architectural standpoint. The width-to-length ratios for the dimensions of the basilica are typical for earlier churches in Palestine (fourth–fifth century), characterized by long, narrow aisles.[50] Admittedly, this type is usually associated with atrium rather than narthex. But it was also suggested that narthex, which probably evolved from the eastern portico of the atrium, appears in the ecclesiastical architecture around the mid-fifth century, and often together with an atrium.[51] Although at Petra the term atrium is not considered technically suitable for the forecourt of the early ecclesiastical phase, that space nevertheless functioned as an integral open-air court of the complex. Other relevant parallels for the early church complex in Petra include those from Syria, where basilicas with the inscribed central apse flanked by quadrangular *pastophoria* are typical for the fifth century.[52]

The major remodeling of the existent complex, i.e., the later ecclesiastical phase, took place in the early–mid sixth century AD. The activities in the church proper included the installation of the side apses in the spaces of the lateral *pastophoria*, and the construction of the elevated *bema* and the *ambo* in the sanctuary. Mosaic floors were laid out in the north aisle and in the eastern part of the south aisle, while the nave was paved with the marble pavement in *opus-sectile* style. The interior received lavish marble furnishing, including screens for the apses and the bema, and the marble covers for the stylobates. The apses' semidomes and the clerestory walls above the arches were decorated with wall mosaics. Benches were installed along the walls. The activities outside the church proper included the westward extension of two of the baptismal rooms (IX and X). New walls improved a delineation of the court in the front of the church, creating an enclosed atrium, which was expanded in size by the total demolition of the narthex. The atrium received a peristyle form with two-floor porticoes on all four sides. A large cistern and a settling tank were constructed in the center of the atrium. A five-tiered, semicircular *synthronon* and, probably, a bishop's throne, were inserted in the space of the interior of the central apse, probably in the later sixth century.

Although the triapsidal churches seemingly occur throughout the Byzantine period, i.e., from the fourth to the seventh century AD,[53] this type is, however, statistically rare before the early sixth century.[54] Unfortunately, some studies fail to recognize a distinction between churches which were built as triapsidal basilicas vs. those which experienced a transformation from mono- to triapsidal churches. The latter is a phenomenon well attested in the neighboring Negev, and the evidence strongly points on the early sixth century as a date of the alteration.[55] This substantial change was postulated to have been linked to the re-emphasis on the cult of martyrs and saints,[56] in association with the veneration and display of relics, and a new, processional character of liturgy. Resulting new architectural arrangements included, as postulated in some cases, the location of relics in the reliquaries in side apses.[57] While the insertion of the side apses is well documented for several churches in the Negev, that transformation in southern Jordan is so far attested only in the church of St. Stephen at Umm ar-Rasas, where it involves the addition of only one, north apse.[58] A transformation example from outside the Negev is the Civic Complex Church at Pella, where the triapsidal phase (2) is dated to 525–550 AD. During this phase, that church, similarly to the Petra church, received a lavish decoration of walls and floors with wall mosaics, colored stonework, as well as marble chancel screens.[59]

The remains found in the church indicate that some sort of renovation or remodeling of the basilica's interior might have been attempted later. Some parts of the church, such as the south aisle, could have been permanently detached from the ecclesiastical function. To facilitate the handling of twenty-one large jars stored in that aisle, a wooden deck was laid over the mosaic there. Construction material, such as wood, flue, and water pipes (south aisle), stone paving slabs and hematite bits (nave) were found during the excavations. Door wings and metal fittings were presumably removed from some doorways. Alternatively, the church might have been in the process of being converted into a storage depot for useful construction material, and the stripping of some of its ecclesiastical furnishing had begun. The planned changes were never fully implemented because a disastrous fire had destroyed the church and caused its abandonment at the end of the sixth–beginning of the seventh century AD. The nave and aisles were strewn with burnt wood and ash, but the church was still structurally sound. Room I was burned too, and the charred remains of wooden ceiling covered the carbonized scroll archives. The atrium and the baptismal rooms were seemingly less affected by the fire, if at all. Limited acts of vandalism might have occurred in the church proper immediately before the fire. An attractive but routine explanation usually given in such cases would point to a destruction, which resulted from a hostile takeover of Petra, followed by an abandonment of the ecclesiastical complex and the robbery of its valuable or useful furnishings. One could not entirely exclude some elements of such a scenario; the Persian and Muslim invasions of the Near East are chronologically close to the proposed date of the church's destruction. Nevertheless, this simplistic explanation is not favored here. The fire could have had a natural cause or been related to an accident. Furthermore, the notion of continuity of intention, represented by the selective removal of the church's furnishings, as observable for the periods immediately before and after the fire, as well as the lack of evidence for a wholesale destruction and exploitation of the church remains, speak against the invader theory. In addition, historical evidence is silent about a conquest of Petra by the Persians, while archaeological data from the sites in the Near East do not support the alleged wholesale destructions of Christian edifices during the Muslim conquest or afterward.[60]

The Post-Ecclesiastical Phases Although the structural stability of the gutted church was not affected by fire, the basilica was neither restored nor re-utilized for its ecclesiastical function. Instead, the non-ecclesiastical occupation was established in the atrium area, primarily in the southwest corner where some domestic use installations were erected, and in the rooms of the baptismal complex. The conspicuous absence of a massive ash and charcoal debris layer in the nave must be explained as a result of post-fire human activity, which included an almost total removal of the marble *opus-sectile* pavement of the nave and chancel (fig. 261). Also, wall-mosaic tesserae and glass were collected for reuse or melting. Glass-paste cakes presumably made of re-melted multicolored components (glass tesserae and shards) were found in Room IX. This occupation certainly continued into the Early Islamic period (after 635 AD) when the derelict church suffered a partial collapse of walls, and columns, probably due to a seismic event, judging from the pattern of collapse. However, the semidomes over the apses might have survived. Following the first earthquake, a limited clearance of the atrium was attempted once again. No evidence of habitation can be associated with this phase. Instead, enigmatic activities took place in Room I and in the north apse, presumably in search of the water channel, which ran from the north under these structures. Also, the north half of the *synthronon* was probably removed during these activities, which can be generally dated to the later seventh–early eighth century AD. In addition to the process of natural deterioration and decay of its ruins, the complex was certainly subjected to at least one more substantial seismic-related destruction. Casual and temporary later occupations, dated to the Abbasid, Ayyubid-Mamluk, and early Ottoman periods (eighth–eighteenth century) are indicated by the presence of late ceramics and glass at the site. Simple stone enclosures were erected in the atrium area to prevent its from being filled with collapsing stones. Limited farming andgrazing could have begun in some parts of the ruined complex.

The Finds The excavations of the church complex provided a plethora of finds related to the Byzantine period. Thousands of iron nails, fasteners, and clamps from the roof construction were recovered. Bronze, iron, and lead elements of the door mechanisms, such as pivots and their mounts, brackets, latches, keys, key-plates, and hinges (some still in situ), provide an unusually clear picture of the doors and their functioning.[61] Many thousands of ceramic sherds were recorded, ranging from small Nabataean sherds through types datable to the fifth and sixth centuries, with limited numbers of seventh-to-early-eighth-century sherds, as well as Late Islamic hand-made pottery.[62] The excavations provided large numbers of glass fragments, primarily from standard liturgical glass oil lamps and windowpanes.[63]

The best preserved among the 4,230 pieces of marble are the complete furnishings of the south apse consisting of a panel, post, two colonnettes, and table, which have been restored and returned to their original position (fig. 274).[64] The identical furnishings of the north apse were less well preserved, while only portions of the badly broken panels and other furnishings from the *bema* and *ambo* were recovered. Four panels with the identical design were used in the side apses and the *bema*, consisting of a central eight-sided cross

273

274

275

276

273. Fragment of wall mosaic; male head. h: 10 cm? The Petra Church. Department of Antiquities, Amman, Jordan.

upper right:
274. Eastern section of mosaic floor of south aisle and marble furnishings of the adjacent south apse (as recently restored). The Petra Church.

275. One of the marble chancel screen panels with cross decoration. The Petra Church. h: 86 cm. Department of Antiquities, Amman, Jordan.

276. View of the Scroll Room during the excavation of the carbonized papyri. The Petra Church.

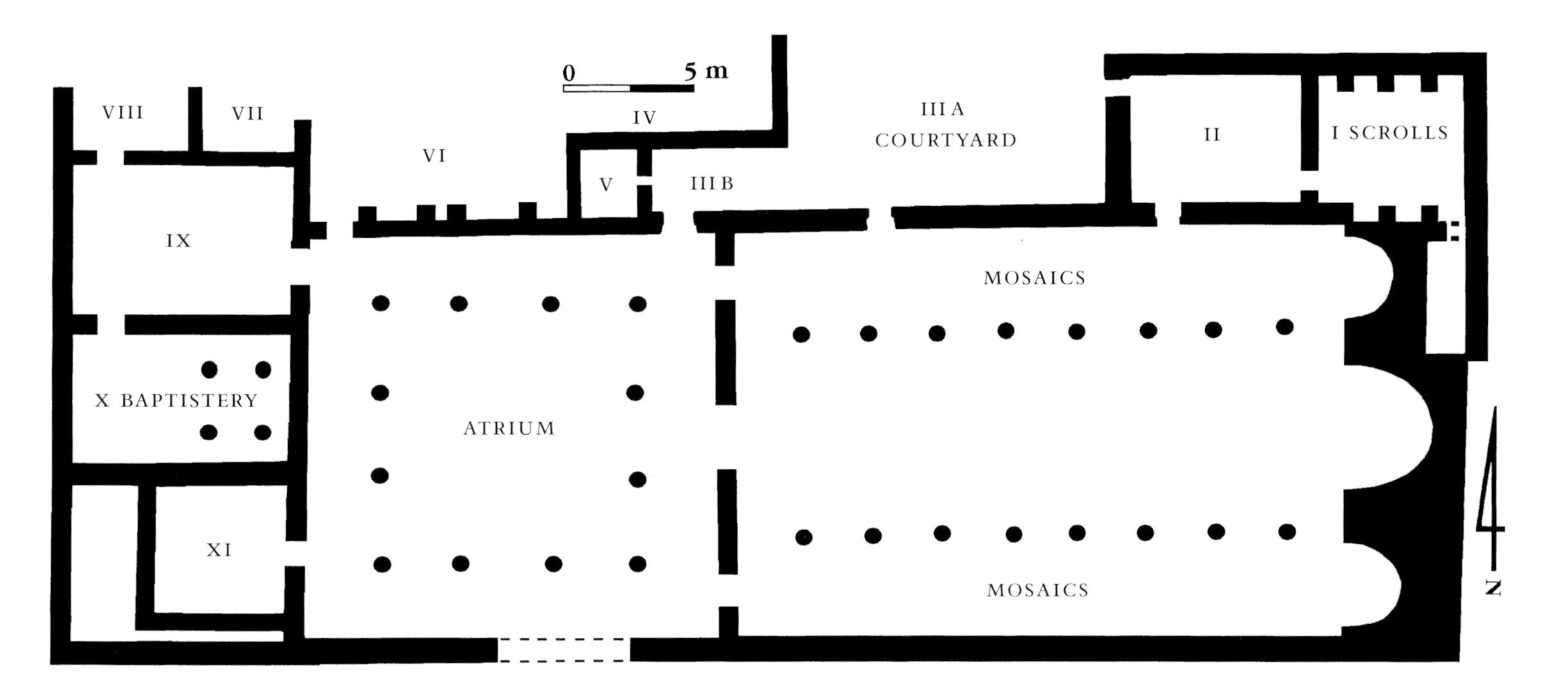

277. Sketch-plan of the Petra Church complex (with numbered rooms).

enclosed by a wreath, with ribbons that curved from the bottom of the wreath, turned up at the lower corners, and terminated in crosses to the sides of the wreath (fig. 275). One open-work lattice screen with a pattern of crosses within circles was found broken up into hundreds of pieces. The broken pieces of a large, footed *kantharos* with two panther-shape handles were found along the middle of the stylobate for the south row of columns (pp. 20, 21; figs. 6, 7). This object, dated to 170–210 AD, was reused in the church, probably for ritual hand washing or the blessing of holy water. A reused limestone water fountain, presumably from a Roman-period building, was found in the atrium.[65]

Unfortunately, no inscriptions directly relating to the church were found. Pre-church inscriptions include a fragmentary Nabataean inscription dated to the reign of King Aretas IV (9 BC–40 AD). A commemorative Greek inscription on a reused block mentions an Aurelius Themos, son of Markianos, who financed an unknown structure/statue (?) related to Aphrodite. The inscription, probably of the third century AD, might have come from the Temple of Aphrodite (*Aphrodeision*) of Petra, mentioned in the Babatha Archive from Nahal Hever.[66] Among the coins found during the excavations, the majority can be dated to the fourth and the sixth century AD. A *follis* of Tiberius II Constantine (578–82 AD) was found in a disturbed post-destruction layer, and an *as* of Trajan, which commemorates the annexation of the Nabataean Kingdom in 106 AD (*Arabia Adquisita*), in a similar context. The discovery of burnt papyrus documents in the Scroll Room in December 1993 turned out to be of utmost importance. The lowermost burnt layer of charcoal and ash contained up to 150 papyrus scrolls or fragments, all completely carbonized. These papyri were probably originally located on a light shelf in the northwestern corner of the room, which must have burned during the fire and then collapsed (fig. 276). In the same room, a second, smaller archive of very poorly preserved papyrus documents was located on the stone shelf between two springers for arches on the southern wall.[67] The contents and the significance of these documents are discussed in Chapter 22 of this volume.

The End of Petra Historically, the seventh century in Petra is totally unknown.[68] The conquest of southern Jordan by the Muslim forces passed without any specific references in either Byzantine or Arab sources. After the initial peaceful capitulations of major towns in the area, such as Aila, Udhruh, and Jarba in 630 AD, no further action seemed to have occurred in southern Jordan. Notably, Petra is neither mentioned in any accounts of the conquest nor in any Early Islamic historical sources. Already at the beginning of the seventh century, some inhabitants of Petra lived among the ruins, as demonstrated in the case of the Petra church. It is possible that the population had gradually moved away from the urban center into outlying rural areas. With the current state of archaeological exploration, it is impossible to chronologically assess the latest phases of the ancient occupation in Petra, but it must have occurred sometime in the seventh or early eighth century, at which time Petra appears to have effectively ceased as an urban center.[69]

22 | Petra in the Sixth Century: The Evidence of the Carbonized Papyri

LUDWIG KOENEN, ROBERT W. DANIEL, AND TRAIANOS GAGAS

In December 1993, a highly unusual find emerged at Petra.[1] During the excavations of a Byzantine church conducted by Zbigniew T. Fiema for the American Center of Oriental Research (ACOR), under the directorship of Pierre Bikai, the remnants of some 140 rolls of carbonized papyri were found (p. 294; fig. 276). After a Finnish team under the leadership of Jaakko Frösén of the Finnish Academy and the University of Helsinki had completed the painstaking conservation work, ACOR assigned the decipherment, edition, and translation of the texts to Frösén's Finnish team and to an American group directed by Ludwig Koenen. The papyri were broken into small fragments, but by assembling the fragments, substantial portions of the rolls have been restored. A total of about forty rolls yield sufficiently coherent pieces of text for publication; the remaining fragments also offer valuable glimpses and will be carefully researched.

Private Family Papers from St. Mary at Petra These rolls, written in Byzantine Greek, belonged to the property-related, private papers of Theodoros, son of Obodianos, from Kastron Zadakathon (modern Ṣadaqa, eighteen miles south-southeast of Petra), where his father had already owned property. Theodoros was born around 514 AD and became a deacon, later archdeacon, in Petra. His work for the church left him enough time and energy to manage his private estate. In 537 AD, after the death of his father and shortly before he came of age, he married his cousin Stephanous, the daughter of Patrophilos. He died probably sometime before 592 AD,[2] and his son and heir added a few more pieces to the family papers. Dated papyri span the period between 537 and 593/4 AD, but caution is needed with regard to this range: Some rolls whose dates have not survived or have not been recognized may date earlier than 537 AD or later than 592/3 AD.

Among the papers, one finds divisions and exchanges of property, receipts for the payment of taxes, and requests for transfer of tax responsibility. The legal importance of such documents is shown in a settlement of 544 or 574 AD, in which the parties present to the judges some documents[3] that were 73, 53, and 40 years old respectively (Inv. 83, or P. Petra H.M. King Hussein bin Talal and H.M. Queen Noor al-Hussein [M. and J. Kaimio]).

Theodoros's papers were found in a storage room of the aforementioned church, which was built after the middle of the fifth century. Early on in the sixth century, it was renovated and sumptuously decorated with marble and superb mosaics (see Chapter 21). This church must have been the one that a papyrus calls the church of "our Blessed and All-Holy Lady, the Glorious Mother of God and Ever-Virgin Mary in Petra" (Inv. 6a, or P. Petra Daniel C. and Nancy E. Gamber [J. Frösén]) and where Theodoros, son of Obodianos, the main figure in the family papers, was deacon and later archdeacon "of the most holy church [of this] Metropolis" (Petra).[4] Archdeacons were assigned to bishops. If so, then St. Mary of Petra was the see of the bishop.

It is not clear whether the papyri were deposited in the storage room of the church one at a time, as they had been written, or all at once around the end of the sixth century. The church was a place to store documents safely. Similarly, private documents seem to have been stored in the monastery of Phoibammon in Egypt.[5] At Nessana in the Negev, about seventy-two miles northwest of Petra, almost all papyri were found in the storerooms of churches. According to Casper J. Kraemer, the editor of the papyri, people stored their papyri in churches when they were no longer of use (Kraemer 1958, pp. 3ff.). This would indicate that people in basically oral societies viewed their written documents with such an awe that they did not destroy them even after they finally lost relevance. But in contrast to these cases, as far as we can tell, the documents found in the storeroom of the Petra church were private papers of only one family. In his capacity as deacon and then archdeacon, Theodoros, the main owner of these papers, had direct access to this room. The same may have also been true for his heir. But despite their efforts to keep the family papers in a safe place, the church burnt down in the early seventh century. Ironically, this fire was responsible for the carbonization of the papyri and, thus, preserved part of them, albeit imperfectly.

The find has opened a new chapter in the history of Petra under the Byzantine Empire. Where we once had blank pages that we tried to fill with generalities as best as we could, we now have real and unexpected information. Petra's destruction by an earthquake in 551 AD, reported as fact in histories and guidebooks, now turns out to be an untenable scholarly theory. Most importantly, the new papyri offer unique evidence for aspects of the social and economic life of the city, of its hinterland, and of (at least) one large and relatively wealthy family over much of the sixth century. This information, however, is one-sided, as the evidence reflects the interests of a well-to-do family rather than those of members of the economically and socially weaker classes and of the community as a whole.

We must add another note of caution: relocation of fragments, progress in decipherment, and study of papyri, which have received only initial attention, may change many details of the picture that is forming. As long as decipherment and historical research are not completed, all conclusions must remain preliminary.

A Wealthy Family in a Changing Economy Theodoros, son of Obodianos, whose own papers are the core of the Petra papyri, belonged to a large and wealthy family of landowners. Male members of this family and other men mentioned in the Petra papyri added the Roman gentilic name Flavius to their names—in his case, Flavios Theodoros, son of Obodianos. In Petra as well as in Egypt and elsewhere, "Flavios" served as a status designation. It marked its bearer as a member of the elite as it related him to the *gens* (family) of the Flavii and, more specifically, to the fourth-century second Flavian dynasty of Constantine the Great (Flavius Valerius Constantinus). The wealth of Theodoros's family may be illustrated by three examples.

(1) Evidence for the economic status of Theodoros's extended family comes from a document written between 527 and probably 537 AD (Inv. 10, or P. Petra Khaled & Suha Shoman). It regulates and details a division of property among three brothers who had largely inherited it from their father. They probably were Theodoros's cousins. The roll was originally some 3.02 m long; about 2.59 m have been reconstructed (see figs. 278, 279). The oldest brother participating in the division was a priest or deacon, for he is called "reverend" (*eulabestatos*). The procedures are close to those we know from Byzantine papyri found at Nessana. The brothers first divided the property into three equal shares without knowing who would receive which share. Then they cast lots that assigned the pre-divided shares to their new owners. Thus, fairness was in the hands of God, and at the end of the document the brothers swear by the Trinity and Imperial Salvation that they will abide by the terms of the division. The results were definitive and unquestionable.

A substantial amount of the property was in Petra, the village Serila, and a large area called Ogbana. The land under cultivation amounts to at least 134 *iugera*, of which forty-four *iugera* were vineyards and ninety were grain land. The 134 *iugera* represent almost eighty-four acres if we assume the standard size *iugerum*.[6] In addition, the brothers divided a total of twenty-one or twenty-two apartments with courtyards, towers, and other structures: twelve in Petra (one a stable), and nine or ten in Serila. Some of the apartments in the city as well as in the village came with small orchards, in Greek *xerokēpia*;[7] and the brothers' property in Petra also included a larger orchard unattached to an apartment. The word *xerokēpia* means literally "dry-garden," which suggests that they did not need irrigation. In Inv. 10, the Arabic term for "dry-garden" is *ganna*, a word which usually refers to an orchard or garden dominated by shade-providing trees. In addition, two of the brothers received a couple of slaves each.[8]

(2) In 537 AD, Theodoros had temporarily moved from Petra to Gaza, where he participated in a property settlement presumably after the death of his father, Obodianos (*P. Petra* I 2 [ed. J. Frösén], also called P. Petra P. E. MacAllister). Among the place-names mentioned appears Eleutheropolis (Beit Jibrin/Bet Guvrin, 28 km northeast of Gaza, halfway to Jerusalem). It would seem that, at some point at least, the family had owned property west of Wadi Araba and as far away as Gaza.

(3) After his marriage to his cousin Stephanous in 537 AD, Theodoros received a dowry and extra gifts valued together at 6½ Roman pounds or 2.128 kg (Inv. 65+63, or P. Petra W. Egan and V. Egan, written in 539/40 AD). Such numbers can be fictitious, but in the present case we see no indication for overstating the amount.

Despite the prosperity of Theodoros's family, we should be cautious in speculating about the general health of Petra's economy. It should, however, be obvious that Petra in the sixth century was still a place where wealthy people could live quite well. While the city in the sixth century was no longer a significant hub in East-West trade, it was still a proud city of local importance. The Petra papyri are silent about trade, but they are focused on agriculture. The landowners leased many of their fields to vintners, farmers, and planters of new vineyards. We may generalize that they derived their income from agriculture, especially from wine, grain, and the fruits of their

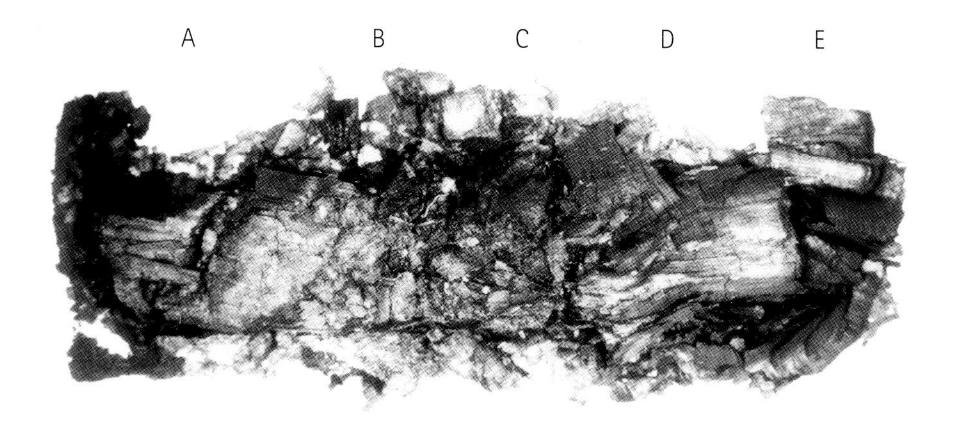

278. P. Petra Inv. 10 (P. Petra Khaled and Suha Shoman) before preservation. The roll was broken up in five sections (A–E). The Finnish conservator separated them into five parallel stacks of layers of papyrus (likewise A–E). In each stack the upper half of the layers of the side with writing faced down, while the written side of the lower layers faced up. In the middle was a layer where writing faced writing. Here each stack was separated into two half-stacks. Then in each half-stack the layers of papyrus were separated from each other and stabilized by pasting each of them on Japanese paper with the written side up and readable. After this was done for the two half-stacks, let us say, of D, the conservator interlaced the layers from these half-stacks, thus producing the entire D section of the original roll. The same was done for the A, B, C, and E sections. Finally the full roll was reconstructed to the extent that was possible by placing the opened and reconstructed sections side by side.

279. The end of P. Petra Inv. 10 (P. Petra Khaled and Suha Shoman), lines 191-208 *(?)* One can still recognize the sections A-E now put together as part of the roll. The E section is now fairly complete, although much of it had to be retrieved from separate and broken-off stacks of fragments (contrast the E-section of pict. 1). Most likely, the roll had fallen on its right side (E) when the "bookshelves" collapsed. The writing is well preserved on the right side (D-E), while the traces of writing on the left side are hardly recognizable on the photograph. There the surface is damaged by a fine web of cracks in a c. 1–2 mm. mesh. The papyrus is partly decomposed. The different states of preservation are the result of the fire. The right side of the roll was exposed to greater heat and was carbonized more thoroughly, while the left side was carbonized less thoroughly and hence retained more organic matter that decomposed over time. – Lines 1 off. from the bottom have the oath by the emperor: το παραπαν επομωσαμενοι αλληλ(οις) τον φρικοδεστατ[ο]ν ορκον | θεεικην αγιαν τριαδα και βασιλικην σωτηριαν (see p. 261)

"dry-gardens." The same products were also grown at Nessana in the more arid Negev. Agriculture has a long tradition in the area. While the Nabataeans were renowned traders, they were also engaged in agriculture from the time they had entered known history. Later, the agricultural economy suited the growing Romanization. In the Roman, as well as in the Byzantine Empire, land ownership was prestigious.

As is attested in Inv. 10 (fig. 279), the brothers divided a larger dwelling complex in Petra, a "villa" (see below), into smaller units by creating new entrances and blocking old ones so that the new units became privately accessible. Archaeological evidence shows the same strategy of dividing a larger house into smaller units in another part of the city some 200 years earlier.[9] People may have had good reasons for such remodeling. The need to divide inherited property was certainly one of them, as is clearly illustrated in Inv. 10. Yet, if we take this development as part of a general process, we may suspect that the depopulation of parts of the city, indicated by archaeological evidence, was compensated by greater density in another part of the city.

The fact that agriculture continued to flourish in the area of Petra has other implications. In the area, profitable agriculture is only possible when terraces are maintained and water management functions. The expenses of maintenance may have been borne by the city or by private owners. In addition, to live in Petra required the continued conveyance of water into the city. If the papyri offer evidence for an economic decline, we have not yet found it. It must have been a slow process.[10]

Petra, a Proud City of the Roman and Byzantine Empire in the Sixth Century In Byzantine society people used honorific titles that underlined their social standing and importance. We mentioned already the use of "Flavios" before personal names as a status indication. Moreover, people used a host of honorific titles, some general, some restricted to office-holders and persons of important professions or of high social standing. It is sufficient to mention a few: "most honorable" (*eudokimōtatos*), "most brilliant" (*lamprotatos*), "most pious" (*eulabestatos*), "most religious" (*theosebestatos*), etc. As individuals were honored, so were cities. Official documents opened with an elaborate preamble stating the date and place where the document was written. In this formulary beginning, Petra was often named by its full honorific titulature, which reflected the city's healthy self-image as an important part of the Byzantine Empire (see p. 259, fig. 281) [Inv. 67, or P. Petra Selz Foundation II]):

> Imperial Colony Antoniana (sic), Distinguished and Holy (?), Mother of Colonies, Hadriana Petra, Metropolis of Tertia Palaestina Salutaris.[11]

The main components of this title are attested elsewhere, but the full collocation appears now in the Petra papyri for the first time. It may be read as a catchword history of the Romanization of the city. After Rome had annexed the Nabataean kingdom, Petra received the title "Metropolis of (the province) Arabia" before or in 114 AD. Some years later Hadrian bestowed the title "Hadriana" upon Petra, probably in connection with his visit to the city in 129/30. About ninety years later, Elagabalus, officially called M. Aurelius Antoninus (218–22), honored the city with the status of Roman Colony: hence "Imperial Colony Antoniana [*sic*]." Bosra, Petra's rival city among the Nabataean cities, as well as other cities of the Roman East were also called "Hadriana" and "Imperial Colony" (*Augustokolonia*). Petra's following title, "Mother of Colonies," is already attested to in an earlier inscription from the area of Petra. This title was also used for several cities in the East. It transforms the Greek concept of "metropolis," literally "mother-city," which denotes the main, or one of the main, cities of a province. While the first part, "mother," was retained, the second part, "polis," turned the Greek concept of polis into Roman "colony." The result was a hybrid term[12] in the distinctively Roman terminology of colonization. But "Mother of Colonies" does not replace "Mother-City." It rather supplements it, as both titles stand side by side. Thus, the two names together are historical markers for the polarity of the Greek and Roman cultures as they established themselves in the eastern part of the empire.

Even the title of the province, Tertia Palestina Salutaris, "Third Palestine the Beneficial," sounds grandiose. Hitherto we knew the province either as Palaestina Tertia or as Palaestina Salutaris. The rhetorically combined accumulation of the three components is a new, probably local phenomenon. New too are the epithets "Distinguished" and "Holy" (?), *episēmos* and *euagēs*. But the latter is an uncertain reading as this word is damaged in all its occurrences (see *P. Petra* I 1.4 comm. [Frösén, Arjava and Lehtinen 2002]). The use of this word would be particularly significant. While, before the fourth century *euagēs* would have been understood as "conspicuous," this term, understood with a long *a,* assumed the meaning of "holy" during the Christian epoch. In the Petra papyri and elsewhere, the Greek term *euagēs* marks churches, chapels, monasteries, and other buildings used by the church. Hence, the epithet "holy" could be regarded as an emblem of Christian Petra.

The documents have not yielded much substantial information on the city government and its relation to the imperial government. We presently know the names of seven *politeuomenoi* of the cities of Petra and Augustopolis (Udruh).[13] The evidence for the use of the Greek term corresponds to Latin *curiales,* a term which denotes members of the families from which the councilors of the city's high council were taken as well as active councilors. But the occurrence of the term *politeuomenos* does not attest a functioning city assembly. By the fifth century, these city assemblies had lost their importance throughout the eastern provinces.[14] Nevertheless, the class of the *curiales* remained important in the eyes of the emperors. The members of wealthy families, once the backbone of the city assemblies, retained administrative functions in their home provinces, and continued to be involved in the collection of taxes.[15] They were those who were financially able to guarantee the assigned amount with their private property. They also retained the title of *politeuomenoi*. The same should apply to sixth-century Petra: the *politeuomenoi* belong to wealthy families whose ancestors may have sat in Petra's city assembly (*boulē*). Their names usually begin with the status designation Flavios, as has already been mentioned. We find both father and son as *politeuomenoi* twice, as this title marked their belonging to that class. At least four of the seven *politeuomenoi* mentioned are tax officials (*hypodektai*, *chrysypodektai*). Many *politeuomenoi* remained deeply involved in the system that still functioned as it was designed to function: members of landowning families continued to collect and guarantee the tax income. But this does not imply that Petra still had a city assembly that could manage the city and make its own decisions.

Its responsibilities had passed from the city body to private families and, presumably, to the church and the military.

The last remarks imply that the Byzantine tax system continued in Petra. Each year, the communities were assessed the amount of taxes they had to contribute. Theodoros's family papers show that the assessment of land taxes was based on the total of land (*homas*) registered in Petra and Augustopolis. The city's committee of tax collectors and its individual members (*hypodektai, chrysypodektai*) collected these taxes on land. Most of the agricultural land was subject to the communal taxing authority. This land, and the fruits from it, were called "free" (*eleutherika*), meaning free from obligations to the fiscal administration of the Imperial House, which levied the taxes from land under its charge (*patrimonalia*). The same division between the communal financial administration of the free land (*eleutherika*) and the emperor's fiscus (*tamiaka*) was hitherto known from only two other places: Cappadocian Caesarea and Syrian Cyrrhus.[16] In Egypt, for example, the authority of tax collection was not split in this way. In the case of Petra and Augustopolis, the same municipal authorities collected the taxes on all land. We, therefore, do not know whether the division into "free" and "patrimonial" land had any practical implication for the tax rate (as it had in Caesarea and Cyrrhus) and for the use of these taxes.

There was certainly a continued presence of the Byzantine military in the camps of Zadakathon (Ṣadaqa, see above) and, probably, Ammatha (now Hammam, twenty-four miles southeast of Petra, fifteen miles east of Ṣadaqa). While the previous view held that these military *castella* no longer functioned in the sixth century, the papyri inform us about the private and civic activities of military officers of Kastron Zadakathon as late as in 593/94 AD (Inv. 44a, or P. Petra Joanne Cotsen). The camp had *priores* and *embathmoi*, the latter attesting an entering rank hitherto known only from Nessana.[17] Two hundred years earlier, the military commander of Palestine (the *dux Palaestinae*) had native cavalry stationed at Kastron Zadakathon under his command. These units had been extracted from regular legions (*not. dign.* I.34.24 p. 73 Seeck). As we see, at the end of the sixth century there were still (or again) local troops of the regular Byzantine army stationed at Kastron Zadakathon. This conclusion is corroborated by the new papyri, a Nessana papyrus (*P. Ness.* 39 [Kraemer 1958]) and a small group of inscriptions (e.g. *SEG* 8.282) stating that the taxes for the maintenance of the army (*annona militaris*) continued to be collected in the area of Petra and the rest of Palestine as well as in other provinces. In Palestine these payments in money and in kind served both the regular Byzantine army (hence, also the troops and *priores* in Kastron Zadakathon) and its Arabic allies (*foederati*). Under Arabic rule, this tax, now called *rizḳ*, was defined by Arab jurists as "food provisions for Muslim soldiers and fighters."[18] In the Petra papyri, we hear nothing about soldiers of the *foederati*. Whether this lack of information is accidental or historically significant is presently unknown.

These remarks bring us to the additional military and administrative power of the Ghassanids, the leaders of the Arab federates of the Byzantine State (*foederati*). A settlement of a long-fought legal dispute in 544 AD, Inv. 83 (see above, with n. 3), deals with a number of issues, one of which concerns the sale of a vineyard in Kastron Zadakathon. This part of the dispute had once been submitted to judgment or mediation by the Ghassanid Abu Karib ibn Jabala (see below). Justinian had appointed Abu Karib as ruler of the Arab tribes of Palestine (*phylarch*) after he had made Abu Karib's brother, Harith ibn Jabala, a Roman patrician in 529 AD and had given him the rank (*axiōma*) of a ruler over all Arab allies in Palestine and Arabia.[19] Both brothers were paid by the emperor, and in return, they provided military protection in Palestine. What has been suggested is now confirmed: Abu Karib's power extended to Petra and Palestina Tertia. He almost certainly exercised his influence in his own ethnic tradition, and this would imply that his activities were not restricted to providing military protection. The parties of Inv. 83 might have turned to him because the case concerned a place outside the metropolis in Kastron Zadakathon, a settlement with a military *castellum*. In any case, power was shared by the imperial and community administrations, the military, and by Arab leaders in alliance with the emperor.

Multicultural Petra: Nabataeans, Arabs, Greeks, and Romans As we have stated, all the papyri from the Petra church are written in Greek, except for a few lines of Latin (in Inv. 6a). The Greek was naturally mixed with a number of Latin terms transliterated into Greek. People used not only the Roman land measure of the *iugerum*, but also Semitic land measures such as the *koriaia* (*kor*), *satiaia* (*se'ah*) and *kabiaia* (*kab*). These measures are also found at about the same time at Nessana and, 400 years earlier, in the archives of Babatha and Salome from the Dead Sea (*P. Yadin* 16, 21, 22 and *P. Naḥal Ḥever* 62 [Cotton and Yardeni 1997]). In sixth-century Petra, members of the upper class began their name with the Roman gentilic name Flavius (see above). In a few cases this status designation was followed by historically Nabataean names, but more frequently by names that primarily sound Greek, Roman, or specifically Christian. Already this mixture of names, used by the elite, points to the culture of a city that once was the capital of the Nabataean kingdom, but that had come under Greek cultural influence and Roman power, and finally had converted to Christianity. But a closer look points to a particularly strong Arabic influence.

At this point we need to bear in mind that the language of the inscriptions and papyri written by the Nabataeans is largely Aramaic, while their spoken language contained strong and increasing Arabic elements. This view is based on Nabataean personal names, most of which are analyzable as Arabic rather than Aramaic. But by the time of the new papyri, the Aramaic written language used by the Nabataeans had long ceased to be used. While Arabic became the language that people spoke, when it came to writing official documents and inscriptions, Greek had replaced Aramaic. Hence, the Arabic that we meet in names of the Petra papyri is written in Greek letters, but represents a spoken form of pre-Islamic Arabic especially and recognizably characterized by the Arabic definite article *al* and the formation of diminutives and plural forms ("broken plural"). Since Greek has specific letters for vowels and uses them in Arabic names, we gain information about the pronunciation of Arabic words in the sixth century, even though this information needs to be approached with great caution.[20]

Some of the names used in the large family of Theodoros were unquestionably Nabataean and Arabic. Theodoros's father as well as another family member, perhaps his brother, were both named Obodianos (this is the name of another two people in the archive). It is derived from the name Obodas, the Greco-Latin form of *'bdt*, a name which was borne by three different Nabataean kings of the first century BC, by a well known city, and possibly by a Nabataean god.[21] A great-uncle of Theodoros was named Dusarios. This Grecized form was based on the name Dushara (Greek *Dusarēs*), a Nabataean god. Finally, Theodoros's grandmother was named Thaaious, Aramaic *Tayayye*, also appearing in at least two other Nabataean names. This name is derived from the name of an Arabic tribe, which, like "Saracens," became a general term for nomadic Arabs.[22]

Other names look Greco-Roman, but were probably chosen because they had meaning in two languages. For example, Dusarios had a brother named Alpheios (another common name in the archive), and this name corresponds to Latin Alfius. But the name appears so frequently in Petra and the late ancient Near East that the Latin name alone does not seem to be a sufficient explanation. Scholars have therefore suggested that Alpheios (Alfius) reflected the common Arabic and Nabataean name *Ḥlfw*, "successor," and Semitic cognates.[23] The father of Alpheios and Dusarios was named Valens (at least ten other men of this name are mentioned in the Petra papyri). This man, who gave his two sons Arabic/Nabataean names, seems to bear a good Roman name. Again, the popularity of this Roman name in the Roman and Byzantine Near East indicates that it must often have been regarded as rendering a Semitic name, probably Arabic *W'l* ("he who takes refuge") or *W'l* ("buck" or "stag"), but Latinized with the ending *-ens, -entis* (Greek *-ēs, -entos*).[24] The name Bassus was borne by two men who were presumably a grandfather and a cousin of Theodoros. This is also at first sight nothing other than the Roman name Bassus. But once again, the name is so common throughout the late ancient Near East that it has frequently been suggested that it renders the common Semitic and Arabic name *Bss* meaning "cat."[25]

In light of the foregoing, other Greek names used in the family may have been regarded as equivalents of local Arabic names. Presumably, a brother of Theodoros's father Obodianos was named Leontios (there are seven other men of this name in the archive). Leontios is a Greek name based on the Greek word for lion. The name became popular among Christians because there was a cult of the Holy Martyr Leontios. It would nevertheless seem that when the name occurs in a local family from Petra it may have been regarded as a translation of the Arabic and Nabataean name *'Asad,'* still common today, which means "lion."[26] In Inv. 83 (see above) a man named Abdallas (Arabic *'Abdallāh* with a Greek ending) called his son Leontios. There is finally the name of Theodoros himself (at least eight other men with the same name occur in the archive). This Hellenistic Greek name meaning "gift of God" was borne by many Christians. In Petra it had special meaning since a Christian martyr, Theodoros, was venerated in much of the East and, as we learn from a Petra papyrus, at Ammatha near Petra. At the same time, the name may have recalled common Arabic/Nabataean personal names such as *'Ausallāh*, "gift of Allah,"[27] but now with a specific Christian nuance. All in all, the names in the family of Theodoros, son of Obodianos, reflect several intersecting worlds: the local, traditional Semitic, the Greco-Roman, and the Christian.

Place-names attest personal names used in previous generations. An example of a man's name is supplied by the toponym *Māl Amar al-Sarwa*. The first term, *māl*, means "livestock," "money," "property," etc. in Arabic. We were familiar with it already from the Greek papyri from Nessana. There, for example, the toponym *Māl Alkani* probably means "the property (of a man named) al-Kanī" and the toponym *Māl Zēmarche* "the property (of a man named) Zēmarche" (likely a Thracian name). Now the Petra papyri supply at least a dozen more such toponyms that have *māl* as a first element. In *Māl Amar al-Sarwa*, the *Amar* is probably the common Semitic name *'Amr* or *'Āmir*. The following *al-Sarwa* is not so obvious, but it might be a nickname meaning "the manly one" or "the generous one."[28] Names of women also appear in toponyms. A place named *Math Osaina* and another called *Math Lela* are mentioned several times in Inv. 10. The first term in both toponyms may be an old Semitic word meaning "land" or "estate" that entered the Arabic of our region via Aramaic. Since Greek in the papyri usually does not indicate aspiration (see n. 21), *Osaina* can be regarded as the female personal name Ḥusaina, the "beautiful one" (a diminutive feminine form; the masculine counterpart is *Ḥusein*, the diminutive of *Ḥasan*). Similarly, in *Math Lela*, the second term is probably the common Arabic female name *Laila* (which literally means "night") known, for example, from pre-Islamic Arabic poetry.[29]

An example of the name of a clan or tribe is provided by "Ogbana," the name of a geographical area in Inv. 10 (see above). This area is not designated as a town or village, and the text suggests that it was rather a more amorphous rural area. It is tempting to see in the name a reference to a tribe that once was well known in Southern Jordan, the *banī 'Uqba*. For the region around Petra, the tribal name is attested to in the medieval chronicle of Nuwairī about the voyage of Sultan Baibars from Cairo to Karak in the year 1276, during which he passed by Petra and reached Shaubak, where princes of the *Banī 'Uqba* tribe attended on him.[30] This tribe was a subtribe of the Ǧudām that entered our area in the pre-Islamic period, possibly already in the third century. Moreover, according to ethnographic studies of the first half of the twentieth century, tribal disputes in what is now southern Jordan were submitted to the arbitration of elders of the *Banī 'Uqba,* who then lived in southern Palestine. Older residents of Wadi Musa still recall this. Nevertheless, there need not be an historical link between the medieval *Banī 'Uqba* of Southern Jordan and the area of sixth-century Ogbana around Petra. The name occurs also in the second-century *P. Euphr.* 2.2 (D. Feissel and J. Gascou 1995) in the combination *beirya Okbanvn* for which the editors refer to the related names *Ocbanes* and *Ocbanas* (*P. Dura* 98, 100 and 101[Wells, Fink and Gilliam 1959]) and translate: "fortress of (the tribe) Ocbanoi." Hence the name of the area near Petra was probably derived from a person's or family's or a tribe's name, but not necessarily the same clan or tribe that once was living on the Euphrates. Either way, this family or tribal name reflects the cultural and social past, as the names of many toponyms do.

Not only did people in Petra own farmland in a landscape that was defined by Arabic toponyms, the very dwellings that they lived in also had Arabic names. Again Inv. 10 provides the evidence. Names of houses and apartments begin with (a) *dāra* corresponding to Greek *aulē*; or with (b) *bait* translated as Greek *oikos*; or with (c) *'illīyya,* Greek *hyperōon*. The text uses the Greek and, as part of names, the corresponding Arabic words side by side. For example, there is an *aulē* called the *Darat al-Ebad*. The Arabic word *dāra* (like its more common masculine counterpart *dār*) refers to a "villa." This is usually a main building or group of buildings with one or more adjoining courtyards, and all usually enclosed by a wall. The same must be meant by the Greek *aulē*, which usually means "courtyard," but can also mean "villa."[31] The full meaning of the name of the villa *Darat al-Ebad* is "the villa of the servants (of god)," whether this reflects the Christian or Nabataean religious tradition. One of the sub-units of a villa (*aulē*) is Greek *oikos*, in Arabic *bait*. The Arabic terms *bait* and *dāra* have the same relationship to each other as Greek *oikos* and *aulē*. They are forerunners of the use of the terms *bait* and *dār* in early Islamic housing, the former a sub-unit of the latter. Greek *oikos* translates *bait,* when it is used in a Petraean context, and therefore means "apartment," not "house," but also not "room." The third Arabic term for a part of a house occurs, e.g., in the mention of the *hyperöon* called *Elliat Aphthonis*. Greek *hyperōon* renders Arabic 'illīyya (transcribed in Greek as *Elliat*), just as the same Greek word in the Septuagint renders the closely related Hebrew word *'ilyah*. In the case of *Elliat Aphthonis*, the name Aphthonis is originally a Greek name, but is now part of an Arabic name phrase: "the roof-apartment of Aphthonios."[32] Similarly, in the name of the apartment *Bait al-Kellar*, the second element is not originally a Semitic word or name. It is almost certainly a loanword from Latin *cellarium* or *cellarius,* "storage room(s)" or "keeper of storage room(s)," respectively. The originally Latin word might have entered Arabic directly from Latin or indirectly, either from Greek *kellarios/kellarion* or from Aramaic. It is interesting to find the same Latin word working its way into the East as well as into the West, where it produced, for example, English *cellar* and German *Keller*.

From this short survey of a selection of Semitic and mainly Arabic personal names, toponyms, and names of dwellings, it should be clear that the language generally spoken in the streets of Petra and in the countryside was mainly Arabic. But Greek had replaced the earlier written language of Nabataean Aramaic, as we mentioned above. Greek was also the language of the imperial government as well as the official language of the local administration. Moreover, Greek was the official language of the Church. But it was Arabic that was the more deep-seated language in the region. Hence, it was even able to determine the meaning in which some Greek terms for buildings were used in the area.

Oral and Written Cultures The coexistence of Greek as the language for writing administrative and contractual documents, spoken by a large part of the population, has further implications. On the one hand, there was an administrative system based on written documentation, and on the other, there existed the tradition of transacting business orally. For comparison we may recall that in Egypt the Greek and Roman administrations were based on paperwork in Greek and, hence, on literacy in Greek, but there were also mechanisms that enabled people who were almost or totally illiterate in Greek to produce written Greek documents as needed.[33] The normal signature under documents began with "I, so and so, son of so and so" and then recapitulated the essential details of the contract. But if, during the Roman and Byzantine periods, the person was illiterate in Greek (*agrammatos ōn*, "being unable to write") or barely literate (*bradeōs graphōn*, "being a slow writer"), he would ask someone else to write the entire subscription, namely signature and summary of the contract, for the illiterate party; or the almost illiterate person would write the entire subscription in clumsy characters or just her or his name, leaving the rest to somebody else. Similar practices are now found in the Petra papyri. An example is the following subscription at the end of a contract in which one Flavios Nonnos signed for a woman named Arista: "For your security [... I have made out (this) document] which is signed through the hand of Flavios Nonnos son of Auxon..., [who has been requested (?) by me] to write [the subscription] on my behalf since I am an unpracticed writer (*oligogrammatos*)."[34] This is precisely the practice that we know from Roman and Byzantine Egypt, but the terminology is different. The Petraean scribe's word for "unpracticed writer" (*oligogrammatos*) is very rare.

Another case is even more remarkable. When in 559 AD a priest of a church or monastery in Kastron Ammatha (Hammam, see above) bought a piece of land from Theodoros, son of Obodianos, he, as well as Theodoros, requested the transfer of the responsibility for the annual taxes from the seller to the buyer. The priest (third hand) wrote: "I PHILOUNENOS SON OF GERONTIOS, PRIEST," and then another person, Flavios Sosamon (fourth hand), continued the subscription on behalf of Philoumenos: "I the aforementioned have requested the relief of the person, estate, and the account of the most God-loving Theodoros, son of Obodianos, deacon ... whereby, after with my own hand I have placed my and my father's name at the beginning, I make use of the hand of Flavios Sosamon son of Alpheios who has been (so) requested by me, because I cannot write with precision, cannot add (the rest) and am very slow, writing letter-by-letter."[35] The words that we have printed in capital letters were written by Philoumenos, indeed letter-by-letter, in block letters that resemble those of a schoolboy learning to write. Philoumenos even misspells his own name as "Philounenos." He must have trained himself to write his name, just as Petaus, an Egyptian "village scribe" (*kōmogrammateus*) in the second century did on a piece of papyrus: He wrote his signature in clumsy letters twelve times, "I Petaus, village scribe, submit," one signature under the other. Once he had made a mistake, he copied that mistake in all the following lines.[36] In the Petra papyrus it is not the head of the village administration, but a priest, who is next to illiterate in Greek. At about Philoumenos's time, fifty-one inhabitants of Aphrodite in Upper Egypt wrote a petition to the empress Theodora. Fourteen, including two priests, were illiterates using a proxy (*P. Cairo Masp.* III 67383[Maspero 1916]). They probably were illiterate in Greek but surely knew how to write Coptic. But was there another language in which Philoumenos wrote? Or did he live in a completely oral culture? Illiterate priests seem remarkable only because the church represents a religion that, by and large, is based on the written word. Doubtless, Philoumenos was able to perform his duties.

Petra in the Byzantine Empire: A Legal Culture of Arbitrations and Negotiations Throughout this essay, we have seen that Petra's administrative, military, and political ties with Constantinople continued in the sixth century. Byzantine-Roman culture was part of the cultural fabric. The city was proud of her history as "Roman Colony," and members of the upper classes called themselves Flavii; parents chose names for their children, many of which were or sounded Greek and Roman, even though they also reflected Arabic traditions in name-giving. Moreover, the handwriting of the scribes is quite similar to hands that we know from Byzantine Egypt (figs. 279, 280). This reflects the influence of the imperial chancellery and perhaps of the training of notaries in law schools. The documentary terminology is, by and large, very similar to that used in Byzantine Egypt, and, so far as we can tell, it is Roman law that governs the land. But this Roman law was very tolerant of local traditions.

It is a characteristic of Byzantine society in the eastern provinces that people avoided courts and preferred negotiations. The same tendency appears in Theodoros's family papers. Formulas in cessions and settlements disclaim "the right to sue" and actions "in and out of court," as they do in Byzantine Egyptian papyri. "Court-houses" are mentioned, but the reality behind the formulaic language remains unclear. The most interesting example is provided by a papyrus roll of 6.50 meters' length, one of the longest ancient Greek documents that have survived, albeit in fragmentary condition (inv. 83, see above with n. 3).[37] In 544 or 574 AD, two "judges" (*dikastai*), Theodoros son of Alpheios, then archdeacon of the diocese of Petra (see n. 4), and Thomas, son of Boëthos, a military *prior* presumably of the *castellum* of Zadakathon (see p. 254), wrote a report protocoling their proceedings and judgment in a suit that Theodoros, son of Obodianos had brought against Stephanos, son of Leontios, another deacon and his neighbor in Kastron Zadakathon. The process concerned mainly various pieces of property and property rights, such as a vineyard, parts of a building, an enclosure, a courtyard, each party's rights to water collection and to collect water from the opponent's roofs. as well as to have construction work done at a dung depository and to make use of it. By the time that the "judges" presided over the present proceedings, the families had been trading accusations against each other for twenty-seven years, beginning in 517 AD, when the fathers of the present opponents controlled the properties and Theodoros, son of Obodianos, was still a toddler. The mutual accusations had turned personal. Theodoros even accused Stephanos of having damaged property and having stolen building materials such as wood, doors, and stones. There had been at least two attempts by preeminent people to settle parts of the case on earlier occasions: one by Sergios, son of Basileios, a priest and "rural bishop" (probably in charge of Kastron Zadakathon),[38] and another by the phylarch Abu Karib, whom we mentioned earlier.

Each of the parties (the *antidikoi* or *diadikoi*) presented written proofs and submitted its version of the case history (*hypomnēstikon*). The countercharges contained in Stephanos's written presentation led to Theodoros's oral reply in which he also referred to witnesses. "After much dispute," the judges issued their final decision "with the agreement of both parties" (*kata synainesin amphoterōn*), as they had been charged at the beginning to "reconcile (the parties) and [issue a final decision] in writing" (*dialysai kai eggrafōs [typōsai*). In practical matters they took the middle ground between the claims of the parties. For example, the dung-storing facility very close to their houses was jointly owned by several parties. The judges assigned a third of this facility to the parties of the present arbitration. Two thirds of this third were to be owned by Stephanos, the remaining third by Theodoros.[39] The facility seems at the time to have been under (or in need of) repair and construction, and Stephanos and Theodoros were allowed to build a dividing wall. Another part of the decision concerned the water-drainage systems on the roofs of the houses of Theodoros and Stephanos. The judges permitted both parties to draw water, as it seems, (from the draining system) of the other party's roof, "according to old practice." However, these and other practical orders, agreed upon by the parties, did not solve the mutual accusations of a more personal nature. In order to settle them, the judges required each of the parties to administer to the other an oath that he is innocent. The oath was composed by the judges and was to be sworn on the Holy Scriptures in the Holy Chapel of the Martyr St. Kyrikos in Zadakathon. If, however, one or both of the litigants would admit his guilt under oath, then he should give satisfaction to the other. Such an oath is not only a procedure to find the truth, but can be an essential step in the healing process. It would facilitate the beginning of a new, friendly relationship. At the end, in their subscriptions, both parties agree to the written agreement (*apallagē*), and stipulate a symbolic fine of only one solidus for future violation, as is characteristic for

280. P. Mich. Aphrod. 74-81 (ed. T. Gagos and P. van Minnen) of c. 537 AD, from Aphrodite in Upper Egypt. Comparison with the handwriting in fig. 279 shows the similarities between hands of scribes in different parts of the Byzantine Empire (see p. 257). Lines 77–79 (here, lines 4–6) contain the oath by the emperor: επωμοσαμην την τε αγιαν και ομοουσιον τριαδα και | την ευσεβειαν και νικην του καλλινικου δεσποτου της οικοουμενης Φλ(αιυιυ) Ιουστινιανου...(see p. 261)

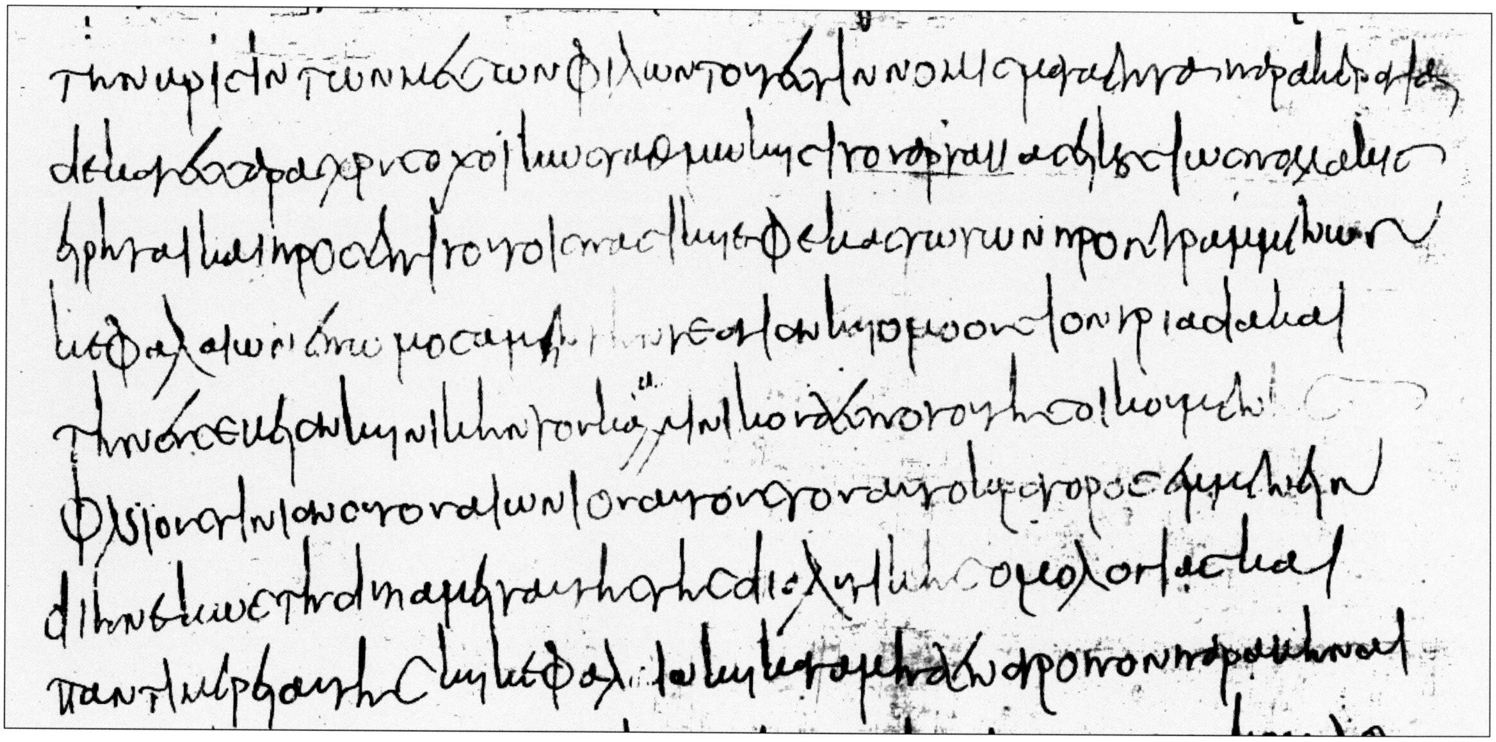

281. P. Petra 67, lines 1-5 (Ol.c.f 8/22/545): 1–3 contain the dating formula, 2–3 the titulature of Petra. For the text see n. 11.

agreements, not court procedures. The small fine was the result of a special mediation.[40]

The two "judges" have other professions: one is an archdeacon[41] of the see church in Petra, the other is a military officer in the local barracks. We do not know how they were selected for this case, but they were surely prominent in their community, one representing the church, the other the military. The parties agreed to the judgment, which, only after their agreement at the end of the document, was binding. Although similar to a protocol of court proceedings, the text reflects the negotiations and compromises of settlements, as we know them from Egypt. The "judges" acted as arbitrators.[42] There are, however, substantial differences between the document from Kastron Zadakathon and the settlements of the Egyptian papyri. For example, an oath by the Trinity to abide by all terms of the contract, as was customary in Egypt, is lacking in Inv. 83. While we see no specific reason for this absence, there are other differences for understandable reasons. They include (i) the oath of innocence (or, as the case could have turned out, the confessions of guilt) on the holy scriptures in a local chapel; (ii) the small fine for violations of the terms of the settlement; and (iii) the absence of the signature of a notary.[43]

The first two differences may have resulted from the particulars of the case and its religious setting. (i) In the present case, the oath of innocence was required, as there was no other evidence for the facts on which the mutual accusations were based.[44] (ii) The low symbolic fine depends surely on the ecclesiastical setting of the case. Both parties were deacons. Thus the archdeacon, sitting on the bench, was their superior. Of the two people trying to resolve the case, or part of the case in earlier phases, one was a priest and one a bishop. An additional mediator, who negotiated the fine, was also a priest (see n. 40). In this environment, the financial punishment could be pro forma. (iii) The third deviation mentioned, however, points to a procedural and structural difference. The absence of the signature of a notary is striking and instructive. The judges/mediators were charged to produce the written judgment, and, as we already stated, the entire process resembled court procedures, for which no notary could have final responsibility. To this we will return.

The church must have been interested in restoring law and order in its ranks. A rural bishop had already attempted to settle the part of the present procedures that concerned the water rights. Likewise, the phylarch Abu Karib (see above) had tried to resolve the conflict concerning a vineyard. We do not know what his precise competence was. But since the case concerned a family feud in the rural hinterland of Petra, he may very well have been approached and may have acted, in his capacity as ruler of the Arabs in Palestine, like an overlordly sheikh. In this capacity, he would have followed the custom of the land. From the point of view of the Arab population, it makes little sense to distinguish between his official duties, as they may have been perceived by Constantinople, and his private actions as a citizen acting in the traditions of the area.

Settling conflicts through external arbitration went hand in hand with resolving conflicts through internal negotiations. In 537 AD, Theodoros, son of Obodianos, then still a minor, married his maternal first cousin, Stephanous, daughter of Patrophilos (see p. 251[3]). A marriage contract is not extant (or has not yet been recognized). There may not have been one.[45] In Byzantine Egypt, marriage contracts in the strict sense were rare. What mattered was not the marriage contract in the Greek social and legal tradition, but agreements concerning the marriage-related transfer of property. Such documents could be written and executed before, at, or after the marriage. Indeed, two years after the marriage, in 539/40 AD, Patrophilos, Theodoros, and two guarantors, one for each party, signed a sworn and secured deed, mutually agreed upon, by which they stipulated the value of the dowry and marital gifts (Inv. 65+63, see p. 251[3]). This deed was preceded by other contracts, including another deed of 537 AD, the year of the wedding (*P. Petra* I 1, or P. Petra Thomas and Francesca Bennett [eds. A. Arjava and C.A. Kuehn]). The latter deals with several property-related issues involving the families of Theodoros and Stephanous and, in case-by-case scenarios, determines who, after the death of one or more interested parties, would receive the properties that Patrophilos had ceded to Theodoros.[46] The ceded properties are not itemized, but are described in general terms. They included (a) the dowry of Theodoros's mother which, after her death, Theodoros had returned to Patrophilos, her brother, and (b) all that Patrophilos and Theodoros had agreed upon in an oral settlement (*dialysis*).[47] The use of this term indicates that there had been a conflict between Patrophilos and young Theodoros, which, at least in part, had resulted from the death of Theodoros's mother and the return of her dowry to her brother, Theodoros's uncle. The present document aimed at safeguarding the claims of all people involved, but in particular of the young bride. Both families seem eager to prevent a repetition of misunderstandings and difficulties such as had occurred at the death of Theodoros's mother. Thus, the wedding was accompanied by contractual agreements that cleaned up the old problems between the families before, two years later, the dowry and gifts for Stephanous were put in writing.

The two documents related to the marriage of Stephanous and Theodoros are not settlements, but they point to extensive, amicable, and private negotiations between Patrophilos and Theodoros. This is stressed through traditional linguistic markers, such as "they both agreed" or "they both considered it fit that..." As we have argued, the proliferation of out-of-court settlements by private means is a social and cultural phenomenon that Petraean society seems to have shared with other parts of the Eastern provinces. This tendency is well established for Egypt after the fourth century (see n. 42) and, as the Petra papyri seem to suggest, settling out of court may be a broader Mediterranean phenomenon. People avoid courts due to economic, cultural, and religious constraints. Rabbinical, Christian, and Bedouin traditions and literature strongly discourage people from litigation, but such avoidance appears to have been further augmented by Roman legal traditions. In particular, the so-called *stipulatio Aquiliana* (a settlement agreement introduced by the Roman jurist Aquilianus) gives individuals the option of settling privately, thus creating a legal frame that local legal traditions could use.

Ancient writers, documents recently published, and studies on pre-Islamic jurisprudence all support the contention that the preference for negotiation and arbitration had deep roots in Petra and, by extension, in the provinces of Palestine and Arabia. The geographer Strabo, writing in the first century BC, reports that Athenodoros, a philosopher and companion of his, was much impressed when he visited the city of Petra: "Athenodoros... used to describe their government with admiration, for he said that he found both many Romans and many other foreigners sojourning there, and that he saw that the foreigners often engaged in lawsuits both with one another and with the natives, but that none of the natives prosecuted one another, and that they in every way kept peace with one another" (*Geography* XVI.4.21). Although this sentence sounds like ethnographic idealization, it may reflect some reality. In the second-century Greek papyri from the Judaean desert (*P. Naḥal Ḥever* [Cotton and Yardeni 1997]), no courts are mentioned—save for that of the governor. According to the editors, "It is a remarkable fact that no court, Jewish or non-Jewish, other than that of the Roman governor of Arabia, is mentioned in any of the documents from the Judaean Desert, a great many of which... are legal documents. We should not therefore conclude, however, that the governor's court was the only one in operation in a Roman province. Nonetheless, the absence of any reference to other courts is disturbing, especially in view of the host of reference in rabbinic sources to courts of different sizes in towns and villages" (introd. p. 154).

The same caution applies to Petra. The evidence for court-like settlement procedures seems to indicate that most matters could be solved without government-appointed courts. The absence of a final signature by a notary in the settlement of Kastron Zadakathon has also alerted us to the possibility that this is a structural difference from settlements as we know them from Egypt. The procedures in Inv. 83 combine the trappings of court procedures with what essentially was a settlement procedure. What we see in Kastron Zadakathon may be a local court at work.

It may surprise us that, by and large, the agreements seemed to have worked without enforcement through government-appointed courts. The agreements had bite in several ways. One of them was usually a substantial fine for breach of contract (albeit not so in the settlement of Kastron Zadakathon). In the case of Inv. 65+63 (see p. 251[3]), the fine was 23 gold coins (104.3 grams of gold). In the property division among three brothers, Inv. 10 (see p. 252[1]), the fine amounted to twenty gold coins, or *solidi* (91 grams of gold).

The second bite was even more frightening in its personal, societal and religious consequences. Both parties had to forgo violations of the agreement by swearing "the most horrifying oath by the Divine Holy Trinity and the Imperial Salvation." This phrase first occurs in a Petra papyrus dated to 527–37 AD (Inv. 10, see p. 252, fig. 279) and is attested three times.[48] The closest parallels are found in two Nessana papyri from the years 562 and 566, respectively: "by the Holy Trinity and the Imperial Salvation."[49] At the same time, around 537 AD, the Trinity emerged in Egypt as part of the oath formula, but it did so in the form of the "Consubstantial Trinity": "by the Holy and Consubstantial Trinity and the Victory and Permanence of our Lord..." This type of the Trinitarian formula became popular in Egypt,[50] while in Petra we find it only once (Inv. 86r, or P. Petra P. M. Bikai [M. Lehtinen]).

The consubstantiality of the Trinity was stressed for religious as well as political reasons. It harks back to the fourth century, when at the insistence of Athanasios, the consubstantiality of God's Son (Logos) was expanded to the consubstantiality of the Holy Ghost. In the fourth century Basilios said: "we baptize in the consubstantial Trinity." The stress on the consubstantiality also recalls the Council of Chalcedon in 451 AD, which was to determine religious-political debates for centuries. According to Chalcedon, the God Son contains in one person both the divine nature of the Trinitarian Logos, consubstantial with the Father, and the human nature, capable of Christ's suffering and consubstantial with man. The consubstantiality of the Trinity is the theological consequence of the consubstantiality of Logos/Christ. Thus the oath formula invoking the Consubstantial Trinity reassured against monophysitism, which held that Christ had only one nature. Justinian was himself suspected of monophysitic tendencies, and thus found reason to defend his orthodoxy and to denounce fourth- and fifth-century heresies precisely by echoing the formula of Chalcedon and stressing consubstantiality.[51] He, therefore, may have favored the invocation of the Consubstantial Trinity in the oath formula. It provided him with theological cover while he favored a rapprochement with the monophysites. In sum, the confession of consubstantiality through the oath formula as became popular in Egypt after the first third of the sixth century had a definite theological and political flair. Whether this applies also to the partial avoidance of the term "consubstantial" in the Petra and Nessana papyri[52] remains an open question. Monophysitism was strong in the area.[53]

Be this as it may, both the substantial fines as well as the oath by Trinity and Emperor reinforced negotiated agreements and helped to make them work. The oath invoked, and threatened punishment by, the two most forceful and frightening institutions, Church and state, both numinous and all-present. In the belief and value system of the times, violators would find themselves outside the social and religious order of their community. They would appear guilty of perjury and, therefore, be subject to prosecution. This oath is indeed "most horrifying," as is said with a Greek word (*phrikodestatos*) that, as an epithet for an oath became popular in Egypt only in papyri of the second half of the sixth century.

The discussion of the oath, in agreements has brought us back to contemplation of essential features of the Byzantine state. The growing importance and self-consciousness of the new elite in local communities, as well as in the church, should not be understood as a weakness of the state. Rather it was a strength that kept the multiethnic and multicultural Byzantine state intact in the sixth century. Despite all the damage that the Petra papyri suffered, they provide not only a host of totally new information, but they also invite us to contemplate broader historical questions that still resonate in our times.

Endnotes

CHAPTER 1

1. Wenning 1992 and 1994.
2. Negev, Naveh, and Shaked 1986 (Obodas the god). *Papiri della Società Italiana* 771. (Bosra).
3. On the episode in 312 see Bowersock 1983. For alliances of the Nabataeans see the same work, chapter 2. On the expedition to South Arabia, see below in the present article.
4. Tacitus, *Ann*. 2. 57. 4. It would be interesting to know where the banquet was held, since the Nabataean king was unlikely to have hosted an event outside his kingdom and Germanicus is not known to have gone to Nabataean Arabia. See my speculations in Joukowsky 1998: 45, n. 45.
5. Diod. Sic. 19. 96-98.
6. See P. Parr's chapter 2 in this volume. Also Graf 1990.
7. On Glaucus, Bowersock 1997a.
8. Bowersock 1983: 17-18. Cf. Cantineau 1932: 43 (Elusa text).
9. Cantineau 1930. But see Macdonald 2000, arguing forcefully against Arabic as the spoken language of the Nabataeans. He notes the predominance of Arabic elements, such as *al* or *ibn*, in the Sinai and argues that these should not be called Nabataean. He believes that the Nabataeans spoke a dialect of Aramaic.
10. Negev, Naveh, and Shaked 1986. See also M.C.A. Macdonald's chapter 3 in this volume.
11. Strabo 16. 4. 21-26.
12. Clermont-Ganneau 1895.
13. Cf. Starcky 1966: 939.
14. Sidebotham 1986a and b. Bowersock 1997b: 551-52.
15. Bowersock 1983: 51, n. 25.
16. Abbadi 1996. The Safaitic graffito is of importance for providing a rare date among the vast store of such graffiti.
17. Meshorer 1975: 43-44.
18. Above all Healey 1993. See also Balty 1983 and Schmidt-Colinet 1983b.
19. Bowersock 1997c.
20. II *Corinthians* 11. 32.
21. Casson 1989: 7.
22. Cf. Cantineau 1932: 22 (*A'râ, dieu de notre maître, qui [habite] dans Bosra*).
23. Zayadine 1981.
24. Wenning 1993.
25. Bowersock 1983: 76-89.
26. Fiema 1988; Haensch 1997: 238-44.
27. Tracy 1999.
28. Milik 1958: 244-45. The Nabataean text (*bšnt tlt lhprk bṣr'*) is rendered somewhat differently in the Greek text of this bilingual as *etous tritou eparcheias*.
29. Lewis, Yadin and Greenfield 1989; Bowersock 1991; Isaac 1992.
30. Tracy 1999: 56-58.
31. Unpublished at the time of writing, but see the discussion of this and related documents in Bowersock 2001.
32. Bowersock 1975.
33. Bowersock 1976.
34. Joukowsky 1998 and the same author's contribution to the present volume. A new Nabataean inscription from Petra and dated to AD 2/3 actually mentions a theater: Jones and Bowersock 2001.
35. Andrew Oliver has referred me to the interesting parallel of four elephant *protomai* on a porphyry capital, of unknown provenance, in the Vatican (H. von Hesberg, *Jahreshefte des Oesterreichischen Archäologischen Instituts* 53, Hauptblatt 1981/2: 44ff.).
36. Bedal 2001.
37. Bowersock 1999: 553.
38. Herrmann 2001.
39. Bowersock 1986a.
40. Bowersock 1990a.
41. Negev, Naveh, and Shaked 1986.
42. Bellamy 1985; Cf. Bowersock 1986b: 114-15.
43. Bowersock 1971: 242, n. 165; Epiphanius, *Panarion* 51. 22. 11: references to an Arabic dialect may indeed refer to Arabic, not Nabataean.
44. Koenen 1996a and b; Frösén, Arjava and Lehtinen 2002.
45. Cf. L. Koenen's chapter 22 in this volume.
46. Bowersock 1984-1985: 72-73. Cf. Lib., *Orat*. 24. 6.
47. Bikai and Egan 1999: 510. From the photograph one can read *teichea* and *kai ptoliethron esōse* and also *Palaistinas Salou* [. . .
48. Bowersock 1997a: 180-85, with obvious typographical errors, which the author would have corrected if he had been shown proof.

CHAPTER 2

1. In a recent conference paper (Retsö 2000) Jan Retsö throws doubt on the generally accepted opinion that Hieronymus's account refers specifically to Nabataeans. He points out that Diodorus's text - the sole authority for the account - has itself only come down to us through much later versions. He argues that in the most reliable of these versions the Arabs to whom Hieronymus refers are not called νομάδες but simply Ναβαταῖοι, or nomadic shepherds. For Retsö the word "Nabataean" is a later term which had no ethnic connotation but was used to designate a social class within the kingdom governed from Petra. This is an interesting suggestion which no doubt will be subjected to scholarly scrutiny, but even if correct it does little to undermine the traditional view that the Arabs Hieronymus describes were the most likely forebears of those who settled in Petra and created the "Nabataean" state.
2. However, Avraham Negev long ago pointed out that the distances given by Hieronymus in connection with the Greek campaigns do not fit well with Petra and rather indicate a location to the west rather than to the east of the Wadi Araba. This is also where Negev would place the main territory of the Nabataeans at this time (Negev 1976b: 127-28; Bartlett 1990: 32). Retsö (2000: 116-17) also adduces information given in Agatharchides of Cnidus' book on the Red Sea (late second century BC), to support the argument that the "Rock" of the Arabs was west of the Araba. (See also note 6.)
3. The Nabataean attitude is remarkably similar to that of the nomadic beduin of Kerak in 1834, when the Ottoman authorities attempted to persuade them to settle down and become farmers: "They laughed and replied that they would surely die if they were to remain in one place for two months." (Quoted by Lewis 1987: 3.)
4. Graf 1990: 51-53; Roche 1994: 39-40.
5. Hammond 1959.
6. For Dushara see Starcky 1966: 986-87, and for his precise role in Nabataean religion, Knauf 1989: 58-59, and Macdonald 1991: 112-14. Shara is usually identified with the biblical Mt. Seir, which some scholars would locate west rather than east of the wadi Araba. If so, and if the argument about the Nabataean adoption of Dushara as their national deity is accepted, then it would support Negev's view that the Nabataean heartland was to the west of Petra.
7. Knauf 1989: 59.
8. Knauf 1989: 59; Starcky 1966, col. 990-91.
9. Glueck 1965: 4; and many places elsewhere.
10. Milik 1982: 263-64
11. Graf 1990: 46
12. Graf 1997a: 82.
13. See Graf 1990: 55, 59 and 67 for these specific points.
14. Graf 1997a: 82.
15. Healey 1989: 42.
16. Personal communication. I am greatly indebted to Michael Macdonald for discussing these philological matters with me.
17. Starcky 1966: 903; Bartlett 1979: 62-63.
18. Negev's attempt to locate Hieronymus's "waterless region" more precisely in the central Negev (1976: 127-28) is unconvincing, "desert" and "waterless" being terms appropriate to many parts of northern Arabia, Sinai, and the Jordanian plateau as well as to the Negev. The "section which [was] fruitful" would apply best to the western edge of the plateau around Petra and to the northern Negev, though the oases of the Hejaz and Sinai would also qualify.
19. Although far too little archaeological research has been done in either the Hejaz or Sinai to enable a proper analysis of ancient settlement patterns to be made, enough is known from preliminary work to indicate that the above remarks are very probably true.
20. For recent discussions of the history and archaeology of Edom see the various papers in Bienkowski 1992 and Edelman 1995.
21. The severity of the effects of the Babylonian destruction of Edom and the extent to which sedentary occupation continued are much debated questions. See in particular Bartlett 1979 and 1990.
22. Parr 1982: 131-33
23. For recent overviews of the history of the Hejaz in the 1st millennium BC, based on the very inadequate evidence which is all that is currently available, see Parr 1989; Edens and Bawden 1989; Bowersock 1996; Salles 1996.
24. The reasons for this initially surprising action on Nabonidus's part were probably complex, but following as it did immediately after the collapse of the Babylonian client states, Moab and Edom, further north, and in view of the threat the resulting instability must have posed to the security of the Arabian trade route, it can hardly be doubted that the need to strengthen his control over this economically important part of the empire would have been uppermost in his mind.
25. For example by De Geus 1979-1980: 70; Bartlett 1990: 34.
26. For a general discussion of Edomite religion see Dearman 1995: especially pp. 123-27 for Qaws.
27. The present writer finds it hard to accept De Geus's view that "not only is there an increasing amount of information available

about occupation in Edom in Persian times, but precisely the continuity between the earlier Edomite culture and the later Nabataean culture is at present becoming more and more emphasized" (De Geus 1979–1980: 69–70). The suggestion sometimes made – and alluded to by De Geus – that the distinctive fine pottery produced from about the late second or early first century BC by the urban Nabataeans has stylistic and technical affinities with the Edomite pottery of some four hundred years earlier, is completely untenable. Nabataean pottery is exclusively influenced by the Greco-Roman world.

28. In addition to the other places mentioned in connection with Nabonidus's campaign, the oasis of al-Jawf (Adummatu, Dumah) had been one of the main Arab centers in Assyrian times, and was later to become a large Nabataean town, judging from archaeological evidence.
29. See Sahlins 1968: 37.

CHAPTER 3

1. Cosmas Indicopleustes 1864: cols 217–218. For more detail, see Lewis and Macdonald 2002
2. See chapter 11 and Lewis and Macdonald 2002
3. Beer 1840: xvi.
4. Stanley 1862: 58. This statement is not in the first edition of 1856.
5. Levy 1860: 375.
6. Doughty 1891: 18 and Renan on pp. 2–3 of the same work.
7. For details, see below under the sections on these regions.
8. For details of Nabataean inscriptions from these and other peripheral areas see the references in Wenning 1987, 22–24.
9. See below under the section on "The Southern Dead Sea Valley."
10. At Ramm see Savignac and Horsfield 1935: 265–69, and at Petra see, for instance, Zayadine 1974: 148 and pl. LXVI, 1 and 3.
11. The ostraca from Petra have not yet been published, though see Kirkbride 1960: 118 and pl. VIII.1, and the discussion below under "Script." The ostraca and pebbles from the Negev come from the site of Nessana, see Rosenthal 1962: 198–210. nos 1–4 (pebbles), 5–10 (ostraca). See also a pebble from northwest of Beer-Sheba with an incantation text in a formal script very similar to Nabataean (Naveh 1979). For the ostraca at Masada, see Yadin, Naveh and Meshorer, 1989: 44–45, pl. 39, nos 514–15.
12. CIS 2 no. 3973.
13. See Macdonald, Al Muʾazzin and Nehmé 1996: 444–49.
14. For this interpretation of the word *šlm* (rather than the traditional "peace!," or "greetings!"), see Milik and Starcky 1970: 142.
15. That is, there are 874 Nabataean signatures out of the 1069 known inscriptions in Nabataean, Greek and Latin in Petra. See Nehmé 1997b: 126–27.
16. Strabo 16. 4.26.
17. For an excellent analysis of the distribution of the inscriptions of Petra, see Nehmé 1997b, from which the information in the paragraph above is taken.
18. Sartre 1993: 85–87, no. 51.
19. Sartre 1993: 91–94, no. 55. The tomb collapsed in 1847, but the text had already been copied *in situ* by early visitors to Petra.
20. There is a handful of other, mainly fragmentary, Latin and Greek epitaphs, most post-dating the Annexation, see Sartre 1993: nos 52–53 (Latin) and nos 56–69 (Greek). No. 54 is not an epitaph but a claim to have constructed a tomb.
21. See Starcky 1965 a, and 1965 b.
22. CIS 2 no. 350, see Healey 1993: 238–42 and Macdonald and Nehmé in preparation.
23. At Hegra, inscription H 36/9 says that a copy of the inscription was lodged in a temple, and this may well have been the case with the other texts. On the "Turkmaniyah" tomb and inscriptions see Macdonald and Nehmé (in preparation).
24. Quoted by Strabo [*c.* 64/BC to *c.* AD 21] 16.4.21
25. A baetyl is a stylized cult-image.
26. See Nehmé 1997b: 130–31 for these and other examples, and references.
27. See Hammond, Johnson and Jones 1986, and corrections to the reading in Jones 1989.
28. For instance, CIS 2, no. 349 (and see the references in Wenning 1987: 202–3) and CIS 2, no. 354.
29. Sartre 1993: nos. 45–49.
30. See the note to fig. 38.4.
31. Dalman 1912: 101–3, no. 92.
32. See Milik 1976 and, most recently, Healey 1993: 243–44 and references there. The Greek part is a summary of the Nabataean. Although this text is unique in Petra, it is of a type which is quite common elsewhere (see below).
33. These are, from south to north, at Buseirah (Starcky 1975), Khirbet et-Tannur (Savignac 1937), Dhat Ras (Zayadine 1970), Umm al-Raṣāṣ (CIS 2 no. 195), Zizia/al-Jīzah (JSNab 392), Madaba (CIS 2 no. 196, Lyon no. 45/Brussels no. 51, and Milik 1958 no. 6), Beit Ras (*RES* 1098).
34. On these languages and scripts see note 91 below.
35. The ancient name of this place, at least in the Nabataean period was *ʾrm*, as attested in some of the Nabataean inscriptions there. Some of the Mediaeval Arab geographers who deal with the *Ḥismā* mention a place called *ʾIram* and this has generally been identified with modern *Ramm* (see al-Hamdæni and al-Yāqū, conveniently translated in Musil 1926: 315–317). Nabataean *ʾrm* has therefore been vocalized *Iram* by most scholars (see Savignac 1932: 584, n. 1). However, the modern name is "Ramm" (pronounced like the drink "rum").
36. Savignac 1932: 407–11, Nabataean no. 1.
37. On the temple and its inscriptions the principal publications are still Savignac 1932, 1933, 1934 and Savignac and Horsfield 1935.
38. See Zayadine and Farès-Drappeau 1998, though the conclusions they draw from this text should be treated with caution, see Macdonald 2000: 73–74, n. 141.
39. Savignac 1932: 590–94, nos. 1–3. See the plan of the distribution of these texts in Savignac 1934: fig. 1 (with a key on p. 573).
40. H 16 (Healey 1993: 154–62). Translation by Healey with some minor changes.
41. H 36/9. This was probably the case with the others as well.
42. JSNab 43, 54 and 56, all of which are on Qaṣr al-Bint, the isolated rock into which some of the most magnificent tombs are carved.
43. For instance JSLih 66 and 79.
44. For instance, the Nabataean inscription CIS 2 no. 332 (see Healey 1993: 245) from Dedan which says "This is the funerary monument of Ab... son of Muqaymū son of Muqaymʾel which his father built for him. In the month of Elūl, year 1 of Ḥaretat king of Nabaṭū" (the translation is Healey's with minor changes). See also ARNA Nab 16 from Dūmā (modern al-Jawf, in northwest Saudi Arabia), reproduced in Healey 1993, 246.
45. The Bab al-Siq bilingual (Pl. 13.8) mentioned above, under Petra.
46. H 13 which says "This is the burial-niche which Hagarū made for Maslamū her brother and for Maîmiyyat her maternal aunt. May it never be opened over them." The "property inscription" on the façade of this tomb is H 14.
47. For a list of the inscriptions mentioning stone-cutters which are found on these tombs see McKenzie 1990: 27, Table 4.
48. See, for instance, Jaussen and Savignac 1909–1922: nos 201 bis-224, 382–91.
49. See the inscription published by Savignac and Starcky 1957a. For other Nabataean inscriptions from Dūmā and its environs see Theeb 1993: nos. 92–95; 1994.
50. See, for instance, Jaussen and Savignac 1909–1922: nos. 225–80, 317–81 and Theeb 1993, 1995 and 2000.
51. Macdonald 1994. The text is dated to year 17 of Rabbel II, i.e. AD 87/88.
52. Starcky 1985: 172–173. These inscriptions are being prepared for publication in the near future by Laïla Nehmé.
53. Musée de Suweidāʾ inv. 196, see Teixidor in Dentzer and Dentzer-Feydy 1991: 148 and pl. 24.
54. For artists' signatures on the bases of statues, see, for example, Musée du Louvre AO 4991 (Shudu the artisan) and LPNab 10117. For the arch of the niche see Musée du Louvre AO 11079. Lyon no. 43a/Brussels no. 71
55. See, for instance, Milik 1980, Starcky 1978.
56. See, for instance, Milik 1958: 242–43, no. 5, from Muʿarribah, six kilometers west of Bosra. If Milik's reading is correct, the text is very odd. He reads "in year 9 of Malkū [the] Nabataean (?), [it is] Thomas who carved [this]."
57. For instance, LPNab 40, 93, 105 (= fig. 28 here) and Starcky 1985: 180.
58. On funerary monuments in the Hauran, see Starcky 1985: 179.
59. Macdonald and Searight 1982: 172 and Macdonald (in preparation, b).
60. LPNab 101.
61. On Babatha's documents see Yadin 1962, 1963b; Lewis, Yadin and Greenfield 1989 and Yadin 2002; on Salome's see Cotton 1995.
62. One was published in Starcky 1954 (see now the new edition in Yardeni 2001). Editions of another six texts, plus two fragments, can be found in Yadin 2002: 169–268. Cotton, Cockle and Millar noted, but were unable to catalogue, an unspecified number "of Nabataean papyri said to come from Naḥal Ṣeʾelim, but likely in fact to come from Naḥal Ḥever," which are to be published by E. Puech. (Cotton Cockle and Millar: 1995: 215).
63. For Greek documents with signatures and witness statements in Nabataean, see Lewis, Yadin and Greenfield 1989, nos. 12, 14, 15, 16, 20, 22, and Cotton 1995: no. IV.
64. Yadin 2002: 257–67. Another document in Nabataean, *P. Yadin* no. 9, is said to date to AD 122, but the passage containing the date is so badly damaged that no secure conclusion can be drawn from it, see Yadin 2002: 268–76.
65. Thus, for instance, at the end of *P. Yadin* 22 in Lewis, Yadin and Greenfield 1989, Babatha's guardian (*ʾadōn*) who has the Jewish name Yōḥana wrote a five-line statement in Nabataean in what was a transaction between two members of the Jewish community. In the fourth signature on the back of *P. Yadin* 16, the name "Yōḥana son of ʿAbdʿobodat Makoutha" would present an extremely interesting mixture of Jewish and Nabataean names, were it not that all the letters in *ʿbdʿbdt* except the last are uncertain.
66. Similarly, the Shimʿōn who signed his name in the Nabataean form of the Aramaic script on at least one ostracon found at Masada (Yadin, Naveh and Meshorer 1989: 44–45, pl. 39, nos. 514–15), may have been brought up in the Nabataean cultural sphere.
67. See, for instance, Glueck 1956: 23–28, Negev 1963: 122 (which is almost certainly referring to Glueck's site 211, described on p. 25).
68. See, for instance, Jaussen, Savignac and Vincent 1905: 237–42, and Anati 1979 [unnumbered plates]. No readings or translations are given in the latter.
69. For example, Negev reported that "more than two score Nabataean inscriptions were discovered" during the clearance of the site of Oboda/Avdat (1961: 127). Of these, only 16 have so far been published (under 12 numbers, in Negev 1961. and 1963). Note also Stone 1992–1994, vol. 3: 164, nos. 8374–75 (apparently unpublished).
70. These are written on potsherds and pebbles (Rosenthal 1962).
71. The incantation text was found at Ḥorvat Raqiq/Khirbet Abū Raqayiq, near Beer-Sheba, and was published in Naveh 1979. The stela was originally published in Cowley 1914–1915: 146, fig. 59. See Wenning 1987: 141, for later bibliography.
72. Negev 1961: 127–28, no. 1.
73. Negev 1963: 113–17, no. 10. Negev's reading *skrʾ* (which he translates "dam") in nos 7a, 8 and 10 is impossible. The first letter is clearly *m* and the word is probably *mkrʾ*, perhaps from Aramaic *kᵉrāʾ*, *kʳrē* (cf. Hebrew *kārâ*) "to dig, bore," referring to the fact that the objects are troughs hollowed out of single blocks of stone, (though see Naveh 1967: 187–188, for a different reading). Note also that while Naveh's reading *mrzḥ* in line 2 of Negev's no. 7 b is very probable (Naveh 1967: 188), Negev's reading of the same word at the end of line 2 of his no. 10 is doubtful.
74. See Negev, Naveh and Shaked 1986. For the most recent treatment, with references to previous studies, see Kropp 1994.
75. For a definition of Old Arabic see note 92 below.
76. Bellamy suggested that the first hemistich was taken "from a hymn to Obodas" (1990: 79), but it seems more likely that the whole Arabic passage is quoted from a liturgical work (see also Kropp 1994: 171).
77. See Negev 1981.
78. Of the 3851 Nabataean inscriptions listed by Stone as coming from Sinai (1992–1994, vol. 3: 205–8), 3846 are in fact from there (his nos. 7299–301 and 8374–75 are from Oboda in the Negev; but note that nos. 4194–201, 4203–12 which are ascribed to Timnaʿ in the Wadī ʿArabah [Vol. 2, 98–99], are actually from Wadi Berraḥ, in Sinai). This 3846 includes virtually all of the published Nabataean inscriptions from Sinai and large numbers of those recorded by Israeli expeditions in the late 1960s and the 1970s, most which remain unpublished.
79. See, for instance, fig. 16 here, no. 1867, and also CIS 2 nos 1081, 1134, 1216, 2499, 2845, 2846, 3184.

80. For example, CIS 2 nos. 3022, and 3031 (on fig. 16 here).
81. For example CIS 2 nos. 1108, 1666, 1667, 1876, 1882, 1883, 2874, 2875, all shown on fig. 16 here.
82. For example CIS 2 no. 1082, shown on fig. 16 here.
83. It is usually difficult to be sure of this because many names were so popular that the chances are very high of there having been more than one ʾAwshū son of ʿAbd-al-Baʿalī, for instance. However, when both father and son bear less popular names it is possible to suggest (though we can seldom, if ever, be sure) that two or more texts are by the same person, e.g. Ḥirshū son of Ḥugayrū in CIS 2 nos 1665, 1701 and 2227. Unfortunately, the vast majority of the graffiti from Sinai are known only from hand-copies of varying accuracy, and very few photographs have ever been published. Most copyists had their own 'style' and this effectively masks that of the original author (on fig. 16, compare nos 1876, 1882, 1883 which were copied by J. Euting, with the others which are copies by G. Bénédite). This makes it impossible at present to use the "handwriting" of different inscriptions containing the same names as a guide to whether they are by the same person.
84. On the question of nomads and literacy see Macdonald 1993: 382–88, and Macdonald, Al Mu'azzin and Nehmé 1996: 442–43.
85. The only alternative would have been one of the Ancient North Arabian scripts (see below), but the extreme rarity in Sinai of texts in any of these alphabets suggests that in fact this was not an option.
86. Note that on several occasions in Littmann and Meredith 1953 and 1954, the same inscription was published twice from different copies.
87. However, recent photographs of four texts which Littmann and Meredith published from bad hand copies show that they contain some interesting material not found before in Nabataean, see Nehmé 1999. The only date so far identified among the graffiti from Egypt is Littmann and Meredith 1953, 16, no. 46a, where the date appears to be 160 (assumed to be of the Era of the Province), i.e. AD 265/6, though the construction of the dating formula is very odd.
88. See Strugnell 1959: 31–34. This goddess is also the subject of brief dedication from another site in the eastern Delta called Qaṣrawet, near Qaṭiyeh (Littmann and Meredith 1954: 230–232, no. 82 = 83. See Strugnell 1959: 34–35).
89. Jones 1988. Note that the reading of this place-name is not entirely certain since the forms of the *n* and the *p* are unusual and differ from the other examples of these letters in the text.
90. See Fiema and Jones 1990, correcting to the date given in Jones 1988.
91. Ancient North Arabian is a group of dialects related to Arabic, but distinct from it. These were used in central and north Arabia and in southern Syria between about the eighth century BC and the fourth century AD, and were written in a number of different alphabets of the "Arabian" or "South Semitic" script-family (of which the South Arabian and Ethiopic scripts are also members). Some dialects were used by the settled peoples of the oases, such as Dadanitic (formerly called "Dedanite" and "Lihyanite") at Dedān (modern al-ʿUlā) and Taymanitic at Taymāʾ. Others were used almost exclusively by nomads, Safaitic mainly in the deserts east and southeast of the Hauran, Hismaic (formerly called "Thamudic E") in the Hisma desert of southern Jordan and northwest Arabia, and the various scripts lumped together as "Thamudic" with rough divisions into "B," "C," and "D," found throughout the Peninsula. See Macdonald and King 1999 on Thamudic, and Macdonald 2000 and 2002 on Ancient North Arabian in general.
92. The Arabic language is only properly attested from the Rise of Islam (seventh century AD) onwards. In the eighth/ninth centuries AD Arab grammarians produced the normalized and systematic amalgam of dialects known as Classical Arabic which is still the basis of written Arabic today. The term "Old Arabic" refers to the forms of the Arabic language that have survived from the pre-Islamic period *independently* of these early Arab grammarians—i.e. inscriptions and other original documents, but not the pre-Islamic poetry which was written down and possibly "normalized" in the Islamic period. Until the late fifth/early sixth centuries AD, Old Arabic was a purely spoken language with no script "of its own." Thus, on the very rare occasions when someone wanted to write something in Old Arabic they had to "borrow" a script normally used by another language, such as Sabaic (from South Arabia), Dadanitic (in northwest Arabia, see the previous note), Nabataean, and Greek. It was only in the fifth/sixth centuries AD that Old Arabic began to be written on a regular basis, in a late form of the Nabataean alphabet. See Macdonald 2000: 36–37, 48–54, 57–60 and Macdonald (in preparation, a).
93. Dadanitic, possibly Taymanitic, and some of the poorly understood dialects which are lumped together under the label "Thamudic."
94. On immigration into Sinai, Egypt and Gaza from the Arabian Peninsula, see Ephʿal 1982: 101–8, 137–42, 193–201, 206–10.
95. Diod. Sic. 19.94.4–5.
96. However, if one excludes those bilinguals in the Hauran in which the Aramaic section is in the local, rather than the specifically Nabataean, script (see below), the number of examples is not great, e.g. LPNab 31 (al-Ghāriyah); Milik 1958, nos 4 (Jammarīn, near Bosra), 6 (Madaba); Kraeling 1938: 371–73, pl. XCV, see fig. 39 here; JSNab 392/JSGreek 21 (Zizia/al-Jīzah); Milik 1976 (Petra) fig. 128 here; possibly Savignac and Horsfield 1935: 263–64, 269, Greek no. 1 and Nabataean no. 5 (Ramm), if Milik's reconstruction is correct (1976: 145, n. 5). Understandably, Nabataean inscriptions outside the Nabataean cultural area are often bilinguals, e.g. CIS 2, no. 160 (Sidon); Levi Della Vida 1938 (the Greek island of Cos), etc. See Wenning 1987: 22–24. There is also a Nabataean-Latin bilingual at Rome (CIS 2 no. 159).
97. King 1990, nos KJC 380 and Nab 1 (Hismaic) and possibly Jobling 1990: 107–8 (Hismaic); Khraysheh 1994 (Safaitic).
98. I am most grateful to the excavator of Qaryat al-Faw, Professor A.T. al-Ansary, for this information (personal communication). The text will appear in his forthcoming edition of the inscribed material from the site.
99. In many cases such etymologies are very strained and a derivation from Aramaic would be far more plausible, see Macdonald 1999: 256–61, and 273–285 *passim*.
100. To take just one instance among many others, Roschinski 1981: 31 "the Nabataeans' mother tongue was clearly Arabic, as above all their personal names show us."
101. See Macdonald 1998: 187–88; 1999: 254–55; 2000: 47.
102. A curious example of this can be found on an inscribed stone used to close a burial niche in Petra (Lyon no. 46/Brussels no. 52). The deceased's name was *šmʿwn br ʿzyrw* "Simon son of ʿUzayrū." The first name is Jewish and the root of the second is almost certainly Hebrew *ʿ-z-r* (from which the name Ezra is formed and of which the Arabic cognate is *ʿ-ḏ-r*, and the Aramaic is *ʿ-d-r*). Yet this apparently Hebrew root has been used to produce a diminutive of an *Arabic* form, *ʿuzayr* (as noted by Starcky in his commentary).
103. See, for instance, CIS 2, no. 890: *dnh swsyʾ dy ʿbd šʿdlhy br ʾʿlʾ* ("this is the horse which Shaʿad-lahī son of ʾAʿla made"). This is pure Aramaic even though the names are etymologically Arabic.
104. See O'Connor 1986, who isolates approximately 15 such words, and the discussions in Healey 1993: 59–63 and Macdonald 1998: 187; 2000: 46–47.
105. See Macdonald 2000: 47.
106. For a possible exception in H 36/5–6, from Ḥegrā, see O'Connor 1986: 221.
107. These were also Cantineau's conclusions, despite his suggestion that the Nabataeans spoke Arabic (1932: 177–78).
108. See, most recently, Healey and Smith 1989 and the comments in Macdonald 2000: 53–54.
109. Another late text, from about the same period, was found at Umm al-Jimāl in northern Jordan (LPNab 41). This is the tombstone of the tutor of a king of the Arab tribe of Tanūkh. It is in Nabataean and Greek and there are mistakes in both. But here, the errors in the Nabataean cannot be ascribed to Arabic influence, since they would be equally incorrect in Arabic (see the commentary to LPNab 41).
110. This text is unfortunately undated and the date which is usually assigned to it (ca. AD 150) is based on the flimsiest of evidence (see Negev, Naveh and Shaked 1986: 60).
111. See Bordreuil 1997 and Bellamy 1985.
112. *Panarion* 51.22,11 (text in Epiphanius 1980: 286–87; translation in Epiphanius 1994: 51).
113. See Koenen 1996b: 187–88, and chapter 22 in this volume, and Ghul 1999.
114. The fact that other Ancient North Arabian written languages (Safaitic, Hismaic and Thamudic B, C and D) were used more or less exclusively by nomads, can have given them little prestige in the eyes of the settled populations which seem generally to have ignored them.
115. Note that the so-called "Thamudic" inscriptions have no demonstrable connection with the tribe of Thamūd, see Macdonald and King 1999: 436.
116. For this interpretation see Macdonald 1995.
117. See Milik 1971, and Macdonald 1995.
118. The Nabataean is JSNab 17 (on which see, most recently Healey and Smith 1989 and Macdonald 2000: 53) and the Thamudic D text is JSTham 1.
119. See Stiehl 1970.
120. For a history of the development of the Nabataean script see Starcky 1966: 926–37.
121. Diod. Sic. 19.94.4–5, quoting an eye-witness account of the nomadic Nabataeans in 312 BC, only eleven years after the death of Alexander the Great.
122. Diod. Sic. 19.96.1.
123. On the development during this period of different forms of the script for use on hard and soft materials, see Naveh 1970: 21–63.
124. A ligature is an additional line, or an extension of part of a letter used to join it to the one that follows.
125. In the earliest inscription from Petra of 96/95 BC (figs. 18, 38.4) only a few of the letters are joined, mainly in common combinations such as the *n-h* of *dnh*, *ʿ-b-d*, *b-r*, etc. but the majority are still written separately. Compare this with the Turkmaniyah inscription (figs. 17, 38.5) of the first century AD in which the majority of the letters are joined.
126. This does not always happen and, for instance, in both the Aramaic script used by the Achaemenid chancellery, and its Jewish Palestinian derivative, each letter was written separately.
127. Thus, in some of the tomb inscriptions at Hegra the mason has continued some lines onto the frame rather than compress the letters, see, for instance, fig. 27 here (last line) and the plate of H 36 in Healey 1993 (the ends of lines 3 and 5–7). More drastic is the case of H 9 where part of the frame has been removed apparently to accommodate the final letters of lines 4 and 5.
128. For instance, the use of an "archaic" final *ʾāleph* in certain words in texts which elsewhere use the 'looped' form in this position. Thus, for instance, in H 16 of 1 BC/AD (figs. 27 and 38.6) the "archaic" final *ʾāleph* is found in the key words *kprʾ* ('tomb', lines 1, 5, 10), *ktbʾ* ("document," line 10) and the divine name *dwšrʾ* (lines 3 and 8) but the looped form in all other cases (*lʾ* line 7, *ʾlʾ* line 7, and *ʾpklʾ* line 8). Similarly, in an inscription from Petra (CIS 2 no. 354) of AD 20, the 'archaic' final *ʾāleph* is used in the word *ʾlhʾ* "god" and the name of the deity *dwtrʾ*, but the looped form occurs in the word *ṣlmʾ* "statue." Compare fig. 34, the inscription on an altar from Imtān, in the Hauran (dated to year 23 of Rabbel II = AD 93/94) which is in the Nabataean (rather than the local Aramaic) script. Here the "archaic" final *ʾāleph* is used only in the divine name Dūsharā, and the looped form in every other instance.
129. It is instructive to compare the careful professional hand of the Nabataean papyri (e.g. figs. 24, 38.15) with the signature and witness statement (figs. 25, 38.16) of someone from the same community who was 'an experienced writer' but not a professional scribe (Lewis, Yadin and Greenfield 1989: 136).
130. Kirkbride 1960: 118–19 and pl.VIII, 1. They have not yet been published but I am most grateful to the late Mrs. Diana Kirkbride-Helbaeck for showing me photographs of them.
131. Cross aptly described it as "pre-Nabataean" (1965: 207).
132. See Starcky 1966: 930–31; 1985: 169, 173, and the discussion above in the section on 'The uses of writing'.
133. For texts dated by the regnal years of Nabataean kings see, for example, fig. 30 (year 11 of Malichus I = 47/46 BC, see Fiema and Jones 1990: 242 for the year of Malichus' accession); fig. 33 (year 17 of Malichus II = AD 57); fig. 34 (year 23 of Rabbel II = AD 93/94); fig. 35 = 10.12 (year 24 of Rabbel II = 405 Seleucid = AD 94); fig. 36 = 10.11 (year 25 of Rabbel II = AD 95); Starcky 1985: 181, and fig. 3 on p. 177 (year 31 of Rabbel II = AD 101/102). Note

that some of these come from outside the Nabataean kingdom.

134. For texts dated by the regnal years of Herodian rulers see fig. 31 (year 33 of Philip the Tetrarch = AD 29/30), and LPNab 102 (Agrippa I or II).

135. For texts dated by the regnal years of Roman emperors see fig. 34 (year 7 of Claudius = AD 48); Starcky 1985: 180 (year 9 of Claudius = AD 50), and LPNab 27 (year 7 of Hadrian = AD 124). Other inscriptions are dated by the Seleucid era (which began in 312/311 BC), see LPNab 100 (year 280-300 (or 311) Seleucid = 32/31 to 12/11 BC (or 1 BC/AD)); Littmann 1904: 90-93, no. 2 (year 308 Seleucid = 4/3 BC); fig. 35 = 10.12 (405 Seleucid = 24 of Rabbel II = AD 94).

136. Starcky 1966: 930.

137. Similarly, the altar inscription from Imtān (fig. 34, dated AD 93/94) where the letter shapes and the use of ligatures are characteristic of the Petra script, but the more or less uniform height of the letters is a feature of Hauran Aramaic.

138. See, for instance, Cross 1965: 206, "the national scripts of Palmyra, Judaea and Nabataea. . . ."

139. For example on fig. 16, working from top to bottom: nos. 2874 and 2875 form a single, interlinked composition. In 952, the letters of each line are joined along the base and the word *šlm* has been elongated vertically so that it runs down the right hand 'margin' of all three lines. In addition, two diagonal strokes have been added to the elongated flourish of its *m* to match those of those of the *sh* nos. 1882, 1883 and 1876 show three different ways of joining the letters of the name *klbw* (Kalbū). At the end of 1882 the letters are joined along the base, in the first name of 1883 the *l* and the *b* are joined by a ligature halfway down the stem of the *l*, while in 1876 the *k* and the *w* are joined along the base but are not joined to the *l* and the *b* which float together in mid-air (as also in the two examples of *klbw* in 1108). In 1857 the two names are joined by a line along the bases of the letters and the word *br* ("son of") has been reduced to two diagonal lines floating above the last letter of the first name.

140. Tayma': examples of Imperial Aramaic, the Louvre stela fig. 38.1 (CIS 2 no. 113, Gibson 1975: 148-151) and the new stela (Cross 1986). Dedan: Imperial Aramaic, JSNab 390, and Naṣīf 1988: pl. 124a. Between Dedan and Hegra: JSNab 268. Ḥegræ: Imperial Aramaic, JSNab 127: 146.

141. As noted above, the latest inscription in the Nabataean-Aramaic language and script is from Hegra and dates to AD 356, see Stiehl 1970.

142. See Bordreuil 1997 and Macdonald 2000: 59-60.

143. The Greek, Syriac and Arabic inscription on the lintel of a church at Zebed in northern Syria, dated AD 512; the graffito by a soldier of the Ghassanid king al-Ḥārith at Jabal Says (Usays), dated AD 528; and the Greek-Arabic bilingual inscription on the lintel of a church at Ḥarrān, in the Leja, southern Syria, dated AD 568. There are also two undated texts which are usually classed with these, one from Ramm and the other from Umm al-Jimal. Neither has been satisfactorily read. See the bibliography in Gruendler 1993: 13-14, and the discussions in Grohmann 1967-1971: 2, 14-17, with photographs on pls 1 and 2.

144. Stiehl 1970, and note that even JSNab 17 was a partially successful attempt by an Arabic speaker to write Aramaic, rather than an unequivocally Arabic text like the Namārah inscription.

Abbreviations used in the notes to Chapter 3

ARNA Nabataean inscriptions published in Milik and Starcky 1970.
H Nabataean tomb inscriptions of Hegra, republished in Healey 1993.
JSLih Dedanitic (Lihyanite) inscriptions in Jaussen and Savignac 1909–1922.
JSNab Nabataean inscriptions in Jaussen and Savignac 1909–1922.
JSTham Thamudic inscriptions in Jaussen and Savignac 1909–1922.
LPNab Nabataean and other Aramaic inscriptions in Littmann 1914.
P.Yadin Papyri from the Naḥal Ḥever "Cave of Letters" as numbered in Lewis, Yadin and Greenfield 1989 and Yadin et al. 2002. [Note that in Yadin 1962 and 1963, Documents nos. 1–4" = *P.Yadin* 1–4, but that "Document no. 6" = *P.Yadin* 7, and so on.]

CHAPTER 4

1. *ANET*: 305.
2. Lemaire: 1995: 68-69.
3. *CIS* II, 1907: 391.
4. Milik 1982: 263-65.
5. Milik 1982: 264.
6. Graf 1992: 970.
6b. al-Khraysheh 2000.
7. Glueck 1965: 143, pl. 31.
8. Glueck 1965: 315, pls. 1-2.
9. Meunier 1980.
10. al-Kalbi 1924: 18.
11. Yaqut 1955: s.v. 7038.
12. Starcky, 1966: 887.
13. Cantineau 1932: 3-5.
14. *CIS* II, 1907: 218.
15. Cantineau 1932: 22.
16. Cantineau 1932: 46.
17. Parr 1957: 13-14.
18. Starcky, 1966: 990.
19. Bowersock 1990: 21-27.
20. Strugnell 1959: 29-36.
21. Milik 1982: 22.
22. Milik and Starcky 1975: 118.
23. Meyerson 1983: 130-40.
24. Fiema and Jones 1990: 239-48.
25. Oren 1982: 203ff.
26. Harding 1971: s.v.
27. Sourdel 1952: 81.
28. Jaussen and Savignac 1909 : 221, no. 72
29. Littmann 1901: 381-90.
30. Bignasca 1996: 142.
31. *CIS* II, 1907, no 182.
32. Savignac 1933: 411-12.
33. Zayadine 1990a: 40 & pl. 1, 2.
34. Gawlikowski 1983.
35. D. Sourdel, *Les cultes*, 70 and no. 7.
36. *ANET* 1955: 299.
37. Caskel 1954: nos. 13 & 25.
38. Zayadine 1981: 113–18, Pls. (I) 1–3, (II) 1–4; Zayadine 1990b: 163–64
39. Milik and Starcky 1975: 124-26.
40. Dalman 1912: 96.
41. Levi Della Vita 1938
42. Zayadine 1991a: 293-95
43. al-Kalbi, *Kitab*. 25.
44. Healy 1993: index 252 under mnwtw.
45. *CIS* II, 1907, 209.
46. al-As'ad and Teixidor 1985: 286-92.
47. al-As'ad and Teixidor 1985: 287-88.
48. Ryckmans 1980: 193-204.
49. al-Kalbi, *Kitab* 19, who reports that the three goddesses were venerated as the daughters of Allah.
50. See Seyrig 1932: 50-64.
51. Seyrig 1932: pl. 18, 4.
52. Leclant 1986: 341.
53. Witt 1971.
54. Grenfell and Hunt 1915: 197.
55. See Zayadine 1991a: 297
56. Leclant 1986: 343.
57. Meza 1996: 167-176 and fig. 1.
58. Hammond 1990: 115-27.
59. Graf 1988: 171-211.
60. al-Kalbi, *Kitab*, 27-28.
61. Zayadine 1990a: 18-19.

CHAPTER 5

1. Graf 1997b: 45-68; cf. Potts 1992: 223-24.
2. Graf 1983: 555-69.
3 Hiller von Gaertringen 1906: no. 108/168.
4. Graf 1996: 208; cf. Pulleyblank 1999: 76-77.
5. Graf 1996: 209.
6. see N. Groom 1981: 143-48.
7. Casson 1989.
8. Sedov 1997.
9. Ingraham 1981: 76-77; but cf. Gatier and Salles 1988: 186-87; see discussion Sidebotham 1986b: 125-26.
10. Bowersock 1983: 70; Casson 1989: 145.
11. Young 1997; but cf. Healey 1993: 30.
12. Parker 1997: 40.
13 cf. Johnson 1987: 101-3.
14. Crone 1987: 24-25.
15. cf. Johnson 1987: 101-3.
16. Tarn 1929: 15-16; cf. Lorton 1971.
17. cf. Crone 1987: 24 n. 51.
18. cf. Bowsher 1989: 22.
19. Graf 1997b:V; cf. Bowsher 1989.
20. Maraqten 1996.
21. Gawlikowski 1994.
22. Maraqten 1996: 229-30.
23. *RES*: 1088.
24. Graf 1997b:V, 276.
25. Knauf 1990: 177.
26. McKenzie 1990.
27. Healey 1993.
28. Personal communication from U. Bellwald; cf. Knauf 1998: 95-97.
29. Personal communication from U. Bellwald.
30. Bowersock 1983: 13; Graf 1997b: I. 51-54; Bowes 1998: passim.
31. Bowersock 1983: 90-109.
32. Potts; De Maigret 1997; Macdonald 1997.
33. Zayadine 1992; Graf 1997b: II.
34. al-Ansary 1982: 22, 28, 63-64.
35. Potts 1991; Potts 1992: 95-97; Graf 1997b: I. 63-64.
36. Graf 1996: 210.
37. Zarins 1981: 27 and pl. 28, no. 6.
38. Zarins 1983: 32.
39. Stucky 1983: 12 and abb. 10-11.
40. Sedov 1992: 120, 122, fig. 10.
41. *RES*: 4153; Mordtmann 1932: 429-30; cf. Macdonald 1994: 135-36.
42. Macdonald 1994: 136 and n. 30.
43. Macdonald 1994: 134.
44. Gatier and Salles 1988: 181.
45. Bowersock 1983: 48, 57, 59-60.
46. Wenning 1996: 254.
47. Healey 1993.
48. Bowersock 1983: 57; Graf 1997b:V. 283–84, 289.
49. Bowsher 1986.
50. Healey 1993: 27.
51. Winnett 1970: 71-73, 88-93, 113-20.
52. Starcky 1957a.
53. Bowersock 1983: 154-59.
54. Meshel 1973; Zayadine 1985; Graf 1998: 110.
55. Oren 1993 IV: 1215; cf. Oren 1982.
56. Starcky 1955: 156; Tsafrir 1982: 212-14; cf. Clermont-Ganneau 1919; and Jones 1988.
57. Rokéa 1983.
58. cf. Sperber 1976.
59. Starcky 1979: 38.
60. *CIS*: 790; Graf 1997b:V. 283.
61. Graf 1997b:V. 286; XI. 344-45.
62. Roche 1996; Roller 199b: 225, 226-28, 234.
63. Dubois 1907: 99-101, 161-62, 268; Frank 1940: 274; Ostrow 1977: 210, 226 n. 31.
64. *CIS*: II, 1.158; Renan 1873: 380; *CIL* X: 2644 and 2935; Meshorer 1975: 61; *IG*: 926, add. 842a; Roche 1996: 89ff.; De Romanis 1996: 166; Bowersock 1997c: 347-52.
65. Müller 1978; Groom 1981.
66. Sidebotham 1986b: 13.
67. Johnson 1987: 80-84, 87; cf. Bowes 1998: passim.
68. Meredith 1957; Johnson 1987: 75-78.
69. Charbel 1985.
70. Kisnawi 1983: 76-78 and pls. 79-81.
71. Patrich 1984; Goldman 1996; Rosenthal-Heginbottom apud A. Negev 1997: 202-06.
72. Crone 1987: 67-69.
73. Bowersock 1983: 28-44.
74. Sidebotham 1986b: 120-30.
75. Bowersock 1997b.
76. Sidebotham 1986b.
77. cf. Greene 1986: 39-40; Duncan-Jones 1982: 366-69.
78. Sidebotham 1986b: 71 n. 74.
79. Johnson 1987.
80. Sidebotham 1986b: 71-72.
81. Graf 1997b:VI, 2-5.
82. cf. Koenen 1996b: 178-79, 186-87.
83. Clermont-Ganneau 1919; Littmann and Meredith 1954: 227.
84. Green 1909: 320; Winkler 1938: 4, 7, 10; Littmann and Meredith 1953; Littmann and Meredith 1954.
85. Clermont-Ganneau 1919.
86. Hammond 1979: 245-47.
87. Briquel-Chatonnet and Nehmé 1998.
88. C. Toll 1994: 381-82.
89. Winkler 1938: 4,7, Site 24N, 10 summarized in De Romanis 1996: 203-4.
90. Sidebotham 1986b: 94-95.
91. Whitcomb 1982: 67, pl. 21d.
92. Hayes 1995: 38; Hayes 1996: 150.

CHAPTER 6

1. Concise overviews on Nabataean pottery and the history of research with much further bibliography can be found in Wenning 1987: 296-98; 1990: 414; Schmid 1997a; 2000a; 2001a,b,c. In general on the function of pottery for modern archaeology see Orton - Tyers - Vince 1993.
2. On Hellenistic moldmade bowls in general see Rotroff 1982; Kossatz 1990; Hausmann 1996; Rogl 1996; on the Peloponnesian production cf. Siebert 1978; for Ionian bowls Laumonier 1977 and Mitsopoulos-Leon 1991: 67-74; on moldmade bowls from the Black Sea area cf. Kovalenko 1996. For Eastern Terra Sigillata in general see Hayes 1985 and for Western terra sigillata Ettlinger, Hedinger and Hoffmann 1990.
3. On this phenomenon see Schmid 2000a: 111–13; Hannestad 1983: 83-120, both with further references.
4. For the provenience of ESA see Hayes 1985: 10; Schneider 1995.
5. On the date and process of Nabataean sedentarization see Schmid, 2001a; 2001b.
6. The misinterpretation about Petra being a "city of the dead" only with tombs and temples, leading to the misinterpretation of the pottery as being used only for cultic purposes can still be found in Negev 1977: 590f.

On recent research on the Nabataean private architecture in Petra see Kolb 1997; Stucky 1996; Zeitler 1989; Zeitler 1990a; Zeitler 1990b; Zeitler 1993; McKenzie 1990: 105ff.
7. Diod. Sic. 19. 94. 1ff.; Strabo 16. 4. 18; Peripl. M. Rubr. 19; Pliny. Nat. Hist. 12. 32. 63ff.
8. On fusiform *unguentaria* see Schmid, 2000a: chap.V. 4. 21; Negev 1986: 105 nos. 900–2; Murray - Ellis 1940: pl. XXVII no. 54; Horsfield 1942: 119 pl. IX no. 33. 127 pl. XIV no. 70; 190 pl. XLIII no. 379.
9. For the metal vessels probably used as prototypes for the Nabataean painted bowls see Schmid 2000a: 147–50. Vickers 1994.
10. Schmid, 2000a: chap.V. 8.; cf. S. G. Schmid, in Stucky 1995: 303–07; for similar silen's masks see Baratte 1986: 64 left picture; Hübner 1993: 14f. 76ff. pl. 3 no. 19; Abdou Daoud 1998: 116-18 fig. 1a-c no. 1.
11. Schmid 2000a: 147–50.
12. Schmid 2000a: 149–50.
13. Schmid 2000a: 123–25.
14. Strabo 16. 4. 22-24; Raschke 1978: especially 650ff.; Sidebotham 1986a: 48ff. 113ff.; 1986b; 1996; cf. further Eadie 1989; Romanis 1996: 19ff.
15. Wenning 1993: especially 86-93; Wenning 1989: 257f; cf. also Schmid 2000c: 400–2.
16. Schmid, 2000a: chap.V. 6.; Khairy 1982.
17. Contrary to Johnson 1990. There is no reason to believe that the parallels from the wider Mediterranean area quoted by Johnson 1990: 240f. and interpreted as Nabataean unguents are from Nabataean origin. Such vessels belong to the most uniform types in the entire antique world and they could have been produced anywhere. According to the small number found at Nabataean sites, the interpretation proposed here seems more convenient.
18. Schmid 1997; 2000a: 141–46.
19. Schmid 2000a: 38–39; Fellmann Brogli 1996: 240 figs. 844-49.

CHAPTER 7

1. Glueck 1935; Glueck 1937-1939.
2. See e.g., within the area of Dharih and Tannur, McDonald 1988.
3. Flavius Josephus, *Jewish Antiquities*, XIV, 374. These lines were probably quoted by Jospehus from Herod's biographer Nikolaos of Damascus.
4. Broome 1955. Starcky 1957b.
5. Glueck 1937c; 1938.
6. Glueck 1965.
7. Starcky 1968.
8. McKenzie 2001; McKenzie, Gibson and Reyes 2002. Roche 1997. Tholbecq forthcoming.
9. al-Muheisen and Villeneuve 1988; 1994; 2000.
10. Lenoble, al-Muheisen and Villeneuve 2001.
11. Especially in McKenzie 2001; McKenzie, Gibson and Reyes 2002.
12. Alt 1921: 8-10, text n° 2, Berosaba Edictum, s. v. Ellebana.
13. Glueck 1965: 138; Healey 2001: 60-61.
14. Glueck 1938: 12.
15. Glueck 1965: 138.
16. McKenzie, Gibson and Reyes 2002.
17. Lenoble, al-Muheisen and Villeneuve 2001.
18. Reconstruction of the elevation: Lenoble, al-Muheisen and Villeneuve 2001: 108.
19. Glueck 1965: 294; McKenzie, Gibson and Reyes 2002: 61.
20. Healey 2001: 158-59.
21. Blood libations on baetyls are testifyed, for the main temple of Petra, in the tenth century *Lexicon* of Suidas, *s.v.* "Theusarès" (Dusares): *Suidae Lexicon*, ed. I. Bekker, Berlin, 1854: 502 = ed. A. Adler, Leipzig, 1931: t. 2, p. 713
22. Epiphanius of Salamis, *Panarion*, 4. 22. 9-11; edition and translation by F. Williams, Leiden, 1987: vol. 1, p. 51.
23. Glueck 1965: 98-99.
24. Glueck 1937c; 1938.
25. Glueck 1965.
26. McKenzie, Gibson and Reyes 2002.
27. Glueck 1965: 182-84; McKenzie, Gibson and Reyes 2002: 71.
28. McKenzie, Gibson and Reyes 2002.
29. The reconstruction of the Tannur inner enclosure façade given here (fig. 74, cf. McKenzie, Gibson and Reyes 2002 p. 60), despite some uncertainties, must now clearly be preferred to that (without pediment; with a wrong distinction of two distinct façades, one in period 2, one in period 3) drawn by Fisher, Glueck's architect, and presented in Glueck 1965.
30. Tholbecq forthcoming.
31. Starcky 1968.

CHAPTER 8

1. For the journey of Antigonos Monophtalmos, see Diod. Sic. 2. 49; 19. 94-95, and translation by C.H. Oldfather, The Loeb Classical Library, Harvard University Press, II, X, 1961: 94-95; On the credibility of this source, see Hornblower 1981: 144-53 and *passim*.
2. Aharoni 1993: 85.
3. Hornblower 1981: note 184, p. 148: Hornblower writes: "If however, A Negev is right in placing the fourth century nomadic Nabataeans and their 'rock' not on the Transjordanian coast around the famous Petra, but in the NE Negev, this difficulty would be resolved: Negev, loc. cit. especially 529; cf. Negev 1976b: 125 ff."
4. Gichon 1993: 395-99.
5. Tsafrir 1994: 186. Recently Z. Meshel has treated this subject again; Meshel 1995: 40-48. On p. 47, note 20 Meshel notes "If so why did not Negev suggest locating it at the rock of Masada itself, or some other rock further to the south"; see also Negev 1996: 228-30, for a reply.
6. Negev 1993a: 379-83.
7. Negev 1976a: 89-95; Negev 1974a: 153-59.
8. Negev 1989: 129-42.
9. Negev 1993c: 1145-49.
10. Colt 1962.
11. Casson and Hettich 1950.
12. Kraemer 1958.
13. Negev 1991a, *passim* and especially indexes A-E: 130-51.
14. Negev 1993d: 1155-65.
15. Negev 1991b: 62-80.
16. Negev 1997.
17. Negev 1961: 127=138; Negev 1963: 113-24.
18. Negev 1981: 11-23, 26-27.
19. For a slightly different dating of the camp, see Cohen 1980: 44-45.
20. See Patrich 1990a.
21. Negev 1974b.
22. For the types of Nabataean pottery of Oboda, see Negev 1986.
23. Negev 1961: 127-38; 1963: 113-24.
24. Negev 1963, inscriptions nos. 11-12.
25. Negev 1981, inscription no. 13.
26. Negev 1993b: 882-93.
27. Negev 1988a, 1988b.
28. Negev 1993f: 241-64.
29. Negev 1988a: 50-77.
30. Negev 1988a: 77-88.
31. Negev 1988a: 88-109.
32. Negev 1988a: 111-62.
33. Negev 1988a: 181-91.
34. Negev 1988a: 167-87.
35. Negev 1993f: 241-64.
36. Negev 1988a: 30-63.
37. Negev 1990: 337-65.
38. Negev 1971: 110-29.
39. Negev 1974c: 337-42.
40. Negev 1969: 89-106.
41. Negev 1969: 89-106.
42. Negev 1988a: 124-25.
43. Negev 1967: 46–55; Mann 1969: 211–14; Jarret 1969: 215–24.
44. Tsafrir 1988; Tsafrir and Holum 1993: 1274-77.
45. Negev 1993e: 1404-10.
46. Tsafrir and others 1988; Tsafrir and Holum 1993: 1274-77.
47. Negev 1993e: 1404-10.

CHAPTER 9

1. Politis 1998.
2. Bowersock 1986b.
3. Politis 2002: 27.
4. Healey 1995: 189-90.
5. Zayadine 1982b: 366; pl. CXXI, 1.
6. Gascou 1999: 61-73.
7. Politis 2003, forthcoming.
8. Yadin 1963a: 169-279; pls. 59-102.
9. Pfister and Bellinger 1945.

CHAPTER 10

1. The program of the French Archaeological Mission in southern Syria, financed by the Ministry of Foreign Affairs at Bosra (Maison René Ginouvès at Nanterre) has been conducted in collaboration with the Directorate General of Antiquities of the Syrian Arab Republic at Damascus and Bosra, where we have been graciously received, since 1974, by Sleiman al-Mukdad and now by Riyadh al-Mukdad. In this mission it is important to emphasize the primary roles of the architects Henri Broise, Philippe Tondon and Thibaud Fournet, and also of René Saupin, topographical engineer. For a summary bibliography, see below.
2. Starcky 1966; Bowersock 1983; Sartre 1985; MacAdam 1986; Sartre 2001: 372-440.
3. P. Cairo Zenon, 59004; X. Durand, Des grecs en Palestine au IIIe siècle av. J.-C., Paris 1997, no. 4; cf. Orrieux 1983: 44-45; Sartre 2001: 411.
4. Josephus AJ, XIII, 392; BJ, I, 103; Bowersock 1983: 25; Sartre 2001: 412, 416.
5. Bowersock 1983: 61, 73-78; Sartre 1985: 54-56; Sartre 2001: 500.
6. Sartre 2001: 487; Starcky 1966.
7. Sounding on the south rampart conducted by F. Braemer in May-June, 2001, and M. Kadour, Seeden 1983: 77-102; Seeden 1988: 387-412; Seeden and Wilson 1984: 19-34; Seeden 1986: 11-82. New soundings on the south rampart conducted by F. Braemer in May–June, 2001: Braemer 2003 in press.
8. Dentzer 1985; Dentzer, Dentzer-Feydy and Blanc 2001.
9. Dentzer 1984; Dentzer 1986; Dentzer 1988; Dentzer, Blanc and Mukdad 1993; Dentzer, Dentzer-Feydy and Blanc 2001; see also Kader 1996.
10. Starcky 1985: 178; Dentzer, Blanc and Mukdad 1993.
11. Dentzer, Dentzer-Feydy and Blanc 2001; see also Masturzo 1991/2.
12. The early part of the Soouthern Baths has been built later on the same orientation.
13. Dentzer, Blanc and Mukdad 2003 in press.
14. Dentzer, Dentzer-Feydy and Blanc 2001.
15. Masturzo 1991–1992; Nehmé 1998; Dentzer, Dentzer-Feydy and Blanc 2001.
16. Dentzer-Feydy 1986; Dentzer 1985-1986: 387-420.
17. Butler 1907-1919, II A: 393-395, ill. 341; Dentzer-Feydy 1986: 280-83; see also Freyberger 1998; Dentzer-Feydy 2003: 105-9.
18. Macdonald 1993; and in Macdonald 2003: 278-79.

CHAPTER 11

1. The main source for Burckhardt's journey is his *Travels in Syria* (London, 1822) 311-456. Passages in quotation marks in the first part of this chapter are from there. The main source for the journey of Bankes and his companions is his manuscript journal in the Dorset County Record Office, Dorchester (Ref. no. D/BKL: Travel Journals HJ4/19 and 20). There is little difference between the part of the journal which deals with Petra and the parallel section in Irby and Mangles's *Travels in Egypt and Nubia, Syria and Asia/Minor* (London, privately printed 1823, published 1844 and 1868). Quoted words in the second part of this chapter are from one of these two sources with the exception of two identified phrases from G. Finati's *Narrative of the Life and Adventures of Giovanni Finati* (Bankes 1830).
2. Bankes produced over twenty sketches during his two days in Petra, five of which are reproduced above. Many of the others are very rough, faint or damaged. Only one of them (fig. 95) was published in his lifetime and of the rest only one (fig. 96) has been published since. The editor of the book and the author of this chapter are indebted to the National Trust for permitting publication of the plates in this chapter, and to the staff of the Dorset County Record Office at Dorchester (where much of the Bankes collection is now archived) for their help during the preparation of this chapter.

CHAPTER 12

1. "Jerusalem July 13 [1842]," Durham Record Office (subsequently "DRO"), Londonderry Estate Archives, D/LO Acc 451 (D) 44/6. Extract quoted by permission of the Londonderry Estate and the Durham Record Office.
2. Stephens 1837, vol. II: 81.
3. See N. Lewis's chapter 11 in this volume.
4. *Ibid.*
5. de Laborde 1836: 143.
6. Linant de Bellefonds 2001: 193-208. See also de Laborde 1994, with preface and notes by Christian Augé and Pascale Linant de Bellefonds. This re-issue of Laborde's book includes excerpts from Linant's unpublished notebook.
7. See Augé and Linant de Bellefonds, *op. cit.* p. 21.
8. See note 5.
9. Lindsay 1838, vol. II: 61.
10. Stephens 82. 1837, Vol. II: 82.
11. Robinson 1841 vol. II: 534.
12. Finden and Finden 1836. See also the re-issue, with foreword by Charles Newton, by the R.S. Surtees Society, 1998. The four illustrations of Petra are: *Ruins of SELAH (Petra) - Temple excavated out of the Rock*, and *Ruins of SELAH (Petra), No.II*, both sketched by Léon de Laborde, drawn by David Roberts; *EDOM - Arch across the Ravine*, sketched by Léon de Laborde, drawn by Clarkson Stanfield; and *EDOM - Entrance to Petra*, sketch by William John Bankes, drawn by J. D. Harding.

13. On David Roberts (1796-1864), see James Ballantine, *The Life of David Roberts R.A.* Edinburgh, 1866; *David Roberts*, exhibition catalogue compiled by Helen Guiterman and Briony Llewellyn. London, Phaidon and Barbican, 1986; and Krystyna Matyjaszkiewicz, article on David Roberts forthcoming in the *Oxford Dictionary of National Biography*, publication due 2004.
14. David Roberts, Eastern Journal, 1838-39 (transcribed by Christine Bicknell née Roberts), Edinburgh, National Library of Scotland, Department of Manuscripts, Acc. 7223/1-2.
15. *Ibid.*
16. *Ibid.*
17. Roberts 1842-1849.
18. *The Literary Gazette, and Journal of the Belles Lettres*, 26 February 1841: 146.
19. *Literary Gazette, op. cit.*, 21. May 1842: 34; also 1843: 171, 288, 466.
20. Linant de Bellefonds 2001. I am grateful to Mme Linant de Bellefonds for drawing this to my attention.
21. See the illustrations in their respective publications for these and other images cited here.
22. Roberts 1842-1849, vol. III: pl. 101.
23. *Literary Gazette, op. cit.*, 1843.
24. *Entrance to Petra*, inscribed *March 10 1839*, The Cecil Higgins Art Gallery, Bedford, England.
25. *El Deir, Petra*, both inscribed *March 8 1839*, both in a private collection, England.
26. Bartlett 1850: Preface, p.iii. On Bartlett (1809-1854) see A. M. Ross's, *William Henry Bartlett. Artist, Author, and Traveller.* Toronto, 1973.
27. See note 12. The engravings after Bartlett cited here, *The Khasné, The Ravine, Principal Range of Tombs* and *El Deir*, all appear in *Forty Days in the Desert on the Track of the Israelites*, 1848. Bartlett's watercolor, *Principal Range of Tombs, Petra*, is in the Searight Collection, Victoria and Albert Museum, London.
28. Bartlett 1848: 110-43.
29. Antonio Schranz (1801-after 1865). On the Schranz family, see Canon John Azzopardi ed., *The Schranz Artists. Landscape and Marine Painters in the Mediterranean*, exhibition catalogue, The Friends of the Cathedral Museum. Mdina, Malta, 1987.
30. Schranz's drawings, bound in five volumes, were formerly at Mount Stewart, the Londonderry house in Ireland; they are now the property of the National Trust and are housed at Lyme Park in Cheshire. I am indebted to James Rothwell, Assistant Historic Buildings Representative at the National Trust in Cheshire, for his assistance. Groups of watercolors from this and other trips were sold at Sotheby's, 17 May 1995, lots 176-8, and 15 February 1990, lot 232; others are in the Searight Collection, Victoria and Albert Museum, London.
31. Castlereagh 1847: 182.
32. *Ibid.*, pp.182-83.
33. Rowley-Conwy 1998: 108-17.
34. "Jerusalem July 13 [1842]," DRO, D/LO Acc 451 (D) 44/6.
35. Lady Louisa Mary Anne Tenison, née Anson (1809-1882). Watercolors by Lady Louisa Tenison were at Sotheby's 17 May 1995, lots 146-152, and 13 October 1999, lots 132-4, and are also in the Searight Collection, Victoria and Albert Museum, London. For her photography, see *Into the Light: An Illustrated Guide to the Photographic Collections in the National Library of Ireland*. Dublin, 1998.
36. Tenison, *Sketches in the East*. London, 1846: pl. 13.
37. Martineau 1848, vol. III: 6-7, 11, 28, 32.
38. On Edward Lear (1812-1888), see Vivien Noakes, *Edward Lear The Life of a Wanderer*, revised edition London, Fontana/Collins, 1979; Vivien Noakes, *Edward Lear 1812-1888*, exhibition catalogue, London, Royal Academy of Arts, 1985.
39. Letter to Ann, 29 March 1858; quoted in Noakes, *op.cit.*, 1979: 156.
40. Letter to Ann, 23 April 1858; quoted in Noakes, *op.cit.*, R.A., 1985: 111. I am grateful to Vivien Noakes for supplying me with a copy of the transcript.
41. This and the following extracts are from Lear's Journal, first published as "A Leaf from the Journals of a Landscape Painter," in *Macmillan's Magazine*, April 1897, vol. LXXV: 410-30.
42. Both drawings are inscribed *Petra, 13 Apl 1858*; one, numbered *40*, is in the Houghton Library, Harvard University, Boston; the other, numbered *41*, is in the Searight Collection, Victoria and Albert Museum, London. Others are detailed and illustrated in G.W. Bowersock, "Edward Lear in Petra," *Proceedings of the American Philosophical Society*, vol. 134, no. 3, September 1990: 309-20.
43. The drawing, dated *1885*, and numbered *177*, is in the Houghton Library, Harvard University, Boston. An interim drawing, undated, but numbered *(172)*, is in Eton College Library, Windsor (illustrated in Noakes, *op. cit.*, RA, 1985: 111, cat.no. 25a).
44. The two oil paintings are both in private collections. The one of the Eastern Cliffs, in New Zealand: see Bowersock, *op.cit.*, 1990: 317; the other of the Theatre, dated *1859*, in Jordan: see *On the Banks of the Jordan, British Nineteenth Century Painters*, exhibition catalogue, Jordan National Gallery, 1987: cat.no.28, illustrated on front cover.
45. Lear's Journal, 1897, *op. cit.*, p. 421
46. *Ibid.*, p. 426.
47. For William Holman Hunt, *The Scapegoat* and for his landscapes of Egypt and the Holy Land, see *The Pre-Raphaelites*, exhibition catalogue, The Tate Gallery, London, 1984, cat. nos 84, 201, 202, 204.
48. For Thomas Seddon, *The Valley of Jehoshaphat*, see *The Pre-Raphaelites*, 1984, *op. cit.*, cat. no. 83.
49. Frederic Edwin Church (1826-1900). Carr 1994, vol.1: 317-24, 386-98. See also Theodore E. Stebbins, Jr., *Close Observation Selected Oil Sketches by Frederic E. Church*, Washington DC, Smithsonian Institution Press, 1978; Edmonds 1985: 81-4.
50. Edmonds 1985: 84.
51. *Ibid.*
52. From Church's letter to W. H. Osborn, see Carr 1994: 390.
53. See Carr 1994: cat, no. 560.
54. See Carr 1994: 391 and figs. 128 and 129.
55. See note 12.
56. See N. Lewis's, chapter 11 in this volume.

CHAPTER 13

1. Lewis 1997: 12 fig. 5.
2. McKenzie 1990.
3. The position of each tomb can be learned by the maps of Brünnow and von Domaszewski 1904, pls. III-XX. L. Nehmé prepares an Archaeological Map of Petra, which will place the monuments more precisely.
4. Brünnow and von Domaszewski 1904: 137-73. The latest survey in this kind is by Matthiae 1991.
5. Cf. Schmidt-Colinet 1980: 197-200.
6. Ibid.: 201-2.
7. Cf. McKenzie 1990: 33, 117
8. Schmidt-Colinet 1980: 202-5; Hesberg 1994: 100-4, 113
9. Ibid.: 207-9.
10. Cf. McKenzie 1990: pls. 101, 125a with pls. 108a, 150c, 161.
11. Negev 1977: 597f.; Freyberger 1991. The early dating by him is not convincing.
12. Milik 1976; Healey 1993: 243-44.
13. McKenzie 1990: 49, 52.
14. It makes no sense to connect the inscription with two graves on top of the rock.
15. Of course, there could have been some more inscriptions written on the plaster of the façades. Gawlikowski 1975-76 assumed religious aspects for the renunciation of inscriptions, but was not followed by other scholars.
16. Healey 1993: 238-42; Macdonald and Nehmé forthcoming.
17. Wenning 1990a. The earlier attribution of CIS II 351 to tomb Br. 808 seems to have been a mistake.
18. Schmid 1997b: 135. Zayadine 1986: 237, fig. 29. Only sherd no. 57 belongs to the early first century AD.
19. Zayadine 1982b: 365-73.
20. The Nabataean pottery from tomb Br. 70 and tomb Br. 148 is not yet published (Zayadine 1983: 229, 239). Cf. for finds from other tombs Horsfields 1941: 106, 138-67.
21. Hammond 1965: 55-65.
22. Ibid.: 73-78; McKenzie 1990: 35.
23. McKenzie 1990: 11-31, 119-20. For the inscriptions cf. Healey 1993.
24. Cf. Schmidt-Colinet 1987 for the Qasr es-Sane, although various of his arguments are not working.
25. Schmidt-Colinet 1980: 220-223; McKenzie 1990: 85-104, 123-26. It needs to be considered that the Nabataeans transformed their prototypes according their own ideas. Beside the Khazneh it will be difficult to use Nabataean façades for a better understanding of Alexandrian art.
26. The same dating is now reached by Schmid 2000b: 492 with new arguments. Cf. Wenning 2003.
27. Cf. Schmidt-Colinet 1983a; McKenzie 1990.
28. McKenzie 1990: 39, 47-50.
29. Measurements are not sufficient for classification. The composition of a façade needs to be considered as well. The study of McKenzie 1990 suffers of various methodological problems and has been seriously criticized by reviewers. She has accepted datings as basic to her chronology which remain problematic (theatre, Temenos Gate, Colonnaded Street, Florentinus Tomb, Obelisk Tomb). It is difficult to accept her Groups she put forward by attributing façades to stone-cutters because of individual features. Despite all critics her study has enlarged our knowlegde on the façades greatly (cf. Parr 1996).
30. Cf. Wenning 1999.
31. Of special importance is the Urn Tomb which is orientated towards the Qasr al-Bint. There are more such orientations among the large tombs. This corresponds with the choice of a prominent place for the cutting of a façade, and a spectacular view from the tomb.
32. At Hegra many of the Step Tombs are owned by women.
33. It cannot be excluded that parts of the Nabataean society refused to have such Hellenistic tombs. That means we should not exclude to find some wealthy or high ranking Nabataeans buried in "simple" rock-cut tombs.
34. This tomb is now researched in a new project: Schmid 2001d.
35. That the tympanum of Br. 66 once showed a typical funerary meal cannot be decided because the relief is destroyed and the old drawing is not clear enough. It cannot be excluded that the bust relief of the Urn Tomb is set up secondary.
36. Cf. Schmid-Colinet 1980: 226-27.
37. Cf. Dagmar Kühn, Totengedenken bei den Nabatäern und im Alten Testament. PhD Thesis Tübingen 2003.
38. It cannot be proven that this triclinium was used in the festivities in honor of Obodas Theos. Cf. Wenning 1997: 181-93.
39. Urban 1997; Külenthal and Fischer 2000.

CHAPTER 14

1. Paradise 1998b.
2. For the story of map-making in Petra, see Parr, Atkinson and Wickens 1975: 31; Zayadine 1980: 249-50; Zeitler 1980b: 292-96; Parr 1990: 17-19.
3. The German explorer U. J. Seetzen had already proposed this identification but he had not visited the site and thus is not usually counted among the discoverers of Petra.
4. Burckhardt 1822: 435: "Plan of the Lower Part of Wady Mousa."
5. Irby and Mangles 1823: plate opposite p. 419: "Sketch of the Ground Plan of Petra".
6. de Laborde 1830: plate 6: "Pan de la ville de Pétra et de ses environs."
7. Brünnow and von Domaszewski 1904-1909: [Pétra = volume 1, 1904: *Die Römerstrasse von Mâdebâ über Petra und Ofruh bis el-ʿAḳaba*]. A general map of Petra and its surroundings at 1:75,000, is also given on pl. 23.
8. Musil 1907: map at the end of the book: "Umgebungskarte von Wâdi Mûsa (Petra)"; Dalman 1908: map at the very end of the volume: "Kartenskizze zur Übersicht über Petra und seine Felsheiligtümer".
9. A second report on the monuments of Petra was published by him in 1912.
10. Bachmann, Watzinger and Wiegand 1921.
11. Kennedy 1925: map and mosaic of photographs after p. 18. This photographic mosaic was reproduced as the frontispiece in Horsfield 1938 as well as in Kammerer 1929-1930: pl. 27.
12. Canaan 1929.
13. Parr, Atkinson and Wickens 1975.
14. Parr 1969, especially p. 394.
15. Zeitler 1980: 299-300. According to this author, there is, in the map, a gap of 2,5° to the west in comparison with the geographical north.
16. For details of the project, see Gory 1976a: 79.
17. Reference JOR IGN 100 FEB 74.
18. This is a geographical entity which was created by the Jordanian authorities to serve as a framework for a policy on the environment and the archaeological remains of the region.
19. Reference IGN 81 JOR 26.100.
20. Photographs no. 73-77, 84-98, 110-29, 147-52.
21. Gory 1976a: *loc. cit.* p. 85.
22. On the technical aspects of the photoplan, see Gory 1976b; Gory 1978-1979: 60-65. This document, in four sheets, is displayed permanently in the Petra Visitors Center.

23. The numbers for the negatives of the Petra region are 8131, 8138, 8158, 8160 and 8167.
24. *The Tourist Map of Petra*: 1st edition, January 1988 (five colours, no grid, rocks in grey); 2nd edition, July 1988 (colored, alphanumeric grid); 3rd. edition, 1989 = 4th. edition, 1992 (the grid does not correspond to the coordinates anymore).
25. The maps were drawn at the scale of 1:2,500 and *then* enlarged.
26. *Archéologie de la Syrie du Sud et de la zone de Pétra du Chalcolithique à l'avènement de l'Islam*, now member of ArScAn, CNRS, Nanterre.
27. Mainly G. Dalman, G. and A. Horsfield, M. Lindner, M.-J. Roche, Z. al-Muheisen and D. Tarrier.
28. Brünnow's catalogue contains 851 monuments but some of them have subsequently been subdivided, for example the niches no. 60 in the Siq are subdivided into 11 niches numbered 60.1 to 60.11. Moreover, Brünnow mentioned some monuments but did not give them a number. The same is true of Dalman.
29. See Roche 1985a, in which she recorded 44 new monuments, 10 of which are also described by other archaeologists (M. Lindner, J. Milik, P. Parr, J. Starcky, F. Zayadine).
30. See al-Muheisen 1986, in which he recorded seventy-three new cisterns, winepresses, farms, etc., five of which are also described by other archaeologists (M. Lindner, G. and A. Horsfield).
31. See Tarrier 1988, in which she recorded twenty-two new banqueting rooms, two of which are also described by other archaeologists (M. Lindner, F. Zayadine).
32. Plus all the members of his team.
33. Plus all the members of the Swiss team.
34. The Theater and Temple of the Winged Lions are not counted here.
34a. Some of these, when cleared, might prove to be triclinia rather than simple rooms. This is the case for no. 290, the so-called Obodas's Chapel, the excavation of which in 2001 and 2002 revealed the presence of benches.
35. Among these, three have one row of crowsteps and three have two rows of crowsteps and are thus also counted in the statistics of those two categories of tomb façades.
36. Parr, Atkinson and Wickens 1975; Zayadine 1982a.
37. The date of the Theater date is based on a palaeographic analysis of the masons' marks found on column-drums during the excavations (see Salmon 1965) and on Hammond's architectural analysis of the monument and its position in the context of the urbanism of Petra (Hammond 1965: 62). The same date is proposed by J. Starcky in (personal communication to J.S. McKenzie, see McKenzie 1990: 58 n. 37).
38. McKenzie, *loc. cit.*
39. See Bignasca. 1996; Kolb, Keller and Fellmann Brogli 1997.
40. Other free-standing houses had been partially excavated by P.C. Hammond, N. Khairy, P. Parr, F. Zayadine and J.P. Zeitler.
41. For a synthesis of what is known of the rock-cut houses, see Nehmé 1997a.
42. It is not absolutely certain that this spring was channelled as far as the Qasr al-Bint.
43. On Ain Brāq and its canalization system, see Lindner 1997.
44. Joukowsky 1997a.
45. Cf. Strabo, *Geography*, XVI.4.21 and the recent sounding in the lower market made by Bedal 1998.
46. Parr 1960a: 130-31 and pl. 16-24 (see p. 130-31).
47. Zayadine 1979: 185-97, pl. 83-94 (p. 185-87, fig. 1-3 and pl. 83-89); Zeitler 1990a: 403-06. See also previous reports by Zayadine in *ADAJ* 18, 1973 and 19, 1974.
48. Kanellopoulos 1998 (p. 1).

CHAPTER 15

1. McKenzie 1988: 90, 92-93; McKenzie 1990: 40-41, 51, pl. 41-45c, 60-66, 68c, 84-87. See also Lyttelton and Blagg 1990.
2. Paradise 1998a: 161-62.
3. Wright 1968; McKenzie 1990: 41, 51, pl. 60-66.
4. McKenzie 1990: pl. 60-62.
5. McKenzie 1990: 145, pl. 92, 95a, 96a-c.
6. McKenzie 1990: pl. 56a, 58a.
7. McKenzie 1990: pl. 64-66.
8. McKenzie 1990: 168, pl. 160, 161c.
9. McKenzie 1990: pl. 64-65a.
10. McKenzie 1990: pl. 132, 134b.
11. Green 1998: 45.
12. Green 1998: 46, fig. 11a-b.
13. McKenzie 2001: 105.
14. Louvre AO 11077; Dunand 1934: 11-13, pl. 4.1; *LIMC* vol. 7.1, 184 no. 86. Detailed discussion: Dentzer-Feydy 1992: 86-95, 99-101, fig. 29, 33-34.
15. For Hauran sculpture see: Dunand 1934; Dentzer and Dentzer-Feydy 1991.
16. Hammond 1965: 69-70, pl. 40, 41.1-3.
17. Weber 1997: 121 fig. 133a.
18. D. Kreikenbom and T. Weber in press, cited in Bowersock 2001: 75 n. 8.
19. Weber 1997: 124 fig. 137.
20. Weber 1997: 125 fig. 138.
21. McKenzie 1990: pl. 98, 102a.
22. McKenzie 1990: pl. 96d.
23. McKenzie 1990: pl. 119b, 122.
24. For Palmyra sculpture chronology and typology: Colledge 1976: 245-64. See also: Dentzer-Feydy and Teixidor 1993: 155-245; Schmidt-Colinet 1992; 1997.
25. Colledge 1976: 245; Walker and Brierbrier 1997: 14.
26. Toynbee 1964; Weber 1997: 122 fig. 134.
27. Hammond 1990: 128, pl. 1.1-2; Hammond 1996: 126 #13, bottom pl. on p. 138; Meza 1996.
28. Stucky 1996: 337-38, 344 fig. 942; Weber 1997: fig. 126.
29. McKenzie 1990: pl. 86d.
30. Parlasca 1998: 69, fig. 2.
31. Lindner 1988.
32. Patrich 1990a: 50-113, 167-91; Patrich 1990b.
33. Patrich 1990a: 83, ill. 26; Healey 2001: 19, 50, 107, 140-41, 157, pl. 7b.
34. Hammond 1980b; Hammond 1996: 127 #217, bottom right pl. on p. 139.
35. Zayadine 1980a: 116 fig. 9.
36. Zayadine 1990b: 174 fig. 15.
37. McKenzie, Reyes and Schmidt-Colinet 1998: 39, fig. 5c.
38. McKenzie 1990: pl. 135, 136b; McKenzie McKenzie, Reyes and Schmidt-Colinet 1998: fig. 6a.
39. McKenzie McKenzie, Reyes and Schmidt-Colinet 1998: fig. 3.
40. McKenzie McKenzie, Reyes and Schmidt-Colinet 1998: 36-39. A recently discovered relief at Sela' has been used to suggest that Edom was under Babylonian administration in the reign of Nabonidus (555-539 BC): Dalley and Goguel 1997: 172-75, fig. 6-12.
41. McKenzie McKenzie, Reyes and Schmidt-Colinet 1998: 39-41, fig. 7a-9b.
42. Guimier-Sorbets and Saif el-Din 1997.
43. McKenzie, Gibson and Reyes 2002: 66-69, fig. 19a-b, d, 20.
44. Glueck 1965: xi-xii.
45. Detailed discussion: McKenzie, Gibson and Reyes 2002.
46. Relevant photographs from ASOR Nelson Glueck Archive reproduced in: McKenzie, Reyes and Gibson in press.
47. Glueck 1965: 104, pl. 11b.
48. The capital reconstructed on it in Cincinnati museum for many years belongs, as Glueck observed, to Period III. As it is the correct size perhaps it was part of a later repair. Glueck 1965: 105, pl. 174a-b.
49. McKenzie, Gibson and Reyes 2002: 56, fig. 10a.
50. Glueck 1965: pl. 175a-b; McKenzie, Reyes and Gibson in press: fig. 12-13.
51. Glueck 1965: 143, pl. 172a-b.
52. Glueck 1965: pl. 53a-b.
53. Glueck 1965: pl. 55-56.
54. Glueck 1965: pl. 146a.
55. McKenzie 1990: pl. 95a, 96a-c.
56. McKenzie, Gibson and Reyes 2002: 59-63.
57. al-Muheisen and Villeneuve 1999: fig. on p. 46.
58. McKenzie, Gibson and Reyes 2002: 57-58, fig. 11a.
59. McKenzie, Gibson and Reyes 2002: fig. 12; McKenzie, Reyes and Gibson in press: fig. 18d.
60. McKenzie, Gibson and Reyes 2002: 63-64; McKenzie, Reyes and Gibson in press: fig. 11.
61. Glueck 1965: pl. 147
62. Glueck 1965: pl. 27-28.
63. Glueck 1965: pl. 26a, 29a; McKenzie, Gibson and Reyes 2002: fig. 7.
64. Glueck 1965: pl. 174d, 175c.
65. Glueck 1965: pl. 30a.
66. Glueck 1965: pl. 134a–b; McKenzie, Gibson and Reyes 2002: 53–56, fig. 9c.
67. Glueck 1965: pl. 12b.
68. McKenzie, Gibson and Reyes 2002: 64.
69. McKenzie 1990: pl. 42.
70. McKenzie 1990: pl. 37e, 57a, c-d.
71. Results of recent excavations: Fiema 1997; 1998; Kanellopoulos 1998. Summary of basis for date of Temenos Gate and Colonnaded Street based on earlier work: McKenzie 1990: 35-36. There has been general agreement that the gate is later than the street. The date of the Temenos Gate has still not been definitively resolved, despite excavations further east along the Colonnaded Street. The excavations indicate that the eastern end of the Colonnaded Street was constructed in the late first century or early second century AD (Fiema 1998: 419). However, Fiema notes (1998: 417): "it is unknown now to what extent results of the previous work in the western part of the colonnaded street are applicable to the situation at the eastern end of the street." He also observes: "The entire complex appears to be a composite design of different aggregates which could have come into existence anytime between the end of the first century BC and the early second century AD." (Fiema 1998: 398).
72. For Khirbet edh-Dharih see: Dentzer-Feydy 1990; al-Muheisen and Villeneuve 1994. More recent suggestion of date, ca. 100-150 AD: al-Muheisen and Villeneuve 1999: 43.
73. Palmyra: Colledge 1976: pl. 8, 64-65, 74, 146; Dentzer-Feydy and Teixidor 1993: 165 no. 168, 166 no. 169, 220 no. 216, 223 no. 218; Hauran: Dentzer and Dentzer-Feydy 1991: pl. 11 no. 229, pl. 17 no. 578, 18 no. 56.
74. Relationship to Coptic sculpture: Kitzinger 1938: 206; Glueck 1965: 396, 534-35.
75. McKenzie, Gibson and Reyes 2002: fig. 9b-c.
76. e.g., Strube 1993: pl. 47, 85c, 86a-b.
77. e.g., Kitzinger 1938: pl. 71.6, 72.5.
78. Mschatta: Creswell and Allan 1989: fig. 123-24. Other relationships to early Islamic decoration: Glueck 1965: 535-36.
79. Glueck 1937c; 1938; 1952.
80. Starcky 1968.
81. Glueck 1965.
82. Photographs of cult statue *in situ* when excavated: McKenzie in press: fig. 23-25.
83. *LIMC* vol. 3, 355.
84. Glueck 1965: 195-209; Starcky 1968: 226.
85. Healy 2001: 124.
86. McKenzie, Gibson and Reyes 2002: 74-76, 79.
87. *De dea Syria* 30-32, ed., trans., Attridge and Oden 1976.
88. Glueck 1965: 514-515, pl. 196. On Qaws: Starcky 1968: 209; Zayadine 1980a: 113; Tarrier 1990: 198-99.
89. Healey 2001: 61, 140; McKenzie, Gibson and Reyes 2002: 76 with references.
90. McKenzie, Gibson and Reyes 2002: 59-63, 78-79; McKenzie, Reyes and Gibson in press.
91. Glueck 1965: 453-71; Starcky 1968: 232-34.
92. See F. Villeneuve's chapter 7, in this volume.
93. Glueck 1965: 415-430; Starcky 1968: 231-32.
94. Glueck 1937c: 7.
95. Glueck 1938: 12.
96. Neugebauer and Parker 1969: vol. 3, 89–91, 93–95, pl. 46, 50.
97. Glueck 1965: pl. 49a
98. Hachlili 1977: 63 fig. 2; Guidoni Guidi 1979: 139 fig. 5.
99. Hachlili 1977: 64 fig. 3; Guidoni Guidi 1979: 137 fig. 3.
100. Cauville 1997: fig. on p. 27.
101. Hammond 2002: fig. 1.
102. Hachlili 1977: 73 fig. 17; Guidoni Guidi 1979: 146 fig. 9.
103. Hachlili 1977: 66 fig. 5; Guidoni Guidi 1979: 134 fig. 1.
104. Bunnens 1969: fig. 2-3.
105. Bunnens 1969: fig. 3-4.
106. Dolphins: Glueck 1965: 315-19. Fish: Glueck 1965: pl. 2a-b; Starcky 1968: 228.
107. Diod. Sic. 2. 4. 2-3.
108. See F. Villeneuve's chapter 7 in this volume.
109. After the detailed draft reconstructions of the elevations of the Khirbet et-Tannur altar platform and inner temenos enclosure had been prepared, it transpired that Laurent Tholbecq was also preparing reconstructions of them. We had a fruitful discussion and were in agreement as to the placement of most of the major blocks. Tholbecq placed the Nikes in the frieze of the main entablature of the façade of the inner temenos enclosure in the light of the recent discoveries at Khirbet edh-Dharih, a reconstruction that was later also suggested independently by other scholars. I would also like to thank Anna Caiozzo, Amanda Claridge, Jacqueline Dentzer-Feydy, Glenn Markoe, Martina Minas, Andres Reyes, and François Villeneuve. This paper was originally prepared prior to the fieldwork at Khirbet et-Tannur in March 2001 (McKenzie 2002), and the work on the ASOR Nelson Glueck Archive in the Semitic Museum Harvard University in April 2002 (McKenzie in press). The dimensions in the captions for the sculpture at the Cincinnati Art Museum were provided by Glenn Markoe.

CHAPTER 16

1. I have found the following to be the most illuminating and/or useful publications on or including the Khazneh: Dalman 1908: 148-52; Dalman 1911; Bachmann, Watzinger and Wiegand 1921: 12-28; Ronczewski 1932;

Wright 1962; Lyttleton 1974: 70-83; Schmidt-Colinet 1981; Wenning 1987: 210-14; Patrich 1990a; McKenzie 1990: 7, 140-43; Browning 1994: 125-31; Healey 2001: 46-47, 73, 138, 153, 174. For the iconography, comparanda are cited from Kahil, ed., *LIMC* 1981-98.

2. Patrich 1990a: 153-57, however, explains the damage as the result of *Nabatean* iconoclasm.
3. E.g. Browning 1994: 129-30–misunderstanding both the syntax of the façade and the offering basin cut into the threshold of the tomb chamber (see below); and most recently, Ball 2000: 370-75; for others, see Healey 2001: 138, 153.
4. Cf. Patrich 1990a: 122, fig. 40.
5. For the rosettes, see Cahill 1997: 48-57; for the eagles, Mørkholm: 1991: pls. 6, 19-21, 44; and Meshorer 1975.
6. McKenzie 1990: 7 includes a useful table of all previously proposed dates.
7. See esp. Ronczewski 1932 with, e.g., Heilmeyer 1970: pls. 9-10; updated by Schmidt-Colinet 1981: 89-95, 98; and McKenzie 1990.
8. On Aretas III and IV, see most conveniently Negev 1977: 537-41, 567-69; and Bowersock 1983: 24-34, 51-69. Heroon of Obodas: Zayadine 1999a: 52, questioned by Healey 2001: 47, 147-51.
9. Probably not eagles, for unlike the eagles on the façade but like the sphinx from near Petra's triumphal arch (Patrich 1990a: 147, fig. 51c), their wings are raised.
10. Bachmann, Watzinger and Wiegand 1921: 24-28, esp. figs. 17-21. Nielsen 1994: 152 argues for a palace, but none of her comparanda include tholos and statue, which were, however, integral components of contemporary sanctuaries and their representations (fig. 8).
11. See M. Joukowsky's chapter 18 in this volume; also http://www.brown.edu/Departments/Anthropology/Petra/temple/temple.html.
12. On the concept of honor (Greek, *time*) as fundamental to Greek religion, see Mikalson 1991 and 1998: 300-4.
13. On Hellenistic and Roman ruler-cult, see, e.g., Price 1984; for Obodas, see Stephanus of Byzantium 482, 15-17 Meineke (at a place called Oboda, "*Obodas ho basileus, hon theopoiousi, tethaptai*") with, e.g., Bowersock 1983: (supra n. 8) 24 n. 47, 62-63; Zayadine 1999a: 52, with skeptical comments by Healey 2001: 47, 147-51. For Augustus, see Cassius Dio 56.46; Suetonius, *Augustus* 60, 100; *Tiberius* 40; and *Claudius* 2; Tacitus, *Annals* 1.10; Velleius Paterculus 2.124.3; etc.
14. Strabo, a contemporary of Aretas IV and perhaps also of the Khazneh, baldly states that "embossed work, painting, and moulded work are not customary" among the Nabateans (*Geographica* 16.4.26); Patrich 1990a: 36-40 summarizes the controversy.
15. For the best modern publication of the Alexander sarcophagus see Graeve 1970; on its bifurcated address to both Greeks and locals, see Stewart 1993: 294-306.
16. On these divinities and their Greek equivalents see Healey 2001: 100-2, 117-19.
17. Cf. *LIMC* s.v. "Erinyes," passim, and s.v. "Amazones," no. 680, where these figures are identified as Amazons; cf. McKenzie 1990: 142, pl. 84c; on Myrina and her conquests see Diodoros 3.55.4-6, paraphrasing the early Hellenistic mythographer Dionysios Skytobrachion.
18. For the coins and their Ptolemaic-inspired symbols, see Meshorer 1976. For the customary attributes of Demeter and Isis see *LIMC*, q.v.
19. Grenfell and Hunt 1915: no. 1380 (an aretalogy of Isis), lines 91-92 ("*Isis epi tes Petras Soteiran*"), with commentary; cf. Patrich 1990a: 104-5; Zayadine 1991a: 301-6, fig. 19 (1897 photograph); Donner 1995; Parlasca 1998: 64-70, with fig. 2 for Huldu-Isis; Healey 2001: 47, 137-40; also Schluntz 1998 (reference kindly supplied by Victor Gold). Unfortunately, Schluntz overlooks our figure's headdress (see below) and mistranslates *Soteira*, "Savior," as "Protectress."
20. *LIMC*, s.v. "Tyche," nos. 46-75, with no. 49 for the branch; s.v. "Tyche-Fortuna," *passim*. The most recent scholar to identify her thus is Healey 2001: 47.
21. Simon Maccabee: I *Maccabees* 13:25-30; Josephus, *Jewish Antiquities* 13.210-12. Antiochos: Sanders 1996.
22. For the statistics see Patrich 1990a: 117-18.
23. I am most grateful to Glenn Markoe for the opportunity to contribute this essay; to audiences in Sydney, Canberra, and Melbourne for their comments; and to Judith McKenzie for a critique and bibliographical help. Many of its ideas were hatched during a visit of the U.C. Berkeley Tel Dor excavation team to Petra in July, 1997. I thank my companions for listening to and critiquing them; my research assistant Becky Martin for checking them; and especially my student and Dor supervisor Danica Stitz for allowing me to make use of her 1998 honors thesis on the Khazneh. Her study underpins my description of the building; my discussion of its sculpture (the central figure of the façade in particular); and my bibliography.

By coincidence, this essay was completed on the day of King Hussein of Jordan's death, Sunday, February 7, 1999, and is dedicated to his memory.

CHAPTER 17 (Introduction)

1. Zayadine 1985: 164-67.
2. Souda Lexicon
3. Zayadine 1991a: 293-95.
4. Lewis, Yadin and Greenfield 1989: 48-49
5. Parr 1967-1968: 16
6. Parr 1996: 65
7. Parr 1967-1968: 16
8. Parr 1996: 66
9. Starcky and Trugnell 1966.
10. Zayadine 1991a: 292-93
11. Parr 1967-1968: 13
12. McKenzie 1990: 234-38.
13. Kohl 1910: 26
14. Lyttleton 1974: 68.
15. Lyttleton 1974: 69
16. Adriani 1935-1939: 52-53, pl. XIX.
17. Netzer 1991: 78ss and III. 156.
18. Blanc 1983: 51-77

CHAPTER 17 (Architectural Study)

1. Since 1979, the periodic excavations supervised by Dr. Fawzi Zayadine and the Department of Antiquities of Jordan have resulted in the publication of a first volume on the temple's architecture : *Le Qasr al-Bint de Pétra, Fouilles et étude architecturale* by F. Zayadine and F. Larché, ERC 2003.
2. Wright 1961a: 20, fig 10.
3. Wright 1968: 38.
4. al-Muheisen and Villeneuve 1988.
5. Zayadine and Farajat 1991: 289-290.

CHAPTER 18

1. Annual reports can be found in the *Annual of the Department of Antiquities of Jordan*. Our Five Year Report has been published, and those who wish an overview can find it on the World Wide Web: <http://www.brown.edu/ Departments/ Anthropology/Petra/>
2. Dating between 93/94 - 132 AD, the 35 papyrus archives were found in a leather purse in 1961 by Yigael Yadin at the cave of Nahal Hever on the west shore of the Dead Sea. These priceless finds are known as documents from "the Cave of the Letters." See Lewis, Yadin and Greenfield 1989.

CHAPTER 19

1. Hammond 1996.
2. Hammond 1975.
3. Brock 1976: 103–7; Brock 1977; Russell 1980: 47–64; Hammond 1980a.
4. Hammond, Johnson and Jones 1986.
5. Hammond 1992: 115-27.
6. Hammond 1987.

CHAPTER 20

1. Horsefield 1938: 15-42; Zayadine 1974: 135-39; Zayadine 1986: 254-58; Hammond 1977-1978: 8ff.; Hammond 1986; Russell 1980; Zeitler 1989: 307-17; Khairy 1990: 3-6. See McKenzie 1990: 105-8 including a short summary of the state of research.
2. Stucky 1996: 13-49; Kolb 1996.
3. On the sequence of the Nabataean structures on ez-Zantur cf. Stucky 1996.
4. Russell 1985: 42 suggested that the destruction of the early second century in Petra was caused by an earthquake of the year 113/14 AD.
5. See Stucky 1996: 14-17.
6. Some stucco fragments with linear paintings have been preserved. See Stucky 1996: 23 and pl. 1.1.
7. On Marisa refer to Horowitz 1980: 96, fig. 2 and on 104, fig. 7. On Dor refer to Stern 1994: 114-15, figs. 143-44.
8. Kolb 1996.
9. Negev 1988a: 34-37.
10. Kraemer 1958: 70-74
11. The development of an architectural tradition restricted to the mentioned geographical region is elsewhere discussed in detail. See Kolb 2000.
12. A letter, ascribed to bishop Cyrill of Jerusalem (348-386 AD), gives evidence of the fact that Jerusalem and, amongst other towns in Palestine, also Petra suffered from the earthquake in the night of 19th to 20th of May 363. See amongst others Brock 1977; Russell 1980.
13. For reference to the earthquake of 419 see Russell 1985: 42-43.
14. The structures recognizable on the surface were briefly described in the context of a survey conducted in 1990 by the Naturhistorische Gesellschaft Nürnberg. See Lindner, Gasteiger and Zeitler 1993-94: 310-15.
15. For more details on the first results in the preliminary reports of the excavation seasons 1996 and 1997; see Kolb, Keller and Fellmann Brogli 1997, and Kolb, Keller and Gerber 1998.
16. In the rooms mentioned, thousands of fragments of the original wall covering (painting, stucco architecture) were rescued.
17. The marble tiles was plundered at an unknown time. The geometric grouting pattern in the mortar bedding conveys an idea of the earlier elaborate floor decoration. Fragments of six different types of imported colored marble and two of alabaster were recovered.
18. To date, indications of first floor rooms were provided by rooms 1 and 6.
19. The decoration phase 3a ran from approx. 20 AD to 70/80 AD. See summary in Schmid 1997b.
20. See Russell 1980.
21. Foerster 1995: 163, fig. 270; Netzer 1991: 232ff. A very similar room arrangement is annexed, in the north, to the large peristyle in Herod's second Palace in Jericho (approx. 25 BC): Netzer 1996: 37, fig. 2.
22. Heermann 1986; Nielsen 1994: 81-99.
23. See Pesce 1950: pl. 11, rooms 17-18. For the dating of the building see Lauter 1971.
24. Kohl 1910: 15-22, 26-35.
25. Zayadine 1987.
26. On Masonry Style see Andreou 1988; Barbet 1985: 12-25.
27. Zayadine 1987: 139, fig. 17.
28. Barbet 1995: 389.
29. Masada, Western Palace (37-30 BC): Netzer 1991: 232-63; Foerster 1995: 1-12. Jerusalem, Palatial Mansion in the so-called Herodian Quarter: Avigad 1991: 57-67.
30. The cleaning of the murals, carried out during the 1998 excavation campaign, revealed that the east pilaster was not painted in a black and white color scheme as has previously been stated (Kolb, Keller and Fellmann Brogli 1997: 237).
31. The brown color of the capitals probably stands for bronze.
32. The acroteria are reminiscent of Hellenistic shield busts. See Winkes 1969: 10-15.
33. The marbling on the light, colored, partially patterned surfaces indicate that the patterns are intended to represent incrustation. See Kolb, Keller and Fellmann Brogli 1997: 238, note 11.
34. For the 2nd Pompeian Style see Barbet 1985: 36-93.
35. See Carettoni 1983: 23-27, color pls. B-F.
36. Compare the powerfully and virtuously executed architectural façades in the triclinum 14 of Poppaea's villa at Oplontis: De Franciscis 1975: 31, fig. 17 and on 34, fig. 23.
37. Zayadine 1987: 140-41.
38. Zayadine 1987: 140.
39. See e.g. Adriani 1963-1966, pl. 56, fig. 199 with hypogaeum 3 from the third century BC in Mustapha Pasha.
40. Gordon 1977: 266.
41. Standard work: Fittschen 1996.
42. Avigad 1984: 112, fig. 102 and on 114, figs. 104-5; compare Fittschen 1996: 144 (late 2nd or early 3rd Pompeian Style).
43. Adriani 1963-1966: 140-43, no. 89, pls. 61-63.
44. Adriani 1963/6: 135-37, no. 86, pl. 54 fig. 194.
45. Adriani 1963-1966: 192-95, nos. 142-43, pls. 109, 111.
46. Adriani 1963–1966: 192-94, no. 142, pl. 109.

CHAPTER 21

1. *Palaestina Salutaris/Tertia* was one of the three provinces named Palestine, all of which encompassed the territories of modern Israel and Jordan. For views on the administrative changes during the fourth century, see Tsafrir 1986; and Fiema 1991: 128-33.
2. For the economic ramifications of that situation, see Avi-Yonah 1958; and Dauphin 1980.
3. Eusebius 1975: 273.
4. For example, a confusion of Christian theology with Nabataean pagan beliefs is demonstrated in the cult of "Dusares and his Virgin Mother Chaamou..." (Epiphanius (1922: 286-87; II.51.22). Dusares was the chief deity of the Nabataean pantheon.
5. Sozomen 1979: 386 (VII.150)
6. Starcky 1966: 922

7. The Council condemned the Nestorianism, and determined that Christ was one person with two indivisible natures: divine and human (i.e. the Orthodox doctrine)
8. Fedalto 1988: 1040. For the ecclesiastical history of Petra, see Schick, 2001. Piccirillo (1989) discusses the ecclesiastical organization of the region.
9. Such as John Isthemus, an alchemist and forger (John Malalas 1986: 222; XVI.5)
10. Zachariah of Mitylene 1899: 208-9 (VIII.5). The Nestorian doctrine professed the conjunction rather than unity (Orthodox view) of the two natures of Christ. Further, the Nestorians rejected the epithet of *Theotokos* (Mother of God) for the Virgin, in favor of *Christotokos* (Mother of Christ). See Kazhdan 1991b: 1459-60..
11. John of Nikiu 1916: 129-30 (LXXXIX.69-70). Monophysite doctrine was characterized by several variations but basically it emphasized the union of the two natures in Christ, in which the human nature was engulfed by the divine nature (Kazhdan 1991a: 1398-99).
12. John of Ephesus 1923: 188 (XIII)
13. Brock 1977. The archaeological evidence of this disaster is fully presented by Russell 1980.
14. A description of the AD 363 destruction and its aftermath is presented by Parr 1986.
15. The neighboring town of Humeima, being more extensively excavated, yielded several Byzantine churches (Schick 1995a).
16. Brunnow and Domaszewski 1904: 393, no. 722. The Jason inscription is re-published by Sartre 1993: 81-84, no. 50.
17. Frösén 1998; Peterman and Schick 1996.
18. Published reports include Schick, Fiema and ʻAmr 1993; Fiema 1994, and Fiema, Schick and ʻAmr 1995. The final publication of the project (PCP) will be a comprehensive volume including several major contributions.
19. The most extensive treatment of the churches in the Negev is that of Rosenthal-Heginbottom 1982. See also Negev 1974a, 1983, and 1989; and the relevant chapters in Tsafrir 1993.
20. That church is generally dated to the sixth century (Bikai 1996: 482).
21. Tsafrir 1988: 40.
22. A square/rectangular area, usually enclosed, situated directly in the front of the central apse and containing the altar is termed chancel or *bema*. The sanctuary or presbytery may be synonymous with *bema* (Johnson 1991), but often refer to the entire cult officiation area including the apse and the chancel in front of it. For variations in the type and form of *bema*, see Bagatti 1984: 238, and Crowfoot 1941: 46–54.
23. See Colt 1962: 10-11, Ovadiah 1970: 198-99; Negev 1983: 173; and Rosenthal-Heginbottom 1982: 151-54, for Palestinian and the Negev churches. Jordanian examples are discussed by Duval 1994: 193-98.
24. Politis 1992: 281, 282, fig. 2.
25. Oleson, ʻAmr and Schick 1992: 152.
26. Duval 1994: 188-91; Ovadiah 1970: 198.
27. E.g., the Church of the Prophets, Apostles and Martyrs in Jerash, the Memorial of Moses at Siyagha, and the basilica at Kefar Shiloah ((Tzaferis 1983: 10, note 8). The latter is dated to the mid-fifth century (Ovadiah 1970: 90–91).
28. Johnson and Cutler 1991.
29. Chord indicates a straight line which closes the semicircular curvature of the apse.
30. E.g., the benches at the Lower Church at Humeima (Oleson, ʻAmr, and Schick 1992: 152); West Church at Mampsis (Negev 1988b: 61), South Church at Sobata/Shivta (Rosenthal-Heginbottom 1982: 68), or the church of Bishop Sergius at Umm ar-Rasas (Piccirillo 1994: 72).
31. Other churches located in the semi-arid zone of the Negev, which have centrally situated cistern within the atrium include Sobata/Shivta North and Mampsis East and West.
32. Ben-Pechat 1989, fig. 1, Typological Table.
33. E.g., the masonry fonts at the Cathedral Church in Madaba (Piccirillo 1993: 116, 118), and in the Old Diakonikon in the basilica at Mt. Nebo (Piccirillo 1976: 298-99).
34. If accepting the chronology of the baptismal chapels discussed by Piccirillo 1985: 353-54.
35. All examples noted and illustrated in Ben-Pechat 1989: figs. 1 and 2.
36. Bagatti 1984: 307-8.
37. Notably, all four churches with baptisteries in the Negev possess these smaller fonts.
38. Negev 1988b: 48-50.
39. Piccirillo 1994: 77.
40. Ben-Pechat 1989: fig. 1, Typological Table. For description, see Rosenthal-Heginbottom 1982: 174-200.
41. The following description is based upon the instructions of Cyrillus of Jerusalem, as discussed and interpreted by Rosenthal-Heginbottom 1982: 176. See also Ben-Pechat 1989: 166, and Piccirillo 1985: 353.
42. Crowfoot 1938: 179.
43. For a rock-cut niche of the same style located in the Siq of Petra, probably of the first century AD, see Zayadine 1979: 194, 196-97, pl. XCIV.1.
44. The mosaics from the Petra church are fully described and analyzed by Waliszewski, 2001a. The most comprehensive presentation of the Byzantine mosaics in Jordan is in Piccirillo 1993.
45. For the discussion of this design widespread in Byzantine Palestine, and relevant parallels, see Dauphin 1987 and Waliszewski 1994.
46. Waliszewski, 2001a: 242-44, which contains full analysis and parallels.
47. Waliszewski, 2001a: 244-59, especially pp. 258-59 for full description and analysis.
48. Waliszewski, 2001a: 262-65, for full commentary and analysis.
49. A detailed presentation of the phases of development and the stratigraphy at the church complex is presented by Fiema, 2001b, while the architecture of the complex is specifically analysed by Kanellopoulos, 2001.
50. Crowfoot 1941: 54, 61; Smith and Day 1989: 84.
51. Ovadiah 1970: 199-200; Krautheimer 1965: 117. Tzaferis 1985: 9. Narthex by itself also occurs in some churches dated earlier (Ovadiah and de Silva 1984: 151)
52. Butler 1929: 48-82.
53. Ovadiah 1970: 194-95.
54. More precisely, in the second quarter of the sixth century, according to Krautheimer 1965: 120; see also Smith and Day 1989: 88, 90.
55. Negev 1989: 142.
56. For the exhaustive bibliography on the cult of Martyrs and Saints in Palestine, see Margalit 1990: 321-23, and note 6.
57. See discussions by Negev 1989, Margalit 1989, Duval 1994: 157-61, and Tsafrir 1988: 47-49. An alternative view points on the variations in the organization of the sanctuaries and in the deposition of the relics in triapsidal churches, and a resulting difficulty in associating an architectural form—mono- or triapsidal—with particulars of the specific cult and liturgical requirements (Rosenthal-Heginbottom 1982: 223-30, 233).
58. Piccirillo 1994: 89-90.
59. Walmsley 1992: 250.
60. See Schick 1995b, for the discussion of the survival of Christian communities and churches during the Early Islamic period.
61. For comparable material is well-represented in the finds from the Byzantine shops at Sardis, especially from shops E9-11, the "hardware store." (Crawford 1990: 71-78; figs. 366, 368).
62. Early Islamic generally refers to the seventh-eleventh century in the Middle East, while Late Islamic refers to the Ottoman period (16th - early 20th century).
63. For a comparable glass material, see Baur 1938, and Patrich 1988a.
64. The marble furnishing of the Petra church, its restoration and original location are discussed by Kanellopoulos and Schick, 2001. For comparable marble or limestone elements of church furnishings, see Acconci (1994) and Alliata (1994) for Umm ar-Rasas, and Patrich (1988b) for the Northern Church at Rehovot in the Negev.
65. Herrmann, 2001a and b, for both the kantharos and water fountain.
66. Lewis 1989: 48-49. The Petra inscription is discussed by Vihonen and Fiema, 2001: 342-45.
67. For the full presentation of archaeological context of the scrolls, see Fiema, 2001c.
68. For analysis of sources and data, see Fiema, 2001d, and Schick 1992.
69. For the most recent presentation of the Byzantine and post-Byzantine periods at Petra see Fiema 2002.

CHAPTER 22

1. Except for references to papyri published by the Finnish team in *P. Petra* I (Frösén, Arjava, and Lehtinen 2002), and a few bibliographical references, this essay is based on information available up to June, 2000; for a more recent view see Koenen 2003, a follow-up summary on results of our work that covers part of the same ground as the present article, sometimes with the same words but also often in greater detail and occasionally reflecting changes of mind; for previous reports, see Koenen 1996b; Koenen, Fiema, and Zayadine 1997: there pp. 157f. and 171 on the papyri. Several papers on the Petra papyri were published in *Atti Congr. XXII*; and for additional archaeological and historical information on the church see on the Petra Church, Z. T. Fiema's chapter 21 in this volume and R.Ch. Caldwell 2001 and Frösén and Fiema 2002. The work of the American team is mainly supported by the National Endowment of the Humanities (NEH), the University of Michigan and the American Center of Oriental Research (ACOR), the Dorot Foundation and the Eugene and Emily Grant Family Foundations. The present report focuses on findings by the Michigan team, but makes use of the decipherment and research by the Finnish team. J. Frösén has assigned the decipherment of individual papyri to individual members of his team. We acknowledge the responsibility of these individual members by indicating their names in parentheses when their papyrus is mentioned for the first time. Our thanks go especially to M. Lehtinen, whose help was crucial in locating a great number of small fragments of Inv. 10. We are also thankful to Z. T. Fiema, who advised us in archaeological and historical questions and offered careful criticism of an earlier draft of this article. Without the continued help and scholarly advice by the Directors of ACOR, Pierre and Patricia Bikai, and without the support of the Department of Antiquities of Jordan and its former Director General Ghazi Bisheh, our work would not be possible. O. al-Ghul advised us regularly on matters in Arabic philology; H.A. Falahat provided us with a wealth of information on toponyms used today in the Petra and Wadi Musa region; and R. Caldwell researched issues that were needed for this article and for which we did not have the library resources in Amman.
2. In Inv. nos. 85 (E. Salmenkivi) of AD 579/581 and 72+79, also called P. Petra Gladys J. and Frank J. Vocci (M. Vierros), written between AD 582 and 591, Theodoros is still alive, but he seems to have died shortly before 592, as A. Arjava has argued by letter. Theodoros was then about 78 years. His father-in-law Patrophilos must have been over 85 at his death.
3. None of these documents has been identified among the extant papyri. For this document, arguably the most important of the find, see Kaimio 2001. See also the discussion at the end of this paper.
4. Inv. 47; cf. 83 (n. 3) where one of the arbitrators is Theodoros son of Alpheios, once formally styled as archdeacon of "our most holy church," apparently referring to the main church of the diocese. The properties that were subject to the settlement were situated in Kastron Zadakathon (more below).
5. Godlewski 1986: 57. However, monasteries may have also collected papyri for recycling. The private documentary papyri in Greek and Coptic from Nag Hammadi had been worked into the covers of codices (see Shelton's introd. to *P. Nag. Hamm* in Barns, Brown and Shelton 1981) and some quires of Didymos's *Commentary on Ecclesiastes* (*P. Tura*) expected the same fate; numerous pages of these commentaries were palimpsests of documentary papyri (see Koenen 1968: 45-46, no 5 and 9). But such explanations are not applicable to the Petra papyri, since no scriptorium was found in the church. The papyri were found in two sections of the storage room, which was used used for keeping many other things. It did not have windows, and light could enter only through the door open to the next room. For depositing the Petra papyri in the church, see also Fiema 2001a: 148f.
6. We calculate with the standard Roman *iugerum* of about 2523 square meters, setting aside the unclear evidence for the use of a so-called "small" iugerum in the Eastern Mediterranean of about 1261 square meters; on the small iugerum, see Schilbach (1970) 77-80. Only items that are sufficiently recognizable have been counted. We have further assumed that fields with a lost number of *iugera* were at least one *iugerum*. Little is known about the amounts of land allotted to the oldest brother; so we calculate his portion as the mean of what his two brothers receive. The total of 84 acres is an intentionally low estimate, but still may give an impression of what the father of the three brothers (Theodoros' uncle) owned in the area of Petra at the time of his death. 84 acres seem to be modest, but may be substantial by Petra's standards. 133 *iugera* would

be ca 123 *arourai* in Egypt. By comparison, in Egypt around the middle of the fourth century, roughly 11% of landowners living in Hermoupolis and Antinooupolis owned more than 100 *arourai*. They were presumably able to live from their incoming rent; and "every Hermopolitan male holding more than 100 aruras would have to belong to the council for that body to number as much as 100" (Bagnall 1992 and 1993: 69f.; *idem, JRS* 82 [1992] 128-49). But we must keep in mind that the yield of one *aroura* in fertile Egypt was much greater than in the Petra area.

7. Although the text is fragmentary, it preserves information about the apartments allotted to all three brothers. For the present purpose we do not distinguish between main and upper floor units, and, except for orchards, we do not count the appurtenances of the apartments (bedrooms, balconies, yards, stairs, etc.). Included in the division were also three threshing floors and two dung depositories—valuable structures in the ancient economy—and an additional piece of land.
8. One of the pairs consist of a husband and wife, and we restore the second, badly damaged, passage correspondingly. It seems that, in accordance with Byzantine law (*CJ* 3.38.11 [334 (?)]; see also *CTh.* 2.25.1) married slave couples were not separated in the division. For this reason, the third brother did not receive a slave. He may have been compensated for this in another category of goods.
9. This is evidenced by the Swiss Liechtenstein excavation of Ez-Zantur IV. Wenning, Kolb and Nehmé 1997: 66, have pointed to similarities between the architecture of 'Roman house II' (fourth to early fifth century) and the architecture reconstructed from *P. Ness.* (Kraemer 1958) 22. The architecture of buildings in Inv. 10 appears to be in the same tradition.
10. There is no evidence that Petra was directly affected by the Persian Wars of 614-28, which heavily damaged areas west of the Jordan River, particularly Jerusalem. See Schick 1995b: 20-48. But, of course, Petra and its hinterland may have lost military protection when, during the Persian War, the troops were needed elsewhere.
11. In a composite text restored from *P. Petra* I (Frösén, Arjava and Lehtinen 2002:1) 1.4f. (ed. A. Arjava and C.A. Kuehn), Inv. 48, 67, 68, 85+89G) and with adjusted spelling: εν Αυγουcτοκολωνια Αντωνιανη (i.e., Αντωνινιανα) επιcημω και ευαγει (?) μητρι κολωνιων Αδριανη Πετρα μητροπολει τηc Τριτηc Παλαιcτινηc Cαλουταριαc.
12. So called by Millar 1970: 41 and 1993: 308.
13. *e.g. P. Petra* I (Frösén, Arjava and Lehtinen 2002:1) 3.3 and 4.3; Inv. 18, 20, 60.1 and 60.2, 71.1, 71.3; in other cases the name is not or only partially extant. Once the person is characterized as NN *tōn politeuomenōn*, "one of the *curiales*."
14. See, e.g., the introductionary remarks by Justinian in *Nov.* XXXVIII (*CIC* p. 246f.) of AD 536.
15. This remains true although the realities forced Anastasius to shift part of the tax-collection from the *curiales* to the *syntelestai* (Johnson and West 1949: 103. For the historical development, see Jones 1964: 757-63; for Egypt: Bowman 1971: 11; Geremek 1981; Laniado 1997; Worp 1997, also Bagnall 1993: 61. The date of an inscription that seems to attest a councillor of Petra for 516/17 (Fiema 2001d: 426f.) has been challenged for good reason (Sartre, 1993: 68; cf. Koenen 2003: 210f. with n. 21).
16. For the unusual division between communal and imperial administration, not attested in Egypt, see Gascou 1985: 39 n. 229; for Petra, see now *P. Petra* I (Frösén, Arjava and Lehtinen 2002:1) 3-4, introd. p. 76f. (T. Rankinen and M. Vierros); Koenen 2003: 212-14 and Koenen 1996b: 178 n. 6. For imperial estates in the area, see the *Salton Hieratikon* in third Palestine (George of Cypros, a Byzantine geographer, *Descr. orbis Romani* 1057).
17. *P. Ness.* (Kraemer 1958) 24 with Kraemer's note on line 3. Cf. βαθμος in the meaning "rank" (Lampe 1961: 281f.).
18. On *P. Ness.* (Kraemer 1958) 39 and the inscriptions, see the introduction to this papyrus and M.E. Abbadi (1984), who also discusses the *rizk* as defined by Arab jurists. *P. Ness.* (Kraemer 1958) 39 does not identify the tax by name and Abbadi presents his results tentatively, but persuasively. For the use of the *annona* for the confederate Arabic tribes, see Mayerson 1994: 344. In alliances between the Byzantine government and the leaders of the *foederati* the emperor was obliged to specify the amount of *annona* to be given to the Arabic leader and his troops. In *P. Petra* I (Frösén, Arjava and Lehtinen 2002:1) 7, 8 and 9, the annona is hiding behind payments in crop (grain) and both wine and meat (*en te genēmasi kai oinokreois*); cf. Mitthof 2001: I 208-12; Koenen 2003: 215f.
19. See especially Mayerson 1994: 342-46; Caldwell 2001: 111-41.
20. For instance, we must be aware that aspiration before vowels is generally not indicated in Greek script and, in Byzantine times, had long ceased to be spoken. This affects, of course, also the Greek transcriptions of Arabic consonants. Moreover, due to phonetic developments, most Greek vowels sounded quite similar to others, and long and short vowels were no longer distinguished. These facts caused a wide range of spellings. See n. 29, and for another Greek spelling habit, also n. 31.
21. Negev 1991a: 48 no. 827. For the god, see Dijkstra 1995: 319-21. This and the following remarks depend mainly on Daniel 2001; see also al-Ghul 1999; Caldwell 2001: 169-82; Koenen 2003: 219-21.
22. G.W. Bowersock (by letter and Bowersock 1978: 117) compares Thaaious/ *Tayayye* to a man's name derived from *tayy/tayyaye* (Negev 1991a: 31 no. 504 and p. 159 sect. 4) and Libanius, *or.* 24.6.
23. Sartre 1985: 172-73; Stark 1971: 88-89.
24. See especially Sartre 1985: 225-27 referring to Epiphanios of Salamis, who noted that Valēs, the founder of the Valesian heresy, bore an Arabic name.
25. Sartre 1985: 188.
26. Sartre 1985: 183.
27. Sartre 1985: 186-87; also 199 under the name Δωρος, and 202. under the name Ζαβδος.
28. Daniel 1998.
29. In late Greek, due to phonetic developments, *Laila* can be spelled *Lela* and vice versa (see n. 20).
30. For the story, see Zayadine 1985: 170-73; for the tribe of the *Banī ʿUqba* in general, see Oppenheim 1943: 333-35.
31. Cf. German *Hof*, which likewise can mean "courtyard," "farmhouse" or princely residence and court (as in "am Hofe"). In Greek, too, *aulē* can refer to the imperial court. For theta (th) in the Greek transcription of Darath, see n. 20.
32. In Greek, *Aphthonis* is a frequent spelling for *Aphthonios*.
33. In Egypt, there was also the possibility of writing documents in Demotic and Coptic; but only Egyptian priests and members of the native upper class could read and write Demotic. Temples had writing offices, but these were gone in Byzantine Egypt.
34. Inv. 47, or P. Petra (Frösén, Arjava and Lehtinen 2002) M. McCamish from between early AD 565 and early 567:]κ[α]ι προc αcφαλει[αν υμετεραν- - - ταυτην την ομολογιαν πεποιημαι | υπο]γρ[α]φιcαν χειρι Φλ(αουιου) Νοννου Αυςωνοc π [ ]μου α . . . [- - - αξιωθεντοc παρ εμου την υπογραφ]ην υπερ εμου γραψαι ωλιγωγραμματου [ουcηc (?). Some details of the wording remain uncertain.
35. Inv. 64+66 or P. Petra (Frösén, Arjava and Lehtinen 2002) K.W. Russell and W. Steward: (m.3) † [ΦΙΛΟ]ΥΝΕ[Ν]ΟC ΓΕ[ΡΟΝΤΙ]ΟΥ ΠΡΕCΒ(ΥΤΕΡΟC) (m.4) ο πρ[ογεγρα]μμεν[οc επε[cτειλα κο]υφιcθηναι το [π]ρ[οcω]πον και ουcι[αν] κα[ι] λογον του θεοφ[ι]λ(εcτατου) Θεοδωρ[ο]υ - - - χρη[cα]μενοc χειρει Φλ(αουιου) Cωcα[μου] Αλφ[ιο]υ π[α]ρ εμου α[ξιωθ]εντοc, [π]ροταξα[ντ]οc οικ[ι]α μου χειρει την εμ[η]ν και τ[ο]υ εμου π[α]τροc πρ[ο]cηγ[ο]ρ[ια]ν δια το εμε μη ηκριβοcθαι και προcγραφειν και κατα cτ[οι]χιον γραφντα περιβ[ρα]δυνειν.
36. *P. Petaus* (Hagedorn and Youtie 1969) 121; Youtie 1973: 611-27; 629-51; 677-96.
37. The decipherment by M. and J. Kaimio is work in progress. We depend on their readings and reconstructions and acknowledge the help we have received by letter. For the document, see Kaimio 2001 (above, n. 3); Caldwell 2001: 111-41; Gagos 2001.
38. From other parts of the Byzantine Empire, we know the intermediary role of bishops conducting an "episcopal hearing" (*audientia episcopalis*). Cf. Schmelz 2002: 272-88.
39. A division of a dung-storing facility into separate portions occurs also in Inv. 10.
40. We do not know whether the mediator, a priest, negotiated the fine for the present settlement or had already done so on an earlier occasion. If the latter was the case, then the earlier determination of the fine was incorporated in the new settlement.
41. Once he was called deacon.
42. For the general procedures of settlements attested by the Egyptian evidence, see Gagos and van Minnen 1994. For the terminological distinction between "arbitrator" and "mediator," see *ibidem* 30-35. For clerics as arbitrators see Schmelz 2002: 272-84.
43. Mari Mikkola, in her unpublished M.A. thesis (University of Helsinki) on "The Local Administration of the City of Petra in the Light of the Petra Papyri and Comparative Material" (in Finnish, but made available to us in English), considers the possibility that in Inv. 83. the notary's signature could have stood at the lost beginning of the papyrus. This would be surprising in this type of document, but not impossible.
44. Swearing an oath to establish innocence is known from Egypt, although there the oath was on the bones of a martyr. Also in *P. Petra* I 6 (ed. M. Vesterinen) in (Frösén, Arjava and Lehtinen 2002:1), the priest Epiphanios takes the oath from somebody whom he suspected of having stolen several things from him.
45. A. Arjava believes that *P. Petra* I (Frösén, Arjava and Lehtinen 2002:1) 1, p. 24 is based on a preceding marriage contract.
46. The hypothetical scenarios could have come out of some sort of manual of legal provisions, perhaps adapted to fit this family's particular circumstances. Indeed, such "toolkits" existed in the Graeco-Roman world and covered a variety of cases. Individuals trying to bequeath their property in an orderly fashion that conformed both to social norms and to their own specific wishes could manipulate and adapt these strategies to fit their needs. Cf. Gagos 2001, 497-501.
47. 16f. εν τοισ [μ]εταξυ αυτων κατα τον κα[ιρον] | της διαλυσεωc λαλουμενοις. The list of lines 11-17 is damaged and the syntax convoluted, but it should be clear that it contains a list of what Theodoros has received.
48. *P. Petra* I (Frösén, Arjava and Lehtinen 2002:1) 1 (AD 537; see n. 45) and Inv. 63+65 (AD 539/40; see p. 254) add the name of the emperor. In two other damaged occurrences the precise wording cannot be recovered (Inv. 8 and 20). *P. Petra* I 2.29 (Frösén, Arjava and Lehtinen 2002:1) 13 (see above), a document written in AD 538 at Gaza and, therefore, in a different province (Palestina Prima), uses an older non-trinitarian form of an oath by "God Pantokrator and the Piety, Victory, and Perseverance of our all-conquering Lord" (the emperor). For this and the following, see already Koenen 2001: 739-42.
49. *P. Ness.* (Kraemer 1958) 21 and 22. Both Nessana papyri omit the name of the emperor, as does Inv. 10 and a number of Egyptian papyri (cf. n. 45).
50. Gagos and van Minnen 1994: 110 on lines 77-79. For the Egyptian evidence, see Worp 1982.
51. In *De summa trinitate* at the beginning of the *CJ*, the emperor declared that the trinitarian Logos and Christ are not different, but the same (person) is consubstantial with the Father according to his Divinity and consubstantial with men according to his humanity. As he argued, "the Holy Trinity has not received the addition of a fourth person."
52. See above on the one occurrence of the Consubstantial Trinity in an oath (Inv. 86r [M. Lehtinen]); Inv. 86v (M. Lehtinen) mentions the Consubstantial Trinity outside of an oath formula.
53. The Ghassanids were monophysites. The synod of Jerusalem in AD 536, in which Bishop Theodoros of Petra participated, was directed against monophysites as was the synod of Constantinople of the same year. On the Ghassanids, see p. 252.

Abbreviations of Journal Titles

AA	Archäologischer Anzeiger
AAAS	Les Annales Archaéologiques Arabes Syriennes
AAE	Arabian Archaeology and Epigraphy
AASOR	Annual of the American Schools of Oriental Research
ACORN	American Center of Oriental Research Newsletter
ADAJ	Annual of the Department of Antiquities Jordan
AfO	Archiv für Orientforschung. Internationale Zeitschrift für Wissenschaft vom Vorderen Orient
AJA	American Journal of Archaeology
Atlal	Atlal: Journal of Saudi Arabian Studies
BA	The Biblical Archaeologist
BAH	Bibliothèque Archéologique et Historique. Institut Français d'Archéologie de Beyrouth
BAR	British Archaeological Reports. International Series
BCH	Bulletin de Correspondence Hellenique
Berytus	Berytus. Archeological Studies
BIFAO	Bulletin de l'Institut français d'archéologie Orientale
BJ	Bonner Jahrbücher
BSOAS	Bulletin of the School of Oriental and African Studies. University of London
BASOR	Bulletin of the American Schools of Oriental Research
CdE	Chronique d'Égypte
CRAIBL	Compte rendus des séances de l'Academie des inscriptions et belles-lettres
DaM	Damaszener Mitteilungen
GCS	Die Griechischen Christlischen Schriftsteller der Ersten Drei Jahrhunderte
IEJ	Israel Exploration Journal
Iraq	British School of Archaeology in Iraq
JA	Journal Asiatique
JAOS	Journal of the American Oriental Society
JdI	Jahrbuch des Deutschen Archäologischen Instituts
JEA	Journal of Egyptian Archaeology
JEOL	Jaarbericht van het Vooraziatisch-Egyptisch Genootschap (Gezelschap) Ex Oriente Lux
JESHO	Journal of Economic and Social History of the Orient
JJS	Journal of Jewish Studies
JNES	Journal of Near Eastern Studies
JPOS	Journal of the Palestine Oriental Society
JRA	Journal of Roman Archaeology
JRS	Journal of Roman Studies
JSS	Journal of Semitic Studies
Klio	Klio: Beiträge zur Alten Geschichte
Ktema	Ktema: Civilizations de l'Orient de la Grèce et de Rome Antiques
LA	Liber Annuus
Latomus	Latomus: revue d'études latines
Levant	Levant. Journal of the British School of Archaeology in Jerusalem
MEFRA	Mélanges de L'École française de Rome et d'Athènes
QDAP	Quarterly of the Department of Antiquities in Palestine
Qedem	Monographs of the Institute of Archaeology
RA	Revue Archéologique
RB	Revue Biblique
SCI	Scripta Classica Israelitica
SHAJ	Studies in the History and Archaeology of Jordan. Amman
ZDMG	Zeitschrift der Deutschen Morgenländischen Gesellschaft
ZDPV	Zeitschrift des deutschen Palästina-Vereins
ZPE	Zeitschrift fur Papyrologie und Epigraphik

ENCYLOPEDIAS AND LEXICONS

ANET	Ancient Near Eastern Texts Relating to the Old Testament. J. B. Pritchard, ed. Princeton. 3rd edition 1969
OxEANE	The Oxford Encyclopedia of Archaeology in the Near East, E. M. Meyers, ed., New York and Oxford. 1997
ODByz	Oxford Dictionary of Byzantium, A.P. Kazhdan et al., eds., New York and Oxford
NEAEHL	The New Encyclopedia of Archaeological Excavations in the Holy Land. Jerusalem.
LIMC	Lexicon Iconographicum Mythologiae Classicae. Geneva/Zurich

COMPENDIA OF INSCRIPTION SERIES

CIL	Corpus Inscriptionum Latinarum, eds. T. Mommsen, et al. (Berlin: G. Reimerum, 1862-)
CIS	Corpus Inscriptionum Semiticarum. Paris
IGR	Inscriptiones Graecae ad Res Romanas Pertinentes. R. Cagnat et al., eds. Paris
IGLS	Inscriptions Greques et Latines de la Syrie
RES	Repertoire d'épigraphie semitique, C. Clermont-Ganneau et al., eds. Paris
SEG	Supplementum Epigraphicum Graecum

Bibliography

el-Abbadi 1984. M. el-Abbadi. " 'Annona Militaris' and 'riz ' of Nessana." Pp. 1057–62 in *Atti del XVII Congresso Internazionale di Papyrologia*. Naples.

Abbadi 1996. S. Abbadi. "New Safaitic Inscriptions Dated to the Last Quarter of the First Century B.C." [in Arabic]. *Abath al-Yarm,,k*: 1–20.

Abdou Daoud 1998. D. Abdou Daoud. "Evidence for the Production of Bronze in Alexandria." Pp. 115–24 in J.-Y. Empereur, ed. *Commerce et Artisanat dans l'Alexandrie hellénistique et romaine*, BCH Supplement 33. Paris.

Acconci 1994. A. Acconci. "L'arredo Liturgico." Pp. 290–313 in M. Piccirillo and E. Alliata. *Umm al-Rasas – Mayfa'ah, I. Gli Scavi del Complesso di Santo Stefano*. Jerusalem.

Adriani 1935–1939. A. Adriani. Annuaire du Musée Gréco-romain, Alexandria, 1940: 52–53, and pl. XIX.

Adriani 1963–1966. A. Adriani. *Repertorio d'Arte dell'Egitto Greco-Romano*. Serie C. I-II. Palermo.

Aharoni 1993. M. Aharoni. "Arad." P. 85 in *NEAEHL* I.

al-Ansary 1982. A.M. al-Ansary. *Qarrayat al-Faw: A Portrait of Pre-Islamic Civilization in Saudi Arabia*. Riyadh.

al-As'ad and Teixidor 1985. K. al-As'ad and J. Teixidor. "Un culte arabe préislamique à Palmyre, d'après une inscription inédite." *CRAIBL* 1985: 286–93.

Alliata 1994. E. Alliata. "I Reliquiari e Altri Elementi Architettonici." Pp. 312–17 in M. Piccirillo and E. Alliata. *Umm al-Rasas – Mayfa'ah, I. Gli Scavi del Complesso di Santo Stefano*. Jerusalem.

Alt 1921. A. Alt. *Die griechischen Inschriften der Palaestina Tertia westlich der Araba*. Berlin and Leipzig.

Amy 1969. R. Amy. *Mise en valeur de Bosra-Cham (1968)*. Unesco Report no. 1228. Paris.

Anati 1979. E. Anati. *L'Art rupestre . Negev et Sinai*. Paris.

Andreou 1988. A. Andreou. *Griechische Wanddekorationen*. Unpublished dissertation, Johannes Gutenberg-University of Mainz.

Attridge and Oden 1976. H.W. Attridge and R.A. Oden, eds. trans. [Lucian] *De dea Syria*. Missoula, MT.

Avanzini 1997. A. Avanzini. *Profumi d'Arabia. Atti del convegno*. Rome.

Avigad 1984. N. Avigad. *Discovering Jerusalem*. Oxford.

Avigad 1991. N. Avigad. *The Herodian Quarter in Jerusalem*. Jerusalem.

Avi-Yonah 1958. M. Avi-Yonah. "The Economics of Byzantine Palestine." *IEJ* 8: 39–51.

Bachmann, Watzinger and Wiegand 1921. W. Bachmann, C. Watzinger and Th. Wiegand. *Petra*. Wissenschaftliche Veröffentlichungen des Deutsch-Türkischen Denkmalschutz-Kommandos 3. Berlin and Leipzig.

Bagatti 1984. B. Bagatti. *The Church from the Gentiles in Palestine. History and Archaeology*. Studium Biblicum Franciscanum. Collectio Minor 4. Jerusalem.

Bagnall 1992. R.S. Bagnall. "Landholding in Late Roman Antiquity: The Distribution of Wealth." JRS 82: 128–49.

Bagnall 1993. R.S. Bagnall. *Egypt in Late Antiquity*. Princeton.

Ball 2000. W. Ball. *Rome in the East. The Transformation of an Empire*. London and New York.

Balty 1983. J.-Ch. Balty. "Architecture et société à Pétra et Hégra. Chronologie et classes sociales: sculpteurs et commanditaires." Pp. 303–24 in *Architecture et Société de l'archaïsme grec à la fin de la république romaine*. Paris.

Baratte 1986. F. Baratte. *Le trésor d'orfèvrerie romaine de Boscoreale*. Paris.

Barbet 1985. A. Barbet. *La peinture murale romaine*. Paris.

Barbet 1995. A. Barbet. "Les characteristiques de la peinture murale à Petra." Pp. 383–90 in *SHAJ* V.

Barns, Browne and Shelton 1981. J.W.B. Barns, G.M. Browne and J.C. Shelton. *Nag Hammadi Codices: Greek and Coptic Papyri from the Cartonage of the Covers*. (*P. Nag Hamm*.). Nag Hammadi Studies 16. Leiden.

Bartlett 1848. W. Bartlett. *Forty Days in the Desert on the Track of the Israelites*. London.

Bartlett 1850. W. Bartlett. *The Nile Boat, or, Glimpses of the Land of Egypt*. London.

Bartlett 1979. J.R. Bartlett. "From Edomites to Nabataeans: A Study in Continuity." *PEQ* 111: 53–66.

Bartlett 1990. J.R. Bartlett. "From Edomites to Nabataeans: The Problem of Continuity." *ARAM* 2: 25–34.

Baur 1938. P.V.C. Baur. "Glassware." Pp. 505–48 in Kraeling 1938.

Bedal 1998. L.A. Bedal. "Petra: Lower Market Survey." *ACORN* 10 (1): 4–5.

Bedal 2001. L.A. Bedal. "In Search of Petra's Buried Garden." *ACORN* 13 (1): 1–3.

Beer 1840. E.F.F. Beer. *Inscriptiones veteres litteris et lingua hucusque incognitis ad montem Sinai*. Studia Asiatica, fasc. 3. Leipzig.

Bellamy 1985. J.A. Bellamy. "A New Reading of the Namærah Inscription." *JAOS* 105: 31–51.

Bellamy 1990. J.A. Bellamy. "Arabic Verses from the First/Second Century: The Inscription of ¶En ¶Avdat." *JSS* 35: 73–79.

Ben-Pechat 1989. M. Ben-Pechant. "The Paleochristian Baptismal Fonts in the Holy Land: Formal and Functional Study." *LA* 39: 165–88.

Bienkowski 1992. P. Bienkowski, ed. *Early Edom and Moab*. Sheffield.

Bignasca 1996. A. Bignasca, et al. *Petra. Ez Zantur. Ergebnisse der Schweizerisch-Liechtensteinischen Ausgrabungen 1988–1992*. Terra archaeologica 2. Mainz.

Bikai 1996. P.M. Bikai. "The Ridge Church at Petra." *ADAJ* 40: 481–86.

Bikai and Egan 1999. P.M. Bikai and V. Egan. "Archaeology in Jordan – Petra." *AJA* 103: 510–11.

Blagg 1990. T.F.C. Blagg. "Column Capitals with Elephant-head Volutes at Petra." *Levant* 22: 131–37.

Blanc 1983. N. Blanc. "Le courant paysagiste dans la dëcoration en stuc." *RA* 1983: 51–78.

Blanc and Dentzer 1997. P.-M. Blanc and J.-M. Dentzer. "Bosra." In "Archaeology in Syria." *AJA* 101 (1): 113–16.

Bordreuil 1997. P. Bordreuil, et al. "Linteau inscrit: AO 4083 [The Namærah Inscription]." Pp. 265–69 in *Arabie heureuse Arabie déserte. Les antiquités arabiques du Musée du Louvre*. Notes et documents des musées de France, 31. Paris.

Bowersock 1971. G.W. Bowersock. "A Report on Arabia Provincia." *JRA* 61: 219–42, reprinted in Bowersock 1994: 103–27 (with note on p. 431).

Bowersock 1975. G.W. Bowersock. "The Greek-Nabataean Bilingual Inscription at Ruwwâfa, Saudi Arabia." Pp. 513–22 in *Le monde grec: Hommages à Claire Préaux*. Brussels; reprinted in Bowersock 1994: 203–12 (with note on p. 432).

Bowersock 1976. G.W. Bowersock. "A New Antonine Inscription from the Syrian Desert." *Chiron* 6: 349–55, reprinted in Bowersock 1994: 195–201 (with note on p. 432).

Bowersock 1978. G.W. Bowersock. *Julian the Apostate*. Cambridge, MA.

Bowersock 1983. G.W. Bowersock. *Roman Arabia*, corrected reprint 1996. Cambridge, MA.

Bowersock 1984–1985. G.W. Bowersock. "Arabs and Saracens in the Historia Augusta." Pp. 71–80 in *Bonner Historia-Augusta-Colloquium* (published 1987); reprinted in Bowersock 1994: 385–94.

Bowersock 1986a. G.W. Bowersock. "An Arabian Trinity." *Harvard Theological Review* 79: 117–21, also with identical pagination and date as a separate volume entitled *Christians among Jews and Gentiles: Festschrift for Krister Stendahl*, and reprinted in Bowersock 1994: 237–41.

Bowersock 1986b. G.W. Bowersock. "Review of I. Shahîd, Rome and the Arabs and Byzantium and the Arabs in the Fourth Century." *Classical Review* 36: 111–17, reprinted in Bowersock 1994: 395–401.

Bowersock 1990a. G.W. Bowersock. "The Cult and Representation of Dusares in Roman Arabia." Pp. 31–36 in Zayadine 1990a; reprinted in Bowersock 1994: 245–52.

Bowersock 1990b. G.W. Bowersock. *Hellenism in Late Antiquity*. Ann Arbor.

Bowersock 1991. G.W. Bowersock. "The Babatha Papyri, Masada, and Rome." *JRA* 4: 336–44, reprinted in Bowersock 1994: 213–28 (with note on p. 432).

Bowersock 1994. G.W. Bowersock. *Studies on the Eastern Roman Empire*. Goldbach.

Bowersock 1996. G.W. Bowersock. "Exploration in North-West Arabia after Jaussen-Savignac." *Topoi* 6: 553–63.

Bowersock 1997a. G.W. Bowersock. "Jacoby's Fragments and Two Greek Historians of Pre-Islamic Arabia." Pp. 173–85 in G.W. Most, ed. *Collecting Fragments/Fragmente sammeln*. Aporemata 1 (with many topographical errors).

Bowersock 1997b. G.W. Bowersock. "Perfumes and Power." Pp. 543–56 in Avanzini 1997.

Bowersock 1997c. G.W. Bowersock. "Commentarii Breviores: Nabataeans on the Capitoline." *Hyperboreus* 3 (2): 347–52.

Bowersock 1999. G.W. Bowersock. *Late Antiquity: A Guide to the Postclassical World*, edited with P. Brown and O. Grabar. Cambridge, MA.

Bowersock 2001. G.W. Bowersock. "Lucius Verus in the Near East." Pp. 73–77 in C. Evers and A. Tsingarida, eds. *Rome et ses provinces: Hommages à Jean Charles Balty*. Brussels.

Bowes 1998. A.R. Bowes. *The Process of Nabataean Sedentarization: New Models and Approaches*. PhD dissertation, University of Utah.

Bowman 1971. A.K. Bowman. *The Town Councils of Roman Egypt*. American Studies in Papyrology 11. Toronto.

Bowsher 1986. J. Bowsher. "The Frontier Post of Medain Saleh." Pp. 23-29 in P. Freeman and D. Kennedy, eds. *The Defence of the Roman and Byzantine East*. BAR International Series 297. Oxford.

Bowsher 1989. J. Bowsher. "The Nabataean Army." Pp. 19-30 in D.H. French and C.S. Lightfoot, eds. *The Eastern Frontier of the Roman Empire. BAR* International Series 553 (1). Oxford.

Braemer 2003. F. Braemer. "Le rempart de Bosra au 2e millénaire av. n. ère." *Syria* 80 IN PRESS.

Briquel-Chatonnet and Nehmé 1998. F. Briquel-Chatonnet and L. Nehmé. "Graffitti nabatéens d'al-Muwayah et de Bi'r al-Hammâmât (Égypte)." *Semitica* 47: 81-88.

Brock 1976. S.P. Brock. "The Rebuilding of the Temple Under Julian: A New Source." *PEQ* 108: 103-7.

Brock 1977. S.P. Brock. "A Letter Attributed to Cyril of Jerusalem on the Rebuilding of the Temple." *BSOAS* 40 (2): 267-86.

Broome 1955. E. Broome. "La divinité Ras 'Ain La'ban." *RB* 62: 246-52.

Browning 1994. R. Browning. *Petra*. London.

Brünnow and von Domaszewski 1904. R.E. Brünnow and A. von Domaszewski. "Petra." Pp. 125-424 in Brünnow and von Domaszewski 1904-1909.

Brünnow and von Domaszewski 1904-1909. R.E. Brünnow and A. von Domaszewski. *Die Provincia Arabia. Auf Grund zweier in den Jahren 1897 und 1898 unternommenen Reisen und der Berichte früherer Reisender*. 3 vols. Strasbourg.

Brussels 1980. *Inoubliable* Pétra. Le royaume nabatéen aux confines du desert. Catalogue of an exhibition at the Musées Royaux d'Art et d'Histoire, Bruxelles. D. Homès-Fredericq, ed. Bruxelles.

Bunnens 1969. G. Bunnens. "Le zodiaque nabatéen de Khirbet-Tannur, entre les Victoires stéphanophores et les anges caryatides." *Latomus* 28: 391-407.

Burckhardt 1822. J.L. Burckhardt. *Travels in Syria and the Holy Land*. London.

Butler 1907-1919. H.C. Butler. *Ancient Architecture in Syria Div. II, Sect. A: Southern Syria*. Syria, Publication of the Princeton University Archaeological Expedition to Syria, 1904-1905, and 1909; div. II, sect. A. Leiden.

Butler 1929. H.C. Butler. *Early Churches in Syria. Fourth to Seventh Centuries. Part One. History*. E. Baldwin Smith, ed. Princeton.

Cahill 1997. J.M. Cahill. "Royal Rosettes: Fit for a King." *Biblical Archaeology Review* 23 (5): 48-57.

Caldwell 2001. R.Ch. Caldwell. *Between State and Steppe: New Evidence for Society in Sixth Cent. Southern Transjordan*. PhD dissertation, The University of Michigan. Ann Arbor.

Canaan 1929. T. Canaan. "Studies in the Topography and Folklore of Petra." *JPOS* 9: 136-218.

Canivet and Rey-Coquais 1992. P. Canivet and J.-P. Rey-Coquais, eds. *La Syrie de Byzance a l'Islam VIIe-VIIIe siècles*. Actes du colloque international Lyon – Maison de l'Orient Méditerranéen. Paris

Cantineau 1930. J. Cantineau. *Le nabatéen*. Vol. 1: Notions *générales-Ecriture-Grammaire*. Paris.

Cantineau 1932. J. Cantineau. *Le nabatéen*. ffol. 2: Choix detextes-Lexique. Paris.

Carettoni 1983. G. Carettoni. *Das Haus des Augustus auf dem Palatin*. Mainz.

Carr 1994. G.L. Carr. *Frederic Edwin Church Catalogue Raisonné of Works of Art at Olana State Historic Site*. Cambridge, England.

Carrino 1999. R. Carrino. "Bosra. Chiesa dei SS. Sergio, Bacco e Leonzio. Il saggio nel Tetraconco T1 (1995)." *Felix Ravenna* 145-148: 1993 (1-2); 1994 (1-2); 1999: 195-202.

Caskel 1954. W. Caskel. *Lihyan and Lihyanish*. Cologne.

Casson 1989. L. Casson. *Periplus Maris Erythraei. Text with Introduction, Translation, and Commentary*. Princeton.

Casson and Hettich 1950. L. Casson and E.L. Hettich. *Excavations at Nessana 2, Literary Papyri*. Princeton.

Castlereagh 1847. Viscount Castlereagh. *Journey to Damascus through Egypt, Nubia, Arabia Petraea, Palestine, and Syria*. 2 vols. London.

Cauville 1997. S. Cauville. *Le Zodiac d'Osiris*. Leuven.

Cerulli 1978. S. Cerulli. "Bosra, note sul sistema viario urbano e nuovi apporti alla comprensione delle fasi edilizie nel santuario dei Ss. Sergio, Bacco e Leonzio." *Felix Ravenna* 115 (1): 77-120, 133-76.

Charbel 1985. A. Charbel. "Matteo 2, 1-12: I Magi nella corniche del regno nabateo." *Studia Patavina* 32: 81-88.

Clermont-Ganneau 1895. Ch. Clermont-Ganneau. *Etudes d'archéologie orientale* 1. Paris.

Clermont-Ganneau 1919. C. Clermont-Ganneau. "Les Nabatéens en Égypte." *Revue de l'Histoire des Religions* 80: 1-29.

Cohen 1980. R. Cohen. "Excavations at 'Avdat, 1977." *Qadmoniot* 49-50: 44-45 (Hebrew).

Colledge 1976. M.A.R. Colledge. *The Art of Palmyra*. London.

Colt 1962. H.D. Colt, ed. *Excavations at Nessana (Auja Hafir, Palestine)* 1. London.

Cosmas Indicopleustes 1864. Cosmae, aegypti monachi, *christiana topographia*. Col. 9-476 in J.-P. Migne, ed. *Patrologiae Cursus Completus. Series Graeca Prior* 88. Paris.

Cotton 1993. H.M. Cotton. "The Guardianship of Jesus, Son of Babatha: Roman and Local Law in the Province of Arabia." *JRS* 83: 94-108.

Cotton 1995. H.M. Cotton. "The Archive of Salome Komaise Daughter of Levi: Another Archive from the 'Cave of Letters'." *ZPE* 105: 171-208.

Cotton and Yardeni 1997. H.M. Cotton and A. Yardeni. *Aramaic, Hebrew and Greek Documentary Texts from Nahal@ever and other Sites*. Discoveries in the Judean Desert 27. Oxford. (*P. Nahal@ever.*)

Cotton, Cockle and Millar 1995. H.M. Cotton, W.E.H. Cockle and F.G.B. Millar. "The Papyrology of the Roman Near East: A Survey." *JRS* 85: 214-35.

Cowley 1914-1915. A.E. Cowley. (Note on a Nabataean Inscription found at Khalasa/Elusa). Pp. 145-46 in *The Wilderness of Zin (Archaeological Report)* by C.L. Woolley and T.E. Lawrence. Palestine Exploration Fund Annual 3. London.

Crawford 1990. J. Stephens Crawford. *The Byzantine Shops at Sardis*. Archaeological Exploration of Sardis, Monograph 9. Cambridge, MA.

Cresswell and Allan 1989. K.C. Cresswell and J.W. Allan. *A Short Account of Early Muslim Architecture*. Aldershot.

Crone 1987. P. Crone. *Meccan Trade and the Rise of Islam*. Princeton.

Cross 1965. F.M. Cross. "The Development of the Jewish Scripts." Pp. 170-264 in G.E. Wright, ed. *The Bible and the Ancient Near East. Essays in Honor of William Foxwell Albright*. New York.

Cross 1986. F.M. Cross. "A New Aramaic Stele from Tayma'." *Catholic Biblical Quarterly* 48: 387-94.

Crowfoot 1938. J.W. Crowfoot. "The Christian Churches." Pp. 171-263 in Kraeling 1938.

Crowfoot 1941. J.W. Crowfoot. *Early Churches in Palestine*. London.

Dalley and Goguel 1997. S. Dalley and A. Goguel. "The Sela' Sculpture: A Neo-Babylonian Rock Relief in Southern Jordan." *ADAJ* 41: 169-76.

Dalman 1908. G. Dalman. *Petra und seine Felsheiligtümer*. Leipzig.

Dalman 1911. G. Dalman. *The Khazneh at Petra*. London.

Dalman 1912. G. Dalman. *Neue Petra-Forschungen und der heilige felsen von Jerusalem*. Palästinische Forschungen zur Archäologie und Topographie, Band 2. Leipzig.

Daniel 1998. R.W. Daniel. "Toponomastic *Mal* in P. Nessana 82 and P. Petra Inv. 10 (Papyrus Petra Khaled & Suha Shoman)." *ZPE* 122: 195f.

Daniel 2001. R.W. Daniel. "P. Petra Inv. 10 and its Arabic." Pp. 331-41 in Atti XXII Congresso 2001.

Dauphin 1980. C. Dauphin. "Mosaic Pavements as an Index of Prosperity and Fashion." *Levant* 12: 112-34.

Dauphin 1987. C. Dauphin. "The Development of the 'Inhabited Scroll' in Architectural Sculpture and Mosaic Art from Late Imperial Times to the Seventh Century A.D." *Levant* 19: 183-212.

Dearman 1995. J.A. Dearman. "Edomite Religion. A Survey and an Examination of Some Recent Contributions." Pp. 119-36 in Edelman 1995.

Dentzer 1984. J.-M. Dentzer, et al. "Sondages près de l'Arc Nabatéen de Bosra." *Berytus* 32: 163-74.

Dentzer 1985. J.-M. Dentzer. "Céramiques et environnement naturel. La céramique nabatéenne de Bosra." Pp. 149-54 in *SHAJ* II.

Dentzer 1985-1986. J.-M. Dentzer, ed. *Hauran I: recherches archéologiques sur la Syrie du Sud à l'époque hellénistique et romaine 1, 2*. BAH 124. Paris.

Dentzer 1986. J.-M. Dentzer. "Les sondages de l'Arc Nabatéen et l'urbanisme de Bosra." *CRAIBL* 1986: 62-87.

Dentzer 1988. J.-M. Dentzer. "Fouilles franco-syriennes à l'Est de l'Arc Nabatéen (1985-1987): Une nouvelle cathédrale à Bosra." Pp. 13-34 in *XXXV Corso di Cultura sull'Arte Ravennate e Bizantina*. Ravenna.

Dentzer 1990. J.-M. Dentzer. "Neue Ausgrabungen in Si' (Qanawat) und Bosra (1985-1987): Zwei einheimische Heiligtümer in der vorkaiserzeitlichen Periode." Pp. 364-70 in *Akten des XIII. Internationalen Kongresses für Klassische Archäologie*. Berlin.

Dentzer 1997. J.-M. Dentzer. "*Bosra*." Pp. 350-53 in *OxEANE* I.

Dentzer and Blanc 1995. J.-M. Dentzer and P.-M. Blanc. "Techniques de construction et de revêtement dans la Bosra nabatéenne." Pp. 223-30 in *SHAJ* V.

Dentzer and Dentzer-Feydy 1991. J.-M. Dentzer and J. Dentzer-Feydy, eds. *Le djebel al-'Arab. Histoire et Patrimoine au Musée de Suweida'*. Paris.

Dentzer, Blanc and Mukdad 1993. J.-M. Dentzer, P.-M. Blanc and R. and A. Mukdad. "Nouvelles recherches Franco-Syriennes dans le quartier est de Bosra ash-Sham." *CRAIBL* 1993: 117-47.

Dentzer, Blanc and Mukdad 2003. J.-M. Dentzer, P.-M. Blanc and R. Mukdad. "Le développement urbain de Bosra de l'époque nabatéenne à l'époque Byzantine: bilan des recherches françaises 1981-2002." *Syria* 80 in press.

Dentzer, Blanc and Mukdad in prep. J.-M. Dentzer, P.-M. Blanc and R. Mukdad. "Travaux archéologiques à Bosra 1993-1997." *AAAS* forthcoming.

Dentzer, Dentzer-Feydy and Blanc 2001. J.-M. Dentzer, J. Dentzer-Feydy and P.-M. Blanc. "Busra dans la perspective par millénaires: la Busra nabatéenne." Pp. 457-68 in *SHAJ* VII.

Dentzer-Feydy 1986. J. Dentzer-Feydy. "Décor architectural et développement du Hauran du Ier s. avant J.C. au VIIème s. après J.C." Pp. 261-310 in Dentzer 1985-1986.

Dentzer-Feydy 1990. J. Dentzer-Feydy. "Khirbet edh-Dharih. Architectural Decoration of the Temple." *ARAM* 2: 229-34.

Dentzer-Feydy 1992. J. Dentzer-Feydy. "Les linteaux à figures divines en Syrie méridionale." *RA* 1992: 65-102.

Dentzer-Feydy 1995. J. Dentzer-Feydy. "Remarques sur la métrologie et le project architectural de quelques monuments d'époque hellénistique et romaine en Transjordanie." Pp. 161-71 in *SHAJ* V.

Dentzer-Feydy 2003. J. Dentzer-Feydy. "Le sanctuaire." Pp. 40-109 in Dentzer-Feydy, Dentzer and Blanc 2003.

Dentzer-Feydy and Teixidor 1993. J. Dentzer-Feydy and J. Teixidor. *Les antiquités de Palmyre au Musée du Louvre*. Paris.

Dentzer-Feydy, Dentzer and Blanc 2003. J. Dentzer-Feydy and J.-M. Dentzer and P.-M. Blanc. Teixidor. *Hauran II. Les installations de Si'8: du sanctuaire à l'établissement viticole*. BAH 164. Beirut.

Dijkstra 1995. K. Dijkstra. *Life and Loyality. A Study in the Socio-Religious Culture of Syria and Mesopotamia in the Graeco-Roman Period Based on Epigraphical Evidence*. Leiden, New York and Cologne.

Dodinet, Leblanc and Vallat 1993. M. Dodinet, J. Leblanc and J.P. Vallat. "Étude géomorphologique des paysages antiques de Syrie." Pp. 425-42 in P.N. Doukélis and L.G. Mendoni, eds. *Structures rurales et sociétés antiques*. Actes du Colloque international de Corfou, May 1993.

Donner 1995. H. Donner. *Isis in Petra*. Leipzig.

Doughty 1891. C. Doughty. "Documents épigraphiques recueillis dans le nord de l'Arabie." (Edited by E. Renan). *Notices et extraits des manuscrits de la Bibliothèque Nationale et autres bibliothèques* 29: 1-64.

Dubois 1907. C. Dubois. *Pouzzoles Antique (Histoire et Topographie)*. Bibliothèque des Écoles françaises d'Athenes et de Rome 98. Paris.

Dunand 1934. M. Dunand. *Le Musée de Soueïda*. Paris.

Duncan-Jones 1982. R. Duncan-Jones. *The Economy of the Roman Empire: Quantitative Studies*, 2nd edition. Cambridge, England.

Duval 1994. N. Duval. "L'architecture chretienne et les pratiques liturgiques en Jordanie en rapport avec la Palestine: recherches nouvelles." Pp. 149-212 in K. Painter, ed. *Churches Built in Ancient Times. Recent Studies in Early Christian Archaeology*. London.

Eadie 1989. J.W. Eadie. "Strategies of Economic Development in the Roman East: The Red Sea Trade Revisited." Pp. 113-20 in D.H. French and C.S. Lightfoot, eds. *The Eastern Frontier of the Roman Empire*. BAR International Series 553 (1).

Edelman 1995. D.V. Edelman, ed. *You Shall Not Abhor an Edomite for He is Your Brother*. Atlanta.

Edens and Bawden 1989. C. Edens and G. Bawden. "History of Tayma' and Hejazi Trade during the First Millennium B.C." *JESHO* 32: 48-103.

Edmonds 1985. C.L. Edmonds. "The Road to Petra." In *Art and Antiques*. February. New York.

Eph'al 1982. I. Eph'al. *The Ancient Arabs. Nomads on the Borders of the Fertile Crescent 9th-5th Centuries B.C.* Jerusalem and Leiden.

Epiphanius 1922. Epiphanius of Salamis. *Panarion haer.* K. Holl, ed. GCS 31. Leipzig.

Epiphanius 1980. Epiphanius of Salamis. *Panarion* II *haer.* 34-64, (Greek Text). K. Holl, ed. 2nd edition. Berlin.

Epiphanius 1994. Epiphanius of Salamis. *The Panarion of Epiphanius of Salamis*. F. Williams, transl. Vol. 2. Nag Hammadi Studies. Vol. 36). Leiden.

Ettlinger, Hedinger and Hoffmann 1990. E. Ettlinger, B. Hedinger and B. Hoffmann. *Conspectus formarum terrae sigillatae italico modo confectae*. Bonn.

Eusebius 1975. Eusebius, Bishop of Caesarea. *Der Jesajakommentar*, J. Ziegler, ed. GCS 9. Berlin.

Farioli Campanati 1988. R. Farioli Campanati. "Relazioni sugli Scavi e ricerche della missione Italo-Siriana a Bosra (1985, 1986, 1987)." Pp. 45-92 in *XXXV Corso di Cultura sull'Arte Ravennate e Bizantina*. Ravenna.

Farioli Campanati 1999. R. Farioli Campanati. "Bosra: le ricerche della Missione Archeologica Italo-Siriana nel quartiere N.E. Rapporto introductivo e sintesi dei principali interventi nell'ultimo decennio." *Felix Ravenna* 145-148: 1993 (1-2); 1994 (1-2); 1999: 97-144 (with bibliography).

Farioli Campanati and al-Muqdad 1996. R. Farioli Campanati and R. al-Muqdad. "Bosra." Pp. 167-70 in E. Peltenburg, Jerablus-Tahtani, *Syrian-European Archaeology Exhibition: Working Together.* Damascus.

Fedalto 1988. G. Fedalto. *Hierarchia Ecclesiastica Orientalis*. Series Episcoporum Ecclesiarum Christianarum Orientalium II. Padova.

Fellmann Brogli 1996. R. Fellmann Brogli. "Die Keramik aus den spätrömischen Bauten." Pp. 219-81 in Bignasca 1996.

Fiaccadori 1999. G. Fiaccadori. "Nuova dedica a Dusares da Bosra." *Felix Ravenna* 1993 1-2/1994 1-2: 145-48.

Fiema 1988. Z.T. Fiema. "The Era of Bostra. A Reconsideration." Pp. 109-21 in *The Proceedings of the XXXV Corso di Cultura sull'Arte Ravennate e Bizantina. La Siria Araba da Roma a Bisanzio*. Ravenna.

Fiema 1991. Z.T. Fiema. *Economics, Administration and Demography of Late Roman and Byzantine Southern Transjordan*. Ph.D. Dissertation, University of Utah.

Fiema 1994. Z.T. Fiema. "Jordanie: une eglise byzantin a Petra." *Archaeologia* 302: 26-35.

Fiema 1997. Z.T. Fiema. "Petra: Roman Street Project." *ACORN* 9 (1): 8-9.

Fiema 1998. Z.T. Fiema. "The Roman Street of the Petra Project, 1997. A Preliminary Report." *ADAJ* 42: 395-424.

Fiema 2001 . Z.T. Fiema, et al. *The Petra Church*. ACOR Publications 3. Amman.

Fiema 2001b. Z.T. Fiema. "Reconstructing the History of the Petra Church: Data and Phasing." Pp. 7-137 in Fiema 2001a.

Fiema 2001c. Z.T. Fiema. "The Archaeological Context of the Petra Papyri." Pp. 139-52 in Fiema 2001a.

Fiema 2001d. Z.T. Fiema. "Historical Conclusions." Pp. 425-36 in Fiema 2001a.

Fiema 2002. Z.T. Fiema. "Petra and Its Hinterland during the Byzantine Period: New Research and Interpretations." Pp. 191-252 in J. Humphrey, ed. *The Roman and Byzantine Near East: Some recent Archaeological: Some New Discoveries III*. JRA Supplementary Series 49.

Fiema and Jones 1990. Z.T. Fiema and R.N. Jones. "The Nabataean King-List Revised: Further Observations on the Second Nabataean Inscription from Tell esh-Shuqafiya, Egypt." *ADAJ* 34: 239-48.

Fiema, Schick and 'Amr 1995. Z.T. Fiema, R. Schick and Kh. 'Amr. "The Petra Church Project 1992-1994. Interim Report." Pp. 289-303 in J. Humphrey, ed. *The Roman and Byzantine Near East: Some Recent Archaeological Research*. JRA Supplementary Series 14.

Fittschen 1996. K. Fittschen. "Wall Decorations in Herod's Kingdom: Their Relationship with Wall Decorations in Greece and Italy." Pp. 139-61 in K. Fittschen and G. Foerster, eds. *Judea and the Greco-Roman World in the Time of Herod in the Light of Archaeological Evidence*. Göttingen.

Foerster 1995. G. Foerster. *Masada V. The Yigael Yadin Excavations 1963-1965, Final Reports. Art and Architecture*. Jerusalem.

Finden and Finden 1836. E.F. Finden and W. Finden. *Landscape Illustrations of the Bible*, 2 vols. London.

de Franciscis 1975. A. De Franciscis. *The Pompeian Wall Paintings in the Roman Villa of Oplontis*. Recklinghausen.

Frank 1940. T. Frank. *An Economic Survey of Ancient Rome 5. Rome and Italy of the Empire*. Baltimore.

Freeman 1941. R.B. Freeman. "Nabataean Sculpture in the Cincinnati Art Museum." *AJA* 45: 337-41.

Freyberger 1988. K.S. Freyberger. "Zur Datierung des Theaters in Bosra." *DaM* 3: 17-26.

Freyberger 1989. K.S. Freyberger. "Einige Beobachtungen zur städtebaulichen Entwicklung des römischen Bostra." *DaM* 4: 45-60.

Freyberger 1991. K.S. Freyberger. "Zur Datierung des Grabmals des Sextius Florentinus in Petra." *DaM* 5: 1-8.

Freyberger 1998. K.S. Freyberger. *Die frühkaiserzeitlichen Heiligtümer der Karawanstationen im hellenisierten Osten: Zeugnisse eines kulturellen Konflikts im Spannungsfeld zweier politischer Formationen*. Damaszener Forschungen 6. Mainz.

Frösén 1998. J. Frösén, et al. "The 1998 Finnish Jabal Haroun Project – A Preliminary Report." *ADAJ* 42: 420-39.

Frösén 1999. J. Frösén, et al. "The 1998 Finnish Jabal Haroun Project. A Preliminary Report." *ADAJ* 43: 369-410.

Frösén 2000. J. Frösén, et al. "The 1999 Finnish Jabal Haroun Project – A Preliminary Report." *ADAJ* 44: 395-424.

Frösén 2001a. J. Frösén, et al. "The 2000 Finnish Jabal Haroun Project – A Preliminary Report." *ADAJ* 45: 359-76.

Frösén 2001b. J. Frösén, et al. "The 1998-2000 Finnish Jabal Haroun Project – Specialized Reports." *ADAJ* 45: 377-92.

Frösén and Fiema 2002. J. Frösén and Z.T. Fiema, eds. *Petra, A City Forgotten and Rediscovered*, exh. cat. Helsinki.

Frösén, Arjava and Lehtinen 2002. J. Frösén, A. Arjava and M. Lehtinen, eds. *The Petra Papyri* I. ACOR Publications 4. Amman. (*P. Petra*).

Gagos 2001. T. Gagos. "Negotiating Money and Space in Sixth Century Petra." Pp. 459-509 in Atti XXII Congresso 2001.

Gagos and van Minnen 1994. T. Gagos and P. van Minnen. *Settling a Dispute. Towards a Legal Anthropology of Late Antique Egypt*. Ann Arbor.

Gascou 1985. J. Gascou. "Les grands domaines, la cité et l'état en Égypte Byzantine." *Travaux et Mémoires* 9: 1-90.

Gascou 1999. J. Gascou. "Unités administratives locales et fonctionnaires romains. Les données des nouveaux papyrus du Moyen Euphrate et d'Arabie. La pétition de Bostra (P. Bostra 1; 29 mai 260)." Pp. 61-73 in W. Eck, ed. *Lokale Autonomie und römische Ordnungsmacht in den kaiserzeitlichen Provinzen vom 1. bis 3. Jahrhundert. Schriften des Historischen Kollegs, Kolloquien* 42. Munich.

Gatier and Salles 1988. P.-L. Gatier and J.-F. Salles, "Aux Frontières méridionales du domain nabatéen." Pp. 173-90 in J.-F. Salles, ed. *L'Arabie et ses mers bordieres* I. *Itinéraires et Voisinages. Séminaire de Recherche 1985-1986*. Lyon.

Gawlikowski 1975-1976. M. Gawlikowski. "Les tombeaux anonymes." *Berytus* 24: 35-41.

Gawlikowski 1977. M. Gawlikowski. "Le temple d'Allat à Palmyre." *RA* 1977: 266-69.

Gawlikowski 1983. M. Gawlikowski. "Reflexions sur la chronologie du sanctuaire d'Allat à Palmyre." *DaM* 1: 59-67, PLS. 13-14.

Gawlikowski 1994. M. Gawlikowski. "Palmyra as a Trading center." *Iraq* 56: 27-33.

Geremek 1981. H. Geremek. "Les politeuomenoi égyptiens, sont-ils identiques aux bouleutaï?" *Anagennesis* 1: 231-47.

de Geus 1979-1980. C.H.J. de Geus. "Idumaea." *JEOL* 26: 53-74.

al-Ghul 1999. O. al-Ghul. "The Names of Buildings in the Greek Papyrus No. 10 from Petra." *Proceedings of the Seminar for Arabian Studies* 29: 67-71.

Gibson 1975. J.C.L. Gibson. *Textbook of Syrian Semitic Inscriptions*. Vol. 2: *Aramaic Inscriptions including inscriptions in the dialect of Zenjirli*. Oxford.

Gichon 1993. M. Gichon. "En Boqeq." Pp. 395-99 in *NEAEHL* I.

Glueck 1935. N. Glueck. *Explorations in Eastern Palestine* II = *AASOR* 15.

Glueck 1937a. N. Glueck. "A Newly Discovered Nabataean Temple." *AJA* 41: 361-76.

Glueck 1937b. N. Glueck. "Explorations in Eastern Palestine III." *BASOR* 65: 15-19.

Glueck 1937c. N. Glueck. "The Nabataean Temple of Khirbet et-Tannûr." *BASOR* 67: 6-16.

Glueck 1937-1939. N. Glueck. *Explorations in Eastern Palestine* III = *AASOR* 18-19.

Glueck 1938. N. Glueck. "The Early History of a Nabataean Temple." *BASOR* 69: 7-18.

Glueck 1952. N. Glueck. "The Zodiac of Khirbet et-Tannûr." *BASOR* 126: 5-10.

Glueck 1956. N. Glueck. "The Fourth Season of Exploration in the Negeb." *BASOR* 142: 17-35.

Glueck 1965. N. Glueck. *Deities and Dolphins. The Story of the Nabataeans*. London and New York.

Glueck 1978. N. Glueck. "Et-Tannur, Khirbet." Pp. 1152-59 in M. Avi-Yonah and E. Stern, eds. *Encyclopedia of Archaeological Excavations in the Holy Land* IV. Oxford.

Godlewski 1986. W. Godlewski. *Le Monastère de St. Phoibammon, Deir el-Bahari* 5. Warsaw.

Goldman 1996. B. Goldman. "Nabataean/Syro-Roman Lunate Earrings." *IEJ* 46: 77-99.

Gordon 1977. R.L. Gordon. *Late Hellenistic Wall Decoration of Tel Anafa*. Ann Arbor.

Gory 1976a. M. Gory. "Travaux effectués par l'Institut Géographique National de France." *ADAJ* 21: 79-86, pl. 33-38.

Gory 1976b. M. Gory. "Établissement d'un photoplan." *ADAJ* 21: 87-91, pl. 39-40.

Gory 1978-1979. M. Gory. "Travaux de l'I.G.N. (Institut Géographique National) dans la région de Pétra." Pp. 54-65 in F. Baratte, ed. *Un royaume aux confins du désert. Petra et la Nabatène*, exh.cat. Lyon.

Graeve 1970. V. von Graeve. *Das Alexandersarkophag und seine Werkstatt*. Istanbuler *Forschungen* 28. Berlin.

Graf 1983. D.F. Graf. "Dedanite and Minaean (South Arabian) Inscriptions from the Hisma." *ADAJ* 27: 555-69.

Graf 1988. D.F. Graf. "Qura 'Arabiyya and Provincia Arabia." Pp. 171-203 in *Géographie Historique au Proche-Orient Syrie, Phénicie, Arabie, grecques, romaines, byzantines. Actes de la table ronde*. Notes et Monographies techniques 23. Paris.

Graf 1990. D.F. Graf. "The Origin of the Nabataeans." *ARAM* 2: 45-75.

Graf 1992. D.F. Graf. "Nabataeans." Pp. 970-73 in *The Anchor Bible Dictionary* 4. New York.

Graf 1996. D.F. Graf. "The Roman East from the Chinese Perspective." Pp. 199-216 in *Palmyra and the Silk Road*. AAAS 42.

Graf 1997a. D.F. Graf. "Nabataeans." Pp. 82-85 in *OxEANE*.

Graf 1997b. D.F. Graf. *Rome and the Arabian Frontier: from the Nabataeans to the Saracens*. Aldershot, Hampshire, Great Britain and Brookfield, VT.

Graf 1998. D.F. Graf. "Les circulations entre Syrie, Palestine, Jordanie et Sinaï aux époques grecque et romaine." Pp. 107-13 in D. Valbelle and C. Bonnet, eds. *Le Sinaï durant l'antiquité et le moyen age*. Paris.

Green 1909. F.W. Green. "Notes on Some Inscriptions in the Etbai District. II." *Proceedings of the Society of Biblical Archaeology* (December 1909): 319-23.

Green 1998. J.R. Green. "Appendix: A Note in the Classification of Some Masks and Faces from Petra." *PEQ* 30: 43-50.

Greene 1986. K. Greene. *The Archaeology of the Roman Economy*. Berkeley and Los Angeles.

Grenfell and Hunt 1915. B.P. Grenfell and A.S. Hunt. *The Oxyrhynchus Papyri* 11. London.

Grohmann 1967-1971. A. Grohmann. *Arabische Paläographie*. 2 vols. Denkschriften. Österreichische Akademie der Wissenschaften. Wien. Philosophisch-historische Klasse 94.1. Vienna.

Groom 1981. N. Groom. *Frankincense and Myrrh: A Study of the Arabian Incense Trade*. London and New York.

Gruendler 1993. B. Gruendler. *The Development of the Arabic Scripts. From the Nabatean Era to the First Islamic Century According to Dated Texts*. Harvard Semitic Studies, no. 43. Atlanta.

Gualandi 1975. G. Gualandi. "Una città carovaniera della Siria meridionale : Bosra romana e la recente esplorazione archeologica nella cathedrale dei Ss. Sergio, Bacco e Leonzio." *Felix Ravenna* 109-110: 187-239.

Guidoni Guidi 1979. G. Guidoni Guidi. "Considerazioni sulla simbologia cosmica nell'arte giudaica lo Zodiaco." *Felix Ravenna* 117: 131-54.

Guimier-Sorbets and Seif el-Din 1997. A.-M. Guimier-Sorbets and M. Seif el-Din. "Les deuxes tombes de Perséphone dans la nécropole de Kom el-Chougafa à Alexandrie." *BCH* 121: 355-410.

Hachlili 1977. R. Hachlili. "The Zodiac in Ancient Jewish Art: Representation and Significance." *BASOR* 228: 61-77.

Haensch 1997. R. Haensch. *Capita provinciarum. Statthaltersitze und Provinzialverwaltung in der römischen Kaiserzeit*. Mainz.

Hagedorn and Youtie 1969. U. and D. Hagedorn and L.C. and H.C. Youtie. *Das Archiv des Petaus*. Wissenschaftliche Abhandlungen der Arbeitsgemeinschaft für Forschung des Landes Nordrhein-Westfalen, Sonderreihe Papyrologica Coloniensia IV. Cologne and Opladen.

Hammond 1959. P.C. Hammond. "The Nabataean Bitumen Industry at the Dead Sea." *BA* 22: 40-48.

Hammond 1965. P.C. Hammond. *The Excavation of the Main Theater at Petra, 1961-1962. Final Report*. London.

Hammond 1975. P.C. Hammond. "Survey and Excavation at Petra 1973-1974." *ADAJ* 20: 5-30, 145-54.

Hammond 1977-1978. P.C. Hammond. "Excavations at Petra 1975-1977." *ADAJ* 22: 81-101.

Hammond 1979. P.C. Hammond, et al. "Epigraphy." Pp. 243-49 in D.S. Whitcomb and J.H. Johnson, eds. *Quseir al-Qadim 1978 Preliminary Report*. Princeton and Cairo.

Hammond 1980a. P.C. Hammond. "New Evidence for the 4th-Century AD, Destruction of Petra." *BASOR* 238: 65-67.

Hammond 1980b. P.C. Hammond. "Ein nabataïsches Weiherelief aus Petra." *BJ* 180: 137-41.

Hammond 1986. P.C. Hammond. "Die Ausgrabungen des Löwen-Greifen-Tempels in Petra (1973-1983)." Pp. 16-30 in Lindner 1986.

Hammond 1987. P.C. Hammond. "Three Workshops at Petra Jordan." *PEQ* 119: 129-41.

Hammond 1990. P.C. Hammond. "The Goddess of the 'Temple of the Winged Lions' at Petra, Jordan." Pp. 115-30 in Zayadine 1990a.

Hammond 1992. P.C. Hammond. "The Goddess of The Temple of the Winged Lions, at Petra (Jordan)." In "Petra and the Caravan Cities." *Arabesque* 17/18: 115-27.

Hammond 1996. P.C. Hammond. *The Temple of the Winged Lions, Petra, Jordan 1974-1990*. Fountain Hills, AZ.

Hammond 2002. P.C. Hammond. "A Note on a Zodiac Lamp from Petra." *PEQ* 134: 165-68.

Hammond, Johnson and Jones 1986. P.C. Hammond, D.J. Johnson and R.N. Jones. "A Religio-Legal Nabataean Inscription from the Atargatis/Al-'Uzza Temple at Petra." *BASOR* 203: 77-80.

Hannestad 1983. L. Hannestad. The Hellenistic Pottery from Failaka, Ikaros. *The Hellenistic Settlements* 2. Copenhagen.

Harding 1971. G.L. Harding. *An Index and Concordance of Pre-Islamic Arabian Names and Inscriptions*. Toronto.

Hausmann 1996. U. Hausmann. *Hellenistische Keramik*. Olympische Forschungen 27. Berlin and New York.

Hayes 1985. J.W. Hayes. "Sigillate Orientali." Pp. 1-96 in *Atlante delle forme ceramiche II. Ceramica fine romana nel bacino mediterraneo. Enciclopedia dell'arte antica. Classica e orientale*. Rome.

Hayes 1995. J.W. Hayes. "Summary of Pottery and Glass Finds." Pp. 33-40 in S.E. Sidebotham and W.Z. Wendrich, eds. *Berenike 1994. Preliminary Report of the 1994 Excavations at Berenike (Egyptian Red Sea Coast) and the Survey of the Eastern Desert*. Leiden.

Hayes 1996. J.W. Hayes. *Berenike 1995. Preliminary Report of the 1994 Excavations at Berenike (Egyptian Red Sea Coast) and the Survey of the Eastern Desert*. Leiden.

Healey 1989. J.F. Healey. "Were the Nabataeans Arabs?" *ARAM* 1: 31-37.

Healey 1993. J.F. Healey. *The Nabataean Tomb Inscriptions of Mada'in Salih*. JSS Supplement 1. Oxford.

Healey 1995. J.F. Healey. "Death in West Semitic Texts: Ugarit and Nabataea." Pp. 188-91 in S. Campbell and A. Green, eds. *Archaeology of Death in the Ancient Near East*. Oxbow Monograph 51. Oxford.

Healey 2001. J.F. Healey. *The Religion of the Nabataeans. A Conspectus*. Leiden.

Healey and Smith 1989. J.F. Healey and G.R. Smith. "Jaussen-Savignac 17: he Earliest Dated Arabic Document (A.D. 267)." *Atlal* 12: 77-84.

Heermann 1986. V. Heermann. *Studien zur makedonischen Palastarchitektur*. PhD dissertation, University of Erlangen-Nürnberg.

Heilmeyer 1970. W.-D. Heilmeyer. *Korinthische Normalkapitelle*. Römische Mitteilungen, Ergänzungsheft 16. Heidelberg.

Heisenberg and Wenger 1986. A. Heisenberg and L. Wenger, eds (2nd edition by D. Hagedorn). Die Papyri der Bayerischen Staatsbibliothek München, I Griechische Papyri 1-18. Stuttgart.

Hellenkemper-Salies 1981. G. Hellenkemper-Salies. *Die Nabatäer*, exh. cat. Bonn.

Herrmann 2001 . J.J. Herrmann, Jr. "Crater with Panther Handles." Pp. 337-39 in Fiema 2001A.

Herrmann 2001b. J.J. Herrmann, Jr. "Basin and Pedestal." Pp. 340-41 in Fiema 2001a.

Hesberg 1994. H. von Hesberg. *Formen privater Repräsentation in der Baukunst des 2. und 1. Jahrhunderts v. Chr.* Cologne, Weimar and Vienna.

Hiller von Gaertringen 1906. F. Hiller von Gaertringen. *Inschriften von Priene*. Berlin.

Hornblower 1981. J. Hornblower. *Hieronymus of Cardia*. Oxford.

Horrowitz 1980. G. Horrowitz. "Town Planning of Ancient Marisa: A Reappraisal of the Excavations after Eighty Years." *PEQ* 112: 93-111.

Horsfield 1938. G. and A. Horsfield. "Sela-Petra, the Rock, of Edom and Nabatene." *QDAP* 7: 1-60, pl. 1-74.

Horsfield 1941. G. and A. Horsfield. "Sela-Petra, the Rock, of Edom and Nabatene IV. The Finds." *QDAP* 9: 105-204.

Hübner 1993. G. Hübner. *Die Applikenkeramik von Pergamon. Eine Bildersprache im Dienst des Herrscherkultes*. Pergamenische Forschungen 7. Berlin.

Hübner, Knauf and Wenning 1998. U. Hübner, E.A. Knauf and R. Wenning, eds. *Nach Petra und ins Königreich der Nabatäer. Notizen von Reisegefährten. Für Manfred Lindner zum 80. Geburtstag*. Bonner Biblische Beiträge 188. Bodenheim.

Ingraham 1981. M.L. Ingraham, et al. "Saudi Arabian Comprehensive Survey Program: c. Preliminary Report on a Reconnaissance Survey of the Northwestern Province (with a Note on a Brief Survey of the Northern Province)." *Atlal* 5: 58-84.

Irby and Mangles 1823. Ch.L. Irby and J. Mangles. *Travels in Egypt and Nubia, Syria, and Asia Minor during the Years 1817 and 1818*. London.

Isaac 1992. B. Isaac. "The Babatha Archive: A Review Article." *IEJ* 42: 62-75. Reprinted 1998, pp. 159-81 in B. Isaac. *The Near East under Roman Rule*. Leiden.

Jarret 1969. M.G. Jarret. "Thracian Units in the Roman Army." *IEJ* 19: 215-24.

Jaussen and Savignac 1909 and 1914. A. Jaussen and M.R. Savignac. *Mission archéologique en Arabie I-II*. Paris.

Jaussen and Savignac 1909-1922. A. Jaussen and M.R. Savignac. *Mission archéologique en Arabie*. 6 vols. Paris.

Jaussen, Savignac, and Vincent 1905. A. Jaussen, M.R. Savignac and H. Vincent. *'Abdeh* (4-9 février 1904) (suite). RB internationale (N.S.) 2: 74-89, 235-57.

Jobling 1990. W.J. Jobling. "Some new Nabataean and North Arabian Inscriptions of the Hisma in Southern Jordan." *ARAM* 2: 99-111.

John of Ephesus 1923. John of Ephesus. *Lives of the Eastern Saints*. Syriac text edited and translated by E.W. Brooks. Patrologia Orientalis. Vol. XVII. Paris.

John of Malalas 1986. John Malalas. *The Chronicle of John Malalas*. E. Jeffreys, M. Jeffreys and R. Scott, transls. Melbourne.

John of Nikiu 1916. John, Bishop of Nikiu. *The Chronicle of John, Bishop of Nikiu*. Translated from Zotenberg's Ethiopic Text by R.H. Charles. London.

Johnson 1987. D.J. Johnson. *Nabataean Trade: Intensification and Cultural Change*. PhD dissertation, University of Utah.

Johnson 1990. D.J. Johnson. "Nabataean Piriform Unguentaria." *ARAM* 2: 235-48.

Johnson 1991. M.J. Johnson. "Bema." P. 281 in A.P. Kazhdan, et. al., eds. *ODByz* 1.

Johnson and Cutler 1991. M.J. Johnson and A. Cutler. "Synthronon." P. 1996 in *ODByz* 3.

Johnson and West 1949. A.Ch. Johnson and L.C. West. *Byzantine Egypt: Economic Studies*. Princeton.

Jones 1964. A.H.M. Jones. *The Later Roman Empire 284-602*. Oxford.

Jones 1988. R.N. Jones, et al. "A Second Nabataean Inscription from Tell esh-Shuqafiyah, Egypt." *BASOR* 269: 47-57.

Jones 1989. R.N. Jones. "A New Reading of the Petra Temple Inscription." *BASOR* 275: 41-46.

Jones and Bowersock 2001. R.N. Jones and G.W. Bowersock. "Nabataean Inscriptions." Pp. 346-49 in Fiema 2001A.

Joukowsky 1997a. M.S. Joukowsky. "The Water Canalization System of the Petra Southern Temple." Pp. 303-11 in SHAJ VI.

Joukowsky 1997b. M. Joukowsky. In M. Joukowsky and K. Freyberger. "Blattranken, Greifen un Elephanten." Pp. 84-86 in Weber and Wenning 1997.

Joukowsky 1998. M. Joukowsky. *Petra Great Temple. Vol. 1: Brown University Excavations 1993-1997*. Providence.

Kader 1996. I. Kader. *Propylon und Bogentor. Untersuchungen zum Tetrapylon von Latakia und anderen frühkaiserzeitlichen Bogenmonumenten im Nahen Osten*. Damaszener Forschungen 7. Mainz.

Kadour and Seeden 1983. M. Kadour and H. Seeden. "Busra 1980: Reports of an Archaeological and Ethnographic Campaign." *DaM* 1: 77-102.

Kaimio 2001. M. Kaimio. "P. Petra Inv. 83: A Settlement of Dispute. Vol. II." Pp. 719-24 in *Atti del XXII Congresso Internazionale di Papirologia*. Florence.

al-Kalbi 1924. H. Ibn al-Kalbi. *Kitab al-Asnam*. Ahmad Zaki, ed. Cairo.

Kammerer 1929-1930. A. Kammerer. *Pétra et la Nabatène. L'Arabie Pétrée et les Arabes du Nord dans leurs rapports avec la Syrie et la Palestine jusqu'a l'Islam*. 2 vols. Paris.

Kanellopoulos 1998. Ch. Kanellopoulos. "Petra: Colonnaded Street and Shops." *ACORN* 10 (1): 1-4.

Kanellopoulos 2001. Ch. Kanellopoulos. "The Architecture of the Complex." Pp. 152-91 in Fiema 2001a.

Kanellopoulos and Schick 2001. Ch. Kanellopoulos and R. Schick. "Marble Furnishings of the Apses and the Bema, Phase V." Pp. 193-214 in Fiema 2001a.

Kazhdan 1991a. A.P. Kazhdan. "Monophysitism." Pp. 1398-99 in A.P. Kazhdan, et al., eds. *ODByz* 2.

Kazhdan 1991b. A.P. Kazhdan. "Nestorianism." Pp. 1459-60 in A.P. Kazhdan, et al., eds. *ODByz* 2.

Kennedy 1925. A.B.W. Kennedy. *Petra, Its History and Monuments*. London.

Khairy 1982. N.I. Khairy. "Fine Nabataean Ware with Impressed and Rouletted Decorations." Pp. 275-83 in *SHAJ* I.

Khairy 1990. N.I. Khairy. *The 1981 Petra Excavations I. Abhandlungen des Deutschen Pallästinavereins* 13. Wiesbaden.

Khairy and Milik 1981. N.I. Khairy and J.T. Milik. "A New Dedicatory Nabataean Inscription from Wadi Musa." *PEQ* 113: 19-26.

al-Khraysheh 1994. F. al-Khraysheh. "Eine safaitisch-nabatäische bilingue Inschrift aus Jordanien." Pp. 109-14 in Nebes 1994.

al-Khraysheh 2000. F. al-Khraysheh. "An Arabic Inscription written in Thamudic script from Jordan." *Adumatu* 2: 59-70 (in Arabic with an English abstract).

King 1990. G.M.H. King. *Early North Arabian Thamudic E. Preliminary Description Based on a New Corpus of Inscriptions from the Hismae Desert of Southern Jordan and Published Material*. Ph.D. dissertation, The University of London.

Kirkbride 1960. D.V.W. Kirkbride. "A Short Account of the Excavations at Petra in 1955-56." *ADAJ* 4-5: 117-22.

Kisnawi 1983. A. Kisnawi, et al. "Preliminary Report on the Mining Survey, Northwest Hijaz, 1982." *Atlal* 7: 76-83.

Kitzinger 1938. E. Kitzinger. "Notes on Early Coptic Sculpture." *Archaeologia* 87: 181-215.

Knauf 1989. E.A. Knauf. "Nabataean Origins." Pp. 56-61 in M.M. Ibrahim. *Arabian Studies in Honour of Mahmoud Ghul*. Wiesbaden.

Knauf 1990. E.A. Knauf. "Dushara and Shai' al-Qaum." *ARAM* 2: 175-83.

Knauf 1998. E.A. Knauf. "Götter nach Petra tragen." Pp. 92-101 in Hübner, Knauf and Wenning 1998.

Koenen 1968. L. Koenen and W. Müller-Wiener. "Zu den Papyri aus dem Arseniuskloster." *ZPE* 2: 41-63.

Koenen 1996a. L. Koenen. "The Phoenix from the Ashes: The Burnt Archive from Petra." *Michigan Quarterly Review* 35: 513-31.

Koenen 1996b. L. Koenen. "The Carbonized Archive from Petra." *JRA* 9: 177-88.
Koenen 2002. L. Koenen. "The Decipherment and Edition of the Petra Papyri: Preliminary Observations." (In collaboration with R.Ch. Caldwell, R.W. Daniel and T. Gagos.) Pp. 201-26 in L.H. Schiffman, ed. *A Climate of Creativity: Semitic Papyrology in Context. Papers from a New York University Conference marking the Retirement of Baruch A. Levine*. Leiden.
Koenen, Fiema and Zayadine 1997. Z. Fiema, L. Koenen and F. Zayadine. "Petra Romana, Byzantina et Islamica." Pp. 145-63 in Weber and Wenning 1997.
Kohl 1910. H. Kohl. *Kasr Firaun in Petra*. Leipzig.
Kolb 1996. B. Kolb. "Die Spätrömischen Bauten." Pp. 51-88 in *Petra. Ez Zantur I. Ergebnisse der Schweizerisch-Liechtensteinischen Ausgrabungen 1998-1992*. Terra Archaeologica 2. Mainz.
Kolb 1997. B. Kolb. "Petra – eine Zeltstadt in Stein." Pp. 62-66 in Weber and Wenning 1997.
Kolb 2000. L. Koenen. "Die spätantiken Wohnbauten von ez-Zantur in Petra und der Wohnhausbau in Palästina vom 4.-6. Jh. n.Chr. Part 2 in *Petra. Ez Zantur II. Ergebnisse der Schweizerisch-Liechtensteinischen Ausgrabungen*. Mainz.
Kolb, Keller and Fellmann Brogli 1997. B. Kolb, D. Keller and R. Fellmann Brogli. "Swiss Liechtenstein Excavations at ez-Zantur in Petra 1996. The Seventh Season." *ADAJ* 41: 231-54.
Kolb, Keller and Gerber 1998. B. Kolb, D. Keller and Y. Gerber. "Swiss-Liechtenstein Excavations at ez-Zantur in Petra 1997." *ADAJ* 42 —.
Kossatz 1990. A.-U. Kossatz. *Die megarischen Becher*. Milet 5 (1). Berlin and New York.
Kovalenko 1996. S.A. Kovalenko. "Some Notes on the Production of Hellenistic Mould-Made Relief Ware in the Bosporan Kingdom." Pp. 51-57 in G.R. Tsetskhladze, ed. *Colloquia Pontica 1. New Studies on the Black Sea Littoral*. Oxford.
Kraeling 1938. C. Kraeling. *Gerasa. City of the Decapolis*. New Haven.
Kraemer 1958. C.J. Kraemer, Jr. *Excavations at Nessana 3. Non-literary Papyri*. Princeton. (*P. Ness.*)
Krautheimer 1965. R. Krautheimer. *Early Christian and Byzantine Architecture*. Baltimore.
Kropp 1994. M. Kropp. "A Puzzle of Old Arabic Tenses and Syntax: The Inscription of 'En 'Avdat." *Proceedings of the Seminar for Arabian Studies*: 165-74.
Kühlenthal and Fischer 2000. M. Kühlenthal and H. Fischer, eds. *Petra. Die Restaurierung der Grabfassaden*. Arbeitshefte des Bayerischen Landesamtes für Denkmalpflege 105.
de Laborde 1830. L. de Laborde. *Voyage de l'Arabie Pétrée par Léon de Laborde et Linant*. Paris.
de Laborde 1836. L. de Laborde. *Journey through Arabia Petraea, to Mount Sinai, and the Excavated City of Petra, the Edom of the Prophecies*. London.
de Laborde 1994. L. de Laborde. *Pétra Retrouvée. Voyage de l'Arabie Pétrée, 1828. Léon de Laborde et Linant de Bellefonds*. Paris.
Lampe 1961. G.W.H. Lampe. *A Patristic Greek Lexicon*. Oxford.
Laniado 1997. A. Laniado. "Bouleuta et politeuÒmenoi." *CdE* 72: 130-44.
Laumonier 1977. A. Laumonier. *La céramique hellénistique à reliefs. 1. Ateliers 'ioniens'*. Délos 31. Paris.
Lauter 1971. H. Lauter. "Ptolemais in Libyen. Ein Beitrag zur Baukunst Alexandrias." *JdI* 86: 149-78.
Leclant 1986. J. Leclant. "Isis, déesse universelle et divinité locale, dans le monde gréco-romain." *Iconographie classique et identité régional*. BCH Supplement IVX. Paris.
Lemaire 1995. A. Lemaire. "Les inscription araméennes anciennes de Teima sur les pistes de Teima." Pp. 59-72 in H. Lozachmeur, ed. *Présence arab dans le Croissant Fertile avant l'Hégire*. ERC. Paris.
Lenoble, al-Muheisen and Villeneuve 2001. P. Lenoble, Z. al-Muheisen, F. Villeneuve. "Fouilles de Khirbet edh-Dharih (Jordanie), I: Le cimetière au sud du Wadi Sharheh." *Syria* 78: 89-151.
Levi Della Vida 1938. G. Levi Della Vida. "Una bilingue greco-nabatea a Coo. Con una postilla di M. Segre." *Clara Rhodes* 9: 139-48.
Levy 1860. M.A. Levy. "Ueber die nabathäischen Inschriften von Petra, Hauran, vornehmlich der Sinai-Halbinsel und über die Münzlegenden nabathäischer Könige." *ZDMG* 14: 363-484, 594, pl. 1-4.
Lewis 1987. N.N. Lewis. *Nomads and settlers in Syria and Jordan, 1800-1980*. Cambridge, England.
Lewis 1997. N.N. Lewis. "William John Bankes in Petra." Pp. 10-12 in Weber and Wenning 1997.
Lewis and Macdonald 2002. N.N. Lewis and M.C.A. Macdonald. "W.J. Bankes and the Identification of the Nabataean Script, with appendices by M. Sartre, S. Clackson and R.G Hoyland." *Syria* 79.
Lewis, Yadin and Greenfield 1989. N. Lewis, Y. Yadin and J.C. Greenfield, eds. *The Documents from the Bar Kokhba Period in the Cave of Letters: Greek Papyri. Aramaic and Nabataean Signatures and Subscriptions*. Jerusalem. (*P. Yadin*.)
Linant de Bellefonds 2001. P.L. de Bellefonds. "From Cairo to Petra: Léon de Laborde and L.M.A. Linant de Bellefonds, 1828." In P. and J. Starkey, eds. *Interpreting the Orient: Travellers in Egypt and the Near East*. Reading.
Lindner 1980. M. Lindner, ed. *Petra und das Königreich der Nabatäer*. 3rd edition. Munich.
Lindner 1986 . M. Lindner, ed. *Petra Neue Ausgrabungen und Entdeckungen*. Munich and Bad Windsheim.
Lindner 1986 . M. Lindner. "Vom Der-Plateau zu einem nabatäischen Bergheiligtum." Pp. 98-111 in Lindner 1986.
Lindner 1988. M. Lindner. "Eine al-'Uzza-Isis Stele." *ZDPV* 104: 84-91.
Lindner 1997. M. Lindner. "Where Pharaoh's Daughter Got Her Drinking Water From. The Ain Braq Conduit to Petra." *ZDPV* 113: 61-67, pl. 1-12.
Lindner, Gasteiger and Zeitler 1993-1994. M. Lindner, G. Gasteiger and J.P. Zeitler. "Ez-Zantur at Petra – Tower, Palace or Temple?" *AfO* 40/41: 308-19.
Lindsay 1838. Lord Lindsay. *Letters on Egypt, Edom and the Holy Land*. London.
Littmann 1901. E. Littmann. "Deux inscriptions réligieuses de Palmyre." *JA* 2: 381-90.
Littmann 1904. E. Littmann. *Semitic Inscriptions*. Publications of an American Archaeological Expedition to Syria in 1899-1900. Part 4. New York.
Littmann 1914. E. Littmann. *Nabataean Inscriptions from the Southern Ḥaurân*. Publications of the Princeton University Archaeological Expeditions to Syria in 1904-1905 and 1909. Division 4, Section A. Leiden.
Littmann and Meredith 1953. E. Littmann and D. Meredith. "Nabataean Inscriptions from Egypt." *BSOAS* 15: 1-28.
Littmann and Meredith 1954. E. Littmann and D. Meredith. "Nabataean Inscriptions from Egypt-II." *BSOAS* 16, pt. 2: 211-46.
Lorton 1971. D. Lorton. "The Supposed Expedition of Ptolemy II to Persia." *JEA* 57: 160-64.
Lyon 1978. *Un royaume aux confines du desert. Petra et la Nabatène*. Catalogue of an exhibition at the Musèe de Lyon, 18 November 1978 to 28 February 1979. Lyon.
Lyttelton 1974. M. Lyttleton. *Baroque Architecture in Classical Antiquity*. London.
Lyttelton 1990. M. Lyttelton. "Aspects of the Iconography of the Sculptural Decoration of the Khazneh at Petra." Pp. 19-29 in Zayadine 1990a.
Lyttelton and Blagg 1990. M.B. Lyttelton and T.F.C. Blagg. "Sculpture from the Temenos of Qasr el-Bint at Petra." *ARAM* 2: 267-86.
MacAdam 1986. H.I. MacAdam. "Bostra gloriosa." (review article of Sartre 1982, 1985). *Berytus* 34: 169-89.
Macdonald 1991. M.C.A. Macdonald. "Was the Nabataean Kingdom a 'Bedouin State'?" *ZDPV* 107: 102-19.
Macdonald 1993. M.C.A. Macdonald. "Nomads and the Hawran in the Late Hellenistic and Roman Periods: A Reassessment of the Epigraphic Evidence." *Syria* 70: 303-413.
Macdonald 1994. M.C.A. Macdonald. "A Dated Nabataean Inscription from South Arabia." Pp. 132-41 in N. Nebes, ed. *Arabia Felix: Beiträge zur Sprache und Kultur des vorislamischen Arabien. Festschrift Walter W. Müller zum 60*. Geburtstag. Wiesbaden.
Macdonald 1995. M.C.A. Macdonald. "Quelques réflexions sur les Saracènes, l'inscription de Rawwæfa et l'armée romaine." Pp. 93-101 in *Présence arabe dans le Croissant fertile avant l'Hégire*. Paris.
Macdonald 1997. M.C.A. Macdonald. "Trade Routes and Trade Goods at the Northern End of the 'Incense Road' in the First Millennium B.C." Pp. 333-49 in Avanzini 1997.
Macdonald 1998. M.C.A. Macdonald. "Some Reflections on Epigraphy and Ethnicity in the Roman Near East." Pp. 177-90, pl. 16.1 in G. Clarke and D. Harrison, eds. *Identities in the Eastern Mediterranean in Antiquity*. Mediterranean Archaeology 11.
Macdonald 1999. M.C.A. Macdonald. "Personal Names in the Nabataean Realm. A Review Article." *JSS* 44: 251-89.
Macdonald 2000. M.C.A. Macdonald. "Reflections on the Linguistic Map of Pre-Islamic Arabia." *AAE* 11: 28-79.
Macdonald 2002. M.C.A. Macdonald. "Ancient North Arabian." In R.D. Woodard, ed., *The Cambridge Encyclopaedia of Ancient Languages*. Cambridge.
Macdonald 2003. M.C.A. Macdonald. "References to Sī' in the Safaitic Inscriptions." Pp. 278-79 in Dentzer-Feydy, Dentzer and Blanc 2003.
Macdonald forthcoming a. M.C.A. Macdonald. *Old Arabic and its rivals in the Age of Ignorance. Six studies on the emergence of Arabic as a written language*.
Macdonald forthcoming b. M.C.A. Macdonald. "A rock-cut tomb near Dayr al-Kahf, Jordan, with Nabataean and Safaitic inscriptions." In *Fawzi Zayadine festschrift* edited by D.F. Graf and S. Schmidt.
Macdonald and King 1999. M.C.A. Macdonald and G.M.H. King. "Thamudic." Pp. 436-38 in *The Encyclopaedia of Islam* 10. Leiden.
Macdonald and Nehmé forthcoming. M.C.A. Macdonald and L. Nehmé. *The Turkmæniyah Tomb at Petra and its Inscription*. In preparation.
Macdonald and Searight 1982. M.C.A. Macdonald and A. Searight. "The Inscriptions and Rock-Drawings of the Jawa Area: A Preliminary Report on the First Season of Field-work of the Corpus of the Inscriptions of Jordan Project." *ADAJ* 26: 159-72.
Macdonald, al-Mu'azzin and Nehmé 1996. M.C.A. Macdonald, M. al-Mu'azzin and L. Nehmé. "Les inscriptions safaïtiques de Syrie, cent quarante ans après leur découverte." *CRAIBL* 1996: 435-94.
De Maigret 1997. A. De Maigret. "The Frankincense Road from Najran to Ma'an: A Hypothetical Itinerary." Pp. 315-28 in Avanzini 1997.
Makowski 1980. C. Makowski. "Le Nymphée de Bosra: faits et opinions." *Ktema* 5: 113-24.
Mann 1969. J.C. Mann. "A Note on an Inscription from Kurnub." *IEJ* 19: 211-14.
Maraqten 1996. M. Maraqten. "Dangerous Trade Routes: On the Plundering of Caravans in the Pre-Islamic Near East." *ARAM* 8: 213-36.
Margalit 1989. S. Margalit. "On the Transformation of the Mono-Apsidal Churches with Two Pastophoria into Tri-Apsidal Churches." *LA* 39: 143-64.
Margalit 1990. S. Margalit. "The Bi-Apsidal Churches in Palestine, Jordan, Syria, Lebanon and Cyprus." *LA* 40: 321-34.
Martineau 1848. H. Martineau. *Eastern Life Present and Past*. London.
Maspero 1913. J. Maspero, ed. *Papyrus grecs d'époque byzantine*. Catalogue général des antiquités égyptiennes du Musée du Cairo II. (*P. Cairo Masp. II*)
Masturzo 1991-1992. N. Masturzo. "Elementi di disegno urbano a Bosra. Rapporto preliminare sulla zona nord-orientale." *Felix Ravenna* 141-144 (1997): 233-56.
Masturzo 1997. N. Masturzo. "Bosra. Rilievo del tempio e della chiesa numero tre." (Butler) Pp. 453-82 in *Decumano XLIII Corso di Cultura sull'arte Ravennate e Bizantina*. Ravenna
Matthiae 1991. K. Matthiae. "Die nabatäische Felsarchitektur in Petra." *Klio* 73: 226-78.
Mayerson 1994. P. Mayerson. *Monks, Martyrs, Soldiers and Saracens. Papers on the Near East in Late Antiquity* (1962-1993). Jerusalem.
McDonald 1988. B. McDonald. *The Wadi al-Hasa Archaeological Survey 1979-1983. West-Central Jordan*. Waterloo, Ontario.
McKenzie 1988. J.S. McKenzie. "The Development of Nabataean Sculpture at Petra and Khirbet Tannur." *PEQ* 120: 81-107.
McKenzie 1990. J.S. McKenzie. *The Architecture of Petra*. British Academy Monographs in Archaeology, no. 1. Oxford.
McKenzie 2001. J. McKenzie. "Keys from Egypt and the East: Observation on Nabataean Culture in the Light of Recent Discoveries." *BASOR* 324: 97-112.
McKenzie, Gibson and Reyes 2002. J. McKenzie, S. Gibson and A.T. Reyes. "Reconstruction of the Nabataean Temple Complex at Khirbet et-Tannur." *PEQ* 134: 44-83.

McKenzie, Reyes and Gibson in press. J.S. McKenzie, A.T. Reyes and S. Gibson. "Khirbet et-Tannur in the ASOR Nelson Glueck Archive and the Reconstruction of the Temple." *ADAJ* .

McKenzie, Reyes and Schmidt-Colinet 1998. J.S. McKenzie, A.T. Reyes and A. Schmidt-Colinet. "Faces in the Rock at Petra and Medain Saleh." *PEQ* 130: 35-50.

Meredith 1954. D. Meredith. "Inscriptions from the Berenice Road." *CdE* 57: 281-87.

Meredith 1957. D. Meredith. "Inscriptions from amethyst mines at Abu Diyeiba (Eastern Desert of Egypt)." Pp. 117-19 in *Eos Commentarii Societatis Philologae Polonorum* 48 (2). Symbolae Raphaeli Taubenschlag Dedicatae II. Bratislava and Warsaw.

Meshel 1973. Z. Meshel. "The Roads of the Negev according to the Geography of Ptolemy and the Tabula Peutingeriana." Pp. 205-9 in Y. Aharoni, ed. *Excavations and Studies: Essays in honour of Professor Shemuel Yeivin*. (Hebrew). Tel Aviv.

Meshel 1995. Z. Meshel. "The Nabataean 'Rock' and the Judean Desert Fortresses." *Cathedra* 76: 40-48 (Hebrew).

Meshorer 1975. Y. Meshorer. *Nabataean Coins*. Qedem 3.

Meunier 1980. M. Meunier. *Lucient de Samosate, La Déesse Syrienne*. Paris.

Meza 1996. A.I. Meza. "The Egyptian Statuette in Petra and the Isis Cult Connection." *ADAJ* 40: 167-76.

Mildenberg 1996. L. Mildenberg. "Petra on the Frankincense Road?—Again." *ARAM* 8: 55-65.

Milik 1958. J.T. Milik. "Nouvelles inscriptions nabatéennes." *Syria* 35: 227-51.

Milik 1971. J.T. Milik. "Inscriptions grecques et nabatéennes de Rawwafah." Pp. 54-58 in P.J. Parr, G.L. Harding and J.E. Dayton, eds. *Preliminary Survey in North-West Arabia 1968*. Part II: Epigraphy. Bulletin of the Institute of Archaeology 10. London.

Milik 1976. J.T. Milik. "Une inscription bilingue nabatéenne et grecque à Pétra." *ADAJ* 21: 143-52.

Milik 1980. J.T. Milik. "La tribu des Bani 'Amrat en Jordanie de l'époque grecque et romaine." *ADAJ* 24: 41-54.

Milik 1982. J.T. Milik. "Origines des Nabatéens." Pp. 261-65 in *SHAJ* I.

Milik and Starcky 1970. J.T. Milik and J. Starcky. "Nabataean, Palmyrene, and Hebrew Inscriptions." Pp. 139-63 in F.V. Winnett and W.L. Reed. *Ancient Records from North Arabia*. Near and Middle East Series 6. Toronto.

Milik and Starcky 1975. J.T. Milik and J. Starcky. "Nouvelles inscriptions Nabatéennes de Petra." *ADAJ* 20: 118.

Milik and Teixidor 1961. J.T. Milik and J. Teixidor. "New Evidence on the North-Arabia Aktab-Kutba." *BASOR* 163: 22-25.

Millar 1970. F. Millar. "The Roman *Coloniae* of the Near East. A Study of Cultural Relations." Pp. 7-59 in H. Solin and M. Kajava, eds. *Roman Eastern Policy and Other Studies in Roman History*. Societas Scientiarum Fennica, Commentationes Humanarum Litterarum 91. Helsinki.

Millar 1993. F. Millar. *The Roman Near East 31 BC-AD 337*. Cambridge, MA and London.

Miller 1983. D.S. Miller. "Bostra in Arabia. Nabataean and Roman City of the Near East." Pp. 110-27 in R.T. Marchese, ed. *Aspects of Graeco-Roman Urbanism*. BAR International Series 188. Oxford.

Minguzzi 1999. S. Minguzzi. "Bosra. Chiesa dei SS. Sergio, Bacco et Leonzio. Il saggio sud-est del Tetraconco T1 SE (1996)." *Felix Ravenna*, 145-148, 1993 1-2/1994 1-2: 203-6.

Mikalson 1991. J.D. Mikalson. *Honor Thy Gods: Popular Religion in Greek Tragedy*. Chapel Hill.

Mikalson 1998. J.D. Mikalson. *Religion in Hellenistic Athens*. Berkeley and Los Angeles.

Mitsopoulos-Leon 1991. V. Mitsopoulos-Leon. *Die Basilika am Staatsmarkt in Ephesos. Kleinfunde 1. Keramik hellenistischer und römischer Zeit*. Forschungen in Ephesos 9 (2). Vienna.

Mitthof 2001. F. Mitthof. *Annona Militaris, Die Heeresversorgung im spätantiken Ägypten. Ein Beitrag zur Verwaltungs- und Heeresgeschichte des Römischen Reiches im 3. bis 6. Jahrh. n. Chr.* 2 vols. Pap. Flor. XXXII. Florence.

Mordtmann 1932. J.H. Mordtmann. "Ein Nabatäer im Sabäerlande-Dionysos-Orotal." *Klio* 25: 429-33.

Mørkholm 1991. O. Mørkholm. *Early Hellenistic Coinage from the Accession of Alexander to the Peace of Apamea (336-188 B.C.)*. Cambridge, England.

Moughdad 1975. S. Moughdad. "Bosra." *Felix Ravenna* 109-110: 157-62.

Moughdad 1976. S. Moughdad. "Bosra: Aperçu sur l'urbanisation de la ville à l'époque romaine." *Felix Ravenna* 111-112: 65-81.

Moughdad 1978. S. Moughdad. *Bosra. Historical and Archaeological Guide*. Damascus.

Müller 1978. W.W. Müller. "Weihrauch." *Realencyclopädie von Pauly-Wissowa*, Supplement-Band 15: col. 700-77.

al-Muheisen 1986. Z. al-Muheisen. *Techniques hydrauliques dans le sud de la Jordanie en particulier à l'époque nabatéenne*. Unpublished dissertation, University of Paris.

al-Muheisen and Villeneuve 1988. Z. al-Muheisen and F. Villeneuve. "Fouilles à Khirbet edh-Dharih (Jordanie), 1984-1987: un village, son sanctuaire et sa nécropole aux époques nabatéenne et romaine (1er-4è siècles ap. J.-C.)." *CRAIBL* 1988: 458-79.

al-Muheisen and Villeneuve 1994. Z. al-Muheisen and F. Villeneuve. "Découvertes nouvelles à Khirbet edh-Dharih (Jordanie), 1991-1994: autour du sanctuaire nabatéen et romain." *CRAIBL* 1994: 735-57.

al-Muheisen and Villeneuve 1999. Z. al-Muheisen and F. Villeneuve. "Sanctuaire nabatéen près de Pétra." *L'Archéologue* 41: 43-46.

al-Muheisen and Villeneuve 2000. Z. al-Muheisen and F. Villeneuve. "Nouvelles recherches à Khirbet edh-Dharih (Jordanie du Sud), 1996-1999." *CRAIBL* 2000: 1525-63.

al-Muheisen and Villeneuve 2001. Z. al-Muheisen and F. Villeneuve. "Dharih (Khirbet edh-)." Pp. 139-41 in A. Negev and S. Gibson, eds. *Archaeological Encyclopaedia of the Holy Land*. New York and London.

al-Muqdad and Dentzer 1987-1988. R. al-Muqdad and J.-M. Dentzer. "Les fouilles franco-syriennes à Bosra (1981-1987)." *AAAS* 37-38: 224-41.

al-Muqdad, Dentzer and Broise 1996. R. al-Muqdad, J.-M. Dentzer and H. Broise. "Bosra." *Syrian-European Archaeology Exhibition; Exposition Syro-Européenne d'Archéologie, Working together, Miroir d'un partenariat*. Damascus.

Murray and Ellis 1940. M.A. Murray and J.C. Ellis. *A Street in Petra*. London.

Musil 1907. A. Musil. *Arabia Petraea. II. Edom*. Wien.

Musil 1926. A. Musil. *The Northern Ȟeǧâz. A Topographical Itinerary*. Oriental Explorations and Studies, no. 1. New York.

Myerson 1983. P. Myerson. "Eleutheropolis of the New Arabia." *ZPE* 53: 130-40.

Nasif 1988. A.A. Nasif. *Al-'Ulâ. An Historical and Archaeological Survey With Special Reference to Its Irrigation System*. Riyadh.

Naveh 1967. J. Naveh. "Some Notes on Nabataean Inscriptions from 'Avdat." *IEJ* 17: 187-89.

Naveh 1970. J. Naveh. "The Development of the Aramaic Script." *Proceedings of the Israel Academy of Sciences and Humanities* 5/1:1-69.

Naveh 1979. J. Naveh. "A Nabataean Incantation Text." *IEJ* 29: 111-19.

Nebes 1994. N. Nebes, ed. *Arabia Felix. Beiträge zur Sprache und Kultur des vorislamischen Arabien. Festschrift Walter W. Müller zum 60. Geburtstag*. Wiesbaden.

Negev 1961. A. Negev. "Nabataean Inscriptions from 'Avdat (Oboda)." *IEJ* 11: 127-238.

Negev 1963. A. Negev. "Nabataean Inscriptions from 'Avdat (Oboda)." *IEJ* 13: 113-24.

Negev 1967. A. Negev. "Oboda, Mampsis and the Provincia Arabia." *IEJ* 17: 46-55.

Negev 1969. A. Negev. "Seal Impressions from Tomb 107 at Kurnub (mampsis)." *IEJ* 19: 89-106.

Negev 1971. A. Negev. "The Nabataean Necropolis of Mampsis (Kurnub)." *IEJ* 21: 110-29.

Negev 1974a. A. Negev. "Nabataean Capitals in the Towns of the Negev." *IEJ* 24: 153-59.

Negev 1974b. A. Negev. *The Nabataean Potter's Workshop at Oboda*. Bonn.

Negev 1974c. A. Negev. Review of E. Meyers. *Jewish Ossuaries: Reburial and Rebirth. Secondary Burials in their Near Eastern Setting*. In *JSS* 25: 337-42.

Negev 1974d. A. Negev. "The Churches of the Central Negev: An Archaeological Survey." *RB* 81: 400-22.

Negev 1976a. A. Negev. "Survey and Trial Excavations at Haluza (Elusa), 1973." *IEJ* 26: 89-95.

Negev 1976b. A. Negev. "The Early Beginnings of the Nabataean Realm." *PEQ* 108-109: 125-33.

Negev 1977. A. Negev. "The Nabataeans and the Provincia Arabia." Pp. 520-686 in H. Temporini, ed. *ANRW* 2 (8).

Negev 1978. A. Negev. "The Nabataeans and the Provincia Arabia." Pp. 520-686 in *ANRW* II (8).

Negev 1981. A. Negev. *The Greek Inscriptions from the Negev*. Studium Biblicum Franciscanum Collection Minor 25. Jerusalem.

Negev 1983. A. Negev. *Tempel, Kirchen und Zisternen. Ausgrabungen in der Wöste Negev. Die Kultur der Nabatäer*. Stuttgart.

Negev 1986. A. Negev. *The Late Hellenistic and Early Roman Pottery of Nabataean Oboda. Final Report*. Qedem 22. Jerusalem.

Negev 1988a. A. Negev. *The Architecture of Mampsis. Final Report 1. The Middle and the Late Nabataean Periods*. Qedem 26.

Negev 1988b. A. Negev. *The Architecture of Mampsis. Final Report 2. The Late Roman and Byzantine Periods*. Qedem 27.

Negev 1989. A. Negev. "The Cathedral of Elusa and the New Typology and Chronology of the Byzantine Churches in the Negev." *LA* 39: 129-42.

Negev 1990. A. Negev. "Mampsis – The End of A Nabataean Town." *ARAM* 2: 337-65.

Negev 1991a. A. Negev. *Personal Names in the Nabataean Realm*. Qedem 32.

Negev 1991b. A. Negev. "The Temple of Obodas: Excavations at Oboda in 1989." *IEJ* 41: 62-80.

Negev 1991c. A. Negev. "Nabataean Inscriptions from 'Avdat (Oboda)." *IEJ* 11 (1961): 127-138; 13 (1963): 113-24.

Negev 1991d. A. Negev. "Obodas the God." *IEJ* 41: 62-80.

Negev 1993a. A. Negev. "Elusa." Pp. 379-83 in *NEAEHL* I.

Negev 1993b. A. Negev. "Jurnub." Pp. 882-93 in *NEAEHL* III.

Negev 1993c. A. Negev. "Nessana." Pp. 1145-49 in *NEAEHL* III.

Negev 1993d. A. Negev. "Oboda." Pp. 1155-65 in *NEAEHL* III.

Negev 1993e. A. Negev. "Sobata." Pp. 1404-10 in *NEAEHL* IV.

Negev 1993f. A. Negev. "The Mampsis Gymnasia and their Later History: Preliminary Report and Interpretation." Pp. 241-64 in F. Manns and E. Alliata, eds. *Early Christianity in Context. Monuments and Documents*. Studium Biblicum Franciscanum Collectio Maior 38. Jerusalem.

Negev 1996. A. Negev. "Identification of the 'Rock'." *Cathedra* 80: 228-30.

Negev 1997. A. Negev. *The Architecture of Nabataean Oboda, Final Report*. Qedem 36.

Negev, Naveh and Shaked 1986. A. Negev, J. Naveh and S. Shaked. "Obodas the God." *IEJ* 36: 56-60.

Nehmé 1997 . L. Nehmé. "L'habitat rupestre dans le bassin de Pétra à l'époque nabatéenne." Pp. 281-88 in *SHAJ* VI.

Nehmé 1997 . L. Nehmé. "La géographie des inscriptions de Pétra (Jordanie)." Pp. 125-43 in A. Sérandour, ed. *Des Sumériens aux Romains d'Orient. La perception géographique du monde. Espaces et territoires au Proche-Orient ancien*. Antiquités Sémitiques 2. Paris.

Nehmé 1998. L. Nehmé. "Une inscription nabatéenne inédite de Bosrà (Syrie)." Pp. 62-73 in C.B. Amphoux, A. Frey and U. Schattener-Rieser, eds. *Études sémitiques et samaritaines offertes à Jean Margain*. Histoire du Texte biblique 4. Lausanne.

Nehmé 1999. L. Nehmé. "Inscriptions nabatéennes." Pp. 154-56, nos. 40-41 and pp. 167-68, nos. 66-67 in H. Cuvigny, et al. "Inscriptions rupestres vues et revues dans le désert de Bérénice." *BIFAO* 99: 133-93.

Nehmé and Villeneuve 1999. L. Nehmé and F. Villeneuve. *Pétra. Métropole de l'Arabie antique*. Paris. (especially p. 69, 118, 130, 140-43).

Netzer 1991. E. Netzer. *Masada III. The Yigeal Yadin Excavations 1963-1965. Final Reports. The buildings: stratigraphy and architecture*. Jerusalem.

Netzer 1996. E. Netzer. "The Palaces Built by Herod – A Research Update." Pp. 27-54 in K. Fittschen and G. Foerster, eds. *Judaea and the Greco-Roman World in the Time of Herod in the Light of Archaeological Evidence*. Göttingen.

Neugebauer and Parker 1969. O. Neugebauer and R.A. Parker. *Egyptian Astronomical Texts* 3. Providence.

Nielsen 1994. I. Nielsen. *Hellenistic Palaces*. Aarhus.

O'Connor 1986. M. O'Connor. "The Arabic Loanwords in Nabataean Aramaic." *JNES* 45: 213-29.

Oleson, 'Amr and Schick 1992. J.P. Oleson, Kh. 'Amr and R. Schick. *The Humeima Excavation Project: Preliminary Report of the 1991 Season*. Echos du Monde Classique/Classical Views 36, n.s. 11: 137-69.

Oppenheim 1943. M. Freiherr von Oppenheim. *Die Beduinen. 2. Die Beduinenstämme in Palästina, Transjordanien, Sinai, Hedjaz.* Leipzig.

Oren 1982. E.D. Oren. "Excavations at Qasrawet in North-Western Sinai: Preliminary Report." *IEJ* 32: 203-11.

Oren 1993. E.D. Oren. "Qasrawet." Pp. 1213-18 in *NEAEHL* IV.

Orrieux 1983. Cl. Orrieux. *Les Papyrus de Zénon*. Paris.

Orton, Tyers and Vince 1993. C. Orton, P. Tyers and A. Vince. *Pottery in Archaeology*. Cambridge, England.

Ostrow 1977. S.E. Ostrow. *Problems in the Topography of Roman Puteoli*. PhD dissertation, The University of Michigan at Ann Arbor.

Ovadiah 1970. A. Ovadiah. *Corpus of the Byzantine Churches in the Holy Land*. Bonn.

Ovadiah and de Silva 1984. A. Ovadiah and C.G. de Silva. "Supplementum to the Corpus of Byzantine Churches in the Holy Land, III: Appendices." *Levant* 26: 129-65.

Paradise 1998a. T.R. Paradise. "Environmental Setting and Stone Weathering." Pp. 151-66 in Joukowsky 1998.

Paradise 1998b. Th.R. Paradise. "Sandstone Weathering, Petra." *AJA* 102: 576-78.

Parker 1997. S.T. Parker. "Preliminary Report on the 1994 Season of the Roman Aqaba Project." *BASOR* 305: 19-44.

Parlasca 1998. K. Parlasca. "Bemerkungen zum Isiskult in Petra." Pp. 64-70 in Hübner, Knauf and Wenning 1998.

Parr 1957. P.J. Parr. "Recent Discoveries at Petra." *PEQ* 89: 13-14, 151-66.

Parr 1960a. P.J. Parr. "Excavations at Petra, 1958-59." *PEQ* 92: 124-35, PLS. 16-24.

Parr 1960b. P.J. Parr. "Nabataean Sculpture from Khirbet Brak." *ADAJ* 4-5: 134-36.

Parr 1962. P.J. Parr. "A Nabataean Sanctuary near Petra." *ADAJ* 6/7: 21-23.

Parr 1967-1968. P.J. Parr. "Recent Discoveries in the Sanctuary of the Qasr Bint Far'un at Petra, I. Account of the Recent Excavations." *ADAJ* 12/13: 5-19 (=*Syria* 45 (1968): 1-24).

Parr 1968. P.J. Parr. "The Investigation of some 'Inaccessible' Rock-cut Chambers at Petra." *PEQ* 100: 5-15.

Parr 1969. P.J. Parr. "Chronique archéologique. Pétra (Jordanie)." *RB* 76: 393-94.

Parr 1970. P.J. Parr. "A Sequence of Pottery from Petra." Pp. 348-81 in J.A. Sanders, ed. *Near Eastern Archaeology in the Twentieth Century: Essays in Honour of Nelson Glueck*. New York.

Parr 1982. P.J. Parr. "Contacts between North West Arabia and Jordan in the Late Bronze and Iron Ages." Pp. 127-33 in A. Hadidi, ed. *SHAJ* I.

Parr 1986. P.J. Parr. "The Last Days of Petra." Pp. 182-205 in M.A. Bakhit and M. Asfour, eds. *Proceedings of the Symposium on Bilad al-Sham during the Byzantine Period* 2. Amman.

Parr 1989. P.J. Parr. "Aspects of the Archaeology of North-West Arabia in the First Millennium BC." Pp. 39-66 in T. Fahd, ed. *L'Arabie Préislamique et son Environment historique et culturel*. Strasbourg.

Parr 1990. P.J. Parr. "Sixty Years of Excavation in Petra. A Critical Assessment." *ARAM* 2: 7-23.

Parr 1996. P.J. Parr. "The Architecture of Petra: Review Article." *PEQ* 128: 63-69.

Parr, Atkinson and Wickens 1975. P.J. Parr, K.B. Atkinson and E.H. Wickens. "Photogrammetric Work at Petra, 1965-1968. An Interim Report." *ADAJ* 20: 31-45.

Patrich 1984. J. Patrich. "'Al-'Uzza' Earrings." *IEJ* 34: 39-46.

Patrich 1988a. J. Patrich. "The Glass Vessels." Pp. 134-41 in Tsafrir 1988.

Patrich 1988b. J. Patrich. "Architectural Sculpture and Stone Objects." Pp. 97-133 in Tsafrir 1988.

Patrich 1990a. J. Patrich. *The Formation of Nabataean Art: Prohibition of a Graven Image among the Nabataeans*. Jerusalem and Leiden.

Patrich 1990b. J. Patrich. "Prohibition of a Graven Image among the Nabataeans: the Evidence and its Significance." *ARAM* 2: 185-96.

Pesce 1950. G. Pesce. *Il "Palazzo delle Colonne" in Tolemaide di Cirenaica*. Rome.

Peterman and Schick 1996. G.L. Peterman and R. Schick. "The Monastery of Saint Aaron." *ADAJ* 40: 473-80.

Peters 1977. F.E. Peters. "The Nabataeans in the Hawran." *JAOS* 97: 263-77.

Peters 1978. F.E. Peters. "Romans and Bedouins in South Syria." *JNES* 37(4): 315-26.

Peters 1983. F.E. Peters. "City-Planning in Greco-Roman Syria: Some New Considerations." *DaM* 1: 269-77.

Pfister and Bellinger 1945. R. Pfister and L. Bellinger. "The Textiles." In M.I. Rostovzeff, et al. *The Excavations at Dura Europos: Final Report*. IV, Part II. New Haven.

Picard 1937. C. Picard. "Les sculptures nabatéenes de Khirbet et-Tannur et l'Hadad de Pouzooles." *RA* 10: 244-49.

Piccirillo 1976. M. Piccirillo. "Campagna Archaeologica nella Basilica di Mose Profeta sul Monte Nebo Siyagh." *LA* 26: 281-318.

Piccirillo 1985. M. Piccirillo. "I Battisteri Bizantini di Giordania." Pp. 345-55 in V. Janeiro, ed. *Noscere Sancta Miscellanea in Memoria di Agostino Amore OFM (+1982)*. Volume 1. Storia della Chiesa, Archeologia, Arte. I. Roma.

Piccirillo 1989. M. Piccirillo. "Gruppi Episcopali nelle Tre Palestine e in Arabia?" Pp. 459-502 in *Actes du Xie Congres international d'archeologie chretienne 1986*. Vol. I (= Studi di antichita christiana 41).

Piccirillo 1993. M. Piccirillo. *The Mosaics of Jordan*. ACOR Monograph Series 1. Amman.

Piccirillo 1994. M. Piccirillo. "Gli Scavi del Complesso di Santo Stefano." Pp. 69-110 in M. Piccirillo and E. Alliata. *Umm al-Rasas – Mayfa'ah, I. Gli Scavi del Complesso di Santo Stefano*. Jerusalem.

Politis 1992. K.D. Politis. "Excavations at Deir' Ain 'Abata 1991." *ADAJ* 36: 281-90.

Politis 1998. K.D. Politis. "Rescue Excavations in the Nabataean Cemetery at Khirbat Qazone 1996-97." *ADAJ* 42: 611-14.

Politis 2002. K.D. Politis. "Rescuing Khirbet Qazone." *Minerva* 13 (2): 27-29.

Politis 2003 forthcoming. K.D. Politis. "Arabs, Greeks and Jews on the Shores of the Dead Sea." *SHAJ* VIII.

Politis 2004. K.D. Politis, ed. "The World of the Nabataeans." *Proceedings for an international conference held at the British Museum, London, 17-19 April 2001*. Oxbow Monograph Series. Oxford.

Porter 1855. J.L. Porter. *Five Years in Damascus: with travels and researches in Palmyra, Lebanon, the giant cities of Bashan and the Haurân*. London.

Potts 1988. D.T. Potts. "Trans-Arabian Routes of the Pre-Islamic Period." Pp. 127-62 in J.-F. Salles, ed. *L'Arabie et ses mers bordières I: Itinéraires et voisinages*. Lyon.

Potts 1991. D.T. Potts. "Nabataean finds from Thaj and Qatif." *AAE* 2: 138-44.

Potts 1992. D.T. Potts. *The Arabian Gulf in Antiquity 2. From Alexander the Great to the Coming of Islam*. Oxford.

Price 1984. S. Price. *Rituals and Power: The Roman Imperial Cult in Asia Minor*. Cambridge, England.

Puchstein 1902. O. Puchstein, et al. "Zweiter Jahresbericht über die Ausgrabungen in Baalbek." *Jahrbuch d.K.A.I.* 17: 104-24.

Pulleyblank 1999. E.G. Pulleyblank. "The Roman Empire as Known to Han China." *JAOS* 119: 71-79.

Raschke 1978. M.G. Raschke. "New Studies in Roman Commerce with the East." Pp. 604-1076 in *ANRW* II 9, 2.

Renan 1873. E. Renan. "Une nouvelle inscription nabatéenne, trouvé à Pouzzoles." *JA* 7th series, 2: 366-84.

Restle 1971. M. Restle. "Hauran." Pp. 962-1033 in *Reallexikon zur byzantinischen Kunst* 2. Stuttgart.

Retsö 2000. J. Retsö. "Nabataean origins – once again." *Proceedings of the Seminar for Arabian Studies* 29: 115-18.

Rey 1860. E.G. Rey. *Voyage dans le Hauran et aux bords de la mer Morte pendant les années 1857 et 1858*. Paris.

Rey-Coquais 1979. J.-P. Rey-Coquais. "Bostra." Pp. 159 ff. in R. Stillwell, ed. *The Princeton Encyclopedia of Classical Sites* 2. Princeton.

Roberts 1842-1849. D. Roberts. *The Holy Land, Syria, Idumea, Arabia, Egypt & Nubia*. London.

Robinson 1841. E. Robinson. *Biblical Researches in Palestine, Mount Sinai and Arabia Petraea. A Journal of Travels in the Year 1838*. London and Boston.

Roche 1985a. M.-J. Roche. *Niches à bétyles et monuments apparentés à Pétra*. PhD dissertation, The University of Paris.

Roche 1985b. M.-J. Roche. "A propos d'un bas-relief inédit de Pétra." *Syria* 62: 313-17.

Roche 1994. M.-J. Roche. "Les débuts de l'implantation nabatéene à Pétra." *Transeuphratène* 8: 35-46.

Roche 1996. M.-J. Roche. "Remarques sur les Nabatéens en Méditerranée." *Semitica* 45: 73-99.

Roche 1997. M.-J. Roche. "Tannur, Khirbet et-." Pp. 153-55 in *OxEANE* 5.

Rogl 1996. Ch. Rogl. "Hellenistische Reliefbecher aus der Stadt Elis." *Jahreshefte des Österreichischen Archäologischen Instituts* 65: 116-58.

Rokéa 1983. D. Rokéa. "Qasrawet: The Ostracon." *IEJ* 33: 93-96.

Roller 1998. D.W. Roller. *The Building Program of Herod the Great*. Berkeley.

Romanis 1996. F. de Romanis. *Cassia, cinnamomo, ossidiana. Uomini e merci tra Oceano Indiano e Mediterraneo*. Saggi di Storia Antica 9. Rome.

Ronczewski 1932. K. Ronczewski. "Kapitelle des El-Hasne in Petra." *AA* 47: 38-90.

Roschinski 1981. H.P. Roschinski. "Sprachen, Schriften und Inschriften in Nordwestarabien." Pp. 27-60 in *Die Nabatæer*. Catalogue of an exhibition in the Rheinsiches Landesmuseum 1978.

Rosenthal 1962. F. Rosenthal. "Nabataean and Related Inscriptions." Pp. 198-210 in H.D. Colt, ed. *Excavations at Nessana (Auja Hafir, Palestine)* 1. London.

Rosenthal 1970. R. Rosenthal. "Der Goldschumuck von Mampsis und Oboda." Pp. 34-38 in *Die Nabataer. Ein Vergessenes Volk Am Toten Meer 312 v.-106 n. Chr.* Munich.

Rosenthal-Heginbottom 1982. R. Rosenthal-Heginbottom. *Die Kirchen von Sobota und die Dreiapsidenkirchen des Nahen Ostens*. Wiesbaden.

Rotroff 1982. S.I. Rotroff. *Hellenistic Pottery. Athenian and Imported Moldmade Bowls*. The Athenian Agora 22. Princeton.

Rowley-Conwy 1998. P. Rowley-Conwy, et al. "A Honeymoon in Egypt and the Sudan: Charlotte Rowley, 1835-1836." In P. and J. Starkey, ed. *Travellers in Egypt*. London.

Russell 1980. K.W. Russell. "The Earthquake of May 19, AD 363." *BASOR* 238: 47-64.

Russell 1985. K.W. Russell. "The Earthquake Chronology of Palestine and Northwest Arabia from the 2ND through the mid-8TH century A.D." *BASOR* 260: 37-59.

Ryckmans 1980. J. Ryckmans. "Al-Uzza et Lat dans les inscriptions sud-arabiques, à propos de deux amulettes meconnues." *JSS* 25: 193-204.

Sahlins 1968. M.D. Sahlins. *Tribesmen*. Foundations of Modern Anthropology Series. Englewood Cliffs, NJ.

Said 1979. E. Said. *Orientalism*. New York.

Salles 1996. J.-F. Salles. "Al-'Ula - Dédan. Recherches Récente." *Topoi* 6: 565-607.

Salmon 1965. J.M. Salmon. "Nabataean Epigraphic Materials from the Excavations." Pp. 73-78, pl. 47-50 in P.C. Hammond. *The Excavation of the Main Theater at Petra, 1961-1962. Final Report*. London.

Sanders 1996. D.H. Sanders. *Nemrud Dagi: The Hierothesion of Antiochus I of Commagene*. 2 vols. Winona Lake, IN.

Sartre 1982. M. Sartre. *Inscriptions grecques et latines de la Syrie 13 (1) Bostra no. 9001-9472*. BAH 113. Paris.

Sartre 1985. M. Sartre. *Bostra: des origines à l'Islam*. BAH 117. Paris.

Sartre 1993. M. Sartre. *Inscriptions de la Jordanie IV. Pétra et la Nabatène méridionale du wadi al-Hasa au golfe de 'Aqaba*. IGLS 21(4). BAH 115.

Sartre 2001. M. Sartre. *D'Alexandre à Zénobie: histoire du Levant antique IVe siècle av. J.-C. - IIIe siècle ap. J.-C.* Paris.

Sartre forthcoming. M. Sartre. *Bostra et la Nuqra* s.p. IGLS 13 (1), suppl.

Sartre-Fauriat 1983. A. Sartre-Fauriat. "Tombeaux antiques de Syrie du Sud." *Syria* 60: 83-99.

Sartre-Fauriat 2001. A. Sartre-Fauriat. *Des tombeaux et des morts: monuments funéraires, société et culture en Syrie du Sud du Ier s. av. J.-C. au VIIe s. apr. J.-C.* Vol. 1: *Catalogue des monuments funéraires, des sarcophages et des bustes;* Vol. 2: *Synthèse*. BAH 158. Beirut.

Savignac 1932. M.R. Savignac. "Notes de voyage - Le sanctuaire d'Allat à Iram." *RB* 41: 581-97.

Savignac 1933. M.R. Savignac. "Le sanctuaire d'Allat à Iram (1)." *RB* 42: 405-22.

Savignac 1934. M.R. Savignac. "Le sanctuaire d'Allat à Iram (suite)." *RB* 43: 573-89.

Savignac 1937. M.R. Savignac. "Le dieu nabatéen de La'ban et son temple." *RB* 46: 401-16, pl. 9-10.

Savignac and Horsfield 1935. M.R. Savignac and G. Horsfield. "Le temple de Ramm." *RB* 44: 245-78.

Savignac and Starcky 1957a. M.R. Savignac and J. Starcky. "Une inscription nabatéenne provenant du Djôf." *RB* 64: 196-217.

Savignac and Starcky 1957b. M.R. Savignac and J. Starcky. "Y a-t-il un dieu Râs'aïn La'aban?" *RB* 64: 215-17.

Schick 1987. R. Schick. *The Fate of the Christians in Palestine during the Byzantine-Umayad Transition, AD 600-750*. PhD dissertation, University of Chicago.

Schick 1992. R. Schick. "Jordan on the Eve of the Muslim Conquest AD 602-634." Pp. 107-19 in P. Canivet and J.-P. Rey-Coquais, eds. *La Syrie de Byzance a l'Islam VIIe-VIIIe Siecles*. Actes du Colloque international Lyon – Maison de l'Orient Mediterranéen. Paris.

Schick 1995a. R. Schick. "Christianity at Humayma, Jordan." *LA* 45: 319-42.

Schick 1995b. R. Schick. *The Christian communities of Palestine from Byzantine to Islamic rule. A Historical and Archaeological study*. Studies in Late Antiquity and Early Islam 2. Princeton.

Schick 2001. R. Schick. "Ecclesiastical History of Petra." Pp. 1-5 in Fiema 2001a.

Schick, Fiema and 'Amr 1993. R. Schick, Z.T. Fiema and Kh. 'Amr. "The Petra Church Project, 1992-93. A Preliminary Report." *ADAJ* 37: 55-66.

Schilbach 1970. E. Schilbach. *Byzantinische Metrologie*. Munich.

Schluntz 1998. E. Schluntz. "Protectress of Petra': Isis and Popular Cult in Nabataean Petra." Pp. 221-22 in *American Academy of Religion-Society of Biblical Literature: Annual Meeting, 1998, Orlando, Florida: SBL Abstracts*.

Schmelz 2002. G. Schmelz. Kirchliche Amsträger im spätantiken Ägypten nach den Aussagen der griechischen und koptischen Papyri un Ostraka. Archiv für Papyrusforschung, Beiheft 13. Munich and Leipzig.

Schmid 1995a. S.G. Schmid. "Nabataean Fine Ware from Petra." Pp. 637-47 in *SHAJ* V.

Schmid 1995b. S.G. Schmid. *Die Feinkeramik der Nabatäer. Typologie, Chronologie und kulturhistorische Hintergründe*. Terra Archaeologica 3.

Schmid 1997a. S.G. Schmid. "Nabataean Fine Ware Pottery and the Destructions of Petra in the Late First and Early Second Century AD." Pp. 413-20 in *SHAJ* VI.

Schmid 1997b. S.G. Schmid. "Eierschalendünne Tongefässe und grobe Waren." Pp. 131-37 in Weber and Wenning 1997.

Schmid 2000a. S.G. Schmid. *Die Feinkeramik der Nabatäer. Typologie, Chronologie und kulturhistorische Hintergründe. Petra - Ez Zantur II 1. Ergebnisse der Schweizerisch-Liechtensteinischen Ausgrabungen* (=Terra Archaeologica IV. Monographien der Schweizerisch-Liechtensteinischen Stiftung für Archäologische Forschungen im Ausland [SLASA/FSLA].).

Schmid 2000b. S.G. Schmid. "The 'Hellenistic' Tomb Façades of Nabataean Petra and their Cultural Background." Pp. 485-509 in *Graeco-Arabica* VII-VIII (1999-2000).

Schmid 2001a. S.G. Schmid. "The Impact of Pottery Production on the Sedentarization of the Nabataeans." Pp. 427-36 in J.R. Brandt and L. Karlsson, eds. *From Huts to Houses. Transformations of Ancient Societies. Proceedings of an International Seminar organized by the Norwegian and Swedish Institutes in Rome, 21-24 September 1997*. Stockholm.

Schmid 2001b. S.G. Schmid. "The 'Hellenization' of the Nabataeans: A New Approach." Pp. 407-19 in *SHAJ* VII.

Schmid 2001c. S.G. Schmid. "The Nabataeans. Travellers between Lifestyles." Pp. 367-426 in B. McDonald, R. Adams and P. Bienkowski, eds. *The Archaeology of Jordan*. Sheffield, England.

Schmid 2001d. S.G. Schmid. "The International Wadi Farasa Project (IWFP) between Microcosm and Macroplanning – A First Synthesis." *PEQ* 133: 159-97.

Schmidt-Colinet 1980. A. Schmidt-Colinet. "Nabatäische Felsarchitektur." *BJ* 180: 189-230.

Schmidt-Colinet 1981. A. Schmidt-Colinet. "Nabatäische Felsarchitektur." Pp. 62-102 in Hellenkemper-Salies 1981.

Schmidt-Colinet 1983a. A. Schmidt-Colinet. "Dorisierende nabatäische Kapitelle." *DaM* 1: 307-12.

Schmidt-Colinet 1983b. A. Schmidt-Colinet. "A Nabataean Family of Sculptors at Hegra." *Berytus* 31: 95-102.

Schmidt-Colinet 1987. A. Schmidt-Colinet. "The Mason's Workshop of Hegra, Its Relations to Petra, and the Tomb of Syllaios." Pp. 143-50 in *SHAJ* III.

Schmidt-Colinet 1992. A. Schmidt-Colinet. *Das Tempelgrab Nr. 36 in Palmyra*. Mainz.

Schmidt-Colinet 1997. A. Schmidt-Colinet. "Aspects of 'Romanization': The Tomb Architecture at Palmyra and its Decoration." Pp. 157-77 in S.E. Alcock, ed. *The Early Roman Empire in the East*. Oxford.

Schneider 1995. G. Schneider. "Roman Red and Black Slipped Pottery from North East Syria and Jordan. First Results of Chemical Analysis." Pp. 415-22 in H. Meyza and J. Mlynarczyk, eds. *Hellenistic and Roman Pottery in the Eastern Mediterranean. Advances in Scientific Studies*. Warsaw.

Sedov 1992. A.V. Sedov. "New Archaeological and Epigraphical Material from Qana (South Arabia)." *AAE* 3: 110-37.

Sedov 1997. A.V. Sedov. "Sea Trade of the Hadramawt Kingdom from the 1st to 6th Centuries A.D." Pp. 365-83 in Avanzini 1997.

Seeden 1981-1982. H. Seeden. "Busrâ eski-Shâm (Haurân)." *AfO* 28: 215-16.

Seeden 1983. H. Seeden. "Reports of an Archaeological and Ethnographic Campaign." *DaM* 1: 77-102.

Seeden 1984. H. Seeden. "Busrâ eski-Shâm (Haurân)." *AfO* 31: 126-28.

Seeden 1986. H. Seeden. "Bronze age village occupation in Busrâ: AUB excavations on the northwest tell 1983-1984." *Berytus* 34: 11-82.

Seeden 1988. H. Seeden. "Busrâ 1983-1984: Second Archaeological Report." *DaM* 3: 387-412.

Seeden and Wilson 1984. H. Seeden and J. Wilson. "Busrâ in the Hawrân: AUB's ethnoarchaeological project 1980-1985." *Berytus* 32: 19-34.

Segal 1988. A. Segal. *Town Planning and Architecture in Provincia Arabia. The cities along the Via Traiana Nova in the 1st-3rd centuries C.E.* BAR International Series 419.

Seyrig 1932. H. Seyrig. "Monuments Syriens de culte de Némésis." *Syria* 13: 50-64.

Sidebotham 1986a. S.E. Sidebotham. "Aelius Gallus and Arabia." *Latomus* 45: 590-602.

Sidebotham 1986b. S.E. Sidebotham. *Roman Economic Policy in the Erythra Thalassa 30 B.C.-A.D. 217*. Mnemosyne, Bibliotheca Classica Batava, Supplement 91. Leiden.

Sidebotham 1996. S.E. Sidebotham "Romans and Arabs in the Red Sea." *Topoi* 6: 785-97.

Siebert 1978. G. Siebert. *Recherches sur les ateliers de bols à reliefs du Péloponnèse à l'époque hellénistique*. Bibliothèque des Ecoles Françaises d'Athènes et de Rome 233. Paris.

Smith and Day 1989. R.H. Smith and L.P. Day. *Pella of the Decapolis* 2. Wooster, OH.

Sourdel 1952. D. Sourdel. *Les cultes du Hauran à l'époque romaine*. BAH 53. Paris.

Sozomen 1979. Sozomen. *Ecclesiastical History*. A.C. Zenos, transl. Select Library of Nicene and Post-Nicene Fathers of the Christian Church. Second Series. Vol. II (1890). Reprinted in 1979, Grand Rapids, MI.

Sperber 1976. D. Sperber. "Objects of Trade between Palestine and Syria in Roman Times." *JESHO* 19: 113-47.

Stanley 1862. A.P. Stanley. *Sinai and Palestine in Connection with their History*. London.

Starcky 1954. J. Starcky. "Un contrat nabatéen sur papyrus." *RB* 61: 161-81.

Starcky 1955. J. Starcky. "Review of Littmann and Meredith 1953-1954." *Syria* 32: 151-57.

Starcky 1957a. J. Starcky. "Une inscription nabatéenne provenant du Djôf." *RB* 64: 106-15.

Starcky 1957b. J. Starcky. "Y a-t-il un dieu Resh aïn La'ban?" *RB* 64: 215-17.

Starcky 1965a. J. Starcky. "Nouvelles stèles funéraires à Pétra." *ADAJ* 10: 43-49.

Starcky 1965b. J. Starcky. "Nouvelle épitaphe nabatéenne donnant le nom sémitique de Pétra." *RB* 72: 95-97.

Starcky 1966. J. Starcky. "Pétra et la Nabatène." Cols. 886-1017 in H. Cazelles and A. Feuillet, eds. *Supplement au Dictionnaire de la Bible* 7. Paris.

Starcky 1968. J. Starcky. "Le temple nabatéen de Khirbet Tannur: à propos d'un livre récent. " *RB* 75: 206-35.

Starcky 1975. J. Starcky. "The Nabataean Altar." Appendix I (p. 16, pl. VII A) in C.-M. Bennett. "Excavations at Buseirah, Southern Jordan, 1973: Third Preliminary Report." *Levant* 7: 1-19.

Starcky 1978. J. Starcky. "Nabataean inscriptions." P. 540 in F.V. Winnett and G.L. Harding. *Inscriptions from Fifty Safaitic Cairns*. Near and Middle East Series 9. Toronto.

Starcky 1979. J. Starcky. "Les Inscriptions nabatéennes du Sinaï." *Le Monde de Bible* 10: 37-40.

Starcky 1985. J. Starcky. "Les inscriptions nabatéennes et l'histoire de la Syrie du Sud et du Nord de la Jordanie." Pp. 167-81 in Dentzer 1985.

Starcky and Strugnell 1966. J. Starcky and J. Strugnell. "Pétra, deux nouvelles inscriptions nabatéenes." *RB* 75: 236-47.

Stark 1971. J.K. Stark. *Personal Names in Palmyrene Inscriptions*. Oxford.

Stephens 1837 J.L. Stephens. *Incidents of Travel in Egypt, Arabia Petraea, and The Holy Land*. New York.

Stern 1994. E. Stern. *Dor. Ruler of the Seas*. Jerusalem.

Stewart 1993. A. Stewart. *Faces of Power: Alexander's Image and Hellenistic Politics*. Berkeley and Los Angeles.

Stewart 1995. A. Stewart. "Imag(in)ing the Other: Amazons and Ethnicity in Fifth-Century Athens." *Poetics Today* 16: 571-97.

Stewart 1997. A. Stewart. *Art, Desire, and the Body in Ancient Greece*. Cambridge, England.

Stiehl 1970. R. Stiehl. "A New Nabataean Inscription." Pp. 87-90 in R. Stiehl and H.E. Stier, eds. *Beiträge zur alten Geschichte und deren Nachleben. Festschrift für Franz Altheim zum 6.10.1968*. Vol. 2. Berlin.

Stone 1992-1994. M.E. Stone. *Rock Inscriptions and Graffiti Project. Catalogue of Inscriptions*. 3 vols. Resources for Biblical Study, nos. 28, 29, and 31. Atlanta.

Strube 1993. C. Strube. *Baudekoration im Nordsyrischen Kalksteinmassiv* 1. Mainz.

Strugnell 1959. J. Strugnell. "The Nabataean Goddess Al-Kutba and Her Sanctuaries." *BASOR* 156: 29-36.

Stucky 1983. R.A. Stucky. "Eine Reise nach Marib, in die Stadt Königin von Saba." *Antike Welt* 14: 2-13.

Stucky 1995. R.A. Stucky, et al. "Swiss-Liechtenstein Excavations at ez-Zantur in Petra 1994: The Sixth Campaign." *ADAJ* 39: 297-315.

Stucky 1996. R.A. Stucky. "Die Nabatäischen Bauten." Pp. 13-50 in Bignasca 1996.

Tarn 1929. W.W. Tarn. "Ptolemy II and Arabia." *JEA* 15: 9-25.

Tarrier 1988. D. Tarrier. *Les triclinia nabatéens dans la perspective des installations de banquet de Proche-Orient*. PhD dissertation, The University of Paris.

Tarrier 1990. D. Tarrier. "Baalshamin dans le monde nabatéen: à propos de découvertes récentes." *ARAM* 2: 197-203.

Teixidor 1979. J. Teixidor. *The Pantheon of Palmyra*. Leiden.

Tenison 1846. L. Tenison. *Sketches in the East*. London.

Theeb 1993. S.A. al-[al-Dhiy¡b] Theeb. *Aramaic and Nabataean Inscriptions from North-West Saudi Arabia*. Riyadh.

Theeb 1994. S.A. Theeb. "Two Dated Nabataean Inscriptions from al-Jawf." *JSS* 39: 33-40.

Theeb 1995. S.A. al-[al-Dhiyīb] Theeb. *Diræsah taḥlīlīyah li-nuqūš naba īyah qadīmah min šamæl fiarb al-mamlakat al-ʿarabīyat al-saʿūdīyah*. Riyadh.

Theeb 2000. S.A. al-[al-Dhiyīb] Theeb. *Al-muʿjam al-naba ī. Diræsah muqæranah li-l-mufradæt wa-l-alfāz al-naba iyah*. Riyadh.

Theeb 2002. S.A. al-[al-Dhiyīb] Theeb. *Nuqūš jabal umm jafāyif al-nabatiyah. Dirāsah taḥlīliyah*. Riyadh.

Tholbecq 1997. L. Tholbecq. "Les sanctuaries des Nabatéens. État de la question à la lumiére de recherches archéologiques récentes." *Topoi* 7: 1069-95.

Tholbecq forthcoming. L. Tholbecq. *Récherches sur les temples nabatéens*. PhD dissertation Thèse. Louvain-la-Neuve.

Toll 1994. C. Toll. "Two Nabataean Ostraca from Egypt." *BIFAO* 94: 381-82.

Toynbee 1964. J.M.C. Toynbee. "A Bronze Statue from Petra." *ADAJ* 8-9: 75-76.

Tracy 1999. S. Tracy. "The Dedicatory Inscription to Trajan at the 'metropolis' of Petra." Pp. 51-58 in *The Roman and Byzantine Near East 2*. JRA Supplementary Series 31.

Tsafrir 1982. Y. Tsafrir. "Qasrawet: Its Ancient Name and Inhabitants." *IEJ* 32: 212-14.

Tsafrir 1986. Y. Tsafrir. "The Transfer of the Negev, Sinai and Southern Transjordan from Arabia to Palaestina." *IEJ* 36 (1-2): 77-86.

Tsafrir 1988. Y. Tsafrir, et al. *Excavations at Rehovot-in-the-Negev. Volume I: The Northern Church*. Qedem 25.

Tsafrir 1993. Y. Tsafrir, ed. *Ancient Churches Revealed*. Jerusalem.

Tsafrir 1994. Y. Tsafrir, et al. *Tabula Imperii Romani Judaea-Palaestina*. Jerusalem.

Tsafrir and Holum 1993. Y. Tsafrir and K.G. Holum. "Rehovot-in-the-Negev." Pp. 1274-77 in *NEAEHL*.

Tzaferis 1983. V. Tzaferis. *The Excavations of Kursi – Gergesa*. 'Atiqot (English Series) 16.

Tzaferis 1985. V. Tzaferis. "An Early Christian Church Complex at Magen." *BASOR* 258: 1-15.

Urban 1997. T. Urban. "Dokumentation nabatäischer Felsengräber in Petra, Jordanien." Pp. 793-808 in C. Beckel, et al., eds. *Xro&noV.* Festschrift für Bernhard Hänsel. Espelkamp.

Vickers 1994. M.Vickers. "Nabataea, India, Gaul and Carthage: Reflections on Hellenistic and Roman Gold Vessels and Red-Gloss Pottery." *AJA* 98: 231-48.

Vihonen and Fiema 2001. J.Vihonen and Z.T. Fiema. "Greek and Latin Inscriptions." Pp. 342-45 in Fiema 2001a.

Villeneuve 1990. F.Villeneuve. "The Pottery from the oil-factory at Khirbet edh-Dharih (2nd century AD). A Contribution to the Study of the Material Culture of the Nabataeans." *ARAM* 2: 367-84.

Villeneuve 1992. F.Villeneuve. "Le peuplement nabatéen de la Gobolitide (al-Jibal): état critique de la question." Pp. 277-90 in *SHAJ* IV.

Villeneuve 2002. F.Villeneuve. "Le sanctuaire nabatéen des 2e-4e siècles à Khirbet edh-Dharih (Jordanie du Sud)." *RA* 2002: 189-94.

Villeneuve and al-Muheisen 1997. F.Villeneuve and Z. al-Muheisen. "Khirbet adh-Dharih, un sanctuaire nabatéen et son village." Pp. 108-11 in E. Delpont, ed. *Jordanie sur les pas des archéologues*. Paris.

Waliszewski 1994. T. Waliszewski. "La mosaique de Deir el-'Asfur retrouvée: Le motif des "Rinceaux habites" en Judée et dans la Shéphéla." *RB* 101-104: 562-79.

Waliszewski 2001a. T. Waliszewski. "Mosaics." Pp. 218-70 in Fiema 2001a.

Waliszewski 2001b. T. Waliszewski. "Céramique byzantine et proto-islamique de Dharih (Jordanie du Sud)." Pp. 95-106 in F.Villeneuve and P. Watson, eds. *La céramique byzantine et proto-islamique en Syrie–Jordanie, 4ème–8ème siècles.* Beirut.

Walker and Brierbrier 1997. S. Walker and M. Brierbrier. *Ancient Faces, Mummy Portraits from Roman Egypt*. London.

Walmsley 1992. A. Walmsley. "The Social and Economic Regime at Fihl (Pella) and Neighbouring Centres between the 7TH and 9TH Centuries." Pp. 249-61 in Canivet and Rey-Coquais 1992.

Weber 1997. Th. Weber. "Die Bildkunst der Nabatäer." Pp. 114-25 in Weber and Wenning 1997.

Weber and Wenning 1997. Th. Weber and R. Wenning, eds. *Antike Felsstadt zwischen arabischer Tradition und griechischer Norm*. Sonderhefte der Antiken Welt. Mainz.

Wenning 1987. R. Wenning. *Die Nabatäer — Denkmäler und Geschichte. Eine Bestandesaufnahme des archäologischen Befundes*. Novum Testamentum et Orbis Antiquus, no. 3. Freiburg/Schweiz - Göttingen.

Wenning 1989. R. Wenning. "Maskierte Götter? Anmerkungen zum Aufeinandertreffen von Ost und West am Beispiel der arabischen Nabatäer." Pp. 243-60 in K. Rudolph and G. Rinschede, eds. *Beiträge zur Religion/Umwelt-Forschung I*. Geographia Religionum 6. Berlin.

Wenning 1990a. R. Wenning. "Two Forgotten Nabataean Inscriptions." *ARAM Periodical* 2: 143-50.

Wenning 1990b. R. Wenning. "Das Nabatäerreich: Seine archäologischen und historischen Hinterlassenschaften." Pp. 367-415 in H.-P. Kuhnen. *Palästina in griechisch-römischer Zeit, Handbuch der Archäologie* II. Munich.

Wenning 1992. R. Wenning. "The Nabataeans in the Decapolis/Coele Syria." *ARAM* 4: 79-99.

Wenning 1993. R. Wenning. "Das Ende des nabatäischen Königreichs." Pp. 81-103 in A. Invernizzi and J.-F. Salles, eds. *Arabia Antiqua. Hellenistic Centres Around Arabia*. Rome.

Wenning 1994. R. Wenning. "Die Dekapolis und die Nabatäer." *ZDPE* 110: 1-35.

Wenning 1996. R. Wenning. "Hegra and Petra: Some Differences." *ARAM* 8: 253-67.

Wenning 1997. R. Wenning. "Bemerkungen zur Gesellschaft und Religion der Nabatäer." Pp. 177-201 in R. Albertz, ed. *Religion und Gesellschaft I*. Alter Orient und Altes Testament 248. Münster.

Wenning 2003. R. Wenning. "Hellenistische Denkmäler aus Petra." Forthcoming in G. Zimmer, ed. *Neue Forschungen zur hellenistischen Plastik. Festschrift für Georg Daltrop.*

Wenning, Kolb and Nehmé 1997. R. Wenning, B. Kolb and L. Nehmé. "Vom Zeltlager zur Stadt." Pp. 56-70 in Weber and Wenning 1997.

Whitcomb 1982. D.S. Whitcomb. "Roman Ceramics." Pp. 51-115 in D.S. Whitcomb and J.H. Johnson, eds. *Quseir al-Qadim 1980. Preliminary Report*. American Research Center in Egypt Reports 7. Malibu, CA.

Wilson and Sa'd 1984. J. Wilson and M. Sa'd. "The Domestic Material Culture of Nabataean to Umayyad Period Busrâ." *Berytus* 32 (140): 35-147.

Winkes 1969. R. Winkes. *Clipeata Imago. Studien zur Römischen Bildnisform*. Bonn.

Winkler 1938. H.A. Winkler. *Archaeological Survey of Egypt. Rock Drawings of Southern Upper Egypt I. Sir Robert Mond Desert Expedition Season 1936-1937. Preliminary Report*. Loondon.

Winnett and Reed 1970. F.V. Winnett and W.L. Reed. *Ancient Records from North Arabia*. Toronto.

Witt 1971. R.E. Witt. *Isis in the Greco-Roman World*. London.

Worp 1982. K.A. Worp. "Byzantine Imperial Titulature in the Greek Documentary Papyri: The Oath Formulas." *ZPE* 45: 199-223.

Worp 1997. K.A. Worp. "ÖArjante! and politeuÒmenoi in Papyri from Graeco-Roman Egypt." *ZPE* 115: 201-20.

Wright 1961a. G.R.H. Wright. "Structure of the Qasr Bint Far'un. A Preliminary Review." *PEQ* 93: 8-37.

Wright 1961 . G.R.H. Wright. "Petra – The Arched Gate, 1959-60." *PEQ* 93: 124-35.

Wright 1962. G.R.H. Wright. "The Khazneh at Petra: A Review." *ADAJ* 6/7: 30-54.

Wright 1968. G.R.H. Wright. "Découvertes récentes au sanctuaire du Qasr à Pétra, II. Quelques aspects de l'architecture et de la sculpture." *Syria* 45: 24-40 (= *ADAJ* 12/13 (1967-68): 20-29).

Yadin 1962. Y. Yadin. "Expedition D – The Cave of Letters." *IEJ* 12: 227-57.

Yadin 1963a. Y. Yadin. *The Finds from Bar Kokhba Period in the Cave of Letters*. Jerusalem.

Yadin 1963b. Y. Yadin. "The Nabataean Kingdom, Provincia Arabia, Petra and En-Geddi in the Documents from NaÌal Ìever." *JEOL* 17: 227-41.

Yadin 2002. Y. Yadin, et al., eds. *The Documents from the Bar Kokhba Period in the Cave of Letters. Hebrew, Aramaic and Nabataean-Aramaic Papyri*. Judean Desert Studies 3. Jerusalem.

Yadin, Naveh and Meshorer 1989. Y. Yadin, J. Naveh and Y. Meshorer, *Masada I. The Yigael Yadin Excavations 1963-1965. Final reports. The Aramaic and Hebrew Ostraca and Jar Inscriptions. The Coins of Masada*. Jerusalem.

Yaqut 1955. *Mu'jam al-Buldan*. Beirut.

Yardeni 2001. A. Yardeni. "The Decipherment and Restoration of Legal Texts from the Judaean Desert: A reexamination of *Papyrus Starcky (P.Yadin 36)*." Pp. 121-37 in *SCI* 20.

Young 1997. G.K. Young. "The Customs-Officer at the Nabataean Port of Leuke Kome (*Periplus Maris Erythraei* 19)." *ZPE* 119: 226-28.

Youtie 1973. H.C. Youtie. *Scriptiunculae*. Amsterdam.

Zacharias of Mitylene 1899. Zacharias of Mitylene. *The Syriac Chronicle Known as that of Zacharias of Mitylene*. F.J. Hamilton and E.W. Brooks, transls. London.

Zarins 1981. J. Zarins, et al. "The Comprehensive Archaeological Survey Program: a. The Second Preliminary report on the Southwestern Province." *Atlal* 5: 9-42.

Zarins 1983. J. Zarins, et al. "Preliminary Report on the Najran/Ukhdud Survey and Excavations 1982/1402 AH." *Atlal* 7: 22-40.

Zayadine 1970. F. Zayadine. "Une tombe nabatéenne près de Dhat-Râs (Jordanie)." *Syria* 47: 117-35.

Zayadine 1973. F. Zayadine. "Excavations at Petra (APRIL 1973)." *ADAJ* 18: 81-82, PLS. 50.2-3.

Zayadine 1974. F. Zayadine. "Excavations at Petra (1973-1974)." *ADAJ* 19: 135-50.

Zayadine 1979. F. Zayadine. "Excavations in Petra (1976-1978)." *ADAJ* 23: 185-97, pl. 83-94.

Zayadine 1980 . F. Zayadine. "Die Götter der Nabatäer." Pp. 108-17 in Lindner 1980.

Zayadine 1980 . F. Zayadine. "Photogrammetrische Arbeiten in Petra." *BJ* 180: 237-52.

Zayadine 1981. F. Zayadine. "L'iconographie d' Al-Uzza-Aphrodite." *Mythologie gréco-romaine: Mythologies périphériques. Etudes iconographiques*. Colloques du CNRS 593: 113-18. Paris.

Zayadine 1982a. F. Zayadine. "Les forifications pré-helléniques et hellénistiques en Transjordanie et en Palestine." Pp. 149-56 in P. Leriche and H. Tréziny, eds. *La fortification dans l'histoire du monde grec*. Paris.

Zayadine 1982b. F. Zayadine. "Recent Excavations at Petra (1979-81)." *ADAJ* 26: 365-93, pls. 117-144.

Zayadine 1983. F. Zayadine. "Die Felsarchitektur Petras: Orientalische Traditionen und hellenistischer Einfluß." Pp. 212-48 in Lindner 1980.

Zayadine 1985. F. Zayadine. "Caravan Routes between Egypt and Nabataea and the Voyage of Sultan Baibars to Petra in 1276 A.D." Pp. 159-74 in *SHAJ* II.

Zayadine 1986. F. Zayadine. "Tempel, Gräber, Töpferöfen." Pp. 214-69 in Lindner 1986.

Zayadine 1987. F. Zayadine. "Decorative stucco at Petra and other Hellenistic sites." Pp. 131-42 in *SHAJ* III.

Zayadine 1990a. F. Zayadine, ed. *Petra and the Caravan Cities*. Amman.

Zayadine 1990b. F. Zayadine. "The Pantheon of the Nabataean Inscriptions in Egypt and the Sinai." *ARAM* 2: 151-74.

Zayadine 1990c. F. Zayadine. "The God(dess) Aktab-Kutbay and his (her) iconography." In Zayadine 1990a.

Zayadine 1991a. F. Zayadine. "L'Iconographie d'Isis à Pétra." *MEFR* 103: 283-306.

Zayadine 1991b. F. Zayadine. "Les Tobiades en Transjordanie et à Jerusalem." Pp. 5-24 in E. Will and F. Larché. *Iraq-Al-Amir, le Château du Tobiade Hyrcan*. BAH 132. Paris.

Zayadine 1992. F. Zayadine. "L'espace urbain du grand Pétra, les routes et les stations caravanières." *ADAJ* 36: 217-39.

Zayadine 1999a. F. Zayadine. "Petra, le Siq." *Dossiers d'Archéologie* 244: 46-53.

Zayadine 1999b. F. Zayadine. "Le relief néo-Babylonien à Sela' près de Tafileh: interprétation historique." *Syria* 76: 83-90.

Zayadine and Farajat 1991. F. Zayadine and S. Farajat. "The Petra National Trust Site Projects: Excavations and Clearance at Petra and Beida." *ADAJ* 35: 288-95.

Zayadine and Farès-Drappeau 1998. F. Zayadine and S. Farès-Drappeau. "Two North-Arabian Inscriptions from the Temple of Læt at Wædį Iram." *ADAJ* 42: 255-58.

Zeitler 1980. J.P. Zeitler. "Petra – Kartographie und Vermessung in der antiken Stadt." Pp. 292-420 in Lindner 1980.

Zeitler 1989. J.P. Zeitler. "Die Siedlungsabfolge am Fusse des el-Hubta-Massivs von Petra (Jordanien)." Pp. 307-18 in Lindner 1980.

Zeitler 1990a. J.P. Zeitler. "A Private Building from the First Century B.C. in Petra." *ARAM* 2: 385-420.

Zeitler 1990b. J.P. Zeitler. "Houses, Sherds and Bones: Aspects of Daily Life at Petra." Pp. 39-51 in S. Kerner, ed. *The Near East in Antiquity, German Contributions to the Archaeology of Jordan, Palestine, Syria, Lebanon and Egypt* I. Amman.

Zeitler 1993. J.P. Zeitler. "Excavations and Surveys in Petra 1989-90." *Syria* 70: 255-60.

Glossary of Architectural Terms

adyton The inner or most holy room of a temple, generally separated from the cella by a wall with a doorway.
aedicule A small structure used as a shrine.
affix A decorative detail attached, joined, or added, especially to an interior wall.
akroterion The plinths at the angles or apex of a pediment provided to carry figures or ornaments.
anta Pilaster (or corner post) of slight projection terminating the end of the lateral walls of a cella, and usually serving as respond to a column. In the latter case the columns are said to be *in antis*.
apse A semicircular projection at the east end of a church that is usually vaulted.
architrave A lintel in stone or beam of timber carried from the top of one column or pier to another; the lowest member of the entablature.
ashlar A thin squared and dressed stone for facing a wall of rubble or brick.
ambo One of the two pulpits or raised stands in early Christian churches from which parts of the service were chanted or read.
atrium The entrance court of a Roman house, roofed over at the sides, but open to the sky in the center. In an atrium of large size, four or more columns would be introduced to carry the roof.
attic A low wall or story above the cornice of a classical façade, sometimes decorated with bas-reliefs or utilized for an inscription.
baetyl A roughly shaped standing stone held sacred or worshipped as of divine origin.
balustrade A rail and the row of posts that support it, as along the edge of a staircase.
basilica **A**n early Christian church building of oblong rectangular shape, consisting of a nave and two side aisles, with a clerestory and a large high transept from which an apse projects
bema The usually raised part of an Eastern church containing the altar.
biclinium A room with stone benches along two walls of its interior.
cavea The tiered semicircular seating space of an ancient open-air theater.
cella The enclosed chamber or sanctuary of a temple, also known by the Greek term **naos.**
ciborium A vaulted canopy permanently placed over an altar.
clerestory An outside wall of a room or building that rises above an adjoining roof and contains windows.
colonette A small column esp. in a group in a parapet, balustrade or clustered column.
corbel An architectural member that projects from within a wall and supports a weight, especially one that is stepped upward and outward from a vertical surface.
colonnade A series of columns set at regular intervals and usually supporting the base of a roof structure.
cornice The upper member of the entablature subdivided into bed-molding, corona, and sima; a term also employed for any projection on a wall, provided to throw the rain-water from the face of the building.
dentil One of a series of small projecting rectangular blocks in the bed-molding of a cornice, or occupying the place of a frieze, originally representing the ends of joists which carried a flat roof.
distyle Marked by columniation with two columns across the front; see under **portico.**
egg-and-dart The pattern applied to the Ionic ovolo profile, in early times with squarish eggs touching each other and concealing all but the tips of the darts, later with more pointed or oval eggs separated to reveal the darts, which in Roman times are sometimes even arrow-shaped.
entablature A horizontal part in classical architecture that rests on the columns and consists of architrave, frieze, and cornice; in the case of pilasters or detached or engaged columns it is sometimes profiled around them.
exedra A semicircular stone or marble seat, or a rectangular or semicircular recess.
fascia The term given to the planes into which the architrave of the Ionic and Corinthian Orders is subdivided, or to a flat projecting band.
flagstone A flat, fine-grained, hard, even-layered stone split into slabs for use in paving.
frieze The middle member of the entablature between the architrave and the cornice, often sculptured or richly ornamented.
gutter A trough along the eaves to catch and carry off rainwater.
half-column An engaged, semicircular column.
half-pediment A decorative element consisting of half of a pediment, typically employed in opposing pairs on Nabataean tomb façades.
header A brick or stone laid with its end toward the face of the wall; compare **stretcher.**
hexastyle Temple or porch front with six columns.
jamb One of the vertical lateral members of a door or window enframement, supporting the lintel.
kiosk An open gazebo or pavilion.
lintel The horizontal beam covering a door or window opening or spanning the interval between two columns or piers.
monolithic Composed of a single block of stone, in the case of a column extending from the top of a base or stylobate to the bottom of the capital.
môtab A base or altar platform designed to house a sacred standing stone, or baetyl.
narthex The portico of an early Christian church or basilica, originally separated from the nave by a railing or screen.
nave The main part of the columned interior of a church, often consisting of a long narrow central hall that rises higher than the aisles flanking it to form a clerestory.
nefesh A rock-cut funerary memorial, in the form of an elongated pyramid, which symbolizes the deceased.
obelisk An upright four-sided, usually monolithic pillar that gradually tapers as it rises and terminates in a pyramid.
pastophorium Either of the two apartments at the sides of the bema that are found in early Christian churches.
pedestal The support or foot of a late classic or neoclassic column; the base of an upright structure.
pediment A triangular space that forms the gable of a low-pitched roof and that is usually filled with relief sculpture in classical architecture.
pilaster An upright architectural member that is rectangular in plan and is structurally a pier but architecturally treated as a column and that usually projects a third of its width or less from the wall.
plinth A block or slab upon which a pedestal, column, or statue is placed.
portico A colonnade or a colonnaded porch or entrance to a building. The term, when applied to a Greek temple, is classed as distyle or tristyle or tetrastyle *in antis* (two, three or four columns between antae).
pronaos The porch in front of the naos or cella.
quarter-column An engaged quarter-of-column, used to decorated the interior corners of a room.
revetment Applied stone decorative facing, typically applied to interior walls.
rotunda A round building, especially one with a dome.
springer A bottom stone of an arch resting on the impost (the uppermost part of a supporting column or pillar).
stele An upright stone slab used for dedicatory or funerary purposes.
stretcher A brick or stone laid parallel to the face of a wall; compare **header**.
stylobate The upper step of a temple, which formed a platform for the columns.
synthronon A structure in a church combining the Bishop's throne and clergy stalls placed behiund the altar against the east wall.
tessera A small piece (as of marble, glass, or tile) used in mosaic work.
temenos The sacred enclosure in which one or more [Greek] temples stand.
tetrastyle Four-columned; see under **portico.**
tholos A Greek circular building with or without a peristyle.
threshold The piece of wood or stone placed beneath a door; doorsill.
triapsidal Having three apses; see under **apse.**
triclinium A banquet or dining room surrounded on three sides with stone benches.
triglyph A projecting member separating the metopes, emphasized with two vertical channels of V section and two corresponding chamfers or half channels on the vertical sides.
tympanum The recessed, usually triangular face of a pediment within the frame made by the upper and lower cornices.
vestibule A small entrance hall or antechamber between the outer door and the interior of a building.
voussoir A wedge-shaped stone which forms one of the units of an arch.

Index

Numbers in italics refer to illustrations.

Illustration Credits

Archaeological Museum, Istanbul: 197; Augrabung der Universität Basel und der Schweizerisch-Liechtensteinischen Stiftung für Archäologische Forschungen im Ausland (SLSA) in Petra: 230, 231, 233, 234, 235, 236; U. Bellwald: 69; G. Bowersock: 128; D. L. Brill: 216; R. E. Brünnow and A. von Domaszewski, *Die Provincia Arabia*, 3 volumes, 1904–1909: 149 top ; J. L. Burckhardt, *Travels in Syria and the Holy Land*, 1822: 147; T. Canaan, *Journal of the Palestine Oriental Society,* 1929: 150; Trustees, Cecil Higgins Art Gallery, Bedford, England: 122 right; Cincinnati Art Museum: 173 bottom, 174 left, 190; Cincinnati Art Museum. Photo T. Walsh: 116, 118, 126; Colt Archaeological Institute and the British School of Archaeology, Jerusalem: 42 right bottom; Cooper-Hewitt, National Design Museum, Smithsonian Inst./Art Resource, NY: 130; G. Dalman, *Petra und seine Felsheiligtümer*, 1908: 149 bottom; Dharih Archaeological Project (DAP): 95 right, 96 top and bottom left; DAP. A. Chambon: 82 bottom right; DAP. H. Fontaine: 82; DAP. J. Humbert: 88 right, 89; DAP. J. Humbert, A. Omari, Yarmouk University: 88 left; DAP. Y. Ino: 95 left; DAP. R. de La Noue, R. Drizard: 92; DAP. J. Taylor: 94 left; DAP. F. Villeneuve, C. Fenetin, CNRS-ArScAn Nanterre: 85; Editions Gabalda, Paris: 42 left top and bottom; Edward Lear Drawings and Manuscripts, Petra (36), NII.L12 [859], Department of Printing and Graphic Arts, Houghton Library, Harvard College Library: 129 bottom; Equipe Proche-Orient hellénistique et romain, Maison René Ginouvès, Nanterre: 144, 146, 152, 153, 154, 155, 156, 157, 159, 161, 162; Reproduced by permission of the Provost and Fellows of Eton College: 129 top; J. M. Farrant: 106; J. M. Farrant after C. Pickersgill: 107 top left; Z. T. Fiema: 241 left bottom and right, 248 bottom; Peter John Gates FBIPP, ARPS, Ashwell, UK: 1, 12, 15, 17, 20, 21, 23, 24, 38 left bottom, 55, 58, 59, 61, 62, 64, 67, 71, 74, 78 bottom left, 79 left top and bottom, 80 right, 81 left, 86, 93, 94 right, 164, 166, 167, 168, 169, 170, 176, 177, 178, 179, 180, 181 left bottom and right, 182, 183, 184, 185, 187, 188, 189, 195 bottom left, middle and right, 200, 217, 218 top, 219 right, 225, 226, 229, 237, 241 left top, 242, 243, 244, 245, 248 top left, right and middle, 252, 259; S. Gibson: 173 top; P.C. Hammond: 224; K. Horton: 108 top left and bottom; Ch. L. Irby and J. Mangles, *Travels in Egypt and Nubia, Syria, and Asia Minor during the Years 1817 and 1818*, 1823: 148; Israel Exploration Society: 42 top right; A. W. Joukowsky: 215 left bottom and right, 219 left, 220; C. Kanellopoulos: 221; C. Kanellopoulos and Z. T. Fiema: 249; Geraldine King: 39 left; Adrian Kitzinger: 18, 66; F. Larché: 204, 205, 206, 209, 210; F. Larché. Photos digitalized by Antoine Chéné: 201, 202, 203, 211; G. Laron: 103; M. Lindner: 138 bottom; Musée du Louvre, Paris. AO 11077: 191; M.C.A. Macdonald: 38 right bottom, 39 right, 46 bottom, 53; G. Markoe: 90; J. McKenzie: 137, 172, 174 right, 175, 181 top left; Metropolitan Museum of Art, New York: 196; J. Wilson Meyers and Eleanor E. Meyers: 238; Miami University Libraries, The Walter Havighurst Special Collections: 120; University of Michigan (P. Mich. Inv. 6922.88–96): 258; Mission archéologique française en Syrie du Sud: 109, 111; Fergus Moynihan, Ashwell: 4, 5, 140; The National Trust, Lyme Park: 125; Property of The National Trust, London: 113, 114; Laïla Nehmé: 38 right middle, 49 right; Olana State Historic Site, New York State Office of Parks, Recreation and Historic Preservation: 131; Photo Réunion des Musées Nationaux Agence Photographique: 46 top left and middle, 49 top right, 50; P. J. Parr: 26, 29, 31, 34; D. Pitney, L. Traxler, P.C. Zimmerman: 218 bottom; Princeton University, Photo no. S.813–26: 46 right; Private Collection: 121, 122 left, 123; S. G. Schmid: 76, 77, 78 top right and left and bottom right, 79 right, 80 left, 81 right; S. E. Sidebotham: 2, 3, 10; T. Springett: 107 top right and bottom left and right, 108 top right; A. Stewart: 192, 194, 195 top left and right; Trustees of the Victoria and Albert Museum, London: 124; R. Wenning: 8, 38 top, 115, 135, 136, 138 top, 139, 141, 143; R. Wenning, I. Browning (line drawings): 134; F. Zayadine: 60, 63; P. C. Zimmerman: 215 top left.